Approaches to Teaching
The Plum in the Golden Vase
(The Golden Lotus)

This publication was made possible in part by a grant from
the James P. Geiss and Margaret Y. Hsu Foundation,
a private, nonprofit foundation that sponsors research
on China's Ming dynasty (1368–1644).

Approaches to Teaching
The Plum in the Golden Vase
(The Golden Lotus)

Edited by

Andrew Schonebaum

Modern Language Association of America
New York   2022

© 2022 by The Modern Language Association of America
85 Broad Street, New York, New York 10004
www.mla.org

To order MLA publications, visit mla.org/books. For wholesale and international orders, see mla.org/Bookstore-Orders.

The MLA office is located on the island known as Mannahatta (Manhattan) in Lenapehoking, the homeland of the Lenape people. The MLA pays respect to the original stewards of this land and to the diverse and vibrant Native communities that continue to thrive in New York City.

Approaches to Teaching World Literature 159
ISSN 1059-1133

Library of Congress Cataloging-in-Publication Data

Names: Schonebaum, Andrew, 1975– editor.
Title: Approaches to teaching The plum in the golden vase (The golden lotus) /
    edited by Andrew Schonebaum.
Other titles: Approaches to teaching The golden lotus
Description: New York : Modern Language Association of America, 2022.
Series: Approaches to teaching world literature, 1059-1133 ; 159 |
    Includes bibliographical references.
Identifiers: LCCN 2021057628 (print) | LCCN 2021057629 (ebook) |
    ISBN 9781603295444 (hardcover) | ISBN 9781603294126 (paperback) |
    ISBN 9781603294133 (EPUB)
Subjects: LCSH: Xiaoxiaosheng. Jin Ping Mei ci hua. | Xiaoxiaosheng—
    Study and teaching (Higher) | LCGFT: Literary criticism. | Essays.
Classification: LCC PL2698.H73 C5236 2022 (print) | LCC PL2698.H73 (ebook) |
    DDC 895.13/46—dc23/eng/20220318
LC record available at https://lccn.loc.gov/2021057628
LC ebook record available at https://lccn.loc.gov/2021057629

Dedicated to the memory of David Tod Roy
(1933–2016)

I would like to appropriate the moving words of my sometime teacher, David Hawkes, the translator of *The Story of the Stone* (another title for *The Dream of the Red Chamber*), who closed the introduction to his great translation with this statement, which has been a source of inspiration to me over the years: "My one abiding principle has been to translate *everything*—even puns. For although this is . . . an 'unfinished' novel, it was written (and rewritten) by a great artist with his own life-blood. I have therefore assumed that whatever I find in it is there for a purpose and must be dealt with somehow or other. I cannot pretend always to have done so successfully, but if I can convey to the reader even a fraction of the pleasure this Chinese novel has given me, I shall not have lived in vain."

CONTENTS

ACKNOWLEDGMENTS

This volume continues a conversation among friends, the circle of whom happily and gratefully continues to expand. I would particularly like to thank all the contributors for their efforts here and beyond to make the joys and complexities of Chinese literature a bit more accessible to nonspecialists. I am grateful to the James P. Geiss and Margaret Y. Hsu Foundation for its generous support of this project and to Martin Heijdra, who stepped in when Margaret Hsu passed away unexpectedly during the preparation of this book. I thank David Rolston for his attentive reading of the entire manuscript and for sharing his own materials and thoughts, many of which have been adapted and incorporated here. Wai-yee Li organized a symposium in honor of David Roy (1933–2016) at Harvard in 2019, entitled *Jin Ping Mei* and the World: Translation and Transculturation, from which I and this volume benefited greatly. At the Modern Language Association, I would like to thank James Hatch for reprising his role and efforts in seeing this manuscript through to publication, Susan Doose for copyediting work, and Judith Altreuter for production work. Thanks to the University of Maryland for its collegial and material support. I am grateful to Pat Hui, who has been a wonderful facilitator and an inspiration for my studies of Chinese culture all along. Most of all I would like to thank Angus Worthing, Eugene Poon-Kaneko, my parents, and especially Chava Brandriss, Ella, Maggie, and Molly for their support and expertise. I love you.

ABBREVIATIONS FOR COMMONLY CITED EDITIONS

The following abbreviations are used in parenthetical citations when referring to commonly cited editions of *Jin Ping Mei*:

HHJPM *Huiping huijiao* Jin Ping Mei 會評會校金瓶梅 (*Variorum* Plum in the Golden Vase)

JPMCH *Jin Ping Mei cihua* 金瓶梅詞話 (*Plum in the Golden Vase: A Ballad Tale*)

XXP *Xinke xiuxiang piping* Jin Ping Mei 新刻繡像批評金瓶梅 (*Newly Cut, Lavishly Illustrated, and Commented On* Plum in the Golden Vase)

ZZP *Gaohe Tang piping diyi qishu* Jin Ping Mei 皋鶴堂批評第一奇書金瓶梅 (Plum in the Golden Vase: *The First Marvelous Book, with Gaohe Tang Commentary*)

NOTE ON CITATION AND ROMANIZATION

This volume is tied to David Tod Roy's translation *The Plum in the Golden Vase*, and we generally refer to *Jin Ping Mei* as *Plum in the Golden Vase* (or *Plum*). Roy annotates his translation, in the words of the historian Jonathan Spence, "with a precision, thoroughness, and passion for detail that makes even a veteran reader of monographs smile with a kind of quiet disbelief" ("Remembrance"). The degree of intertextuality displayed in *Jin Ping Mei* is part of what makes the text so remarkable, and Roy's translation gives serious students of Chinese culture access to the novel's intertextual references.[1] We refer primarily to Roy's translation, citing the five-volume edition published by Princeton University Press between 1993 and 2013 by volume, chapter, and page number. For example, "(1.5.200)" refers to volume 1, chapter 5, page 200. (When only two numbers appear, the chapter is not given because a different element of the volume, such as a preface, is cited.) Published under the title *The Golden Lotus*, the translation by Clement Egerton and Shu Qingchun—known by his pen name, Lao She—has many virtues, and it would be confusing to use a title other than *The Golden Lotus* when talking about that edition or about movies or older translations available under that title. When citing the Chinese text of the novel, we generally use the digital edition of the *Jin Ping Mei cihua* 金瓶梅詞話 (*Plum in the Golden Vase: A Ballad Tale*) available on the website of the National Central Library. We cite the *cihua* edition by chapter and page (e.g., chapter 79, page 5a is "79.5a" [*a* indicates recto and *b* verso, given that Chinese texts and script are traditionally read from right to left]; when only one number appears, the chapter is not given because a different element of the volume, such as a preface, is cited). When referring to the Zhang Zhupo commentary edition, *Gaohe Tang piping diyi qishu* Jin Ping Mei 皋鶴堂批評第一奇書金瓶梅 (Plum in the Golden Vase: *The First Marvelous Book, with Gaohe Tang Commentary*), we use the digital edition from Waseda University Library (cited by chapter and page) and then supplement this with the corresponding volume, chapter, and page from the Egerton-Lao translation, since Zhang and Egerton were reading the same, or very similar, Chinese editions.[2]

Roy uses the older, Wade-Giles system of romanization of Chinese when transcribing names and places. This system uses apostrophes to distinguish voiced and nonvoiced initials, hyphens to break up bisyllabic compounds, and lots of umlauts. We opt for the standard Pinyin system adopted by the People's Republic of China and UNESCO, which uses apostrophes only to distinguish noninitial syllables that begin with vowels in multisyllabic compounds, and follow the basic rules of Hanyu Pinyin orthography (www.pinyin.info/readings/zyg/rules .html). We use Pinyin rather than follow Roy's historical English spelling of place-names: we use Beijing instead of Peking, Nanjing instead of Nanking, Suzhou instead of Soochow, Hangzhou for Hangchow, Yangzhou for Yangchow, and Guangzhou for Canton, which facilitates finding these places on a current map. Where places or people's names could be pronounced multiple ways, we mark the syllable break with an apostrophe (e.g., Changan could be Chang'an or Chan'gan; Li Pinger is Li Ping'er).

Characters' names are written according to Pinyin orthography—for example, Roy's Hsi-men Ch'ing becomes Ximen Qing, and Ch'en Ching-chi becomes Chen Jingji. (Wade-Giles romanizations are given in parentheses on first mention of a character's name.) The decision to use Pinyin orthography extends to the treatment of quoted matter from Roy's translation, where characters' names have been silently changed to reflect Pinyin spellings. The names of historical figures do not follow any one romanization system but are presented as they would be found on *WorldCat* or using a *Google* search.

Notes on Spelling and Pronunciation

A brief (and approximate) note on the spelling and pronunciation of Pinyin romanization is as follows: $c = ts$, $q = ch$, $x = sh$, $z = dz$, $zh = j$.[3] Chinese syllables are made up of one or more of the following elements:

1. an initial consonant (*b, c, ch, d, f, g, h, j, k, l, m, n, p, q, r, s, sh, t, w, x, y, z, zh*);
2. a semivowel (*i* or *u*); and
3. an open vowel (*a, e, i, o, u, ü*), a closed vowel (*an, ang, en, eng, in, ing, ong, un*), or a diphthong (*ai, ao, ei, ou*).

Possible combinations are as follows:

3 on its own (e.g., *e, an, ai*);
1+3 (e.g., *-ba, xing, hao*); or
1+2+3 (e.g., *xue, qiang, biao*).

Initial Consonants

Apart from *c, z,* and *r,* the only initial consonants whose pronunciation is likely to give nonnative speakers of Chinese much trouble are the two groups *j, q,* and *x* and *zh, ch,* and *sh.* Both groups sound somewhat like the English *j, ch,* and *sh,* but whereas *j, q,* and *x* are articulated much farther forward in the mouth than the English *j, ch,* and *sh,* the sounds *zh, ch,* and *sh* are made in what is referred to as a retroflexed position much farther back. This means that to the ears of an English speaker *j* sounds halfway between the English *j* and the Chinese *dz, q* halfway between the English *ch* and the Chinese *ts,* and *x* halfway between the

English *sh* and the Chinese *s*, while *zh*, *ch*, and *sh* sound somewhat like *jr*, *chr*, and *shr* would sound if all three combinations, and not only the last one, were found in English. If difficulty is experienced in making the distinction, it is always possible to pronounce both groups like the English *j*, *ch*, and *sh*.

Semivowels

The semivowel *i* palatalizes the preceding consonant—that is, it makes a *y* sound after it, like the *i* in *onion* (e.g., Pan Jin**lian**). The semivowel *u* labializes the preceding consonant, which is to say it makes a *w* sound after it, like the *u* in *assuages* (e.g., Han Dao**guo**).

Vowels

Three types of vowels are discussed in this section: open vowels, closed vowels, and diphthongs. Open vowels are sounds produced when the tongue is positioned as far as possible from the roof of the mouth. Closed vowels are sounds produced with the tongue touching the roof of the mouth. Diphthongs are sounds made by combining two vowels.

Open Vowels

a   is a long *ah*, like the *a* in *father* (e.g., Wu Zong**jia**)

e   on its own or after any consonant other than *y*, *e* is like the French sound *ouef* or the English *the* (e.g., Xue'e, Guan'**ge**)

e   after *y* or a semivowel, *e* is like the *e* of *egg* (e.g., Ying Bo**jue**, Li Gui**jie**)

i   after *b*, *d*, *j*, *l*, *m*, *n*, *p*, *q*, *t*, *x*, and *y*, *i* is pronounced like the long Italian *I* or the English *ee*, as in *see* (e.g., **Li** Ping'er)

i   after *zh*, *ch*, *sh*, *z*, *c*, *s*, and *r*, *i* is a growl somewhere between the *u* of *suppose* and a vocalized *r* (e.g., Bu **Zhi**dao, Zhu **Shi**nian)

i   after the semivowel *u*, *i* is pronounced like the *ay* in *sway* (e.g., Li **Gui**jie, Song **Hui**lian)

o   is the *oa* of *oar* (e.g., Ying **Bo**jue)

u   after the semivowel *i* and all consonants except *j*, *q*, *x*, and *y*, *u* is pronounced like the Italian *u* or the English *oo* in *too* (e.g., **Ru**yi)

u   after *j*, *q*, *x*, *y*, *ü*, *l*, or *n*, *u* is like the narrow French *u* or the German *ü*, for which there is no English equivalent (e.g., **Qiuju**, Hua **Zixu**)

Closed Vowels

an   after the semivowel *u* or any consonant other than *y*, *an* is like *an* in the German word *Mann*; it sounds somewhere between *an* and *on* (e.g., **An** Feng**shan**)

an   after *y* or the semivowel *i*, *an* is like the *en* in *hen* (e.g., Pan Jin**lian**, Xia **Yan**ling); *yan* sounds more like *yen*, as in *the Japanese yen*

ang   whatever it follows, *ang* invariably has the long *a* of *father* (e.g., **Pang** Chunmei, **Wang** Liu'er)

en, eng   the *e* in these combinations is always a short, neutral sound like the *a* in *ago* or the first *e* in *believe* (e.g., Xi**men** Qing, **Meng** Yulou)

in, ing   short *i* as in *sin* or *sing* (e.g., Ximen **Qing**, Wu **Yin**'er)

ong   the *o* sounds like *oh* (e.g., **Song** Huilian, Qin **Tong** ["Song" is not pronounced like a song one sings])

un   the rule for the closed *u* is similar to the rule for the open one: after *j*, *q*, *x*, and *y* it is the narrow French *u* of *rue*; after anything else it resembles the short English *oo* of *book* (e.g., Jia **Yun,** Ying-**chun**)

Diphthongs

ai   like the sound in the English *lie*, *high*, or *mine* (e.g., **Cai** Jing, **Dai**'an)

ao   like the sound in the English *how* or *bough* (e.g., Han **Dao**guo, Lai**bao**)

ei   like the sound in the English *day* or *mate* (e.g., **Bei**jing, Pang Chun**mei**)

ou   like the sound in the English *old* or *bowl* (e.g., Meng Yu**lou**, General **Zhou**)

The syllable *er*, sometimes found as the second element in names, is a peculiarity of the Beijing dialect that lies outside this system. It sounds like something between the English *are* and *err*.

Converting between the older, Wade-Giles system of romanization and the now-standard Pinyin system can be confusing. The following are some of the most common proper names that appear in *Plum*, in their older, Wade-Giles forms (used in Roy's translation) and their current, Pinyin forms (used in this volume and in the Egerton-Lao translation [Tuttle, 2011]):

Wade-Giles	*Pinyin*
Auntie Hsüeh	Auntie Xue
Ch'en Ching-chi	Chen Jingji
Cheng Ai-yüeh	Zheng Aiyue
Han Tao-kuo	Han Daoguo
Hsi-men Ch'ing	Ximen Qing
Hsiao-ko	Xiaoge
Hua Tzu-hsü	Hua Zixu
Ju-i	Ruyi
Kuan-ko	Guan'ge
Lai-wang	Laiwang
Lai-hsing	Laixing
Li Chiao-erh	Li Jiao'er
Li Kuei-chieh	Li Guijie
Li P'ing-erh	Li Ping'er
Meng Yü-lou	Meng Yulou
P'an Chin-lien	Pan Jinlian
P'ang Ch'un-mei	Pang Chunmei
Sun Hsüeh-o	Sun Xue'e
Sung Hui-lien	Song Huilian
Tai-an	Dai'an
Wang Liu-erh	Wang Liu'er
Wu Sung	Wu Song
Wu Yüeh-niang	Wu Yueniang
Ying Po-chüeh	Ying Bojue
Yü-hsiao	Yuxiao

We also capitalize the title *Jin Ping Mei*. *Jin Ping Mei* emphasizes the names of the three female characters to which the title refers—Pan **Jin**lian, Li **Ping**'er, and Pang Chun**mei**—while *Jin ping mei* (or *Jinpingmei*) reads the three characters as a phrase—"The plum in the golden vase."

Chinese characters are included in this volume to conform to the Modern Language Association's publication policy of giving quotations from primary texts in the original language as well as to aid those students who are learning Chinese or beginning serious inquiry into *Plum*. Roy has done a remarkable job of translation, and while he translates fully the earliest extant and most complete edition of *Jin Ping Mei*, this was not the edition that most early readers of the novel encountered. For about three hundred years, *Jin Ping Mei* referred most frequently to an edition known as the *xiuxiang* 繡像本 ("the illustrated text"), also known as the Chongzhen edition, the Chongzhen Emperor having reigned between 1628 and 1644, although that dating is based on somewhat flimsy evidence.[4]

NOTES

[1] A more modestly priced student edition that employs Pinyin romanization, with end-notes and appendixes moved online, is forthcoming from Princeton University Press.

[2] Gaohe Tang 皐鶴堂 is the pen name under which Zhang Zhupo 張竹坡 (1670–98) wrote.

[3] Notes on spelling and pronunciation haven been adapted from the edition of David Hawkes and John Minford's *The Story of the Stone* published between 1973 and 1986 (1: 12–14).

[4] For the Chongzhen edition, see Lanling Xiaoxiao Sheng, *Xinke xiuxiang piping* Jin Ping Mei 新刻繡像批評金瓶梅 (*Newly Cut, Lavishly Illustrated, and Commented On Plum in the Golden Vase*).

Part One

MATERIALS

Plum's Infamy and Influence

The Plum in the Golden Vase (*Jin Ping Mei* 金瓶梅) has been known as one of the four great masterworks of Ming dynasty fiction (*si da qishu* 四大奇書) since at least the seventeenth century, but it is also just as if not more famous for its reputation as a dirty book (*yinshu* 淫書). The novel occupies a complicated status as a masterwork and an obscene book, one that assembles practically all Ming dynasty literature into an intricate pastiche of quotations and references. It is also one of the earliest books to deal largely with the lives, pressures, and motivations of women. Prefaces to the earliest known printed editions (1618) and many subsequent editions insist on the virtues of the book, positing that only the most obtuse readers call the book a work of pornography because they read only the sex scenes. A prefatory essay by the commentator Zhang Zhupo 張竹坡 (1670–98), titled "On the First Book of Genius Not Being a Debauched Book" ("Diyi caizi shu fei yinshu lun" 第一奇書非淫書論), defends the novel against accusations of pornography. As Zhang maintains, "Those who see the debauched are themselves debauched" (淫者自見其爲淫耳; my trans.; *ZZP* 1a–2b). As early as 1590, leading writers of the day read the novel in manuscript, sharing it with one another, savoring its vivid descriptions, its nuanced representations of social interactions and the practices of daily life. They marveled at its intricate plots and structure, and they commented on its biting indictment of the immorality and banality of the age. It was not lost on them that the Song dynasty setting—which enabled comparisons of Ximen Qing (Hsi-men Ch'ing) and his six wives to Emperor Huizong and his six evil ministers, who were traditionally blamed for the fall of the Northern Song dynasty (960–1127)—was a surrogate for the contemporary Ming court and its feckless emperor, scheming ministers, and corrupt eunuchs.

Plum's fame as a dirty book has been downplayed at times and foregrounded at others, but this fame has never disappeared altogether. Its reputation as pornography has had as much of an impact on its renown as have its literary achievements. There has been a renaissance of scholarly work on *Plum* in the People's Republic of China (PRC) now that unexpurgated editions are available online, though hard copies are still hard to come by.[1] University librarians in the United States have told me that they used to have a hard time keeping uncensored editions from being stolen. In past decades, students in the PRC with editions that note exactly how many characters have been deleted from a particular passage attempted to guess exactly which words were deleted, and I've heard claims that lists of just those characters expunged from a popular edition circulated, which meant that readers could complete their censored copies. The demand for the complete novel has led to numerous crackdowns ever since the 1980s, when *Plum* could be printed in abridged and officials-only editions. In 2016 a Beijing man was fined ten thousand yuan, or about two years' salary, for privately printing an unredacted version of the novel without a license ("Beijing nanzi"), a mere slap on the wrist compared to Wan Jianquo's 1993 sentence of four years in a Hebei jail for publishing sixty thousand copies (Wolfendale). All other masterworks of Chinese fiction—*Romance of the Three Kingdoms* (*Sanguo yanyi* 三國演義), *Outlaws of the Marsh* (*Shuihu zhuan* 水滸傳), *The Story of the Stone* (*Honglou meng* 紅樓夢), and so on—have been made into television miniseries, but not *Plum*.[2] That *Plum* is an object of both fascination and contestation, a masterwork notorious for its popular iterations, is testified to by such endeavors as the failed Jin Ping Mei Park in Xixinan Village in Huangshan, Anhui, a project that cost twenty million yuan and that seeks to draw tourists to what it claims to be the setting of the novel and to the historical home of the salt merchant Wu Tianxing, who was supposedly the model for Ximen Qing.[3] The failure of the park may be tied to failures of similar ventures associated with sex such as Love Land in Chongqing, shut down by local officials before it opened in 2009, as much as to the implausibility of constructing ruins in Anhui from a fictional novel that does not mention Anhui.[4] While *Plum* has frequently been banned or censored throughout the last century, purportedly because of its licentiousness, it is just as likely that sensitivities are provoked by its representation of official corruption at every level.

Predictably, banning and censoring *Plum* has only done so much to curtail its consumption. In July 2013, for instance, a technician carrying out maintenance on a digital advertising sign near a train station in Jilin did not realize that the huge screen was still connected to his computer, which displayed images to hundreds of viewers on the street while he watched the banned erotic film *New Plum in the Golden Vase* (*Xin* Jin Ping Mei 新金瓶梅) from his room that evening (Blum).[5] Others presumably had similar ease of access to proscribed *Plum* iterations. As a commodity *Plum* reveals a world of unofficial networks and subcultures in modern China, but it also has a storied history of consumption around the world. The dual reality of *Plum*'s status as erotic literature and masterwork gave its licentious aspects gravitas and its masterwork status popular appeal. *Plum* was read in Korea, Vietnam, and Japan in its original Chinese by the educated elite only decades after its initial publication, but it was only at somewhat random moments in modern history that it was translated into the national languages of those East Asian countries.

Plum is rightly compared to *The Story of the Stone*, the other major masterwork of Chinese fiction in the premodern period, but their popular versions contrast markedly: while *Stone* is perceived as the embodiment of the height of Chinese culture, *Plum* is seen as a sexual spectacle that is either decontextualized from Chinese culture or that fetishizes aspects of that culture. Ironically, it was *Plum*'s eroticism that made the work seem to its English readers more modern than *The Story of the Stone*, with its supernatural framework. *Plum* bore the mark of a modern masterwork, namely its frank depictions of sex, and like other such modern masterworks, it was proscribed, banned, and censored in the West. In terms of both its content and form, *Plum* represents a detailed record of almost every aspect of late Ming culture, but that is clearly not why many read the book today.

Plum continues to reflect its enduring influence on Chinese culture. The 2012 satirical novel by Liu Zhenyun 刘震云, *Wo bu shi Pan Jinlian* 我不是潘金蓮 (*I Am Not Pan Jinlian*), available in English under the title *I Did Not Kill My Husband*, was made into a hugely popular film of the same title (the English title of which is *I Am Not Madame Bovary*), directed by Feng Xiaogang 馮小剛 and starring the well-known actress Fan Bingbing 範冰冰. The first scene provides a short, illustrated lecture explaining how in the Song dynasty (the historical setting of the Ming-era novel), Pan Jinlian (P'an Chin-lien) was a fictive beauty whose infidelity led to murder, her name still a byword for devious, faithless femininity. The film's heroine, however, is on a crusade to vindicate herself from the machinations of her ex-husband and his public accusation that she is a "Pan Jinlian." Jinlian, perhaps the most famous female character in Chinese literary history, is often juxtaposed with her chaste rival for that title, Lin Daiyu of *The Story of the Stone*. The former's worldly maneuverings and carnality present a stark contrast to the latter's ethereal romanticism and purity. Modern readings of Pan Jinlian's character have, however, often been more compassionate. Ouyang Yuqian 歐陽予倩 (1889–1962) rewrote Jinlian's status as the archetypal bad woman in his 1928 play *Pan Jinlian* 潘金蓮. Rather than portraying her as a licentious shrew and bloodthirsty villain, Ouyang casts her as the archetype of the free-spirited Chinese woman who is sacrificed to a rigid, male-centered social system.[6] Ouyang played the title role himself. Clara Law's 1989 film, *Pan Jinlian zhi qianshi Jinsheng* 潘金蓮之前世今生 (*Reincarnation of Golden Lotus*), and the 1986 opera by Wei Minglun, *Pan Jinlian: Yige nuren de chenlun shi* 潘金蓮: 一個女人的沉淪史 (*Pan Jinlian: The History of a Woman's Downfall*), similarly recast Pan Jinlian as a Chinese Nora or Emma Bovary, a woman with modern sensibilities, eager to choose her own husband but consistently wronged and trapped by a patriarchal society.[7] The composer Fang Man, with Guo Jie writing the libretto, recently turned *Plum* into *Golden Lily* 金蓮, an opera in three acts. The opera is an ongoing project, sung in English and including traditional Chinese orchestral instruments; portions of it have been performed at a variety of venues, the earliest of which took place in 2015 at the Aix-en-Provence Festival.

Plum's status as risqué literature and masterwork was not always a choice between two opposites—the novel could exist simultaneously on both levels. In 1687 the Kangxi 康熙 Emperor (r. 1662–1722) banned *Plum*, a circumscription that would remain in effect until the end of the Qing dynasty in 1911, but the effectiveness of that ban seems to have been limited. It was in 1695, during Kangxi's rule, that Zhang Zhupo published his commentary edition of *Plum*, which would become by far the most widely read version of the novel until at least the mid–twentieth century. Just over a decade after the publication of Zhang's commentary edition, a Manchu translation of *Plum*, apparently done in circles close to the court, was published in 1708 under the title of *Gin ping mei*

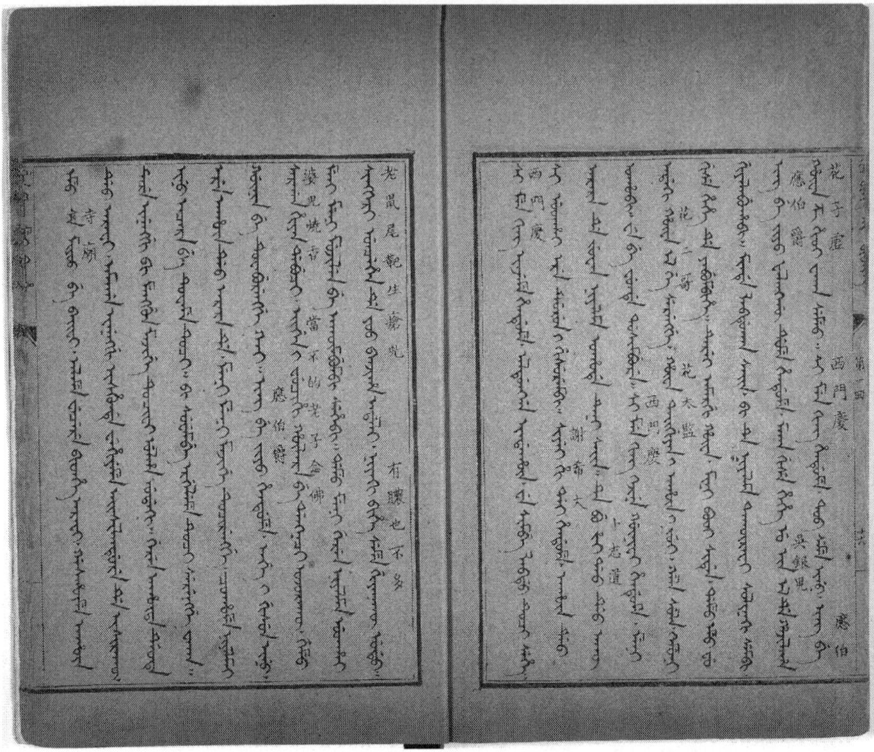

Figure 1. A page from the Manchu translation of *Plum, Gin ping mei bithe* (1708; *Plum in the Golden Vase*). Documentation and Information Center for Chinese Studies, Kyoto University.

bithe. Figure 1 shows a page from this translation with the phrase "But we are like sores on a rat's tail, there's not much pus in them: we don't have much money" (老鼠尾巴生瘡兒: 有膿也不多).[8] Some believe Kangxi's younger brother worked on the translation, others that it was primarily the work of the courtier Hesu 和素 (1652–1718), and it is regarded by some experts as the finest of all Manchu literature (Haenisch 149; Laufer 32). The Manchu translation of *Plum* was an important work, as evidenced by the fact that parts of it were used in the Manchu-Chinese primer *Qingwen qimeng* 清文啟蒙 (*Instructing the Young in the Language of the Qing*; in Manchu: *Cing wen ki meng bithe* [fig. 2; "From the *Jin Ping Mei*"]). It was also the only *Plum* text known to those who had no access to Chinese but were Manchu-literate.

Between the fall of the Qing dynasty and the founding of the PRC in 1949, many "clean versions" (*jieben* 潔本) of *Plum* were openly published. Some argued that these so-called "true editions" (*zhenben* 真本) were closer to the author's original vision because the sex scenes were all added in later. Photo reprints of the *cihua* and Zhang Zhupo editions were made in Hong Kong and

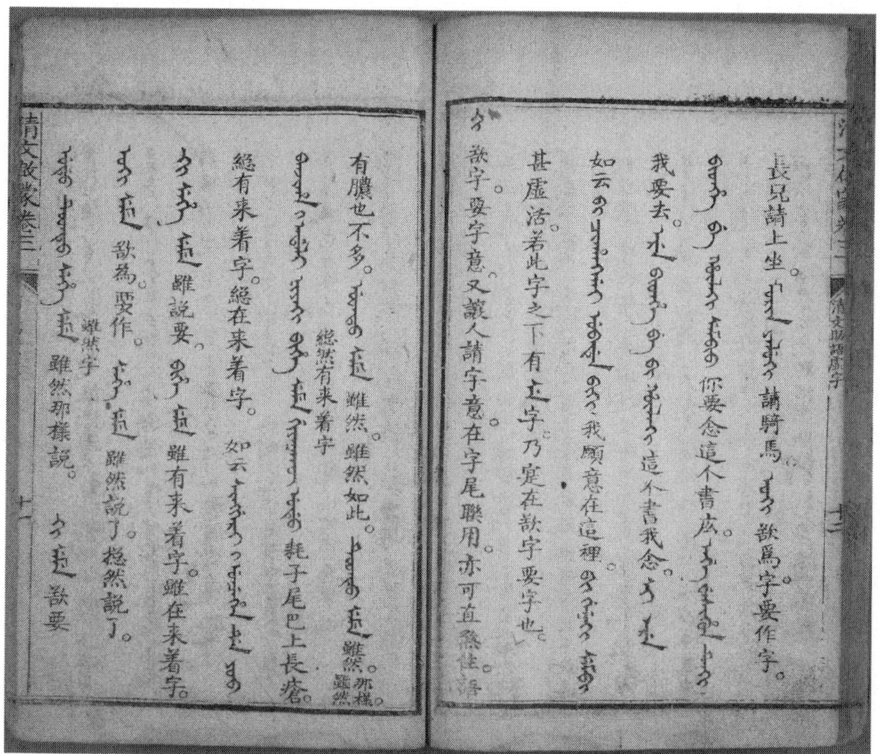

Figure 2. A page from the classic Manchu primer *Cing wen ki meng bithe* (1730; *Instructing the Young in the Language of the Qing*), retranslating the phrase in figure 1 back into Chinese. Harvard-Yenching Library.

Taiwan, where the novel had also been banned for a time. Unexpurgated, type-set editions have only become available in the past few decades, suggesting some resistance because they made reading *Plum* too easy. In mainland China a photo reprint was made in 1957, when Mao Zedong suggested that *Plum* was a good novel for revealing the decadence and depravity of Ming society and was worth reading by provincial party secretaries (Liu Jixing). This reprint was available for purchase by high-level officials only; each of the two thousand copies was individually numbered, and every owner's name was carefully filed.

Serious scholarly attention is once again being paid to *Plum* in China, as evidenced by a swell of publications in the past decades and conferences such as the August 2015 meeting in Xuzhou to celebrate thirty years of conferences on the novel in the PRC, where over seventy-five scholars presented papers. Even so, the effects of centuries of censorship have made the title *Jin Ping Mei* suggestive of lewdness, and few who are not literary scholars admit to having read it (Qi 14).

It was the hard-core realism of the sex scenes in *Plum in the Golden Vase* that interested the first consumers of the novel in English. Those scenes tended to make up the bulk or even the entirety of the earliest adaptations of *Plum*, starting with the illustrated *Adventures of Hsi Men Ching*, privately published (supposedly limited to 750 copies) in New York in 1927 by the Library of Facetious Lore (Wang Feng-Chow). This volume was the subject of Manhattan-based lawsuits brought against booksellers between 1929 and 1931 by the Society for the Suppression of Vice for violating the penal code banning so-called objectionable books. In 1932, for instance, a grand jury refused to indict Miss Frances Stelloff, the owner of the Gotham Book Mart on West 47th Street, for selling (at the price of $4.25, approximately $72 in 2021) *Adventures of Hsi Men Ching* after she successfully defended herself on the grounds that the novel was a classic ("Refuses to Indict"). A Bronx book dealer was convicted on an obscene-literature charge in connection with the sale of *Adventures of Hsi Men Ching* just the year before ("Book Dealer"). Among the subsequent translations and retellings that exclusively focused on the sexual escapades of Ximen Qing and Pan Jinlian were *The Love Pagoda: The Amorous Adventures of Hsi Men and His Six Wives* (1965; reprinted in 1967 and 1987), *Houses of Joy* (1958; reprinted in 1965 and 1968), the illustrated *Don Juan of China* (1960), and *The Harem of Hsi Men* (subtitled *The Complete Adventures of a Dissolute Mandarin, His Six Wives, His Concubines, His Singing Girls and Flower Maidens—Told with Unblushing Frankness and Rich Humor!*). These renderings are consistent with, for instance, the Harry Novak release of Koji Wakamatsu's 1968 Japanese film adaptation *Kinpeibai* 金瓶梅 as *The Notorious Concubines* ("The Golden Lotus"), billed on the film poster as "The rage! The fire! The passion! A thousand year old ribald classic! Banned for 400 years! A love affair from one of the world's best classics of eroticism" but also labeled with an excerpt from *The New York Times Book Review* stating that "it is possible that this is the greatest novel ever written!" (Film poster). For English readers of translations, reviews of translations, and trial proceedings in the first half of the twentieth century, *Plum*'s reputation was that of a racy book, albeit one that evoked in exquisite detail the realism of the bedroom. It was a masterwork, and therefore justified reading, but it was an ancient, foreign masterwork for our time.[9]

This volume is aimed at readers who are aware that *Plum* is, among other things, a major achievement of world literature and who want to teach it, or at least to read it. As David T. Roy writes:

> With the possible exceptions of *The Tale of Genji* (1010) and *Don Quixote* (1615), neither of which [*Plum*] resembles, but with both of which it can bear comparison, there is no earlier work of prose fiction of equal sophistication in world literature. The only other work of Chinese fiction which can be said to be its equal is the eighteenth-century novel *Honglou meng* [*The Story of the Stone*] which is demonstrably in its debt.
>
> ("*Chin P'ing Mei*" 287)

We hope that our readers will become interested in *Plum* not just for its vivid portrayal of characters and its incredibly intricate and entertaining structure but also for its other virtues, such as its depiction of virtually every facet of sixteenth-century life in China, its discussions of connoisseurship, its catalogs of artifacts, and the quality and variety of its poetry.

Part 1, "Materials," seeks to provide interested readers, students, and teachers with information that will aid them in pursuing their own inquiries into *Plum*. Part 2, "Approaches," presents a solid, accessible introduction to most of the major topics teachers might want to cover in the classroom, and indeed, many of the recommended readings are written by contributors to this volume. Part 1 offers a guide to some of *Plum*'s more confusing aspects and suggests topics, questions, and sources to get interested readers and teachers started.

Historical Context

The action of *Plum* takes place between 1112 and 1127, during the reign of Emperor Huizong 徽宗 (r. 1100–25) of the Northern Song dynasty (960–1127). The novel describes the internal collapse of that regime, which culminated in the conquest of North China by the Jurchen Jin dynasty (1115–1234) in 1127. Although the author set his novel in the Song dynasty, close reading reveals that the conditions he describes are really those of his own day—the reigns of the Jiajing and Wanli Emperors of the Ming dynasty. These two emperors sat on the throne from 1521 to 1566 and from 1572 to 1620, respectively, and for nearly a century they were "among the most irresponsible rulers in the history of imperial irresponsibility" (Roy, Introduction xxx). In his introduction to *Plum*, David Tod Roy uses the *Dictionary of Ming Biography*, edited by L. Carrington Goodrich and Chaoying Fang, to provide summaries of the careers of these emperors. Because *Plum* presents such a clever, sustained critique of these rulers, and because this fact is so important to understanding the novel, it bears repeating those summaries here, more fully and with Pinyin romanization to aid teachers and students:

> In the early years of his long reign the [Jiajing] emperor's attention was focused domestically on this struggle [over succession], and in the later years he turned to the cult of religious Daoism in a search for a life without death. Both concerns ruined many able officials and wasted the energy and wealth of the empire. In foreign relations these years saw Mongol bands sweeping across the Great Wall almost at will, raiding and killing from the northwestern frontier to the Liaodong peninsula. Along the southeast coast the [Japanese pirates] caused equal suffering and destruction and erupted just as often. In spite of his concentration on selfish

whims and the menace on his borders, Jiajing never let anyone usurp his power and authority. In his time the rich grew richer and the poor became impoverished, particularly in the lower Yangtze area. Wealth bred leisure, which demanded luxuries and entertainment; it also encouraged the development of theatre, art, literature, and printing. The political vigor of the empire, however, began to decline, and the house of Ming showed signs of senescence.   (Goodrich and Fang 1: 315)

When the [Wanli] emperor died in 1620, the far northeast frontier had been overrun by the Manchus; ruinous tax increases or extortions had driven large numbers of people into banditry or rebellion in all parts of the empire, and state coffers were nevertheless drained; posts in both central and provincial government agencies were vacant as often as not, and officials on duty were locked in partisan antagonisms that almost paralyzed the government; and for a quarter century the emperor had done his best to neglect affairs of state. Extravagance, corruption, and ineptitude had become so normal that post-Ming historians have consistently attributed the collapse of the dynasty in the 1640s to trends that developed in Wanli times, specifically blaming the emperor himself.   (1: 325)

These dictionary entries describe the world of *Plum* and the one that readers find in microcosm in Qinghe, the town in which Ximen Qing works and lives. In hindsight, this corruption, malaise, bickering, and ineptitude at court was the beginning of the end of the Ming dynasty—a view, it seems, that was also held by *Plum*'s author. To fully understand the historical and literary milieu of *Plum*, though, it is useful to consider this impending collapse amid the height of Ming glory. In the late sixteenth century, China's achievements in culture and the arts were remarkable, urban and commercial life were spreading new levels of prosperity, and Chinese skills in printing and the manufacture of porcelain and silk exceeded anything that could be found in Europe at the time. Jonathan Spence puts the glory and fall of the Ming in perspective:

While the West was at this time the hub of global explorations that brought it extensive knowledge of the world as a whole, the Ming rulers not only had drawn back from overseas ventures and the knowledge that might have come from them, but had begun a pattern of self-defeating behavior that within fifty years would bring their dynasty to a violent end. . . . The loosely woven fabric of Ming China's state and economy began to unravel at many points. Falling tax revenues led to failures to pay the army promptly. Troop desertions encouraged border penetration by hostile tribes. A flow of silver from the West brought unexpected stresses in the Chinese economy. Poor state granary supervision and harsh weather conditions led to undernourishment and a susceptibility to pestilence among rural populations. Random gangs of the disaffected coalesced into armies whose only ideol-

ogy was survival. By 1644 all of these elements combined in such a viru-
lent fashion that the last Ming emperor committed suicide.   (*Search* 3)

Spence tellingly begins his well-known book and commonly used classroom text
The Search for Modern China with a chapter on the late Ming—the period in
which *Plum* was written and the period that it both celebrates and excoriates. It
is a complex era that embodied the height of traditional Chinese culture and
power, but also one in which an incipient global modernity was beginning to complicate age-old domestic issues.

Plum, among many other things, is the story of misrule. Like the Wanli court,
the Ximen Qing household is full of schemers and sycophants, with a capricious
and debauched figure at its head. Some readers find in *Plum*'s characters antecedents in powerful ministers or eunuchs at court—famous historical figures
whose venery and greed are blamed for the fall of the Northern Song dynasty.
The practice of using eunuchs—castrated male attendants whose official job was
to supervise the management of day-to-day business in the palace—in Chinese
courts had existed for more than two thousand years. Ming dynasty rulers employed many more eunuchs than their predecessors, though, and by Wanli's time
there were over ten thousand eunuchs in the capital.

From the 1580s onward, the Wanli Emperor began to neglect his official duties, and in his absence, considerable power accrued to court eunuchs. Since the
emperor would not come out from the inner quarters of the Forbidden City, eunuchs were the gatekeepers to imperial power and began to play a central role
in the political life of the country. Their influence grew as Emperor Wanli assigned them to collect revenues in the provinces, often abusing their position.
In some cases they tyrannized wealthy provincial families and used imperial
guards to enforce their will and to imprison, torture, and even kill their political
enemies. The most spectacular example of these abuses occurred in the person of
Wei Zhongxian 魏忠賢 (1568–1627), famous as one of the most powerful and notorious eunuchs in history. Tales of his rise and fall spawned many novels and
plays, starting just years after his death.

As often as they are portrayed as suspicious characters and villains (and occasionally heroes, as with tales of the Ming voyager and diplomat Zheng He
鄭和 [1371–1433]), it is important to remember that eunuchs were also victims
of human trafficking that relied on mutilating and desexing young men. To sell
a son into service, a family must have been extremely poor, given the historical
preference for male progeny. Families would castrate their sons and sell them
into service attending to the emperor and his many sexual partners. Poor families would endanger their own lineage so that their sons could be employed tend-
ing to the emperor's.

Although there may have been as many as ten thousand eunuchs sold into
service to the Wanli court, certainly this number is a fraction of the young
women bought and sold throughout the empire in the same period. The buying
and selling of young people—particularly young women—was common until

the early twentieth century, when the practice was outlawed. Poor families could sell their daughters into service to wealthier ones to ensure their daughters' survival or to concentrate resources on sons. Some sales agreements would allow for daughters to be bought out of service, making their situation similar to that of indentured servants. As they grew older, young women in the service of wealthy households might become concubines to the young men of the family or be married off as the proper wives of manservants. In the world of Chinese domestic workers, there were also hereditary servants, sometimes the descendants of criminals or prisoners of war. It would be hard to argue that their status was significantly different than that of enslaved people. The sexual implications and repercussions of buying and selling young women suffuses *Plum*, as almost every woman who joins the Ximen household does so through a monetary transaction.

Authorship and Origins

Trying to determine the author of *Plum* is important in itself and for its implications about the literary culture in which the novel was written. Tina Lu has pointed out that *Plum* is

> embedded in a textual world, not just because of its relationship with *Water Margin*, but also in the way the novel makes explicit and highly artificed reference to the enormous diversity of late Ming literary life. No other work in the tradition borrows so heavily from other texts: vernacular stories, works of pornography, histories, dramas, popular songs, jokes, and prosimetric narratives, and even texts far outside of the parameters of the literary, such as official gazettes, contracts, and menus. These quotations are not approximate, as they would be if transmitted orally, but precise, and they are deployed with ironic distance. A novel that initially circulated in manuscript, it is also a profound reflection on the fungibility of all texts in print culture. (107)

The author of *Plum* is known only by the pseudonym Lanling Xiaoxiao Sheng 蘭陵笑笑生 ("The Scoffing Scholar of Lanling"), and without new evidence, we may never know his true identity. There is no shortage of theories concerning the authorship of *Plum*, however. Modern scholars writing in Chinese, Japanese, French, and English have proposed over fifty possible candidates with some evidence (Wu Gan 33–43). Some of these—for example, Li Kaixian 李開先 (1502–68), Xu Wei 徐渭 (1521–93), Wang Shizhen 王世貞 (1526–90), Li Xianfang 李先芳 (1511–94), Jia Sanjin 賈三近 (1534–92), Tu Long 屠隆 (1542–1605), Yuan Hongdao 袁宏道 (1568–1610), Dong Qichang 董其昌 (1555–1636), Li Yu 李漁 (1510–80), and Tang Xianzu 湯顯祖 (1550–1616)—are familiar names in Chinese literary history; others are less well known.[10] Many of the proposed possible authors were associated with the circle of literary men who first recorded reading *Plum* in manuscript in the last decade of the sixteenth century. Rather than summarize the scholarly debates surrounding *Plum*'s authorship and attempt some sort of resolution, it may be useful to repeat a famous story—one that is certainly apocryphal though also telling and influential—about how the novel came to be written. Many of the editions of *Plum* available to readers between the seventeenth and twentieth centuries contain prefatory items that serve as apologies for the novel. One of these, by Zhang Zhupo, entitled "Ku-xiao shuo" 苦孝說 ("The Bitterness of Filial Piety"), has traditionally been interpreted as referring to the legend of how *Plum* was created.[11]

This legend of *Plum*'s origin has it that Wang Shizhen, a famous writer and historian, authored the novel. Wang's father had been put to death by the evil minister Yan Song 嚴嵩 (1481–1568; some accounts say it was Tang Shunzhi 唐順之 [1507–60]) for selling the minister what Wang's father was told was the original of a famous painting, which turned out to be a copy. Wang was bent on avenging his father and set his sights on Yan's son, Yan Shifan 嚴世蕃 (1513–65), who had risen in rank and was a model of corruption.[12] Yan Shifan's fatal flaw, so the story goes, was his penchant for licentious literature. Wang, a great Confucian scholar, was capable of incredible literary feats, and so he set himself to writing a novel that would be of interest to Yan. In a matter of weeks (some accounts say three years), Wang finished a novel of one hundred chapters, weaving into it not just pornographic elements but also, through the portrayal of the corrupt protagonist, Ximen Qing, a pitiless satire of his enemy. That Ximen Qing stood for Yan Shifan was a fact that no one could fail to recognize, since "Ximen" means "western gate" and Shifan's style was Donglou, meaning "eastern pavilion." But Wang was not content simply to mock his enemy, so he soaked the pages in poison and hired a merchant to sell the book to Yan. Falling prey to his desires, Yan bought the book. Licking his fingers to turn the pages, he slowly ingested more and more poison until finally, when Yan read to the last page and the story of his own degraded existence was done, he fell dead.[13]

Zhang Zhupo writes elsewhere that he does not believe that *Plum* is a roman à clef, that "hearsay in such matters is generally apocryphal and not to be taken seriously. . . . Therefore I shall ignore the theory that Ximen Qing was intended to represent Yan Shifan" (Roy, "Chang Chu-p'o's Commentary" 119). Yet he alludes to the theory repeatedly, to gesture at the frustrated anguish that the anonymous author must have felt while writing the novel. More remarkable than this most assuredly fictional account is the fact that it endured through so many printings and subsequent editions up to the modern period. The legend must have been widely known, as it was to Lu Xun 魯迅 (1881–1936), known as the father of modern Chinese literature, who taught it at Beijing University and records it in the 1934 printed edition of his lectures (*Brief History* 220–21). The legend points to the contradiction of a pornographic, literary masterwork and the concern that inexperienced or naive readers of fiction could do themselves harm.

That the author crafted *Plum* to appeal to these debauched readers, that they might read themselves to death, and that this was done in the service of filial duty was both an apology for the novel (and the novel form) and an enticement to read it. Zhang's preface "The Bitterness of Filial Piety," which can also be translated as "Frustrated Filial Piety," describes how the author lost his father, probably through some act of injustice, and hence lost all opportunity to fulfill his filial duties. Instead of turning to revenge, the author, as conceived by Zhang, relieved his "frustrated" filiality by writing about filiality in the *Plum*.

Other prefaces to *Plum* put the onus on readers to take away from the novel the correct message through a contemplation of its artistry and constructedness. The author of the dated preface to the *cihua* edition of the novel claimed, and others repeated the claim, that "[h]e who reads the *Jin Ping Mei* and responds with a feeling of compassion is a Bodhisattva; he who responds with a feeling of apprehension is a superior man; he who responds with a feeling of enjoyment is a petty person; and he who responds with a feeling of emulation is no better than a beast" (余嘗曰: 讀《金瓶梅》而生憐憫心者, 菩薩也; 生畏懼心者, 君子也; 生歡喜心者, 小人也; 生效法心者, 乃禽獸耳; 1.6; 1b–2a). *Plum*, in this vision, is like the aphrodisiac that Ximen Qing procures midway through the novel. If taken thoughtfully and in moderation, it has a tonifying effect and can enhance enjoyment, but if abused and taken for granted, it can result in the deterioration of one's vital forces. The potential danger in the legend of *Plum*, and in its possible corrupting influence, was part of the attraction for readers. Even a comment by Zhang Xinzhi 張新之, on the more chaste masterwork of Chinese fiction, *The Story of the Stone*, written centuries later, claims that "*The Story of the Stone* is a literary work that is not only very appealing but, more important, it also carves a deep impression on the mind, moving and transforming one's nature and emotions. It goes even further than *Plum in the Golden Vase* in producing potentially dangerous effects, in that readers are prone to recognize only its immediate surface, failing to perceive what lies on the other side" (Plaks, "How to Read" 323). The legend of *Plum*'s origins is useful to discuss with students because it demonstrates a real concern about the dangers of the novel, its threat to social order, and the battle over who has the authority or ability to read the novel. In addition to a hermeneutic struggle over entertainment literature and pornography, the legend also reveals concerns about official corruption and justice as well as the circulation and vetting of knowledge. I include some accounts that debate the veracity of *Plum*'s origin story at the end of part 1.

Editions of *Plum*

Scholars generally agree that *Plum* was written late in the Jiajing era (1521–67) or early in the Wanli era (1573–1620) of the Ming dynasty. The historian Wu

Han 吳晗 (1909–69) suggested that the Ming reality depicted in *Plum* is most likely a reflection of the period after the death of the important prime minister Zhang Juzheng 張居正 in 1582. Several prominent scholars of the day commented on the novel as it circulated in manuscript in the last decade of the sixteenth century and the first decade of the seventeenth century. It clearly is a work of stupendous concentration and imagination and must have taken many years to write. *Plum* exists in three major recensions: the *Jin Ping Mei cihua* (*Plum in the Golden Vase: A Ballad Tale*); the *xiuxiang* 繡像, or "illustrated," edition, which includes two hundred woodblock prints; and the *diyi qishu* 第一奇書 ("most marvelous book") edition, which contains Zhang Zhupo's commentary.[14] The *cihua* edition (1618) is the earliest extant version.[15] The *xiuxiang* and *diyi qishu* editions are practically identical textually, but the *cihua* and *xiuxiang* versions present important differences. There is no extant urtext of *Plum*. Scholars are starkly divided as to which of the (for sake of simplicity) two recensions is older, which is more authentic, and which is better.[16] Traditional views placed the *xiuxiang* edition later, in the period of the Chongzhen Emperor's reign (1628–44), though that is based on somewhat weak evidence. The Zhang Zhupo commentary edition dates to 1695, and it eclipsed the other two versions in popularity for the next two and a half centuries because of the quality of Zhang's commentary (fig. 3).

Some critical estimates view the *xiuxiang* recension—the one (or one very similar to the one) that Zhang uses for his commentary edition—as tighter, lacking a number of minor characters and details, and greatly reducing the chantefable quality of the *cihua* text, resulting in a more concise style and controlled plotline.[17] The opposite view regards the *xiuxiang* text as far inferior, or even as a bowdlerization of the *cihua* version. Roy, who not only translated into English the *cihua* version, with all its poetry and paratexts, but also added thousands of endnotes explaining intertextual and cultural references, felt strongly that the *xiuxiang* version was an inferior recension of the text, published by an editor

> who not only completely rewrote the better part of the first chapter to suit his own ideas of how a novel should begin, but made significant alterations, including both deletions and additions, on every page of the remainder of the work. It is clear that this editor did not understand certain significant features of the author's technique, especially in the use of quoted material, for much of the poetry incorporated in the original edition is either deleted or replaced with new material that is often less relevant to the context. It is, however, precisely the subtle way in which the author uses poems, songs, snatches of dramatic dialogue, and other types of borrowed material as a form of running ironic commentary on the characters and action of the novel that makes this work unique. The inevitable effect of any tampering with this quoted material is to distort seriously the author's intentions and render the interpretation of his work that much more difficult.
>
> (Introduction xx–xxi)

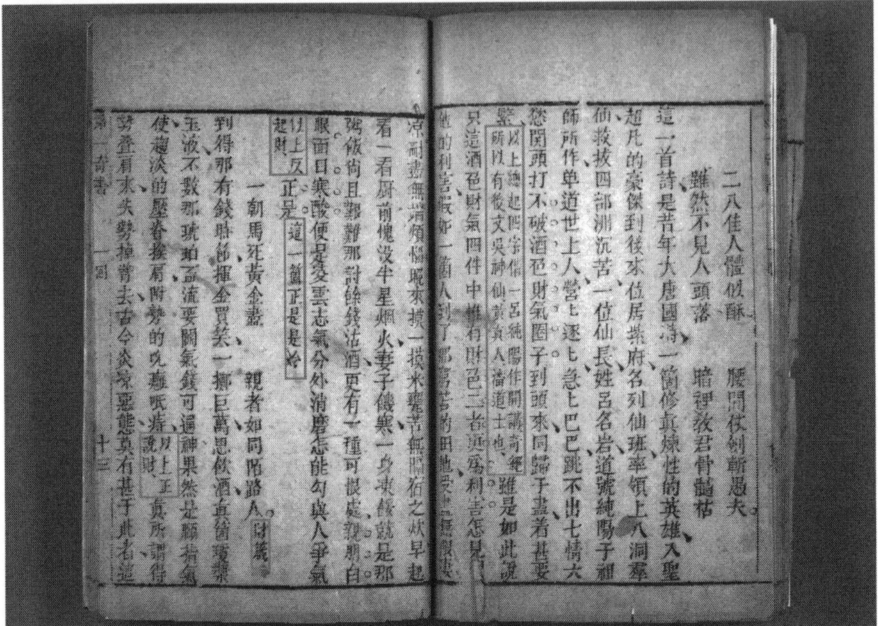

[page 13 verso]: **nothing but dirty looks,** and **his face is covered in humiliation and shame; in** such a situation a man's most noble ambitions would fritter away, and he is certainly in no position to get into passionate rivalry with others, *The above passage brings up wealth negatively.* **Truly:** *This 'Truly' is cold.*

> As soon as one's mount dies and gold used up,
> Kith and kin turn into strangers. *This is a proverb about wealth.*

When a man comes into possession of money, he may spend it like water to purchase the pleasures of romance. The wine he drinks will be like jade elixir, not to mention being poured from precious amber cups. Should he enter into a spirited rivalry with anyone, his wealth will buy him the path to the gods. With a mere nod he can order people about, and people will press forward and flock to him to curry favor. They will even lick his sores and suck the pus out with their tongues. *The above passage describes wealth positively.* It is indeed as they say, 'When a man has power, followers come in throngs; when a man loses power, they leave him without a backward glance.' From past to present, no situation is harder to bear than this change from hot to cold. [page 14 recto, not pictured] Aren't these people victims of the plague of wealth? *The author divides the text here into four branches: one branch is on sex; one branch is on wealth; one branch is on wealth in the eyes of the enlightened man; one branch is on sex in the eyes of the enlightened man. In each of the first two branches, he inserts descriptions of alcohol and of passion, for his true focus is on wealth and sex, but he weaves in alcohol and passion. Thus, his method of branching is lively and not rigid.*

Then there is the plague of sex. Look at today's world: how many men are like **Liu Xia Hui,** who was not tempted even with a maiden in his arms? Or like **the man of Lu,** who closed his doors on a woman coming to him? Or like **Guan Yunchang,** who, with a lighted candle, kept chaste watch over his sisters-in-law till dawn? *These three men who were not intimidated by sexual temptation are positive models.*

It is one thing to have several wives and concubines at home . . .

Figure 3. *Above,* page 13 from chapter 1 of a 1695 Zhang Zhupo commentary edition of *Plum, Gaohe Tang piping diyi qishu* Jin Ping Mei 皋鶴堂批評第一奇書金瓶梅 (Plum in the Golden Vase: *The First Marvelous Book, with Gaohe Tang Commentary*), with Zhang's comments outlined. Courtesy Waseda University Library. *Below,* English translation of that and the following page, with comments in italics and words with *quan* emphasis marks from the original in bold. Translation by Xiaofei Tian, adapted from "*Jin Ping Mei:* The Number One Marvellous Book Noted and Commented on by Gaohetang," *Renditions,* vols. 81–82, p. 45.

Both views presume, as Xiaofei Tian points out, that the *cihua* version was the base text, which may or may not have been the case. Tian defends the literary merits of the *xiuxiang* version as a self-conscious, fully intentional, well-conceived literary construct, no less so than the *cihua* version. Moreover, she makes the case that the two recensions

> show a series of divergences in terms of conceptual framework, narrative style, and characterization. The *cihua* recension is clearly grounded in a social vision and ethic that we recognize in some way as "Confucian," whether or not we tie the values in the text to one particular school of Confucianism. The *xiuxiang* recension's divergences from the *cihua* often soften the strictness of moral judgment, leaving room for compassion, for mercy, and for a discovery of the emptiness of the passions; in short, both in the details of representation and the larger restructuring of the narrative we see Buddhist values, broadly defined, playing a large role in the ideological background of the novel.   ("Preliminary Comparison" 351)

The ending of *Plum*, in both editions, is open to debate, and it is often cast in terms of the moralizing destruction of the Ximen family, its integrity, and its lineage (i.e., in a Confucian light) or as redemptive sacrifice and forgiveness arrived at by means of karmic rebirth (that is, in keeping with Buddhist ideology). For this reason, choosing between one version and the other (or, as we shall see, between one translation and the other) does not necessarily limit hermeneutic or pedagogical options with regard to two of China's most essential religions and philosophies. The author and his preferred text will likely never be known, so we must come to terms with the notion that whichever text we are reading is just as likely to be an augmented version of his vision as it is to be a diminished one.

When considering which version to teach, instructors should be aware of certain differences between editions and between the respective translations of these editions. First, a recension very similar to the *xiuxiang* edition with commentary by Zhang Zhupo was essentially the only version that readers encountered from the middle or late seventeenth century until the mid–twentieth century, when the *cihua* recension, rediscovered in Shanxi in 1932 and purchased by the Beijing National Library, started to be reprinted. That is, for three of the four centuries since it appeared in print, *Plum was* the Zhang Zhupo commentary edition. This edition's first chapters begin with *Plum*'s protagonist, Ximen Qing, and his sworn brotherhood, while the *cihua* edition opens with Wu Song (Wu Sung), the tiger-slaying hero of *Outlaws of the Marsh*. Readers of *Outlaws* know that in that novel Wu Song kills Pan Jinlian and Ximen Qing as revenge for murdering his brother, meaning that expectations when reading *Plum* are likely to focus on retribution for transgression and a comparison of a true hero with a corrupt protagonist. The first part of chapter 1 in the *cihua* edition serves, in Roy's view, as a prologue that, through references to well-known stories, makes it clear that Ximen Qing is meant to be analogous to a benighted ruler and that one of the novel's major themes is the unfortunate consequences, for both society and the individual, of failure to take moral responsibility for one's actions ("Appendix I"). This emphasis is often understood as a type of Confucian moralizing. The *xiuxiang* version opens with an image of Ximen and his brotherhood of rascals and interchangeable sycophants as they indulge in sex, alcohol, and gambling. This emphasis on the emptiness of sex and money alerts the reader to the *xiuxiang* edition's more general leanings toward Buddhism. After dwelling on the true nature of money and sex, the *xiuxiang* narrator concludes:

> Well does the *Diamond Sutra* speak of this foolish life "as dream and as illusion; as lightning and as dew." For though at the end of life all things are vain, during life men cannot bear the loss even of a trifle. We may be so strong that, unaided, we can lift a cauldron or tow a ship, but, when the end draws near, our bones will lose their strength and our sinews their power. Though our wealth may give us mountains of bronze and valleys of gold, they will melt like snow when the last moment comes. Though our beauty outshine the moon, and the flowers dare not raise their heads to look on us, the day will come when we shall be nothing but corruption, and men will hold their noses as they pass us by.   (Egerton and Lao 1.1.32)

> 只有那金剛經上兩句說得好, 他說道: "如夢幻泡影, 如電復如露." 見得人生在世, 一件也少不得, 到了那結束時, 一件也用不著. 隨著你舉鼎蕩舟的神力, 到頭來少不得骨軟筋麻; 由著你銅山金谷的奢華, 正好時卻又要冰消雪散. 假饒你閉月羞花的容貌, 一到了垂眉落眼, 人皆掩鼻而過之.   (*XXP* 1.2b–3a)

Yet, as some have noted, the prologue-esque sections of the first chapter, in which the narrator explicates the novel's primary themes, and the prefatory poems contained in these sections also differ between versions in striking ways. The *cihua* version warns the reader about the danger of *qingse* 情色 ("sexual passions," or "passion and beauty" in Roy's translation), which could be interpreted as having a Buddhist overtone, since the opposite of enlightenment (*kong* 空, or "emptiness") is *se* 色 ("form," "appearance," "passion"). The *xiuxiang* text opens with a poem entitled "Copper Bird Terrace," by Cheng Changwen 程長文, a woman poet who lived during the Tang dynasty. Copper Bird Terrace was built in 210 CE by the military leader and statesman Cao Cao 曹操 (155–220), who ordered his concubines to reside on the terrace after his death, playing music, singing, and dancing to his spirit tablet. In the context of *Plum*, this favorite poetic topic evokes Ximen's dying wish that all his wives remain together in his household. That this wish is inevitably unfulfilled at the end of the novel should be understood a colossal failure given the Confucian emphasis on the stable family as the basis of social order.[18] For all their differences, the two recensions both contain themes and ideals drawn from the entire range of Chinese beliefs and practices. The two editions differ less in terms of meaning than in terms of emphasis. From a pedagogical standpoint, teaching both versions of chapter 1, which is about twenty-five pages long, would allow students to engage and debate these differences.

The two recensions are markedly different in terms of their respective styles. The *cihua* edition conspicuously includes elements characteristic of marketplace storytellers, such as "if you want to know what happens next, pray hear it told in the following session" (畢竟未知後來何如, 且聽下回分解; my trans.; 1.21b). Such elements are entirely absent in the *xiuxiang* edition. If the *xiuxiang* recension used the *cihua* version as its base text, it deleted, rewrote, or abridged about half of the latter's popular songs, dramatic lines, and other verse forms that give the novel the qualities of a chantefable. Still, prose interspersed with verse was a structural convention of vernacular fiction at the time, and the *xiuxiang* edition did not completely depart from that tradition, retaining well over two hundred such pieces (Qi). Perhaps more important, the two editions have vastly different verses that open and close each chapter. The semantic relationship between these prefatory verses and the prose text is difficult to interpret in the *cihua* edition because these verses often seem to have little to do with, and at times even contradict, the events of the chapter that follow (Satyendra 4). Lively debate surrounds these, too, as they seem to indicate very different narrative aesthetics of their respective author-editors. The *xiuxiang* edition seemingly refined or rewrote ninety of the one hundred prefatory verses, making them more consistent in structure and more closely aligned with the events of the chapter that follow. The chapter title couplets are also usually the lines taken as the captions for that chapter's two illustrations.

One last bit of evidence further suggests that the editor of the *xiuxiang* edition was seeking to extricate the text from its attachments to its forebears. It edits out a plot borrowed from *Outlaws of the Marsh* in chapter 84, making the new edition of *Plum* seem somewhat more independent from that source, its meanings, and its legacy.

The Golden Lotus, Translated by Clement Egerton and Lao She

Just as the *xiuxiang* recension of *Jin Ping Mei* was virtually the only edition of the novel available to readers for three hundred years, the Clement Egerton and Lao She translation of that recension, entitled *The Golden Lotus*, was the only complete version of *Jin Ping Mei* in English for most of the twentieth century. (Roy's five-volume authoritative translation, *Plum in the Golden Vase*, was published between 1993 and 2013.) Until Robert Hegel edited and reprinted a two-volume edition of *Lotus* with Tuttle in 2011, *The Golden Lotus* existed only as a four-volume set originally published in 1939 and reprinted in 1953, 1954, 1955, 1957, 1959, 1964, 1969, 1972, and 1995. The early printings translated the racy portions of the novel into Latin to prevent curious youngsters from infiltrating their fathers' libraries and being corrupted by those passages, and even the Latin was missing passages. It was not until the 1972 edition that these passages were finally translated into English.

Like the Roy translation, *Golden Lotus* amplifies aspects of its respective base text. The Egerton-Lao translation was based on a *xiuxiang* or Zhang Zhupo edition of the novel. While the edition it is based on omits a great deal of the poetry found in the *cihua* "chantefable" recension, the translation leaves out even more. *Golden Lotus* therefore magnifies the "written" qualities of *Jin Ping Mei* in a manner (coincidentally?) consistent with the *xiuxiang* editors-authors, changing or omitting much of the poetry, which is often sung, in order to tighten the narrative and clarify the plot. Of the important poems that begin each chapter in the Chinese versions, *Lotus* translates only about half of them, and often incompletely. The text also drops all the epilogue-like poems at the end of every chapter. Further, *Lotus* translates only about a quarter of the poems in the main text of chapters. It might be argued that deleting these poems from the middle of chapters does not seriously threaten the integrity of the novel, but that excising the prologues and epilogues does. For *Plum*—and indeed, for many premodern Chinese novels—prologues and epilogues are a crucial part of the structure (Qi 164). To be sure, the poems in *Plum* are of varied quality—many have little literary value as poems, some are virtual masterpieces, and others are borrowed from famous poets. No matter the quality, however, the poems serve the narrative and characterization and are meant to be interpreted within the context of the novel. The poems that Egerton does translate are often rendered in prose, while others are expressed in free verse, as Roy does with almost all the poems in *Plum*.

For all that is lost, it must be said that the Egerton-Lao translation was prepared with readers of English literature in mind. It is fluent and, some believe, the best of the two complete translations at retaining the humor of the dialogue. Most of the praise given to the Egerton-Lao translation, though, relates to the fact that it is "without serious errors" (Hsia 153). It is generally more conversational and freer than the Roy translation, though it also smooths over the heteroglossia of the novel—the many different registers of language in the text, both in terms of dialogue and intertext.

The revised version of the translation, which appeared in 2011, was done under the direction of Robert Hegel, one of the world's foremost experts on premodern Chinese fiction. Hegel's editing has given the Egerton-Lao translation new life. Perhaps most important in Hegel's edition is his foregrounding of Lao She's contribution to the translation. Lao She 老舍, the pen name of Shu Qingchun 舒慶春 (1899–1966), was a major figure in twentieth-century Chinese literature, recognized above all for his novel *Rickshaw* (*Luotuo xiangzi* 駱駝祥子), also known as *Rickshaw Boy* and *Camel Xiangzi*, and his play *Teahouse* (*Chaguan* 茶馆). How much Lao She contributed his expertise and voice to the translation of *Golden Lotus* is a matter of debate. For those for whom Chinese is a second language, it seems natural to suspect the contribution was considerable, especially since Egerton states in the preface to the translation that he had only been studying Chinese for three years when he undertook the translation. Egerton makes it clear that Lao She's involvement was significant, but he does not specify its nature or extent. Whatever the case, Lao She's contribution to the Egerton translation increases its value and deserves greater acknowledgment than it has received.

Hegel's edition of *The Golden Lotus* is also more accessible than previous editions because it uses standard Pinyin romanization, which will be more familiar to students of Chinese than the previous Wade-Giles system is. This version also transliterates female names, making them seem less exotic or caricatural than previous versions of the translation do: Li Ping'er (Li P'ing-erh) is no longer "Lady of the Vase." Wu Yueniang (Wu Yüeh-niang) is no longer "Moon Lady." Teachers may want to seriously consider using Hegel's edition of *The Golden Lotus* in the classroom, especially given its brief but masterful introduction, its succinct character list, and its reduced cost and bulk. Although many of the structural or generic differences between a Chinese novel (*changpian xiaoshuo* 長篇小說) and an English novel are obfuscated in the Egerton-Lao translation, teachers who wish to focus on the story, its depictions of daily life and practice in seventeenth-century China, or the novel's place in literary history, or who are simply willing to make concessions for a briefer, cheaper text, may find *The Golden Lotus* appealing.[19]

The David Tod Roy Translation

The Roy translation of *Plum*, finished in 2013, is a masterwork of the art of translation and a marvel of scholarship. Its publication has been the primary motivation for putting this volume together, since Roy's translation enables a full range of pedagogical approaches to the novel in English. Part of the problem in making selections and choosing pedagogical approaches, apart from the translation's sheer length (3,672 pages), is the quantity of ancillary and scholarly materials presented in it.[20] Roy's translation will appeal to those who want to stay closer to the oldest extant version of the novel and who would like to gain a deeper understanding of this masterpiece of entertainment literature. In addition to the extensive reference matter, the thorough introduction, and the valuable, complete list of characters (which is more of a summary of character biographies), Roy's translation also includes the two hundred woodblock prints found in the *xiuxiang* editions but not included in the Egerton-Lao translation (fig. 4). In his five-volume translation, Roy presents many important aids to the reader. Since instructors rarely teach all five volumes of *Plum*, and since the notes are a forest of scholarship only very intrepid readers dare wander into, I discuss some of those aids here so that they can be more fruitfully and efficiently utilized.

Roy's introduction to volume 1 of *The Plum in the Golden Vase*, subtitled *The Gathering*, discusses the origins and meaning of the title *Jin Ping Mei*, common readings and misreadings of the novel, editions in Chinese and English, the nature of the story, generic conventions particular to Chinese novels, *Plum's*

Figure 4. Two woodblock prints from a 1695 edition of *Plum*, Jin Ping Mei *diyi qishu* 金瓶梅第一奇書 (Plum in the Golden Vase: *The First Marvelous Book*). Courtesy Waseda University Library. *Right*, Wu Song causes a ruckus in the tea shop. *Left*, he is arrested and exiled. Roy reprints these in chapter 10 of his translation.

especially dense intertextuality, and the novel's creative use of traditional formulaic material (Introduction). Roy's is the only English translation of the earlier, fuller, more complex *cihua* edition of *Jin Ping Mei*, and his translation includes all the prefatory material in the *cihua* edition, while the Egerton-Lao translation does not include any prefatory material. Roy explains the importance of these prefatory items, particularly the first, in which the "Master of Delight" claims that the author of *Plum* is a friend of his (Introduction xxii). Scholars have gone to great pains to identify the author, though none of their theories has been compelling enough to gain wider acceptance. The author's pseudonym, Lanling Xiaoxiao Sheng 蘭陵笑笑生 ("The Scoffing Scholar of Lanling"), is an important part of Roy's argument that the author aligned himself with the general philosophical orientation of Xunzi 荀子 (third century BCE), who scoffed at the disorder of the world and attributed it to the evil of human nature. An important Confucian scholar, Xunzi was once the magistrate of Lanling, a county in the eastern province of Shandong on the Yellow Sea. While foundational, Xunzi's thought lost out in popularity and influence to that of Mencius (fourth century BCE), which became fundamental to later neo-Confucianism, a philosophy that some scholars see reflected in *Plum*.[21] In giving his reasons for this assertion, Roy explains his belief that the novel's setting, the district town of Qinghe 清河 ("Clear [Yellow] River") is ironic, given the ancient Chinese idea that the waters of the Yellow River will run clear only if a true sage sits on the throne, and given the novel's consistent and elaborate social and political criticism. Roy points out that the real historical model underlying the description of *Plum*'s locales is neither Qinghe nor any of the other sites in Shandong Province that have been proposed but rather the city of Beijing, which served as the capital of the Ming Empire from 1421 to 1644. Scholars such as Wu Xiaoling 吴晓鈴 have demonstrated that many of the places and institutional names mentioned in the novel correspond to places and institutions peculiar to sixteenth-century Beijing. This is consistent with the author's rhetorical strategy of using the microcosm of a household in a provincial town to suggest macrocosm of the empire and its administrative center in the capital city.

Roy's translation of *Plum*'s prefatory materials and his discussion of the prologue in chapter 1 provide instructors with fodder for teaching the conflicts when it comes to apologies for the novel. All agree that this is an important work, one that does not (necessarily) corrupt, but all explain its workings differently. If an instructor or moderator were to include in class readings Zhang Zhupo's essay "How to Read the *Chin P'ing Mei*" or Zhang's commentary on the first and final chapters of *Plum* (Rolston, "Introduction") along with materials related to the legend of *Plum*'s origins, initiates would get a sense of the stakes—intimated by the coercive hermeneutics of publishers, censors, apologists, and devotees.[22]

As Roy states toward the end of his introduction, his philosophy of translation was to translate everything. The text of *Plum in the Golden Vase* "is characterized by an amazingly dense network of internal, as well as external, allusions, verbal repetitions, resonances, cross-references, and patterns of incremental repetition or replication," which Roy strove to render "in exactly the same way whenever they occur or recur" (Introduction xlviii). He admits that his approach at times produces a slight awkwardness in English, but that is a small sacrifice to help readers better understand one of the salient features of the text.

What at first glance may seem a whimsical inclusion of poetry or song can play a significant role in foreshadowing events or offering ironic commentary. A savvy reader will realize, for instance, that a song's reference to a faithless brother prefigures the way in which Ximen Qing's close friends will rob his widow blind right after his funeral.[23] Roy's decision to mark verse (songs and poetry) as well as aphorisms and idioms in classical Chinese by indenting them is one of his translation's important contributions to the classroom.

Plum was written in vernacular Chinese, but all the proverbial sayings, stock couplets, formulaic language, parallel prose, poetry, and song that it includes are written in classical Chinese, vaguely analogous to the relative importance of and relationship between modern Italian and classical Latin. The most cursory explanation of the important differences between classical and modern Chinese would probably begin with the former's incredible degree of succinctness. Classical Chinese is a language of few words, each of which has much meaning. While modern Chinese is a largely disyllabic language, classical Chinese is much more monosyllabic, especially in the formative classical period of antiquity. For example, *qizi* 妻子, which in modern Chinese means "wife" (with the meaningless noun suffix *zi* 子), in classical Chinese means "wife and children," where both syllables retain their full meaning. Words in classical Chinese slip readily from one part of speech into another. For example, *dong* 東, which means "east," can also mean "to go east," or it can function as an adverb, meaning "eastward." In classical Chinese, "blue" is also a verb—"to be blue" or "to become blue." The reader who encounters "sky blue" (*tianlan* 天藍) in poetry needs to understand through context if the meaning is "a clear day," or if "dawn is breaking" and the sky is becoming blue. The word *mu* 目 ("eye") in classical Chinese can also serve as a verb, meaning "to eyeball" something, "to regard it," and by extension, "point of view" or "judgment." The noun *lin* 林 ("forest") could mean "a veritable forest of something" or "many and more."

Plum contains a whole spectrum of linguistic registers in the Chinese original, registers belonging both to classical Chinese and to vernacular Chinese that are often juxtaposed in meaningful or humorous ways. Chinese vernacular texts would often indent poetry or parallel prose—as is the case for *Plum*—but other uses of classical Chinese in the text are not offset in the original. Roy chooses to indent these bits of classical language because they would have been conspicuous to readers of Chinese (Qi 165). These snippets of text, now easily identifiable because they are set off from the rest of the narrative and dialogue, are the locus of much of the humor in the novel, often because of their ironic misappropriation. They also frequently serve as literary devices or as a means of fleshing out characters who use or misuse quoted text.

Roy's translation strives to give the Western reader some idea of the lineation of Chinese poetry by attempting to translate every line of the original into only one line in English. Chinese poems tend to have either five-character lines or seven-character lines. If the original line is seven characters long, Roy's translation is at times longer than a single line, but Roy strove to make all lines equal in length (Qi 170). In short, Roy was committed to providing English-language readers with a feel for reading the original novel in Chinese and to preserving everything he found there. The text of *Plum* is marked by an incredible degree of intertextuality—allusions, parallel prose, verse, song, common phrases, and quotations from every kind of printed text available in the late Ming. Roy's translation seeks to make the novel's intertextual elements visible by either setting them apart from the narrative and dialogue or by explaining them in endnotes. Roy writes that he did this, despite the fact that readers may find it strange or annoying, to effect in the reader a sense of defamiliarization that highlights the novel's intertextual density and alerts the reader to the subtle counterpoint of different linguistic voices in the original. For modern readers, it can be difficult to detect some of the themes, structures, patterns, and humor in *Plum*, but if reading it in English, the Roy translation gives one a fighting chance.

Most of Roy's six hundred pages of endnotes are devoted to tracing the proximal or ultimate origins of quotations and references. The overall effect of such scholarly attention is an appreciation of the text's embeddedness in a complex literary world and of the author's genius not only in accessing such an incredibly broad range of material but also in using it advisedly—often ironically or humorously. One of the more obvious examples of this ironic deployment of famous quotations is when the author appropriates Confucius's first analect, "is it not delightful to learn and at times, to practice what one has learned?" (學而時習之 不亦說乎) as auto-commentary on his lurid descriptions of sexual encounter— "is it not delightful?" (不亦說乎; 1.13.266; 13.8a).

At the end of volumes 1 and 2, Roy translates what might be called supplementary material—mostly song suites that are said to be sung by a character in the main text but that are not quoted in the text. These references show the incredible degree to which the author uses texts in the tradition to help define character or mood, and they show Roy's devotion to conveying the author's art to readers. Another important teaching text that might go overlooked is an appendix to volume 1 titled "Translator's Commentary on the Prologue." The prologue, not designated as such in the original text, is set off in the Roy translation with ellipses, constituting pages 12–16. Roy makes a compelling case that the references in this prologue to historical figures and places are so carefully selected to adumbrate "all of the major issues raised in the body of the novel and must be regarded not only as an integral part of the work, but as essential to any interpretation of the author's intended meaning" ("Appendix I" 436). This appendix could be a way for instructors to give students an idea of how *Plum* engages the literary-cultural tradition.

There is not, as far as I can see, an easy way to deal with the great quantity of endnotes in *Plum*. More than half of them trace the origins of a quotation and thus would be interesting primarily to scholars whose research focuses on those literary or linguistic connections. The remainder of the reference material is a virtual history of Chinese literature, or a literary history of China, in disorganized fragments. To point out that each volume of the Roy translation has an extensive index and comprehensive bibliography is to state the obvious, but both are invaluable to scholars. If these were digitized and made available (and searchable) online in Pinyin romanization, as is the plan for a forthcoming student edition, such resources would be useful for students writing a research paper, leaving a cheaper, more streamlined text for classroom use. Another seemingly obvious yet often overlooked feature of the Roy translation is the list of characters at the beginning of each volume. It bears noting that this list is more like an indexed biography of every character in the novel. Since the list is the same in each volume, it also contains a fair number of plot spoilers, disclosing everything about a character whom a reader may have only just been introduced to.

Resources for Teaching

Ideally, *Plum* would be taught in its entirety. Because of the novel's length and complexity, however, this is not an opportunity that many instructors, schools, or departments can offer. This section is designed to give teachers some ideas about how *Plum* might be abridged or supplemented, with limitations of time and finances in mind.

Aside from the present volume, Roy's introduction to his translation in volume 1 of *Plum* and Robert Hegel's introduction to *Golden Lotus* are the most important general introductions, though Perry Link's and Jonathan Spence's reviews of Roy's translation in *The New York Review of Books* are also outstanding. One of the most interesting pairings with *Plum* is *The Story of the Stone*, which is demonstrably in *Plum*'s debt, but which has outstripped *Plum* for the title of greatest work of premodern Chinese fiction. An earlier volume in the same MLA series as this one, *Approaches to Teaching* The Story of the Stone (Dream of the Red Chamber), edited by Andrew Schonebaum and Tina Lu, aims like this volume to offer a comprehensive introduction to one of the most important Chinese novels. Mary Scott's essay in the current volume discusses the affinities between these two masterworks.

Another possible pairing is with what might be called the only sequel or piece of fan fiction published for *Plum*, available in English translation as *Flower Shadows behind the Curtain* (Ding Yaokang).[24] One of the prefaces to *Plum*, written by Dongwu Nongzhuke 東吳弄珠客 ("The Pearl-Juggler of Eastern Wu")—possibly a pseudonym of Feng Menglong 馮夢龍 (1574–1646), the famous connoisseur and purveyor of vernacular stories—argues that it is the reader's responsibility to interpret the novel correctly by focusing on *Plum*'s artistry, not by attempting to emulate its characters. Other prefaces also express concern for readers and their abilities to properly understand *Plum* without being harmed by its portrayals of avarice, deception, and lust. Ding Yaokang 丁耀亢 (1599–1669) wrote *Xu* Jin Ping Mei 續金瓶梅 (*Sequel to* Plum in the Golden Vase) in 1660, in another attempt to help readers understand *Plum* correctly. Ding published his sequel sixteen years after the Ming dynasty fell and the Manchus took over Beijing. Soon after it was banned in 1665, a revised version of it, titled *Gelian huaying* 隔簾花影 (*Flower Shadows behind the Curtain*), was published, strategically deleting the passages with political associations, such as those concerning the Jurchen invasion that caused the fall of the Northern Song dynasty in *Plum*.[25] This sequel to *Plum* is also a reading of *Plum* and seeks to correct the original version based on the idea that its readers hitherto had not clearly understood its moral of worldly retribution for indulgence, depravity, and treachery. A preface to *Flower Shadows* by Xihu Diaoshi 西湖釣史 ("Angling Historian of West Lake") argues that since *Plum* depicted so much sumptuousness and depravity, its modern readers often "witnessed its descriptions without knowing its hidden meanings, saw its recklessness without knowing its restraint, and enjoyed its showing off without knowing its satire" (今人觀其顯不知其隱見其放不知其止喜其誇不知其所刺; my trans.; Ding Yaokang, *Xu* Jin Ping Mei 2b). *Flower Shadows* is consequently more obviously didactic than its predecessor, indicating a concern that readers are not sophisticated enough to understand *Plum*.

Another difference between *Sequel to* Plum and *Flower Shadows* is the names of characters. While *Sequel to* Plum retains the original names of the characters, *Flower Shadows* changes these names to names that thinly mask the originals. *Flower Shadows* changes certain place-names as well. There is little agreement as to why these changes were made. Lengthy passages of historical and philosophical reflections were excised in the writing of *Flower Shadows*, and the discussion of retribution is reduced compared with that of the original, though it is obvious that karma is still the governing theme of the work.

Flower Shadows follows most of the main characters of *Plum* through their subsequent incarnations to witness all the troubles that befall them as karmic punishment for their actions in the original novel. The travails of Ximen Qing's primary wife, Wu Yueniang, who survives *Plum*, make up a large part of the story, though the reader also learns the fates of Ximen Qing, Pan Jinlian, and others. *Flower Shadows* ignores the details of the characters' new names and families presented in the last chapter of *Plum* in favor of more explicitly undesirable circumstances: Ximen Qing is reborn as a blind boy who becomes a beggar, Li Ping'er's new family is tricked into selling her into a brothel, and Pan Jinlian is reborn into a military family, loses her father when he dies in battle, and marries the man to whom she was betrothed at age six, who is now poor and paralyzed from a blow to the head.

Flower Shadows states explicitly in the first few pages that the characters' early deaths in *Plum* have not served as adequate atonement for their sins. An important distinction is made between retribution that happens during a lifetime and the workings of karma that follow particularly evil persons into the next life. This represents a fundamental difference between *Plum* and its sequel: in *Plum* characters simply die early for their misdeeds, but in *Flower Shadows* they must go on paying for them in a second, more miserable incarnation. *Flower Shadows* presents a simple reversal of fortune to depict the workings of karmic retribution. What was done by a character in *Plum* is done to that same character in *Flower Shadows*. Those characters that were rich or lustful in a previous lifetime are denied wealth and intimacy in this one.

In addition to its more explicit moral didacticism, *Flower Shadows* presents fewer instances of sexual intercourse than does *Plum*, and those that it does represent are depicted using flowery, indirect language. While *Plum* at times seems to revel in some of the scenes of sexual debauchery, including lyrical descriptions of anatomy and occasional vulgar terms, the sequel seems to present sex primarily either as something for which the character will later have to atone or as karmic punishment in the form of violence, as is the case with one of the more explicit sex scenes in which Li Ping'er sleeps with the coarse but wealthy man to whom she has been married. Unlike *Plum*, *Flower Shadows* does not employ sexual metaphors of combat or economy. The general lack of sexual interaction in *Flower Shadows* seems misleading given the title, which implies catching fleeting glimpses of beautiful maidens hidden behind a screen and the subsequent lust that such an image would normally produce.

Ding Yaokang relies heavily on Daoist and Buddhist texts to advise and warn his readers. As Siao-Chen Hu explains:

> *Xu Jin Ping Mei* develops along two plot lines. The first narrates the story of the original characters who are still living, such as Yueniang, Xiaoge, and Dai'an. The second plot line describes how characters such as Ximen Qing, Ping'er, and Jinlian, who died in the original, return to their next lives and pay their karmic debts. The two plot lines sometimes merge, and historical figures such as Emperor Huizong, Zhang Bangchang, and Qin Hui also appear in certain episodes. When the Jurchen army invades China, Yueniang and her son experience many difficulties while trying to escape. They return home to live in peace only after both mother and son have converted to Buddhism. In the meantime, the dead also continue their stories. Ximen Qing is reincarnated as the son of a wealthy family. He squanders all his fortune and dies a beggar. Ping'er in her next life is sold into prostitution. She commits suicide after being betrayed by her lover. Jinlian in her reincarnation marries an impotent cripple, who is the reincarnation of Chen Jingji. Jinlian becomes a "stone woman" after a demonic sexual encounter and decides to become a nun. Chunmei in her next life becomes the concubine of a Jurchen. She is tortured badly by the first wife and finally becomes a nun. The first wife turns out to be none other than the reincarnation of Sun Xue'e, whom Chunmei had mistreated and tortured in the original novel. Although the major characters of *Jin Ping Mei* continue their stories, either in this life or in the next, it is easily noticeable that the sequel diverges from *Jin Ping Mei* in its tone, style, and concerns. (76)

Flower Shadows also seems to grant the characters ultimate escape from the wheel of karmic retribution, as most pay penance for their misdeeds and attain enlightenment.

These sorts of sequels—and Ding's in particular, which has recently started receiving increased attention in English-language scholarship—are a way of understanding readers' responses to the novel. If teachers were to present even the first few chapters of *Flower Shadows*, despite the shortcomings of the English translation, students would get some insight into how *Plum*, a product of the late Ming, was read by people in the early Qing period, and a sense of how the new Manchu dynasty and its top-down moralizing affected culture. *Flower Shadows* could be usefully paired with prefatory materials in *Plum*, which have also motivated readings of the novel, and students could discuss coercive hermeneutics and apologies for entertainment literature.

Following is a list of the names of major characters from *Plum* (in both Pinyin and Wade-Giles romanization) as they are rendered by the translator Vladimir Kean in *Flower Shadows*:

Ximen Qing (Hsi-men Ch'ing) is "Little Gold Brother"

Wu Yueniang (Wu Yüeh-niang) is "Moon Lady"

Li Jiao'er (Li Chiao-erh) is Li Kiao

Pan Jinlian (P'an Chin-lien, also known as Golden Lotus) is
    "Cinnabar-Cinnamon"

Pang Chunmei (P'ang Ch'un-mei) is "Fragrant Jewel"

Li Ping'er (Li P'ing-erh) is "Silver Vase"

Approaches to Teaching Plum

One of the most productive ways of teaching *Plum*, or any work of world literature, is to place it in its historical and cultural contexts. Approaching *Plum* as a keyhole through which students can view late Ming culture complements an approach to *Plum* as a stand-alone masterwork with its own complicated language and structures. The latter approach might consider literary contexts, for which Judith Zeitlin's entry on *xiaoshuo* 小說 ("novel") and Andrew Plaks's chapter in Franco Moretti's edited volume *The Novel* would be useful introductions to some aspects of the Chinese novel and readership (Zeitlin, "*Xiaoshuo*"; Plaks, "Novel"). Teachers might also ask students to discuss the *cihua* prefaces in Roy's translation and Zhang Zhupo's prefatory essay "How to Read *Jin Ping Mei*," which not only argue the aesthetic innovations and importance of *Plum* but also, in their defensiveness, reveal the competing anxieties that *Plum* and its genre provoked. A wonderful example of traditional Chinese criticism, Zhang's essay is included in David Rolston's *How to Read the Chinese Novel* (202–43), which also contains an authoritative, descriptive bibliography of extant *Plum* editions (456–84). Tina Lu's "The Literati Culture of the Late Ming (1573–1644)" provides an in-depth discussion of *Plum* and its innovations—a work that reflects the lives of, appealed to, and was associated with the new social and economic merchant class.

While *Plum* is itself a comprehensive introduction to virtually every idea, issue, and detail of daily life in premodern China, past students of mine have said that an introduction to the basic tenets of Confucianism and Buddhism would have been useful prior to reading the novel. There are many ways to do this, and while any short distillation of such huge, complex topics is bound to have problems and detractors, the following resources may be useful: the entries for "Confucius" and "Chan Buddhism" in the *Stanford Encyclopedia of Philosophy* (plato.stanford.edu/index.html) or, if time permits, selections from Daniel Gardner's *Confucianism: A Very Short Introduction* (1–48) and Damien Keown's *Buddhism: A Very Short Introduction* (1–56).

A course focused on Confucianism in context or on the Ming dynasty would be a great place for *Plum*. I have taught a role-playing game about the succession crisis of the Wanli Emperor using Gardner and Mark C. Carnes's *Confucianism and the Succession Crisis of the Wanli Emperor, 1587*, part of the Norton series Reacting to the Past. In the game, most students assume the roles of members of the Grand Secretariat of the Hanlin Academy, the body of top-ranking graduates of the civil-service examination who serve as advisers to the Wanli Emperor. Some Grand Secretaries are what might be called Confucian purists, who hold that tradition obliges the emperor to name his firstborn son as successor; those who support the most senior of the Grand Secretaries maintain that it is within the emperor's right to choose his successor; and still others, as they decide this matter, continue to scrutinize the teachings of Confucianism for guidance about pirates on the southern coast, incursions on the northern frontier, and other pressing issues confronting the empire. The game requires students to engage with the *Analects* on an intense level and to see how Confucian precepts were applied and creatively construed. The game, like *Plum*, is usefully supplemented with Ray Huang's *1587: A Year of No Significance*, which gives a fascinating account of the Wanli crisis, its encapsulation of and contribution to the decline of the Ming dynasty, and what it was like to be an emperor—the daily rituals, strictures, and debates. Timothy Brook's book *The Confusions of Pleasure*, which, like Huang's book, is well-written and accessible, looks at changing attitudes to the interrelationship of commerce, culture, and leisure activities throughout the Ming dynasty. Brook quotes from a wide variety of sources, many of which were narratives of the authors' journeys in the Ming Empire. Such firsthand accounts provide insight into the operation of the courier and postal services and the Grand Canal, modes and costs of travel, the printing industry, maritime trade, the circulation of silver and copper, the cotton and silk industries, the employment of women, and other fascinating topics that illuminate daily life in Ming China and that resonate with or explain many aspects of *Plum*.

Plum is one of the first narrative works in Chinese literature, and therefore in world literature, to focus on women, their internal lives, and their motivations. Some readers feel that this portrayal is extremely negative, but others see sympathy (on the part of the author) in the portrayals of women. As Plaks writes:

> Coming to *Jin Ping Mei* we plunge into one of the most profoundly negative investigations of feminine psychology in all of world literature but still one that reveals great insight into the existential truth of women trapped in the demeaning reality of concubinage, unchecked patriarchal authority, and the absolute imperative of producing male heirs—insight far more penetrating than a cursory reading of the book's notoriously explicit sexual passages alone could possibly reveal.   ("Novel" 204)

All the women in *Plum* contend with strictures that limit their agency and mobility. To understand the forces that shaped women's lives in different late Ming social milieus, teachers may want to consider assigning three articles from El-len Widmer and Kang-I Sun Chang's edited volume *Writing Women in Late Imperial China*. Brothel culture and courtesans feature prominently in *Plum*, and the lives and ideals of courtesans form the subject of these articles: Wai-yee Li's "The Late Ming Courtesan: Invention of a Cultural Ideal," Dorothy Ko's "The Written Word and the Bound Foot: A History of the Courtesan's Aura," and Paul S. Ropp's "Ambiguous Images of Courtesan Culture in Late Imperial China."

Plum employs themes of jealousy, mismanagement, and retribution strategically, conflating health and coin in terms of a sexual economy. The novel's themes and conceits are drawn largely from the corpus of fictional, medical, and sexual texts of its day. It incorporates and develops rhetoric from previous works of fiction, particularly in those passages that describe the body in detail. It also appropriates older notions from medical texts that warn of the dangers of female sexuality. A few works that instructors may want to incorporate into classes that approach *Plum* through the lens of the history of women and their representation in premodern China include the following: Naifei Ding's *Obscene Things: Sexual Politics in* Jin Ping Mei, Victoria Cass's *Dangerous Women*, and Wai-yee Li's translation of two memoirs about courtesans, Plum Shadows *and* Plank Bridge. Two important anthologies of writings by women are *Under Confucian Eyes: Writings on Gender in Chinese History*, edited by Susan Mann and Yu-Yin Cheng, and *The Red Brush: Writing Women of Imperial China*, by Wilt L. Idema and Beata Grant. A fascinating and accessible book about medical views of women's bodies and reproduction is Yi-Li Wu's *Reproducing Women: Medicine, Metaphor, and Childbirth in Late Imperial China*.

After this, instructors could have students discuss same-sex encounters in *Plum*, their precedents, and the implications of homosexual desire in Chinese society. Giovanni Vitiello's "Exemplary Sodomites: Chivalry and Love in Late Ming Culture" and Matthew Sommer's "The Penetrated Male in Late Imperial China: Judicial Constructions and Social Stigma" are important articles in the field and can help students challenge certain paradigms. Teachers might ask students to consider the represented body by selecting one of Charlotte Furth's many important articles on medicine, such as "Androgynous Males and Deficient Females: Biology and Gender Boundaries in Sixteenth- and Seventeenth-Century China," or Schonebaum's chapters "Diseases of Sex" and "Diseases of Qing" in his book *Novel Medicine: Healing, Literature, and Popular Knowledge in Early Modern China* (122–73).

With respect to specific aspects of daily life, teachers may want to focus on material culture. Craig Clunas's *Superfluous Things: Material Culture and Social Status in Early Modern China*—particularly chapter 6, "Anxieties about Things: Consumption and Class in Ming China" (141–65)—provides a way to discuss the many lists and elaborate descriptions of things in *Plum*. James Cahill's book *Pictures for Use and Pleasure* discusses a large and important but understudied subset of Chinese paintings that has been ignored and even scorned by traditional Chinese critics and collectors because these paintings were functional rather than self-expressive. These include, among others, pictures of the kind one would purchase or commission for such occasions as birthdays, New Year's celebrations, and weddings; family pictures, narrative pictures, and pictures of *meiren* 美人, or beautiful women; and erotic pictures, chiefly albums. Cahill's book deals with erotic albums and with paintings of scenes in *Plum* (1–31, 99–148). Chapter 1 of Susan Naquin's *Peking: Temples and City Life*, "Introducing Peking" (3–18), would give students some geographic orientation as well as some background on the functioning of cities in sixteenth-century China. Naquin's book also discusses the temples and Ming dynasty city life that are so central to Ximen Qing's story (19–287).

Plum features and is often associated with the printing impulse that created sexual manuals popular in the sixteenth and early seventeenth centuries, manuals that paired images with verse. An example of this type of manual, *Huaying jin zhen* 花營錦陣 (*Brocade Battle Formations from the Flowery Compound*), is available in English translation as *The Fragrant Flower: Classic Chinese Erotica in Art and Poetry*. *Plum* is clearly indebted to what is thought to be the earliest and most well-known piece of narrative erotica with graphic sexual depictions, *The Lord of Perfect Satisfaction* (*Ruyijin zhuan* 如意君傳), which first appeared in the early sixteenth century. Charles Stone wrote the definitive study in English on this work and translated the novella in *The Fountainhead of Chinese Erotica:* The Lord of Perfect Satisfaction (Ruyijun zhuan).

The Peony Pavilion

The Peony Pavilion (*Mudan ting* 牡丹亭)—likely the most famous play in all Chinese literature, and certainly the most famous play in the late Ming—is an excellent text to pair with *Plum*. The play gives students an introduction to Chinese drama and to late Ming concerns. It was written at approximately the same time as *Plum*, is also unusually dense and poetic, and was incredibly popular in its day. Indeed, parts of it are still performed today. *Peony Pavilion* was written by Tang Xianzu 湯顯祖, who has been proposed as a possible author of *Plum*, but the play's vision of love is different than the one encountered in *Plum*. Desire and women's lives are presented more romantically and tragicomically, and perhaps more satirically, than they are presented in *Plum*, which relies instead on hard-core realism and political commentary. Completed in 1598, *Peony* was long even by the standards of southern-style drama of its day; its fifty-five scenes would have taken several days to perform before a birthday or festival audience that would have been free to wander in and out as the musical or comic scenes succeeded each other. More often, however, selected highlights would have been performed, and this history of selection or abridgment makes teaching just a few scenes from *Peony* an authentic project if an instructor is short on time.

Peony Pavilion tells the story of a young maiden, Du Liniang, who is visited by a handsome young scholar, Liu Mengmei, in a dream in which the two make love under the peony pavilion. Overcome with longing when she awakens, Du Liniang falls ill with a wasting disease, and after painting her self-portrait, she pines away and dies. Grief-stricken, her parents establish a shrine to consecrate her memory. But the dead woman's desire is so strong that three years later she returns as a ghost to the land of the living. Near her shrine she finds the scholar of her dream and enters into a passionate union with him. After they pledge their undying love for each other, she admits to him that she is a ghost, imploring him to exhume her remains so that she may be resurrected. Liu Mengmei digs up her corpse, which has suffered no decay. Once he brings her back to life, they elope, and after a series of complications (including Mengmei being accused of grave robbing), he passes the highest palace examination. Liniang's father finally accepts the match once her resurrection and their secret marriage are officially sanctioned by imperial decree.

Peony Pavilion is available in a readable and widely available translation by Cyril Birch (*Peony Pavilion: Mudan ting*). Some of the most commonly performed scenes, and the ones most often anthologized, are scene 7, "The Schoolroom" (24–30); scene 10, "The Interrupted Dream" (42–52); scene 14, "The Portrait" (66–71); scene 20, "Keening" (97–109); scene 26, "The Portrait Examined" (143–47); and scene 28, "Union in the Shades" (155–65).[26] *Renditions* magazine has made the first ten scenes—the most popular scenes for teaching—available for free download (Birch, Peony Pavilion; *or,* Return of the Soul).

Written in enchantingly beautiful but often elusive lyrics, *Peony Pavilion* celebrates the power of passion and was part of a new, humane current of thought that appeared during the waning years of the Ming dynasty. The schoolroom scene is one of the play's most famous scenes and one of the few that is still performed (Birch, *Peony Pavilion: Mudan ting* 24–30). It depicts the subtle psychological changes a young woman yearning for love undergoes on viewing a brilliantly flowering spring scene in a deserted garden. *Plum*, by contrast, is largely about the lives of women, but their psychology—their interiority—is rendered only obliquely. As Mary Scott discusses in this volume, *The Story of the Stone* (also known as *Dream of the Red Chamber*), the only Chinese novel more famous than *Plum*, is indebted to both *Plum* and *Peony*. In the famous scene in *Stone* in which she buries fallen flower petals, Lin Daiyu quotes *Peony* self-referentially, tacitly drawing a parallel between herself and Du Liniang, who dies of love but is also resurrected through its power. As Scott illustrates, *Stone* also makes use of *Plum*'s darker vision of the effects of love and sex on women's lives.

Whether or not one chooses to pair *Plum* and *Peony*, two articles about commentary editions of *Peony*—one that romanticizes the play's reading by women, one that reads it erotically for them—provide historical and hermeneutic context for *Plum* as well. The first of these is Judith Zeitlin's "Shared Dreams: The Story of the Three Wives' Commentary on the *Peony Pavilion*," which will interest students who are curious about portrayals of women's engagement with entertainment literature, reading, illness, and criticism. Zeitlin discusses the 1694 commentary edition of *Peony*, titled *The Three Wives of Wu Wushan's Commentary on* The Peony Pavilion (*Wu Wushan sanfu heping* Mudan ting *huanhunji* 吳吳山三婦合評牡丹亭還魂記). Purportedly, the wife of Wu Wushan 吳吳山 (1647–1704?), a Hangzhou literatus, fell in love with reading the play and added her own commentary to it but took ill and died while doing so. Wu's second wife found the first wife's commentary and vowed to finish it but also died before she was able to complete it. Wu's third wife completed the commentary, which was subsequently published and celebrated as a real-life example of the power of love to both kill and revive—that is, through the ability of works of art to transcend death.

Zeitlin discusses the paradoxical reception of the commentary edition of the play. While Du Liniang's longing and desire are ultimately fulfilled in *Peony Pavilion*, virtually every story about women's responses to the play involves their overidentification with the heroine, sickness, and untimely death, which leads Zeitlin to explore the following question: "How does a play, a romantic comedy at that, which celebrates the triumph of life over death and the triumph of love over social constraints, induce such a response?" ("Shared Dreams" 130). Zeitlin argues that the recurrent cultural myths about the deaths of readers, commentators, and actresses who encountered *The Peony Pavilion* point to an infectious danger emanating from the play. The allure of women dying young, and the exquisite pleasure and pain produced in contemplating those deaths, was part of the play's enduring popularity. The power of the play to trigger a fatal response in women, and the elevation of those deaths to the level of art—an art that was savored by male readers, whose sensibilities were seen as more refined and sophisticated—marked *Peony Pavilion* as a transcendent masterpiece and cultural phenomenon.

Wei Hua's "How Dangerous Can the *Peony* Be? Textual Space, *Caizi Mudan ting*, and Naturalizing the Erotic" is another fascinating article that discusses a rare and unconventional commentary edition of *Peony Pavilion*. Published as *Caizi* Mudan ting 才子牡丹亭 (*The Genius* Peony Pavilion), this commentary edition was printed by Wu Zhensheng 吳震生 during the Yongzheng reign (1723–35). The annotator, known by the pseudonym A-bang 阿傍, was Wu's wife, Cheng Qiong 程瓊. This edition includes commentaries on *The Peony Pavilion* by both husband and wife and is unique for its encyclopedic nature (to the extent that it incorporates notes on other plays), its thoroughly erotic reading of *Plum*, and its explicit concern to address the interests of women readers.

Hua pays particular attention to the interplay of corporeal or vulgar readings of sex (*se* 色) and more refined readings of passion and sentiment (*qing* 情). The topic of *seqing* 色情 ("sexuality," "eroticism," or "sexual love") often appears in the commentary of *The Genius* Peony, partly because the play itself deals with romantic love, and partly because the commentators were interested in explicating the indomitable power of sensual passion and its relevance to human existence. As a hermeneutic, *The Genius* Peony commentary can be seen as a reaction against the resurgent moralistic teachings of neo-Confucian orthodoxy in the early Qing dynasty, but much of its import, aside from its incorporation of a wide cross section of learning, lies in its erotic reading of the play (by a woman, no less) and its explicit interest in directing the play to a female readership.

In addition to discussing *seqing* and paying close attention to female consciousness and sociocultural criticism in the commentary, Hua considers the tradition of dramatic criticism by women and in particular the relation of *Genius* Peony to the *Three Wives* commentary. *Genius* Peony, for instance, seems to base its text of the play on that of the *Three Wives* commentary, although it also excises certain notable passages. Hua maintains that the *Three Wives* commentaries belong, more or less, to one of four categories: characters' personalities and psychology, the theme of love, plot structure, and the play's artistic use of language. By contrast, the *Genius* Peony commentary eroticizes the text of the *Peony Pavilion* and does so partly in response to the brevity and inadequacy of the *Three Wives* commentary, which was particularly popular at the time. The making of *Peony Pavilion* into an erotic text may have been driven by editorial and commercial considerations, but as Hua argues, it also made the text strange and unfamiliar, enabling new readings by women.

Commonly Taught Selections from Plum

Plum is not found in many anthologies of literature in English.[27] In general, when *Plum* is taught in a survey of Chinese literature, instructors tend to require the first volume of Roy's translation and teach either the whole of that volume or selections from it (for instance, chs. 1–6, 9, 12, and 15; chs. 1 and 12; chs. 9–14; or chs. 9–18). This approach is essentially an introduction to Pan Jinlian, one of Chinese literature's most famous characters, and to some of the pressures and realities she and other women face in this late Ming household. These early chapters, in particular chapters 1–2 and 5–6, have also been assigned in courses that survey Chinese history; these chapters show some of the structures, the decadence, and the corruption that have become emblematic of the late Ming. Another strategy is to focus on Pan Jinlian's story, including Ximen's famous death scene in chapters 78–79 and Pan Jinlian's death at the hands of a vengeful Wu Song in chapter 87. I have taught, with mixed success, most of *Plum in the Golden Vase* in an undergraduate course devoted to the novel, providing students with plot synopses for the chapters we skipped. Students tended to focus on what they missed, though, and some students insisted on reading the whole novel (about 175 pages per week). I have also taught the entirety of *The Golden Lotus*, supplementing it with passages from *Plum* to focus on poetry or cultural references, or as a means of obtaining a more detailed or alternative account of important moments of death and divination. The virtue of this approach, for me, was the ability to discuss with students in detail the last twenty chapters, which tend to be ignored. Students noticed the inversion of gender roles evinced in the characters of Pang Chunmei (P'ang Ch'un-mei), the maid who becomes the de facto head of a powerful family, and Chen Jingji (Ch'en Ching-chi), who ends up prostituting himself because of his squandering of money and goodwill. Using the Egerton-Lao translation made it possible for students to read the entire novel, giving them a better sense of its structure, but it also repeatedly drew conversations to characterization and plot at the expense of what the novel can teach us about aspects of culture, something that is more apparent in the Roy translation and its accompanying notes.

If instructors cannot commit to teaching all of *Plum*, the next best thing would be to teach all of *The Golden Lotus*; the latter's full plot and character arcs allow students to see how the author expands the *Outlaws* episode, and how he goes beyond it.[28] Students crave endings, and teaching the last chapter of *Plum* or *Lotus* not only satisfies that craving but also provides fodder for lively debate since each ending complicates the reader's understanding of some of the characters and of the overall moral. If using the Egerton-Lao translation, teachers could supplement this with Xiaofei Tian's translation of Zhang Zhupo's commentary (Zhang Zhupo, *"Jin Ping Mei"*). One might also choose to teach the entire first volume of Roy's translation, which includes chapters 1–20. Chapters 1–10 and 11–20 form an excellent contrast with each other, the first ten chapters focusing on Pan Jinlian's entrance into the Ximen household and the second ten on Li Ping'er's. To understand more of what makes a Chinese novel unique—the intertextuality, the structures, the verse, the more literal language—students should be asked to do a close reading of the text beyond the plot. The following plot summary should orient students to the various story arcs while also allowing them to move beyond these arcs. Broken into ten-chapter segments to illustrate the structure of those segments, this plot summary will prove useful no matter how *Plum* is incorporated into the classroom.

Structure, Pattern, and Plot

Attentive readers will note that *Plum* is structured as ten-chapter segments and that the narrative usually features a twist in the seventh of each of these ten chapters, reaches a climax in the ninth chapter, and concludes in the tenth chapter, which also introduces the events that follow. *Plum* can also be neatly divided into two textual hemispheres. The rise of Ximen's economic, political, and sexual power along with his acquisition of material objects, wives, lovers, and offices in the first half of the book reaches a climax in chapter 49 when he acquires a magical aphrodisiac. This drug marks the beginning of his self-destruction. He loses his favorite wife and son, and he ultimately loses his own life. Soon after he dies, he loses the loyalty of most of his wives, lovers, and friends, and many of them perish as well. Finally, he loses his reputation: his household is diminished, his house run down, and he is deprived of his legacy when his last son disappears with a mysterious Buddhist monk. In a number of passages, Zhang Zhupo refers to this fundamental structural division as a key to understanding the work. The preface to the *cihua* edition claims that "[f]rom its beginning to its end the strands of the plot are as intricately articulated as the conduits of the circulatory system and are like a myriad skeins of silk that flutter in the wind without ever becoming entangled" (如在目前始終, 如脈絡貫通, 如萬系迎風而不亂也; 1.3; 11a).[29] To better understand the author's achievement in creating these patterns, and to assist teachers in making selections from *Plum* for courses that are unable to accommodate the entire novel, I have provided, with the help of Katherine Carlitz, a plot synopsis in ten-chapter increments. Chapter 100, the culmination of the narrative, is summarized separately.[30]

Chapters 1–10

Plum begins with a discussion of *qing* 情 ("passion") and *se* 色 ("beauty" or "sex") and of the dangers that women pose to men. A purported summary of the novel is then given, describing it as a tale of the ruin a certain licentious woman brought to all who desired her. We are told that this novel is set during the reign of Song Huizong (1100–25) and that the empire is under the sway of evil ministers, whose rapacious rule causes misery among the people and has brought forth various rebel leaders.

The narrative proper then begins with the story of Wu Song (Wu Sung) and his older brother, the simple and small Wu Da (Wu the Elder). A local landowner marries Wu Da to Pan Jinlian (P'an Chin-lien), who has been raised in the landowner's household as an entertainer, and whom the landowner has deflowered. Beautiful, vain, and accomplished, Pan Jinlian is contemptuous of her husband, and when the pair are joined by Wu Song, who has established a reputation as a hero by killing a tiger on his travels to visit them, she is attracted to him. He rejects her, earning her enmity, and soon after leaves on a commission for the local magistrate. In his absence, Jinlian begins an affair with the merchant Ximen Qing (Hsi-men Ch'ing), and with his help murders her husband in order to marry Ximen. Ximen Qing is presented as wealthy, boorish, and tyrannical, feared by local commoners and officials alike. At the beginning of the novel, his income derives from a medicine shop and from his business as a pawnbroker. He has two wives, Wu Yueniang (Wu Yüeh-niang) and a former singing-girl (courtesan) named Li Jiao'er (Li Chiao-erh), and during his courtship with Pan Jinlian, he marries another widow, Meng Yulou (Meng Yü-lou), and a former maid in his household, Sun Xue'e (Sun Hsüeh-o). Jinlian thus becomes the fifth of his wives. Wu Song returns, learns of his brother's death, and, correctly assuming the identity of the murderers, attempts to avenge his brother by killing Ximen Qing. Ximen escapes, however, and Wu Song is taken into custody for the murder of a court runner who has been killed in a fracas.

Ximen Qing bribes local officials to sentence Wu Song to death, but the prefect plans to prosecute Ximen Qing, Pan Jinlian, and their associates in the murder of Wu Da. Making use of the fact that his daughter, Ximen Dajie (Hsi-men Ta-chieh), is related by marriage to the minister at the capital, Yang Jian (Yang Chien), Ximen Qing prevails on the chief minister, Cai Jing (Ts'ai Ching), to have the indictment against himself quashed. Wu Song is exiled, and Ximen Qing returns to the comfort of his family, where he begins a sexual relationship with Jinlian's maid, Pang Chunmei (P'ang Ch'un-mei). Pan Jinlian arranges for Chunmei to have privileges beyond those allowed the other maids, and a relationship of loyalty, rather than competition, is thus established between them.

Chapters 11–20

Ximen Qing deflowers a young singing-girl, Li Guijie (Li Kuei-chieh), the niece of his second wife, Li Jiao'er, who thus becomes his official favorite outside the household. Jealous sparring begins between Pan Jinlian and Li Guijie over Ximen Qing's favors.

Ximen Qing also begins a liaison with Li Ping'er (Li P'ing-erh), the wife of his friend, neighbor, and sworn brother Hua Zixu (Hua Tzu-hsü). When Hua is imprisoned over the inequitable distribution of certain family property, Li Ping'er gives much of their wealth to Ximen Qing for safekeeping and has him intervene for her husband's life. Once again Ximen Qing intercedes through Cai Jing, and Hua is released. He is now penniless, however, and is forced to persuade Ximen Qing to purchase his house. Li Ping'er claims she has spent all their money securing his release, and Hua grows ill and dies of exasperation and anger. Li Ping'er implores Ximen Qing to marry her without delay, but his wife Wu Yueniang insists that he wait until Li Ping'er's ritual period of mourning is over, and Ximen Qing wants to first complete work on the elaborate garden he is now able to build by joining Hua's property to his own.

Ximen Dajie, Ximen Qing's daughter by a deceased earlier wife, now arrives to join the household with her husband, Chen Jingji (Ch'en Ching-chi). A relative of Yang Jian, the minister at the capital who has recently been impeached, Chen Jingji is also under investigation. Fearing for Chen and himself, Ximen Qing sends a subordinate with gifts to Cai Jing's son, Cai Yu (Ts'ai Yu), and learns that Yang is to be spared punishment. Ximen Qing's gifts also ensure his own safety.

In the meantime, Li Ping'er despairs of Ximen Qing's intention to marry her and marries her doctor, whose sexual abilities she finds inadequate compared with Ximen Qing's. Ximen Qing has the doctor beaten, and Li Ping'er, now despising the doctor still more, drives him away. After this, Ximen Qing finally brings Li Ping'er into his household as his sixth wife. He ignores her for several days to humble her and then beats her for attempting to hang herself. Finally, however, the sight of her body arouses him, and the two are reconciled. Ximen Qing's obvious preference for Li Ping'er ignites the jealousy of both Pan Jinlian and Wu Yueniang, who vows to have nothing to do with her husband henceforth.

Chapters 21–30

A devout Buddhist, Wu Yueniang prays for her husband to mend his ways and give one of his wives a child; her prayers are overheard by Ximen Qing, who is moved to reconcile with her. Pan Jinlian and Meng Yulou discuss Yueniang's secret capitulation as an example of her abuse of her position as first lady in the household.

A new maid, Song Jinlian (Sung Chin-lien), enters the household as the wife of Laiwang (Lai-wang), one of Ximen Qing's employees. Her name is changed to Song Huilian (Sung Hui-lien) to avoid confusion with Pan Jinlian, but in fact her behavior mirrors Jinlian's to an extreme degree, and she uses Ximen Qing's sexual attraction to her to extract favors and clothing that allow her to rise above her station. In doing so, she excites Pan Jinlian's jealousy and unfavorable comments on the part of Ximen Qing's other wives as well as the jealousy of her fellow servants. She flaunts Ximen Qing's promise to marry her but is then overcome by remorse and contrition when Ximen Qing entraps her husband and has him sentenced for attempted murder. Her husband is exiled, and Song Huilian hangs herself. A shoe of hers, found among Ximen's possessions and mistaken for one of Pan Jinlian's, causes an outburst of sadistic jealousy on Jinlian's part.

When he learns that Li Ping'er is pregnant, Ximen Qing begins to show her more attention, thereby intensifying Jinlian's jealousy. Jinlian betrays, with sarcastic remarks, that she has overheard the news of Ping'er's pregnancy, which leads to a torrid love scene between Ximen Qing and Pan Jinlian beneath the grape arbor that includes bondage.

Ximen Qing is approached by a neighbor, Qiao (Ch'iao), and asked to intercede with Cai Jing on behalf of an imprisoned salt merchant. Ximen Qing's negotiation is successful.

A Daoist sage, Immortal Wu, tells the fortunes of various members of the Ximen household. Immortal Wu says that Ximen Qing will flourish but warns him of a disease closely resembling the one he eventually contracts by his thirty-sixth year. He warns him against sexual excess. He calculates that he will have two sons, and that he will lose a wife. He also forecasts that within ten days Ximen Qing will be promoted and that within a year he will have a son. He predicts that Wu Yueniang will prosper and give birth to a son and that she will aid her husband and be an effective manager of the household. He predicts that Li Jiao'er will marry three times. She will enjoy good food and fine clothing but will either end up in reduced circumstances or die young. Meng Yulou's fortune is the most favorable. Immortal Wu predicts that she will enjoy prosperity throughout her life. Initially, Pan Jinlian is unwilling to have her fortune told. When she consents, Immortal Wu observes that she is excessively lewd, will harm her husband, and will die young. She will upset human relations, and, although she will live in a wealthy household, she will be unable to achieve peace of mind. Li Ping'er will give birth to a son and be loved by her husband, but she will often be ill. Before the age of twenty-seven, she will have cause for grief, and therefore she must be careful. Immortal Wu predicts for Sun Xue'e a fate of relatively low social status; in fact, she might become a mere servant. He foretells that Ximen Dajie will be tormented. She will lack food and clothing and experience difficulties by her twenty-seventh year. Even if she does not meet an untimely death, she will still experience trials and tribulations. Pang Chunmei will marry a wealthy man and give birth to a son. She will enjoy rank and prosperity. She will assist her husband in advancing his fortunes and be loved and respected by him. Ximen Qing does not take these predictions seriously since, as he says, one can divine fate but not predict human behavior.

Immortal Wu's prediction that Ximen will be promoted to a government position is fulfilled when, in return for birthday gifts sent to him by Ximen Qing, Cai Jing confers on Ximen his first official appointment. (The narrator comments explicitly at this point that the evil ministers who control the empire are selling offices and rank.) Ximen Qing and his wives begin to wear insignia of rank higher than that to which they are entitled and to violate sumptuary laws. In chapter 30 Li Ping'er gives birth to Ximen Qing's first son with the help of a midwife named Cai (Ts'ai). The boy is named Guan'ge (Kuan-ko), or "Official Elder Brother," a reference to Ximen's recent appointment.

Chapters 31–40

Perceiving Ximen Qing's new power, the singing-girl Li Guijie comes bearing presents, requesting that Wu Yueniang accept her as her goddaughter. Having accomplished her mission, Li Guijie immediately puts on airs in the presence of her fellow courtesans. Ximen Qing's continued favoritism toward Li Ping'er exacerbates Pan Jinlian's jealousy, who complains that Li Ping'er is being treated as though she had given birth to the crown prince. Left alone with the baby at one point, Pan Jinlian frightens it, causing it to fall ill. Yueniang, who is about to give birth to a child of her own, invites the other wives to a reading of Buddhist scriptures and afterward joins them in examining the construction in progress at the house of their neighbor Qiao. There, Yueniang slips and falls. She has belly pains and calls for Dame Liu, who attends to her and says that she is more than five months pregnant, but they cannot save the fetus. Yueniang takes medicine to induce miscarriage of what would have been a son. She swears the others to secrecy and Ximen does not hear word.

Ximen Qing is given a servant boy whom he names Shutong (Shu-t'ung) and with whom he has sexual relations. Han Daoguo (Han Tao-kuo), the newly hired shop clerk, is cuckolded by his own brother, who has been having an affair with his wife, Wang Liu'er (Wang Liu-erh). Wang Liu'er sends Han Daoguo off to sleep in the store. She and her brother-in-law are caught in flagrante delicto by the neighbors. Han Daoguo boasts of his intimacy with the affairs of Ximen Qing when he is informed of the embarrassing arrest of his wife and brother. Han Daoguo asks Ximen's crony and sworn brother Ying Bojue (Ying Po-chüeh) to intercede on his behalf with Ximen Qing, who hears the case and releases Wang Liu'er from custody. He turns the tables on the accusers and has them beaten and jailed for their illegal entrance into Wang Liu'er's house at the time of the adulterers' arrest. The relatives of the arrested accusers now approach Ying Bojue to intercede with Ximen Qing to obtain their release. Having already spoken on Han Daoguo's behalf, Ying Bojue decides to work through Shutong to avoid the appearance of a conflict of interest. Shutong asks Li Ping'er to intercede with Ximen, and the men are let off. Shutong invites the other boys to share the wine he has received for his pains. Ximen Qing's servant Ping'an (P'ing-an) is inadvertently left out of the party, and in his resentment he tells Pan Jinlian of the relations between Ximen Qing and Shutong, earning himself a beating when this is discovered by Ximen Qing.

Ximen discusses with Yueniang a court case he has decided involving the brother of a eunuch-official surnamed Liu. (The brother has illegally used timber from the imperial forests, and Ximen has made him tear down his house.) Work begins on the elaborate buildings to be constructed at the Ximen family tombs; tiles are to come, illegally, from the imperial tileworks.

Ximen Qing receives a letter from Zhai Qian (Chai Ch'ien), the majordomo of Cai Jing's household, inquiring about the progress of the search on Zhai's behalf for a wife, a task Ximen Qing has completely forgotten. The letter also requests that Ximen host the *zhuangyuan* 狀元, the recipient of the highest score on the highest level of the imperial examination, who happens to be passing through Ximen Qing's district. (Here the narrator informs us that the recipient, an adopted son of Cai Jing, has been falsely awarded this honor, the real prize having originally gone to An Chen [An Ch'en]) Because of his connections to an out-of-favor clique, An Chen has not been officially recognized but has been given a post in the Board of Works, the government body that oversees weights, measures, construction, mining, and infrastructure. Ximen chooses Han Aijie (Han Ai-chieh), the daughter of Han Daoguo and Wang Liu'er, to be Zhai's wife. Ximen then begins an adulterous liaison with Wang Liu'er. Wang Liu'er and Han Daoguo decide that she will use the affair to gain as much as she can from Ximen Qing. Ximen opens a cloth store on Lion Street and installs the couple on the same street. When he wants to sleep with Wang Liu'er, Han Daoguo sleeps in the shop. Zhai Qian now addresses Ximen Qing as "kinsman."

An inappropriately elaborate Daoist naming ceremony is held for Guan'ge, and Ximen attends it wearing insignia of rank to which he is not entitled. He misses a birthday celebration for Pan Jinlian, who is forced to spend the occasion listening to the reading of Buddhist scriptures arranged by Yueniang. Jinlian remarks again that Guan'ge is being treated like a crown prince. Yueniang learns of a fertility potion prepared by Nun Xue (Hsüeh) and requests it for herself.

Chapters 41–50

Wu Yueniang and the other wives attend a party at the home of their neighbor Qiao, and at this gathering the women betroth Guan'ge to the Qiaos' infant daughter. Ximen Qing agrees to the betrothal when he is informed of it, but he is displeased at the disparity in rank between the Qiaos and himself.

Much is made of the little Daoist suit made for Guan'ge's naming ceremony; he is jokingly referred to as the "little priest." The courtesan Wu Yin'er (Wu Yin-erh), a former favorite of Li Ping'er's deceased husband, has herself adopted by Li Ping'er.

A golden bracelet is stolen from Ping'er's room by one of Li Jiao'er's servants. The servant is beaten and threatened with expulsion, and only the intercession of Li Guijie saves her. Guijie is incensed at the difference between the treatment her aunt's servant is given and the more lenient treatment received by a servant of Li Ping'er's in a previous similar incident. Li Ping'er keeps Wu Yin'er with her for the night and complains of the jealousy the others feel for her; she gives Yin'er a great deal of clothing, making Wu Yueniang and the others even more jealous of Li Ping'er's independent wealth. Ximen Qing's cronies whisper that Li Guijie is involved with another young man, Wang Sanguan (Wang San-kuan).

Ximen Qing's wives leave the household to visit Yueniang's sister-in-law, and several of the more prominent maidservants are invited to a party hosted by the wife of Ximen Qing's employee Ben the Fourth (Pen the Fourth). The maidservants are treated to entertainment and the sort of elaborate politeness usually reserved for their social superiors. When the servants are sent back to the Ximen household for the ladies' fur coats, the maidservants cause difficulties by standing on their own perceived differences in rank and, because of their quibbles, are slow in bringing the fur coats. Pan Jinlian is embarrassed by having no fur coat of her own and having therefore to wear one that has been taken in pawn by Ximen. The women's fortunes are told, and Li Ping'er learns that she is in danger. Pan Jinlian scoffs at the prediction, claiming that although one can interpret horoscopes, it is impossible to predict people's behavior.

A rogue named Miao Qing (Miao Ch'ing) murders his master and is exposed by a fellow servant, and Ximen Qing, who has been bribed to free Miao Qing, is impeached with his associate. Gifts are sent to Zhai Qian with a request for intervention by Cai Jing, and Zhai sends a reassuring answer; the impeachment is suppressed. Cai Jing's recommendations to the court for reorganization of the economy are adopted. These recommendations further Ximen Qing's growing financial interest in the salt trade.

Guan'ge suffers a severe fright on his return from ritual observances at the newly completed Ximen tombs. Ximen Qing once again gives an elaborate feast for the *zhuangyuan*, Cai Yun (Ts'ai Yün). Ximen accompanies Cai Yun as far as a nearby temple on the latter's departure. At the temple Ximen meets a monk who is described by the narrator in phrases that evoke the description of a penis. The monk gives him a powerful aphrodisiac but warns him to be cautious in its use.

Wu Yueniang receives the fertility drug she has requested. She has Buddhist nuns visit to celebrate Li Ping'er's birthday. Ximen spends the day with Wang Liu'er, where his aphrodisiac proves extremely powerful. His absence rouses Wu Yueniang's suspicions. While Ximen is with Wang Liu'er, his servant Dai'an (Tai-an) visits a brothel. On his arrival home, Ximen insists on having intercourse with Li Ping'er against her wishes. Because she is menstruating, he violates a ritual taboo. Jealous of Li Ping'er, Pan Jinlian foments a quarrel between Li Ping'er and Wu Yueniang.

Chapters 51–60

Wang Sanguan and several other revelers are arrested at Li Guijie's brothel. A warrant is out for Li Guijie's arrest. Ximen Qing has her name expunged. She swears that she has had no personal dealings with Wang and will have none. Nun Xue instructs Wu Yueninang concerning the proper day for use of the fertility drug. Ximen Qing is angered at Yueniang's dealings with Nun Xue, whom he has earlier ordered defrocked and punished for her part in arranging an illicit meeting between two young lovers.

Pan Jinlian is left to watch Guan'ge during a family party. She leaves the baby unattended to keep an assignation with Chen Jingji. Others appear before the couple's adulterous plans are realized, and the baby is found screaming, menaced by Jinlian's cat.

Ximen Qing sleeps with Wu Yueniang on a day propitious for the working of the fertility drug. Li Ping'er, worried about her son's ill health, promises Nun Xue to have scriptures printed as a way of storing up merit and thus protecting the boy. Ximen visits the capital for a celebration of Cai Jing's birthday.[31]

Ximen Qing hires a secretary, Wen Pigu (Wen Pi-ku, Warm-buttocks Wen, Pedant Wen, or Licentiate Wen), and visits an elegant singing-girl, Zheng Aiyue (Cheng Ai-yüeh). The crudity of his sexual demands distresses her. Li Ping'er gives money to Nun Xue for the printing of scriptures without demanding an accounting; Pan Jinlian and Meng Yulou both criticize her improvidence and note that money cannot purchase immortality. Pan Jinlian's cat, whom Jinlian has trained to jump at meat wrapped in a red cloth, pounces on Guan'ge one day while he is lying on the kang, having been dressed in a red shirt by Li Ping'er.

The baby suffers another severe fright and falls ill. Remedies are desperately tried, and the newly printed scriptures arrive. Li Ping'er dreams of her former husband, Hua Zixu, who demands her son. The baby dies. He is buried in the arms of Ximen Qing's deceased first wife. Li Ping'er dreams that Hua Zixu knocks her down when she refuses to follow him and Guan'ge. She becomes ill. Ximen Qing opens another shop and continues to lend money.

Chapters 61–70

One afternoon Ximen Qing has intercourse with Wang Liu'er, exhausting himself, and then has intercourse with Pan Jinlian on his return home. He is unable to have intercourse with Pan Jinlian without resorting to the use of his aphrodisiac. Li Ping'er hemorrhages repeatedly. Doctors are called in and give useless (and in one case absurd) diagnoses. Immortal Huang (Master Huang), a fortuneteller who is called in when Immortal Wu cannot be located, states that Li Ping'er's case is hopeless. Li Ping'er tells Ximen Qing of more dreams in which she is menaced by Hua Zixu. An exorcist, Daoist Master Pan (Taoist Master P'an, Demon-catcher P'an), is summoned. Through ceremonial and ritual performances, he determines that Li Ping'er committed a serious offense in a former life and that a complaint has been lodged against her with the officials of the netherworld. He further states that her current illness is not the result of some malevolent possession that can be exorcized. She is bound to die, and Pan declares that he is incapable of successfully intervening on her behalf. Li Ping'er warns Ximen Qing that he must mend his ways, warns Wu Yueniang to be careful of her own child when it is born, and dies. Ximen Qing remains disconsolate for many weeks, refusing to eat anywhere other than Li Ping'er's room and weeping whenever she is mentioned. His grief is extreme enough to elicit a warning from his otherwise sycophantic friend Ying Bojue that he will make the other women jealous, as indeed he does. He begins to sleep with Guan'ge's wet nurse, Ruyi (Ju-i), who had been kept on to serve Li Ping'er after Guan'ge's death.

An elaborate series of funeral observances is held, with rites conducted by a Daoist priest, Master Huang, who is en route to offer official sacrifice for the empire. News of another official promotion for Ximen Qing arrives during the ritual. Ximen finds time to entertain the visiting Grand Marshal Huang at the request of a powerful censor with whom Ximen is acquainted. Yueniang and Jinlian notice that the wet nurse Ruyi is acting above her station.

During a visit of condolence made by two prominent eunuch-officials to Ximen's household, recent ill omens at the court are discussed. These omens occurred in conjunction with the arrival of the Jin (also known as "Jurchen" or "Tartar") ambassador and his request that the Chinese court turn over three important Chinese garrison regions to Jin control. The eunuchs dismiss all this as personally inconsequential since they are not in the capital.

Ximen is asked by local merchants in his debt to intercede on behalf of relatives who have been arrested; his intervention is successful, and the men are released. Ximen grows progressively more exhausted by the rituals and entertainments in which he has had to take part. He complains of pains in his lower back and dreams that Li Ping'er warns him to slow his pace; Pan Jinlian scoffs that "dreams just tell you what you're already thinking" (夢是心頭想; my trans.; 67.16a). Ximen sleeps with Ruyi, who asks him for clothing.

An Chen, the deposed *zhuangyuan* whom Ximen Qing entertained earlier, describes to Ximen in two separate conversations the difficulties brought on the people by the upriver shipment of marble for construction of Song Huizong's Genyue, a pleasure park in Kaifeng.[32]

Pan Jinlian obtains Nun Xue's fertility drug. The courtesan Zheng Aiyue tells Ximen that Li Guijie, whom Zheng Aiyue views as a rival, is still involved with Wang Sanguan and suggests that Ximen Qing get the better of Wang by seducing both Wang's mother, a widow, and Wang's neglected and unhappy wife. Ximen Qing is delighted with these suggestions, since they will lead to sexual conquests of a higher order than any he has previously experienced. He visits Wang's mother, Lady Lin, who urges him to take her dissolute son in hand; by the time he leaves, Ximen Qing has seduced Lady Lin and become the adoptive father of Wang Sanguan. Ximen sends for further news of the promotion he has been promised. He receives his appointment and is entertained lavishly in the capital; at a presentation ceremony he receives special recognition by the corrupt minister Zhu Mian (Chu Mien).

Chapters 71–80

Still at the capital, Ximen Qing listens to a play about the founding of the Song dynasty, wearing a borrowed robe whose insignia is that of a rank higher than his own, and dreams again of Li Ping'er, who warns him about his conduct. Sexually aroused by his dream, he has intercourse with his servant Wang Jing (Wang Ching), the younger brother of his mistress Wang Liu'er.

He arrives home to a household racked, in his absence, by quarrels over which of his wives has the greatest access to him. Wu Yueniang invites nuns to recite scriptures for Meng Yulou's birthday, which Ximen Qing ignores until Yueniang forces him to go to Yulou, causing him to miss an opportunity to sleep with Pan Jinlian on the day propitious for the working of the fertility drug she has obtained from Nun Xue. Pan Jinlian's claims on Ximen's sexual favors are by this time nearly exclusive among his wives. Yueniang quarrels with Jinlian, a quarrel that is mediated by Meng Yulou. Pan Jinlian remains jealous of Ximen's attentions to the wet nurse Ruyi and to a new maid, Lai Huilian (Lai Hui-lien), whose appearance recalls the dead Song Huilian and with whom Ximen Qing predictably begins a sexual liaison.

At this point jealousy also exists among the courtesans, as Li Guijie protests Zheng Aiyue's slander of her to her adoptive mother, Wu Yueniang. Ximen Qing's physical powers are further taxed by an almost ceaseless round of official visiting and entertaining, including a reception for the ninth son of Cai Jing. During these official gatherings Ximen Qing makes a great many recommendations for posts, all of which succeed. He obtains an imperial commission to supply works of art for Song Huizong's Genyue.

It is discovered that Ximen Qing's secretary, Wen Pigu, has been forcing one of the servant boys to have sexual intercourse with him; Wen is immediately removed from the household. The ladies of Ximen's household are invited to visit the wife of his crony Ying Bojue, and in their absence, the maidservants have a party, during which Chunmei displays her sense of self-importance by ordering a blind singer, originally hired by Wu Yueniang and presently in Yueniang's rooms, to come and sing for them. When the singer refuses, Chunmei drives her from the house. Ximen begins an affair with the wife of his employee Ben the Fourth, as does his servant Dai'an. Ximen plans the seduction of the socially prominent young wife of a new colleague. Ximen's friends comment on his growing debilitation. He visits Wang Liu'er one afternoon, exhausting himself sexually. On his drunken return home, a shadowy figure darts out at him from under a bridge and startles his horse. (Is this Hua Zixu's spirit pursuing him, as Li Ping'er tells Ximen Qing when she visits him in a dream?) Once home, he passes out in Jinlian's rooms. Jinlian feeds him an enormous dose of his aphrodisiac and engages him in sexual intercourse while he is barely conscious, whereupon he finally ejaculates—first semen, then blood, and finally cold air. (Here the narrator comments that nothing awaits him now but death.) His penis and testicles swell; doctors diagnose sexual exhaustion, but their remedies fail to save him. Immortal Wu predicts his imminent death. Ximen Qing sees visions of Wu Da and Hua Zixu, who demand payment of a debt. Ximen Qing expresses to Wu Yueniang his desire that his wives keep the household, including the coming child, intact. He also gives orders to sell off some of his stores. Ximen Qing dies. At nearly the same time, Yueniang gives birth to a son, whom she names Xiaoge (Hsiao-ko, "Filial Elder Brother"). Ximen Qing's associates and his second wife, Li Jiao'er, immediately begin to steal from the household.

Chapters 81–90

Ximen Qing's band of sworn brothers has a eulogy written to be read at his funeral; it turns out to be a eulogy on his penis. Han Daoguo and Wang Liu'er abscond with the proceeds from the unauthorized sale of Ximen Qing's silks to their daughter's home with Zhai Qian in the capital. The Ximen family's cloth stores are closed down. Other employees steal from the household. Pan Jinlian flirts openly with Ximen Qing's son-in-law, Chen Jingji; the two write verses to each other and express their feeling in operatic arias. They begin a sexual liaison.

Li Jiao'er provokes a quarrel with Yueniang and returns to the brothel. Wu Yueniang makes a pilgrimage to the temple of the Princess of Azure Clouds on Mount Tai to fulfill a vow made during Ximen Qing's last illness. The Daoist monk at the monastery is in league with a highway man and routinely waylays beautiful women so that the bandit can sexually assault them. Yueniang escapes to the abode of a hermit, the Buddhist priest Pujing (P'u-ching), who promises her safety on condition that she give her son, Xiaoge, to him as a disciple when the boy reaches the age of fifteen. She agrees for the sake of convenience but does not take the agreement seriously.

In Yueniang's absence, Pan Jinlian becomes pregnant by Chen Jingji but aborts the child, attempting to dispose of it in the sewer, where it is discovered by the sewer cleaner. On her return, Yueniang first expels Chunmei, who acted as a go-between, and then Chen Jingji and Pan Jinlian. Pang Chunmei leaves the household with her head held high and without shedding a tear. Yueniang gives her the sixteen taels of silver she arrived with but no extra clothing. Pan Jinlian is distraught at being separated from her closest companion and confidante.

Chunmei is married by a matchmaker to Major Zhou Xiu (Commandant Chou Hsiu), a wealthy and powerful former associate of Ximen Qing's, and Chen Jingji gallops off to his parents' home to borrow the bride-price of one hundred silver taels required for Pan Jinlian.[33] (Here we briefly return to the original story, borrowed from *Outlaws of the Marsh*, in which Wu Song returns, kills Jinlian, and then flees to join the rebels.) Wu Song, the brother of Pan Jinlian's first husband, Wu Da, returns to Qinghe District. He claims he wants to marry Pan Jinlian. Pan Jinlian believes this. Old Lady Wang (Dame Wang) goes to Yueniang with the proposal. Wu Yueniang does not intervene to stop the marriage, although she feels that Pan Jinlian is surely doomed by it. (Wu Song has been freed as part of an amnesty granted when Song Qinzong 宋欽宗 [1100–61] is declared heir apparent to Emperor Song Huizong.) Pan Jinlian's original attraction to Wu Song revives, and she is pleased when he offers the required bride-price. He takes her home and promptly disembowels her with a dagger as part of a grisly sacrifice to his deceased brother, Wu Da. He also kills Old Lady Wang for her part in the murder. He then flees, becomes a monk, and finally joins the bandits on Mount Liang.

On reaching home, Chen Jingji finds his father dead and immediately returns to Qinghe. Pan Jinlian's spirit appears both to him and to Chunmei in dreams, asking for burial. Chunmei arranges for Jinlian's entrails to be returned to her body cavity, which is then sewn up. Pan Jinlian is buried in the graveyard at Eternal Prosperity Temple. The matchmaker who married Chunmei to Commandant Zhou reports to Yueniang and the remaining wives that Chunmei is well and pregnant. The women are silent and jealous. Yueniang sends Ximen Dajie in mourning garb and with appropriate sacrificial articles to pay a daughter-in-law's respects to Chen Jingji's late father. Jingji refuses to accept either his wife or the articles and turns them away. Dajie is forced to continue living in the Ximen household. The women of the household visit Ximen's grave on Tomb-Sweeping

Day; there they see Chunmei, in all her splendor, who has come to sacrifice for Pan Jinlian. She behaves very courteously to members of her former household and is particularly careful not to put on airs as a result of her newly elevated status. Without mentioning Pan Jinlian's name directly, Chunmei indicates that she has come to offer sacrifice to her "mother" (俺娘; 5.89.170; 89.11a). Yueniang fails to understand what "mother" Chunmei is referring to. Meng Yulou does and goes to offer her own sacrifices to Pan Jinlian.

Laiwang and Sun Xue'e, Ximen Qing's fourth wife, renew their affair and begin to remove stolen valuables from the Ximen household. The stolen goods are recognized, the two are arrested, and Sun Xue'e is returned to Yueniang by the magistrate to do with her as she sees fit. Yueniang sells her as a maid to Chunmei, who puts her to work in the kitchen as revenge for their former enmity.

Chapters 91–99

Meng Yulou is married with great pomp to Li Gongbi (Li Kung-pi), the son of a local magistrate. When Chen Jingji threatens Yueniang with a lawsuit, alleging that she is keeping property of his, she sends him Ximen Dajie and her trousseau. On a purchasing trip, Chen Jingji wastes much of his money and takes a concubine named Feng Jinbao (Feng Chin-pao), leaving little left of Dajie's trousseau and his mother's money with which to open a cloth store. The news of this second marriage and dissipation causes his mother's death. An associate of Chen Jingji's absconds with the remains of his capital and goods. Chen Jingji attempts to blackmail Meng Yulou with a hairpin of hers that he once found; she and her husband try to entrap Jingji and bring him before the law, but he proves persuasive in court, and the resultant embarrassment causes Magistrate Li to exile his son and Yulou to the Li family's properties in the north. Chen Jingji finds Feng Jinbao and Ximen Dajie quarrelling and beats Dajie, who hangs herself. Yueniang brings legal action against Chen Jingji for murder, but Chen Jingji bribes the court and has the sentence reduced from strangulation to exile. Feng Jinbao is ordered by the court to resume her former profession as a prostitute. Jingji is required to pay for Dajie's burial and finds himself destitute.

Jingji falls in with beggars but is eventually taken in hand by a Daoist benefactor and installed in a local temple. Here he survives among the corrupt monks by means of sexual favors and is allowed to conduct the temple business at the wharf, where he once again meets Feng Jinbao. After a brawl, Chen Jingji and Feng Jinbao are brought before Chunmei's husband, Commandant Zhou. Chunmei has Sun Xue'e sold into a brothel to keep her from exposing the truth about her past with Jingji and then claims that Jingji is her cousin. She has him installed in the Zhou household, where the two begin an adulterous affair. Chunmei, who has borne a son and daughter and gained ascendance over Yueniang, asks her husband to intercede in Yueniang's favor after a false accusation of adultery is lodged against her. Now the two women relate to one another as social equals. When Chunmei visits with gifts on Xiaoge's birthday, there is a striking contrast between her prosperity and the present state of the once elaborate Ximen garden, which has since fallen into disarray. A post and a wife are found for Chen Jingji. He is married with great pomp, though he continues his sexual relationship with Chunmei. He uses money given to him by Commandant Zhou to sue the associate who stole the proceeds of his cloth business. The suit is successful; he is now prosperous and his former associate destitute. He opens an inn at the wharf, where he maintains a swaggering presence. Han Daoguo, Wang Liu'er, and their daughter, Aijie, take rooms at the inn; they have been forced to leave the capital as a result of Cai Jing's fall from favor. The family is supported by the prostitution of the mother and the daughter. Chen Jingji falls in love with Han Aijie.

A relative of one of Commandant Zhou's retainers causes a brawl at the inn, and Chen Jingji vows vengeance; his vows are overheard by the retainer, who kills him. The retainer is arrested and sentenced to death. Sun Xue'e hangs herself for fear of being implicated in the case. Han Aijie insists on maintaining chaste widowhood after Jingji's death and goes to live with Chunmei and Chen Jingji's legitimate wife, Ge Cuiping (Ko Ts'ui-p'ing).

Chapter 100

Han Daoguo and Wang Liu'er join a merchant on his return to Huzhou. Han Aijie and Chen Jingji's wife keep each other company, and both maintain their chaste widowhood for Chen Jingji. Bored and fretful, Chunmei unsuccessfully attempts to seduce one of her husband's servants. On a military expedition, Commandant Zhou sends for Chunmei, their children, and their servants. Aijie and Cuiping are left behind with relatives. Chunmei seduces the son of one of her husband's retainers, Zhou Yi (Chou I).

Battles and invasions erupt everywhere, and Commandant Zhou is killed. Chunmei and her servants return home with his ashes; the whole country is now at war. Pang Chunmei completely abandons herself to pleasures of the bed with Zhou Yi. Wasting away, she dies while having sex with him. A frightened Zhou Yi steals jewelry and money but is soon arrested and beaten to death.

Meanwhile, Jingji's wife, Cuiping, is taken back by her family, and Han Aijie sets out to find her own family. A chance meeting with her uncle leads her to her mother, and she discovers that her father, Han Daoguo, has died. Her uncle, Han the Second, and mother, Wang Liu'er, marry (the two previously had an affair) and succeed to the property on which they have been living, when Wang Liu'er's patron dies. Han Aijie refuses to marry any of the local gentry, becomes a nun instead, cuts off her hair, blinds herself, and joins a temple, where she falls ill and dies at the age of thirty-two.

Wu Yueniang, her second eldest brother, and her son, Xiaoge, set out with their remaining servants to escape the Jin invaders. Yueniang plans to make her way to the home of Yun Lishou (Yün Lishou), a sworn brother of Ximen Qing's whose daughter she has betrothed to her son, Xiaoge, who has just turned fifteen. En route, however, they meet Pujing, the priest to whom Xiaoge had been promised as an infant, who demands the boy. When they refuse, he conducts them to the Eternal Prosperity Temple, where they spend the night. As the others sleep, Yueniang's maid Xiaoyu peers through a crack in the old priest's door and sees Pujing speaking to the ghosts of those who have died in the Ximen household, promising them his intercession to mitigate the penalties of karma. All, including Ximen Qing, announce their imminent reincarnation in the Eastern Capital (a term commonly used in the novel to refer to Kaifeng, the capital of the Northern Song dynasty) as sons and daughters of families of rank approximately equal to that held in life.

Meanwhile, Yueniang dreams that she and her company reach the household of Yun Lishou. In the dream Yun Lishou's wife has died, and he proposes to Yueniang. She refuses and calls for her brother. Yun Lishou declares that he has already killed her brother and Dai'an and has their heads brought in to prove it. Thus threatened, Wu Yueniang agrees to the marriage on the condition that her son first be married to Yun Lishou's daughter. The children are married at once. After the marriage Wu Yueniang refuses to let Yun Lishou have his way with her. Angered at her attempt to deceive him, he cuts off Xiaoge's head. Wu Yueniang awakens from her dream in a fright. When she wakes, she and Xiaoyu recount what they have seen to each other and are silent and fearful. In the morning, Pujing explains that their meeting is the result of Wu Yueniang's piety. He asks whether she has become enlightened or not, and she says that she has. He then repeats his demand for Xiaoge, saying that the boy is in fact a reincarnation of Ximen Qing, who has come back to life to repair the damage he caused. Pujing touches Xiaoge with his wand, and the boy turns into Ximen Qing; he touches the boy a second time, and he is Xiaoge once again. Convinced of the truth of the old priest's words, Yueniang weeps and gives up her son. Pujing then announces that peace is at hand, and that the family must return to Qinghe. He then disappears with Xiaoge.

The Jin Empire is established in the north, and the first emperor of the Southern Song dynasty ascends the throne to rule over his diminished territories. On their return home, Yueniang changes the servant Dai'an's name to Ximen Dai'an and makes him heir to her diminished property so that he can maintain her in her old age.

While no plot summary can do justice to the narrative texture of such a complex work as *The Plum in the Golden Vase*, a synopsis allows one to identify patterns within that texture. Despite *Plum*'s almost exclusive focus on the daily life of the Ximen family, attentive readers will notice certain parallels between the life of that family and the world outside the household: the fall of the Ximen household parallels that of the Northern Song Empire, and both the household and the empire are reestablished only in reduced form. Ximen Qing's six wives seem to correspond to the six evil ministers misgoverning the empire. Ximen's corrupt and tyrannical behavior matches that of the court, whose corruption and tyranny are brought to our attention by *Plum*'s narrator at strategic points throughout the novel. There are no obvious one-to-one correlations, though. Ximen Qing's pattern of interceding with officials to achieve his aims matches the pattern established for the evil minister Cai Jing 蔡京, whose name is homophonous with *cai* 財 ("money") and *jing* 精 ("semen"). Within this pattern of macrocosm and microcosm is one of models and imitators, of masters and servants, of main characters and their shadows. Pan Jinlian, for instance, has Song Huilian and then Lai Huilian. Chen Jingji learns to be like Ximen, who in turn is like a little Cai Jing. Pang Chunmei learns to monopolize information like Jinlian and indulge in sexual excess and taboo violation like Ximen Qing. And she dies just like he does.

Early Modern Comments
on *Plum* and Its Origins

The following are some selected comments that teachers may find useful as a means of initiating discussion. Most of these comments wrestle with the notion that *Plum* was written to entice and destroy a particular kind of reader. It is, of course, challenging and perhaps even unfair to compare works of such disparate times and places, but given the apocryphal tale attached to the writing of *Plum*, the tale's focus of poison and revenge, its persistence as claim or rumor, and its implication that the book is both literally and metaphorically poison, teachers may find a comparison with Umberto Eco's *The Name of the Rose* useful for sparking discussion. As Eco says in the postscript to his novel, "[B]ooks always speak of other books, and every story tells a story that has already been told" (489). Is *Plum* a roman à clef? Does it (can it?) speak to our own time? Does *Plum* prefigure the postmodern idea that all texts perpetually refer to other texts rather than to external reality? Does *Plum*, like *Name of the Rose*, also hearken back to the notion that the citation of books was inherently necessary to write new stories? In China, fiction (*xiaoshuo* 小說) evolved out of official histories and their inclusion of "unofficial histories" (*waishi* 外史). Does something similar happen in Eco's book? Eco mentions that his novel ends with irony: "[V]ery little is discovered and the detective is defeated" (564). After unraveling the central mystery, in part through coincidence and error, William of Baskerville concludes that there was no pattern. Eco undoes the central attempt to untangle the threads of the plot, leaving resolution partly the result of accident and arguably without meaning. How do we read the ambiguity of *Plum*'s ending? How do we read its beginning as a subplot of another novel? Does the ending derive its meaning from a Confucian or Buddhist interpretation, do they cancel each other out, or does the novel's incessant intertextuality prevent any one meaning from taking precedence over others? Just as *Plum* says in its prefaces, critics say that this (fictional) novel (really) corrupts real people. What is *Plum*'s relationship to truth and fiction? What relation do the stories of *Plum*'s creation have to its reception, availability, or meaning? The following comments from the seventeenth (and eighteenth?) century address some of these issues and the legend of *Plum*'s origin.

From "Miscellaneous Notes on Drama and Song" ("Guqu zayan" 顧曲雜言), by Shen Defu 沈德符 (1578–1642)

Yuan Hongdao wrote in his "Drinking Games" that *Plum in the Golden Vase* was an extension of and a companion volume to the famous novel *Outlaws of the Marsh*. I am very sorry that I have not been able to read it. When I visited Hongdao at his residence in the capital in 1606, I asked him if he had a complete copy of the book. He told me at that time that he had only read several chapters of it, and that he found them quite extraordinary. . . . However, three years later, when Hongdao's brother Zhongdao came to the capital to sit for the *jinshi* examination, he brought a complete copy of the book with him, which I borrowed and copied for myself. My friend Feng Youlong was so impressed and delighted when he read it that he approached a bookstore with the suggestion that they purchase it from me at a high price and publish it. Another friend of mine, Ma Zhongliang, Superintendent of Taxation in Suzhou at the time, also tried to persuade me to accept the bookseller's offer, explaining that it would alleviate some of my financial difficulties. I told him, "A book of this nature will sooner or later find its way into print. But once it becomes available, it is certain to be widely read, and people are bound to be corrupted by it. When I am brought to trial in the court of the King of Hades, how shall I answer the charges put to me? Is it worthwhile suffering the tortures of hell, in exchange for the petty profits to be gained from having it printed?" Ma was in complete agreement with me, and so I kept the book securely locked up in my cabinet. Before long, however, *Plum in the Golden Vase* was enjoying brisk sales in Suzhou.[34]

From "Jottings from Cold Flower Cottage" ("Hanhua'an suibi" 寒花盦隨筆)

It is generally believed that the novel *Plum in the Golden Vase* is from the brush of Wang Yanzhou (Shizhen), and that it was written to criticize Yan Shifan. The character of Ximen Qing in the novel is a faithful image of Yan Shifan. Yan's childhood name was Qing, the same as that of the character in the book. Shifan's courtesy name was Donglou [東樓 ("eastern pavilion")] while that of the character in the book is Ximen [西門 ("western gate")]. The two names are exactly antithetical.

Others say that the novel was written by a filial son to avenge his father's death. The son was aware that his father had been murdered by an official whom he knew. He tried to wreak vengeance upon that man repeatedly, but with no success. Then, through secret inquiries, he learned that the man had the habit of turning the pages of whatever book he was reading with a finger moistened with saliva. The filial son spent three years writing the novel, and when it was finished, put poison on the corner of every page. He then hired a man to offer the book for sale in the marketplace at the very moment when that official was passing by in his sedan chair. The hired man cried out, "This is the most extraordinary book in the whole world [*tianxia diyi qishu* 天下第一奇書, the title by which many later Zhang Zhupo editions became known]." The official took the book and began to read it in his sedan chair, and by the time he got home, he had finished it. He was so impressed that he wanted to find the person who sold it to him and enquire about its price, but he was nowhere to be found. At this point he suddenly realized that he had been the victim of a plot and attempted to save himself. But it was too late. He had already been fatally poisoned and died soon after. Examining this matter now, both of the remarks above appear to be correct.

The filial son was really Wang Fengzhou [Wang Shizhen] and the official Tang Jingchuan 唐荆川 [also known as Tang Shunzhi 唐順之 (1507–61)]. Wang Shu, Shizhen's father, died as a result of the scheming of the Yans [Yan Song and his son, Yan Shifan], though Tang Jingchuan's slandering was the underlying cause of the entire affair. In Yao Pingzhong's *Essential of the Chronicles*, mention is made of the death penalty imposed on the imperial inspector Wang Shu. The following is found in a note: Yan Song was eager to acquire an ancient painting in the possession of Wang Shu. Since Wang was reluctant to part with it, he gave Yan a copy of the painting. When a connoisseur pointed this out, Yan Song became enraged and put Wang to death on the grounds of a false charge that he had leaked an important military secret. Though the name of the connoisseur is not revealed, someone with knowledge of the event said it was none other than [the anthologist] Tang Jingchuan, and that the painting in question was the celebrated scroll "A View of the River at the Qingming Festival" *Qingming shanghe tu* 清明上河图.

Harboring bitter and deep-seated hatred for Tang Jingchuan, Wang Shizhen swore his revenge. He sent his men several times to spy on Tang, but Tang guarded himself carefully against all attempts on his life. One evening, Tang was reading alone in his room when an assassin grabbed him by the hair from behind. The assassin was just about to stab him when Tang said, "Though I cannot escape my bitter fate, please allow me to write a letter to my family." The assassin stood by his side as Tang penned a few lines. Suddenly the tip of his writing brush became detached from the stem. Making out as if to repair it, Tang held the stem near a candle. The stem actually concealed a miniature crossbow fitted with poison arrows. The heat of the candle released the trigger, and the assassin died instantly as one of the arrows pierced his throat. The news of this left Wang in deep despair.

One day, he met Tang while waiting for an audience with the emperor. Tang said, "Since I have not seen you for a long time, you must be busy writing something." Wang replied that he was engaged in writing a novel called *Plum in the Golden Vase*, but in fact he was not writing anything, and was only trying to deceive the other man. Tang Jingchuan pressed him for a look at his new book, so when he went home, Wang hired a great corps of workers to carve the woodblocks, and as he wrote the novel, each chapter was carved as soon as he had finished it. Wang had the book printed with a mixture of ink and poison and delivered it to Tang when it was completed. Tang immersed himself immediately in the book and read it in great haste. Since it was freshly printed and the ink particularly sticky, some of the pages were stuck together, and Tang had great difficulty separating them. In order to read it, then, he separated the pages with a finger moistened with saliva. By the time he finished reading the novel, he had ingested so much poison that he died.

Some claim that the victim of this poisoning was actually Yan Shifan, not Tang Jingchuan. However, Yan Shifan was executed after receiving the death sentence, so that the poisoned man must have been Tang. The details pertaining to "the dutiful son spending three years writing the novel" and "the official reading the book in his sedan chair," are merely different versions of the same story. It is hard to understand why an outstanding scholar like Tang Jingchuan would be willing to serve the base needs of the Yans and be forced to pay for all the trouble he caused with his own life.[35]

From "The Notebook of an Anonymous Scholar" ("Queming biji" 缺名筆記*)*

Plum in the Golden Vase is one of "four marvelous books" of Chinese literature. It is said that it was written by Wang Shizhen as a way of avenging his father's death at the hands of the Yan family. . . . Some say that the perpetrator was actually Tang Jingchuan, who, while holding the post of Imperial Inspector of Jingyou, framed a charge against an innocent person which led to this person's execution. The innocent man's son then tried every possible means of taking his revenge, but to no avail. At this time Tang retired from his official post and returned to his hometown. He was a great collector of curious books which he took great relish in reading. When the dead man's son learned about this, he wrote the novel *Plum in the Golden Vase* in a very short time, applied arsenic to the pages of the manuscript and presented it to Tang, since he knew that Tang had the habit of turning the pages of his books with a finger moistened with the tip of his tongue. Tang finished reading the entire book in one night. The next morning, his tongue felt numb and sluggish, and he saw in a mirror that it had turned a dark color. Realizing that he had been poisoned, Tang summoned his son and said, "People are plotting against me. After my death, you must allow no one except our closest relatives to enter my room."

Sure enough, Tang died shortly afterwards, and within a matter of hours, a man wearing a white mourning gown rushed into the Tang's home crying loudly in lamentation. The man fell to his knees before Tang's son, and told him that he owed the deceased an inestimable debt, and hoped that he would be allowed to pay his last respects to his benefactor before the coffin was sealed. Tang's son, moved by the man's sincerity, gave his permission, and the visitor entered Tang's room and cried bitterly over his corpse. After making repeated bows, he left. When it came time to dress the corpse for burial, it was discovered that one of the arms was missing, whereupon they realized that the "mourner" was actually the author of the novel. One surmises that since his own father had been beheaded, the author would not rest content with poisoning Tang, but disguised himself to facilitate his maiming the dead man. Both of these stories are in circulation, yet it is hard to say which is true. In Yuan Zhonglang's 袁中郎 [Hongdao's] book *Jinfan ji* 锦帆集 [*The Embroidered Sail Collection*] one comes across the statement: "I read *Plum in the Golden Vase* in bed and found it full of vivid descriptions. Even the famous essay 'Qi fa' 七發 ['The Seven Exhortations,' by Mei Sheng 枚乘 (d. 141 BCE)] cannot vie with the book in terms of excellence." *Plum in the Golden Vase* has been well-known for ages, but it is actually an indecent book, full of trash, with little merit. It is not only a matter of the absurdity of its concluding scene, wherein all the main characters in the book are reincarnated.[36]

From "Notes from Qiushui Studio" ("*Qiushui xuan biji*" 秋水軒筆記)

The biography of Tang Shunzhi [also known as Jingchuan] contains the following information about his death: In the 39th year of the Jiajing reign [1561], during the flood season, Tang made a trip by boat on the Yangtze River despite his declining health. He got past Jiaoshan, but when he reached Tongzhou, he expired at the age of fifty-four. I received notice of his death and attended his funeral. Like myself, Tang was a native of Wujin prefecture, and enjoyed a fine reputation as a scholar. At the same time it was rumored that an enemy of Tang's acquired the original copy of the novel *Plum in the Golden Vase* by paying a fabulous sum. This person had dipped the pages of the manuscript in liquid arsenic and then presented the book to Tang. Tang was an avid reader, and finished the book in a short time, turning the pages with a finger moistened with saliva. By the time he came to the end of the book, his tongue was stiff and numb, and he soon after died of poisoning. When one compares these two stories, it becomes obvious that the rumor circulating among the people cannot stand up to the official record. The latter includes the following: "Tang Shunzhi was a man of broad learning. He was well-read in the fields of astronomy, music, geography, military science, archery, geometry, the black arts, animals and birds." This remark is not unfounded. A story has been handed down in my hometown to the effect that Tang's home in Qingguo Street was called the Pangu Tower, and contained winding staircases so confusing to the uninitiated that it was very difficult to gain access to the central part of the building. Tang had concealed crossbows placed among his furniture and on his desk from which arrows could be released to prevent potential assassins from causing harm to his person. The residence now belongs to the Lin family. Whenever I walk past it, I fondly recall the great scholar who is now no longer among us.[37]

From the Biography of Zhang Zhupo, Written by His Younger Brother, Zhang Daoyuan 張道淵

My brother read so quickly it seemed as if he could take in ten lines of text with every glance. Occasionally I would see him browsing through works of fiction like *Outlaws of the Marsh* and *Plum in the Golden Vase*; the leaves of the book would turn as quickly as fallen leaves blown by the wind. Before long, he would already be finished with his reading. He once said to me, *"Plum in the Golden Vase* is a very finely constructed work but since the death of Jin Shengtan [commentator on *Outlaws of the Marsh* and other major novels] there are few people alive who know about this. I am going to pick out all of its fine points and make them manifest." Thereupon he closeted himself in his room and in a little more than ten days his commentary was finished. Someone said to him, "If you sell your manuscript to a book publisher, it would fetch a very good price." My brother said, "Do you think that I wrote this for money? I intend to have it published so that all the people of the realm can also enjoy the beauty of its composition. Is this not a good enough reason?" Therefore, he had the blocks cut for printing, and then took them to Nanjing. People came from far and near to purchase copies and his fame spread widely. Of the famous literary men who came to Nanjing, the number of them who paid visits to my brother in a single day could be counted by the tens. Zhupo was by nature very fond of society, and even though he was staying in rented lodgings, his parlor was always crowded with guests. However, his income was just enough to cover his expenses. One day he exclaimed, "How can a real man allow himself to be tied down by this!" He then turned over the printing blocks for the edition to his landlord and set out for the North empty-handed.[38]

NOTES

[1] In 2004 an application from Bu Jian and Bai Weiguo was approved to make a new annotated edition of the unexpurgated *cihua* edition, and in 2015 the government permitted an increase of the run from one thousand to three thousand copies, although it still ordered that buyer eligibility be restricted to selected experts and academics.

[2] In the 1990s Chen Jialin managed to get a permit to film the novel, but as he was about to shoot, a notice arrived ordering him to stop the movie and return the permit.

[3] This claim is made by a local, self-taught *Plum* scholar, Pan Zhiyi.

[4] Despite *Plum*'s fictional setting, two towns in Shandong Province make rival claims as the book's true historical location.

[5] Onlookers reported that this was the 2008 Hong Kong film known in English as *The Forbidden Legend: Sex and Chopsticks*.

[6] This play is available in English translation (see Swatek). Braester argues that in modern plays Pan Jinlian is rewritten as a feminist heroine who seeks happiness but is tragically killed because of social intolerance (56–72).

[7] Wei Minglun's play is available in two English translations; see Wei, *Pan Jinlian: The History* and *Pan Jinlian: The Story*.

[8] This same phrase appears in the *Muwa gisun* (*Plain Talk*), a schoolbook belonging to Leping, an eleven-year-old boy learning Manchu, possibly in the late eighteenth century ("From the *Jin Ping Mei*"). The book is in the collection of the Harvard-Yenching Library.

[9] Aside from the earliest English translations of *Plum* that focus only on the sex scenes, Franz Kuhn's abridged German translation of *Jin Ping Mei* was retranslated into English by Bernard Miall and published in 1939 under the title Chin P'ing Mei: *The Adventurous History of Hsi Men and His Six Wives* (later editions appeared in 1940, 1942, 1947, 1950, 1952, 1959, 1960, and 1982). While this book carried the scholarly weight of an introduction by the well-known sinologist and translator Arthur Waley (1889–1966), and while it did not focus on erotic scenes, that it shared a subtitle with translations meant to sell on the erotic fiction market must have made distinguishing between the pornography and the masterpiece somewhat challenging to interested readers.

[10] In his introduction to *Plum*, Roy briefly discusses the case for the playwright Tang Xianzu's authorship (Introduction xlii–xliii). Roy discusses this in more detail in "The Case for T'ang Hsien-Tsu's Authorship of the *Jin Ping Mei*."

[11] See Zhang Zhupo, "How to Read the *Chin P'ing Mei*." An earlier version using Pinyin appeared in *Renditions*; see Zhang Zhupo, "How to Read *Jin Ping Mei*." Roy's quite early "Chang Chu-p'o's Commentary on the *Chin P'ing Mei*," although in need of updating with regard to newer information about Zhang himself, remains a good brief introduction to Zhang's commentary in English that quotes from a variety of prefatory items in the extensive front matter of Zhang's commentary edition of the novel.

[12] There is a similar story about Yan Shifan in *Yipeng xue* 一捧雪 (*A Handful of Snow*), a play by the Suzhou dramatist Li Yu 李玉 (ca. 1591–ca. 1671). The story involves a priceless jade cup that Yan wants but that the aristocrat Mo Huaigu tries to keep by giving him a facsimile. When the forgery is discovered, Yan has Mo arrested. When the time comes to behead Mo, at the last minute, his servant substitutes himself for his master and is executed instead. Scene 18 is available in English translation (Li Yu, "Handful").

[13] Arthur Waley details other versions in his account of this legend in his introduction to Chin P'ing Mei: *The Adventurous History of Hsi Men and His Six Wives*.

[14] To translate *cihua* as "ballad tale" or "chantefable" is not really fitting, since the novel is not at all similar to works that are more properly labeled *cihua*. The *xiuxiang* and later versions omit *cihua* from the title. Presumably the term referred to the large number of popular songs incorporated into the *cihua* text that do not appear in other editions.

[15] The *cihua* edition is dated based on one of its prefaces, which includes a date that encompasses a couple days in 1617. Since most of the dates are from 1618, we use 1618 for convenience.

[16] Xiaofei Tian provides a clear comparison of the two major recensions and makes a compelling argument for the *xiuxiang* version in her article "A Preliminary Comparison."

[17] A chantefable is a medieval tale that consists of alternating verse and prose.

[18] Xiaofei Tian makes these contradistinctions and many more in her article "A Preliminary Comparison."

[19] For more on the differences between *changpian xiaoshuo* and novels, see Shang Wei's essay in this volume.

[20] A student edition of Roy's translation is planned. This edition will move the reference material online and use Pinyin to transliterate proper nouns.

[21] Andrew Plaks discusses the novel's neo-Confucian leanings in *The Four Masterworks of the Ming Novel* (55–180).

[22] The version of Zhang's "How to Read" essay published in *Renditions* reinstates complete translations of Zhang's commentaries in the first and hundredth chapters of the novel and includes attempts to reflect the emphatic punctuation of the original. The essay is available for free download on the journal's website; see Zhang Zhupo, "How to Read *Jin Ping Mei*."

[23] Perry Link makes this observation in his review of Roy's translation. Link's review also offers an excellent introduction to *Plum*.

[24] Many scholars are averse to calling sequels written by later authors *fan fiction*, largely because most authors of sequels are well-known authors or scholars in their own right, but the difference between sequels and fan fiction is certainly worth discussing in the classroom.

[25] Siao-Chen Hu writes, "The narrator's discussions of karmic retribution are also omitted. In doing so, the editor of *Gelian huaying* actually moved away from the fundamental concepts of Ding Yaokang. However, before long it too was banned. Perhaps more interestingly, a new version titled *Jinwu meng* (*Dream of the golden chamber*) came out in 1915, less than four years after the last Manchu emperor abdicated the throne. This was a time when people were trying to promote nationalism and anti-Manchu sentiments. The editor Sun Jing'an therefore based his work on Ding's *Xu Jin Ping Mei* and restored all those 'sensitive' passages related to history and politics. The retribution part is further reduced in this version, something understandable given the fact that this was a time obsessed with science and reason" (94n4).

[26] Stephen Owen translates scene 10, "Waking Suddenly from a Dream" (882–92); scene 26, "Looking Over the Portrait" (892–96); and scene 28, "Secret Union" (896–914) in *An Anthology of Chinese Literature*.

[27] I know of only one, which excerpts chapter 12 to show the clever, sometimes vicious competition among the many women who vie for Ximen's attention; see Mair 981–97.

[28] The *Shuihu zhuan* episode is available in English; see Shi and Luo, *Outlaws and Marshes*.

[29] Unless otherwise noted, parenthetical citations refer to Roy's translation, *The Plum in the Golden Vase*, and to *Jin Ping Mei cihua* 金瓶梅詞話 (*Plum in the Golden Vase: A Ballad Tale*).

[30] The plot synopsis provided here relies heavily on Carlitz's *The Role of Drama* (15–26). The synopsis has been borrowed with permission, and with some changes.

[31] The events described in this paragraph are inferred from the title couplets of chapters 53–57, chapters that in both the *cihua* and *xiuxiang* versions seem to have

been written by another author, perhaps because that portion of the manuscript had been lost while being circulated among the small circle of its initial readers before it was completed. More detailed discussions of editions and variants can be found in Rolston, *How to Read* 439–46 and Hanan, "Text."

[32] Most of the precious rockery, rare trees, and unusual flora that embellished the environs of Emperor Huizong's pleasure park, Genyue (Northeast Marchmount), built between 1117 and 1122, were shipped to Kaifeng from the far regions of the empire. The corruption and waste that characterized much of that operation, the hardships and burdens it put on the common people, and its huge drain on the national treasury have all been criticized severely by traditional and modern historians alike and are cited as a major, collective cause of the collapse of the Northern Song dynasty in 1127 (Hargett 6).

[33] For a discussion of trafficking and relative prices, see Siyen Fei's essay in this volume.

[34] For the original Chinese, see Jiang Ruizao 71–75. The English translation, by Yang Qinghua, has been adapted from Lévy 116.

[35] For the original Chinese, see Jiang Ruizao 57–58. The English translation, by Yang Qinghua, has been adapted from Lévy 118–119.

[36] For the original Chinese, see Jiang Ruizao 58. The English translation, by Yang Qinghua, has been adapted from Lévy 118–119.

[37] For the original Chinese, see Jiang Ruizao 58–59. The English translation, by Yang Qinghua, has been adapted from Lévy 122.

[38] For the original Chinese, see Zhu 89. The English translation is from Zhang Zhupo, "How to Read *Jin Ping Mei*" 64.

Part Two

APPROACHES

Introduction

Andrew Schonebaum

The Plum in the Golden Vase (*Jin Ping Mei* 金瓶梅), also known as *The Golden Lotus*, is widely regarded as a breakthrough for the traditional Chinese novel. Believed to have first been published between 1617 and 1618, it was the first novel in the Chinese tradition that did not rely on an extant body of folklore, as did earlier novels like *Outlaws of the Marsh* (*Shuihu zhuan* 水滸傳), also known as *Water Margin*; *Romance of the Three Kingdoms* (*Sanguo yanyi* 三國演義); and *Journey to the West* (*Xi you ji* 西遊記), known also as *Monkey*. *Plum* was one of the first, possibly the first, long work of Chinese fiction to be written by a single (anonymous, unidentified) author, who employed complex structural features to an unprecedented degree. This "authored" quality—by which I mean *Plum*'s conspicuous constructedness—is apparent in many of the novel's features but especially in its embeddedness in an elaborate textual world. Most of the novel takes place inside another novel—*Outlaws of the Marsh*. The illicit relations between Pan Jinlian (P'an Chin-lien) and Ximen Qing (Hsi-men Ch'ing), their murder of Jinlian's husband, and the subsequent revenge taken by the dead man's brother, Wu Song (Wu Sung), is told in chapters 23–27 of the hundred-chapter *Outlaws of the Marsh*. *Plum* begins with this story (chs. 1–9) but delays Wu Song's revenge, telling in its own hundred-chapter story of the rise and fall of Ximen Qing, his career and exploits, and the many wives, concubines, and servants in his household. While *Plum* self-consciously inserts itself into an earlier work, it also makes ingenious use of practically the entire range of texts of the late Ming dynasty (1369–1644): vernacular stories, erotic fiction, histories, dramas, popular songs, jokes, prosimetric narratives (i.e., narratives made up of prose and verse), and works far outside the boundaries of the literary, such as medical works, gazetteers, contracts, and daily-use encyclopedias. These texts are deployed in many ways but almost always with precision, and often with irony. That *Plum* was written by a single author also enables it to have a detailed and highly structured plot. This structure is perhaps *Plum*'s most significant innovation. Every chapter contains two main events, which thematically contrast with each other. These events are often referred to in separate halves of the couplets that begin each chapter. Every ten chapters covers one major plot development, such as Pan Jinlian's entry into Ximen Qing's household, followed in the next ten chapters by the entrance of Li Ping'er (Li P'ing-erh). The penultimate ten chapters deal with the dissolution of Ximen's household after his death, and the final ten chapters reveal the fates of the remaining characters.

The original title, *Jin Ping Mei cihua*, works on several levels. It includes parts of the names of three main female characters, Pan **Jin**lian ("Golden Lotus"), Li **Ping**'er ("Vase"), and Pang Chun**mei** (P'ang Ch'un-mei, "Spring Plum"). If *Plum* is a story that highlights the arcs of these three characters, among many others, and the significance of characters' deaths, then the title gives the sense that this novel is ultimately about taboo violation, excess, and retribution for misdeeds: *Jin Ping Mei* sounds, homophonously, like "money, (wine) bottle, and beauty," three of the obsessions and excesses that lead to Ximen Qing's ruin. The title also puns with three near homophones, sounding like "the glory of entering the vagina," making explicit the symbolism inherent in a literal reading of the title as "The Plum in the Golden Vase." There is much more to the novel than the sexual escapades of Ximen Qing and three of the many women in his life, however, and this is gestured at by the addition to the original title of the generic term *cihua*, meaning approximately "a ballad tale" or "chantefable" that celebrates the inclusion of many poems and songs and the novel's resulting philosophical and narrative complexity.

The Plum in the Golden Vase is the first Chinese novel to focus on the domestic sphere and the mundane details of daily, albeit elite, life. Together with *The Story of the Stone* (*Honglou meng* 紅樓夢), *Plum* is the greatest of the premodern Chinese novels. *Plum*'s story centers on the rich merchant Ximen Qing, the many characters who populate his household, and the many others who are employed by it, have business with it, or are menaced by it. The novel describes in lavish detail the physical surroundings and material objects of the household and its denizens while also relating the interactions of its cast of characters with an unprecedented degree of psychological and emotional realism. Indeed, "[t]his image of a family in which the many wives squabble over the unavailable husband, each attempting to gain the upper hand in the household, as the procreative energies of all are squandered on sensuality rather than being engaged in the production of children, became emblematic of late imperial decadence in the eyes of many modern writers. But this impression owes everything to *The Plum in the Golden Vase*" (T. Lu 108).

The first twenty chapters of *Plum* describe the formation of the Ximen household as the novel's major characters are gathered together. The cast of characters comprises Ximen Qing and his wives—his principal wife, Wu Yueniang (Wu Yüeh-niang, "Moon Lady"); Pan Jinlian; Li Ping'er; Meng Yulou (Meng Yülou, "Tower of Jade"); a former prostitute named Li Jiao'er (Li Chiao-erh, "Picture of Grace"); and Sun Xue'e (Sun Hsüeh-o, "Beauty of the Snow"), a former maid of his deceased first wife. In addition to the wives are the many maids, servants, and locals, the most important of whom are Pang Chunmei, Pan Jinlian's maid and coconspirator; Li Guijie (Li Kuei-chieh, "Cassia"), Ximen's current favorite prostitute; and the coterie of sycophants Ximen Qing surrounds himself with. The following sixty chapters, culminating in Ximen Qing's death (ch. 79), are concerned with intrigues, jealousies, and power struggles within and beyond his household. Information about other characters—what they say and do—is an important source of power in the Ximen household for those who do not have access to regular sources of power but who are good at manipulating such information—for instance, Jinlian. Hence, what may seem like casual indelicacies of voyeurism, eavesdropping, and gossip rise to the level of information and influence—power—often wielded in an indelicate or nearsighted manner. Li Ping'er emerges as Ximen Qing's favorite wife, especially after she gives birth to his first son (ch. 30), named Guan'ge (Kuan-ko) because Ximen Qing had recently bribed his way into office (*guan*). Consumed by jealousy, Pan Jinlian brings about the death of Guan'ge (ch. 59). Li Ping'er dies of grief and a mysterious female ailment brought on by sexual transgressions and the avenging ghost of her dead husband (ch. 62).

Ximen Qing's own rise and fall is told in these middle sixty chapters. He becomes rich as a merchant and uses that wealth to secure for himself an official career, accepting and offering bribes to gain power and influence. Midway through the book, he escapes punishment despite indictment by Zeng Xiaoxu (Tseng Hsiao-hsü), the only righteous official in the entire novel (ch. 48), and in the following chapter receives a mysterious aphrodisiac from an Indian monk, who is described as the personification of a penis. The structure of the novel thus reiterates the intertwining of sex, money, and power—public and private economies. Ximen's increased power and wealth is matched by increasing numbers of sexual encounters—with his male and female servants, with the wives of his servants, and with underlings, prostitutes, Guan'ge's wet nurse, and the widow of an official. He dies after Jinlian gives him an overdose of the Indian monk's aphrodisiac and engages him in a rigorous sexual encounter. This death is ostensibly from exhaustion and depletion, but it is also a form of retribution, of demon haunting, and the result of mismanagement of bodily resources. At the moment of Ximen's death, Wu Yueniang gives birth to a son, Xiaoge (Hsiao-ko; literally, "Filial Brother").

In the last twenty chapters, Ximen Qing's household disintegrates, and the tone of the narrative becomes more hurried and sensational. Jinlian and Chen Jingji (Ch'en Ching-chi), Ximen Qing's son-in-law, consummate their long-running adulterous flirtation, and Chunmei joins them as a third partner. All three are evicted or sold when Yueniang discovers the affair. Wu Song finally catches up with Jinlian and exacts his revenge (ch. 87). With the exception of Yueniang, who remains as ineffective head of household, all Ximen's wives leave: Li Jiao'er returns to her former brothel, Meng Yulou remarries, and Sun Xue'e runs off with a former servant. Former employees compete to pilfer from Ximen's estate. Chunmei is the only one whose fortune rises, albeit only briefly, after the fall of Ximen's house. She eventually becomes the primary wife of a military official. Chunmei hires Chen Jingji, who has fallen into poverty, and resumes her relationship with him. Both come to a disgraceful end, however: Chen is murdered, and Chunmei dies of sexual excess and depletion. In chapter 100, the invading Jin army brings about the collapse of the Song dynasty. Wu Yueniang and the fifteen-year-old Xiaoge seek refuge in a Buddhist temple. The Buddhist monk there performs sacrifices for the dead, and the novel's dead characters appear, each explaining the significance of their death and the karmic justice of their rebirth. The monk convinces Yueniang that Xiaoge is Ximen Qing's reincarnation, and she allows Xiaoge to become the monk's disciple. The book thus concludes with the destruction of Ximen's biological line and the take-over of his household by a posthumously adopted heir—a terrible Confucian fate—and, at the same time, with the vision of Buddhist salvation.

Plum has been controversial from the first due to its explicit sexual descriptions. It was banned as pornography during the Qing dynasty (1644–1911), and until recently only expurgated editions were available. In this work of approximately one million words, however, the proportion of sexually explicit passages is insignificant, especially when compared with many late Ming works of erotic literature. Prefaces to most editions of *Plum* defend the novel against accusations of licentiousness on the grounds that characters who indulge themselves to such a degree should arouse in the reader feelings of aversion rather than desire. While some critics consider the novel's explicit sexual descriptions titillating spectacle, others see in them critical gestures and moral seriousness. Some praise such passages as key to the book's project of unflinching realism, others examine ironic disjunctions as signs of moral judgment, and some note the subversive potential of such passages in undermining conceptions of order and authority. These passages are frequently unoriginal, since many use clichés common to late Ming erotic literature. The second half of *Plum*, however—with its dark accounts of perversions, its turn from playful sex to mechanical, violent, and purely manipulative sex, often involving pain and humiliation—stakes out new territory. Late imperial erotic literature is rife with poetic justice and moral exhortations, but *Plum* is unique in linking desire and death in the most graphic and gruesome manner. Stanley Fish's *Surprised by Sin*—which argues that John Milton's *Paradise Lost* purposefully seduces the reader into at least partially identifying with Satan and then makes the reader's susceptibility to this seduction apparent—is a useful analogue to what happens with Ximen Qing and the reader in *Plum*.[1]

The sex and corruption featured in *Plum* function, at least in part, as a form of social and political critique. The traditional, Confucian idea of the family in premodern China as the cornerstone of social order implicated politics. Family and state, both of which were hierarchical and patriarchal, mirrored each other. At the same time, the polity was made up of and sustained by families. The selfishness, overindulgence, and taboo violation of the Ximen family has been thought to stand in for the immorality of the late Ming Wanli court, and Ximen Qing and his conniving wives thought to represent the emperor and his bickering ministers. Or perhaps it is the Ximen family's depravity, and that of other families like theirs all over the empire, that is the ultimate cause of the dynastic fall depicted at the end of the novel.

Nearly everything a person could buy in a prosperous late Ming town is described in *Plum*: clothing, food, art, handcrafts, medicine, games, money. The novel's whole focus is on urban life. All traces of rural life—which in traditional Confucian thought was the moral foundation of society—are conspicuously absent. The world of civil examinations and officialdom is similarly relegated to the margins. The almost complete lack of moral behavior by *Plum*'s characters has led some critics to believe, despite the novel's pervasive realism, that *Plum* has an uncompromising moral vision, aligned with that of the philosopher Xunzi (third century BCE), that human nature is evil and can be redeemed only through moral transformation. That vision is challenged by the complicated end of the novel in which all the most transgressive characters are redeemed and reincarnated at the hands of a sympathetic Buddhist monk.

The Plum in the Golden Vase is one of the most sophisticated works in Chinese literature, in terms of not only its language and ideas but also its profound relationship to Chinese literature and culture as a whole. Because the novel is filled with details relating to furniture, medicine, food, poetry, and other aspects of the quotidian lives of late Ming literati, readers actually used it as an encyclopedia. However, the novel is often perceived as being too complex to teach in literature or culture courses. At over 2,500 pages in translation, with thirty major characters and over three hundred minor ones, *Plum* is a complex text, rich in cultural, historical, and literary references and so dense in its highly allusive language that many professors, specialists and nonspecialists alike, tend to shy away from it. Without explanatory essays and extratextual materials, the novel is difficult to teach, and much specialized knowledge is required to understand even the first hundred pages or so. This is a sad contradiction. A novel that teaches so much about Chinese literature and culture is not taught because it teaches too much. There are no guides to *Plum* in English. This volume seeks to address these issues.

This volume offers scholarly interpretations of some of the major questions raised by *Plum* and provides background that we hope will allow teachers to come up with their own approaches in the classroom. Each essay in this volume deals with a major issue, the many sides of which students may productively argue. Our contributors have taught *Plum* in courses dedicated solely to it; in surveys of Chinese, East Asian, and world literature; and in courses on the novel, on Chinese and East Asian civilization, on gender, and on Chinese history. The essay topics are interconnected. By assigning groups of them as reading material to students, teachers can use *Plum* in a variety of classes. Essays are grouped into four sections—"Reading *Plum*," "Historical Contexts and Affects," "Women, Gender, Marriage, and Sex," and "*Plum* and the Literary Tradition"—but there are many other themes that unite these essays, such as practices and artifacts of daily life, retribution and identity, the law, and *Plum*'s relationship to history. We hope that readers and instructors will discover a web of connections among the essays presented in this volume.

Early modern editions of *Plum* included many prefatory essays and much commentary meant to aid understanding. At times, these editions also suggested particular readings of the novel. Some prefaces advocated traditional approaches while others championed new entryways into the text. Some defended the novel against accusations of pornography; others provided guides to reading, common questions and answers, long lists of characters with descriptions and commentary, and so on. As yet there are no editions that translate the front matter, back matter, and marginal and interlineal commentary that so many early readers of the novel experienced as part of the text.[2] Our volume takes a step toward providing the reader of *The Plum in the Golden Vase* or *The Golden Lotus* in English with an experience similar to the experiences Chinese readers had for three hundred years. Commentary editions were so popular in part because they turned first-time readers into second-time readers without the necessity of re-reading the book. I hope that our volume will serve that purpose as well.

NOTES

[1] Thanks to David Rolston for this insight.

[2] There is, however, a translation of the Zhang Zhupo commentary for chapters 1 and 100; see Rolston, "Introduction."

Interiority in *The Plum in the Golden Vase*

Tina Lu

A comparison of *The Plum in the Golden Vase* (*Jin Ping Mei* 金瓶梅) with vernacular short stories, or *huaben* 話本, in particular those from the 1620s, reveals some important continuities and one glaring difference.[1] Both *Plum* and these *huaben* are filled with descriptions of the material world, in particular the corporeal world (specifically what bodies look like) and the world of consumerism. *Plum* and *huaben* differ, however, in their treatment of the individual. Like eighteenth- and nineteenth-century European fiction, *huaben*—and all the major fictional works that follow in Chinese literature—expend a great deal of energy and space depicting the individual from the inside; to readers who are used to Jane Austen or Émile Zola, *huaben* feel familiar. Physical sensation is often couched in interoception, the mind's reflection on stimulus (e.g., "she noticed she felt cold" as opposed to "she was cold"), and internal states are meticulously depicted, sometimes in passages that take up the better part of a page and might take as long for the reader to read as for the character to have felt.

None of this is present in *Plum*, which was written only about twenty years prior to the rise of *huaben*. In *Plum*, bodies are depicted from the outside. There is little internal monologue and often only enough to keep the narrative going. Even in moments of enormous physical suffering—an illness that leads to death, for example—we are given virtually no description of what the suffering feels like to the patient beyond what they tell others. In some respects, the novel's depiction of interiority aligns much more closely with theatrical and cinematic depictions, which makes sense given the fact that the novel's heavy use of songs, present in their entirety in virtually every chapter, suggests its close affiliation with a play. Our interpretation of characters' motivations and emotions retains theatrical qualities, meaning that a character's surface becomes a slate for reading. We read what they say and do so that we might understand what they are thinking; they read one another; they and we read their readings of one another.

This essay focuses on interiority—that is, the depiction of what transpires inside a character's mind and is not visible to others, but more precisely, what might be considered the gradient between what is visible to one person but unknown or invisible to another. Although sometimes I come close to this terrain, my concern in this essay is not emotion. In fact, the novel quite regularly imputes emotion—especially anger and joy—to characters. What it does not do is transform those emotions into inner monologue.

Both *huaben* of the 1620s and *Plum* are deeply concerned with matters that were almost never written about before, and certainly not in such detail, specifically the world of commerce and its main actors. Sinologists often categorize these people as merchants, but in the world of *Plum* such a word does not do justice to the thriving and diverse ecosystem of people seeking to make money—ranging from men like the novel's protagonist, Ximen Qing (Hsi-men Ch'ing), who at their zenith are more powerful than officials, to managers, storekeepers, peddlers, middlemen and middlewomen, and all their consumers. No one exists outside this matrix of self-interest—not clergy, not high officials, and certainly not women. One of *Plum*'s critical, and seemingly revolutionary, points is that the difference between a buyer and a seller is only situational. Buyers can become sellers and vice versa, depending on the circumstances in which they find themselves. As a result, interactions between characters in *Plum* are largely negotiations.

In some respects, the first real episode of *Plum*, as independent from *Outlaws of the Marsh* (*Shuihu zhuan* 水滸傳), takes place in chapter 7, when Meng Yulou (Meng Yü-lou), a wealthy young widow, first considers and then accepts Ximen Qing's marriage proposal. The reader is thrown into the midst of a family feud: one of Meng Yulou's relatives, Aunt Yang, advocates for Ximen Qing, while another, Zhang the Fourth (Chang the Fourth), pushes Meng Yulou to accept the offer of Provincial Graduate Shang, the son of a prefectural judge. Each party acts out of self-interest: Aunt Yang is being paid by Ximen Qing, while Zhang the Fourth hopes to gain access to the fortune of Meng Yulou's late husband. Much of the chapter consists of lists of items and quantities of silver—what Ximen Qing offers to the matchmaker, Auntie Xue (Auntie Hsüeh); what Meng Yulou will bring to her new household; and those gifts Ximen Qing offers to the household of Meng Yulou's brother-in-law.

We are never told what Meng Yulou really thinks, not in the sense of an authoritative interruption to the narrative. Nonetheless, by the conclusion of chapter 7, readers are able to surmise Meng Yulou's preferences. Virtually all extant materials on late Ming China make it clear that an elite family like the Shangs—

the father an official, the son a successful examination candidate—would generally have been far more socially desirable than Ximen Qing's, so to a late Ming reader the choice of Ximen Qing as a husband over Provincial Graduate Shang would have been particularly glaring; the reader is, in other words, encouraged to find out why Meng Yulou has made this decision. What might be motivating her—though never voiced—is nonetheless revealed. The following lines are all we have to make a conjecture, but they would have been perfectly intelligible to the late Ming reader:

> Ximen Qing no sooner saw her than his heart was filled with delight. Auntie Xue made haste to hold aside the portiere over the doorway in order to facilitate her entrance. The woman came in and neither correctly nor precisely bowed and uttered a word of greeting, after which she sat down in a seat directly across from that which occupied her visitor. Ximen Qing scrutinized her from head to toe with such intensity that the woman lowered her head. (1.7.134)

> 西門慶一見, 滿心歡喜. 薛嫂忙去掀開簾子, 婦人出來, 望上不端不正道了個萬福. 西門慶把眼上下不轉睛看了一回, 婦人把頭低了. (7.6b)[2]

The two stare at each other, and in a way that would have struck a sixteenth-century reader as heterodox to the point of kinkiness. Meng Yulou clearly likes what she sees.

Even so, there are no moments of selfhood outside of a context of personal interest, no moments of thought that stand outside this dynamic matrix of interaction, which strongly resembles market negotiation. We are led to believe that Meng Yulou's preferences themselves are not static. Instead, if the deal had changed—if the provincial graduate had been a more highly ranked capital graduate, if the Shang family were significantly richer, or if Ximen Qing himself had not been so good-looking—Meng Yulou would have chosen differently. Instead of interiority conceived of as internal monologue, we might be better off understanding it—both here and elsewhere, as the novel seems to intimate—as the caprice of desire and as the calculations involved in determining whether that desire will be temporarily satiated.

Throughout this enormous novel, there are no instances in which interiority functions outside this matrix of negotiation. Motivation is only able to be perceived through the prism of other people's motivations. This is perhaps most vividly enacted in the interruptions that take place during sex, an activity that to some might seem a privileged sphere, or at the very least one of concentration and focus. In the novel, though, negotiations often take place during the sex act. The following example is taken from one of the first trysts between Ximen Qing and Song Huilian (Sung Hui-lien), the ambitious social climber and rival to Pan Jinlian (P'an Chin-lien):

While down below the woman grasped his organ in her hand, up above she took a sip of wine and transferred it into the mouth of her companion. "Father," the woman said to him, "if you've got any breath-sweetening lozenges give me a few more. The ones you gave me the other day are all gone." "I also owe several mace [of silver] to Auntie Xue for trinkets," she went on to say. "If you've got any money handy give me a little so I can pay her." (2.23.49)

婆娘一面用手攫著他那話, 一面在上噙酒哺與他吃. 老婆便道: "爹, 你有香茶再與我些, 前日你與的那香茶都沒了. 又道我少薛嫂兒幾錢花兒錢, 你有銀子與我些兒." (23.4a)

Even sex is not a space that is safe from negotiation, meaning a constant reading of the other party's mental state to try to elicit the best deal one can get.

Out of this ceaseless positioning—the negotiation that constantly takes place between parties, in which each attempts to maximize their own profit, where each jockeys constantly for their own interests—emerges the novel's version of psychology. Our readings of these negotiations construct our sense of characters' motivations. A character says something, and we can only read the statement situationally: What circumstances would make a person say or do this? But the novel's characters are also always reading others in context; everything they do or say is in response not just to their own motivations but also to their readings of others' motivations.

This is one reason why so many scenes are constructed around the use of quotations, in which one character cites another, subtly twisting the first character's words to suit their own motivations. The first instance of quotation may take place spontaneously. Thereafter, however, it is used in the service of other characters' interests and motivations, and each time the quotation is transformed by a new set of social pressures. Take, for example, chapter 25, the climax of several chapters' worth of conflict between Song Huilian and Pan Jinlian. The action in this chapter consists largely of gossip passing from one person to another until it reaches the ear of Ximen Qing. Because character after character relays information, much of what each one says simply quotes the previous character. But the reader can only understand the import of what is taking place by considering each person's quotation in context—information that the novel itself does not directly offer up.

When Song Huilian's husband, Laiwang (Lai-wang), returns home from a business trip, Sun Xue'e (Sun Hsüeh-o) "secretly confides" (背地告訴) that much has changed since he left: "Ever since you went away, during the last four months or so, your wife has been carrying on an affair with Ximen Qing. It all started with Yuxiao playing the role of pander and delivering a gift of silk. They've used Jinlian's quarters as their nest" (自從你去了四個月光景, 你媳婦怎的和西門慶勾搭, 玉簫怎的做牽頭從鍛子起, 金蓮屋裡怎的做窩; 2.25.85; 25.4b). These key bits of information—the blue silk given by Yuxiao (Yü-hsiao), the role played by Pan Jinlian—will return again and again, often in sentences that are virtual copies of one another.

So how do we read others with specificity even when different people are saying virtually the exact same things? We consider how characters may benefit from what they say. In other words, we understand the social world through the prism of the market.

Things begin to escalate when Laiwang gets drunk and embarks on a long rant, first about Ximen Qing's cuckolding him:

> And I know how, later on, they set it up so they could sleep together all night long, and how Pan Jinlian provided cover for them. Well, so much for that. But he'd better not fall into my hands, that's all I can say, or it'll be a case of "a white blade going in, and a red blade going out."   (2.25.89)

> 後來怎的停眠整宿, 潘金蓮怎做窩主由他, 只休要撞到我手裡. 我教他白刀子進去, 紅刀子出來.   (25.6a)

Laiwang then proceeds to air his grievances with both Ximen Qing and Pan Jinlian. He has been one of Ximen Qing's fixers before, and now he lays out that history. Laiwang knows exactly what it has taken for Pan Jinlian to enter the Ximen household as the fifth wife:

> [H]e'd better not fall into my hands, that's all I can say, or it'll be a case of:
> > A white blade going in, and
> > A red blade coming out.
>
> For better or for worse, I might as well kill that whore named Pan into the bargain. Come to think of it, when that whore named Pan was still in her own house, she killed off her first husband, Wu the Elder. And when her brother-in-law Wu Song came back and lodged a complaint against her, who was it she has to thank for going off to the Eastern Capital to fix things up for her and getting Wu Song condemned to military exile? Now that she's got both feet on level ground again, you'd think she'd be content to enjoy it, but instead she encourages my wife to commit adultery. My enmity for her is as big as the sky.   (2.25.89)

> 只休要撞到我手裏; 我教他白刀子進去, 紅刀子出來. 好不好, 把潘家那淫婦也殺了, 我也只是出來做的出來! 潘家那淫婦, 想當一個他在家擺死了他頭漢子武大, 他小叔武松因來東京打點, 把武松墊發充軍去了? 今日兩腳踏住平川路, 落得他受用, 還挑撥我的老婆與他結的有天來大!   (25.6a–6b)

As he says this, Laiwang is overheard by Laixing (Lai-hsing), another one of Ximen Qing's manservants, who quickly passes on what he has heard to Pan Jinlian.

But in the transmission, Laixing subtly transforms the main elements of Laiwang's rant. Compare Laixing's version of the knife with Laiwang's original. In Laixing's recounting, a metaphorical knife (an old saw really, the way Laiwang uses it) has been transformed into an actual one, and a hypothetical plan for murder into an actual plan: "He's had a knife made for himself and threatens to kill Father [Ximen Qing] and you, saying it would be a case of 'a white blade going in, and a red blade coming out'" (他打下刀子, 要殺爹和五娘, 白刀子進去, 紅刀子出來; 2.25.92; 25.7b). In Laixing's version, Laiwang is not simply relating Pan Jinlian's sordid past but is furious with her for the lack of gratitude she has shown him for saving her life: "He said that you were now requiting kindness with enmity" (說五娘如今恩將仇報; 2.25.92; 25.7b). These transformations are understandable only in the context of Laixing's rivalry with Laiwang. A manservant of the same rank as Laixing, Laiwang has received plum assignments that would otherwise have been Laixing's. Without taking into account the two men's shared history, it would seem only that Laixing is somewhat inaccurately quoting Laiwang. But knowing how Laixing stands to gain from Laiwang's downfall helps us decipher the true meaning of Laixing's words, superficially so similar to Laiwang's. We are left with what is unspoken, Laixing's plot against Laiwang.

Readers must attend to the social context of everything articulated. Consider, for instance, the way in which Pan Jinlian carefully stages a conversation with Ximen Qing: "[W]hen Ximen Qing came home, he found Jinlian in her room with her cloudy locks in disarray and her fragrant cheeks wrinkled from sleep, while her eyes were bleary with weeping. When he asked the reason for this, she told him all about Laiwang's drunken tirade and his threats to kill his master" (西門慶至晚來家, 只見金蓮在房中雲鬢不整, 睡損香嗯, 哭的眼壞壞的. 問其所以, 遂把來旺兒酒醉發言, 要殺主之事訴說一遍; 2.25.95; 25.10a). Pan Jinlian persuades Ximen Qing—using the same information that Laixing passed to her—that he must get rid of Laiwang.

At the same time, there is also much that we are not privy to. After Ximen Qing leaves Pan Jinlian's room, he speaks to Song Huilian, who convinces him that the proper solution is to send Laiwang away on a lucrative new assignment. But Ximen Qing is easily swayed, and after that he speaks to Pan Jinlian, a conversation that ends one chapter and begins the next: "The story goes that on hearing Jinlian's argument, Ximen Qing changed his mind" (話說西門慶聽了金蓮之言, 變了卦兒; 2.26.100; 26.1a). It is only in watching the plot unfold—and in retrospect—that the reader can return to the end of chapter 26 and understand what must have happened in the conversation that takes place between Ximen Qing and Pan Jinlian in the space between chapters 26 and 27. We understand that Laiwang has been framed only when he himself does, when he is dragged to the main reception hall in the middle of the night and presented with the knife that had been planted on his person (2.26.103).

But why did Sun Xue'e tell Laiwang about the affair in the first place? What was *her* interest in setting these events in motion? It isn't simply that Sun Xue'e and Laiwang are also illicit lovers. The reader presumes it is largely because Xue'e and Pan Jinlian have long hated each other. I have done here what any careful reader who wants to make sense of the text must do, tracing each step of information backward by putting into context what each character knew and what the personal interests of each were.

As readers we see partial fragments of a breadcrumb trail of information, out of which we are able to construct a plot that entails and depends on thoughts to which we have no privileged access. Could an average reader have pieced together all these details? Perhaps not, but they would have a sense of unspoken machinations and wheels within wheels. Each incident trains the reader how to approach the next, how to understand each character in context. Lacking any special access to what these characters are thinking, the reader has something of the same experience as the characters themselves have, except that the reader can go back and reread the text.

As Lisa Zunshine has written, fiction often provides us an assurance of others' motivations that real life lacks almost entirely ("Theory"). A hand trembles, and the narrator explains that it is violent emotion barely repressed—not illness, not cold, not exhaustion. But such assurances are withheld from the reader of *Plum*, a novel in which the reader quite frequently remains in the dark as to why characters behave in certain ways, even as we long to know with certainty. In fact, however, the narrative foregrounds precisely that which we cannot know. This idea of not knowing is foregrounded most strikingly in the characters of Song Huilian and Wang Liu'er (Wang Liu-erh), two of Ximen Qing's lovers. Neither mistress can speak frankly, in part because both are underlings, not just socially but also within the semicorporate structure of the Ximen household and business. As Zunshine suggests elsewhere, however, their position as social inferiors also makes more acute their abilities to read other people, especially their social superiors ("Think What You're Doing").

Consider, for instance, Song Huilian's death. Pan Jinlian and Ximen Qing conspire to entrap Huilian's husband, Laiwang, who after being accused of theft and attempted murder is arrested, tortured in jail, and finally exiled. While Laiwang is incarcerated, Song Huilian is kept in the dark concerning his fate. Ximen Qing promises her that he will pay to have Laiwang released, but when one of Ximen Qing's servants, Dai'an (Tai-an), lets slip that Ximen Qing has been lying and that Laiwang has already been sent away, Song Huilian kills herself, saying, "While you [Laiwang] are on the road, I don't know whether you're alive or dead, I can't tell whether you'll survive or perish. They might as well have put a water crock over my head, for all I knew about it!" (你在路上死活未知, 存亡未保, 我如今合在缸底下一般, 怎的曉得; 2.26.116; 26.11a).

Song Huilian is an adulterous woman and a liar, maintaining to her husband that she is innocent of adultery with Ximen Qing; when Laiwang rifles through her trunk and sees blue silk, she lies to him: "[T]he mistress noticed I was wearing a violet jacket along with a skirt I had borrowed from Yuxiao that did not match" (娘看見我身上, 上穿著紫襖, 下邊借了玉簫的裙子穿著, 說道: 媳婦子怪刺刺的, 甚麼樣子不好; 2.25.87; 25.6a). Like so much of the speech repeated throughout this chapter, Song Huilian's explanation of the silk tweaks earlier versions; the person who noticed her clothes and gave her silk was Ximen Qing. Nonetheless, Song Huilian's suicide makes us guess at internal motivations to which we have no access. What was she thinking all along? Perhaps she killed herself out of despair because she felt loyalty to and love for her husband, Laiwang. Perhaps she felt responsible for his exile. Or perhaps we are meant to understand what she says literally: she kills herself because it turns out that everyone else is a liar just like her, and because Ximen Qing did not tell her the truth. But death is irrevocable, and so we understand her suicide as something different from her social climbing and her ceaseless negotiations. Everything she said before might not have been meant to be taken at face value, but the suicide must be some statement of incontrovertible sincerity. But what does such a statement actually mean? That we cannot know.

Song Huilian's death forces onto the reader a sense of the inaccessibility of others' secret thoughts and feelings, even when it comes to Ximen Qing. He barely reacts to the news of her death, although his principal wife, Wu Yueniang (Wu Yüeh-niang), worries that he will respond explosively: "'She was just a foolish woman,' said Ximen Qing, 'who was not destined to be happy'" (他恁個拙婦, 原來沒福; 2.26.125; 26.17a). He never mentions her again. A chapter later, however, Pan Jinlian happens to find Song Huilian's shoe while searching for her own (2.27.155). It has been stowed away in Ximen Qing's letter case, along with invitations and stationery—seemingly a keepsake, an external marker of sentiment. But what does it mean? Had the shoe been hidden there during Song Huilian's lifetime and simply been forgotten? Does it signify that Ximen Qing misses her? Or is the shoe a token of sexual conquest, since the smallness of her feet—smaller than Pan Jinlian's own remarkably small feet (2.23.53)—was always a quantifiable marker of her desirability? We do not know. We cannot know. The shoe niggles at Pan Jinlian, just as it niggles at us, a sign that one cannot know another's mind.

This sense of uncertainty appears again in the figure of Wang Liu'er, who assumes Song Huilian's position later in the novel; she too is the wife of Ximen Qing's employee. As in his relationship with Song Huilian, part of Ximen Qing's pleasure stems from the fact that he is cuckolding his own underling, in this case Han Daoguo (Han Tao-kuo). A sexual relationship with Ximen Qing provides Wang Liu'er—as it did for Song Huilian—the opportunity to overhaul her whole look, upgrading her clothes, hair, and makeup. Like Song Huilian, and unlike Ximen Qing's other sexual partners, Wang Liu'er retains submissive elements in her behavior to Ximen Qing.

But unlike Song Huilian's husband, Wang Liu'er's husband knows that his wife is sleeping with Ximen Qing and seems to treat the affair with equanimity. When Han Daoguo returns from a business trip, Wang Liu'er immediately shares the news of her new relationship with their boss. She tells Han Daoguo that she has earned money from her affair, that this is how they are now able to afford a slave girl, and that she thinks she has even talked Ximen Qing into buying them a house. Her husband says he now understands why Ximen Qing asked him not to spend his earnings, and he urges her not to let Ximen Qing know that he knows anything. Han Daoguo even says, seemingly with admiration, "Don't be remiss in your treatment of him, but cater to his every whim. It's not all that easy to make money these days. How did you ever happen on this way of doing it?" She responds jokingly, "You're certainly proficient enough at 'eating the bread of idleness.' You don't have any idea what your old lady has had to put up with" (休要怠慢了他, 凡事奉他些兒! 如今好容易賺錢, 怎麼趕的這個道路! 老婆笑道: '賊強人, 倒路死的! 你倒會吃自在飯兒, 你還不知老娘'; 2.38.392; 38.7b). The temptation is to take this moment at face value: it seems as though the two are being perfectly honest with each other and that they are plotting together. Perhaps within the context of what appears to be a harmonious, companionate marriage we have finally encountered a space in which—unlike everywhere else in the novel—what people say is what people think. If this is the case, however, the irony is that what seems to be transparent communication takes place between an adulterous wife and a cuckolded husband.

But that sense of security is shaken when the reader situates what Wang Liu'er says within the context of her interests. When she says to her husband that sex with Ximen Qing constitutes hard work, is she telling the truth? Is she joking? Is she lying to preserve marital harmony? After all, she will repeat this version of her relationship with Ximen Qing immediately following his death, when she tells Han Daoguo that it is entirely justifiable for the two of them to run away with Ximen Qing's money "[g]iven the way [Ximen Qing] has taken advantage of me in the past" (他占用著老娘, 使他這幾兩銀子不差甚麼; 5.81.7; 81.3b). Everything is read in the context of competing personal interests. In the case of Wang Liu'er and Ximen Qing, that means understanding every aspect of their interaction as colored by the stark differences in their respective social standings. Can anything she says to him be considered truthful? Even during sex, she is solicitous, eager to provide the best of all possible customer service experiences: "I'm afraid your legs will start to hurt if you squat that way. Pull the pillow over so you can sit on it, and let this whore of yours do the moving. I'm afraid you're not really comfortable," she went on to say. "Why don't you try fucking me with one of my legs suspended? How would that be?" ('我只怕你蹲的腿酸, 拿過枕頭來, 你墊著坐, 等我淫婦自家動罷!' 又道. '只怕你不自在, 你把淫婦腿吊著 入日, 你看好不好?'; 2.38.388; 38.6b).

The narrator tells us about Wang Liu'er's orgasms, and we learn more about her sexual quirks than we do about those of any other female character, including the fact that she can achieve orgasm only with anal sex and manual clitoral stimulation; we also learn that this is the kind of sex she engages in both with Ximen Qing and with her husband. Seemingly transparent access to her sex life—a litany of sexual peccadillos—still does not allow us to know exactly what those sexual relationships mean to her, whether they are burdensome or pleasurable, whether they are work, the degree to which they are purely transactional. That kind of information is precisely what the novel withholds from us while also signaling its importance.

Then there is the matter of Han the Second, Han Daoguo's brother and Wang Liu'er's illicit lover when we first meet her. After Wang Liu'er replaces Han the Second with Ximen Qing, a visit by Han the Second leads to an altercation between the former lovers. Han the Second drinks the wine Ximen Qing has given Wang Liu'er, and she pushes him down with some violence. He uses the same threat against her that Laiwang used against Ximen Qing: "A white blade going in, and a red blade coming out." She grabs a laundry bat and chases him out of the house. Ximen Qing sees him leaving the house and promises to deal with him. The next day Han the Second is arrested and tortured.

When Wang Liu'er relates these events to her husband, she is not altogether truthful. Han the Second didn't know his place, she says, and "he happened to run into him [Ximen Qing] and ended up being dragged off to the yamen, where he was beaten to a stinking pulp" (被他撞見了, 拿到街門裡打了; 2.38.391; 38.7b).[3] The version she presents to her husband, in other words, carefully elides her own participation (when she pushes Han the Second down and beats him with a bat, for example). Even in the context of seeming marital harmony, she frames her words carefully, understanding that her husband's interests might lie in protecting his brother, while hers are to minimize her own role. In this version of emotional intimacy, confiding to another person does not mean that what both parties say is now a reliable conduit to some true inner self; instead, it simply means that two people have come together, perhaps only temporarily, for the purpose of deceiving a third. Here, too, we do not know what Wang Liu'er really thinks. In place of any certainty we have what she says: a form of expression that is modulated by Wang Liu'er's interpretation of her interlocutors' self-interest. The commentator for the *xiuxiang* edition shares both my curiosity about what is really on her mind and my sense that we can never know. Above their last sex scene together he writes the following: "I cannot tell whether what Liu'er says is sincere or not. But to exchange what she loves for something that she doesn't love, that's a constant of human nature" (六兒之言不知果真心否? 然而以其所不愛, 易其所愛, 是人情之常; my trans.; 79.62a).

But, for the moment, let us pretend that Wang Liu'er does not have a history of gaming her husband. To the reader, other scenes between them come as something of a relief. One person confides in another in a way that seems transparent, without calculating what they might gain from that interaction. Such communication is the closest that *Plum* comes to permanent, fixed notions of interiority that it otherwise never provides.

The novel provides many indications that what Pan Jinlian wants more than anything in her relationships is to share knowledge, to participate in something like the alliance of interests shared by Han Daoguo and Wang Liu'er. When Ximen Qing is engaged in an affair with Li Ping'er, Pan Jinlian offers to help him, but on three conditions. Ximen Qing must give up prostitutes, he must obey her, and, most important, he must tell her of his sexual indiscretions: "The third condition is that when you go over to sleep with her, when you come home, you must tell me all about it, without deceiving me by so much as a single word"

(你過去和他睡了來家, 就要告我說, 一子不許你瞞我; 1.13.271; 13.10b). That words do not deceive, that they function not as a source of coercion, that they reveal something of the inner self—that remains something of an unattainable ideal in the novel.

In other words, impossible as it is, transparency remains tantalizing. In chapter 23, Pan Jinlian faces off with Song Huilian, whose affair with Pan Jinlian's husband has just begun. In the chapters that follow, the two women continue to jockey for dominance, each asserting her power over the other, at times expressed in their incessant comparisons of foot size and shape, at others in the differential in their social status. Pan Jinlian has overheard Song Huilian's pillow talk with Ximen Qing in which she disparages Pan Jinlian, and now Pan Jinlian is on the offensive. Pan Jinlian claims that sex is not real intimacy, which anyone who has read any chapter of the novel can only agree with. Real intimacy, she asserts, is when someone tells you everything:

> Do you think I'd have the patience to eavesdrop on you? Let me tell you something. Not even ten wives could hope to satisfy a man's every desire. Even though your father has these several wives of his at home, every time he chooses to entertain a powdered face outside, when he comes back he conceals nothing from me, but gives me a word by word account of everything that happened. (2.23.58)

> 傻嫂子, 我閑的慌, 聽你怎的? 我對你說了罷, 十個老婆買不住一個男子漢的心. 你爹雖故家裡有這幾個老婆, 或是外邊請人家的粉頭, 來家通不瞞我一些兒, 一五一十就告我說. (23.10a)

Of course, what is sadly ironic is that this is all a lie. Pan Jinlian's husband has told her nothing, and in fact he will continue to lie about his relationship with Song Huilian; everything Pan Jinlian knows, she knows because she was eavesdropping. She has no power because she can only understand everything as readers do, suspiciously interpreting everything and giving no one the benefit of the doubt.

NOTES

[1] It is difficult to speak of the vernacular short story—hereafter referred to as *huaben*—as a single corpus, since a number of authors and editors were involved, but it is fair to say that these stories share important consistencies.

[2] Unless otherwise noted, parenthetical citations refer to Roy's translation, *The Plum in the Golden Vase*, and to *Jin Ping Mei cihua* 金瓶梅詞話 (*Plum in the Golden Vase: A Ballad Tale*).

[3] A yamen was the office of local bureaucrats. These offices sometimes also contained storerooms, prisons, and courts of law.

Buddhist-Inflected Patterns of Characterization in *The Plum in the Golden Vase*

Maram Epstein

The superficial parallels between *The Plum in the Golden Vase* (*Jin Ping Mei* 金瓶梅) and the Western novel of manners raise a number of basic interpretive issues for modern readers who look, whether consciously or unconsciously, for similarities between the Western realist novel and narrative works from other traditions. Thanks to translation, modern reading habits all over the world have been formed by the norms of the nineteenth-century realist novel. Indeed, one of the real pleasures of reading works from other places and times is armchair tourism: reading a good novel can open a window onto a world filled with exotic colors and beliefs. Travelers experiencing a new culture for the first time frequently try to make sense of the unfamiliar by domesticating it—that is, by translating it through their own native conventions. However, such an approach to reading the late-sixteenth-century Chinese novel *Plum* risks obscuring some of the text's more unusual aesthetic features. Like the essay in this volume by Tina Lu, this essay takes up the topic of characterization in *Plum*. However, rather than analyze *Plum* through a modern lens that focuses on the construction of characters with interiority and psychology—that is, characters that anticipate the modern individual—this essay reads *Plum* as a text that reflects sixteenth-century Chinese anxieties about the construction of a self that is motivated by desires.

A feature that predisposes modern readers of *Plum* to interpret it according to the conventions of the Western realist novel is that the fictional world of the novel centers on the lives of a small group of protagonists. Historians of the Western novel have long recognized the close ideological relationship between the development of the novel and the emergence of the modern individual. As Nancy Armstrong has argued, "[T]he history of the novel and the history of the modern subject are, quite literally, one and the same" (3). Although scholars of non-European literatures may object to the way Armstrong universalizes the British novel, her assertion is a useful reminder that many modern readers, even in China, read fiction through the conventions of the Western novel, meaning that we unconsciously focus on what is most easily recognizable to us, individuals with psychological interiority and with legible (read: familiar) desires and motivations. Because of *Plum*'s frank exploration of libidinal desires and sexual experience, the sensibilities of the characters are recognizable to modern readers. As Patrick Hanan wrote in an early article on *Plum*, "[The characters in *Plum*] seem to us a fairly naturalistic representation of actual types of people," and in *Plum* "we are at last confronted with women of a satisfying, indeed astonishing degree of complexity" ("Landmark" 327). Andrew Plaks refers in much the same way to the novel's "convincing mimetic representation of worldly experiences" (*Four Masterworks* 136).

When compared with other works of late Ming fiction, *Plum* stands out with respect to its representation of contemporary culture and an economy fueled by new-world silver (Ma 52–53). Indeed, when compared with other premodern Chinese novels, *Plum*'s rich descriptions of domestic life, material culture, and the realm of the private, including the sexual, often tempt modern readers to approach it as a work of realism. As has been widely noted, there are striking parallels between *Plum* and the Western novel of manners. The novel of manners typically makes use of a variety of discursive conventions associated with realism to create the effect that it is describing life as it is. Among these conventions is a focus on ordinary middle-class life that is rooted in the domestic but still creates a sense of a thick social texture; the use of naturalistic details that expose the private lives of characters (as opposed to their public masks) and that provide readers the privilege of eavesdropping on characters' private thoughts and actions; the inclusion of what is understood as authentic contemporary detail; and a concern with social change. In the introduction to his translation of *Plum*, David T. Roy makes this approach to reading the novel overt when he quotes a lengthy description of Dickens's *Bleak House*, substituting the Chinese title *Jin Ping Mei* for every reference to Dickens's novel of manners (Introduction xxvii–xxix).

Although *Plum* was groundbreaking for its inclusion of so much reliable information about the material and popular cultures of late Ming China, literary realism as an aesthetic mode that peaked in the nineteenth-century Western novel did not exist in premodern Chinese literature. While the ability of a writer or artist to capture the essence of a subject was highly prized in premodern China, realism was not. The art historian Richard Vinograd has discussed an example of the famous literatus Yuan Mei 袁枚 (1733–99), who rejected a strikingly individualized portrait of himself because it was unrecognizable to his family members. To modern eyes, the portrait is less idealized, with more particularizing details than was conventional, and thereby reads as more realistic (Vinograd 84–91). Today's readers should not assume that because *Plum* contains accurate and detailed descriptions of certain aspects of material and domestic culture that all its representations of late Ming society and manners are historically representative. While certain pockets of late Ming society were noted for their cultivation of decadent tastes, especially the wealthy salt merchants (Ho 155–57), all people who were literate enough to read *Plum* would have been steeped in the norms of neo-Confucian ritual. Neo-Confucianism, which was the hegemonic ideology of late imperial China, taught that all individuals were responsible for cultivating themselves through what were referred to as the Five Cardinal Relationships: loyalty to the emperor and the state, filial obedience to one's parents, chaste loyalty to one's husband, fraternal love between brothers, and trust between friends. As is immediately apparent to any reader of *Plum*, almost every scene presents a caricature of how social relations were supposed to be. As much as readers might enjoy the transgressive interactions depicted in *Plum*, it is clear that much of the novel is a parody of ritual norms.

Even as *Plum* engages ideological concerns that anticipate the modern—such as the importance of the libidinal unconscious as the foundation of identity and the idea that people are formed by their material conditions rather than by cultural ideals—this essay explores the characters in *Plum* as symbolic constructs that illustrate the Chinese Buddhist concept of "illusion" (*se* 色) rather than as attempts to represent the individual self. The aesthetics of late imperial Chinese fiction were deeply influenced by the *Heart Sutra* (*Xinjing* 心經), one of the central texts of Mahayana Buddhism. The sutra concerns itself with the illusory nature of sensory perception (Lopez 23–24). Unlike Western Enlightenment philosophies, which prize the ability of the mind to use reason to transcend subjective desires, Buddhism treats the mind as one of the six sensory organs that trap people in the world of desires; the Chinese term for *mind, xin* 心, literally means "the heart" and is the site of both thought and desire. As explored in the late Ming novels *Journey to the West* (*Xiyou ji* 西遊記) and its sequel *The Tower of Myriad Mirrors* (*Xiyou bu* 西遊補), as a sense organ, the mind, once engaged, actively creates its own subjective reality. By attempting to think through a problem, the rational mind starts to spin further and further out of control (Dong Yue 16–18, 38; A. Yu 1: 455–58, 3: 76–117).

The *Heart Sutra* addresses the Buddhist paradox that the desire for enlightenment is a form of desire; to evade the trap of logic, the *Heart Sutra* rejects the binary categories of illusion and enlightenment and posits that they are the same. By internalizing the Buddhist concept of nonduality, in which all distinctions are erased, Buddhist practitioners are able to actualize their Buddha nature and gain enlightenment. The Chinese terms used in the *Heart Sutra* for "illusion" and "enlightenment" are the common words for "color" (*se* 色) and "empty" or "hollow" (*kong* 空), respectively. In pre-Buddhist classical Chinese, *se* was often used metaphorically to refer to the beauty (the external coloring) of sexually desirable women and men; following this, *se* became a metonym for *lust*. In Buddhist writings, *se* was the term used to represent sensory illusion, and it can also be translated as "material reality" or "form." Because the semantic field associated with *se* is so broad, fiction writers exploited its metaphoric possibilities as shorthand for the linked concepts of anything visually colorful that dazzles and deludes the mind and the internalized desires that these colorful objects incite. Naifei Ding's rendering of the Chinese concept of *se* as "se(x)" brilliantly captures the range of meanings associated with *se* (221). Late imperial Chinese literature conventionally refers to the colors red and green as common metonyms for sexual desire. The fact that *se* is both external to the self and an internalized desire is captured in the common Ming expression "Beauty does not delude people, people delude themselves" (*se bu mi ren, ren zi mi* 色不迷人, 人自迷; 1.3.63; 3.1a).[1] Without self-control, people will be trapped by their desires.

Before turning to specific scenes in *Plum* that illustrate how various female characters are used to embody the concept of *se*(x), it is first necessary to discuss how characterization is conventionally used in other late imperial novels to achieve a didactic goal. Classical Chinese literature is stocked with exemplary characters, both good and bad. One of the techniques this literature borrows from early Confucian texts is the concept of "showing the good as good and the bad as bad" (*shanshan e'e* 善善惡惡) so that readers learn to emulate the good examples and criticize the bad. Educated readers knew to read fiction looking for figuratively similar characters or incidents in order to group them as a basis for moral judgment (Rolston, *Traditional Chinese Fiction* 146–47). As Plaks has discussed, Ximen Qing (Hsi-men Ch'ing), the central male protagonist in *Plum*, should be read as a microcosm of the emperor (*Four Masterworks* 157–67). The emperor's primary function was to ensure that the intertwined ritual and political functions of the state were well regulated. The emperor is symbolically situated at the center of the five phases, the active aspect of the five elements (Earth, Water, Wood, Fire, and Metal). The emperor is positioned at the center, associated with the Earth element and the heart/mind, the position charged with anchoring the orderly progression through the cyclical phases. The five-phases allegorical structure ties the temporal and spatial order to the five elements; arranged around the Center/Earth in the North are winter, Water, and the color black; in the East are spring, Wood, and the color green; in the South, summer, Fire, and the color red; and in the West, autumn, Metal, and the color white. When the self is properly regulated—that is, if energies flow harmoniously according to the season—this positive energy extends order outward to the political and cosmic environments. If the self is not properly regulated, this internal chaos results in political and cosmic disorder (Plaks, *Archetype* 50–53). Rather than center and regulate the fictional world of *Plum*, Ximen Qing's constant pursuit of his material desires (*se*[x]) destabilizes any hope for order.

Even though it is possible to read certain characters in *Plum* as moral foils that delineate good and bad, *Plum* uses an unusual style of characterization that erases meaningful distinctions between the different characters in such a way that challenges the ability of readers to make moral judgment. For example, the first ten chapters set up an explicit comparison between Pan Jinlian (P'an Chinlien) and Meng Yulou (Meng Yü-lou) in terms of how they are brought into the household of Ximen Qing: Jinlian murders her husband in order to marry Ximen Qing, while Meng Yulou meets him after she is widowed (chs. 5–9). However, once the two are married to Ximen Qing, they are paired together so often that they seem more alike than different. Even though Pan Jinlian ("Golden Lotus") is the central female protagonist, her individuality as a character is repeatedly called into question. The first example of this occurs when Jinlian is introduced along with the short-lived character Bai Yulian (Pai Yü-lien, "Jade Lotus"). In addition to the similarity of their names, which evoke the common pairing of jade and gold, the two young concubines play similar stringed instruments, the balloon guitar and the psaltery (1.1.26; 1.10b). The pairing of the two has no lasting significance beyond establishing an aesthetic pattern of similarity and conflict; Yulian dies on the same page on which she is introduced. The aesthetic pattern of doubling is repeated with the paired introductions of the maids

Yuxiao (Yü-hsiao, "Jade Flute") and Xiaoyu (Hsiao-yü, "Little Flute") and the maids Chunmei (Ch'un-mei, "Spring Plum Blossom") and Qiuju (Ch'iu-chü, "Autumn Chrysanthemum"; 1.9.171; 9.2a). This pattern repeats with the introduction of the servants Laiwang (Lai-wang) and Laixing (Lai-hsing; 2.25.94–95; 25.9b–10a). In all these examples, the characters are locked in bitter and often deadly rivalries with their doubles.

Whereas specific details are typically used in realist narratives to create a sense that a character is unique and recognizable, *Plum* presents such a profusion of repeated details that it erases not only the boundaries that keep individual characters distinct from each other but also those that distinguish humans from objects. It is this erasure of stable categories of meaning and identity that I refer to as Buddhist-inflected characterization based on the concept of nonduality. Nonduality rejects the logic of binary or any other categorical thinking; Zen koans, such as the riddle about the sound of one hand clapping, are designed to reveal the limits of the rational mind and allow for a transcendent vision of enlightenment. The continuous and excessive pattern of discursive doubling in *Plum* frustrates the desire of any reader to construct a stable meaning for the text.

Chinese fiction writers often take advantage of the semantic associations of characters' names. This feature of Chinese language is made possible by names that are composed of recognizable lexical items. For example, *Jinlian*, literally "golden lotus," can refer to a gold-colored lotus flower, a woman's bound feet, the intricately embroidered slippers that women with bound feet wore, and the fictional character Pan Jinlian. *Plum* exploits this rhetorical feature of Chinese language to an unprecedented extent. Two episodes featuring Jinlian, the ultimate embodiment of *se*(x), illustrate the way that *Plum* presents such densely textured layers of detail that they form arbitrary patterns of variations that ultimately obscure rather than reveal meaning.

Both episodes illustrate the aesthetics of *se*. The first of these is the celebration of the Lantern Festival (also known as the Yuanxiao 元宵 [Yuan-hsiao], or "Primal Night," Festival) in chapter 15. The Lantern Festival is held on the first full moon of the Chinese New Year. The historical origins of the Lantern Festival are complex, but the holiday—like the Chinese New Year itself, which is held on the new moon of the first lunar month—marks a cosmic transition from winter, when the cosmos is dominated by yin energy, to spring, when cosmic yang energy gradually becomes ascendant. Under the logic of Chinese cosmological symbolism, yin is associated with the moon, the feminine, night, cold, illness, death, sexuality, passive receptivity, and chaos. By analogy, yang is associated with the sun, the masculine, day, heat, health, life, self-regulation, active initiating, and order. Within metaphysical discourse, such as that articulated in the *Yi jing* (*I ching*) 易經 (*Book of Changes*), yin and yang are mutually complementary and fluidly interdependent forces; generation, regeneration, the process of change, and the full range of experiences and phenomena depend on a free and endless mixing of these two energies (Wilhelm and Baynes 280–87). At various points of a person's life or the calendrical cycle, one energy or the other will gain force until it is dominant; after peaking, this energy begins to recede until the other is dominant. Confucian ritual texts, however, use a moral framework that valorizes the qualities associated with yang as inherently good and views those associated with yin as morally negative (Epstein 31–35). The light of the lanterns and the noisy explosions of the fireworks that are traditionally set on Primal Night symbolically bolster the emergent yang energy of the new year. As Victoria Cass has discussed, the festival was also the setting for what was referred to as the Walk of the One Hundred Illnesses, an exorcistic rite in which women would parade through city streets to drive out the baleful influence of yin energy that lingered after the cosmic transition from winter to spring ("Revels" 225). Since late imperial China practiced the strict cloistering of women, the rare appearance of women from all walks of life out on the streets along with the colorful and chaotic atmosphere created by the decorated lanterns established the Lantern Festival as a literary trope representing "an urban rite of spring" (225). *Plum* exploits these associations of the festival, but it also refers to the Buddhist iconographic representation of the full moon as a symbol of enlightenment and the Daoist allegory of the lamp as a symbol for human life. In this common allegory, the oil lamp burns brightly until its oil is used up; the brighter it burns, the more energy it expends, and the more quickly one's life force is extinguished.

It should be noted that by the late Ming, these multiple symbolic layers of belief and symbolism had become part of a common cultural vocabulary. Literary evocations of these symbols should by no means be understood as doctrinal expressions of commitment to a specific religious or ideological belief system. Similarly, in contemporary practices of the United States, dressing as a ghost or witch for Halloween in no way connotes any belief in, nor even an understanding of, occult practices.

The setting for the Lantern Festival in chapter 15 is the apartment on Lion Street belonging to Li Ping'er (Li P'ing-erh). The holiday falls shortly after the death of Ping'er's twenty-three-year-old husband on the last day of the eleventh month of the lunar year (1.14.285; 14.8a). Like the other concubines who enter Ximen Qing's harem, Li Ping'er fails to observe the ritually mandated twenty-seven-month mourning period for her husband. Instead, she immediately pursues marriage with Ximen Qing and invites his wives over to celebrate Primal Night with her. Rather than serve its traditional exorcistic function of driving off the baleful effects of yin energy, this holiday celebration initiates a temporary period of yin setbacks for both Li Ping'er and Ximen Qing. Shortly after this chapter, Li Ping'er is haunted by fox spirits, a specifically sexual form of spectral energy symbolically related to the many tigers, lions, and cats that appear in the novel (1.16.326, 1.17.349; 16.6b, 17.7b); on the verge of death, she marries the doctor Jiang Zhushan (Chiang Chu-shan; 1.17.355; 17.10b).[2] Ximen Qing, who enjoys a mostly uninterrupted period of accumulation of wealth, power, and sexual partners for the first half of the hundred-chapter novel, learns that he and his powerful patrons have been swept up in a purge of corrupt officials; he uncharacteristically closes himself off inside his home while his servants bribe their way along a chain of officials until they reach the office of Li Bangyan (Li Pang-yen), who tampers with the imperial decree that lists the names of all corrupt officials who are to be exiled so that Ximen Qing's name, 西門慶, now reads Jia Lian (Chia Lien 賈廉; 1.18.360; 18.3b–4a). These setbacks present only a temporary retarding of the narrative's forward motion, and by chapter 20, Ximen Qing has resumed his upward trajectory and Li Ping'er finally marries into his household as his sixth wife. As brilliant as the display of light during the Lantern Festival is, it fails to shift the cosmic *yinyang* balance until the New Year is celebrated again in chapter 23.

One of the effects of this layering and repetition of details in the description of the Lantern Festival in chapter 15 is that the semiotic boundary between Ximen Qing's wives and the lanterns becomes blurred. Ximen Qing's wives sit outside admiring the lanterns; the concubines Li Jiao'er (Li Chiao-erh), Meng Yulou, and Pan Jinlian are all dressed identically "in white satin jackets and blue silk skirts" (白綾袄兒藍段裙; 1.15.300; 15.2a), and only a splash of green and red (the metonymic colors of *se*[x]) in their vests distinguishes Yulou from Jinlian. The women themselves are adorned with lanterns: "from just behind the hair over their temples, there dangled innumerable pendant earrings in the shape of miniature lanterns of every description" (鬢後挑着許多色燈籠兒; 1.15.300; 15.2a). Immediately following this, the long descriptive poem evocatively mentions the presence of "Golden Lotus lanterns" (*jinlian deng* 金蓮燈) and "Tower of Jade lanterns" (*yulou deng* 玉樓燈). "Golden Lotus lanterns" could plausibly refer to the beautifully embroidered shoes (*jinlian*) that women wore over their bound feet, but since a "Tower of Jade" (*yulou*) lantern is also mentioned, readers are immediately alerted to the fact that these linguistic signs refer to two distinct and equally plausible signifieds: the women, Jinlian and Yulou. The descriptive poem concludes with references to "the twin perfections / of plum blossom [the maid Chunmei's name means 'Spring Plum Blossom'] and moonlight [Yueniang's name means 'Moon Lady']" (梅月之雙清; 1.15.303; 15.3a).

The list of lantern types mentioned in the descriptive poem, although encyclopedic in scope, challenges any sense of rational order: dragon and crane lanterns quickly morph into Golden Lotus and Tower of Jade lanterns, followed by flowers, types of people, animals, fish, and objects including carved lacquer and mother-of-pearl bed lanterns reminiscent of the two Nanjing beds that figure so prominently in Meng Yulou's dowry (1.7.126; 7.1b). In short, the descriptive poem is a visual distillation of the entire fictional world of *Plum* as seen through the eyes of Ximen Qing, who is conspicuously missing from the list of character types figured on the lanterns.

The absence of a Ximen Qing lantern suggests that the scene is being staged for his benefit. The significance of the focalization of this scene through Ximen Qing's gaze becomes apparent in the final repetition of the Lantern Festival topos in chapter 79, when Ximen Qing returns to Lion Street to view the lanterns and then engages in so much sexual excess that it leads to his death. Following what seems like an endless flow of semen (semen being a man's yang life force stored in his bone marrow), Ximen Qing ejaculates blood and then cold air: "When its oil is used up the lamp goes out; When his marrow is drained a man will die" (油枯燈滅, 髓竭人亡; 4.79.639; 79.10a). The lesson about the illusory nature of *se*(x) has been lost on its primary intradiegetic target.

It is worth remembering that when Meng Yulou was first introduced, she was described as being "pretty as a figure on a decorative lantern" (就是個燈人兒; 1.7.126; 7.2a). In asserting the analogy between a beautiful woman and a painted lantern, the narrative does more than make the obvious point about the superficial and illusory nature of beauty (*se*). No matter how stunning the lanterns in chapter 15 are, the gaze of the crowds on the street is quickly turned on Yulou and Jinlian, who are on display above the crowds, leaning out the windows, distinguished again by their "brocaded green vest" (綠遍地金背比甲的) and "brocaded scarlet vest" (大紅遍地金比甲兒; 1.15.304; 15.4a). The women are fungible with the fantastic lanterns. Jinlian "laughs uproariously" when "a sudden gust of wind blew up and tore a gaping hole in the abdomen of the old lady lantern" (忽然被一陣風來, 把個婆子兒燈下半截刮了一個大窟攏; 1.15.303; 15.3b), and in so doing, she encapsulates one of the central messages of the novel— namely, that the willful ignoring of the many teachings about the dangers of expending all one's energies in the pursuit of the four Buddhist vices of drunkenness, lust, avarice, and anger, which can also be translated as "ego," will lead to one's death.[3] The ripping open of a "gaping hole" (*kulong* 窟攏) in the old woman lantern prefigures Jinlian's own death when Wu Song returns from exile, purchases her from the same Dame Wang who helped Ximen Qing seduce her in the beginning of the novel, and cuts open "a blood-filled cavity" (*xue kulong* 血窟攏) in her chest (5.87.128; 87.9b).

In creating an analogy between the central female characters and the lanterns, the novel again illustrates the Buddhist concept of nonduality, which teaches that all distinctions are a product of false perception. The enlightened mind perceives that underlying the welter of ephemeral manifestations that construct the false world of sensory perception is an ultimate unity. As stated in the *Heart Sutra*, "*Se* [color, passion, sex, the illusion of form] is nothing more than emptiness [enlightenment]" (*Se ji shi kong, kong ji shi se* 色即是空, 空即是色; Lopez 23). Unlike more simplistic renderings of Buddhist thought that distinguish between illusion (*se*) and enlightened truth (*kong*), the *Heart Sutra* teaches that the mental effort made in distinguishing the two is a product of the unenlightened mind; the enlightened mind recognizes that any distinction is arbitrary. *Plum* alludes repeatedly to the meaninglessness of the distinction between surface, or form, and emptiness. Not only are the women no different than the brilliantly lit but hollow lanterns, Ximen Qing is also described as "solid without, but hollow within" (裡虛外實; 1.7.139; 7.10b), and the formerly fearsome tiger (a foil for Pan Jinlian as she is presented in the first chapter) lies dead and hollow "on the ground like an embroidered bag" (躺岱著卻似一個綿布袋, 動不得了; 1.1.20; 1.6a). In "How to Read the *Jin Ping Mei*," the great Qing commentator Zhang Zhupo notes that "sex [*se*] and money are empty [*kong*]" (財色兩空) and that the author's "message is that everything is empty" (蓋其傳教人空也; "How to Read the *Chin P'ing Mei*" 213, 235; *ZZP* 8b, 26a). As Zhang suggests in his descriptions of each chapter of the novel as composed of hot and cold scenes, or more complexly heat within cold, or cold within heat, the heat of *se* is integral to the cold insight of enlightenment ("How to Read the *Chin P'ing Mei*" 204–05; *ZZP* 11a–11b). As described by Andrew Plaks, "the dual nature of illusory reality and emptiness (*se-kong*) [are] worked out in the novel as two sides of the same coin" (*Four Masterworks* 180).

A separate episode presents an even more complex illustration of the Buddhist concept of *se*(x). In chapters 22–28, Pan Jinlian is paired with the minor character Song Huilian (Sung Hui-lien). With her avaricious ambition, cruelty, sexual appetite, and florid use of abusive language, Pan Jinlian is among the most memorable characters in the novel. Even though she is endowed with a seemingly realistic and rounded characterization, Jinlian is in no way unique.[4] In chapter 22, one of Ximeng Qing's servants acquires a wife whose name is Song Jinlian (Sung Chin-lien, "Golden Lotus"). To avoid the taboo of using the name of a master, her name is immediately changed to Song Huilian ("Orchid Lotus"). Both Jinlians have exquisitely shaped feet, the ultimate symbol of a woman's sexuality in late imperial China and in this novel. As soon as Song Huilian enters the household, it becomes known that her feet are even smaller than those of Pan Jinlian, and Jinlian quickly comes to resent her as a rival. For her part, after only a month of working in the kitchen, Huilian begins to affect the mannerisms and fashionable styles of the mistresses, especially those of Jinlian: "[Huilian] built up her chignon under her fret until it became higher and higher, affected a bouffant hairdo, and adorned her temples with two long spit curls" (他把鬆鬌墊的高高的, 梳的虛籠籠的頭髮, 把水鬢描的長長的; 2.22.32; 22.2a). She also adopts Pan Jinlian's habit of spitting out cracked melon seeds, a sign of empty fertility. Pan Jinlian spits out cracked melon seeds on the heads of the crowd gathered below during the first Lantern Festival (1.15.303; 15.3b); Huilian spits out seeds all over the ground as the members of Ximen Qing's household gather for another celebration of the Lantern Festival (2.24.63; 24.1b).

Dolled up in the latest styles of the day, Huilian quickly catches Ximen Qing's ever-roving eye. Ximen Qing is a master of *se*, here meaning both "sex" and "color," and so he begins to remake her in the latest styles. He sends the servant Yuxiao to Huilian with a bolt of blue silk and coaches Yuxiao to say the following:

> The other day Father saw you serving wine at the party wearing a violet skirt along with a red jacket, a combination that was most unbecoming and really didn't do you justice. I told him that the violet skirt was one you had borrowed from me. He opened up the clothes cabinet, just now, and took out this bolt of silk which he sent me over to give you to make into a skirt.
>
> (2.22.33)

爹昨日見你酒席上斟酒, 穿著紅袄, 配著紫裙子, 怪模怪樣的不好看. 說這紫
裙子還是問我借的, 爹纔開廚櫃拿了這疋段子, 使我送與你, 教你做裙子穿.
(22.3a)

Huilian unwraps the cloth and admires the intricate pattern of "turquoise blue
silk, figured with roundels of flowers from each of the four seasons and pairs of
magpies face-to-face, a rebus for the words 'happy reunion'" (一疋翠藍四季團花
兼喜相逢段子; 2.22.33; 22.3a). Similar to the descriptions of the lanterns "striped
with colors / Producing brocade effects that dazzle the eye" (掠彩燈, 錦誘奪眼;
1.15.302; 15.3a), the intricately patterned textiles that adorn the bodies of Huilian and Jinlian overwhelm and confuse the readers' ability to imagine the scene.
Although it becomes clear in chapter 26 that Huilian is ultimately a positive foil
to Jinlian, when Huilian hangs herself after realizing that her affair with Ximen
Qing has caused her husband's death (2.26.116, 123–24; 26.11a, 16a), the two
women are nonetheless symbolically reduced to *jinlian*, the intricately embroidered shoes that are intimate tokens of the women who made and wore them.

The semantic erasure of any distinctions between people, and between objects and people, continues in the chapter after Huilian's death, when Jinlian
allows Ximen Qing to amuse himself at her expense in what is one of the most
pornographic scenes in the novel. In a gesture reminiscent of Huilian's death by
hanging, Ximen Qing suspends the naked Jinlian by her foot-bindings in the
grape arbor (2.27.144; 27.10b). Jinlian almost passes out from the violence of Ximen Qing's sexual thrusting, and when she is helped out of the garden, she loses
one of her embroidered shoes. One of her maids eventually finds a *jinlian* hidden away inside Ximen Qing's study and gives it to Jinlian:

> The woman took it in her hand and then picked up her other shoe to com-
> pare with it. They were both embroidered shoes of scarlet silk, figured with
> flowers from each of the four seasons and the symbolic representations of
> the "eight treasures," with flat, white satin soles, green heel lifts, and blue
> hook and eye fastenings. Only the chain stitching of the two shoes was
> slightly different. One was chain stitched with sand-green thread, and the
> other with turquoise-blue thread. Without careful scrutiny they could not
> have been told apart.　(2.28.155)

> 婦人拿在手內, 取過他的那隻鞋來一比, 都是大紅四季花嵌八寶段子白綾平
> 底繡花鞋兒, 綠提根兒, 藍口金兒. 惟有鞋上鎖線兒差些, 一隻是紗綠鎖線兒,
> 一隻是翠藍鎖線, 不仔細認不出來.　(28.4a)

This shoe belongs to Huilian, and Jinlian correctly surmises that Ximen Qing is
holding on to it as a token of his dead lover. In the very last appearance of Huilian's shoe, Jinlian treats it as a metonym for Huilian herself. As her servant carries the shoe out of her room, Jinlian orders, "Fetch me a knife so that I can chop

that whore into pieces and throw them into the privy" (取刀來, 等我把淫婦剁做幾戳子, 掠到毛司裡去; 2.28.164; 28.9b). The confusion of *jinlians* continues when Pan Jinlian's lost shoe reappears only to fall into the hands of her son-in-law, Chen Jingji (Ch'en Ching-chi), and then serves as the catalyst for their incestuous relationship (2.28.156; 28.5a).[5] This chain of *jinlians* exemplifies the pattern in *Plum* whereby seemingly unique characters and objects are duplicated and refracted into a proliferation of variations. The golden lotus, the ultimate symbol of *se*(x), signifies the sexualized female form, the embroidered shoe, and the characters Pan Jinlian and Song Jinlian / Huilian. Are any of the manifestations of *jinlian* more real than any other? The fungibility of these categories parallels another discursive pattern in *Plum*—the repeated use of "that woman" to refer to many of the female characters. This erasure of any individual identity under the rubric of "that woman" points to the female characters' shared identity as projections of *se*: they are ephemeral consumables, designed to titillate, and differentiated only by variants of surface pattern and color.

One of the qualities that makes *Plum* endure as a great work of literature is that it can be read on many different levels and using many different approaches. The reading I have offered here explores how the characterizations in *Plum* reflect the Buddhist paradox of the nonduality of form and emptiness, *se*(x) and *kong*. This reading challenges the desire of many scholars to read *Plum* as an anticipation of modern constructions of an autonomous individual marked by interiority and libidinal desires. While many aspects of *Plum* certainly parallel the Western novel of manners that is structured around the life of a central, individualized protagonist, *Plum*'s techniques of characterization undermine any sense of the autonomous individual. Rather than naturalize subjective desires as a defining feature of the individual self, *Plum* explores how immersing oneself in desires (*se*) ultimately destroys the boundaries of the self. This Ming novel ultimately resists the attempts of readers to interpret it as a celebration of the subjective desires at the core of modern identity. Moreover, unlike Western realist fiction that creates verisimilitude by superimposing details that flesh out a physical and temporal setting (e.g., nineteenth-century London), many of the references to authentic material culture in *Plum* are so densely layered that they undermine mimesis.

NOTES

[1] Unless otherwise noted, parenthetical citations refer to Roy's translation, *The Plum in the Golden Vase*, and to *Jin Ping Mei cihua* 金瓶梅詞話 (*Plum in the Golden Vase: A Ballad Tale*).

[2] For more on the symbolic relationship between tigers, lions, cats, dogs, and fox spirits, see Plaks, *Four Masterworks* 99–101.

[3] See the prefatory "Lyrics on the Four Vices" ("*Sitan ci*" 四貪詞; 1.10–11; 2a–3b).

⁴ Pan Jinlian's many shadows (*yingzi* 影子) are linked by various combinations of simi-larities of name, ranking as Number Six (six being the numerological equivalent of yin), avarice, ambition, cruelty, physical attributes, and a predilection for certain nonprocre-ative sexual acts. Among Jinlian's most important shadows are Song Huilian; Wang Liu'er ("Wang Number Six"), with whom Ximen Qing indulges himself before Jinlian gives him an overdose of aphrodisiac; and Jinlian's maid Chunmei.

⁵ The commentator Zhang Zhupo cannot resist punning: "Because Pan Jinlian begat a Song Jinlian, and because Pan Jinlian lost her '*jinlian*,' this caused Song Huilian to leave behind her '*jinlian*'" (因潘金蓮生一宋金蓮，又因潘金蓮之遺失 '金蓮，' 引出宋金蓮之遺下 '金蓮'; my trans.; *ZZP* 30.1a).

Borrowed Time and Infinitude: Narrative, Media, and the Body in *The Plum in the Golden Vase*

Ling Hon Lam

We tell ourselves stories, not just to record or entertain but also to reconcile contradictory experiences of time alternately perceived as the serialization of points, which only registers "before" and "after," and as a past-present-future overlap, without which we could have no memories and hopes (Ricoeur, *Time* 3: 12–22). This aporia of temporality became manifest in the early modern regime of capital, as Terry Eagleton's reading of *Macbeth* suggests: on the one hand, the Macbeth couple represents "an endless expansion of the [bourgeois] sense of the self in a single trajectory"; on the other hand, this unilinear direction of progress is haunted by "the cyclical time" epitomized by "the subversiveness of the witches"; the chaos and ruins left behind in the trail of the bourgeois transgression ultimately catches up, and all the apparent progress "lapses into nothing" (4–5). And yet, in his recent rereading of Karl Marx, Moishe Postone argues that the infinite expansion of capital cannot be exhaustively understood in terms of linear time and therefore is not necessarily contradicted by cyclical time; rather, linearity itself has to be embedded in a larger context of circularity because, in order to maximize itself, capital "ceaselessly generates what is new while regenerating what is the same" (40). In Marx's own words, "By describing its circle [capital] expands itself as the subject of the circle and thus describes a self-expanding circle, a spiral" (*Grundrisse* 746).

Postone maintains that he is referring to the universal logic of capital, which has reshaped the West as much as other parts of the globe (29). Written roughly around the same era as *Macbeth* in response to the global flux of silver (Glahn 113–41; Ma 1–78), *The Plum in the Golden Vase* (*Jin Ping Mei* 金瓶梅) demonstrates a rather different kind of articulation between linearity and circularity, which Marx himself dismissed too quickly. The dual temporality of capital in this peculiar incarnation provides a key to understanding afresh both the sexual economy depicted in this domestic novel and the textual economy in which the novel was produced. Ultimately, *Plum* may allow us to catch a glimpse of what is looming large on the horizon of our current socioeconomic crisis.

Borrowed Time: Between Media and Narrative

It is well known that *Plum* extracts the Pan Jinlian (P'an Chin-lien) and Ximen Qing (Hsi-men Ch'ing) episode from chapters 23–27 of *Outlaws of the Marsh* (*Shuihu zhuan* 水滸傳)—also known as *Water Margin* and *The Marshes of Mount Liang,* first published in the early sixteenth century—and expands it into a full-length domestic novel (Shi and Luo, *Marshes* 2: 1–115). Instead of being slain by Wu Song (Wu Sung), the tiger killer who attempts to avenge his elder brother's murder, the illicit lovers survive and lead a flamboyant life while the hero is arrested and exiled. What makes possible this expansion of an otherwise short-lived affair is blind luck in timing. The first major deviation from *Outlaws* takes place in the second half of chapter 6—a brand-new segment not found in the original novel or other sources—that relates a seemingly uneventful scene in which Dame Wang goes to fetch wine for the couple and runs into rain (1.6.119–20; 6.6a.).[1] As Zhang Zhupo 張竹坡 (1670–98) comments, however, it is that rain that continues for the whole summer and delays Wu Song's return from his business trip, opening up a narrow window for Jinlian to move out before Wu Song has a chance to seize her (*ZZP* 6.10a). Just like *Sliding Doors*—a 1998 film divided into two alternative story lines contingent on whether the female protagonist (played by Gwyneth Paltrow) slips through the subway train's closing doors in time or not—*Plum* opens up a parallel world of what-ifs by having Wu Song stranded in rainfall and letting Jinlian slip away.

It is tempting to see *Plum*'s world not just as one that is opened up right in time, as it were, but also as one that is bounded by an extended loan of time: what is being loaned for a period of time is nothing other than that particular time period, hence setting a limit on the characters' lifetimes. The postman always rings twice, and the bogeyman is due to collect the debt however long the detour he takes. The transgression of the couple—allegorically understood as the ever-increasing expansion of capital—is thus apparently capped by a doomsday destined to end the whole cycle. But this preliminary reading stumbles over two facts, those being that Ximen dies long before Wu Song's return and that the novel does not end with Wu Song's murder of Jinlian.[2] Cyclical time does not quite result in nothingness, nor does it fully explain the premature demise of Ximen. The premise that human activities and enterprises wax and wane in a big cycle is therefore an inadequate means of explaining *Plum*'s temporal structure.

Linearity and cyclicity are interwoven in a sophisticated way by the time readers get to the second ten-chapter arc. Having acquired in chapter 7 bountiful dowries from his marriage to Meng Yulou (Meng Yü-lou), Ximen accelerates the rise of his fortune through an affair with Li Ping'er (Li P'ing-erh). Ping'er smuggles all the silver ingots belonging to her husband, Hua Zixu (Hua Tzu-hsü), over the wall to Ximen, who lives next door and eventually makes Zixu's house into part of his expanded garden. The seriality of sexual, financial, and territorial conquests, however, is punctuated by intermittent disruptions that take the form of recurrent cycles throughout the arc. The arc begins with the debut of the new courtesan Li Guijie (Li Kuei-chieh) under Ximen's patronage. Then comes the first cycle, which showcases itself succinctly in chapter 12, where Ximen spends his days in Guijie's licensed quarter, leaving the lonely Jinlian home to commit adultery with the page boy Qintong (Ch'in-t'ung), only to come back to discipline her. The rest of the arc then runs through this three-stage cycle—

Table 1. Structure of Chapters 11–20

	CHAPTER 11	CHAPTER 12	CHAPTERS 13–16	CHAPTERS 17–19	CHAPTER 20
0. Grand opening	Ximen Qing patronizes the new courtesan, Li Guijie.				
1. Man's absence		Ximen frequents the brothel.	Hua Zixu frequents the brothel and later becomes involved in a lawsuit.	Ximen gets into trouble when a relative of his son-in-law's family loses the emperor's favor.	After marrying Li Ping'er, Ximen seldom visits Guijie.
2. Woman's transgression		Pan Jinlian commits adultery with the page boy Qin-tong.	Li Ping'er commits adultery with Ximen Qing.	Ping'er marries the doctor Jiang Zhushan and finances his pharmaceutical store.	Guijie betrays Ximen when she receives another patron behind his back.
3. Woman's punishment (endings)		Jinlian is punished and forgiven by Ximen.		Jiang Zhushan is beaten up by Ximen's thugs; Ping'er marries Ximen, receiving insults and forgiveness from him.	Ximen and his associates storm Guijie's brothel (grand conclusion).

the man's absence, the woman's transgression, and finally her punishment—almost three more times. "Almost" because the second cycle (chs. 13–16) witnesses Hua Zixu's visits to the brothel and Li Ping'er's adultery, yet without any immediate penalty for Ping'er, thus indirectly reflecting her adulterer Ximen's ability to get away. Before long, however, punishment befalls Ping'er in the third cycle (chs. 17–19): she marries her physician out of despair when Ximen holes himself up to survive a political storm, and she is eventually manipulated to get divorced and marry Ximen under severe humiliation before they reconcile. The incomplete second cycle is therefore completed by the third one; the two form a bigger unit that accounts for seventy percent of the arc, driving home the prominence of Ping'er in these ten chapters. But Ximen's keen attention to Ping'er means a decline in the attention he shows to the courtesan Guijie, and when he finds out in chapter 20 that Guijie is entertaining another male client during his absence, Ximen and his gang storm her brothel and deal her career a heavy blow. This constitutes the fourth cycle and brings the whole arc to a grand ending. The patterns formed among the four cycles and mapped onto the second ten-chapter arc can be visualized with the help of table 1.

Once laid out for examination, the striking symmetry and balance of the whole picture, the intriguing correspondence and reversal of local details, and the well-orchestrated variation of pace and rhythm all bear out the observations made in traditional commentary on Chinese novels in general and *Plum* in particular, namely, that a full-length work of vernacular fiction can be read as a coherently patterned piece of writing. Propagated in fiction and drama criticism by Jin Shengtan 金聖嘆 (1608–61) and then applied to *Plum* by Zhang Zhupo (Rolston, *Traditional Chinese Fiction* 66–73), such traditional literati aesthetics endeavor to uncover textual patterns anywhere down to the most imperceptible link across hundreds of pages and ascribe this compositional beauty to the literary mind of a genius author (Plaks, "Toward a Critical Theory").

More recently, this literati view of vernacular novels as belles lettres has been reproved for its elitist bias toward an abstract notion of writing, which tends to ignore the materiality of mediums. Such powerful critiques come from two opposite directions. On the one hand, recurrent patterns, which Jin Shengtan claimed to find in such early Chinese novels as *Outlaws* and lauded as a writerly design, are now ascribed to oral storytellers' mnemonic techniques and improvisational engine (Ge 90–92). On the other hand, Zhang Zhupo's commentary to *Plum*, modeled after Jin Shengtan's approach, is criticized for the opposite reason: rather than a legacy of orality, patterning is questioned as a figment of the imagination of the elite commentator who fails to understand the potpourri nature of the text, which on numerous occasions copies verbatim from a wide range of texts made available to the writer by print—a compositional procedure that seems to render the overarching coherence envisioned by Zhang impractical and pointless (Shang, "'Jin Ping Mei'" 195).

However, between the recurrent patterning as the techne of oral storytelling, on the one hand, and the unstructured openness as a collage effect of print, on the other, the tightly knit picture seen in table 1—which exemplifies how every ten chapters of *Plum* form a coherent arc, a unique structure among novels of the Ming dynasty (Plaks, *Four Masterworks* 73–74)—reveals a gray zone in which resides what I would call "the repetition in print." Here repetition derives neither from the bodily rhythm of orality (Saussy 156–71) nor from the modern technology of mechanical reproduction (Benjamin) but from the heightened structuration of the print medium—the woodblock page frame—within which all otherwise irregular verbal elements now neatly fall in place.

Characterized by its meticulous articulation, repetition in print is evidently nothing like in oral forms of repetition. In *Outlaws of the Marsh*, which preserves the modus operandi of oral storytelling, narrative sequences sharing a recurrent pattern are sporadically distributed, interspersed irregularly by other patterns or elements; conversely, even when two different patterns are repeatedly articulated together, their adjacency is motivated by the need for improvisation and without much narrative justification. Take the original Wu Song story for example: if, allegorically, the episode in which Wu Song beats up a tiger on his way home (ch. 23) only barely relates to the ensuing episode in which he slays his unfaithful sister-in-law Pan Jinlian (chs. 24–26)—women are as fatal as tigers, the elimination of both being the very condition of masculinity (N. Ding 143–52)—their joint repetition almost twenty chapters later renders this allegorical association even more flimsy and uncertain. This time it is the Black

Whirlwind Li Kui who plays the tiger-killing hero on his homecoming trip in chapter 42, and then another hero, Shi Xiu, sees to it that his own sworn sister-in-law receives the ultimate punishment in chapters 43–45. Li Kui's and Shi Xiu's tales each retell and parody one of the Wu Song episodes,[3] but the arbitrary juxtaposition of Li Kui and Shi Xiu, who do not cross each other's path at this point, reveals that the concatenation of their stories is motivated not so much by allegorical association but by mnemonic invocation. In the Wu Song story cycle, the slaying of the tiger is followed by the execution of the sister-in-law, so when Li Kui slays a family of tigers, another sister-in-law's downfall is automatically triggered, even if this takes place under circumstances that have nothing to do with Li Kui. This metonymic arbitrariness in the way stories are strung together in *Outlaws* is not careless storytelling but storytelling in its true form, and that form is defined by a distinct kind of repetition—a distinct way in which past, present, and future overlap—that is absolutely free of what Ricoeur calls "followability"—the retrospective understanding of causality, of the past as the cause, only from the perspectives of the present and future—which he presumes to be the rule for all kinds of narratives to make sense of time (1: 66–67, 149–55). In oral storytelling, however, time makes sense in a different fashion than Ricoeur understands it.

By contrast, the second ten chapters of *Plum* meticulously weave even the most random repetition into followability. Each of the four cycles is inaugurated by the disequilibrium brought about by the man's absence, and one absence unwittingly leads to another absence. The followability of repetition, among all the cycles, coalesces into a coherent system that subjects circular time to the service of linear progression. Ximen's absence from home and stay in the brothel provides another man the opportunity to sleep with Jinlian, but it also means that Ximen's sworn brother Hua Zixu frequents the brothel with him, leaving the latter's home wide open for Ximen to steal his wife, Ping'er. Ximen's obsession with Ping'er eventually leads to his absence from the brothel, making Guijie available for other male clients. The only instance of contingency strikes when Ximen is suddenly plunged into a high-profile political drama far away in the imperial court, which forces him to lay low and release Ping'er to other romantic encounters, but by this point the pattern has taken off and explained itself: it does not matter why the man is absent or where he is. Rather, the overall picture shows us how a social system works on the expansion of desire beyond the physical limit of the body. Hence a recurrent pattern of lacunae: the more women and territories a man occupies, the more ground he fails to cover and leaves open for other men to infiltrate. It is not the zero-sum moral economy suggested in the preface written by Xinxinzi 欣欣子, the Master of Delight (1.3–5; 5a), and further intensified in Li Yu's 李漁 mid-seventeenth-century *Rou putuan* 肉蒲團 (*Carnal Prayer Mat* [28–29, 296–97]), where those who steal other men's wives and daughters must suffer the same loss in return. Rather, it is an economy of capital (*benqian* 本錢) that expands through circulation (M. Huang 96–97).[4] The point is not that Ximen's punishment takes the form of other men stealing his women but that, for Ximen to have as many women as he wishes, he has to exchange his own women for those of other men, even though he does not want to do so. His jealousy and impulse for revenge are beside the point; what matters is that he epitomizes the triumph of capital despite himself.

At the level of content of this first full-length domestic fiction, the amalgam of circular and linear time coalesces in the prominent image of the Chinese courtyard house, whose porous boundaries facilitate the circulation of money and sex in and out of the household but at the same time delineate an ever-growing private property. The simultaneous dissolution and reconfirmation of privacy is at the core of libidinal economy and is succinctly summed up in a voyeuristic scene in which a maid pokes a hole in the paper window and peeps on Ximen and Ping'er's lovemaking (1.13.264–66; 13.7b–8a).

At the level of media, a similar amalgam of circular and linear time can be seen in the form of printed books. On the one hand, the self-sufficient integrity of a book reveals itself as a grand illusion when one considers the trafficking and circulation of blatantly copied-and-pasted materials made available by print. On the other hand, such revelation is re-velation: the illusion of books as reified objects has never been so powerful, precisely because print, owing to its "control of space" that "locks words in position," "encourages a sense of closure, a sense that what is found in a text has been finalized, has reached a state of completion" (Ong 120, 119, 129). Intertextuality, which describes the connections among identifiable texts alluding to one another, is a direct product of this reification of books as discrete entities—of which the meticulous organization of *Plum* is a symptom—rather than of their disintegration. Table 1, through which we have visualized that meticulous organization, draws on the same power of spatial control as a printed page does. The way that words are locked in position on a printed page thus enables at higher levels *Plum*'s narrative structure as well as our reading practice.

Infinitude: Before the Big Bang

Lurking behind its protean incarnations as both houses and books, capital undergoes linear expansion through circular time. Despite its overt moralistic overtone, *Plum* is a celebration of this two-faced temporality of capital. Traditionally, the novel has been read as a warning that desire mortally drains our bodies, as the narrator says: "[T]he vitality of the individual is finite. . . . Ximen Qing sought only his own sexual gratification but did not realize that when its oil is used up the lamp goes out; when his marrow is drained a man will die" (一己精神有限. . . . 西門慶只知貪淫樂色, 更不知油枯燈滅, 髓竭人亡; 4.79.639; 79.9b–10a). Taking this admonition literally, modern readers tend to see *Plum* set a biological limit on sexual capital but not on financial capital. Mixing up these "two kinds of capital"—which are said to be two distinct "forms of materiality"—and as a result overindulging himself in sex allegedly costs Ximen his life (M. Huang 96–98; Ma 76). Deep down in this modern interpretation, such material distinctions do not hinge so much on the biological limit (because obviously even financial capital cannot grow without recourse to living bodies) as on a dubious notion of desire. Ximen's sexual conquest is now ascribed to a "subtlest aspect of desire" named *qi* 氣. A yearning for domination that is neither tangible nor measurable, *qi* is said to be far more insatiate and thus unsustainable than his pursuit of money, which is at least countable (M. Huang 103–10).[5] Ironically, what started as an analysis of materiality ends up with an immaterialist mystification of desire.

Any essential distinction between sexual and financial capital is therefore materially untenable. Something that the two kinds of capital seem to share—and this is also what underlies both traditional and modern interpretations—is the presumption of biological life in terms of circular time, as a cycle of life and death. No matter how successful Ximen has been in accumulating money and women, his downfall is inevitable and can only be accelerated by his material success. Ximen's mortality thus reinforces the overarching theme of borrowed time: after all, his life is just on a short-term loan, due on the return of the hero Wu Song. And maybe Ximen should be considered lucky since he escapes the violent death at the hands of Wu Song by first overspending himself to death in sweet jouissance. However, this conventional account of Ximen's death falls short of taking into consideration the temporal structure of capital to see how it modifies the temporality of the body in the novel as a result. Andrew Schonebaum has recently reopened Ximen's case of "death from excess" and stresses that it is "not so cut-and-dried. . . . The vector of his illness is not well defined" (*Novel Medicine* 123, 125). I propose a peculiar vector of illness in view of capital's dual temporality.

To regard overspending as the culprit of Ximen's death is to slip back to the moral of agrarian economy without heeding the opposite advice repeated in the novel. In chapter 7, when faced with the possibility that the recently widowed Meng Yulou will marry Ximen Qing and thus have her dowries taken away, Meng Yulou's uncle-in-law slanders Ximen, maintaining that the latter is deep in debt and prone to spend all her money quickly. She retorts with a rather liberal view on money: "Money in this world is a thing that comes and goes by itself / Where is the family that is long rich or forever poor?" (世上錢財倘來物, 那是長貧久富家; 1.7.140; 7.9b). Yulou's name literally means "jade tower," a symbol of towering treasure, and if Yulou manages to remarry once more after Ximen's death and remain affluent to the end, it is not because she is good at amassing wealth, turning it into immobile real estate, or simply keeping it all to herself; rather, it is because Yulou, as a woman who repeatedly remarries, is the perfect embodiment of ever-migrating possessions—a moving castle of dowries, so to speak—in sharp contrast to the uncle who represents a naive desire to keep money close to home.

It is only in the light of Yulou's unchallenged economic notion—namely, that money never stays in one place—that Ximen's spirit of charity in chapters 56–60 starts to make sense. Ximen first gives his poorest sworn brother, Chang Shijie (Ch'ang Shih-chieh), twelve taels of silver and promises to buy him a four-room house of Chang's own choosing (3.56.378–79; 56.4a–4b); next, Ximen donates money to a Buddhist temple (3.57.406–07; 57.7b); finally, in addition to keeping his word and covering the cost of Chang's house, Ximen gives Chang 150 taels to start a business (3.60.503; 60.8a)—which is extraordinary, given that one chapter earlier, Chang asks Ximen to pay the tab at the worst possible time, when the latter's infant son, Guan'ge, is about to die (3.59.475; 59.14b).[6] These episodes can be viewed as dramatizing a culture of gift exchange that normatively constitutes social relationships but at the same time perversely destabilizes the social order (Volpp, "Gift" 137–38). Here we catch a glimpse of something growing out of and beyond the circuit of reciprocity. In chapter 56, Ying Bojue (Ying Po-chüeh), another sworn brother of Ximen, comes to seek financial help on Chang Shijie's behalf. Whereas Ying still subscribes to the cliché of retribution in moral economy through a vulgar reading of the Daoist maxim "The Way of Heaven favors reversion" (*tiandao hao huan* 天道好還), Ximen retorts with an ontology of money echoing what Yulou has said in chapter 7:

> Money is something which likes movement and dislikes inertia. It will not allow itself to be immured in any one place. And it is designed by Heaven for human use. For every person who accumulates a surplus there will be another who suffers a deficiency. It is wrong, therefore, merely to pile up wealth and valuables. (3.56.381)

> 兀那東西是好動不喜靜的, 曾肯埋沒在一處? 也是天生應人用的, 一個人堆積, 就有一個人缺少了. 因此積下財寶, 極有罪的. (56.4b–5a)

As Martin Huang argues, Ximen's remark suggests that "[m]oney will only reproduce more money or wealth will only multiply when it is in circulation or in the process of exchange" (95–96). We need to explore what this view implies for the history and theory of political economy, and ultimately how Ximen's death should be reappraised in regard to this serious crime (*zhi youzui* 極有罪) of piling up wealth. What Ximen describes is tantamount to what Western economists call "the paradox of thrift," which means expanding the availability and utility of an otherwise limited amount of currency by way of circulation (L. Yang 37). This argument for growing wealth through spending rather than miserly saving, though it remained marginal throughout China's imperial history (Chin 109–24), was fully articulated in an essay by Lu Ji 陸楫 (fl. ca. 1540) and used to explain the prosperity of cities like Suzhou, Hangzhou, and Shanghai in the Jiangnan region (L. Yang 50–52). Given the intensified trend of commodification in the second half of the sixteenth century, it should be no surprise that similar ideas found their way into a novel written during the period, despite the overtly conservative tone of the storyteller, who recycles hackneyed warnings against prodigality.

According to Marx, this partial, mercantilist view that capital permanently self-multiplies through circulation alone (*Capital* 1: 256) is a mirage advocated even in "scientific economics," a misguided belief that "capital possesses a mysterious source of self-valorization that is independent of its production process and hence of the exploitation of labor and derives rather from the sphere of circulation" (2: 204). But such a picture fits, at least in part, with historical conditions in late Ming China. Even in the most commercialized areas of Jiangnan, capital (in merchants' hands) only took control of the exchange market between producers (e.g., between spinners and weavers) and not of the production process per se; beyond Jiangnan, the highly developed transregional network of commerce coexisted with rather than obliterated the infra-economy of self-sustenance at local levels (Brook 198–201). In this respect, the fictional world of *Plum*, which centers on a merchant's accretion of capital through selling, buying, and lending—in short, through "the sphere of circulation"—is not an illusion but a snapshot of the white-hot monetary economy driven by the flow of silver in late-sixteenth-century China.[7]

Once the novel's economic iconoclasm against the traditional advice "to pile up wealth and valuables" is clarified, we are now in a better position to see that Ximen's death is not really caused by libidinal overspending but by an explosion resulting from overhoarding. What makes the aphrodisiac Ximen acquires from the mysterious Indian monk dangerous is not that it indulges Ximen's desire and empties out his vitality. Quite the contrary, the drug blocks his ejaculation and makes it impossible for him to spend, so to speak. According to the monk, the aphrodisiac sustains the erection so well that a man can "handle ten women in one night" and "his essence will never be damaged" (*qi jing yong bu shang* 其精永不傷; 3.49.200–01 [trans. modified]; 49.16b), meaning that he can potentially postpone ejaculation forever (the Chinese word *jing* 精 connotes both "essence" and "sperm"). But perennial erection without spending is not at all a preferable condition—a red flag that is hard to miss as the monk boasts of the drug's power:

> If you are not able to believe these claims,
> Mix it in with rice and feed it to your cat.
> For three days it will indulge itself without restraint;
> On the fourth day it will be too overheated to stand it.
> A white cat will be transformed into a black one,
> Its excretory functions will stop and it will die.
> In the summer months you should sleep in the breeze,
> In the winter you should submerge yourself in water;
> But should you ever be unable to ejaculate,
> Your hair will drop out and leave you bald.   (3.49.200)

恐君如不信, 拌飯與貓嘗.
三日淫無度, 四日熱難當.
白貓變為黑, 尿糞俱停亡.

夏月當風臥, 冬天水里藏.
若還不解泄, 毛脫盡精光.   (49.16b)

The endless phallic power predicated on withholding semen is ironically compared to the poor cat's death from blockage. The monk must therefore introduce a remedy to lift the blockage:

If you should ever lose interest in the battle [of lovemaking],
Wishing to retire your warriors from the field,
Swallow a mouthful of cold water,
The yang energy replenishes with no damage to the essence.
(3.49.201 [trans. modified])

有時心倦怠, 收兵罷戰場.
冷水吞一口, 陽回精不傷.   (49.16b)

The last line, which I have modified from David Roy's translation as "the yang energy replenishes with no damage to the essence" (*yang hui jing bu shang* 陽回精不傷), seems to repeat a previous line, "his essence will never be damaged" (*qi jing yong bu shang* 其精永不傷), but they convey opposite meanings. Whereas in the latter not damaging one's essence means avoiding ejaculation by taking the aphrodisiac, the same expression in the former refers to resolving the built-up, harmful tension—that is, releasing the semen by taking in "a mouthful of cold water." The whole point of drinking cold water is to unblock, not to hold back, semen, as clearly shown one chapter later when Ximen has intercourse with Li Ping'er under the influence of the drug. To end the act, "he reached out for the tea on the bedside table and swallowed a mouthful of cold tea. Instantaneously, his semen arose and he ejaculated like a geyser" (呷了一口冷茶, 登時精來, 一泄如注; 3.50.219; 50.10b).

This proper measure is missing from the fatal chapter 79. One chapter earlier, Ximen reports, "[T]oday I don't seem to have any energy, and keep dozing off" (今日只是沒精神, 打睡; 4.78.624; 78.29b). It is not, however, the exhaustion of his energy but the blockage of pent-up energy that ultimately kills him. When Ximen dozes off in chapter 79, Jinlian administers the drug on his behalf. Without knowing the Indian monk's instruction, she not only overdoses him with all three remaining pills but also, and more important, fails to serve him a bowl of cold water in time. Throughout the night she has multiple orgasms, "but Ximen Qing did not ejaculate," his blocked, swollen organ graphically ominous and on the way to a gruesome "Big Bang":

His turtle head had swollen larger than ever and turned the color of purple liver. Its distended blood vessels were all exposed, and it was as hot as fire to the touch. It was gorged with blood, and though he told the woman to remove the band that was tied around its root, it continued to swell without ceasing. He told her to suck it, and so she crouched over his body, engulfed his turtle head with her ruby lips, and proceed to move it, back and forth without stopping. She continued for as much time as it would take to eat a meal, until the semen in his urethra spurted out en masse like mercury pouring into a bucket. She tried to catch it in her mouth and swallow it but she wasn't quick enough. The emission went on and on. . . . When the flow of semen ceased, it was followed by blood; when the flow of blood stopped, nothing came out but a discharge of cold air.

(4.79.638–39)

龜頭越發脹的色若紫肝, 橫筋皆現, 猶如火熱. 一回〔會〕, 害籟脹的慌, 令婦人把根下帶子去了; 還發脹不已, 令婦人用口吮之. 這婦人扒〔趴〕伏在他身上, 唇吞裹其龜頭, 只顧往來不已. 又勒勾約一頓飯時, 那管中之精, 猛然一股邀將出來, 猶水銀之瀉筒中相似, 忙用口接, 嚥不及, 只顧流將起來.... 精盡繼之以血, 血盡出其冷氣而已.

(79.9a–9b)

Exhaustion (*jin* 盡) is therefore not the actual cause of death but merely the result of unspent surplus—the real culprit. To keep one's energy replenished, one must first spend, discharge, ejaculate—this is the teaching of the Indian monk. Ximen bursts to death simply because Jinlian misses the timing of properly releasing his semen. If there is any moral lesson in *Plum*, it is one opposite to what many readers expect: libido and capital are the same. They need to be spent, let go, circulated like clockwork, only to come back in heightened abundance but to benefit mostly a small number of people who already have capital to start with. Again, circularity does not spell the end of the borrowed time; rather, it suggests and supports the latter's linear infinitude.

This ultimate fantasy of undying capital—the more we spend, the more it grows—channels a shed of historical reality in *Plum*'s time, but capital's reification as a supersexual organ in the story reveals that undying capital remains very much a fantasy, a "what if" opened up by the sliding door. The fantasy lingers on and has become at once both more real and more illusory than ever in our modern-day society: real because, today, governments of states play unprecedented roles in spending on the common good and mass destruction; illusory because circulation has turned into a cover-up for the exploitation of surplus value in capitalistic production, giving rise both to the bogus trickle-down economics that absurdly expect capitalists' mercy of spending more on hiring and to a class of happy consumers who feel like spending for the good of the economy—no more urgently than in the era of COVID-19. In our global capitalist era, such reality and illusion intertwine at the top of the food chain, both symbolic and literal, where we find giant retailers such as Walmart. While apparently reminiscent of seventeenth-century Chinese merchants who profited from circulation without seizing control of production, Walmart has in effect forced its suppliers, by suppressing their pricing, into ruthless labor exploitation and massive environmental destruction (Petrovic and Hamilton).[8]

But things are now blowing up in our faces: unequal distributions, worsened by increasingly unbearable hiccups in economic cycles, have fueled the angriest citizens across the globe. Just as circulation—now a sham of exploitation—is cited to explain and justify the self-propagation of capital, spending—not inequality—plays the red herring that takes the heat of people's misplaced anger. Politicians are obsessed with debt issues, budget cuts, sequestration—a trend not so much mitigated as aggravated in the wake of huge stimulus packages amid economic downturns—only to wrongfully target expenditures on the common good (Žižek 403)—public education, health care, safety nets—things the underprivileged cannot afford to lose. In light of *Plum*, one thing is nonetheless certain in this darkest hour: the spell of undying capital is now broken, and infinitude is meeting the Big Bang soon.

NOTES

This essay is dedicated to the memory of Professor David T. Roy and Professor Moishe Postone.

[1] Unless otherwise noted, parenthetical citations refer to Roy's translation, *The Plum in the Golden Vase*, and to *Jin Ping Mei cihua* 金瓶梅詞話 (*Plum in the Golden Vase: A Ballad Tale*).

[2] The point is clarified when one compares *Plum* with the first Chinese novel, *The Romance of the Three Kingdoms* (*Sanguo zhi tongsu yanyi* 三國志通俗演義), prefaced 1494, whose temporal scope is delimited by a cycle of division and reunification. The last main character, Zhuge Liang (Kongming), dies in chapter 104, but the novel does not end until sixteen chapters later, at the conclusion of the civil war. As Kongming himself puts it, he "dies in the middle of the way" (中道喪亡) toward unifying the country, and therefore his death is not expected to bring an end to the narrative (Luo Guanzhong, *Three Kingdoms* 806 [trans. modified]; *Sanguo yanyi* 2: 864). By contrast, while the world of *Plum* is opened up by the deferral of Wu Song's revenge, the novel deviates from the cycle completed by the return of Wu Song not only because the story does not conclude with the revenge but also because Ximen Qing's premature death allows him to once again evade Wu Song's wrath.

[3] Whereas Wu Song establishes his fame in the underworld by killing the tiger, the undercover Li Kui tries but fails to run away from the renown he has earned as the tiger killer, which epitomizes a more general problematic of name and identity that mixes up Li Kui and his impostor and ultimately obliterates the boundaries between humans and animals. Li Kui's consumption of his impostor's leg connects to the tigers that eat his mother's leg—"Hungry man, starved tigers—both live for their mouths" (餓人餓虎皆為嘴; Shi and Luo, *Marshes* 2: 431 [trans. modified]; *Shuihu zhuan* [Zhonghua shuju] 1: 574). Shi Xiu also subverts Wu Song's original story by flipping one key element of the latter: whereas Wu Song is directly involved in the drama with Pan Jinlian except during his absence from town (Jinlian tries to seduce him but gets rejected; he comes back to kill her after she murders his brother), the hero Shi Xiu regresses to the role of voyeur, an onlooker of the seduction drama between his sworn sister-in-law (also surnamed Pan) and a Buddhist monk, and then acts as a facilitator and a witness to the woman's execution by her husband's hands (*Marshes* 3: 26–31, 53–59).

[4] The novel's analogy between libidinal and monetary economies is ubiquitous: as Ximen's sexual spoils grow with his capital, the small business capital (*benqian*) of the impotent Jiang Zhushan is destroyed when he is forced to divorce Li Ping'er, his financial benefactor (1.19.385, 391; 19.6a–6b, 10a). The analogy is foregrounded in Li Yu's *The Carnal Prayer Mat*, which uses the size of *benqian* ("capital" or "endowment") as a metaphor for surgically adjustable penis size (95–98, 122–23).

[5] The presumed equivalence between immateriality and insatiability of desire is questionable. As Marx argues, capitalists' desire runs amok not because their object of desire is now intangible and immeasurable but, quite the contrary, because the object of desire becomes purely quantitative, adopting the form of exchange value without qualitative differences (*Capital* 1: 254–55). Avarice becomes boundless only when what one desires is not something better or nicer but simply more. By the same token, if Ximen's desire to dominate (*qi*) is insatiable, it is because the dominance he pursues is always as measurable (by scope, duration, and frequency) and hence as materialistic as sex and money are.

[6] It has been noted that chapters 53–57 commit multiple continuity mistakes in relation to the chapters that precede and follow this segment and therefore might have been written by someone else (Hanan, "Text" 14–27). The discussion here is less concerned with textual corruption than it is with a higher level of continuity that can be shown between the probably interpolated chapters (56 and 57), on the one hand, and the other parts of the novel (chs. 7, 59–60), on the other.

[7] According to Harry Harootunian, "In *Capital*, time is divided among production, circulation, and reproduction: the time of production, abstract, measurable, divisible, is linear; circulation relates to the rotation of value, is circular or cyclical; and reproduction consists of an organic union of production and circulation, reproducing them repetitively but always with a difference" (25; see also Harvey 136). But Harootunian loses no time pointing out that such a depiction of temporality in Marx's analysis only presents a logic of capital that remains schematic and abstract until it comes across historical contingency (26). If in capital's abstract logic the reunion of linear and circular time resides in reproduction, in the late Ming context it was at least partially fulfilled in the domain of circulation despite Marx's objection to mercantilism.

[8] Anna Lowenhaupt Tsing has coined the term "salvage accumulation," by which she means that late capitalists, now increasingly detached from actual production, must rely on the production chains beyond capitalism, thus opening up the dominant system to some sort of otherness (62–70). But the Walmart example, which Tsing cites, shows how the "beyond" may just be an extraterritorial zone under the power of capital.

Recalcitrant Things
in *The Plum in the Golden Vase*

Wai-yee Li

The Plum in the Golden Vase (*Jin Ping Mei* 金瓶梅) is chock-full of things. A character's appearance is usually accompanied by a detailed description of their articles of clothing, jewelry, and shoes—not only when we first meet them, but on nearly every occasion. No repast seems insignificant enough not to merit a listing of all the dishes. Almost all gifts and bribes are carefully itemized, sometimes with details about their market value. There is often close attention to the decor of certain kinds of interior or enclosed spaces (e.g., rooms, halls, gardens), with occasional excursus on the particularities of furniture (notably the bed). What does this obsessive devotion to the world of things signify? What is the function of such a level of attention? How should we situate it in terms of Chinese cultural and literary history? On the most obvious level, such an obsession with materiality confirms what historians tell us about the abiding concern with consumption, extravagance, and the material markers of status and power in late Ming society. In symbolic terms, *The Plum in the Golden Vase* stands alone in the literary tradition in its relentless commitment to depicting characters defined by their material desires. In the process they are not only "transformed by things";[1] they are almost dehumanized and transformed into things.

Let us begin by indulging in a piece of counterfactual literary history: imagine a reversal in chronology of *Plum* and the eighteenth-century masterpiece *The Story of the Stone* (*Honglou meng* 紅樓夢), also known as *Dream of the Red Chamber.* If *Plum* were responding to the romantic and aesthetic sensibility of *Stone*, we would have been justified in regarding the materiality of things in *Plum* as the product of deliberate demystification. As it were, we confront instead another intriguing proposition: How and why does *The Story of the Stone* charge the world of things with lyricism and symbolic meaning, even as it inherits *Plum*'s fascination with material and mundane details? The question suggests a productive juxtaposition. Things inviting subjective illumination, symbolic construction, and sentimental association in *Stone* provoke us to ponder opposite processes in *Plum*, as we confront recalcitrant things that seem to resist translation into emotional, moral, or religious meanings.

People as Things

Stone's lyrical worldview toys with the idea that the self can defy social norms and assign value to things. In chapter 27, Tanchun tells her half brother, Baoyu, to buy her "interesting things" when he leaves their garden and family compound:

"Just like last time, when you got me the willow-branch basket, the incense box carved out of bamboo, or the little clay burner. I really liked them. But the others fancied them too and looted them as if they were treasures." Baoyu laughed. "So you want those things—they are not worth much. Just give a few strings of coins to the lads and they will bring you cartloads of them." Tanchun said, "What would the lads know! You could pick out the interesting and uncommon items—just bring me lots of them."[2]

"怎麼像你上回買的那柳枝兒編的小籃子, 整竹子根摳的香盒兒, 膠泥垛的風爐兒, 這就好了. 我喜歡的什麼似的, 誰知他們都愛上了, 都當寶貝似的搶了去了." 寶玉笑道, "原來要這個. 這不值什麼, 拿五百錢出去給小子們, 管拉一車來." 探春道, "小廝們知道什麼. 你揀那樸而不俗, 直而不拙者, 這些東西, 你多多的替我帶了來." (Cao Xueqin 1: 281)

Such a mode of reasoning would be unthinkable in *Plum*, where everything can be bought and sold and monetary value reigns supreme. No character would dream of elevating the value of "interesting things" by going against market consensus.

Almost everything has a price tag in *Plum*. No maid is bought or sold without mention of the price.[3] Pang Chunmei (P'ang Ch'un-mei), an orphan who starts out as the maid of Wu Yueniang (Wu Yüeh-niang), the principal wife of Ximen Qing (Hsi-men Ch'ing), but eventually becomes the maid and confidante of his concubine Pan Jinlian (P'an Chin-lien) as well as his unofficial concubine, is bought and sold for sixteen taels (5.85.86; 85.9b). Some comparisons in prices are in order here. Ximen pays five taels for Xiaoyu (Hsiao-yü), the maid who replaces Chunmei in Yueniang's rooms. Qiuju (Ch'iu-chü), bought to serve Jinlian, costs six taels, perhaps on account of her presumed culinary skills, or more probably because Ximen has a greater passion for Jinlian than for Yueniang (1.9.171; 9.2a).[4] Gratified by the sexual proclivities of his new paramour Wang Liu'er (Wang Liu-erh), the wife of his underling Han Daoguo (Han Tao-kuo), Ximen uses four taels to buy a maid, Jin'er (Chin-erh), to serve her (2.37.373; 37.9a). After leaving the Ximen household, Chunmei's fortunes soar as a result of her marriage to the commandant Zhou Xiu (Chou Hsiu), and she buys the cheapest maid in the book, paying three and a half taels for Jinqian'er (Chin-ch'ien-erh), one tael less than the asking price (5.97.345; 97.10b–11a). What does it mean that Chunmei costs about three or four times as much as an average maid? She has a higher market value because of her beauty, wit, and cleverness (1.10.204; 10.9a). For all that, she can still be bought and sold. Wu Yueniang makes a point of adhering to the price of purchase when she puts Chunmei up for sale to indicate that Chunmei's years in the Ximen household do not matter—they have done nothing to enhance or diminish her value (5.85.86; 85.9b).[5]

Pan Jinlian was sold at age nine for an unspecified amount to the household of Imperial Commissioner Wang, where she learned embroidery and acquired various musical skills that enabled her mother to resell her at age fifteen to a rich man, Zhang (Chang), for thirty taels. Under pressure from his jealous wife, Zhang sends Jinlian away, but he marries her to an impoverished and ugly dependent, Wu Da (Wu the Elder), so that he can continue his liaison with Jinlian. The adultery of Ximen Qing and Pan Jinlian and their murder of Wu Da is of course the story from *Outlaws of the Marsh* (*Shuihu zhuan* 水滸傳), also known as *Water Margin*, that becomes the opening act of *Plum*. The almost immediate revenge taken by Wu Da's younger brother, Wu Song (Wu Sung), in *Outlaws of the Marsh* is delayed for eighty chapters in *Plum*. One of the reminders that we are in a different fictional universe is Jinlian's price, which draws attention to the question of her agency or lack thereof. Wu Da gets her for free but continues to pay, so to speak, by acquiescing to Zhang's continued access to his wife. In the aftermath of Wu Da's murder, Ximen Qing delays his marriage to Jinlian, being distracted by the prospect of marrying a concubine, Meng Yulou (Meng Yü-lou), with a handsome dowry and by paying for the deflowering of the courtesan Li Guijie (Li Kuei-chieh). Jinlian is no longer linked to the thrill of acquisition and can wait. Ximen Qing's wedding with Jinlian has minimal pomp, paling in comparison with the ceremonies that surround his union with Meng Yulou and Li Ping'er (Li P'ing-erh).[6] After Ximen Qing's death and the exposure of Jinlian's affair with her son-in-law, Chen Jingji (Ch'en Ching-chi), Yueniang sends Jinlian away with some veneer of respectability (she leaves in a sedan chair, taking with her some trunks) but in effect puts her up for sale, through the go-between Dame Wang, for a hundred taels. Yueniang is not willing to settle for less because Ximen Qing expended more than enough money on her "to cast a silver figurine to match her dimensions" (打個銀人兒也還多; 5.86.111; 86.14a). Jinlian and Chunmei become close allies because of their shared fate of being bought and sold as things. Modern interpretations taking a more sympathetic view of these characters see Chunmei's pride, Jinlian's jealousy, and both characters' temper, ruthlessness, and vindictiveness as a form of resistance against that fate.

Women with financial resources are just as susceptible to this web of buying and selling. Ximen Qing decides to marry Meng Yulou before setting eyes on her. He is easily swayed by the matchmaker's account of Yulou's dowry and her late husband's wealth. We know the exact value of the bribe Ximen pays to Auntie Yang, the paternal aunt of Yulou's late husband—an initial offering of a bolt of cloth and four baskets of food, followed by two more bolts and a hundred taels. It is a good investment: with Auntie Yang's support, Yulou's beds, curtains, and trunks are carted out with whirlwind efficiency to Ximen's house, foiling the self-serving designs of the maternal uncle of Yulou's late husband. The farcical scene depicting the competing claims over these possessions shows that legal or poetic justice is elusive or irrelevant. In Li Ping'er's case, the things she owns are connected to the highest echelons of political power. She was the concubine of the privy councilor Liang Shijie (Liang Shih-chieh), and when Liang's household was ravaged by the avenging fury of Li Kui (Li K'uei), another character and plot detail from *Outlaws*, she escaped the carnage and took with her "a hundred large Western Ocean pearls and a pair of sapphires weighing two taels" (一百顆西洋大珠, 二兩重一對鴉青寶石; my trans.; 10.7a).[7] Eunuch Hua then arranges Li Ping'er's marriage to his nephew, Hua Zixu (Hua Tzu-hsü). There are broad hints that the eunuch had illicit relations with Ping'er, which would explain why his trunks of valuables, which include objects from the imperial palace as well as insignia of office such as python robes and jade belts, end up in her keeping. (Ping'er claims that Hua Zixu does not know about their existence, but he alludes to them.) The sexual toy (the Burmese bell) and the pornographic album that Ping'er enjoys with Ximen Qing—objects that he then uses with Jinlian—retain the aura of things originating from the imperial palace. One may question Ping'er's rights to these things, but their original owners also have only dubious claims to them. We are in a fictional universe where the frenetic quest for things moves the plot but in which no rightful ownership can be established to restore equilibrium. The transference of Ping'er's possessions to Ximen Qing's household—clandestinely transported over the garden wall and endlessly paraded through the streets—engages as much narrative attention as her own move into the household. Ping'er tries to buy favors and acceptance with her possessions, but she is diminished rather than empowered by these possessions. Her very entry into the Ximen household fulfills this logic. After the transference of her things is complete, Ximen humiliates her and drives her to despair. The issue is not Ximen Qing's greed per se—he is quite generous with his sycophants—but rather the identification of desire with inner void and the obsessive need for acquisition.

Ximen Qing pays fifty taels and four sets of clothing for the privilege of deflowering the courtesan Li Guijie (ch. 11). In that sense, marriage and concubinage share the transactional logic of the "licensed quarter" (*jiaofang* 教坊 or *yuanli* 院裡). Courtesans socialize with Ximen Qing's wives; two of them adopt Wu Yueniang and Li Ping'er as "mothers" (chs. 32, 42). Ximen Qing claims to be visiting courtesans when he is in fact having a clandestine rendezvous with Ping'er, prompting Jinlian to mock him: "The other night when that cuckold of hers [Hua Zixu, Ping'er's husband] supposedly invited you to join him for an excursion into the licensed quarter, it was his own home that was the licensed quarter, wasn't it?" (你還哄我老娘! 前日他家那忘八, 半夜叫了你往院裡去, 原來他家就是院裡; 1.13.269; 13.10a). During Ping'er's liaison with Ximen Qing, one of his sycophants refers to her as "a tart outside, not inside, the quarter" (不是裡面的, 是外面的婊子; my trans.; 15.6b). Pan Jinlian comments on different "styles of shoes favored by those inside the quarters" (裡邊的樣子) and "styles favored by those outside" (外邊的樣子; my trans.; 58.6b), but "those outside" also try to emulate the style of "those inside the quarters," as Wang Liu'er does in chapter 42 and Pan Jinlian does in chapter 52. Ximen complacently exclaims when he sees Pan Jinlian and Meng Yulou dressed in finery, "They look just like a pair of painted faces, and they'd cost a pretty penny too" (好似一對兒粉頭, 也值百十銀子; 1.11.207; 11.2a). Value is enhanced through the thrill of purchase; perhaps that is why Pan Jinlian dresses up as a maidservant newly bought for sixteen taels to "market her favor" (市愛) and counter the ascendancy of Li Ping'er.[8] Value is also perceived as the pleasure of appropriating what belongs to others; that is why Ximen Qing can be as excited by his liaison with a social superior like Madame Lin, the widow of a commissioner, as he is by his affair with Ruyi (Ju-i), the former wet nurse of his dead son, so long as she cries out about being another man's wife during intercourse (4.78.603; 78.16a).

The transactional nature of sex is on full display in the numerous scenes of intimacy or intercourse in which the woman asks for things. The maidservant Song Huilian (Sung Hui-lien), who agrees to a rendezvous after Ximen Qing sends her a bolt of blue silk (ch. 22), plies him with requests, from tea to a fret for her hair (chs. 23 and 25). Pan Jinlian interrupts the fellatio she is performing on Ximen Qing to ask for the fur coat that belonged to Li Ping'er, which according to Ximen Qing is worth sixty taels (ch. 74). Sexual acts associated with pain, violence, and perversion are sometimes accompanied by the most specific requests. Jinlian asks for "a drawnwork silk skirt of glossy gosling-yellow with silver stripes, and an inset of gold-spangled sheepskin, trimmed with varicolored thread" sported by Li Guijie and "purchased in the licensed quarter" while enduring bloody sodomization (那玉色線掐羊皮金挑的油鵝黃銀條紗裙子倒好看, 說是裡邊買的; 3.52.257; 52.2a). After burning moxa on Ruyi's body (a practice confirming a man's sexual conquest), Ximen Qing offers her "a patterned vest of jet color satin" (玄色緞子妝花比甲兒; 4.78.604; 78.16b). A tryst that begins with Ruyi's wish for a gold "tiger-shaped tiara" (金赤虎; 4.75.461; 75.4b) is punctuated by Ximen's offer of a bolt of red chiffon and his promise of promoting Ruyi to the status of concubine should she bear a child and ends with Ximen urinating in her mouth (4.75.464; 75.6b), an indignity she is induced to bear because he boasts of a similar act performed by Jinlian (ch. 72) as a mark of her abject devotion.

As if to underline the connection between sex and economic calculations, Ximen Qing, while having intercourse with Li Ping'er, discusses business with his servant Dai'an (Tai-an) as the latter stands outside the window while Ximen Qing explains his calculations to Ping'er (ch. 16). Among Ximen Qing's sexual partners, Wang Liu'er, the wife of his underling Han Daoguo (Han Tao-kuo), is the most businesslike. They go over details of his business arrangements in coitus (ch. 50). While burning moxa on Wang's body, they reach an agreement that her husband should become Ximen's buyer and manager down south (ch. 61). Enumerating her gains through the liaison, Wang explains to her husband: "It's all owing to my willingness to surrender my body to him. We might as well take advantage of the opportunity to get what we can out of him and improve our life-style" (也是我輸了身一場, 且落他些好供給穿戴). Han heartily agrees and urges his wife to "cater to his [Ximen's] every whim" (凡事奉承他些兒; 2.38.392; 38.7b). After Ximen's death, Wang suggests to Han that they abscond with the thousand taels of silver in Han's keeping: "Given the way he has taken advantage of me in the past, for us to make use of these few taels of his silver is hardly wrong" (他占用著老娘，使他這幾兩銀子不差甚麼; 5.81.7; 81.3b). Unlike Song Huilian and Pan Jinlian, whose desire for things is bound up with pride, self-worth (or lack thereof), and in Jinlian's case jealousy and insatiable sexual needs, Wang Liu'er sells her body with purposeful and methodical calculation.[9] Her acquisitiveness is unburdened by compulsion or obsession. Ironically, she ends up the winner, enjoying a measure of financial security by inheriting the property of her last paramour, Magnate He (Magnate Ho), even as the Song dynasty collapses and chaos ensues (ch. 100).

The measure of a man lies in the things he consumes. Li Ping'er considers Ximen Qing vastly superior to Jiang Zhushan (Chiang Chu-shan), the quack doctor to whom she was briefly married after the death of Hua Zixu, because of Ximen's fine clothes and attendants; "even the delicacies that constitute your daily fare are such things as he would never see, were he to live for hundreds of years. How can he be compared to you?" (只你每日吃用稀奇之物，他在世幾百年還沒會看見哩! 他拿甚麼來比你?; 1.19.399; 19.15b). Ximen Qing claims that even divine clemency can be bought with "good works" after sexual transgression against goddesses because the Buddhist heaven and hell depend on economic contributions from humans: "I've heard it said of the Buddha's heavenly realm that it was no more than a matter of paving the ground with gold; and that even in the Ten Courts of the underworld, one needs paper money to get things done. As long as I use what I own to do a lot of good works, even if I were to rape Chang E, fornicate with the Weaving Maid, abduct Xu Feiqiong, or steal the daughter of the Queen Mother of the West, it would do nothing to diminish the Heaven-splashing wealth and distinction that I now possess" (咱只消盡這家私廣為善事，就使強姦了嫦娥，和姦了織女，拐了許飛瓊，盜了西王母的女兒，也不減我潑天富貴; 3.57.411; 57.9b–10a). Lives, sexual favors, affection, position, and apparently everything else that defines being human can be bought and sold. In that sense, people are no different from things. A person is often referred to as "a thing" (huo 貨 or hanghuo 行貨, literally "merchandise"), a term conveying disdain or jocularity.[10]

This logic of objectification extends beyond the women: Ximen Qing is also strangely objectified. His obsession with sexual prowess reduces him to an instrument of sexual gratification—his penis is described in greater detail than any other part of his body. Dependent on, and almost enslaved by, his aphrodisiac and bag of "sexual implements" (yinqi 淫器), he is strangely pathetic even as he revels in his power. It is fitting that the Indian monk who gives him the aphrodisiac should appear as the personification of the male sexual organ,[11] and that Ximen's death should be followed by an absurd eulogy from his sycophants filled with puns and double entendres depicting the penis (ch. 80). Phallic potency is matched by the loss of agency;[12] this is most evident in the lurid scene in which Jinlian administers an overdose of the Indian monk's aphrodisiac and straddles the unconscious Ximen Qing (ch. 79).

Love tokens (biaoji 表記) belong to a wonted convention in Chinese fiction and drama. In Plum, such exchanges are either perfunctory, as when Ximen Qing and Jinlian exchange a hairpin and a handkerchief at the urging of Dame Wang (ch. 4), or merely provocative, as when Jinlian gives Chen Jingji a handkerchief in return for her red shoe, which Jingji picked up in the garden (ch. 28). In any case, no love token is described with as much detail about its making as the white satin band that Jinlian sews, with aphrodisiac backstitched securely inside "with her extremely deft technique" (甚是細法; 4.73.385; 73.1b) and Wang Liu'er's final gift to Ximen Qing: "a lock of her dark-black glossy hair, bound into a circlet with variegated satin displaying the motif of 'joined hearts,' and with two brocade straps attached to it, so that it could be fastened around the root of his chowrie handle" (却是老婆剪下一柳黑臻臻光油油的青絲, 用五色絨纏就的一個同心結托兒, 用兩根錦帶兒拴著, 安放在塵柄根下; 4.79.630; 79.3a). Both objects are supposed to enhance Ximen Qing's sexual performance, and both are linked to the image of bondage, perhaps echoing the foot-binding cloth with which Ximen Qing ties up both women in earlier sexual games (chs. 27, 79). Paradoxically, self-aggrandizement ends in objectification. Ximen Qing becomes a mere thing, a sexual organ subjected to manipulation.

Potentially Sentimental Things

The objectification of humans raises the question of the possibility of humanizing things. Meng Yulou has a hairpin engraved with lines that encode her name, which means "jade tower": "The golden-bridled horse neighs among fragrant grass, / The one on the jade tower is drunk in apricot blossom season" (金勒馬嘶芳草地, 玉樓人醉杏花天; my trans.; 8.7b). Contrary to expectation, no symbolic connection between the character and her hairpin develops. We first hear of it when Pan Jinlian finds it in Ximen Qing's topknot, but the scene of Yulou giving the hairpin to Ximen Qing is elided. In the throes of a passionate affair with Jinlian that has led to the murder of Wu Da (Wu the Elder), Ximen Qing nevertheless stops visiting Jinlian while he arranges his financially advantageous marriage with Yulou. Unaware of this development, Jinlian mistakes the hairpin as a gift from a courtesan. Indeed, the lines evoke the image of a romantic encounter and recur in fiction, drama, song lyrics, and vernacular songs from the Song dynasty through the Qing dynasty, sometimes in the context of a courtesan-literati romance. The hairpin is mentioned again when, after Ximen's death, Jinlian consummates her adulterous affair with her son-in-law, Chen Jingji, and finds Yulou's hairpin in his sleeve (4.82.302; 82.8a–8b). Chen has merely picked it up in the garden, but his possession of it later allows him to threaten Yulou with false accusations after she remarries. In other words, the hairpin functions as a means of narrative progression rather than as something that provides insight into Yulou's character.

In the same episode in which she discovers Yulou's hairpin in Ximen Qing's possession, Jinlian gives Ximen a hairpin in the shape of a double lotus, one among several birthday gifts. It is engraved with a quatrain professing love and devotion: "I have a twain-bloom lotus, / A gift for holding your topknot. / In all things be twain and one: / Do not easily cast me aside" (奴有並頭蓮, 贈與君關鬢. 凡事同頭上, 切勿輕相棄; my trans.; 8.8b). Ximen Qing is delighted by this display of cleverness since the quatrain has presumably been composed by Jinlian; they rekindle their passion, and shortly thereafter Jinlian enters Ximen's household. But for Ximen this mark of enhanced value—very much like Yulou's skill with the moon guitar—does not preclude pursuit of other objects of desire. The chapter is preceded by his marriage to Meng Yulou and followed by his liaison with the courtesan Li Guijie and his prolonged absence, which in turn leads to Jinlian's abortive affair with one of the young male servants. The hairpin with the quatrain is a would-be symbol of love in a world that negates such symbols.

If Yulou's hairpin merely moves the plot forward and Jinlian's becomes a flawed symbol, the hairpins Li Ping'er gives to Ximen Qing show how power negotiations overtake sentimental value. At the beginning of her affair with Ximen, when she is still married to Hua Zixu, Ping'er takes two gold hairpins from her chignon and puts them in Ximen Qing's hair, saying to him: "If you should go into the licensed quarter, don't let Hua Zixu see them" (若在院裡, 休要叫花子虛看見; 1.13.267; 13.8b). She wants this token of their secret bond to be hidden from her husband but also more generally from the prying eyes of others. When Jinlian finds out about the affair, however, Ximen Qing does not hesitate to offer the hairpins to placate her, pretending that Li Ping'er intended them as a gift to Jinlian: "Taking them into her hand and looking them over, Jinlian saw that they were a pair of gold, openwork pins, in the shape of the character for long life, which had been deeply chased in intaglio and inset with azurite. It was obvious from the extraordinary intricacy of the craftsmanship that they had been manufactured for imperial use and came from the palace" (金蓮接在手內觀看, 却是兩根番紋底板石青填地金玲瓏壽子簪兒, 乃御前所製造, 宮裏出來的, 甚是奇巧; 1.13.270; 13.11a). Jinlian then happily acquiesces to the clandestine affair and even promises to assist Ximen Qing. It is fitting that we should see the hairpins through Jinlian's eyes: she appreciates their material value as well as their symbolic value as the facilitator of triangular desire. Powerless to stop Ximen Qing, Jinlian reclaims lost ground through information and repetition—she reenacts Ping'er's sexual acts with Ximen Qing, down to the use of the pornographic album and the Burmese bell. When Ximen's wife Wu Yueniang remarks on the hairpins as Ping'er's gift to Jinlian at Jinlian's birthday party, Ping'er betrays no unease (has she just found out that Ximen Qing has transferred her gift to Jinlian?) and offers to give Yueniang and the other concubines sets of the same kind of hairpin (1.14.292; 14.11a–11b). A private love token becomes a tool for preparing Ping'er's entry into, and management of the power balance within, Ximen's polygamous household.

Jinlian's and Ping'er's hairpins demonstrate how sentimental objects can become embroiled in rivalries and power negotiations. But there are also examples—admittedly rare—of objects as symbols of unalloyed emotional attachment. Not surprisingly, these are linked to the relationships that come closest to emotional attachment: the relationship between Li Ping'er and her infant son, Guan'ge (Kuan-ko); between Ximen Qing and his favorite wife, Li Ping'er; and between Pan Jinlian and her maid, Chunmei. After Ping'er marries Ximen Qing, she gives birth to a son, Guan'ge, who dies not long after his first birthday as a result of Jinlian's machinations. Unable to part with Guan'ge's coffin, Ping'er is overcome with grief when she sees the clapper-drum he used to play with (ch. 59). The toy is first mentioned as one of the items in a list of congratulatory gifts that Eunuch Xue (Hsüeh) presents to Ximen Qing when Guan'ge is born. In "a pair of square lacquer gift boxes decorated with inlaid gilt designs," we find "a bolt of red government-quality shot silk, four gold-plated silver coins bearing the characters for 'good fortune,' 'long life,' 'health,' and 'tranquility,' a toy clapper-drum decorated with a varicolored, gold-flecked portrait of the God of Longevity, and two taels worth of silver trinkets in the shape of 'eight treasures'" (戧金方盒拿了兩盒禮物, 爛紅官鍛一疋, 二福壽康寧鍍金銀錢四個, 堆金瀝粉彩畫壽星博郎鼓兒一個, 銀八寶貳兩; 2.32.244; 32.2a–2b). Eunuch Xue tactfully checks whether his close associate, Eunuch Liu, has also sent a gift; his main concern is how he compares with his potential rival. In this sense, the clapper-drum is a mere marker of social transactions and obligations, just like most other gifts that feature in *Plum*. For a fleeting moment, however, Li Ping'er endows a social object with affective significance, since that object triggers her mournful remembrance of Guan'ge.

Scenes involving sentimental objects that evoke a longing for the dead or absent beloved are, however, quite rare in *Plum*. Ximen Qing commissions the painter Han to paint one half-length and one full-length portrait of Li Ping'er after her death. Han must create the likenesses based on the corpse and on his memory of a past encounter. Instead of dwelling on the pathos of tenuous connection between the person and the image, the narrative quickly shifts attention to the image's social significance. The countenance depicted in the half-length portrait is said to be "pale and fragrant" (白馥馥; 4.63.94; 63.7b). If that seems vague, it is because the hair ornaments and gown of figured scarlet material are described in all their particularity (ch. 63). The half-length portrait invites the comments of Ximen's other wives and is admired by the guests at the funeral. Ximen Qing asks Han to lavish even greater attention to the full-length portrait. In an earlier comment Ximen stipulates the style for both portraits: "She must be depicted in both cases in bright blue and green style, with pearls and trinkets adorning her chignon, wearing a scarlet full-sleeved variegated brocade robe, over a flower-sprigged skirt. And it should be mounted on patterned damask, with ivory knobs on the ends of the roller" (俱要用大青大綠, 珠翠圍髮冠, 大紅通袖五彩遍地金袍兒、百花裙. 衢花綾裱, 象牙軸頭; 4.63.88; 63.4a). Again, external paraphernalia seem to be more significant than verisimilitude or expression. The novel provides a detailed description of the garb of the Daoist who presides over the ceremony and who displays and dedicates the full-length portrait of Li

Ping'er, and Chen Jingji, Ximen's son-in-law, in the role of the filial son, intones an elaborate but scarcely heartfelt eulogy of Li Ping'er in front of the portrait in a faintly ridiculous scene (ch. 65).

For a moment, Ximen is overwhelmed with emotion as he watches a funereal drama performance that mentions a character bequeathing her self-portrait (ch. 63). There is also a scene in which Ximen Qing looks at the portrait as he spends the night in Li Ping'er's room in front of her spirit tablet. A conventional poem describes the sadness of bereavement. However, mourning soon becomes another sexual orgy as Ximen Qing starts an affair with Ruyi, Guan'ge's erstwhile wet nurse who stays on in Ping'er's room (ch. 67). The social and ritual functions of Li Ping'er's portraits are fully delineated, but the affective meaning of the portraits for Ximen Qing is easily superseded by another sexual adventure. Li Ping'er's lavish funeral takes up four chapters. We know all the details of the ceremony, the amount Han is paid for the portraits, the mourners' gifts, and the gifts given in return. Ximen Qing's grief is extravagantly displayed, but somehow the reader feels a lack of access to his inner life. He has no deep communion with Li Ping'er's portraits, the objects most likely to arouse sentimental associations. After Ximen Qing's death, his principal wife, Wu Yueniang, has the portraits unceremoniously burned.

If Li Ping'er's portraits seem enmeshed in social and ritual functions, even as they may appear to have sentimental value for Ximen Qing, Pan Jinlian's bed, which Chunmei tries to recover as a memento, shows the pressure of economic transactions. The bed is featured in the rivalry between Li Ping'er and Pan Jinlian. Pan Jinlian "induced Ximen Qing to spend sixty taels of silver in order to buy a balustraded bedstead of inlaid mother-of-pearl for her" because Li had a similar bed (婦人旋教西門慶使了六十兩銀子, 也替他也買了這一張螺鈿有欄杆的床; 2.29.187–88; 29.12b).[13] The bed is described in great detail: the narrative lingers over the side panels, whose mother-of-pearl designs depict "towers and terraces, halls and chambers, flowers and foliage, birds and animals" (樓臺殿閣, 花草翎毛; 2.29.187; 29.12a); the motifs of pines, bamboos, and plum blossoms on the three comb-back-shaped backrests; and the purple gauze bed curtains with brocade sashes and silver hooks. The bed is the setting for a seduction scene: clad in nothing but a bodice of red chiffon and red slippers, Pan Jinlian "had secretly mixed the stamens of jasmine blossoms with butterfat and face powder and rubbed the mixture over her entire body" until it was "white and glossy, shiny and smooth" (就暗暗將茉莉花蕊兒攪酥油定粉, 把身上都搽遍了. 搽的白膩光滑; 2.29.188–89; 29.12b), in the hope of besting her rival Li Ping'er, whose fair skin entranced Ximen Qing (ch. 27). The bed is but the symbolic extension of the body; both belong to the same scheme of sexual competition and insatiable desire. As Jinlian's loyal ally and the conspicuous third party in her sexual exploits,[14] Chunmei replicates Jinlian's desires and aversions, especially after the latter's death. It is fitting, therefore, that Chunmei should seek to recover Pan Jinlian's bed after Jinlian is eviscerated by her nemesis Wu Song (ch. 87)—in some ways Chunmei is recovering part of herself. In the wake of a reversal of fortune, Chunmei, now the wife of Commandant Zhou, visits the declining Ximen household after Ximen's death, where she finds general dilapidation and asks about Jinlian's missing bed. Ximen Qing had taken the gilt lacquer "Nanking bed with retractable steps" (南京拔步床) that Meng Yulou had brought with her as part of her dowry and given it to his daughter, Ximen Dajie (Hsi-men Ta-chieh), as part of her trousseau when she married into the Chen family (1.7.147; 7.1b). When Meng Yulou remarries Li Gongbi (Li Kung-pi) after Ximen Qing dies, Wu Yueniang turns over Jinlian's bed to Meng to make up for the Nanking bed (ch. 91). A potential sentimental object turns out to be a link in a chain of substitution. Objects are replaceable because of consensual monetary value. Chunmei accepts this inexorable economic logic and asks about the fate of the other beds. Yueniang reclaims Ximen Dajie's bed (the reason for the loss of Jinlian's bed) after Dajie's suicide (ch. 92) and sells it for a mere eight taels of silver. Li Ping'er's bed, which had inspired the competition, was sold for thirty-five taels of silver. Chunmei remembers that it originally cost sixty taels and regrets the cheap resale: "If I had known that you were getting rid of it, I would have been willing to pay you thirty or forty taels of silver for it. I would have really liked to have it" (早知你老人家打發, 我倒與你老人家三四十兩銀子, 我要了也罷; 5.96.316; 96.5a). In other words, her mind is quickly diverted from the sentimental value of Jinlian's bed to the monetary value of the beds related by substitution and association. She would not have minded paying for Li's bed the amount that Yueniang sold it for. It would have been a bargain.

Appreciating Things: The Vulgar Connoisseur

If things usually do not command sentimental or emotional value, and if the logic of the marketplace reigns supreme, what are we left with? Do we see the objectification of people as the index to moral collapse?[15] Is oppressive materiality a self-subverting proposition that necessarily implies its own vacuity and meaninglessness? Alternatively, can we find meaning beyond negation and critique? In other words, does *Plum*'s implied author seem to take pleasure in lingering over this plethora of things? Is it possible to imagine that the author appreciates the things being described?

The character that articulates the most fulsome appreciation of things is the sycophant Ying Bojue (Ying Po-chüeh), one of Ximen Qing's sworn brothers. Having gained the office of assistant judicial commissioner through lavish gifts to the grand preceptor, Cai Jing (Ts'ai Ching), Ximen Qing revels in the paraphernalia of office. He shows off a new girdle to Ying Bojue, who is predictably impressed and exclaims:

> Regarding the rest of them, enough said; but as for this girdle with its decorative plaque of rhinoceros horn, and this one of "crane's crest red," you couldn't find the like in the entire metropolis, though you had the money

in hand. . . . [T]his is the horn of the water rhinoceros, not the horn of the
dry land rhinoceros. The latter is not worth anything. The horn of the water
rhinoceros is called "Heaven penetrating rhinoceros horn." If you don't believe me, bring a bowl of water, put the rhinoceros horn in it, and it will
divide the water in two. This is a priceless treasure. Moreover, if you ig-
nite it at night it will illuminate an area of a thousand li, and the flame will
not be extinguished the entire night.   (2.31.216–17)

別的倒也罷了, 只這條犀角帶并鶴頂紅, 就是滿京城拿著銀子也尋不出 ... 這
是水犀角, 不是旱犀角. 旱犀角不值錢. 水犀角號作 "通天犀," 你不信, 取一碗
水, 把犀角安放在水內, 分水為兩處, 此為無價之寶. 又夜間燃火照千里, 火
光通宵不滅.   (31.2b)

For Ximen Qing, the girdle matters because of its price (a hundred taels) and its
provenance "from the household of Imperial Commissioner Wang on Main
Street" (是大街上王招宣府裡的帶; 2.31.217; 31.2b), whose financial straits seem
to render the Wang family's superior status available for appropriation.[16] The
Wang household commands the arc of Ximen Qing's desire, being the place
where Jinlian started out as a maid (ch. 1) and where Ximen revels in the illusion of power in sexual encounters with a social superior, Lady Lin, the widow
of Imperial Commissioner Wang (chs. 69, 78). Ying Bojue, for his part, is flatter-
ing Ximen Qing as a preamble to requesting a loan on behalf of their crony Wu
Dian'en (Wu Tien-en). Again, money and status are the real issues; the thing itself does not seem to matter much. Zhang Zhupo 張竹坡 (1670–98) scoffs at
Ying Bojue for being a "fake connoisseur" (*jia zaihang* 假在行), and there is some
evidence of a mix-up in his information.[17] However, it is also possible that the
author simply enjoys dilating on the lore of the "Heaven penetrating rhinoceros
horn"; it testifies to his "broad learning about things" (*bowu* 博物) even as it lends
urgency to the undercurrent of transgression and doom.[18]

Ying's connoisseurship is a unique blend of virtuosic knowledge and vulgarity. When Eunuch Director Liu, the manager of the imperial brickyard, sends
Ximen Qing twenty pots of chrysanthemums, attention shifts quickly from the
flowers to the pots. Zhang Zhupo comments, "The emphasis is on the pots: this
is how vulgar people of the marketplace love flowers" (反重在盆, 是市井人愛花;
my trans.; *HHJPM* 3.61.1213). Yet Ying's knowledge about the pots is a tour de
force: "[T]hese pots are double-banded wide-mouthed flowerpots, manufactured
from the finest clay in the imperial kilns, and are both long-lasting and water-
repellent. They are made from clay that has been strained through silken sieves
and kneaded underfoot until it becomes a thick paste, just like that used in
the firing of the finest quality of bricks in Suzhou" (這盆正是官窯雙箍澄漿盆,
又吃年代, 又禁水漫. 都是用絹羅打, 用腳趾過泥, 纔燒造這個物兒. 與蘇州澄漿磚
一個樣兒做法; 4.61.23; 61.13b). David T. Roy points out that there was indeed an
imperial brickyard located in Suzhou during the Ming dynasty that made bricks
for palace construction (4.698n47). The chrysanthemums may have traditional

symbolic associations, but Ying is right that the economic and political signifi-cance of the gifts lies with the pots, which have a more immediate connection with the giver. His excursus on the making of the pots would not be out of place in the manuals of taste prevalent in the late Ming.

Sycophancy does not preclude heartfelt appreciation. Thus, Ying Bojue's song on tea (1.12.228; 12.3b) and his paean to shad: "This fish of yours from Jiangnan is only in season once a year. If it gets stuck in the cracks between your teeth, when you manage to extricate it, it is still fragrant. It's not easy to come by. To tell the truth, I doubt if it is available even at court. Where else are you likely to find it except at Brother's place here?" (你們那裡曉得, 江南此魚, 一年只過一遭兒, 吃到牙縫兒裡, 剔出來都是香的. 好容易! 公道说, 就是朝廷還没吃哩, 不是哥這裡, 誰家有?; 3.52.278; 52.14b).[19] He also recommends a recipe for its prepara-tion (2.34.288; 34.5a). His effusive appreciation of the butterfat "abalone shell" sweets prepared by Li Ping'er (3.58.434; 58.10a) and by the courtesan Zheng Aiyue (4.67.182; 67.12b) elevates delectable taste as a transformative experience, even while callously implying that women are replaceable. (After Ping'er's death, Ying Bojue can continue to enjoy the delicacy because Zheng Aiyue is equally adept in preparing it.)

If the implied author seems to intermittently speak through Ying Bojue's sen-sual appreciation despite the latter's vulgarity, it is because there is no counter-vailing standard of elegance in *Plum*. Or rather, elegance itself becomes vulgar. As Ximen Qing amasses wealth and power, the paraphernalia of refinement, such as calligraphy, painting, zithers, and antiques, come to grace his surroundings. Using a kind of free indirect style, Ying Bojue offers one of the most detailed descriptions of Ximen's summerhouse, Kingfisher Pavilion, which is graced by such markers of elegance:

> Ying Bojue observed that facing each other on the upper and lower ends of the room were ranged two rows of six low-slung, bow-back, folding arm-chairs of the type called Dongpo chairs, embellished with Yunnan ag-ateware lacquer, gilt nails, and wickerwork rattan seats. On the two side walls were hung four landscape paintings by well-known artists, mounted on ultramarine patterned damask with white satin borders. On one hand there stood a side table, the cabriole legs of which were carved in the shape of protruding "mantis belly" that tapered down into "dragonfly feet," and the top of which was inlaid with an oblong, letter-shaped, slab of marble, chosen for its pictorial quality. On this table was displayed an antique bronze incense burner in the shape of a gilded crane. In the center of the back wall there hung a plaque emblazoned with the three characters for Kingfisher Pavilion, with a pair of framed hanging scrolls suspended to the left and right, on the coated paper of which was inscribed the couplet:
>
>> The breeze is tranquil, shadows of locust trees purify the courtyard;
>> The day is long, fragrance from an incense burner suffuses the
>> latticework.

. . . Ying Bojue wandered into the inner study, where he found standing on the floor a black lacquer summer bedstead with incised gold ornamentation and a decorative marble panel, and fitted with bed curtains of blue silk. To either side of this were painted lacquer bookcases adorned with gold tracery, which were filled with conventional presentation gifts of privately printed books with brocade wrappers and bolts of fabric. There was also a desk, piled high with writing implements and books. Under the green gauze window there stood a black lacquer zither stand and a solitary folding chair inlaid with mother-of-pearl. A letter case was also visible containing Ximen Qing's social correspondence, calling cards, and lists of people with whom Mid-autumn Festival gifts have been exchanged.

(2.34.284–85)

伯爵見上下放著六把雲南瑪瑙漆減金釘藤絲墊矮矮東坡椅兒, 兩邊掛四軸天青衢花綾裱白綾邊名人的山水, 一邊一張螳螂蜻蜓腳、一封書大理石心璧畫的幫桌兒, 桌兒上安放古銅爐、鎏金仙鶴, 正面懸著 "翡翠軒" 三字. 左右粉箋吊屏上寫著一聯: "風靜槐陰清院宇, 日長香篆散簾攏." . . . 伯爵走到裡邊書房內, 裡面地平上安著一張大理石黑漆縷金涼床, 挂著青紗帳幔. 兩邊彩漆描金書廚, 盛的都是送禮的書帕、尺頭, 几席文具書籍堆滿. 綠紗窗下, 安放一隻黑漆琴桌, 獨獨放著一張螺鈿交椅. 書篋內都是往來書東拜帖, 并送中秋禮物帳簿.

(34.2b–3a)

This passage appears only in the *cihua* edition. The editor of the Chongzhen edition would have been justified in cutting it, for it contributes nothing to the plot. Yet it is a remarkable embodiment of vulgarized elegance. Ying does not pause to offer details on the paintings, lingering instead on the material for mounting them. The mood of contemplative detachment suggested by the couplet and the incense burner is belied by the ornate side table and the chairs. The gold tracery on the bookcase seems to demand greater attention than do the books, which are notable more for their brocade wrappers as vanity projects than they are for their content. Ying's attention is drawn to the list of gifts exchanged because transactions override all other modes of human connections in *Plum*. It is fitting that Kingfisher Pavilion should be the setting for sexual trysts, monetary negotiations, and maneuverings that bypass legal constraints.

Despite their veneer as learned men, the scholars and officials who supposedly embody ideals of refinement are every bit as vulgar as Ximen Qing and his cronies. The way Censor Song Qiaonian (Sung Ch'iao-nian) transparently hankers after Ximen Qing's "gilded Eight Immortals Tripod" (流金八仙鼎) is no different from the calculations of the marketplace (4.74.430, 4.75.464; 74.7b, 75.6b). The mansions of the grand preceptor, Cai Jing; his steward, Zhai Qian (Chai Ch'ien); and Imperial Commissioner Wang may boast of possessing more precious objects and cultural artifacts than Ximen Qing does, but one does not have the impression that these mansions fulfill higher standards of elegance. Indeed, the grandest and most ambitious aesthete of all may be the Huizong emperor, but his Mount Gen Imperial Park is seen as the source of suffering and corruption rather than as the realization of an aesthetic ideal. In Ximen's dealings with scholar-officials, he affects elevated speech and uses cultural allusions. The result is not so much the exposure of his déclassé pretensions but the implicit castigation of all parties involved and the degradation of high culture. When Ximen Qing and Principal Graduate Cai (Ts'ai) compare themselves to famous Eastern Jin epitomes of lofty spirits like Xie An and Wang Xizhi, standard literati justifications of sensual pleasures through the appeal to such analogies are brought into question (1.49.185–86; 49.8a–8b). If Ximen's relationships with courtesans are unabashedly crass, those of Principal Graduate Cai or Wang the Third are not any better, even though they may be dignified by the conventionally sentimental poems that those two write for their lovers (3.49.190, 4.77.560–61; 49.8a, 77.9b–10a).[20]

If there are no higher standards of elegance and good taste (and the traditional ornaments of literati culture certainly do not seem to represent them here), what we are left with is a frank wallowing in sensual reality. Instead of seeing the endless descriptions as markers of moral outrage, readers can imagine an author fascinated by the multifarious sensual appeal of clothing, food, and decor. The author may be mocking Ying Bojue for failing to dwell on the famous landscape paintings in Kingfisher Pavilion but, like Ying, may find the cabriole leg of the side table well worth absorption and detailed description.

Contexts of Literary History

No other works of Chinese fiction before *Plum* show the same obsession with material reality. Of all Chinese genres, *fu* 賦, translated as "rhapsody" or "poetic exposition," displays the most sustained focus on exhaustive description. Some of the genre's most famous examples—such as Sima Xiangru's "*Fu* on Shanglin Park" and "*Fu* on the Great One," Ban Gu's "*Fu* on the Two Capitals," and Zuo Si's "*Fu* on the Three Capitals"—also encompass a grand inclusiveness and aspire to evoke a sense of plenitude. Numerous *fu* on objects tirelessly list the attributes and history of objects. It could be that Chinese fiction, in trying to summon the illusion of totality, draws from the penchant for descriptive details endemic to *fu*. Indeed, there are numerous passages in parallel prose—often announced by the phrase *danjian* 但見 ("behold") and devoted to subjects as various as a person's appearance, the decor of a room, gardens, natural scenery, storms, temples, a matchmaker's wiles, sexual intercourse, the Lantern Festival, feasts, and funerals—that are in effect mini-*fu*. Couched in somewhat categorical and formulaic language, descriptive passages like these are also found in earlier works of Ming vernacular fiction. Where *Plum* diverges from its precedents is in its enumeration of less tidy lists of attributes built into the narrative and its attention to contemporary particularities that engross the narrator (and sometimes characters like Ying Bojue).

The aesthetic ideal of *fu* is to "give form to (or embody) things" (*tiwu* 體物). Even this implied principle of externalization, however, comes to presume a true understanding of the meaning of things or the communion with things. Poetry that takes things as its objects of attention also upholds the primacy of the affective meanings of things and blurs the boundaries between the poet and their object. Following this lyrical reasoning to its logical conclusion, Baoyu in *The Story of the Stone* declares, "Not only plants and trees, but all things that have a reason for being are just like humans: when they find someone who truly understands them, they become absolutely numinous" (不但草木, 凡天下有情有理的東西, 也和人一樣, 得了知己, 便極有靈驗的; Cao Xueqin 2: 877). The opposite logic unfolds in *Plum*. Things are not humanized; people are objectified.

In willfully declaring the sentience of all things, Baoyu knows that he must deal with the incredulity of others. The project of privately defining values is often implicitly oppositional. Responding to the saying "When the host is refined, the guests come calling often" (主雅客來勤), Baoyu protests, "Have done! Have done! I am but the most vulgar of the vulgar! I do not want to spend them with these people [i.e., the guests]!" (罷, 罷! 我也不過俗中又俗的一個俗人罷了, 並不願和這些人來往!; Cao Xueqin 1: 336). Defying the boundary between refinement and vulgarity is affirmed but also sometimes called into question in *Stone* because the general discontent with conventional standards of judgment is connected to a nagging unease with the implications of inventing one's own values.[21] Such conundrums do not exist in *Plum*, yet the novel also provides a de facto exploration of the meanings of vulgarity and refinement. Conventionally refined things seem vulgar, yet no one is interested in defying the consensus and following different rules of taste. Vulgar things resist moral and spiritual meanings, yet they are deeply human and invite immersion in pleasures of the senses.

Things in *Plum* resist the imposition of emotional, moral, and spiritual meanings. They even resist their own negation. Interpretations of *Plum* that are based on a stringent moral or religious vision presume revulsion against the venality and futility of the novel's material surface, yet the implied author has an undeniable fascination with all its details. Recalcitrant things possess a momentum that drives the narrative. Think, for instance, of Pan Jinlian's shoes and their function in numerous scenes of flirtation, sexual orgy, jealousy, and rivalry. It may be precisely because these things do not have deeper meanings that they are so evocative of desires and fears as lived experience. *Plum*'s characters may be defined by their material existence and sometimes reduced to mere things, but they are not thereby dehumanized. On some level we still empathize with their desire for or reliance on things, despite the fatuousness of such desire, as the basic struggles of the human condition.[22] The paradox of *Plum in the Golden Vase* lies in how it entrances with its plethora of things and shows their connection to human drama while withholding their consistent connection to a moral or religious system.

NOTES

[1] "For things can move human beings in countless ways, and if the likes and dislikes of humans are not regulated, then things come and humans are transformed by things.

Humans being transformed by things means that heavenly principles are extinguished as human desires are pushed to their limits" (夫物之感人無窮, 而人之好惡無節, 則是物至而人化物也. 人化物也者, 滅天理而窮人欲者也; my trans.; Zheng Xuan et al. 10a–10b [*juan* 37]). For a discussion of *juan* 卷, a term denoting the internal divisions common in books of the late imperial period, see endnote 4 of Carlitz's essay in this volume.

[2] Translations of passages from *Honglou meng* are my own. In passages from *Jin Ping Mei* when I am not quoting Roy's *Plum*, my translations are based on *Jin Ping Mei cihua* 金瓶梅詞話 (*Plum in the Golden Vase: A Ballad Tale*) and *Huiping huijiao* Jin Ping Mei 會評會校金瓶梅 (*Variorum* Plum in the Golden Vase).

[3] Servants, including maids, were bond servants, but they were not legally confined to that status. They still had basic rights. In some cases, a maidservant could become a concubine or even a principal wife. Interestingly, the price of male servants is rarely mentioned. However, Ximen Qing's page boys and catamites, Shutong (Shu-t'ung) and Wang Jing (Wang Ching), come to him by means of a network of favors sought and bestowed, a process akin to pricing (chs. 31, 55).

[4] It is ironic that Qiuju, the constant object of Jinlian's sadistic ire, should cost more than Xiaoyu, who by marrying Dai'an, Ximen's trusted servant and eventual inheritor of what remains of his wealth (5.100.419; 100.16b), rises in the world by default.

[5] As Ximen Qing's unofficial concubine, Chunmei is entitled to some clothing and jewelry when she is sold. Yueniang gives her nothing because of her role in facilitating the affair between Pan Jinlian and Ximen Qing's son-in-law, Chen Jingji. The go-between, Auntie Xue (Auntie Hsüeh), makes a tidy profit when she resells Chunmei to the commandant Zhou Xiu for fifty taels.

[6] Jinlian is brought to Ximen Qing's house in a sedan chair accompanied by four lanterns (ch. 9). Yulou comes in a large sedan chair and four pairs of gauze lanterns (ch. 7). For Ping'er, Ximen Qing sends a large sedan chair, a bolt of red satin, four pairs of red lanterns, and four servants (ch. 19).

[7] Roy translates *yaqing* 鴉青 (rendered here as "sapphires") as "onyx" (1.10.200), probably taking his cue from its literal meaning as "crow black." According to various miscellanies, *yagu*, *yaguqing*, and *yagu qing yagu* are transliterations of an Arabic or Persian word that means "jewel," of which the most prized kind is blue. Note that Li Ping'er's string of pearls are said to be foreign.

[8] Roy translates "to market favor" (a phrase in the titular couplet for chapter 40) as "to court affection" (2.40.438).

[9] In that sense, Jinlian's acquisitiveness is less about wealth or the things themselves than about her own obsessive desire. The Chongzhen edition commentator notes the dismissive way Jinlian refers to the powerful eunuch Huang Jingchen, defender-in-chief of the palace command: "The words 'Eunuch Huang' are uttered so coldly. Thus one can see that in the hearts of truly passionate women and truly lustful women, wealth does not matter" (金蓮 "黃內官" 三字寫得冰冷. 可見真正情婦人、淫婦人胸中原無富貴; my trans.; *HHJPM* 4.73.1498).

[10] The term also refers to the penis, as in "donkey-member-sized merchandise" (*lü da xinghuo* 驢大行貨; my trans.; 3.1a), which Roy translates as "member of a donkey" (1.3.62). Other vernacular novels use the terms *huo* and *hanghuo*, but much less frequently than in *Jin Ping Mei*.

[11] Both the Chongzhen edition commentator and Zhang Zhupo note the resemblance (*HHJPM* 3.49.970–71). All the dishes in the feast for the monk are based on overt or covert sexual puns, as Zhang Zhupo implies by his repeated comments, *qu* 趣 ("clever") and *xiang* 像 ("look alike"; my trans.; *HHJPM* 3.49.973–74).

[12] The late Qing critic Wen Long notes Ximen Qing's lack of agency in general and enumerates the occasions when he is manipulated by Dame Wang, Auntie Xue, Pan Jinlian, Li Guijie, Ying Bojue, and Shutong (*HHJPM* 2.35.737).

[13] This bed presumably replaces the "black lacquer bedstead, elaborately adorned with gold tracery" that Ximen Qing purchased for Pan Jinlian for sixteen taels when she entered his household (1.9.171; 9.1b).

[14] Chunmei is made to watch Pan Jinlian and Ximen Qing's coitus and sexual games (chs. 18, 27), and she has intercourse with Chen Jingji in front of Pan Jinlian (ch. 82).

[15] See, for example, Roy's reading, which construes the implied author's stringent moral critique from the perspective of Xunzi's thought (Introduction xxvi, xxxvi). For Andrew Plaks, the book ironically unmasks moral vacuum by drawing on sixteenth-century "learning of the heart and mind" (*xinxue* 心學; *Four Masterworks* 159). Sophie Volpp's discussion of objects in *Jin Ping Mei* also focus on the idea of transgression and moral collapse ("Gift").

[16] The Wang household also pawns a fur coat (ch. 46), which Pan Jinlian does not deign to accept, arguing instead that she must have the fur coat that belonged to Li Ping'er (ch. 74).

[17] None of the sources mention that the "Heaven penetrating rhinoceros horn" comes from "water rhinoceros." The association here might have arisen because of its supposed attribute of dividing water. It is not clear whether the author is responsible for the confusion or whether he is mocking Ying Bojue for the inaccurate association. By contrast, Ying's elaborate praise of Li Ping'er's expensive coffin boards named "Peach Blossom Cavern," designed to impress Eunuch Xue, is an obviously incongruous jumble of stories based on free associations with an essay by Tao Qian titled "Peach Blossom Spring," a well-known account of entry into a world of peace beyond human strife and historical turmoil (4.64.112–13, 4.710n13).

[18] According to Roy, the locus classicus of the "Heaven penetrating rhinoceros horn" is found in *Master Embracing Simplicity* (*Baopuzi* 抱朴子; 2.528n9). It is mentioned in poetry, prose, historical texts, and Song and Ming miscellanies, in addition to the sources cited by Roy.

[19] Despite endless enumeration of dishes in the book, there are only a few discussions of taste. Aside from Ying Bojue's remarks, see also Ximen Qing's description of the "coated plums" (4.67.191). Recipes are also uncommon—exceptions include Huilian's way of cooking pig's head and the crabs prepared by Chang Shijie's wife (ch. 23, ch. 61).

[20] Ximen Qing's sobriquet is Siquan ("Four Springs"); those of Cai and Wang are Yiquan ("One Spring") and Sanquan ("Three Springs"), respectively. This similarity implies a sense of affinity. After Wang becomes Ximen's adopted son, he fears that such closely linked nomenclature may imply disrespect and changes his sobriquet to Xiaoxuan ("Little Studio"). Ximen Qing regards Wang's deference as a significant social victory (ch. 77).

[21] The dangers and paradoxes of being obsessed with refinement or setting one's own standards are evident in the scene in which Baoyu and his cousins savor tea prepared by the nun Miaoyu (ch. 41). When Baoyu explains to Qingwen that the raison d'être of a fan may lie in its sound of tearing—that is, so long as one is following one's feelings in "appreciating things" (*aiwu* 愛物; Cao Xueqin 1: 328)—there are also echoes of death and destruction.

[22] Sun Shuyu sees sympathy for human weaknesses and failures as the distinct achievement of *Jin Ping Mei*. Among the traditional commentators, the Chongzhen commentator seems least judgmental.

I Lie, Therefore I Am

Lisa Zunshine

Lying is fundamental to the construction of fictional consciousness. Some genres, such as the picaresque novel, the detective story, and the comedy of manners, are built around characters who intentionally deceive one another. Others, such as the eighteenth- and nineteenth-century psychological novel, thrive on their protagonists' self-deception. Yet others, such as postmodernist metafiction, present characters that deceive us, the readers, concerning the ontological status of other characters, while also leaving open the possibility that they themselves may be figments of other characters' imagination.

As a cognitive literary critic, I think of lying in the context of our mind-reading ability, also known as our theory of mind—that is, our evolved cognitive predisposition to perceive our own and other people's observable behavior as caused by mental states, such as thoughts, feelings, desires, and intentions. I have argued elsewhere that fiction exploits our readiness to intuit the mental states that underlie behavior: we make sense of what we read by attributing thoughts and feelings to characters, narrators, authors, and (implied) readers (Zunshine, *Why We Read Fiction* and "From the Social"). Different genres foreground different aspects of mind reading, speeding up and slowing down the process, encouraging wrong attributions of mental states, and resolving (or refusing to resolve) ambiguous social situations by revealing characters' feelings. Given the productive instability surrounding mind reading in fiction, it's not surprising that lying—as a deliberate or an unwitting misrepresentation of one's true intentions—remains a staple of fictional subjectivity.

If we want to use a cognitive literary perspective to take a closer look at what lying can do for a writer in a particular genre—in addition, that is, to merely reflecting and magnifying our real-life mind-reading uncertainties—we would do well to turn to an early paradigm-setting specimen of that genre. *The Plum in the Golden Vase* (*Jin Ping Mei* 金瓶梅) fits this description well. Written in the last decades of the sixteenth century, it is considered "the first Chinese novel that was wholly the creation of one author and had no antecedent in the oral tradition" (Schonebaum, Introduction 63). It tells the story of an upwardly mobile merchant, Ximen Qing (Hsi-men Ch'ing), and his six wives and concubines, whose lives are steeped in "deception, bribery, blackmail, profligacy, flamboyant sex, and even murder" (Link). Among those familial pastimes, lying occupies pride of place. Every couple chapters, a new intrigue blossoms, often starting with a sexual transgression and snowballing as characters keep eavesdropping on and framing one another. Let us consider one such episode in some detail to see what is gained by viewing it through a cognitive lens.

Jinlian Drives a Servant to Suicide

In chapter 25, when Ximen Qing's purchasing agent, Laiwang (Lai-wang), comes back from a business trip, he learns from Ximen Qing's concubine Sun Xue'e (Sun Hsüeh-o) that, while he was away, Ximen Qing started an affair with Laiwang's wife, Song Huilian (Sung Hui-lien). Laiwang confronts his wife, but she claims that her enemies made up this story, which seems to placate him (1.2.87).[1] (It may help that by now Laiwang has started his own affair with Sun Xue'e.)

Another one of Ximen Qing's retainers, Gan Laixing (Kan Lai-hsing), who has a grudge against Laiwang, overhears Laiwang, in his cups, railing angrily against Ximen Qing and one of his wives, Pan Jinlian (P'an Chin-lien), who, as Laiwang has been told by Sun Xue'e, has provided cover for the affair between Song Huilian and Ximen Qing. Laixing goes to Pan Jinlian, tells her (falsely) that Laiwang tried to pick a fight with him, and gives her an exaggerated account of Laiwang's threats. The incensed Pan Jinlian reports this to Ximen Qing. Ximen Qing questions Song Huilian, but she swears that Laiwang "never said any such thing" (他可是沒有這個話) and that Laixing has "made up this story out of whole cloth" (平空做作出來; 2.25.96; 25.11a). Ximen Qing believes her and promises to send her husband off on another long-term business trip. Song Huilian and Ximen Qing then agree on a lie that she will tell when others notice a present that Ximen Qing is about to give her.

When Pan Jinlian learns that, instead of punishing Laiwang, Ximen Qing plans to trust him with another prestigious errand, she convinces Ximen Qing that Song Huilian lied to him about her husband's intentions and that, sooner or later, Laiwang will take revenge on his master. Ximen Qing decides to drive Laiwang away. He frames him and has him imprisoned. What follows is a long series of lies aimed at making Song Huilian believe that her husband is doing fine when, in fact, he is being severely beaten in jail.

Song Huilian eventually learns the truth and kills herself. To avoid an official investigation of her death, Ximen Qing bribes the court magistrate and concocts a story in which Song Huilian is put in charge of the household's silver utensils and hangs herself in fear of retribution when a cup goes missing.

What are we to make of this swarm of lies? We can view them as integral to the author's larger critique of the corruption of the contemporary imperial court. For, while the story "is set during the reign of Emperor Huizong of Song (1101–1126 CE)," as a political allegory it "points clearly to contemporary Ming rulers as well" (Link). Or we can consider the characters' eager intriguing as a warped expression of "competing claims of individual feeling and the constraints of conventional morality" (Scott 266). Or, along with the seventeenth-century commentator Zhang Zhupo 張竹坡 (1670–98), we can appreciate the elaborate architectonics of the three-thousand-page novel, in which every little detail becomes a "structural device" used by the author "to accomplish his aims without leaving a trace" ("How to Read the *Chin P'ing Mei*" 204, 206). For instance, the "author needs Song Huilian . . . in order to bring out as completely as possible the viciousness of Pan Jinlian," for it is Pan Jinlian's "double-tongued troublemaking between Sun Xue'e and Song Huilian" that precipitates both Laiwang's "narrow escape from death and the needless suicide of Song Huilian" (211).

Embedded Mental States in Fiction

To see how a cognitive perspective may complement these insights, consider the role of deception in generating complex embedments of mental states. As I have argued elsewhere, fiction as we know it today, as well as some literary nonfiction, constantly embeds mental states on at least the third level (i.e., a mental state within a mental state within yet another mental state). This is in direct contrast both to expository nonfiction—which may contain complex embedments now and then but can also wholly subsist on just the first and second level—and to our routine social interactions. For, occasional drama and intrigue notwithstanding (e.g., "I *don't want* him to *know* that I *forgot* his birthday"; "I *wonder* if she *knows* what they really *have in mind* for her"), thinking about thinking about thinking (i.e., third-level embedment) "occurs in interpersonal cognition in real life less frequently" than, for instance, thinking about thinking (i.e., second-level embedment) does (Miller et al. 622). The former, as the cognitive psychologist Patricia Miller and her colleagues put it, "has a lower ecological plausibility" (622).

In fiction, we make sense of what we read by processing a steady stream of third- and fourth-level embedments, associated with characters, narrators, (implied) authors, and (implied) readers, in a vast variety of combinations. For instance, in *Story of the Stone* (*Honglou meng* 紅樓夢), by Cao Xueqin 曹雪芹, while visiting her aunt, Mrs. Xue, Lin Dai-yu scolds a maid who brings her a hand-warmer, because she *imagines* that someone may *think* that she *thinks* that her hosts are not taking good care of her. She explains this to the surprised Mrs. Xue as follows:

> You don't understand, Aunt. . . . It doesn't matter here, with you; but some people might be deeply offended at the sight of one of my maids rushing in with a hand-warmer. It's as though I thought my hosts couldn't supply one themselves if I needed it. Instead of saying how thoughtful the maid was, they would put it down to my arrogance and lack of breeding.
> (Hawkes and Minford, *Story* [Fan Shengyu] 1: 193)

> 姨媽不知道. 幸虧是姨媽這裏, 倘或在別人家, 人家豈不惱? 好說就看得人家連個手爐也沒有, 巴巴的從家裏送個來. 不說丫頭們太小心過餘, 還只當我素日是這等輕狂慣了呢.
> (1: 124)

In "A Madman's Diary" ("Kuángrén Rìjì" 狂人日記), by Lu Xun 魯迅 (1881–1936), the protagonist laughs uproariously at the doctor's suggestion that he should rest quietly for a couple days. Both the doctor and the protagonist's brother turn pale in response, which leads the protagonist to think that they are "awed" by his "courage and integrity" (老頭子和大哥, 都失了色, 被我這勇氣正氣鎮壓住了; *Madman's Diary* 19; 24). That is, he *thinks* that they *know* that he *has seen through their plot* to fatten him up and eat him. The reader *knows*, however, that the protagonist *doesn't realize* that the reason that the two men turn pale is that they *think* that his laughter is a sure sign of his *insanity*. Or, to put it differently, the (implied) author *wants* the readers to *realize* that the mad protagonist *misinterprets* the body language of his visitors.

Of course, these are my formulations, but if you try to come up with one of your own you may discover that, if you want to capture the complexity of the situation conjured up by Lu Xun, simpler descriptions of mental functioning—such as "they *think* that he is *insane*" or "we *know* that he *doesn't realize* why they turn pale"—won't do. Even worse, such descriptions misrepresent the situation until you find a way to connect them, as in "we *know* that he *doesn't realize* that they *think* that he is *insane*." It seems, in other words, that however you choose to phrase it, you will have to recursively embed mental states on at least the third level. While we do not explicitly articulate them to ourselves when we read, something in us must keep track of these complex intentionalities, otherwise we would miss the ironic effect of this scene.

Complex embedments can be explicitly spelled out (as in the above example from *Stone*) or implied (as in "A Madman's Diary"), or they can be a combination of the two. These types of embedments appear as far back as *The Epic of Gilgamesh* (ca. 2100 BCE), *The Iliad*, and *The Odyssey* (ca. 800 BCE), although they don't appear nearly as frequently in those texts as they do in later works (e.g., the eleventh-century Japanese novel, the sixteenth-century Chinese novel, the eighteenth-century English novel, or the nineteenth- and twentieth-century memoirs concerned with imagination and consciousness, such as William Wordsworth's *Prelude* or Vladimir Nabokov's *Speak, Memory*).

Moreover, it appears that the further back in time one goes, the likelier it is that third-level embedments in fiction are created chiefly by portraying characters who intentionally deceive other characters. For instance, in *Gilgamesh*, Ea *wants* dwellers of Shuruppak to *think* that they are *loved* by a god and hence should *expect* abundance to rain on them, when, in fact, they are about to be wiped out by a flood (85). On another occasion, Gilgamesh *wants* Utnapishtim to *think* that he (Gilgamesh) has been awake for six days and seven nights—when, in fact, he has slept for a week—and in response, Gilgamesh is shown seven loaves of bread that Utnapishtim's wife baked for each day that Gilgamesh slept, for they had expected that Gilgamesh would lie to them—that is, they *had known* that Gilgamesh *would want to make them believe* that he had not slept at all (92). In contrast, in more recent works, complex embedment is generated by a much wider variety of representational means, which include but are not limited to deception (Zunshine, *Secret Life*).

Given that *Plum* marks an important threshold in Chinese literary history, its pattern of embedment deserves special attention. To see how *Plum* uses deception to generate complex embedment, we start with the sad story of Laiwang and his wife. When Laiwang first confronts Song Huilian about her affair with their employer, she *wants* him to *believe* that her enemies *wanted* him to *think* that she has been unfaithful: "[S]ome backbiting . . . person . . . must have put you up to abusing your old lady" (是那個嚼舌根的沒空生有、枉口拔舌 調唆你來 是那沒根基的貨, 教人就欺負; 2.25.87; 25.5a). Later, Laixing *wants* Pan Jinlian to *think* that Laiwang *intends* to kill her, and then Pan Jinlian, in her turn, *wants* Ximen Qing to *think* that Laiwang is *keen on revenge*. Then, when Laiwang is in jail, Ximen Qing *doesn't want* Song Huilian to *know* that he *intends* to force Laiwang to run away by making his life unbearable. Finally, after Song Huilian kills herself, Ximen Qing *wants* the magistrates to *think* that the young woman was *afraid* of being punished for misplacing a silver cup.

Note that although I speak of Ximen Qing's *intention* to shape the magistrates' *thinking* about the reason a young woman in his household would *want* to kill herself, it falls to the reader to reconstruct these and other mental states. The novel itself offers almost no explicit references to characters' thoughts and feelings. Instead, as Tina Lu observes in her essay in this volume, "In *Plum*, bodies are depicted from the outside. There is little internal monologue." What we have, instead, are implied embedments. That is, characters' interiority emerges from what Lu refers to as a "matrix of negotiation" in which "[m]otivation is only able to be perceived through the prism of other people's motivations."[2]

There are many other examples of such types of embedments, both in Song Huilian's story and elsewhere in the text. At every turn of the plot, another one springs to life. To make sense of what is going on, readers must constantly keep in mind what one character wants another character to think about their or someone else's intentions.

Uncovering this pattern allows for an exploration of various ways in which it is used by the novel. We can say, complementing insights of the other scholars, quoted earlier, that it serves to present Ximen Qing's household as rotten to the core and thus deserving an awful retribution that awaits them, that it critiques the corruption of contemporary rulers, and that it shows what twisted forms individual initiative can assume when, as in the case of women in the patriarchy, it has no better outlet than selfish intriguing. But even as we commit to any of those existing interpretations, it is important to acknowledge the role of the "cognitive" factor in structuring our response to the story. For while lying in fiction does not always call for moral condemnation,[3] it does open the door to a complex embedment of mental states and, with it, to a pointed and energetic engagement with readers' theory of mind.

Cognition and History

To speak of deception as a long-traveled road to complex embedment begs the larger question of why embedded mental states have become so integral to the representation of fictional consciousness. To answer this question is to consider an interplay of cognitive and historical factors. On the one hand, given the centrality of mind reading and misreading to human communication, it may not be terribly surprising that writers would intensify this aspect of human sociality to render their narratives more engaging. As Patrick Colm Hogan puts it:

> Successful authors are unusually proficient at simulating and communicating simulations. Such processes are largely unselfconscious, a matter of implicitly understanding patterns in human relations and conveying that implicit understanding representationally, which is to say, through the depiction of situations that manifest the patterns—usually in a heightened or more salient form than we would encounter them in ordinary life.   (26)

On the other hand, while the "ordinary life" of every human society may depend on people's capacity to embed their own and other people's mental states, not every society openly acknowledges this dependence or foregrounds it in their stories. For instance, in a number of Melanesian cultures, it is considered unacceptable to talk about people's intentions. This has led some ethnographers to assume that in those cultures "it is impossible or at least extremely difficult to know what other people think or feel" (Robbins and Rumsey 408). A closer look reveals, however, that the taboo against attributing intention reflects the local notion of personal integrity and inviolability, according to which the loss of ability to keep one's feelings hidden—as, for instance, during confession, after conversion to Protestant Christianity—is considered shameful. As Webb Keane explains:

> It is not that inner thoughts are inherently unknowable but that they ought to be unspeakable, or at least, it matters greatly who gets to speak these thoughts. . . . [Thus, it] is not the case that [the Melanesians] have no capacity to read minds or invent fictions: rather, these capacities serve ethical thought, leading to emphatic denial of something that they are in fact doing. . . . To reiterate, if Theory of Mind and intention-seeking are common to all humans, how these get played down or emphasized can contribute to quite divergent ethical worlds. Elaborated in some communities, suppressed in others, these cognitive capacities appear as both sources of difficulties in their own right and affordances for ethical work.
>
> (127–31)

After a talk I once gave about embedded mental states in *Story of the Stone* at the China Cognitive Poetics Conference at Guandong University of Foreign Studies in Guangzhou, an audience member asked me the following question: Is it possible, she wondered, that Chinese literature is more invested in the representation of complex embedments than other national literatures are because people in China are "obsessed," as she put it, with each other's mental states? At the time I disagreed with her. I was convinced that no culture is exempt from this obsession, and that the presence of works of fiction characterized by intensified mind-reading patterns is only one of several cultural forms that this obsession may take. Today, however, I am more open to her argument. While I would oppose any grand pronouncement about what kind of fictional narratives can or cannot thrive in a community in which capacities for mind reading are downplayed, I think we can safely assume that communities in which mind-reading capacities are emphasized offer their members more contexts for explicitly representing various shades and hues of intentionality.

To this broadly conceived set of historical circumstances congenial to sustained representation of embedded mental states in fiction we can add other, more specific ones. As Haiyan Lee has argued, "[S]tranger sociality, cosmopolitanism, and social mobility," which structure "modern commercial societies," encourage exercise of theory of mind, removing from it the "tinge of opprobrium" that may be attached to it in societies characterized by "kinship sociality that presumes relatively stable identity and . . . effortlessly [embodied] socially shared values" ("Measuring the Stomach" 205; see also Lee, *Stranger*). The availability of the vernacular literary language and advanced means of textual reproduction may further contribute to generic diversification and dissemination of imaginative narratives shot through with mind-reading opportunities.

A critical inquiry into complex embedment generated by lies is thus not just a cognitive project but also a historicist project (Zunshine, "What Mary Poppins Knew" 11–16). Fictional characters deceived each other for millennia—take, for instance, "Scholar T'an" ("Tán shēng" 談生), by Cao Pi 曹丕 (187–266), which dates to the late second or early third century, or "Scholar Ts'ui" ("Cuī shūshēng" 崔書生), by Niu Seng-ju 牛僧孺 (779–847), from the early ninth century (Zunshine, *Secret Life*)—but not on a scale comparable to what we find in *Plum*. In recognizing the steady stream of lies that runs through this novel as a cognitive literary innovation, we open a conversation about the historical circumstances, both long-term and immediate, that made this form of experimentation with our daily mind-reading patterns acceptable and possible.

A Mind-Reading Profile of Plum

Lest we think that lying is the only pathway to complex embedment in *Plum*, let us consider a few others, starting with a concern for one's dignity. As Lee has shown, the notion of face, or dignity, is in itself an effective generator of complex embedment in fiction because it conjures the perspective of a character thinking about how they would be perceived by an imagined observer ("Response"). In *Plum*, given Ximen Qing's social ambitions, the possibility of losing face is an ever-present worry. Thus, during an earlier debacle in chapter 12, when Pan Jinlian first fools around with a page boy and then claims that it never happened and that her enemies cooked up the whole story, her loyal servant, Pang Chunmei (P'ang Ch'un-mei), exploits Ximen Qing's fear of losing face with his neighbors if he punishes Pan Jinlian on false premises. As she puts it, "This is all something fabricated by someone who is jealous of Mother and me. Father, you ought to think what you're doing, or you'll only make an ugly reputation for yourself, which won't sound any too good when it gets abroad" (這個, 爹, 你好沒的說! 和娘成日脣不離腮, 娘肯與那奴才? 這個都是人氣不憤俺娘見們, 作做出這樣事來. 爹, 你也要個主張, 好把醜名兒頂在頭上, 傳出外邊去好聽?; 1.12.237; 12.10a).

Pang Chunmei *wants* Ximen Qing to *imagine* what other people will *think* when they find out about his rash behavior. Her manipulative invocation of those judgmental others adjoins a lie—for, in the same breath, she also *wants* Ximen Qing to *believe* that his other wives *want* to bring Pan Jinlian down.

Does a lie gain in persuasiveness when thus paired with a reminder of one's social vulnerability (i.e., one's dependence on other people's opinions)? This seems to be the case, given how often appeals to a character's face are connected to lies in *Plum*. When, in chapter 25, Pan Jinlian *wants* Ximen Qing to *believe* that Laiwang *considers him his enemy*, she makes Ximen Qing *worry* about what other people will *think* about him. Thus, she refers to "allegations" that Laiwang makes "in front of people" and assures Ximen Qing that "such allegations would not redound to [his] credit" (怎說在你臉上也無光了; 2.25.95; 25.10b). Similarly, when Pan Jinlian *wants* Ximen Qing to *think* that Song Huilian is *concealing* from him the true extent of the *enmity* that Laiwang bears him, she once again brings in public opinion: "Whatever that woman has had to say for some time now has only been spoken on behalf of that slave of yours" (老婆無故只是為他; 2.25.99; 25.13a). If Laiwang defrauds Ximen Qing of his money—and Pan Jinlian implies that he intends to do this—Ximen Qing will be too embarrassed to "accuse him of anything" (頭一件你先說不的他; 2.25.99; 25.13a), because everybody will know that he has stolen Laiwang's wife.

Again, when Laiwang is already in jail, tortured for a crime he didn't commit, and Pan Jinlian learns that Ximen Qing is writing a note to the judge asking for his release, she lobbies for "polish[ing] off this slave once and for all" (把奴才結果了; 2.26.111; 26.8b) by planting an image of jeering neighbors in Ximen Qing's mind. Laiwang, she claims, will always hold a grudge against his master, even if Ximen Qing were to go as far as marrying him to someone else to make up for having taken Song Huilian from him. For instance, if Laiwang were to "report something" (回話) to Ximen Qing and see him with Song Huilian, wouldn't Laiwang get "angry" (氣)? And would Song Huilian then have "to stand up" (站起來) to greet her ex-husband (2.26.111; 26.8b)? Wouldn't that be embarrassing for Ximen Qing? As Pan Jinlian puts it, "Just to start out with, this alone wouldn't look right. If it got around, not only would your neighbors and relatives laugh at you, but even the members of your own household, high and low, would not be able to take you seriously" (先不先只這個就不雅相, 傳出去休說六鄰親戚笑話, 只家中大小, 把你也不著在意裡; 2.26.111; 26.11a).

Strategic appeals to face constitute just one aspect of the psychological manipulation that *Plum*'s characters practice on one another. When Laiwang is finally driven away, just as Pan Jinlian hoped he would be, she goes between Sun

Xue'e and Song Huilian, reporting lies that can't fail to stir up a "sense of grievance and desire for revenge" (有個不懷仇忌恨的; 2.25.152; 25.7a). First, Pan Jinlian *wants* Sun Xue'e to *think* that Song Huilian *knows* that Sun Xue'e told Laiwang about Song Huilian's affair with Ximen Qing (which is not true) and that Song Huilian blames Sun Xue'e for making Ximen Qing angry and for making him want to get rid of Laiwang. Then Pan Jinlian goes to Song Huilian. Pan Jinlian *wants* Song Huilian to *believe* that people in the compound *think* that she has never *cared* about her husband. Pan Jinlian lies to Song Huilian, saying that Sun Xue'e tells everyone that Song Huilian is an "old hand at inveigling" her masters "into adultery" and that the tears that she sheds about her husband "are only crocodile tears" (是蔡家使喝了的奴才, 積年轉主子養漢 . . . 說你眼淚留著些 腳後跟; 2.26.121; 26.15a). These lies precipitate an ugly standoff between Song Huilian and Sun Xue'e, which pushes Song Huilian over the brink and leads her to commit her second, and this time successful, suicide attempt.

Yet another way in which *Plum* generates complex embedment is through its frequent references to songs, poems, and sayings, each of which presupposes an elaborate give-and-take between the implied author and their audience. Were we to spell it out—which we don't do, of course, for it happens below the level of our conscious awareness—we could say that the author *expects* that readers would *appreciate* the author's *intention* of drawing readers' *attention* to a particular aspect of a given situation. For instance, when Song Huilian wants to convince Ximen Qing that her husband would never curse and threaten Ximen Qing behind his back, she asserts that, were Laiwang to do such a thing, he would effectively be biting the hand that feeds him, and he is not that stupid. As she puts it:

> If he should:
>> Live off King Chou's largesse,
>> And yet call King Chou a villain,
> on whom could he depend to make a living?   (2.25.96)

又吃紂王水士, 說紂王無道! 他靠那裡過日子?   (25.11a)

Song Huilian's mention of King Chou comes close on the heels of an earlier reference to the ancient *Book of Documents* (*Shu-ching* 書經). That reference, according to an endnote provided by *Plum*'s translator, David Tod Roy, tacitly likens Ximen Qing to King Chou, the "evil last ruler" of the Shang dynasty (2.25.494n31). While Song Huilian seems to want to emphasize the implausibility of her husband bad-mouthing Ximen Qing, she accomplishes the opposite with her quotation: she herself bad-mouths Ximen Qing since, as Roy explains, the "unmistakable implication" of what she says "is that Ximen Qing himself is an evil last ruler" (2.25.494n32; see also Plaks, *Four Masterworks* 163–64).

That neither Song Huilian nor Ximen Qing are aware of this implication makes their mutually pleasing exchange profoundly ironic. The implied author wants the implied reader to know that the author considers Ximen Qing evil, but the author also wants us to know that Ximen Qing doesn't realize that the argument that he apparently finds convincing is a classical reference that condemns him. Nor is he aware of the grave innuendo of being likened to the last ruler— something than the implied author wants us to keep in mind as we follow the household's rejoicing at the birth of Ximen Qing's son, Guan'ge (Kuan-ko). Finally, when Song Huilian unwittingly calls her lover a villain, we know that she doesn't know that he is about to behave like one toward her and her husband— another nuance in the ongoing give-and-take between the implied author and the implied reader.

Scholars of *Plum* have long been aware of some "serious intention" behind the text (Plaks, *Four Masterworks* 132). Andrew Plaks cites the earliest critical responses to the novel, which contain such observations as "the author definitely has his own intentions" and "there is an object to [the text's] ironic stabs" (132). Plaks himself discusses at length "the possibility of hidden intentions" (128) implied by the author's use of "borrowed material," such as songs and poems, as well as the role that "frequent interpolations of authorial asides" play to periodically remind "the reader of the presence of the narrator somewhere between himself and the story" (123). One insight that the cognitive perspective adds to this ongoing conversation is that the reader's awareness of the narrator's, or implied author's, intention, which must vary quite widely, depends on that reader's processing of mental states embedded within one another on at least the third level.

Plum's mind-reading profile thus combines deception, psychological manipulation of one character by another, and ironic stabs, the full meaning of which is often available to the implied reader but not to the characters themselves. Such moments of deception, manipulation, and irony ensure that the reader keeps steadily embedding mental states on a high level. Later works, such as *The Scholars* (*Rulin waishi* 儒林外史 [1750]), by Wu Jingzi 吳敬梓 (1701–54), and Cao's *Story of the Stone*, will amplify these methods. The latter in particular will drastically expand the novel's repertoire of strategies for complex embedment by afflicting its male protagonist with the "lust of the mind" (*yiyin* 意淫)—that is, with a passionate need to understand and share the emotions of girls and young women (Zunshine, "From the Social" 179), something that's hard to imagine in the universe of Ximen Qing. Still, as we think of *Plum*'s "sophisticated use of narrative rhetoric," which makes it "a model of the literati novel genre maturing in the sixteenth century" (Plaks, *Four Masterworks* 120), we acknowledge its unprecedentedly innovative appeal to late Ming readers' theory of mind.

Approaches to Teaching Plum

An analysis of *Plum in the Golden Vase* from a cognitive perspective allows for the inclusion of the novel in a relatively wide spectrum of courses, albeit not in its entirety. Having taught the first volume of David Hawkes's translation of *The*

Story of the Stone in a sophomore-level seminar titled Introduction to Literature in my university's English department, I can easily imagine including instead a lengthy excerpt from *Plum*—for instance, chapters 22–26, which, at just under one hundred pages, tell the story of how Pan Jinlian drives Song Huilian to suicide. The same selection could be integrated into a course on the history of the novel or into a variety of special topics courses, such as (to still draw on my own teaching experience) Social Minds in Fiction and Lying Bodies: Pretense, Performance, and the Novel.

Given the rapid growth of the field of cognitive literary studies over the last decade (Zunshine, "Introduction" 1), seminars on critical theory and narrative theory increasingly feature units on cognitive approaches. Particularly if the instructor has comparativist inclinations and does not want to limit themself to just one national literary tradition, chapters 22–26 of *Plum* can be used as a focal point for exploring complex embedment in literature. One option would be to pair *Plum* with other texts that similarly foreground both deception and authorial intention—for instance, with a sixteenth-century picaresque novel, such as *Lazarillo de Tormes* or Mateo Alemán's *Guzmán de Alfarache.*[4] Another option would be to follow a unit on *Plum* with texts that illustrate the evolution of lying in literature (i.e., from deception to self-deception to unreliable narration). On the whole, a cognitive take on *The Plum in the Golden Vase* contributes to the ongoing project of situating this novel in the context of the millennia-long experimentation with the representation of fictional consciousness.

NOTES

[1] Unless otherwise noted, parenthetical citations refer to Roy's translation, *The Plum in the Golden Vase,* and to *Jin Ping Mei cihua* 金瓶梅詞話 (*Plum in the Golden Vase: A Ballad Tale*).

[2] For a discussion of psychological interiority in classical Chinese texts, such as the *Analects* of Confucius, see Slingerland.

[3] In fact, we can be made to feel sympathy for the liar. For instance, Utnapishtim does not judge Gilgamesh for attempting to deceive him; he sees that behavior as only too human. As he puts it to his wife, "Since the human race is duplicitous, he'll endeavor to dupe you" (*Epic* 92).

[4] For a cognitivist reading of the early modern Spanish picaresque novel, see Simon 19.

The Ximen Household as a Warning to a Doomed Dynasty

Katherine Carlitz

The household depicted in *The Plum in the Golden Vase* (*Jin Ping Mei* 金瓶梅) consists of the master, Ximen Qing (Hsi-men Ch'ing), and his six ladies, one wife and five concubines, most of whom entered the household illegitimately: Pan Jin-lian (P'an Chin-lien) and Li Ping'er (Li P'ing-erh) murdered their former husbands, Li Jiao'er (Li Chiao-erh) is an erstwhile prostitute who takes up her trade again at the end of the novel, and Meng Yulou (Meng Yü-lou) was a widow who ignored the ideal of widow chastity when she became Ximen Qing's Third Lady and will remarry again when he dies. Once assembled, the wife, Wu Yueniang (Wu Yüeh-niang), and the five concubines compete for Ximen Qing's attention, while Ximen Qing himself amasses a fortune through a combination of business deals and bribes. As David Roy points out in his introduction to *Plum*, the structural parallel between the court, with its emperor and six ministers, and the ethically challenged Ximen household, with its husband and six ladies, implicitly links corruption in the household to bad governance at the top (Introduction xxxi). By setting *Plum* at a time when the Song dynasty rulers were losing half their territory to non-Chinese tribesmen, the author was warning that the Ming dynasty could suffer a similar fate.

How plausible did the warning look to its intended governing-class audience? Some clues are offered by Ming dynasty epitaphs, which show us the rules of conduct that the Ximen family routinely disobeys. The standard epitaph discussed here is a *mu zhi ming* 墓誌銘, which consists of a biographical essay (*zhi* 誌) and a poem of praise (*ming* 銘), written for the construction of or as an addition to a tomb (*mu* 墓). When Ming literati wrote epitaphs for governing-class wives, they praised the wives for strengthening the families they had married into and overcoming difficulties like the ones the Ximen women create for one another. Since the moral standards of the epitaphs were familiar to all members of the governing class, readers who saw them flouted by the Ximen household and the ruling court would have known that both were in trouble.

Here I first examine the allegorical structure linking the Ximen household to the Ming court. Next I investigate the rich body of Ming epitaph literature to demonstrate how badly behaved the Ximen household would have looked to an educated audience. Epitaphs contemporary with *Plum* show us the culturally approved way to handle betrothal, money, jealousy between household women, and grief at the death of a wife. The more we know about what was understood as the right way to do things, the more we can enjoy the brilliance of *Plum*'s author at showing us the wrong way.

Imperial Allegory in Plum in the Golden Vase

The court in *Plum* is nominally that of the hapless Song dynasty emperor Huizong (r. 1082–1135), who lost the northern half of the empire, located in present-day Manchuria, to the Jurchen tribes. But the novel's allusions to historical Ming figures keep us focused on the Ming, which is the novel's actual concern (Roy, Introduction xxix–xxx).

Plum's allegorical dimension is immediately evident in the unusual structure of the Ximen family. The Ximen family is not at all typical of the actual Ming dynasty governing class, whose sons would have been educated to seek office in the imperial bureaucracy, and whose daughters would have been betrothed to those office-seeking sons. Nor is the family depicted in *Plum* typical of upwardly mobile merchant families, who sought respectability by modeling themselves on the gentry. The typical sixteenth- and seventeenth-century Chinese family consisted at all social levels of three generations: elderly parents, their adult sons and daughters-in-law, and the children who were being raised by those sons and daughters-in-law. This standard configuration is nowhere to be seen in *Plum*. Instead, we see a husband with a wife and five concubines, mirroring the emperor with his six ministers.

To the educated reader—and Roy argues forcefully in his introduction that *Plum* was written for educated readers—the imperial configuration seen throughout the book would have carried an unmistakable message. The educated classes in Ming dynasty China were steeped in the teachings of the five relationships (the relationship between emperor and subject, father and son, husband and wife, elder brother and younger brother, and elder friend and younger friend), and students learned by heart the classic known as the *Great Learning* (*Daxue* 大學). These teachings, which reached their final form during China's first long-lived dynasty, the Han (206 BCE–220 CE), had been central to the all-important civil-service examination system since at least the tenth century CE. The key segment of the *Great Learning* reads as follows:

> The ancients who wished clearly to exemplify illustrious virtue throughout the world would first set up good government in their states. Wishing to govern well their states, they would first regulate their families. Wishing to regulate their families, they would first cultivate their persons. Wishing to cultivate their persons, they would first rectify their minds. Wishing to rectify their minds, they would first seek sincerity in their thoughts. Wishing for sincerity in their thoughts, they would first extend their knowledge. The extension of knowledge lay in the investigation of things. For only when things are investigated is knowledge extended; only when knowledge is extended are thoughts sincere; only when thoughts are sincere are minds rectified; only when minds are rectified are our persons cultivated; only when our persons are cultivated are our families regulated; only when families are regulated are states well-governed; and only when states are well-governed is there peace in the world.   (W. Chan 115)

> 古之欲明明德於天下者, 先治其國. 欲治其國者, 先齊其家. 欲齊其家者, 先修其身. 欲修其身者, 先正其心. 欲正其心者, 先誠其意. 欲誠其意者, 先致其知. 致知在格物. 物格而後知至. 知至而後意誠. 意誠而後心正. 心正而後身修. 身修而後家齊. 家齊而後國治. 國治而後天下平.   (Wang Guoxuan 5)

The message of the *Great Learning* is the unbreakable continuum of state, family, and individual, with corresponding responsibilities at each level. As we watch Ximen Qing's rise in power and wealth, we see what happens when he neglects these responsibilities. In chapter 21, a visiting nun reminds us of the *Great Learning* continuum by joking that Ximen Qing is like the head clerk of a yamen, the county government whose six local offices represent the imperial government's six bureaus. A clerk "has the run of all Six Chambers" (如何六房裡都串到), which immediately calls to mind the chambers of the six women of Ximen Qing's household as well as the six bureaus through which the emperor governs (2.21.24; 21.14a).[1] By chapter 30, when Ximen Qing obtains the positions of local magistrate and battalion vice-commander, he becomes the undisputed local face of imperial power, both civil and military (2.30.211). The disorder of Ximen Qing's own six chambers, however, suggests the author's mistrust of the Wanli Emperor's six chambers.

Ximen Qing is appointed to these positions just as his first son, Guan'ge (Kuanko, "Official Brother"), is born, and the novel hints at the parallel between household and court by repeatedly referring to the baby as a "crown prince." Shortly after Ximen Qing's sixth wife, Li Ping'er, gives birth to Guan'ge, the jealous Pan Jinlian complains to Ximen Qing that "[e]ver since she gave birth to this seedling, you've been treating her just as though she'd produced the crown prince!" (自從養了這種子. 恰似他生了太子一般; 2.31.229; 31.11a). In another veiled allusion to the court, Jinlian's speech in chapter 27, when she learns of Ping'er's pregnancy, is dotted with quotations from *The Lord of Perfect Satisfaction* (*Ruyi jun zhuan* 如意君傳), a Ming tale about the Tang dynasty empress Wu Zetian (2.27.507–09 [nn 45, 60, and 61]). And after Guan'ge is betrothed to the daughter of the neighboring Qiao family, their senior relative Mme Qiao (Ch'iao) gives the Ximen family a bolt of brocade "of the kind purveyed for use in the palace" (捧過一端宮中; 3.43.60; 43.11b).

Mme Qiao hints at danger to the Ming when she tells the Ximen ladies that the emperor's Consort Zheng (Cheng) is her own niece (3.43.60; 43.11a). Emperor Huizong of the Song dynasty did indeed have a Consort Zheng, but so did the Ming dynasty Wanli Emperor, who was on the throne when *Plum* was published. The Ming dynasty Consort Zheng was the Wanli Emperor's favorite, but she was a disruptive force, agitating to have her own son displace the empress's son as crown prince. Ultimately the Wanli Emperor was persuaded to follow protocol and elevate the son of his empress, but Consort Zheng and her brother were widely thought to have orchestrated an attempt to assassinate the empress's son in the notorious affair known as the "attack with the club."[2]

Thus, the betrothal of Guan'ge to a relative of Mme Qiao is one of many hints that the Ximen family and the Ming rulers are putting themselves in harm's way. The little "crown prince" will be murdered by Pan Jinlian, and though Wu Yueniang finally bears a son just as Ximen Qing is dying (ch. 79), that son will become a celibate monk, signaling the end of the Ximen family (ch. 100). The simultaneous doom of family and court is in keeping with another myth that had grown up around imperial rule, that of the "bad last emperor," as Arthur Wright called this recurring figure.[3] Dynasties had been rising and falling for many centuries before the Ming, and by Ming times a standard explanation had evolved, namely that dynasties began with an explosion of vigor and then gradually declined until a "bad last emperor" brought them to an end. These emperors neglected government, oppressed their subjects, and, in the most outrageous cases, gave themselves over to spectacular sexual excesses, just as Ximen Qing does. To the extent that Ximen Qing is conceived in *Plum* in the mold of a "bad last emperor," his excesses tell us that the Ming is doomed right along with his own household.

Plum *and the World Portrayed in* **Ming Dynasty Epitaphs**

Ming dynasty epitaphs were written by prominent literati. If one's wife or parent died, one paid for the most prominent writer one could afford and gave the writer a précis of what one wanted others to know about the deceased. The writers and the families of the deceased were generally of the same social standing: these writers were landowners, scholars, and officials, writing for one another as well as for the wealthy merchants who aspired to join the governing class. In the Ming dynasty, epitaphs were carved on stone or porcelain and placed in the tombs of the deceased to announce them to the guardians of the afterlife. But since epitaphs were a prestigious literary genre that could display the talent and the social connections of the writer, these epitaphs were also published in the collected works of their authors to reflect well not just on the deceased but also on the writers.

These epitaphs also represented what families wanted others to know about the deceased. The results could be remarkably revealing, with epitaph writers sometimes divulging information that family members had originally kept hidden from one another. But revealing these secrets, so to speak, in an epitaph was not really a breach of confidence: family members themselves had supplied the information because they felt it reflected well on the deceased.

Here I focus on epitaphs by the prominent Ming scholar-official Li Mengyang 李夢陽 (1473–1529). His popularity as a writer of epitaphs shows us that his values were representative of the Ming dynasty governing class, the intended readers of *Plum*. The epitaphs below focus on clothing as a marker of status and on marriage, money, jealousy, and grief, all of which are key issues for the protagonists of *Plum*.

Clothing and the Culture of Display

Li Mengyang's turbulent life saw him alternately in high positions or in jail, first for offending the Hongzhi Empress (r. 1488–1505); next for offending the powerful eunuch Liu Jin 劉瑾 (d. 1510); then for arousing the suspicions of officials in the city of Nanchang in Jiangxi Province, where he had been sent to report on the state of education; and one final time after an accusation that he had joined a rebellious clique. For brief periods he enjoyed the life of a respected official, and in retirement he became a well-known poet. He was devoted to his wife, and his son achieved success as an official. His arrests did nothing to harm the fame that had been growing since he passed the highest civil-service examination at the age of twenty ("Li Mengyang"). Governing-class families clearly felt that a word from Li Mengyang would ensure the good reputation of the deceased.

Moreover, the epitaphs he wrote for his own family members allowed him to praise himself as well as his subjects, as we can see from the epitaph he wrote for his beloved wife, Mme Zuo. Her mother and grandmother had initially rejected him as a suitor, and Li Mengyang is not shy about reminding them of the great success he went on to achieve:

> Initially, when matchmakers sought a betrothal for Li Mengyang [Li refers to himself here in the third person], they were not successful, since the Zuo family matriarch felt that "the tutor [Li's father] is insignificant and poor." Only the Ceremonial Companion [Li's father-in-law, referred to here by his court-bestowed title] was happy. He went to talk to his mother

and wife about it. Both of them were against the marriage, saying: "Isn't [Mengyang] the son of Tutor Li? He is insignificant and poor!" But the Companion said: "the Li son has talent," and in the end the marriage was arranged. At this time, Li was 19 years old. In the following year, the *xin hai* year of the emperor's reign [approx. 1491], Mme Zuo gave birth to a son named Zhi.

初李子妁婚妁咸不之婚也. 曰教授微而貧. 及妁左氏儀實則顧獨喜. 入白其母並郡君氏. 母郡君乃亦咸不之婚也, 曰夫非李教授兒邪. 微而貧. 儀實曰李氏子才. 竟婚李氏. 是時李子生十有九年矣. 明年為治辛亥左氏生子枝.

(Li Mengyang 45.7b)[4]

The epitaph goes on to say that when Li was sent to deliver rations to the troops in Ningxia, he took his wife with him and they stopped at her natal home. As Li describes the visit, his delight in his vindication is clear, and for our purposes the value of the epitaph is to show us how important clothing was for indicating status, which can help us make sense of the constant descriptions of clothing in *Plum*:

At that time, the Ceremonial Companion and his mother had died; no one was left except the Commandery Mistress [Li Mengyang's mother-in-law]. My wife entered with a stately gait, wearing a pheasant-plume headdress, kingfisher ornaments, and a multilayered skirt that was flowing with pearls. The Commandery Mistress was delighted and wept at the sight of her, saying to a servant: "As a student Li was insignificant and poor, but now look at this!" And, deeply moved, she repeated the Ceremonial Companion's words.

是時儀實母儀實亡矣. 獨郡君. 而左氏翟冠翠翹揚帔曳裙見焉. 其行于于也. 皙而顧瞋而流珠. 郡君喜已而泣顧謂侍人曰向謂李生微而貧乃今若此矣. 因道儀實語慟.

(Li Mengyang 45.8a)

We see this same sort of vindication in chapter 89 of *Plum*. By this chapter, Ximen Qing has died of sexual exhaustion and Pan Jinlian has been murdered, but Pan Jinlian's former maid, Pang Chunmei (P'ang Ch'un-mei), has risen in rank, becoming the wife of Ximen Qing's erstwhile colleague Commandant Zhou. Even in her glory, Chunmei sacrifices faithfully at Pan Jinlian's grave, which leads to an unexpected meeting with her former mistresses Wu Yueniang and Meng Yulou. The two Ximen wives happen to visit the temple where Pan Jinlian is buried, and Chunmei, unaware of them, enters to speak to the abbot. Wu Yueniang and Meng Yulou, peeking through the door blind, see that Chunmei now seems taller, larger, more dominant, her coiffure now covered in pearls, her clothing embroidered in scarlet, her "kingfisher-patterned skirt" showing off her "minuscule golden-lotus" slippers (翠紋裙下映金蓮小; 5.89.166; 89.8b). Here, just as in

Li Mengyang's epitaph for his wife, description of clothing is what the author uses to show us how the lowly have risen and the mighty fallen. Wu Yueniang and Meng Yulou, embarrassed to meet Chunmei with their fortunes now so clearly reversed, try to leave unobtrusively but in the end are compelled to sit through an uncomfortable dinner with Chunmei and the abbot (5.89.166; 89.8b).

Betrothal: Family and Community Connections

From the time of China's earliest written records, marriage was a matter to be arranged by parents using the services of a go-between to prevent a young couple from taking matters into their own hands and going against their parents' interests. Betrothal was supposed to proceed through a series of six rituals, starting with checking the birth dates of the couple to make sure that their horoscopes were compatible. Infant or childhood betrothal was the norm. It has long been understood that some of these rituals existed only in ancient texts, but the basic principles were clear and unvarying: parents were the ones who should choose spouses for their children, ideally as a means of creating advantageous family alliances.

Guan-ge's betrothal to the daughter of the neighboring Qiao family is a lively affair that takes place during a visit by the Ximen ladies to the Qiao family compound. However, the betrothal fails to meet the requirement that both families should benefit socially. The betrothal is described in chapter 41 as follows:

> Yueniang got up and retired to the inner room to change her clothes and redo her makeup. Meng Yulou also followed suit. When they arrived in their hostess's bedroom, what should they see but the wet-nurse Ru'yi who was looking after Guan'ge. She had put him down on a little sleeping-mat that was spread out on the kang frame, where he was lying right next to Zhangjie, the newborn daughter of their host. The two of them were playing happily at:
> You hit me a blow and I'll hit you one back,
> which tickled Yueniang and Yulou [to] no end.
> "The two of them are just like a couple," they exclaimed.
> On seeing Wu Kai's wife come in after them, they said to her, "Come and take a look. The two of them are really like a little couple."
> "That's true," said Wu Kai's wife with a smile. "The way the children on the kang are:
> Reaching out their hands and kicking their feet,
> playing at:
> You hit me and I'll hit you,
> makes them look like a predestined little couple."　　　　　　　(3.41.4)

月娘就下來往後房換衣服. 勻臉去了. 孟玉樓也跟下來. 到了喬大戶娘子臥房中. 只見奶子如意兒. 看守着官哥兒. 在炕上鋪着小褥子兒倘着. 他家新生的長

姐也在旁邊臥着. 兩個你打我下兒. 我打你下兒. 玩耍. 把月娘玉樓. 把月娘
玉樓. 見了喜歡的要不得. 說道他兩個. 倒好相兩口兒. 只見吳大妗子進來. 說
道大妗子. 你來瞧瞧. 兩個倒相小兩口兒. 大妗子笑道. 正是孩子每. 在炕上
張手兒. 蹬腳兒的. 你打我. 我打你. 小姻緣一對兒耍子.   (41.3b)

Right after this the other guests come in for a look, and after each family has
politely declared itself unworthy of the other, they exchange information about
the children's dates of birth, which are found to be compatible. Afterward,

> [w]ithout permitting any further explanation, the whole group insisted on
> dragging Qiao Hong's wife, Wu Yueniang, and Li Ping'er to the front re-
> ception hall, where the matrons of the two households formalized the be-
> trothal of the children by exchanging cuttings from the lapels of their
> blouses, while the two singing-girls played and sang to entertain them.
>   (3.41.5–6)

于是不由分說把喬大戶娘子. 和月娘李瓶兒拉到前廳. 兩個就割了衫襟. 兩個
妓女彈唱着.   (41.3b–4a)

But when Ximen Qing arrives home and learns of this impromptu ceremony, he
is displeased. The wives have not thought through the implications of the betrothal for the families' future social interaction. As Wu Yueniang admits, the
betrothal was spontaneously arranged "[w]ithout premeditation or forethought"
(不因不由), leading Ximen Qing to point out that while both families are currently
wealthy, he has achieved official rank while neighbor Qiao has not (3.41.11; 41.6a).
This is bound to cause awkwardness later on, says Ximen Qing, since the baby's
future father-in-law will not be able to wear the official insignia to which Ximen
Qing is now entitled: "How will he be comfortable," asks Ximen Qing, "associ-
ating with an official family such as ours?" (與俺這官戶, 怎生相處?; 3.41.11;
41.6a). The betrothal soon leads to insults and recriminations within the Ximen
household: Pan Jinlian wisecracks that no one really knows who sired Guan'ge,
causing a volley of curses from Ximen Qing that leaves her in tears.

This unhappy affair contrasts sharply with Li Mengyang's joint epitaph for
Subprefectural Magistrate Bian Jie and his wife, Dong ruren.[5] Here we see betrothal done right, with appropriate attention to what will benefit both families:

> By the time [Bian Jie] reached the age of 6 or 7, everyone could tell that
> he was quite out of the ordinary. Dong Jie [Dong ruren's father] was a no-
> table of Li City and had long respected Vice-Prefect Bian [Bian Jie's
> father]. He respected the Vice-Prefect even more highly when he saw his
> remarkable son and wanted to join the families in marriage. One day, the
> Vice-Prefect gave a banquet, and as it happened, Dong found himself
> seated next to young Master Bian. Dong took the boy onto his lap and said:
> "Call me Father-in-law!"

"Father-in-law!" said the boy.

"I'll call you son-in-law!" said Dong.

"Son-in-law!" answered the boy.

They repeated this three times, and Dong looked over at the Vice-Prefect and laughed. The entire hall burst out laughing, and all the guests raised their glasses in congratulation, while the two gentlemen made a "cutting the garments agreement" [to betroth their children]. The two gentlemen laughed again, followed by all the guests, and the party ended with everyone pleasantly tipsy.

即六七歲時. 見者業識其非常兒云. 董傑者歷城豪也. 故善治中. 及見治中郎異. 則益敬治中. 思與婚. 一日治中大置酒會. 有董公邊郎立偶徬董公. 董公抱之起坐膝上曰呼我邊郎應聲曰舅我呼汝甥邊郎應聲曰甥如是者三董公顧治中大笑滿堂皆笑於是客盡起觴兩公賀而交其襟割之盟兩公復笑客各復笑醉乃罷散去. (44.17b)

This, one of Li Mengyang's most affectionate epitaphs, displays spontaneity while also maintaining appropriate boundaries of gender, class, and status.

Money

In chapter 11, we learn that the Ximen family finances are being handled by Li Jiao'er, a former and future prostitute.[6] Since household finance was conventionally a first wife's responsibility, handing it over to a former prostitute serves to remind us yet again of the Ximen family's corruption. The first wife, Wu Yueniang, is frequently ill, and therefore unable to take on this conventional responsibility. Having a wife act as household "bursar," to use Joseph McDermott's term, was the norm by Ming times: wives' financial role had grown significantly during the Song dynasty (960–1279), and domestic financial management was generally accepted as women's domain by the Ming (McDermott). Married women in the Ming dynasty retained control over a portion of their dowries, though this could be contested, and as long as both spouses were still living, wives controlled household expenditures. If a husband predeceased his wife, the widow would manage her deceased husband's share of the family wealth. This lent wives a certain degree of independence and, more to the point, authority. They were able to make important decisions about projects the family might undertake, and they could lend money to other family members, male or female.

The epitaph for Bian Jie and Dong ruren shows Dong ruren making such a loan without asking anyone's permission:

Initially, Bian Zhizhong [Bian Jie's father], concerned that Bian Jie was his only son, also adopted Cheng, the nephew of his wife Mme Wang. Mme Dong therefore treated Cheng as she would have treated a younger brother, and when Cheng married, she treated Cheng's wife as she would have treated a younger sister. When Bian Zhizhong died, Cheng asked permission to leave. Mme Dong knew that Cheng had some private savings, but she did not expose him, and did not tell her husband. When Mme Dong became ill and died, Cheng's wife came from Li City [Cheng's original home] to prostrate herself at Mme Dong's grave.

初治中以子孤也取王宜人弟之子城子之. 孺人即弟城猶弟也. 城有婦. 孺人即又娣城婦猶娣也. 治中歿也城求去. 城有私畜. 孺人知之竟不發. 亦不以語邊公. 後孺人病且死. 會城婦自歷城來匍匐於終事.   (Li Mengyang 45.15b)

Moreover, the epitaph shows that Dong ruren was supported by the most senior woman in the household, namely her husband's mother, Mme Wan. When her father-in-law, Bian Zhizhong, died, the family demanded the gold that Dong ruren retained from her dowry. But Mme Wan—whose great age gave her the final say in all domestic matters—rebuked them harshly: "The new wife is virtuous—and now you even want her gold?" (治中亡厥金求焉. 治中母萬太君者叱止之曰. 新婦賢. 不愈獲金乎?; 45.15b). After that, Dong ruren was able to keep the gold.

In another epitaph, we read that Mme Hou,[7] the wife of Gao Jin, was able to use her financial authority to resolve a tragic case involving the murder of her own son:

> Mme Hou was the daughter of Hou Yan. She served her mother-in-law just as her husband served his mother, and she served her two elder sisters-in-law just as her husband served his elder brothers. When her sister-in-law's son murdered Mme Hou's son Lu, Mme Hou considered the matter and said to her husband, "Fortunately, we still have our other son, Xun. But your brother's family will have no posterity at all [if his son is executed]!" Then she paid one hundred *jin* to have the murderer released from jail. Upon his release, the grateful murderer attempted to recompense Gao Jin, but Gao Jin refused to accept any money. When the murderer visited Mme Hou she also refused, saying: "Did I pay to have you released just to benefit myself?"

侯氏者巖之女也. 事姑猶夫事母. 事二嫂猶夫事二兄. 嫂之子提殺璐也. 侯與處士計曰. 吾幸尚有珣. 奈何令伯氏無後. 卒出之獄以百金. 詣處士謝. 處士不受. 詣侯謝. 侯亦不受. 曰. 吾利而金出汝邪.   (Li Mengyang 45.15b)

Dong ruren and Mme Hou make their financial decisions with the good of the entire family in mind. When Dong ruren protects her brother-in-law, Cheng, she insures his loyalty to the Bian family. When Mme Hou pays to get her son's murderer out of jail, she is acting on the standard belief that all branches of her husband's family require descendants to carry out the ancestral sacrifices that will keep the family safe from harm or want. But nobody takes this kind of care in *Plum*. Chapter 43 is a prime example, mixing realistic description—for example, the cumbersome use of silver ingots to pay large debts—with cosmological references (why are the gold bracelets "cold"?), all within a narrative of the Ximen family's typical disorganization.

The discussion of money in *Plum* clearly situates the Ximen family in the Ming dynasty, despite the novel's ostensible setting in the Song. The Song dynasty had pioneered the use of paper currency, which became quite popular, but by Ming times paper currency was dangerously inflated, and China was awash in silver from the New World (Von Glahn). The Ximen family is very obviously operating in a silver economy. In chapter 43, when two contractors repay the money that Ximen Qing lent them to supply tea and wax to the royal palace, they do so by shaving silver from the ingots they carry. We see Chen Jingji weigh it out with a steelyard to make sure the amount is correct. A drama troupe arrives to entertain the ladies, and they too are paid in silver. And in chapter 64, the servant Dai'an (Tai-an) laments the death of Li Ping'er, recalling that she never used to weigh the nuggets of silver she gave him to shop for her but instead just laughed and hoped that he would keep the change and put it to good use.

After the silver has been weighed and the contractors paid, chapter 43 transitions smoothly to the language of symbols and portents. Here money is transmuted into danger: the two contractors do not have quite enough silver to repay Ximen Qing, so they make up the difference by adding in four gold (*jin* 金) bracelets. As soon as Ximen Qing returns home with the bracelets, he gives them to the baby Guan'ge to play with. But as Li Ping'er immediately realizes, and as Wu Yueniang later agrees, these are dangerous toys: not only are the bracelets heavy, but they may also give the baby's hands a chill. In traditional *Wuxing* 五行 ("five phases") cosmology, metal in general is designated by the character *jin* 金, the same character used in everyday speech for *gold*. The cosmological *jin* is associated with *yin*, of the familiar pair *yin* 陰 and *yang* 陽. *Yang* is associated with heat, brightness, and growth, while *yin*, the complementary opposite of *yang*, is associated with cold, autumn, winter, death, and decay. (Thus, executions are carried out in the autumn, not in the spring, so as not to violate the season of new growth.) There is no need for the wives to explain their fear that Guan'ge will catch a chill, since the extended meaning of *jin* was common knowledge.

In any case, trouble immediately ensues. Li Ping'er is inattentive, and temptation being what it is, Li Jiao'er's maid, Xiahua (Hsia-hua), makes off with one of the gold bracelets, causing a round of accusations and recriminations. The baby is then menaced by gold for the rest of the chapter. While the ladies are drinking tea, the maid Yingchun brings him in to show him off; he is wearing a gilt-ridged satin cap and sporting little gold bracelets. And when Mme Qiao, the aunt of the emperor's Consort Zheng, comes to share a meal with the Ximen ladies, she gives the baby another pair of gilded bracelets. Nothing in the plot requires these last two references to gold; they seem to be placed at this point in the chapter simply to keep the motif of dangerous gold fresh in our minds. And in chapter 59 we learn why, when Pan Jinlian ("Golden Lotus" Pan) trains her cat to kill the baby.

Jealousy

By chapter 20 Ximen Qing has acquired his wife and all five of his concubines, and the household becomes a hotbed of jealousy centered on money, status, and sex. The Fourth Lady, Sun Xue'e, who entered the household as the maid of Ximen Qing's deceased first wife, works in the kitchen and is resentful that she is never treated as well as the others. On Li Ping'er's first visit to the house, for example, Wu Yueniang says that Li Ping'er needn't kowtow to Sun Xue'e as she does to the other wives; a mere bow will do. Sun Xue'e and the Second Lady, Li Jiao-er, are both jealous of Ximen Qing's attraction to Pan Jinlian, so they tell Wu Yueniang that Jinlian has been sleeping with the page boy Qintong (Ch'in-t'ung), which almost earns Jinlian a whipping—until Ximen Qing is aroused by the sight of her naked body. When the other wives organize a little party in chapter 23 and ask for contributions, Sun Xue'e resentfully plays up her poverty by saying that they can treat one another all they want, but she cannot afford to take part. And when the wives are invited to the Qiao family compound where the baby Guan-ge will be betrothed, Pan Jinlian complains that she has nothing to wear and makes Ximen Qing call in the tailor to sew new clothes all around, with the best outfit reserved for her

Nothing, however, compares to Jinlian's jealousy of Li Ping'er. Ximen Qing has frequent (and sometimes sadistic) sex with Pan Jinlian, but only Li Ping'er has his heart. When he learns in chapter 27 that Ping'er is pregnant, he is overjoyed. But given the intensity of Pan Jinlian's jealousy, this good news seals Li Ping'er's doom. Jinlian is particularly enraged when she overhears Ximen Qing growing lyrical about Li Ping'er's "white bottom" (白屁股兒; 2.27.134; 27.6a). Jinlian trains a cat to jump at meat wrapped in a red cloth, and later, when the baby Guan'ge is briefly left alone with her in chapter 59, she wraps him in that same red cloth, and the cat leaps at him and frightens him to death. In despair, Ping'er dreams of her first husband, whom she murdered; he threatens retribution, and, shortly thereafter, she dies.

How could this all have been avoided? Once again, epitaphs show us the preferred Ming way to deal with jealousy in the women's quarters. In the idealized world of epitaphs written by Ming literati, jealousy between wives and concubines was thought to be one of the greatest possible dangers to family harmony. The wife had a huge array of household tasks to manage, while concubines were free to serve the husband's pleasure. Still, concubines might well resent their lower status, and this could cause friction with the wife. In the epitaph that Li Mengyang wrote for Shen yiren 申宜人 ("Lady of Suitability," a title for women married to high-ranking officials), Shen calms a resentful concubine and earns the whole community's respect. This is what Wu Yueniang ought to have done in the Ximen household:

Originally, Vice-Commissioner Dong had taken a wife from the Li family, but as Mme Li was sickly and had no sons, he took a concubine from the Chen family. Shortly thereafter, Mme Li died, and Dong took Mme Shen as his new principal wife, to succeed Mme Li. Concubine Chen felt greatly wronged by this, and she protested vigorously, saying: "I am the daughter of a scholarly family! My father and brother only gave me to you as a concubine because they knew that Mme Li was sick and without sons. Day and night they repeated to me that if Mme Li should, by some misfortune, happen to die, I would succeed her. And now you're marrying Shen, are you?" When Vice-Commissioner Dong's relatives and members of the community heard this, they worried on his behalf, saying that when Shen entered the household the two women were bound to compete, and wouldn't that put the Dong family in dire straits?

初董娶於李. 病而無子. 乃更娶陳氏. 居無幾李卒. 於是繼娶於申. 而陳氏則大不平. 鬧曰. 吾儒門女也. 父兄謂李病無子. 乃始副室於君. 然恒日夜念曰李或不幸卒. 吾女其繼之矣. 乃今繼申氏女邪. 於是宗族鄉黨聞之. 私為董憂曰. 申入門二女必鬥爭. 董之家其索乎.　　　　　　　　　　　　　(Li Mengyang 44.13a)

But soon, Li Mengyang writes, Concubine Chen began to accord Mme Shen the deference due to a principal wife. The two became like sisters, and the relatives and community members were all delighted, saying to one another that Dong was a happy man to have obtained two such sage and virtuous wives. Shortly thereafter, however, the process of Chen's erasure began. In Ming dynasty families, the principal wife was the ritual mother (*dimu* 嫡母) of all the husband's children, and standard praise for a principal wife was that even when children were born to a concubine, the family ran so smoothly that no one would be able to tell:

After about a year, Chen bore a son Lan. Mme Shen held him in her arms and treated him as though he were her own. Chen bore another son Run, and then a daughter. Mme Shen treated all of them as her own, and none of them knew that she was not their mother. Someone teased them, saying: "You are not really Mme Shen's children!" The children did not believe it, and when finally they did learn the truth, they felt all the more strongly that Mme Shen was their real mother.

年餘. 陳生子瀾. 申抱之. 育為己子已. 又生子潤暨女. 申又咸抱之. 育為己子. 諸子女乃咸亦不自知其非申出. 或唆之曰. 汝曹實非申出. 諸子女不信也. 已而知之. 乃顧益母申.　　　　　　　　　　　　　(Li Mengyang 44.13b)

Thereafter, Concubine Chen disappears from the record. Mme Li (posthumously) and Mme Shen were each given the title of *yiren* 宜人, or "lady," delighting the relatives and community members again, and when Mme Shen died at the age of thirty-nine, she was buried with Mme Li so that the two of them could await their husband together. In another remarkable coincidence, we learn that these two principal wives had the same childhood name, *qijie* 七姐 ("Seventh Sister"). "Even I," marveled Li Mengyang, who had been a close friend of the family, "had no idea that the two sons were not Mme Shen's children!" (猶不知二子非申出; Li Mengyang 44.13b).

Modern-day readers may well find this outcome unfair, since it is Chen who provides progeny for the family, while Shen, who "treat[s] all of them as her own," produces no babies at all. Why then is Shen praised and Chen erased? The answer is that Shen is the legitimate wife, who has been introduced to the ancestors during the marriage ceremony, and who is thus responsible for continuing her husband's family line. As long as she raises the children, it does not really matter which concubine her husband used to produce them. Since she occupies the position of *dimu*, the children are brought up to think of her as the mother who matters. This arrangement was intended to produce harmony and clarity regarding the family line.

We see the devotion men could feel for their *dimu* very clearly in the case of the painter and poet (and sometimes official) Xu Wei 徐渭 (1521–93). Xu Wei did know his *shengmu* 生母, or birth mother; he provided for her during her lifetime and carried out an appropriate burial when she died (Carlitz, "Mourning" 47). But his deepest emotion was reserved for his *dimu*, Mme Miao, who died when he was only fourteen. In adulthood, he wrote the following passage in a passionate *mu zhi ming* for her: "She protected, loved, and instructed me, such that if I called on all the cosmic transformations, summoned all the gods and spirits, ran up expenditures in the hundreds, and exhausted all of my physical and mental powers, covered hundreds of sheets of paper, and pulverized my body one hundred times, I would not be able to repay her" (其保愛教訓渭則窮百變致百物散數百金竭終身之心力累百紙不能盡渭粉百身莫報也.; my trans.; Xu Wei).

Grief

Li Mengyang's deepest emotion is reserved for the death of his wife, which gives us some context for Ximen Qing's grief at the death of Li Ping'er as well as for Ping'er's grief at the death of her son. In Li Mengyang's epitaph for his wife, he turns the conventional formula of good household management into an eloquent cry of loss:

Weeping, I said to someone: "Only now when my wife has died do I know my wife!" This person asked how that might be? I replied: "Previously I studied and took office, and paid no attention to household matters. But now if I don't keep track of things they don't get done. When I had guests, food and drink suitable to their needs were supplied. Now no more guests come, or if they do, nothing is suitable. Previously, I used things without any attention to where they belonged. Now, everything gets thrown about and nobody puts anything away, but everyone's good at breaking things! Previously, we never lacked for pickles and sauces and salted beans—now, it's not like before! Chickens, ducks, sheep, and pigs were all fed at the proper time—now, they're not fed at the proper time and they are too thin![8] When my wife was alive, there was no whispering and giggling inside. If I went out, the door was not barred when I came back at night. Now the door is barred and inside I hear that giggling! Before, I had no idea what dirty clothes were. Now, if I don't order them washed, they don't get washed. As for sewing, cutting, drawing and embroidery, my wife was a model teacher, never just depending on others to do her work. Now we no longer have that good model, and everyone sloughs the work off onto someone else! When friends visited we would groan about troubles old and new, but when I tired of my friends I could talk to my wife. Now when I come home, I have no one to talk to. That's why I say: only now when my wife has died do I know my wife!

李子哭語人曰. 妻亡而予然後知吾妻也. 人曰何也. 李子曰. 往. 予學若官不問家事. 今事不問不舉矣. 留賓酒食稱賓至. 今不至矣. 即至弗稱矣. 往予不見器處用之. 具今器棄擲弗收矣. 然又善碎損. 往醢醬鹽豉弗乏也. 今不繼舊矣. 雞鴨羊豕時食. 今食弗時瘦矣. 妻在. 內無嘻嘻. 門予出即夜弗扃也. 門今扃. 內嘻嘻矣. 予往不識衣垢. 今不命之澣不澣矣. 縫剪描刺. 妻不假手不襲巧. 咸足師. 今無足師者矣. 然又假手. 人往予有古今之憽. 難友言而言之妻. 今入而無與言者. 故曰妻亡而予然後知吾妻也.　　　　　　　　　　　　　(45.10a)

Though Li laments the state of the laundry, he does not consider his wife a mere servant or housekeeper. A wife's household management was idealized by the educated elite as complementing a husband's governance in the public sphere, and so, by speaking of the pickles and the pigs, Li is praising his wife as a fully realized moral person.

At the same time, the Ming dynasty romantic ideal of married love had a great impact on the way men wrote about their deceased wives. It became conventional to say that grief for one's deceased wife was so great that it overstepped ritual bounds. This enabled widowers to understand themselves as men of deep feeling, an important literati value in the middle to late Ming. The irrepressible Li Meng-yang was convinced that in his grief he had been vouchsafed a miracle: on the day following his wife's death, he wrote that the family sacrificed in her honor. When the intestines of the sacrificial animal were boiled, they spontaneously coiled in such a way as to weave themselves into the shape of the written characters *yin* 陰 and *yang* 陽 (45.9b). For Ming Chinese, the intestine was the seat of emotion, and to be broken-hearted was to "split the intestine" (*duanchang* 斷腸). *Yin* and *yang* symbolize the complementary union of the genders, and for Li Mengyang, only the symbolic union remained; the actual union was tragically gone forever.

Li Mengyang's epitaph for the wife of his close friend Zhao Ze displays the same romantic ideal. Li Mengyang knew Zhao well, having "lived in the same lane, and traveled together for [their] studies, worked toward the same objectives, and frequently slept in the same bed" (居趙同巷焉游同學焉謀同道焉寢嘗同榻焉; 22.2a). Zhao's wife, Mme Wen, served Zhao's parents diligently and brought up their five sons and one daughter while Zhao studied for the all-important government civil-service examinations, though his career as a low-ranking instructor shows that he was only marginally successful. Mme Wen died when they had been in Kaifeng for only five years. Like Li Mengyang, Zhao experienced a miracle when his wife died and wrote a song to commemorate it. At her funeral, "[a] magpie landed on her coffin and gave a despairing cry. Zhao said: 'If this is not her spirit, what else could make that sound?' Thereupon he looked up to heaven and gave way to his grief, and crumpled to earth, weeping" (有鵲立棺首喈喈鳴趙君曰嗟匪妻之靈孰為斯鳴於是仰天大慟頓地哭已; 22.2a). Li Mengyang gives the text of Zhao's "Magpie Song" and says that Zhao also wrote a "Mourning Song" of several hundred words, and rare were those who heard it and did not weep. Li Mengyang closes by defending Zhao Ze's overpowering grief: "If you are virtuous, your emotion will exceed bounds. If your emotion exceeds bounds, then you will overstep the Rites. If you overstep the Rites, then your song is bound to be sad. Therefore I say: Zhao was virtuous toward his wife; she was not alone in being virtuous!" (賢之則情必過情過則禮必踰禮踰則歌必哀故 曰趙之於溫也賢之也非獨妻也; 22.2a).

What these *mu zhi ming* show us is that Ming dynasty culture approved of extreme grief, in appropriate circumstances, and, most importantly, by appropriate people. Li Mengyang and Zhao Ze lament in ways that earned deep approval from their literati peers. This extreme grief is the cultural model that the author of *Plum in the Golden Vase* follows when he describes Li Ping'er's feelings at losing her beloved baby son (ch. 59), and Ximen Qing's feelings when he loses Li Ping'er (ch. 62). But since these *Plum* protagonists are radically inappropriate people, can we take their grief as seriously as we take the grief expressed in literati *mu zhi ming*? After all, Ximen Qing and Li Ping'er essentially tortured her husband, Hua Zixu, to death, and the baby Guan'ge owes his very existence to Ximen Qing's and Li Ping'er's adulterous, murderous relationship. Thus, although Ximen Qing and Li Ping'er are described as consumed by grief, we could also read their suffering as a parody of the grief seen in the literati examples above.

And yet their grief comes across as real and moving, especially in the case of Li Ping'er. In chapters 61 and 62, Li Ping'er's grief is such that she literally disintegrates. The descriptions spare us nothing: Li Ping'er suffers vertigo as she voids what feels like all her inner organs into the commode (ch. 61). She loses her balance and falls frequently (ch. 61). Ximen Qing's demise is yet to come, as he depletes himself sexually over the next seventeen chapters, requiring larger and larger doses of his aphrodisiac until he finally expires after intercourse (ch. 79). At almost the same time, his wife Wu Yueniang gives birth to a son, but as noted, this son will become a celibate monk and will not carry on the family line.

What is the larger message of these tragic moments in the demise of the Ximen family? The Song dynasty supposedly depicted in *Plum in the Golden Vase* is actually a stand-in for the Ming dynasty, making the book a warning that the Ming is on track to suffer the same fate as the Song. Can we read Li Ping'er's painful death as hinting at the author's own pain, watching his beloved culture on the road to disaster?

NOTES

[1] Unless otherwise noted, parenthetical citations refer to Roy's translation, *The Plum in the Golden Vase*, and to *Jin Ping Mei cihua* 金瓶梅詞話 (*Plum in the Golden Vase: A Ballad Tale*).

[2] In 1615 a man with a club was apprehended at the residence of the heir apparent and, though suspected of murderous intent, was never executed; see Ray Huang, "Lung-ch'ing and Wan-li Reigns" 554–56. Given the 1618 publication date of the *Jin Ping Mei cihua*, this would have been a very late addition to the plot.

[3] The stereotype of the "bad last emperor" is analyzed in Arthur Wright's classic article "Sui Yang-ti: Personality and Stereotype" (*Confucian Persuasion* 47–76).

[4] Li Mengyang's epitaphs, all translations of which are my own, are cited by *juan* and page number. In general, printed books in the late imperial period consisted of a number of separately bound volumes (*ce* 冊), but books had their own internal divisions, *juan* 卷, which often did not correspond with their physical divisions. Books in the Ming and Qing were commonly divided into a certain number of *juan*, a term that connotes "roll" and derives from the time when a roll of stitched-together strips of bamboo was the standard form for books. *Juan* is most often rendered into English as "fascicle," "scroll," "chapter," or "volume," which is misleading, as there were often multiple *juan* in one physically bound book. *Juan* usually correlates with "chapter," but in some cases a *juan* may contain several chapters. Very long chapters can also stretch over several *juan*.

[5] *Ruren* 孺人, which means "child nurturer," was a title given to women whose husbands had reached the seventh of nine total ranks for civil-service officials.

[6] Li Jiao'er was originally an entertainer from the "licensed quarter," meaning that she could be legally hired for a variety of services, including sex. Like the Japanese geisha, such women were often valued for a wide variety of skills, but given the services that Ximen Qing typically seeks, it makes sense to call her a prostitute. In chapter 59, for example, when Ximen Qing first visits a high-class brothel, he wants to cut short the standard preliminaries, like the elegant meal, and go straight to bed.

[7] Wives in traditional China retained their birth surnames; unless their titles are germane to the discussion, I generally refer to them using the title *Mme*.

[8] Here the classically educated Li Mengyang is echoing the writings of the philosopher Mencius, who maintains that breeding and planting at the proper season are essential to a benevolently governed state (I.A.3).

The Case in the Vase:
Legal Process, Legal Culture, and Justice in *The Plum in the Golden Vase*

Michael Szonyi

Law and justice may not be the first things that most readers notice about *The Plum in the Golden Vase* (*Jin Ping Mei* 金瓶梅), but they are important if often overlooked themes of a book that actually devotes much attention to legal matters. The text mentions more than thirty separate legal disputes, and some half dozen court cases receive detailed treatment. *Plum* is not only a valuable source for learning about law and legal culture in premodern China; thinking about law in *Plum* may also be productive for reflecting on the relationship between law and society in modern-day China and perhaps even elsewhere.

The main goal of this essay is to help students appreciate more fully the legal dimensions of *Plum* and better understand the role of law in Chinese history. How do *Plum*'s descriptions of legal processes compare with formal Ming law? What can the text tell us about Ming legal culture, about what people knew of the law and what they expected from it? What can it teach us about how Ming judges reached their verdicts—that is, about Ming legal reasoning?

Two frames of reference may be helpful in guiding student engagement with the legal aspects of the novel. The first is the long history of Western views of Chinese law. At roughly the same time *Plum* was written, some thinkers of the early European Enlightenment were expressing admiration for the Chinese legal system. Their views were shaped less by a thorough knowledge of Ming law than by their strategy of using an idealized version of China as a foil for aspects of their own European society that they wished to criticize. This positive assessment largely disappeared in subsequent centuries. By the nineteenth century most Western scholars described Chinese law as brutal, punitive, and arbitrary. Indeed, for some, China had no law, and certainly no justice. These views were informed by the Confucian prejudices of China's own intellectuals, who often denigrated criminal law as inferior to moral teaching, even as some of these intellectuals applied law in their professional lives as government officials. But probably even more important in shaping these views were imperialist designs on China, missionary impulses to "civilize" the Chinese people, and efforts to justify the legal practice of extraterritoriality.[1] This limited awareness of, and even more limited appreciation for, China's long legal tradition still casts a shadow over the study of premodern Chinese law.

How does a careful reading of *Plum* reinforce or challenge existing prejudices about Chinese law? Certainly, no one could finish the book and still think premodern China was without law. The world described in the novel has a sophisticated legal system with elaborate formal laws and processes. But just as critics have charged, this does not mean that the Ming legal system delivered justice. The novel does suggest, however, that people in Ming China had other ways of thinking about justice besides as the outcome of a formal legal system.

A second useful frame of reference is the notion of law and justice in popular culture. Though most college students today have never been in a courtroom, they may already have strong ideas—not all of which are necessarily accurate—about how the legal system operates in their society. Much of what people think they know about the justice system they learn from novels and television shows about solving crimes and prosecuting criminals—a genre known in the entertainment business as the procedural.

Seventeenth-century Ming China had its own version of the procedural. The case narrative (*gong'an* 公案) is a genre with a long tradition in China.[2] The stock elements in *gong'an* cases are not so different from those in modern TV procedurals: a crime, an investigation and trial, and a hero who solves the case. One difference is that in historical Chinese case narratives, the protagonist was ordinarily not a detective or a prosecutor but rather a judge. The most famous literary judge was Judge Bao, an insightful and perspicacious investigator who was based on a historical figure, Bao Zheng 包拯 (999–1062). Judge Bao was the star of a huge number of story collections and plays, some of which are available in English translation (Comber; Idema; Shi Yukun). Case narratives were popular in the late Ming; indeed, one of the cases in *Plum*, the murder of Miao Tianxiu (Miao T'ien-hsiu), is adapted from a published collection of Judge Bao stories from 1594, *Baijia gong'an* 百家公案 (*The Hundred Cases [of Judge Bao]*), by An Yushi 安遇時. The case narratives in *Plum* belong to this larger literary tradition, the Chinese equivalent of detective fiction.

Fiction and drama were not the only sources of information about the Ming judicial system. Legal trials were conducted in public spaces and sometimes drew large crowds. Elite male readers, *Plum*'s main intended audience, would have known about the judicial system because it had been part, albeit a small part, of their own education, which was aimed at passing the civil examinations and ultimately becoming an official. Other readers would also have known something about the judicial system through sources such as household encyclopedias and through the imagery and rituals of popular religion. As a result, like the modern viewer of TV procedurals, the typical reader of *Plum* probably also knew—or at least thought they knew—a lot about the judicial system in their society. This might have encouraged the author to describe that system realistically lest readers be troubled by the discrepancies between the text and their own knowledge. But it might also have provided opportunities to exaggerate or satirize the real system for dramatic or comedic effect. It can be a challenge for modern readers to tell the difference.

Legal Process

The descriptions of legal cases in *Plum* vary in length and detail. In some cases, the novel's protagonist, Ximen Qing (Hsi-men Ch'ing), is involved as a litigant or plaintiff; in others he is the judge. There are others in which he does not appear at all. But virtually all references gesture in some way to the legal process, to the way in which the law was supposed to operate. (For more detailed descriptions of the legal cases depicted in the novel, see the appendix.)

One question that needs to be dealt with briefly is which legal process is described in the book. *Plum* was written in the Ming dynasty (1368–1644), but it is set in the Song dynasty, some three centuries earlier. For the purposes of this essay, I accept the position of *Plum*'s translator, David Roy, that the author employed a deliberate anachronism that readers at the time would have been aware of. Roy writes that despite the setting in the Song, "the conditions that [the author] described in it were really those of his own day"—that is, the late Ming (Introduction xxix).

In the legal systems of many societies, it is judges who are responsible for applying the law. Let us unpack this sentence to ask what it meant in Ming China. First, who were the judges? The very term *judge* is something of a misnomer. The Ming did not have specialized judges in local government. The basic administrative unit in Ming government was the county, and every county was presided over by a magistrate. Conducting investigations, holding trials, and passing sentence were simply part of the magistrate's slate of responsibilities. This is not to say that there were no legal specialists in Ming government. The magistrate's office, known as the yamen, employed clerks who specialized in legal matters, and, at higher levels of government, specialized judicial offices reviewed cases and sentencing. But in general, the functions we think of as being performed by a judge were simply part of the overall duties of the local official, though they were often described as the most consequential of those duties.

Ximen Qing is first appointed to a judicial position in chapter 30; he is then promoted to a higher position in chapter 70. The titles of his posts do not correspond exactly to any official titles in the Ming bureaucracy nor, for that matter, in that of the Song. But the text suggests that Ximen Qing works in a judicial supervisory office, where his job is to monitor and review cases handled at lower bureaucratic levels, to deal with official misconduct, and sometimes to hear cases brought to his court directly.

What was the law that Ming judges applied? The Ming had an explicit legal code that was compiled early in the dynasty. The code consists of a set of rules about how state and society should operate, with criminal sanctions and punishments to be used when necessary to ensure compliance. Each of its 460 articles defines a crime and its applicable punishment. The full code is available in a recent translation by Yonglin Jiang. The code was supplemented with memorials and case reports that, after making their way up the chain of command all the way to the emperor and receiving his approval, came to have the force of law.

What did it mean to apply the law in Ming China? What was the role of the judge? It does not take a very careful reading of *Plum* to realize that Ximen Qing's work as a judge is not his top priority. But we can still learn something about what people in the Ming thought about the judge's role, even from a negligent judge like Ximen Qing. Some of the information is very specific. One day, "finding himself at leisure, [Ximen Qing] went to the yamen, where he took his place on the bench, held roll call, reheard the cases of all the defendants who had been brought to court for the crimes of rape, assault, gambling, or larceny, and took the time to sign the documents that had accumulated during his absence" (那日清閒無事, 且到衙門裡升堂畫卯, 把那些解到的人犯, 也有姦情的、鬥毆的、賭騁的、竊盜的, 一一重問一番. 又把那些投到文書, 一一押到日押僉了一會; 3.55.367; 55.12b).[3] This is indeed more or less what Ming judges did—manage staff members, hear cases, and sign documents—though they were expected to take the job more seriously than Ximen Qing does.

Chapter 94 provides an account of the physical setting in which a judge worked. There was no dedicated courtroom, and legal matters were handled in the main hall of the yamen:

> [The judge] came in and took his place on the bench. The functionaries, soldiers, and jailers were neatly arrayed to either side in strict formation. Behold:
> The walls are decked with crimson silk;
> The tables covered with purple drapery.
> At the head of the chamber are suspended red hangings;
> On all four sides there hang kingfisher-hued screens.
> The judge adheres strictly to the law;
> The admonitory stone tablet is incised with four lines in the emperor's hand.
> The officers are meticulous and honest;
> Beside the external abatises are displayed two of the commandant's standards.
> The soldiers and jailers stand sedately;
> The functionaries are arrayed imposingly.
> Holding their staffs, they stand before the steps ready to perform their duties;
> With writing materials in hand, they wait on the sidelines to hear the judgment.
> Though only the officers of one region; they resemble a courtroom full of gods.
> (5.94.274)

不一時, 只見裡面雲板響, 守備升廳, 兩邊僚掾軍牢森列, 甚是齊整. 但見
耕羅緻壁, 紫緩卓圍. 當廳額掛茜羅, 四下簾垂翁翠. 勘官守正, 戒石上刻御製
四行. 人從謹 廉, 鹿角旁插令旗兩面. 軍牢沉重, 僚掾威儀. 執大棍授事立增
前, 挾文書廳旁聽發放. 雖然一 路帥臣, 果是滿堂神道.　　　　(94.3b–4a)

In the novel as in real life, cases were generally, though not always, initiated when someone brought an accusation or lawsuit to the magistrate. We see a stylized representation of this in the image of "Wu Yueniang creat[ing] a stir in the district yamen" (5.92.238; fig. 1). In theory, anyone could bring a lawsuit to the magistrate. The novel suggests that at least some ordinary people had enough knowledge of the legal system to do this. Even a lowlife like Crudcrawler Tao is said to be "well versed in the law" (你老人家深通條律; 2.33.279; 33.11b). The clerks in the yamen try to dissuade Wu Song (Wu Sung) from bringing a suit because he "seem[s] to be ignorant of the law" (不省得法度; 1.9.182; 9.8a), by which what they really mean is that he ought to know better. But while ordinary people might threaten to take their enemies to court, more specialized knowledge was generally needed to bring a lawsuit. This is what lies behind the seemingly cryptic remark that Wu Song "went to Master Chen's house for assistance in drafting a formal complaint" (先在陳先生家, 寫了狀子; 1.9.181; 9.7b). This is almost certainly a reference to Wu's need for the services of a legal expert or pettifogger who knows how to produce the necessary documents to bring a lawsuit to court. Indeed, the document that Wu Yueniang (Wu Yüeh-niang) is holding, and which is reproduced in full on the page facing the image, is clearly the work of a professional.

Figure 1. "Wu Yueniang creates a stir in the district yamen." *Qinggong zhenbao bi meitu* 清宮珍寶祕美圖 (*Two Hundred Beautiful Paintings [Formerly] Treasured in the Qing Palace*), vol. 4, Qizhen gongshangshe, 1985?

What kinds of matters might generate a lawsuit? Obviously, crimes such as "rape, assault, gambling, or larceny" that are explicitly prohibited in the code were one type of offense. Another type of offense involved infringements of what we would call civil law. The Western legal tradition makes a basic distinction between criminal law, which concerns itself with violations of state laws, and civil law, which deals with disputes between private individuals or entities. There is no explicit Ming law comparable to civil law in the West. Lawsuits in the Ming, as in other dynasties, had to be framed in relation to a specific violation of the code. This has long led many scholars to assume that premodern China had no civil law, only criminal law. But a careful study of the cases in *Plum* shows that this view is problematic. There are many cases that are clearly disputes between people, such as those involving inheritance, debt, marriage, and property (chs. 14, 19, 88). These are clearly matters that belong to what we would call the category of civil law. The Ming code included provisions to punish those found to be in the wrong in such disputes, and this is how the case is framed, but the primary goal of the case is clearly not to punish the guilty—as in more straightforward criminal cases—but to resolve a dispute between two parties.

The Ming code also includes sanctions against officials who violated administrative regulations. Cases of impeachment for dereliction of duty—for example, when Ximen Qing's patron Cai Jing (Tsai Ching) and his supporters are accused of conspiracy (chs. 17–18)—were initially handled much like any other court case. Had Ximen Qing not bribed an officer of the court to take his name off the list of the accused in this case, we might not have the remaining eighty percent of the novel. Ximen Qing's own impeachment case over corruption in the investigation of the death of Miao Tianxiu in chapter 48 is likewise handled as an ordinary case, at least until Ximen enlists Cai's support to make the case go away.

Ximen Qing notes that once a magistrate receives a case, he is required to pursue it to its conclusion (2.38.383). The first step is the investigation. The magistrate orders yamen staff members—the clerks, runners, lictors, and constables—to gather all relevant information, including both physical and forensic evidence. This process occurs several times in the text—for example, after Song Huilian's suicide, when the magistrate dispatches his clerks to examine the corpse (2.26.125). Ming law had clear standards of evidence, a point that is understood by several characters in *Plum*. A court official reminds Wu Song that "[i]n any case involving an accusation [of murder or manslaughter] there are five prerequisites that must be possessed by the prosecutor before he can proceed to trial: the corpse of the victim, the wound, the medical cause of death, the weapon, and evidence that implicates the accused" (但凡人命之事, 須要屍傷病物踪, 五件事俱完, 方可推問; 1.9.183; 9.8b).

The next step, to borrow a phrase from another corrupt official in a different context, was to "round up the usual suspects." Everyone involved in a lawsuit—the accused, the accuser, and any witnesses—could be detained for the period of the investigation. Ming code required that detainees be treated well and be fed, but *Plum* suggests repeatedly that this rule did not count for much in practice. After Laiwang (Lai-wang) had been in detention "for half a month or so without any money of his own, . . . his body was lacerated, his clothes were tattered, and he had nowhere to turn" (在監中, 監了半月光景, 沒錢使用, 弄的身體狼狽, 衣服藍縷, 沒處投奔; 2.26.112; 26.9a). It is little wonder that the judge allows Wu Yueniang, the widow of an official, to be excused from detention. He orders a household servant detained in her place (5.94.240). For similar reasons, Ximen Qing writes a note to the judge in the hope of persuading him not to detain Li Guijie (Li Kuei-chieh) when she is implicated in a criminal matter (3.51.230).

When the evidence had been gathered and the parties involved assembled, it was time for the trial. Ming administrative regulations gave clear instructions for the conduct of a trial. The judge interrogated first the accuser, then the accused. If the accused did not confess, then the judge turned to the witnesses. If any inconsistencies remained, torture was permitted as a means of uncovering the truth. Torture could be used to secure a confession as well as to attain unanimity and consistency in testimony. There is no explicit statement in Ming law about the instruments of torture, but it seems that three methods of torture that appear often in *Plum*—beating with a stick as well as two gender-specific forms of torture—were ubiquitous in real Ming courtrooms. Men could be tortured with ankle-squeezers and women with finger-squeezers (Xu and Du 43–46). Both implements consisted of sticks or boards connected by ropes, which were wrapped around the ankles or between the fingers and then pulled or rapped with a stick to inflict pain. Though the judges in *Plum* use torture at the drop of a hat, the threat of torture was probably more common in Ming justice than was its actual use. Ming law had guidelines about how much torture could be applied to persons of different ages and genders to elicit truth while avoiding false statements (Y. Jiang 230–31, 240). Judging by how often they call for the use of torture, the judges in *Plum* seem unaware of these guidelines or, if they are, don't take them very seriously. It is not clear whether the frequent and indiscriminate use of torture in the novel is meant to mirror such usage in real-life judicial proceedings or is intended as an exaggerated contrast with the real world.

Once the facts were clear, the judge had to reach a verdict. (I leave discussion of this issue to the section below, on legal reasoning.) For major crimes, the judge's sentence was provisional and subject to review by superiors all the way up the hierarchy to, in theory, the emperor. We see the review process most clearly in the case of Wu Song. In minor matters, the magistrate's decision was final but could in principle be appealed.

After the initial verdict was reviewed, approved, and returned to the original judge, he delivered the final verdict and ordered the appropriate punishment be imposed. The case was then closed for all but the convicted, who would be taken off to be punished. This phase is represented in *Plum* by the image entitled "Laiwang is sent under penal escort to Xuzhou" (2.26.114; fig. 2). The range of legal

Figure 2. "Laiwang is sent under penal escort to Xuzhou." *Qinggong zhenbao bi meitu* 清宮珍寶皕美圖 (*Two Hundred Beautiful Paintings [Formerly] Treasured in the Qing Palace*), vol. 2, Qizhen gongshangshe, 1985?

punishments, from corporal punishment to penal servitude to internal exile to capital punishment, are specified clearly in the first article of the Ming code (Y. Jiang 5). Many punishments could be commuted on payment of a fine. So the law had different consequences for the rich than it had for the poor.

At every stage, from the initial plaint to the final verdict, strict rules of documentation had to be observed. The author of *Plum* includes several legal documents in full:

> Wu Song's plaint against Ximen Qing (1.9.182);
>
> a forensic report on Li Waichuan (Li Wai-ch'uan), dead by Wu Song's hand (1.10.189);
>
> a case report on Wu Song's guilt, submitted for review (1.10.192);
>
> a witness report about the fight between Han the Second and his lover's tormenters (2.34.290); and
>
> a lawsuit filed by Wu Yueniang against Chen Jingji (Ch'en Ching-chi) for killing of Ximen Dajie (Hsi-men Ta-chieh; 5.92.238).

These look very much like the texts of actual legal documents that survive from the Ming, and models for such documents were available in household encyclopedias that were widely available during this period. Literary scholars today debate what to make of this intertextual verisimilitude and why *Plum*'s author chose to copy entire legal documents into the text. Their inclusion may be one reflection of a broader interest in proceduralism—evident also in popular religion—that does seem to be a new phenomenon of the Ming.

Legal Reasoning

How did Ming judicial officials reach decisions? The Ming code, as mentioned above, consists of descriptions of different types of crimes and the punishments that are applicable to each. Because of this, some scholars have argued that the judge's task was a simple one: he had to identify the crime and apply the sentence befitting that crime. In other words, the act of sentencing was the judge's central concern. This view is supported by the fact that judges were required to cite the relevant article of the code when issuing a sentence. If no article of the code was obviously appropriate, then the judge was expected to reason by analogy to the nearest applicable one (Y. Jiang 238).

There is plenty of evidence in *Plum* of judges taking this approach to judicial reasoning. For example, in the case report on Wu Song's initial trial we read that, "[i]n cases of involuntary manslaughter resulting from an affray, no matter whether the fatal injury be inflicted by hand, foot, other object or metal blade, the penalty shall be strangulation. Wu Song should be sentenced to death by strangulation" (擬武松依鬥毆殺人, 不問手足他物金兩, 律絞; 1.10.192; 10.3b). The first phrase is a direct quotation from the legal code; the second is the application of the relevant sentence. Asking students to find relevant laws in the code and compare the text of the code with its application in the novel could make for an interesting classroom exercise.

Today legal scholars are expanding the study of Ming law beyond the code to a variety of sources, including casebooks written by famous magistrates, handbooks for the edification of would-be officials, a small number of surviving Ming legal archives, and even fiction.[4] As a result, the prevailing scholarly view of judicial reasoning has become more complex. A more recent approach to Ming legal reasoning holds that judges tried to balance the law (*fa* 法) with circumstance (*qing* 情; Jiang and Wu). We also see evidence of judges adopting this approach in *Plum*. The honorable prefect of Dongping, Chen Wenzhao (Ch'en Wen-chao), reduces Wu Song's sentence for the crime of "deliberate homicide of an innocent person" (故殺平人) on the grounds that Wu is "a man of honor, motivated by righteous indignation" (有義的烈漢) seeking to avenge the wrongful death of his brother (1.10.193; 10.4a). The code is straightforward, but Chen takes extenuating circumstances into account. As a follow-up to the exercise above, students might be asked to consider how law and circumstances interact in judicial reasoning in the more detailed case narratives, which are identified with an asterisk in the appendix.

While legal scholars today debate whether judges simply identified and applied the relevant law or took other factors into account, Ximen Qing was driven primarily by a concern of a different kind—what was best for Ximen Qing. But even he must balance multiple considerations in reaching verdicts. Indeed, he takes a kind of perverse pride in his performance, comparing himself with judges who do not even try to make themselves look good. His colleague Xia Yanling (Hsia Yen-ling) intends to trump up a charge against a member of the Chen family because the family's wealth makes it a promising target for extortion. But Ximen Qing puts a stop to this (2.34.302–03). He says of Xia that "when cases come before him, without so much enquiring into the blue or red, black or white of the situation, if money comes into his hands, he frees the parties concerned. What sort of justice is that?" After all, he continues, "we are charged with the administration of justice and ought to have some regard for appearances" (有事不問青水皂白, 得了錢在手裡就放了, 成什麼道理! 我便再三扭著不你我雖是個武職官兒, 掌著這刑條, 還放些體面才好; 2.34.289; 34.6a). Thus, even for a judge as venal as Ximen Qing, the judicial process involves the balancing of multiple factors. But none of these factors has much to do with justice.

Other Realms of Law and Justice

The case narratives in *Plum* suggest a legal process that is highly bureaucratized, formalized, and consistent with the Ming code and other related administrative regulations. Decision-making was not just arbitrary but also rested on a foundation of legal reasoning, though we may debate the content of that reasoning.[5]

But in *Plum*, the formal process is subverted at every turn. What drives the judicial process is less the pursuit of justice than the pursuit of self-interest—by the plaintiffs, the judges, and anyone involved. Wealthy people like Ximen Qing try to influence judges' decisions. They pay bribes or invoke personal relationships to affect the verdict; to persuade the judge to make an arrest or to pursue a case; to improve or worsen the conditions under which detainees are held, to use torture and corporal punishment or the threat thereof; to show leniency or reduce the sentence when a conviction is inevitable or to threaten more severe treatment in the future; and to trump up a charge so that someone else can get off.

Judges also take every opportunity to enrich themselves. Everyone from the judge down is on the take. When Laiwang is sentenced to penal exile, the guards who escort him to the place of exile clearly expect a gratuity, for he tries to raise enough money to "compensate [them] for [their] trouble" (謝二位; 2.26.113; 26.9a). According to Ming law, officials who exonerated the guilty or implicated the innocent were subject to serious punishment, even execution (Y. Jiang 233–35). Such concerns do not seem to influence the judges in the novel.

Thus, what the case narratives in the novel actually demonstrate is flawed proceduralism. The system was easily susceptible to manipulation by people with wealth, power, and connections. Ming China may have had a complex and elaborate legal system, but it did not necessarily produce justice.

But the justice of the courtroom is not the only type of justice—or injustice—in the book. There are at least three other ways in which *Plum* reflects on the theme of justice, and these can help us better understand the broader legal culture of the society in which *Plum* is set and was written. To today's readers, none of the matters described below are self-evidently legal cases, but I will suggest—or try to make the case, so to speak—that seeing them as such would have made sense to readers at the time.

Ximen Qing often seems to bring his job home with him. On one occasion, Xiahua (Hsia-hua), a maidservant, is found in possession of a missing gold bracelet. A drunken Ximen studies the evidence (the stolen bracelet) and interrogates the accused (Xiahua). He orders she be tortured to encourage her to confess. The implements of judicial torture are available in his own home. He sends for the finger-squeezers, which are applied to poor Xiahua, and then has her beaten with a sturdy stick (3.44.74). This obviously isn't the first time he has used such methods: earlier in the text he calls for those among his servants who have experience at administering punishment to apply their expertise (2.35.319).

Even the language that Ximen uses at home reflects the spirit of the courtroom. He threatens that those who disobey him will be "sentenced" to a beating (決打二十板; 2.26.113; 26.9b). When Song Huilian (Sung Hui-lien) commits suicide in the compound, Ximen Qing writes a note to the magistrate explaining that she must have been afraid that Ximen would "investigate and punish her" (查問見責; 2.26.125; 26.17a)—that is, that he would play the role within his own house that he does in court. In other words, he sees parallels between the way a judge resolves issues in the courtroom and the way the head of a household resolves issues in the household.

The parallels between the courtroom and the home were certainly evident to the illustrators of *Plum*. Compare, for example, the many visual similarities between the courtroom scenes and the image of Ximen Qing punishing his page boy Ping'an (P'ing-an) for admitting visitors in violation of his orders (2.35.321; fig. 3). We should not assume that these parallels are simply a matter of public law being emulated in private. Rather, we should recognize that in Ming China the values and practices of the family were widely seen as homologous to the values and practices of the state, and the distinctions between private and public were less obvious and self-evident than they may seem today. Whether the self-conscious parallels in the novel between the formal justice system and the justice of the household reflect social reality or function as a literary device intended for satirical effect is open to debate.

Not only do the private and public realms of legal process resemble one another, they sometimes interact. In chapter 87, the servants of Zhou Xiu (Chou

Figure 3. "Harboring resentment, Ximen Qing punishes Ping'an." *Qinggong zhenbao bi meitu* 清宮珍寶甋美圖 (*Two Hundred Beautiful Paintings [Formerly] Treasured in the Qing Palace*), vol. 2, Qizhen gongshangshe, 1985?

Hsiu) hope to persuade Dame Wang to accept his offer for Pan Jinlian (P'an Chin-lien). When Dame Wang demands more money, one of the servants suggests to his master that he should have her arrested and tortured. Philip Huang has argued that the formal legal system in premodern China operated alongside and in constant interaction with a system of informal community mediation (11–13). We certainly see signs of this in *Plum*, though the servant's proposal to use the threat of involving the formal legal system as a way to pressure Dame Wang into making a deal is not exactly what Huang had in mind.

Recall in the description of the courtroom above that the imposing figures are said to resemble "a courtroom full of gods" (果是滿堂神道). This is an image that would have made perfect sense to Ming readers since it was generally thought that the gods and the dead had their own court system, with many parallels with the legal system of the living. In Chinese popular religion, the term used by scholars for the diffuse ideas and practices of the vast majority of Chinese people, the world of gods, spirits, and the dead had long been imagined as resembling closely the world of the living, and this resemblance extended to the legal realm. The dead were thought to pass through a series of courts, each overseen by a judge, who rendered judgement and imposed punishment based on the ill deeds that the person had committed while alive. King Yama, who makes several appearances in *Plum*, was the most senior judge of these courts (Teiser 5–7, 11–15, 177). The parallels went even further: it was possible for the souls of those who had suffered harm at the hands of the living to bring lawsuits against the living in the courts of the dead. The same legal process was thought to apply in both judicial systems. Both used identical documents written in standardized language. Images from other Ming novels and instructions for set design in Ming drama show that the two courtroom systems were thought to be physically identical. We can label this legal system the supernatural legal system in contrast to the secular system of the living.

There was a widespread assumption in Ming China of a continuum between supernatural and secular justice. Judge Bao is able to solve some of his most difficult crimes only with the help of a supernatural agent. But this is not a prominent element in *Plum*; the only example that comes to mind is in chapter 48, when a whirlwind suddenly appears in front of an official on horseback. The official orders his servants to follow the whirlwind until it stops, which leads them to the discovery of the corpse of a murder victim (3.48.150).

In chapter 62, a Daoist master, or priest, summons a spirit from the world of the dead, who relays the information that the illness that Li Ping'er (Li P'ing-erh) suffers from—which will ultimately prove fatal—arises from a court case in the courts of the dead. Were Li Ping'er's troubles caused by evil spirits, it might be possible for the priest to take measures to placate them. Unfortunately, the situation is more serious, and the priest's hands are tied. As the priest explains, "[T]his woman is being sued in the court of the underworld by someone who suffered an injustice at her hands in a former existence. . . . In the case of an enemy or a creditor from a previous existence . . . it is up to the plaintiff himself. If he is willing to drop the case, it may be dropped; but even the authorities of the underworld cannot force him to do so" (此位娘子, 惜乎為宿世冤您所訴于陰曹 . . . 冤家債主, 須得本人可捨則捨之, 雖陰官亦不能強; 4.62.63; 62.15a). In other words, the courts of the underworld, like the courts of the living, have their due process, and that process must be respected. Later, Li Ping'er's enemy will appear before her and mock her husband's efforts to save her. Since his lawsuit has already been accepted by the court, she cannot escape (4.62.68). Sure enough, she dies.

Her spirit then appears to Ximen Qing in a dream and reports that as a result of the lawsuit lodged against her, she has been detained in prison and is now "dripping with blood, befouled by my own filth, and suffering torments" (血水淋漓, 與穢污在一處, 整受了這些苦). It seems that the prisons of the underworld are no better than those of our own world. But Ximen's efforts on Li Ping'er's behalf do lead to a reduction in the charges against her. This angers her accuser, who now intends to lodge an accusation against Ximen Qing himself. Li warns Ximen Qing not to become the "unexpected victim of [the accuser's] venomous skullduggery" (一暗遭他毒手; 4.67.199; 67.16b). She is of course warning him that he may suffer the same fate as those on whom he himself has practiced "venomous skullduggery" in the human world.[6]

We hear no more of Li Ping'er's lawsuit in the courts of the dead. But we will soon learn that her warning was prescient, for things begin to fall apart for Ximen and his whole household. His infant son is already dead at the hands of his lover. Ximen himself will die as a consequence of his excessive behavior. And because fate is cruel, his second son, born after Ximen's death, will be spirited away to become a Buddhist monk, ensuring that the family line will be cut off forever. Even his daughter, abused and ignored by her own husband, will commit suicide. All that remains of the family estate will eventually go to Ximen's former servant Dai'an (Tai-an).

No judge, human or spirit, presides over a courtroom to determine Ximen Qing's fate. But Ming readers would likely have interpreted the novel's conclusion as a kind of justice, the justice of a neutral, dispassionate Heaven that ensured that immorality eventually reaps its just rewards. This form of justice may not operate quickly or in obvious ways. As the novel tells us, "Good people do not live long; the wicked live a thousand years" (好人不長壽, 禍害一千年; 4.73.397; 73.8a). But ultimately, inexorably, the good are rewarded and the evil punished, and the universe remains in balance. This represents a fourth mode of justice in *Plum*, a kind of abstract justice. As one character sings, "Murder may be excused / but reason cannot be evaded / No fickle deed escapes the eye of Heaven" (論殺人可恕, 情理難饒, 負心的天鑒表; 2.38.398; 38.10a). While the novel may be more satirical dystopia than transparent representation of reality, both the fate of the Ximen household and the fall of the ruling dynasty at the end of the novel are intended to convey to readers the widely held view that Heaven's impartial justice will, or at least ought to, eventually judge us all.

It is easy to overlook the fact that *Plum* is, among other things, a novel about law and justice and about how people in late imperial China thought about the relationship between the two. Just as television shows like *CSI* or *Law and Order* can tell us something about how people in our society think about the law, the detailed narratives in *Plum* can teach us something about legal culture in Ming China. Asking students to rewrite the cases in the novel in the form of a modern TV procedural is a classroom exercise that should bring this point home to them.

Of course, *Plum* is not a sociological study of Ming society. It is a novel, and one that is richly satirical. Students will almost certainly be struck by the seeming deficiencies of the legal system in the novel. They may need to be reminded that no legal system delivers justice with absolute reliability. As United States Court of Appeals Judge Richard Posner writes, "[T]he frequent discontinuity between the spirit and the letter of the law, or between law's general aim and its concrete application, is one reason law so often strikes laypersons as arbitrary" (33). When we think about law in any premodern society, we should be mindful to compare it not only with modern law but also with what the law was like in other societies at that time. Students who hope to make more informed judgments about law in Ming China should be encouraged to learn more about European legal and judicial systems of the sixteenth and seventeenth centuries. They should also be reminded of the pitfalls of comparing the theory of one system with the practice of another.

The role of law in the novel goes well beyond descriptions of court cases. It is a rich and widely understood source of imagery. The seriousness of the Daoist master is conveyed by the phrase "just as if he were hearing a case in court" (恰似問事之狀; 4.62.63; 62.15a). The law is used as a convenient plot device several times—for example, in Chen Jingji's explanation that he came to the Ximen household because of his parents' legal problems (1.20.421). It is used as a framing device for jokes, puns, and ribaldry (e.g., 2.35.338, 3.51.239, 3.54.327). All these examples give us insight into the place of law within the broader culture of the time, something we could not possibly learn from the legal code alone.

But I think the book's main contribution to the study of legal culture lies in its treatment of the legal process. The accounts of trials in the novel are remarkably faithful to the actual legal procedures of the Ming dynasty. Unlike the detailed laws and regulations in official publications, these accounts suggest that the formal procedures, no matter how elaborate, were frequently subverted. Readers of the novel—and people in Ming society more broadly—understood their legal system to be process-bound, bureaucratized, elaborate, and formal but also deeply flawed. The wealthy, the powerful, and the well-connected could exploit the system to their advantage. Law was not necessarily a path to justice. This does not mean that the secular legal system in Ming China lacked all legitimacy to people in that society—if that was the case then no one would ever have brought a lawsuit. Nor do the pervasive failings of the legal system mean that there was no justice in the world. But to supplement the flaws of the formal judicial process, *Plum*'s author and its readers imagined a more abstract, normative sense of justice that people in Ming China thought, or at least hoped, would eventually win out.

These themes have some echoes in China today, where concern about judicial and police corruption and about flawed proceduralism is widespread. There is an ongoing internal debate about whether the judiciary should be independent from or subject to the authority of the ruling Chinese Communist Party. The official position of the party-state is that China must find its own way to rule of law, or rule of law with Chinese characteristics, and that the principle of an independent judiciary is a Western import that is not suited to China's distinctive needs. Not everyone agrees. In a widely circulated but subsequently censored 2017 blog post, the legal scholar He Weifang cited the Judge Bao stories as evidence that the aspiration for judicial independence is rooted in Chinese tradition and history (Forsythe). One could read the discussion of legal culture in *Plum* as making a similar point from a different perspective. The judges in the novel are corrupt almost without exception; the existence of strict rules of procedure do nothing to constrain them. There is no justice in the courtroom. But this is not to say that people do not yearn for justice to be done, for the guilty to be punished, and for the legal system to protect ordinary people from arbitrary power.

The subversion of justice by money and power is of course unique neither to *Plum* nor to Ming China. Nor is its exaggerated depiction in fiction or other genres of entertainment. Students might find it interesting to think about these issues not only as they are described in a Ming novel but also in other contexts. How does the legal system of the world in which students live treat rich and poor differently? This would open up the possibility of using the novel in the classroom to discuss the complex and delicate relationship between law and justice not just long ago and far away but also in our own society today.

NOTES

I thank William Alford, Wilt Idema, Joo-hyeon Oh, Jonas Ruegg, Karen Thornber, and the students in my 2020 seminar on Ming legal history, especially Kangni Huang, Chao Lang, Dengyang Liao, Shumo Wang, and Wenyu He, for their helpful advice and comments on this essay.

[1] Extraterritoriality is the principle that foreign nationals in China should not be subject to Chinese law but rather to the laws of their own country and to trial by their compatriots. In the nineteenth century Western colonial powers and Japan forced the government of China to accept this principle.

[2] The Chinese term *gong'an* is equivalent to the Japanese term *koan*, an anecdote or riddle used in Buddhist teachings to provoke enlightenment.

[3] Unless otherwise noted, parenthetical citations refer to Roy's translation, *The Plum in the Golden Vase*, and to *Jin Ping Mei cihua* 金瓶梅詞話 (*Plum in the Golden Vase: A Ballad Tale*).

[4] The surviving legal archives of the dynasty that followed the Ming, the Qing (1644–1911), are much richer and have therefore been the subject of more research.

[5] For a more detailed introduction to Ming law, see Langlois.

[6] The courts of the underworld are also referenced indirectly on two occasions (3.51.239, 3.54.327).

APPENDIX

LEGAL CASES IN *JIN PING MEI*

More detailed case narratives are identified with an asterisk. The "Comments" column includes the applicable law, or "holding," when it is stated explicitly in the text, is especially relevant, or can be matched with the Ming code. References to the code can be found in Y. Jiang. This appendix was inspired by a table in Xu Zhongming (45–48).

ID NUMBER	CHAPTER(S)	MATTER	COMMENTS
1*	9	Homicide of Wu Zhi	Complainant: Wu Song Accused: Pan Jinlian, Ximen Qing Presiding judge: District magistrate Outcome: Case declined by presiding judge Based on *The Water Margin* Note plaintiff's use of pettifogger to write the suit
2*	9–10	Homicide of Li Waichuan	Accused: Wu Song Presiding judge: Li Tianda Reviewing judge: Chen Wenchao Applicable law: "In cases of involuntary manslaughter resulting from an affray, no matter whether the fatal injury be inflicted by hand, foot, other object, or metal blade, the penalty shall be strangulation" (compare code article 313) Outcome: Accused sentenced to death, reduced to military exile on review Reviewing judge reduces sentence on grounds of defendant's character and circumstances of crime
3	14	Dispute over inheritance of estate of Eunuch Director Hua	Complainant: Hua Ziyou et al. Accused: Hua Zixu Presiding judge: Yang Shi Outcome: Estate is ordered sold and proceeds divided up among plaintiffs
4	17–18	Dereliction of duty	Complainant (memorialist): Yuwen Xuzhong Accused (official): Cai Qing; Wang Fu, Yang Jian, and their associates, including Ximen Qing Presiding judge: Three Judicial Offices (investigation ordered by emperor) Applicable law: "Malfeasance in regard to military commands" Outcome: Wang Fu and Yang Jian impeached and sentenced to death; associates sentenced to public exposure in the cangue for one month, followed by military exile Ximen Qing arranges to have his name removed from list of those impeached Full text of impeachment memorial included
5	19	Failure to repay a debt	Complainant: Lu Hua Accused: Jiang Zhushan Presiding judge: Xia Yanling Outcome: Accused flogged and ordered to repay debt
6	20	Unknown	Accused: Family of Chen Jingji Chen Jingji was forced to take refuge in the home of his father-in-law, Ximen Qing, because of his family's involvement in this case

ID NUMBER	CHAPTER(S)	MATTER	COMMENTS
7	22	Homicide of Jiang Cong	Accused: Unnamed kitchen worker Presiding judge: Vice-magistrate Outcome: Accused is convicted of a capital crime and executed This case sets up the entry of Song Huilian into the Ximen household
8	26	Larceny	Complainant: Ximen Qing Accused: Laiwang Presiding judge: Xia Yanling Applicable law: "Servant coveting his master's property and attempting to murder him with knife in hand" (compare code article 307) Outcome: Accused sentenced to forty strokes and military exile Note repeated use of torture Ximen Qing launches this suit to get back at Laiwang, who is angry at Ximen because of Ximen's affair with Laiwang's wife, Song Huilian
9	25, 27	Unknown	Accused: Salt merchant Wang Sifeng and eleven others Outcome: Accused released
10*	26, 27	Extortion relating to suicide of Song Huilian	Complainant: Ximen Qing Accused: Song Ren (victim's father) Presiding judge: Qinghe magistrate Applicable law: "Attempting a shakedown, relying on the corpse of the deceased to extort money" Outcome: Defendant sentenced to twenty strokes, ordered to desist from his accusations This suit arises from Ximen Qing's wish to forestall Song Ren's plan to launch a suit against him for "using coercion to cause others to die" (code article 322)—that is, for pressuring Song Huilian to commit suicide
11*	33–35	Adultery between relatives	Complainant: Four local hoodlums including Che Tan Accused: Wang Liu'er and Han Ershu Presiding judge: Xia Yanling, Ximen Qing Applicable law: "In cases of fornication with . . . brother's wives, the punishment is strangulation" (code article 215) Outcome: Case dismissed Complainants ("upon whom Ximen Qing turns the tables by abusing the judicial system") threatened with "further trial" but eventually released
12	34	Illegal appropriation of timber from Imperial Lumber Depot	Accused: Company Commander Liu Presiding judge: Xia Yanling Outcome: Liu's servant Liu the Third sentenced to twenty strokes in his master's place
13*	34, 51	Illicit fornication leading to death of Ruan the Third	Complainant: Parents of Ruan the Third Accused: Ms. Chen, Ms. Chen's mother, Nun Xue Presiding judge: Xia Yanling, Ximen Qing Outcome: Ms. Chen sentenced to twenty strokes on finger-squeezers; Ms. Chen's mother convicted of action "detrimental to public morals" and sentenced to twenty strokes on finger-squeezers; Nun Xue convicted as accessory to the fact, beaten twenty strokes and ordered to return to the laity and married
14	35	Illegal appropriation of land	Accused: Xiang the Fifth Presiding judge: Military Intendant of the State Farms Circuit
15	38	Larceny	Complainant: Ximen Qing Accused: Han the Second Outcome: Accused sentenced to ankle-squeezers and twenty strokes Multiple procedural requirements are ignored in this case (probably because the complaint was brought by the presiding judge). The defendant is sentenced "without permitting any further explanation"

ID NUMBER	CHAPTER(S)	MATTER	COMMENTS
16*	47–48, 49	Homicide and robbery of Miao Tianxiu	Complainant: Antong Accused: Miao Qing, Chen the Third, Miao the Eighth Presiding judge: Ceng Xiaoxu, Shandong Regional Investigating Censor Outcome: Case dismissed This case is adapted from the late-sixteenth-century work *Baijia gong'an* 百家公案 (*The Hundred Cases [of Judge Bao]*). Dismissal of the case gives rise to the impeachment proceedings in case 18
17	48	Homicide and robbery of unknown victim	Accused: Monks of Temple of Compassionate Wisdom Presiding judge: Ceng Xiaoxu Outcome: Dismissed This case is dismissed when it is learned that the victim is Miao Tianxiu, the subject of the murder case above
18	48	Obstruction of justice	Complainant (memorialist): Ceng Xiaoxu Accused (official): Xia Yanling, Ximen Qing Outcome: Dismissed Full text of memorial of impeachment included From a legal perspective, this case is separate from the case of Miao Tianxiu, which gives rise to it
19	51	Unknown (consorting with prostitutes?)	Complainant: Defender-in-Chief Huang Jingchen Accused: Blabbermouth Sun, Pockmarked Chu, Trifler Chang, Li Guijie Outcome: Dismissed
20	67	Homicide of Feng Huai	Complainant: Feng the Second Accused: Sun Qing, Sun Wenxiang Presiding judge: Lei Qiyuan Applicable law: "Both [parties] sustained injuries as a result of their affray, and . . . the ensuing death . . . took place after the period of responsibility for the crime had already expired" (compare code article 326) Outcome: Sun Wenxiang is required to pay ten taels to cover victim's funeral expenses
21	69	Unknown	Auntie Wen is forced to sell her house due to her involvement in this suit
22	69	Inveigling young men into consorting with prostitutes	Complainant: Ximen Qing Accused: Trifler Chang and others Presiding judge: Xia Yanling, Ximen Qing Outcome: Accused are given twenty strokes, released with a warning
23	69	Extortion of Wang the Third	Complainant: Ximen Qing Accused: Trifler Chang and others Presiding judge: Ximen Qing Outcome: Accused released with a warning This may not qualify as a separate case; Trifler Chang and the others are hauled into Ximen Qing's residence, where he warns them if they do not desist he will have them incarcerated and tried
24	76	Fencing of stolen goods	Accused: He the Tenth and several thieves Presiding judge: Ximen Qing Applicable law: Fencing stolen goods Outcome: He the Tenth is released; monk from Honghua temple is arrested in place of He the Tenth on charge that he sheltered the thieves; thieves are beaten

ID NUMBER	CHAPTER(S)	MATTER	COMMENTS
25	76	Fornication between mother-in-law and son-in-law	Accused: Song De, Ms. Zhou Presiding judge: Ximen Qing Applicable law: Fornication between a son-in-law and mother-in-law, thus falling within the fifth degree of mourning relationships; the penalty for both parties is strangulation (compare code article 392) Outcome: Accused are convicted, sentenced to strangulation; case submitted for review
26	87	Beating of Jiang Menshen	Accused: Wu Song Outcome: Accused is beaten, sentenced to military exile in Anping Stockade Based on *The Water Margin*
27	87	Homicide of Jiang Menshen, Military Director Chang, and their families	Accused: Wu Song Outcome: Dismissed because of proclamation of general amnesty on appointment of heir apparent Based on *The Water Margin*
28	87–88	Homicide of Pan Jinlian and Dame Wang	Accused: Wu Song Local constabulary are too afraid of Wu Song to arrest him; magistrate puts up notice of reward for his capture, inspects corpses as required Wu Song flees to join outlaw gang
29*	90	Fornication between Zheng Wang and Sun Xue'e; larceny	Accused: Zheng Wang (also known as Laiwang), Sun Xue'e, Qu Tang Presiding judge: Magistrate Li Changqi Applicable law: Zheng Wang: servant fornicating with his employer and stealing her goods; Qu Tang: larceny Outcome: Zheng Wang convicted, sentence commuted to five years' penal exile Sun Xue'e subjected to squeezers, then arranged to be sold Qu Tang subjected to squeezers; confesses, convicted, sentence commuted to five years' military exile Goods confiscated
30	92	Larceny	Accused: Chen Jingji, Chen An Presiding judge: Prefect Xu Feng, Assistant Prefect Li Changqi Outcome: Convicted, beaten ten strokes, then punishment suspended; presiding judge investigates further; case eventually dismissed Meng Yulou and her husband, Li Gongpi, invent this accusation to rid themselves of trouble
31*	92	Death of Ximen Dajie	Complainant: Wu Yueniang Accused: Chen Jingji, Feng Jinpao Presiding judge: Qinghe magistrate Huo Dali Applicable law: Husband beats wife to death (compare code article 316) Outcome: Chen convicted, but crime reduced to coercing someone to death; sentence commuted Feng sentenced to one hundred strokes Full text of accusation appears in text Note forensic examination of corpse Judge also issues restraining order forbidding Chen from ever visiting the premises of the complainant

ID NUMBER	CHAPTER(S)	MATTER	COMMENTS
32*	94	Brawling	Complainant: Liu the Second Accused: Chen Jingji, Zheng Jinbao Presiding judge: Commandant Zhou Xiu Applicable law: Brawling (compare code article 14) Outcome: Chen Jingji sentenced to twenty strokes and revoking of his ordination certificate Zheng Jinbao sentenced to fifty blows on the squeezers and returned to the brothel Chen's punishment interrupted halfway, through the intervention of the commandant's wife Cheng seems to be sent back to the brothel without a beating This case was manufactured by Liu the Second, who was angry at Chen Jingji for consorting with the singing-girl Cheng; although the complaint appears to have been for brawling, Judge Chou also holds Chen accountable When Abbot Ren learns that he is also going to be held accountable for his disciple's misdeeds, he dies of fright
33	95	Theft	Complainant: Longfoot Wu Accused: Ping'an Presiding judge (?): Police Chief Wu Dian'en Wu is not empowered to hear cases, which leads to the next case
34	95	Larceny	Complainant: Wu Yueniang Accused: Police Chief Wu Dian'en Presiding judge: Commandant Zhou Xiu Outcome: Accused confesses; case dismissed with a warning
35	98	Theft	Complainant: Chen Jingji Accused: Yang Guangyan and Yang Erfeng Presiding judge: Provincial Surveillance Commission judges Outcome: Accused are convicted, sentenced to be beaten, incarcerated, and ordered to make good the stolen property
36	98	Dereliction of duty (?)	Complainant (memorialist): Chen Tung Accused (official): Cai Jing and five other officials Outcome: Accused are impeached, stripped of office, sentenced to military conscription and exile; Cai Jing's son is executed and his property confiscated
37	99	Homicide of Chen Jingji	Complainant: Li An Accused: Zhang Sheng Presiding judge: Commandant Zhou Xiu Outcome: Accused is convicted, sentenced to one hundred strokes of the bamboo; beating leads to his death Commandant takes advantage of the case to also order the arrest and execution of Liu the Second
Supernatural Court Cases			
38	62	Unknown	Complainant: Unknown spirit Accused: Li Ping'er
Jokes Involving Court Cases Real or Supernatural			
39	35	Illicit sexual intercourse	Joke told by Ben the Fourth about a magistrate interrogating a suspect
40	51	Unknown	Joke told by Ximen Qing about King Yama turning a dead man into a donkey; assessors discover that he still has years allotted to his life, therefore he is returned to the land of the living
41	54	Unknown	Joke told by Ying Bojue about King Yama investigating a dead man's claims to have been a vegetarian

Nation, Brand, Afterlives:
The Plum in the Golden Vase in
Early-Twentieth-Century China

Y. Yvon Wang

The Plum in the Golden Vase (*Jin Ping Mei* 金瓶梅) has reappeared in some surprising forms since its debut as a manuscript in the luxurious studies of late-sixteenth-century gentlemen-scholars. An examination of the novel's unexpected reincarnations raises important questions about the relationship between literature and politics: How have canonical literature and modern ideas about nations, identities, and desires shaped one another? How have governments, markets, scholarly experts, and readers conceived of and enforced (sometimes contradictory) ideas about what should and should not count as literature?

In Shanghai, which was under Japanese occupation during World War II, *Plum* was illustrated as a multivolume comic book, combining art nouveau elegance, folk-art simplicity, and titillating nudity (Stember). During a meeting in 1957, likely during the short-lived Hundred Flowers campaign of political, social, and cultural critique launched by Mao Zedong 毛澤東 (1893–1976), the chairman himself said that "*Plum* can be used for reference; it's just the parts disrespecting women that are bad. The Party Secretaries of each province can take a look" (qtd. in Cai 63). In 1993 a journalist and rising *Plum* researcher and two collaborators were arrested for making 2,800 unlicensed copies of an unexpurgated early edition of the novel (He 297–99). They planned to sell each for up to 150 percent of one month's pay for the average worker (National Statistics Bureau). In the twenty-first century, *Plum*'s permutations seem to have mushroomed ever more rapidly: in early 2004 a Nanjing chain restaurant offered a *Plum*-themed banquet at a range of prices up to about one hundred US dollars to attract families and even tourists from Hong Kong during the Lunar New Year holiday ("*Jin Ping Mei* yan liangxiang Nanjing"). In 2006 *Learning Management from Ximen Qing: Breaking the Code of* Plum in the Golden Vase (*Guanli xiang Ximen Qing xuexi: Pojie* Jin Ping Mei *mima* 管理向西門慶學習:破解金瓶梅密碼) went on sale on amazon.cn.

In short, *Plum* has been a powerful, profitable brand name in China's cultural marketplace—even though unexpurgated copies of the book remain difficult for readers outside officialdom to access on mainland China. Moreover, as this volume exemplifies, the novel is increasingly recognized as an emblem of Chinese cultural tradition abroad, a position it has held for decades among literary specialists (Link). But at the heart of *Plum*'s enduring power as China's very own great novel is something even more difficult to embrace than the book's enormous scale, its sometimes patchy plot, or its myriad allusions: it is, instead, the novel's wide-ranging, lurid descriptions of sex.

Without a doubt, *Plum* is not only a pornographic book. Its literary merits and rich documenting of late imperial material life are indisputable; by raw numbers, those passages regarded by some as objectionable occupy only a little over nineteen thousand characters—about three percent of the book (Yang Muzhi).[1] Yet it is this salacious sliver of *Plum* that has, since the turn of the twentieth century, made the book into a commercial brand at home and a representative of traditional Chinese civilization around the world. The book's role in the reinvention of China from an all-under-heaven empire to part of a global assembly of competing nations is inseparable from its licentiousness.

Plum's story at the turn of the twentieth century is the tale of complex and at times contradictory interactions among an accelerating and expanding media market, the quest for a unique national culture, and struggles, both open and violent as well as more subtle, for cultural authority. In the transition between empire and republic, these conjoined forces made *Plum* into a text of national heritage as well as a brand that was more profitable than ever. Despite the avowedly revolutionary sociopolitical goals of the Chinese Communist Party and its efforts to control media—including sexually explicit imperial fiction—that was deemed politically incorrect and socially destabilizing, patterns and trends set in motion for *Plum* in the years before the party's victory in 1949 seem to have continued to this day. After the late 1970s, with individuals again free to openly pursue profit and the post-socialist state clinging to legitimacy in the relatively ideologically neutered terms of Chinese nationalism and modernity, *Plum* has once more become one of the most lucrative brand names in the Chinese canon.

The Late Imperial Canonization of Plum

Plum in the Golden Vase first became a powerful presence in the Chinese cultural landscape well before the twentieth century. The novel began its career in the ranks of the empire's top cultural celebrities, but it soon escaped their orbit. The trickling down of *Plum* during the final imperial dynasties to less-than-elite audiences through print markets was central to the novel's enduring appeal throughout the upheavals of the twentieth century. Through adaptions into other genres, *Plum* became a byword for all things licentious (*yin* 淫) in late imperial China. The fact that *Plum* became known as a dirty book across the social spectrum—among the highest officials and best-known men of letters as well as among ordinary villagers—made elite readers eager to defend their taking pleasure in the novel. Educated commentators argued that their aesthetic insights insulated them from the filthiness of the text, making their enjoyment totally different from that of the country folk, who suppressed giggles and arousal as they watched traveling actors reenact the amorous exchanges of Pan Jinlian (P'an Chin-lien) and Ximen Qing (Hsi-men Ch'ing).

Throughout the four hundred years that followed, this text—and more importantly, the idea of this text—passed into the hands (as well as the ears and eyes) of enthusiastic consumers. Many early elite readers of *Plum* wrung their hands about the novel's potential to corrupt less sophisticated audiences even as such elite readers lauded the novel as extraordinary.[2] But nearly as soon as the book was circulated in manuscript, its plotlines and characters were translated into dramatic, visual, and oral storytelling forms that began to traverse the boundaries of region and class. *Plum* has been the basis for at least a dozen adaptations into different narrative and performance genres, including opera and short songs; the earliest sequel to *Plum*, starring reincarnated versions of the protagonists, dates to the 1640s.[3] Literati who continued to buy, borrow, and read *Plum* during the late Ming (ca. 1590–1644) and Qing (1644–1911) periods repeatedly defended the book and their own connoisseurship of its artistic sophistication and moral significance, contrasting this with what they believed to be *Plum's* corruptive influence on the ignorant masses. The karmic retribution met by the cast of characters was supposed to be a warning against following their paths; going one step farther, the late-seventeenth-century scholar Zhang Zhupo claimed that it was written as a tool of filial vengeance, its intoxicating pages literally smeared with poison to kill a corrupt official (Epstein 48–49; N. Ding 120–24).

A moral reading of *Plum* was problematic, however, because the book's ethical thrust and even its alleged use as righteous assassination weapon hinged on its extensive, explicit depictions of sexual excess. Late imperial consumers of *Plum*, operating in a milieu in which elites were assumed to be more culturally discriminating than non-elites, could use this hierarchy to insulate themselves from the self-contradictions inherent in their enjoyment of the novel. By the first years of the twentieth century, however, it became increasingly difficult to take this superiority for granted because of the rise of two linked ideas: first, the value of popular culture as the counterpart of participatory politics and, second, the notion of sexuality in its modern sense—dictated by evolutionary biology as *the* foundation of a universal human nature on which identity, family, society, and the state rested.

The Problem and Promise of Plum *for the New Culture Movement*

The year 1912 heralded the final demise of the Qing monarchy and the enshrinement of a Chinese nation whose territory was no longer to be the patrimony of an imperial clan but instead the shared property of individuals bearing the privileges and responsibilities of citizenship.[4] After World War I, urban intellectuals called for a New Culture in which science, democracy, and other Enlightenment values would supersede the old, Confucianist thinking associated with the imperial past. These political and intellectual transformations had been emerging for at least an entire generation. Late Qing state and society had begun to adapt to the incursions of foreign powers as well as to the demands of imperial subjects for change.[5]

Emancipating what was understood as a more natural sexuality was a central objective for late Qing and early Republican political and social reformers. Arranged marriages and the oppression of women by means of foot-binding, sequestration, and expectations of chaste widowhood were, to these reformers, leading examples of Chinese backwardness. By contrast, the mingling of the sexes and the free pursuit of heterosexual romance were taken as the hallmarks of modern civility and progress. The agitation of these reformers, known as the New Culturalists, for a different view of sexuality, gender, and family left institutional and ideological legacies that are still evident in the twenty-first century. Nevertheless, many facets of Republican Chinese society and culture, from people's everyday routines to the actual workings of political, economic, and military power, continued precedents from the Qing. Most leading figures among reformers, even the self-appointed iconoclasts of the New Culture movement, were not sexual anarchists. They considered a heterosexual, reproductive, monogamous couple most natural and therefore ideal. In this as in many other regards, the New Culturalists were perhaps less icon-smashers than they were icon-replacers.[6]

The tension between old and new was deeply felt and of central concern for many in this era of transition, and evaluations of *Plum in the Golden Vase* by leading commentators reflected the depth of this tension. *Plum* continued to be praised for its artistic value: Lu Xun 魯迅—the pen name of the iconic writer, translator, and critic Zhou Shuren 周樹人 (1881–1936)—declared the novel's panoply of narrative devices and piquant, detailed social critique to be "unsurpassed by any other fiction of its time" (同時說部, 無以上之; my trans.; "Ming zhi renqing xiaoshuo" 686). Like late imperial literati, early-twentieth-century critics understood *Plum* as a moral piece. However, out of profound concern for the future of their polity, many in the late Qing and early Republic emphasized *Plum*'s ability not just to admonish individuals but also to rescue and simultaneously define the Chinese nation.

In 1917, Chen Duxiu 陳獨秀 (1879–1942), then the dean of Peking University (the institutional heart of the New Culture movement) as well as the founder of *New Youth* (*Xin qingnian* 新青年), the movement's flagship publication, wrote of *Plum* to his colleague and ally, Hu Shi 胡適 (1891–1962), calling the book "refreshing, healthy, and natural" in its "description of the evil [old] society" down to "every detail" (此書描寫惡社會 ... 無微不至; my trans.; qtd. in Zhong 48). One of Chen and Hu's colleagues at the university, Zheng Zhenduo 鄭振鐸 (1898–1958), who included *Plum* in his edited series of world literature, likewise concluded that the book was "an exceptionally noble masterpiece" because it revealed the "naked, uninhibited expression of the sickness in Chinese society" (一部很偉大的寫實小說, 赤裸裸的毫無忌憚的表現著中國社會的病態; my trans.; 73, 75).

In an age when the old hierarchies of legitimacy seemed no longer tenable, the New Culturalists' praise of *Plum* also served as part of their bid for cultural authority. Like Ming-Qing literati fans of *Plum*, Chen, Zheng, and their allies argued that it took a special kind of insight to see the merits of the book beyond its sexual depictions; by implication, they were possessed of this insight. As Qian Xuantong 錢玄同 (1887–1939), another prominent member of the New Culture circle, put it, "If we cast aside all conventional notions and use only the eyes of literature to observe it, then *Plum in the Golden Vase* certainly is also among the first rank" (若拋棄一切世俗見解, 專用文學的眼光去觀察, 則《金瓶梅》之位置亦在第一流也), but, unfortunately, "in those days in which morality had not yet evolved and bestial fleshly desires were still so powerful" (往昔道德未進化, 獸性肉慾猶極強烈之時), writers devoted their attention to salacious details, and readers also focused their reading on these passages; immature youths "were especially poisoned" (尤受其毒; my trans.).

What was more, *Plum*'s age, length, and complexity could be compared favorably to the fiction of other nations, especially as the vernacular, realistic novel became the preeminent genre of literary modernity. From the late Qing through the early Republic, reformers and conservatives alike saw salvaging national tradition as essential to claiming China's place in the modern world, and *Plum* was rapidly becoming one of the best-known pieces of that tradition. As Yang Jiyun noted, "If China has anything that could be said to be a realistic novel, then *Plum in the Golden Vase* is the first. Its value is no less than Hugo's *Les Misérables*, Charles Dickens's *Oliver Twist* and Zola's *Nana*" (如果中國夠得上稱有寫實小說的話, 金瓶梅實是第一部, 其價值當不下於囂俄的孤星淚, 卻爾斯迭更斯的賊史, 和左拉的娜娜; my trans.; 59–60). Commentators lauded the book as a venerable example of the very type of literature that cultural reformers were calling for: "On one hand, it looks like we are debating, promoting, and innovating [in popular-language literature], but on the other hand, we have had [such literature] since long ago" (一方面看來是正在討論, 提倡, 發端 [大眾語文學];一方面我們卻早已有了; my trans.; 59).

But for all *Plum*'s merits, it could not shake the infamy of its catalog of sex acts, or "unclean descriptions" (不乾淨的描寫), as Zheng Zhenduo dubbed them. This was not merely because these descriptions were so numerous that they resembled "summertime flies, refusing to scatter no matter how one swats at them" (夏天的蒼蠅似的, 驅拂不盡; my trans.; 75). That had, of course, been just as true in the early seventeenth century as it was in the twentieth. Instead, precisely because Zheng and his New Culture comrades had linked the open discussion of love and sex to democracy, science, and modernity itself, they were less able than ever before to swat away *Plum*'s flies, so to speak. Unlike late imperial commentators, who operated in a world where the hierarchies of cultural authority were taken for granted, the New Culturalist readers of *Plum*, by paying homage to egalitarianism, risked being condemned as moralizing feudal hypocrites if they tried to downplay *Plum*'s teeming eroticism. As putatively natural sexuality gradually became more visible than ever in the urban cultural and commercial life of Republican China as well as widely discussed across academic and artistic disciplines, attempts to read positive aesthetic and political value into *Plum* grew likewise more precarious.

Plum *as Best-Selling Brand*

If we turn to a view of *Plum* focused on ground-level media markets and consumers, the records of early Republican law enforcement suggest a real expansion of the cultural egalitarianism that New Culturalists argued for—though not always in ways that they would have condoned. Late Qing China already possessed lucrative, extensive markets for books and images; in the fin de siècle, new technologies like the lithograph enhanced the power of this trade. Treaty ports and foreign concessions, established through accords with foreign powers, gave producers and distributors a degree of legal cover from censorious authorities, whether imperial or Republican. All these factors enabled *Plum*, in increasingly diverse formats, to reach ever-greater numbers of consumers and to become synonymous with the erotic to a degree that had not been seen before. But the rapid and extensive circulation of *Plum* in the Republican era was not simply a continuation of the trickle-down process that took place in the Ming and Qing. The acceleration and growth of media markets in the late Qing and Republican periods were unprecedented, and, in tandem with the race to define a uniquely Chinese national literary canon and new frameworks for thinking about sexuality, cemented *Plum*'s place as a patriotic cultural brand name. At the same time, the collision of new ideas with more sophisticated networks and tools for conveying those ideas enabled a wider range of individual consumers to use the newly empowered language of sexuality, democracy, and nationalism to defend their own enjoyment of *Plum*. The demand of non-elite consumers for *Plum* also contributed to making the book an emblematic part of the Chinese cultural landscape.

In higher-end urban book markets, there was much continuity between the late Qing and the Republican period. Late imperial woodblock editions of *Plum* remained available on a semicovert basis in antique dealers' stocks, as they had long been. Rare, high-quality recensions were desirable enough to command high prices. Those with money could still find *Plum* in the shops of Beijing's Liulichang neighborhood, renowned since the eighteenth century for expert bookdealers who formed close relationships with cultivated, wealthy patrons. Yet securing a genuine late imperial copy of *Plum* remained a measure of bookhunting skill. Seeking *Plum* could even count as a part of a collector's connoisseurial education. As the editor and bibliophile Zhou Yueran 周越然 (1885–1962) put it, because "this book is sold secretly and bought in silence, so that you are necessarily duped many a time before securing a rare edition," those who successfully bought a valuable edition of *Plum* "will definitely have no trouble acquiring serious classics and histories" (因此書偷偷而賣, 默默而買, 獲得善本者非

經過多次 "上當" 不可.... 有購《金瓶梅》之經驗且得到善本者, 其求取正經正史 絕無困難; my trans.; ("Yu zhi" 284–85).

Indeed, Zhou's first brush with *Plum* in the early 1930s was likely representative of how the high-end Republican markets in which *Plum* was bought and sold functioned: an intimate, expensive, homosocial dance between customer and seller, pitting profit against discernment. One day, when he was still at a stage where he could only stand before bookshelves "gazing dumbly" (向架上呆看), Zhou asked a bookseller for a copy of *Plum* and was queried in return, "Is that the kind of book that I can just pull out for you in the open like that?" (這種書 可在大庭廣眾中拿出來麼?). Instead, the merchant delivered the book in person to Zhou's home the next day. Quoted a hefty 160 yuan (about one hundred times the price of a brand-new popular romance or martial-arts novel at the time), Zhou paid immediately.[7] Two months later, the same dealer appeared at Zhou's door with another copy of *Plum*: "Sir, that one you bought earlier is on good paper but there are lots of wrong characters. It's not nearly as nice as this one. Look at this picture" (先生, 你從前購的, 紙張雖好, 訛字很多, 不及這一部好. 你看這個圖), the dealer said, pointing at one of the novel's more explicit illustrations, "isn't it nice?" (好不好?). The asking price was a staggering six hundred yuan; eventually, Zhou bargained the man down to 450 yuan. Zhou's triumph was short-lived, as he recollected with rue; afterward, he learned that the market price for that edition was at most 250 yuan (my trans.; "Yu zhi" 283–84).

While highbrow buyers' focus on provenance, condition, and authenticity perpetuated the old, intimate networks of *Plum*'s circulation, the role of middle- and lowbrow buyers was at least as crucial in making a durable brand out of the novel. In turn, it was the novel's (in)famous reputation and the eagerness with which consumers pursued it that created opportunities for wily media marketers to charge high prices for inferior editions or, better yet for their bottom lines, sell items only tenuously related to *Plum*.

Learning to see through sellers' tricks was not just a central part of the connoisseurial education described by Zhou but also a common hurdle at all tiers of the media market. Sellers freely spliced together the contents of different books in unauthorized compilations; a book might appear under a new name if it were not selling well. Longer books might be rebound and sold as separate titles to maximize profit.[8] Moreover, the more widespread use of new print technologies in the Republican era directly affected the prices of older editions. Not all pre-Republican copies of *Plum* available on the early-twentieth-century market were such luxuries as those sought after by Zhou. Lithography and modern movable type could replicate text and images with great crispness and speed; even small-format books could now have uniformly printed characters and clear punctuation that made them easier to transport and easier to read—not to mention more affordable. By spurring a proliferation of new editions of the text, these state-of-the-art technologies greatly accelerated the pace of *Plum*'s assimilation as a cultural brand.

It was because of movable type that the first twentieth-century version of *Plum*, based on a late Qing edition from which the most graphic passages had been removed, appeared in 1916 (He 452). As early as 1920 consumers could buy the book in "foreign binding" (*yangzhuang* 洋裝), likely thicker volumes with a glued (if paperback) or sewn (if hardcover) spine, as opposed to thinner paperback fascicles with traditional thread binding (Beijing Municipal Police [BMP], file number J181-019-57016). This did not mean that the old format was necessarily incompatible with new print technologies: in 1921 a lithographic press in Shanghai released an unexpurgated, thread-bound version that included Zhang Zhupo's commentary and late imperial woodblock illustrations. A copy of a woodblock-printed edition from the Wanli era (1572–1620), the oldest known complete version of the novel, was discovered in 1931 and sold for a princely sum to the Beiping Library,[9] but the Republic's biggest publishing houses soon put out censored, typeset versions of this edition that were much more affordable, giving *Plum* pride of place in book series intended to popularize and reinforce a national canon like the "Rare Books of National Studies" (國學珍本叢書) and the "Library of Precious Literature" (文學珍本文庫; He 455). In a vast array of formats, *Plum* continued to suffuse the market in the 1930s, as advertisements in Shanghai's prominent *Shenbao* newspaper reveal; one could purchase *Plum* in a single volume or more than twenty; a cheap new copy at one of more than a dozen established bookshops might cost as little as one-tenth of a finer edition (Zhao and Zhao 179). Zhou confirms this trend: by 1935, new reprints of *Plum* could be bought for just twelve yuan, triggering a drop in the prices of late Qing editions with cheaply made illustrations or no illustrations at all to only sixteen or twenty yuan apiece; meanwhile, "miniature" (袖珍) versions could be had for a mere eight yuan ("Yu zhi" 284).

What was more, these myriad editions only represented the legally published and more or less complete versions of the novel, selling at prices affordable by people of at least middling means. Legally published editions from known publishers were only a small part of the Republican-era market for *Plum*. Early-twentieth-century police files from Beijing recording the arrests of book peddlers for selling untoward titles suggest that those in Republican China who were less well-off also craved a taste of *Plum*, which they could get through the many titles that riffed on the original in addition to various versions of the text itself. Again, the pursuit by nameless middle- and working-class consumers of these low-end print goods claiming to be *Plum in the Golden Vase* and its sequels did at least as much as favorable appraisals by connoisseurial enthusiasts to consecrate the novel's canonical position in Chinese literature.

Nestled in crates hung from shoulder poles and in sacks slung over shoulders, set out on the ground on busy streets and in crowded markets, most of these down-market editions of *Plum* were created by unlicensed, small-time printers and sold by street-side vendors. It is hard to say for sure what titles like *Interesting Tales of the New* Plum in the Golden Vase (*Xin* Jin Ping Mei *qushi* 新金瓶梅趣史), located by police among a vendor's wares in 1922, actually contained. But we do know that this particular seller, a fifty-two-year-old man named Liu, was of humble background and probably low literacy: he was from a village a dozen miles outside Beijing and had started his life in the city as a household servant.

The fact that such dealers sold books purporting to be *Plum* at very low prices—in this case, between five and seven strands of copper coins, about 0.5 to 0.7 yuan—suggests just how well-known and lucrative a brand name *Plum* had become by the early twentieth century (BMP, file number J181-019-35958). A host of similar cases confirm the variety of spin-offs of *Plum* available on Republican Beijing's low-end print market and the tenacity with which sellers trafficked them. Sixty-two-year-old Gao Jie, from the capital's suburbs, was caught hawking *New* Plum in the Golden Vase (*Xin* Jin Ping Mei 新金瓶梅), which he carried in a box on his back along with ten other titles that law enforcement deemed salacious (J181-019-22190); the police of Japanese-occupied Beijing detained Lang Baoqi, an unmarried, unemployed twenty-six-year-old ex-chauffeur living with his parents in 1938, when he was caught trying to sell nine volumes of *Addenda to* Plum in the Golden Vase (Jin Ping Mei *buyi* 金瓶梅補遺) to a bookstall near his home (J181-023-04473).

These men were uniformly aware of the demand for *Plum* despite their likely inability to read more than simple texts, and they pursued the novel and its spin-offs as opportunities to make a profit despite the risk of confiscation, detention, and fines. Liu told police interrogators that he had begun selling books in 1909 at various night markets and claimed that he had acquired his "licentious books" (淫書) from a "box-carrying bookseller" (背箱賣書人) earlier that year because his own stock had not been selling well. He had his two copies of *Interesting Tales* confiscated and his fine of three yuan changed to three days' detention because he could not afford to pay (BMP, file number J181-019-35958). Gao received four days for the same reason; meanwhile, the hapless Lang, who confessed that his father had told him that the *Addenda to* Plum were "licentious" (淫) and had ordered him to burn them, was detained for a full week (J181-019-22190; J181-023-04473). Some unlucky enough to be punished for peddling *Plum* and other so-called licentious books nevertheless persisted, like twenty-five-year-old Zhang Peilin, hailing from the forested hills of Ji County about sixty miles east of the capital (J181-019-22193). Police files indicate that Zhang, who ran a relatively well-appointed shop in the bustling Dong'an Market, an enclosed shopping center with both fixed retail shops and transient hawkers, was first brought in for interrogation in mid-December 1918 with a large trove of books for rent and sale, including late imperial titles well known for explicit sexual detail like *Candlestick Monk* (*Dengcao heshang* 燈草和尚). Despite a lengthy interrogation, Zhang was arrested again less than six months later in the same Dong'an shop, this time for carrying *Plum*. Judging that he "clearly knew" the book to be "licentious," the authorities confiscated it and detained him for five days (J181-019-29847).

In much the same way as the common experience of reading the novel had been a homosocial bond among late imperial literati, using *Plum*'s reputation for profit was apparently a common experience among early-twentieth-century Beijing's hundreds of low-end booksellers, most of whom were sojourners known as bare sticks, men without land, property, or wives, viewed by Chinese law and law enforcement as the default criminal type from the imperial era into the twenty-first century.[10] These men, coming to Beijing from across the capital's hinterlands as well as more distant areas of the coalescent nation like Anhui or Shandong, seem to have formed a social network of sorts around the selling of *Plum* and similar books (BMP, file number J181-019-57016; J181-019-22193). Though *Plum* was not found in Zhang Peilin's shop after his initial arrest in 1918, his testimony set off a chain of investigations that brought eight colleagues scattered in markets and bookstall-dense neighborhoods around Beijing under police scrutiny. Investigators subsequently discovered multiple copies of books labeled as *Plum in the Golden Vase* at three of these retailers and found Zhang himself carrying *Plum* just a few months later. These petty merchants tended to cluster in proximity to one another, as seen in the case of those turned in by Zhang Peilin: while police rifled through one stall in the enclosed Qingyunge Market, a neighboring seller, hearing the commotion, tried to hide one of his own books but was caught in the act. The members of book-peddling networks were not only competitors but also business partners; some were even related. Two of the men implicated by Zhang were brothers who had opened one of the earliest permanent bookshops in Dong'an Market. They seem to have been prosperous enough that their franchise included at least three locations. Peddlers furthermore worked with printers and larger-scale distributors. Under interrogation, some dealers described how Beijing print shops used letterpresses to replicate the products of other cities, especially Shanghai, where extraterritoriality created an overlapping legal situation that provided some shelter to those avoiding official scrutiny. Persistent plainclothes officers following these leads turned up many offending typeset blocks on the premises of one such print shop and bookstore (BMP, file number J181-019-22193).

The buyer's side of the story for cheap books marketed as *Plum in the Golden Vase* is less clear. Very few consumers appear in the case record, and middle- or working-class fans—as far as we know—did not leave chapter-by-chapter annotations or memoirs about their experiences like their literati counterparts did. By the early twentieth century, however, *Plum* had become such a ready synonym for eroticism that it was used as a way to contextualize the foreign and the unfamiliar for Republican China's domestic consumers, even as the book was also being newly reproduced in Western-imported formats, and even as its characters and plotline had been journeying to the West since at least the early nineteenth century.

Plum: *A Chinese Brand for the World*

In 1816 Jean-Pierre Abel-Rémusat, the first chair of sinology at the Collège de France, wrote that he "knew only by reputation" ("je ne connais que de réputation cet ouvrage") of *Plum* as a "famous novel said to be in its licentiousness above, or, to put it better, beneath any that corrupted Rome or that are produced in modern Europe" ("un roman célèbre, qu'on dit au-dessus, ou pour mieux dire au-dessous de tout ce que Rome corrompue et l'Europe moderne ont produit de plus licencieux"; my trans.; 59). An early-nineteenth-century copy of *Plum* featuring Zhang Zhupo's commentary was added to the British Library's holdings in 1856 (Liu Cunren 168–69), and the earliest known European-language translation of the entire novel, based on the early-eighteenth-century Manchu version, was completed between 1862 and 1869 by the German aristocrat and linguist Hans Conon von der Gabelentz and his son, the far more famous sinologist Hans Georg Conon von der Gabelentz.[11] As scholars have recently begun to explore in greater depth, European contact with the erotic cultures of places like China, the Middle East, and India was central to the emergence of sexology—a modern science of sexuality that viewed erotic feelings and behaviors as the most primal and universal aspects of human identity. More than ever, the scientific epistemology of sexology opened these fundamental drives, which belonged to each individual citizen, to government scrutiny and regulation, in symbiosis with the transition from monarchies to nation-states. As described by theorists like Michel Foucault, the formation of modern sexuality was a messy process in which ideas, textual commodities, and canons moved in sometimes circular patterns. While *Plum* was not solely responsible for catalyzing the rise of sexology, it was certainly one of the cultural mediators essential to the global ascendance of sexual science, which brought with it new notions of sexual nature and ideas about sexual citizenship.

From at least the 1910s, middle- and lowbrow media merchants began carrying sexology books—or at least publications that used the terms of sexual science, like *Mandatory Knowledge for Sexual Hygiene* (*Nannü weisheng xuzhi* 男女衛生須知)—alongside *Plum in the Golden Vase* (BMP, file number J181-019-22193). The provenance of many sexological titles is nearly impossible to trace for the same reasons that the contents of the spin-offs of *Plum* found in book peddlers' stocks are uncertain: dealers altered titles and freely made private printings in an effort to make more money and avoid detection. Even official advertisements by licensed publishers evidenced the interchangeability between self-consciously modern sexological tracts and distinctly traditional erotic fiction. Books like *Chunü weisheng lun* 處女衛生論 (*A Treatise on the Hygiene of Virgins*) were said to supply "richness and concentration of flavor and precision of scholarship truly beyond the wildest dreams of the conventional mind" (qtd. in Zhang Zhongmin 159).[12] Nonetheless, at least some of the scientifically flavored books confiscated from street-side vendors were based on state-of-the-art sexological texts freshly translated from Japanese, German, and English.

A survey conducted by a Beijing-based, politically progressive periodical of its young readers' favorite books in the mid-1920s suggests that Republican consumers, even New Culture followers, found late imperial novels with romantic and sexual content like *Plum* and translated imports dealing with similar topics, like the British-born eugenics and contraception advocate Marie Stopes's *Married Love,* to be of comparable interest. In fact, old fiction seems to have been far more popular than newfangled sexology was. *The Story of the Stone* (*Hong-lou meng* 紅樓夢), an eighteenth-century novel repeatedly condemned as licentious by Qing authorities (Sommer, "Scandal"), appeared on 183 of 308 ballots; *Married Love* was named on just twenty-four. Though only thirteen readers around the country claimed *Plum* as a favorite, that score put the novel on par with *The Works of Henrik Ibsen*, whose titular author, the Norwegian playwright, was much admired by the New Culturalists.[13]

Further reflecting the experiences of readers who moved among late imperial fiction, sexual science, and treatments of sexuality in modern fiction are the memoirs of the sociologist Pan Guangdan 潘光旦 (1898–1967), who translated the monumental *Studies in the Psychology of Sex*, by the pioneering British sexologist Havelock Ellis. In his preface to the translation, Pan relates his experiences as a curious child in the 1910s and 1920s who had sought out books about "sexual questions" (性的問題). Dissatisfied with "the odd bit of hearsay" (偶有聞見) from peers and unable to consult his elders, he turned to print, of which "eight or nine out of ten were traditional novels that had to do with sex and love. . . . From around age ten to age twenty or so, I remember looking at truly a lot of such things" (十之八九是性愛的說部 . . . 記得在十歲前後, 到二十歲的光景, 這一類的東西著實看得不少; my trans.; 205).

As books claiming to be *Plum*—licensed and unauthorized, cleaned of explicit language or not—continued to multiply on Republican markets, *Plum* became a way to directly translate sexology and other erotic imports from the West. Shortly after the end of World War II, Shanghai law enforcement found mail-order books with "licentious Western portraits" (淫蕩西像)—photographs, that is—that were being advertised as "ten times as rakish as *Plum in the Golden Vase*" (比金瓶梅風流十倍; Shanghai Social Bureau [SSB], file number Q6-12-170-39) as well as advertisements for book dealers that listed *Western* Plum in the Golden Vase (*Xiyang* Jin Ping Mei 西洋金瓶梅) alongside *The Best of* Plum in the Golden Vase (Jin Ping Mei *jinghua lu* 金瓶梅精華錄), presumably a selection of choice passages (Q6-12-170-14).

The application of *Plum* to foreign titles as a synonym for explicit writing was not limited to low-end media markets and the police who regulated them. *Plum* had also become a byname for infamously explicit Western books among intelligentsia and in the press of the 1930s and 1940s. For instance, a newspaper column about peddlers selling "Western-translated *Plum in the Golden Vase*" (西譯金瓶梅) on the streets became a tip for Shanghai police in 1946 (SSB, file number Q6-12-170-14). Following details recounted in the article, investigators seized a large batch of explicit foreign novels frequently banned in the West, including D. H. Lawrence's *Lady Chatterley's Lover* and Henry Miller's *Tropic of Cancer*. The Chinese vendors, some hailing from cities as distant as Fuzhou, claimed that they had ordered these books from some Jews and White Russians. Evidently, "Western-translated *Plum*" did not signify translations of that novel into non-Chinese languages but instead books understood to be of comparable content and status. The prominent translator and writer Lin Yutang 林語堂 (1895–1976), for instance, penned a short essay in the form of a dialogue, in which one speaker asks the other how D. H. Lawrence differs from *Plum in the Golden Vase*. The other replies, "*Plum in the Golden Vase* is bold and has high technique, but it's different from Lawrence—I naturally am speaking of *Lady Chatterley's Lover*. Lawrence is also bold and has high technique, but it is a different sort of technique" (金瓶梅有大膽, 有技巧, 但與勞倫斯不同—我自然是在講他的《查泰萊夫人的情人》. 勞倫斯也有大膽, 也有技巧, 但是不同的技巧; my trans.; 311).

Plum was not merely compared to or used to translate foreign flavors of eroticism; in the early decades of the twentieth century, as China seemed to languish in the grip of war, poverty, and natural disaster, *Plum* emerged as a rallying point for Chinese cultural nationalism on the international stage; it remains such today. As Zhou Yueran wrote in a 1944 essay titled "Waiguo *Jin Ping Mei*" 外國金瓶梅 ("Foreign *Plum in the Golden Vase*"), the novel "is a Chinese specialty—a monumental work of lovely prose, the grandest licentious book" (是中國的特產—是一部文章極美的巨作, 是一部篇幅最大的淫書). Zhou maintained, moreover, that "Western and Eastern society are of such different situations, how could they [Westerners] possibly write a *Plum in the Golden Vase*" (東西洋的社會情形這樣不同, 他們那裡能夠寫金瓶梅)? Westerners, having taken a great interest in "our life, and our society—especially in ancient times" (他們西洋人很喜歡研究我們的生活, 我們的社會情形—尤其是古代的), had already produced multiple translations of *Plum*, but the book "is a creative work, and a Chinese person was its creator" (是創作, 創作金瓶梅者是中國人; my trans.; 77). Thus, Zhou concluded triumphantly, the West would now and forever lack its own *Plum*.

It was *Plum*'s potent presence in late imperial and early Republican print markets that gave it a representative position in the literary canon, and it is that prominence that has in turn allowed *Plum* to so frequently stand for all things explicit. *Plum*'s synonymy with pornography has made it a ready translator for foreign works of explicit sexual content, and it is because *Plum* has been through such comparisons with the non-Chinese that this sixteenth-century novel has become the cultural touchstone it is today, a powerful brand name with an appeal that is both pornographic and patriotic. Perhaps the insistence on "setting up literary civilizations as rivals," as Perry Link points out, "only gets in the way of readers enjoying imaginative works." But our contemporary world order, from markets to national governments, has been built on repeated attempts by peoples to defensively stake out claims on their unique cultural greatness, and moving beyond this defensiveness will not be easy, as long as translations are made.

NOTES

[1] In 1985 the People's Literary Publishing House edition deleted 19,174 characters; subsequent editions removed as few as 4,300 characters—less than one percent of the entire text.

[2] For the gendered cultural politics of literati commentaries and scholarship on *Plum*, see N. Ding, especially chapters 5–7 (144–223).

[3] For examples of opera and folk ditties based on *Plum*, see Hu Wenbing 271–76 and Huang Lin 73–74; Hou and Wang's compendium of *Plum*-related materials reprints several prefaces to the sequel (459–60).

[4] For two volumes of scholarly essays that address this key transition, see Fogel and Zarrow; Goldman and Perry.

[5] See, for instance, David Wang's work on the late Qing as an era of "repressed modernities."

[6] For the new discourse of sexuality, see, for example, Diköter; for the sometimes ironic degree to which self-professed radicals ended up sounding like their conservative rivals, see, for example, Hockx on the cultural economy and politics of the movement and Lee on the New Culturalists' moral politics around love (*Revolution*).

[7] The yuan (圓) was the standard currency of the Republican period despite significant fluctuations during that time. For living standards, currency, and prices in the Republic, see the American sociologist Sidney Gamble's *Peking: A Social Survey*; see also Meng and Gamble.

[8] For Beijing as the epitome of the "recycling" economies—teeming with secondhand and even stolen goods, and full of petty sellers' tricks—within Republican cities, see M. Dong; for booksellers' tricks, see Zhang Zhongmin 155–56, 248–50.

[9] *Beiping* became the new name for Beijing after the relocation of the Republican capital to Nanjing in 1928.

[10] For the bare stick as rebel, rapist, and all-around threat to the social order, see Perry; P. Kuhn; and Sommer, *Sex* and *Polyandry*.

[11] See Gimm's monograph as well as Miao and Song's 2015 article on the father-son duo and their translation.

[12] This advertisement appeared in a November 1902 issue of *Xinmin congbao* 新民叢報 (*New Citizens Journal*). Zhang's monograph offers numerous examples of such advertising language.

[13] The survey results were published in a special issue of the supplement to the *Beijing Daily* (*Jingbao fukan* 京報副刊) in March 1925 by its editor, Sun Fuyuan. The issue was titled *What Youths Love to Read* (*Qingnian aidu tekan* 青年愛讀書特刊).

Divination and Retribution
in *The Plum in the Golden Vase*

Andrew Schonebaum

The religious traditions of China extend beyond what is encompassed by Confucianism, Daoism, and Buddhism. These other traditions, with which the more well-known religions in China often overlap, are usually grouped together under the rubric of "Chinese folk religion," "the popular religion," or simply "Chinese religion." Chinese religion is rarely named among the religious traditions of China, which is ironic, especially given that it undergirds the daily behaviors of so many. (By some accounts, it is the world's third largest religion.) Chinese religion includes an expansive pantheon and various practices, the goal of many of these being to attract good fortune and avoid bad luck. To do so, one might worship local gods of rivers or city walls, kitchen gods, or dragons. One might post talismans on one's front door, perform rituals to expel demons, or call back a wandering soul; divine the future by consulting an oracle, foretell if a venture will have a favorable outcome by reading an almanac, or compare dates and times of birth to ascertain if an engagement will result in a lasting marriage. Chinese religion creates a holistic worldview, a systematic cosmos—but the workings of that cosmos are assessed through a wide variety of practices and implied beliefs. Another aspect that makes studying it challenging is that while many of the practices of Chinese religion have accompanying texts (some of which are identified as Daoist), it is neither a liturgical religion nor one that is based on any particular scripture.

For these reasons, long domestic novels that record the practices of daily life in premodern China are an important source for understanding how some of these practices were performed (often out of public view) and what some (admittedly fictional) characters and authors thought of them. Ming and Qing dynasty novels drew heavily on all manner of printed materials, not the least of which was drama and poetry. In the same sense that realism captured and represented aspects of daily life, this high degree of intertextuality and borrowing makes premodern novels compendiums of vernacular knowledge and values. Novels also borrowed and quoted extensively from practical texts—medical handbooks, carpentry guides, almanacs, divinatory manuals, and almost every other companion to daily life (Shang, "Making"). Novels reveal the extent to which many practices were woven into the fabric of everyday life, casually described without explanation, and in some cases are the only known records of some practices. Novels like *The Plum in the Golden Vase* (*Jin Ping Mei* 金瓶梅) were written by highly educated authors but in a (mostly) vernacular language accessible to a variety of readers, which enables us to glimpse the polarizing nature of some practices, like divination, across gender and class lines and the evolving attitudes toward concepts like fate and retribution.

As divinatory practices touch on practically all aspects of life in China in the premodern period, it will not come as a surprise that all genres of literature in China reflect the influence of such practices. *Plum*'s polytextual and polyphonic nature makes it inclusive of almost every kind of practice. An examination of a seemingly highbrow novel such as *Plum* gives us the opportunity to evaluate attitudes toward these supposedly low- or middlebrow practices while also revealing how divinatory ideas can be employed as literary figures. That mantic arts are consistently and sometimes thoroughly represented in premodern fiction seems to valorize these practices, or at least the cosmic structures that underlie them.

Divination in Literature

Divination in China is as old as, if not older than, Chinese writing itself. By the third millennium BCE at the latest, specialists in reading stress cracks in the bones of deer, sheep, pigs, and cattle had already emerged as a distinct occupational group in North China's neolithic cultures. During the Shang dynasty (ca. 1600–ca. 1050 BCE), the use of these oracle bones reached a high degree of sophistication, often recording in the earliest forms of Chinese characters the answers to questions both weighty (e.g., those relating to birth and harvest) and quotidian (e.g., a toothache). Many of the foundational texts in the Chinese tradition attest to the importance of divination in China throughout the Zhou period (ca. 1050–256 BCE).

The *Book of Changes* (*Yijing* 易經 or *I Ching*), originally an oracle and divination manual and later viewed more as a book of wisdom, is certainly the most influential divinatory text in Chinese history.[1] The evolution of the *Book of Changes* from oracle to philosophy is just one example of the ways in which literature and divination in China are intertwined. Temple oracles tended to be accompanied by poems, which then had to be interpreted by a diviner.

Poetry in general was thought to encode truth in some manner, whether because it was closer to the language of nature or because it was ancient, mystical, or carrying the weight of its authors' intelligence. The phrase "there is a poem as proof" (*you shi wei zheng* 有詩為證), for instance, is found in texts of all kinds. The links between literature and divination extend all the way back to the earliest signs of written language, to the first surviving Chinese characters written on oracle bones, and continue well into the modern period in the form of written talismans that copy out characters with embellishments and flourishes and "spirit writing," or "planchette writing" (*fuji* 扶箕), taking dictation from the dead.

Divining Fiction and Fictional Divination

Just how much can we learn about divination by looking at even one of these long, vernacular novels of the premodern period, especially one that quotes from every kind of extant text, as does *Plum*? Such an investigation would require far more room than the current essay would allow, to say nothing of how an understanding of divination illuminates the ways in which novels create meaning. Thus, let us consider, with some examples, the kinds of things such an investigation might uncover.

Plum represents all sorts of mantic and apotropaic practice, from women "walking off the hundred ailments" (走百病兒去了; 2.24.74, 3.45.93; 24.6b, 45.5b) on the night of the Lantern Festival to the prognostications of Yinyang Master Xu (Yin-yang Master Hsü).[2] Sometimes characters or the narrator make it clear that they think apotropaic methods are spurious, but often it is a wariness of practitioners, especially professional ones, rather than a belief that the narrator or author espouses. The narration also addresses the reader directly on a number of occasions as "gentle reader" (*kanguan* 看官). These fall generally into one of two categories—either the narrator is explaining or pointing out complicated aspects of the plot or the narrator is giving the reader advice on aspects of daily life. The advice does not seem ironic, if only because it is in keeping with prevailing literati attitudes of the time and because it is fairly consistent throughout the novel. The warnings are invariably about the deceitfulness of humans, particularly women. *Plum* warns the reader against those who seek only money—hangers-on, sing-song girls (courtesans), monks, and nuns who expect payment—but it does not suggest that the world of demons is not real or that the workings of the cosmos cannot be glimpsed through divination. On the contrary, some *kanguan* passages warn that they are real: "Gentle reader take note: Black magic and sorcery have existed since ancient times. . . . [C]an the existence of such [mantic] arts be doubted?" (看管聽說: 巫蠱魔味之事, 自古有之 . . . 豈能不信哉; 1.13.272; 13.12a–12b). But *Plum* has a complicated stance toward these practices. The novel warns the reader about female medical practitioners, including those who prescribe demonological and herbal remedies, but it also presents mantic masters as real, even final, authorities on the course of disease.

One practice in the heterodox medical tradition, "divination of the cause" (*zhuyou* 祝由), which also includes a prediction of the outcome of the disease, is well represented in *Plum*. The text even preserves one of the earliest accounts of a particular *zhuyou* practice in print. There are a variety of ways to divine a disease: by counting days, as Celestial Master Zhang Daoling (Chang Tao-ling) does in an exorcistic play performed at Li Ping'er's funeral in chapter 65, or using other methods found in eighteenth- and nineteenth-century medical manuscripts like the "demon valley method" (*guiguzi zhibing fa* 鬼穀子治病法), the "eight trigrams method" (*bagua* 八卦), or the method of "enumerating the diseases caused by demons in a sixty-day cycle" (*huajia shogun* 花甲說鬼).[3]

Another little-known method of divining the outcome of a disease is detailed in a medical manuscript titled *Luma ding sheng sijue* 祿馬定生死訣 (*Instructions on How to Determine Survival or Death by Means of Emolument and Horse*). The meaning of "emolument and horse" (*luma* 祿馬) has to do with "official reward and fate" (*luming* 祿命) following the movement of the "heavenly steed" (*tianma* 天馬) with a fixed regularity. It is not clear when the emolument-and-horse method was first used to predict the course of an illness, but a story in *Shagou ji* 殺狗記 (*Record of Killing a Dog*), an early Ming *nanxi* drama by Xu Zhen 徐畛 (fl. 1377), may be the first: "On the previous day your sister-in-law was ill, and you asked me to go and consult a bamboo slip for prognosis. The Daoist said: There is a clear sign that there will be no harm. Emolument and horse are not upside down" (淨] 前日你每阿嫂有病. 教我去求籤. 那道人說. 大像不妨. 祿馬不倒; my trans.; 43). Little about the emolument-and-horse method is recorded in any literature between this story and its mention in *Plum*, and these fictional accounts are some of the only records of this practice anywhere, which is remarkable for a couple reasons. One is that because of the simplicity of this practice, we might imagine that it was popular. This method of prognosis without diagnosis relies on calculations carried out on a table of four columns of ten characters each composed of the alternating characters *ma* 馬 ("horse") and *lu* 祿 ("emoluments"). The two characters are written in one of three possible positions: upright, slanted, and upside down. The doctor-diviner then counts the number of days from the beginning of the month to the date of the illness's onset, moving his finger down or up the chart depending on the month. How the character he lands on is written—whether upright, slanted, or upside down—allows him to predict the course of the illness. The medical manuscripts indicate that if "emolument and horse are not upside down," as was noted in *Record of Killing a Dog*, then the patient was expected to recover. If they were upside down, the disease would become serious and unresponsive to treatment, but if they were slanted, a talented physician would be able to cure it. This method of predicting the outcome of a disease is important because it is unusual—independent of the whimsy of gods, demons, and ancestors but distinct from natural laws like *yinyang* and *Wuxing* 五行 ("five phases") cosmology, the notion that there is a systematic correspondence between bodily organs and fundamental elements and their properties, upon which most medical practice was based. This method is essentially an individual, secular medicine that is tied to the regular occurrence of certain events. The emolument-and-horse method is a way of revealing that regularity, but it is only a way of reading—it cannot influence events, nor can it explain them (Unschuld and Zheng 174; figs. 1 and 2).

This is precisely how the *luma* is used in *Plum*. When one of his wives, Li Ping'er (Li P'ing-erh), is ill, Ximen Qing (Hsi-men Ch'ing) calls in a great number of doctors to diagnose and prescribe for her. Another one of his wives, Wu Yueniang (Wu Yüeh-niang), tells him:

> You ought to be sparing in the medications you give her. She has already stopped eating and drinking, so what is there left in her stomach? If you insist on continuing to medicate her, it is likely to exhaust her vitality. Formerly, that Immortal Wu predicted that during her twenty-seventh year

she would suffer a bloody catastrophe, and this just happens to be her twenty-seventh year. You ought to send someone to look for that Immortal Wu and have him prognosticate on her behalf to calculate if the *lu* and *ma* are up. 　　　　　　　　　　　　　　　　(4.61.40 [trans. modified])

你也省可裡與他藥吃. 他飲食先阻住了, 肚腹中有甚麼兒? 只顧拿藥淘漾他. 前者那吳神仙算他二十七歲有血光之災, 今年均不整廿七歲了? 你還使人尋這吳神仙去, 教替他打算算, 這祿馬數上看如何. 　　　　　(61.24b–25a)

Emolument and horse and the fiction that depicts this practice were ways of ordering the chaos of contemporary medical practice. With different doctors giving different diagnoses and prescriptions, it made sense to have a fixed way to determine the outcome of the disease and to limit the possible meanings of an oracular text. That this practice survived as part of the doctor's repertoire into the modern period speaks to the continued heterogeneity of the medical field and to the anxiety that robust systems of knowledge could provoke in patients suffering from illness. Novels like *Plum* ordered vernacular knowledge and functioned as a guidebook for those who did not practice or understand

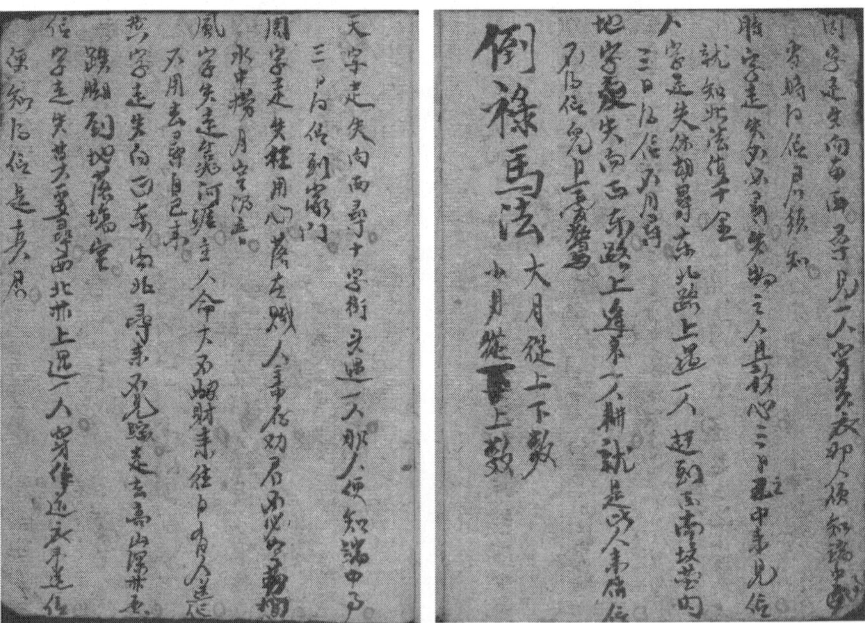

Figure 1. Emolument-and-horse diagnostic method from an early-twentieth-century manuscript, *Yaoshu fang* 藥書防[方] (*Book of Pharmaceutical Recipes*). East Asia Department, Berlin State Library, Prussian Cultural Heritage Foundation (Staatsbibliothek zu Berlin—Preussischer Kulturbesitz), Slg. Unschuld 8472.

elite medicine. That the practice of prognosticating with horse and emolument is recorded in fiction suggests something about the heterogeneity of literati practice as well. These two kinds of texts, novels and practical medical handbooks, the writers of which clearly read very broadly and did not seem to draw harsh distinctions between the logic of fiction and verifiable truth, are the only instances I have found that record this divinatory practice. *Plum's* narrator may argue against employing Buddhists and Daoists, but the author was certainly intimately familiar with these figures and their practices, along with the already copious and varied knowledge in the novel culled from elite life and literature.

Good Fortune, Bad Math

A visit made by the physiognomist Wu Shenxian (Wu Shih), otherwise referred to as Immortal Wu, to the Ximen household in chapter 29 marks an essential moment in *Plum's* story. His visit is represented in the title of the chapter,

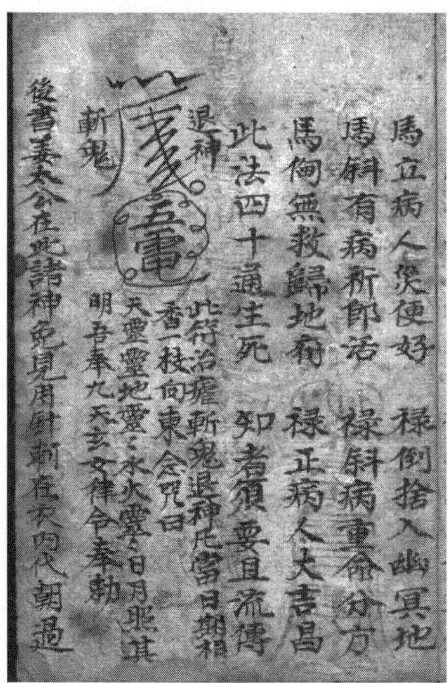
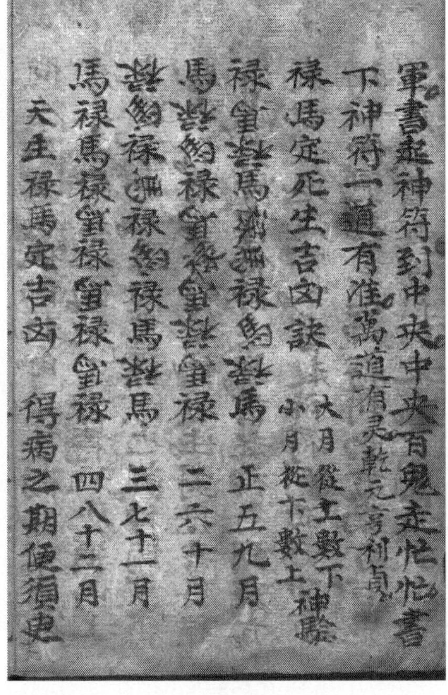

Figure 2. Handbook showing *lu* and *ma* prediction tables from a nineteenth-century medical manuscript, *Zhuyou chaoben* 祝由抄本 (*Manuscript on Apotropaic Healing*). East Asia Department, Berlin State Library, Prussian Cultural Heritage Foundation (Staatsbibliothek zu Berlin—Preussischer Kulturbesitz), Slg. Unschuld 8806.

Figure 3. "Immortal Wu physiognomizes the exalted and the humble." *Qinggong zhenbao bi meitu* 清宮珍寶皕美圖 (*Two Hundred Beautiful Paintings [Formerly] Treasured in the Qing Palace*), vol. 2, Qizhen gongshangshe, 1985?

"Immortal Wu Physiognomizes the Exalted and the Humble" (吳神仙冰鑒定終身), and the corresponding woodblock print in the *xiuxiang* edition of the text (fig. 3). During his visit, Wu predicts—correctly, of course—the fortunes of all the main characters. Immortal Wu is a complicated figure and can bear a great deal of scrutiny. For the most part, all prognostication in fiction is accurate, serving as a type of foreshadowing and a reminder that individual action has little effect on the machinations of fate. Fortunes are always significant in fiction, but fortune-tellers are often scorned. Yet Immortal Wu's first visit adumbrates almost the whole of the novel in certain essential points, and his image is presented as stately, mysterious, and powerful. Wu Shenxian is described as follows:

> Master of the discriminating mirror of physiognomy,
> Adept at interpreting the rules of Xu Ziping;
> By examining celestial phenomena [*qiankun* 乾象] he understands the
>   yin and yang,
> By perusing the *Dragon Canon* he can assess geomantic conditions
>   [*fengshui* 風水].

Profoundly conversant with the Five Planetary Features [*wuxing* 五星],
Deliberating to himself upon the Three Fates [*sanming mi tan*
　三命秘談];
By scrutinizing the astrological circumstances [*geju* 格局],
He can determine the success or failure of a lifetime;
By observing the humor and the complexion [*qise* 氣色],
He can decide the good or evil of one's allotted years.
If he is not Chen Tuan, the realized adept who sojourned on
　Mount Hua,
He must be Yan Junping, who sold fortunes in the market of Chengdu.
(2.29.117; 29.4b)

This is all to say that Immortal Wu is not a hack, and the author knows at least something about these arts, their believers, and their practitioners. Wu was sent by Commandant Zhou Xiu (Chou Hsiu) to Ximen's house, so Ximen is obliged to invite Wu in and allow him to ply his trade, despite Ximen's initial reluctance. Before doing so, he inquires about which schools of *yinyang* Wu is familiar with and which varieties of physiognomy he practices. Wu's replies indicate that he has achieved a very advanced level of skill and knowledge, and moreover, because he distributes medicine to the poor and does not accept payment for his services, he is described as the kind of amateur expert prized by elites. Initially hesitant, Ximen is now impressed by the discourse and demeanor of the diviner and has him predict his future, first from the date and time of his birth, which Immortal Wu silently calculates on his fingers, and then from the features of his face. Wu then uses physiognomy to predict the fates of Ximen's primary wives. Although the fortune-telling jargon employed here and elsewhere in the novel is quite authentic, the horoscopes provided for the characters are calendrically impossible, which suggests that the author did not intend his readers to take these horoscopes too seriously. Readers with a rudimentary knowledge of the calendrical system would likely have noticed this impossibility, as did the anonymous commentator on the *xiuxiang* edition of the novel: "These 'four pillars' are entirely out of keeping with Song [dynasty] fate calculation" (四柱俱不合想宋时算命如此; my trans.; *XXP* 29.35b). It is a mystery why the author would have employed accurate lexicon but absurd math in his representation of diviners predicting fortunes that come true. Is it a kind of code? Is it a desire to disparage the practice or profession? The author was clearly familiar enough with such practices and theories and could have easily looked up the correct dates in an almanac, so why signal to the reader that the fortune-tellers are anything less than reliable? Perhaps the math is off out of respect for living people, for readers who might have dates in their own horoscopes identical to *Plum*'s ill-fated characters. Perhaps the author simply copied from an almanac (*rishu* 日書, *lipu* 曆譜, *lishu* 曆書, *tongshu* 通書), a divinatory manual, or a daily-use encyclopedia (*riyong leishu* 日用類書), all of which began to circulate in huge quantities at the same moment that vernacular novels became immensely popular.[4] These practices were all common well into the modern period, though it seems, based on the attitudes of Ximen and his wives, that they appeared more often in middlebrow circles. The complex representation of divinatory practice points to the robustness of *Plum*'s contents—the author not only quotes from the classics, from poetry, and from drama but also makes extensive references to common knowledge, to practices of the marketplace, and to the logic that undergirded them—however spurious this logic was in the eyes of literati.

Prognostication, Retribution, and Agency

Historical fiction is always prognosticative since the reader knows how it all ends. In the case of *Plum*, the dangers invited by the text's social and political critique of the Ming dynasty are obfuscated by its Song dynasty setting. And yet the years leading up to the invasion and collapse of the Northern Song are implicitly part of the novel's contemporary critique of the Ming court, which even casual readers would have noticed. The collapse of the Song dynasty foretells the collapse of the Ximen household and, not incidentally, the collapse of the Ming dynasty, which occured thirty years after *Plum*'s publication. *Plum*'s setting is also doubly indebted to the past and beholden to its course since it expands into eighty chapters an episode that happens in chapters 23–26 of *Outlaws of the Marsh* (*Shuihu zhuan* 水滸傳). Readers know that, in actual history, the Northern Song fell and that, in literary history, Ximen Qing and Pan Jinlian (P'an Chin-lien) were killed by Wu Song (Wu Sung). Thus, when Immortal Wu predicts that Jinlian is inclined to wantonness and assured of a premature death, readers know he is trustworthy.

Ximen Qing's wives and concubines have their fortunes told again in chapter 46, when, out of boredom and whimsy, they invite in an itinerant woman who is capable of divining with the "tortoise oracle" (*linggui* 靈龜). She is unnamed—an "old country woman who made her living telling fortunes by means of the tortoise oracle and trigrams [i.e., the *Book of Changes*]" (鄉裡卜龜兒卦兒 的老婆子), and, unlike the finery of Immortal Wu, she is wearing a simple blue cotton skirt and patchwork jacket (3.46.122 [trans. modified]; 46.16b). The woman asks the years of their birth, each in turn, and then gives the tortoise oracle a toss (一擲; in later divinations it is a "spin" [卜轉龜兒]). The tortoise (shell?) lands on an image on her board (portrayed as a circle in the woodblock print in the *xiuxiang* edition), and each of the images bears the name of one of the so-called palaces (*gong* 宮) found on the face, according to some schools of physiognomy (figs. 4 and 5).[5] Her predictions tally with those of Immortal Wu, which also combine physiognomy with other divinatory strategies, simultaneously justifying both methods of divination, both kinds of diviners, and establishing the predictions as verified evidence.

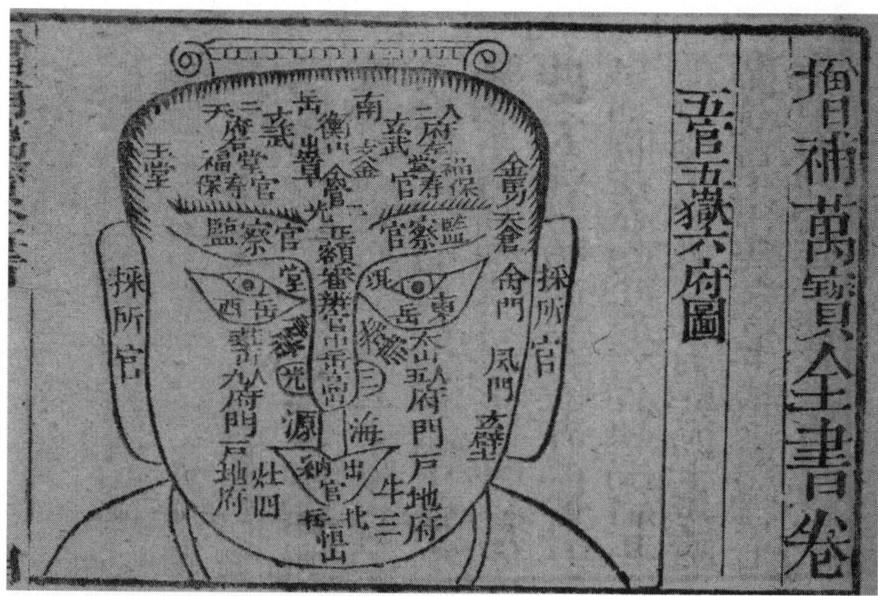

Figure 4. Image showing the location of the various palaces on the face from the daily-use encyclopedia *Zengbu wanbao quanshu* 增補萬寶全書 (1823; *Augmented, Complete Book of Myriad Treasures*). Harvard-Yenching Library.

Figure 5. "Wife and concubines laughingly consult the tortoise oracle." *Qinggong zhenbao bi meitu* 清宮珍寶皕美圖 (*Two Hundred Beautiful Paintings [Formerly] Treasured in the Qing Palace*), vol. 2, Qizhen gongshangshe, 1985?

Plum takes a complicated stance toward prognostication. While it foreshadows the various fates of the primary characters by means of fortune-telling, it repeatedly speaks directly to the reader about the immutability of fate:

> Truly:
> The myriad affairs are things that one cannot argue with;
> One's whole life is entirely determined by one's destiny.
> There is a poem that testifies to this:
> Gan Luo's success came early, while [Jiang] Ziya's came late;
> Pengzu and Yan Hui attained longevities of differing length.
> Fan Dan was impoverished, while Shi Chong was a rich man;
> However calculated, the differences were only in the timing.
>
> (3.46.128)

> 萬事不由人計較, 一生都是命安排
> 有詩為証:
> 甘羅發早子牙遲,
> 彭祖顏回壽不齊;
> 範單家貧石崇富,
> 算來各是只爭時.
>
> (46.18a–18b)

Both the couplet and the poem are borrowed from other pieces of vernacular literature, and the poem makes references to other stories that were common knowledge. Yan Hui and Shi Chong, both of whom are mentioned in the poem, are characters featured in the legend of Fan Dan, in which Confucius sends Yan to borrow some grain from Fan. Before Fan lends it, however, he asks Yan difficult philosophical questions. Yan's answers, which please Fan, are about the evils of money and the scarcity of upright people. Fortune-telling in *Plum* is accurate but futile, given the narrative's fatalistic attitude toward destiny. However, this reference to Fan Dan—a man who chose to endure a life of poverty and support himself by fortune-telling rather than compromise his integrity by acquiescing to the corrupt values of his time—seems meant to valorize lesser trades, especially in the face of the official corruption and personal decadence consistently and mercilessly decried in the novel.

Plum's attitude toward fortune-telling is further complicated by Pan Jinlian, who is late to the gathering and does not have her fate predicated by the divine tortoise. When told that she has missed her chance, she remarks that on a previous occasion the diviner had predicted that she would suffer a premature death (*duanming* 短命). "Who needs it?" she asks, since "[i]t only serves to make one depressed. What will be, will be" (説我短命哩、怎的哩! 說的人心裡影影的). She reiterates that fortune-telling is not for her, maintaining that "I will not have my fortune told by her," and then cites the common phrase "You may predict a person's fate, but you can't predict his conduct" (我是不卜他. 常言算的著命, 算不著行; 3.46.127; 46.18a).[6] This is the idea that resolves the tension between the narrative's insistence on destiny, the story's characters who either do not believe in fate or do not believe in prognostication, and the story's plot, the very length of the novel, which would not exist if the reader were simply to accept foreknowledge of characters' ends as fact. On the one hand, people have some agency, some chance to change their fates, but on the other hand, people are more whimsical than invisible patterns of nature.

While prognostications in *Plum* are accurate, particularly in the case of Jinlian, who the reader knows is doomed based on extratextual sources, such prognostications are not undisputed. All the characters who have died in the novel reappear, in ghostly form, in the last chapter to report on the cause of their deaths and the manner of their reincarnations. One of the primary themes of *Plum* is retribution—immediate, long-term, and karmic—though who gets what and when and why is less clear. Some characters who are conniving and licentious die early deaths, while others make it to nearly the end of the novel. The Chan (Zen) master Pujing (P'u-ching) recites a spell to dispel enmity, and the ghosts of the major characters appear to him. Li Ping'er says that she died from a bloody landslide. Some events corroborate this diagnosis. She suffered from long-term uterine bleeding after giving birth to her son; unadvisedly had intercourse with Ximen while menstruating, which led to semen entering her blood; and was harangued incessantly by Jinlian after the death of her infant son. Yet characters' accounts of their own deaths are somewhat at odds with the narrative. In the case of Li Ping'er, the reader knows that she had an affair with Ximen Qing, stole her husband's money, and caused her husband to die of anger and desperation, transgressions which might be expected to invite retributory punishment. Her former, deceased husband appears to her repeatedly in her dreams, holding her deceased son, and demands that she join them in the underworld, and when she does not, he lodges a case against her. When Ping'er is on her deathbed, all manner of healers are brought in. Doctors prescribe several medicines, but her symptoms only worsen. The feeling of urgency increases and Ximen sends for supramundane healers. They all predict ominous outcomes for her illness, confirming Immortal Wu's prediction that she would meet with difficulties at the age of twenty-seven, her present age. Unable to find Immortal Wu to update his prediction, they invite Daoist Master Pan (P'an). Through ceremonial and ritual performances, he determines that Li Ping'er committed a serious offense in a former life and that a complaint has been lodged against her with the officials of the netherworld. He further states that her current illness is not the result of some malevolent possession that can be exorcized. She is bound to die, and Priest Pan declares that he is incapable of successfully intervening on her behalf (ch. 62).

What are readers to make of Li Ping'er's own claim, made as a ghost in the last chapter of the novel, that she died of blood loss? She knows her crimes, at least the ones committed in this life, and she has dreamt of her former husband accusing her of them in the underworld. These karmically retributory (previous life) or distally retributory (murdered husband's revenge) explanations seem to hold more authority than proximal retribution (blood loss for lasciviousness), yet the revenant must know how she truly died. Pan Jinlian's claim that you can predict a person's fate but not their actions is a key to explaining this case. Li Ping'er's fortune is contingent. As the tortoise diviner says to her, "This year the planet Ketu impinges on your fate, meaning that you may suffer a bloody catastrophe. Only if you can avoid hearing the sound of weeping in the seventh and eighth months, will you be all right" (你老人家今年計都星照命, 主有血光之災. 仔細七八月, 不見哭聲才好; 3.46.127; 46.17b).[7] Her fortune takes the form of "only if you . . . will you be all right." Fate makes room for behavior. Yet because Jinlian is determined to make Li Ping'er miserable, there is much weeping in the household, and Li Ping'er is not able to escape her bloody catastrophe. Most of the prognostications in *Plum* are contingent on human action, and many are specific about time but vague about the mechanism of fate. Li Ping'er is predicted to suffer a bloody calamity in her twenty-seventh year, but the future is in motion—the divination allows for the possibility that Li Ping'er can change her fate enough to survive it, though, inevitably, neither she nor her sister wives do.

Ximen Qing repeats the old saying "One can calculate fate; but one cannot calculate behavior" (算的著命, 算不著行; 2.29.222; 29.10b). And he elaborates by saying that "[t]he physiognomic marks, following the heart [i.e., internal conditions], are produced; the physiognomic marks, according with the heart, disappear" (相逐心生, 相隨心滅). Significantly, this latter quote repeats what Immortal Wu himself had said to explain physiognomy: "As for physiognomic marks, there are those who have the heart without the marks. In this case the marks, following the heart, are produced. There are those who have the marks without the heart. In this case the marks, according with the heart, depart" (夫相者, 有心無相, 相逐心生. 有相無心, 相隨心滅; 2.29.213; 29.9b). That is to say that physiognomic features are not physical markers of an immutable fate, but that both physical features and the fate they point to change with behavior and intention.

Using poems, sayings, and asides, the novel suggests that Heaven controls everything and there is nothing to do but accept the inevitabilities of change and fate. But this is not reflected in the attitudes of the characters, none of whom show a profound belief in fate or fate calculation but only differing degrees of skepticism. They seem to be convinced of the primacy of behavior over fate and of the heart over external physiognomic marks. That each character fulfills their destiny, no matter how meager, is a testament to their normalcy, their unremarkable willpower, and their willful ignorance of prescient warnings. These characters are, essentially, poor readers of their own lives.

If divining the outcome of illness is prognosis without diagnosis, then in the novel it helps reveal much about characters, given the strong, recurring motif of retribution in *Plum*. If a character dies from an illness that they have a chance to survive, according to the mantic tables or the "little black book" (*heishu* 黑書) of Yinyang Master Xu (Hsu), then the reader can judge the relative strength or weakness of their fate or the tolerance of their fate for immoral or unwise acts.

Their death is an indication of the severity of their actions and the degree to which they have tempted fate. This kind of prognostication is similar in aim to the novel's *kanguan*, or "gentle reader," passages, which point the reader not to truths they should glean from fiction but show them instead how to decipher the complexity, relationships, and morality articulated by the text. Moreover, mantic arts in life essentially read the relative strength of fate, and in fiction simple practices like *luma* read it for the reader.

Practitioners of traditional Chinese medicine and divination often considered a patient's moral behavior a significant factor in determining that person's health and well-being. Clients of both doctors and diviners were therefore advised to cultivate good thoughts and to banish selfish desires, and both doctors and diviners shared prescriptive approaches undergirded by theories of "retributory correspondence" (*ying* 應 or *xiangying* 相應), which involved considerations of time, place, and demonology as well as notions of physiology and personality (Smith 688).

The demands of realistic fiction complicate diagnosis and prognosis. Divining fortune presents a problem in a novel that is fundamentally about retribution. Many readers struggle to make sense of *Plum*'s last chapter, in which we learn the status of all the main characters in their subsequent incarnations. Most are happily reincarnated into well-to-do families, and thus the Chan master Pujing is seen as a figure of redemption. Yet he also has made a deal to adopt as his acolyte the only remaining son of Ximen Qing, thereby extinguishing the Ximen line, the ultimate retribution for Ximen's wrongdoing. Is the novel ultimately, then, about Buddhist salvation or Confucian retribution? Or is it about the difficulty of adapting to the vicissitudes of life and the even more difficult task of avoiding one's fate?

Divination in and of Fiction

Fictional practitioners usually do not go into detail about why they practice one method of divination over another or why there are multiple kinds of divination. Presumably, each divinatory method accesses the same cosmic information, so why is there a need to have more than one method? We see in *Plum* that Xu Ziping's method provides more detail about the future than does the physiognomic method, whereas the emolument-and-horse method seems to provide little more than a "yes," "no," or "maybe" to a given question. Undoubtedly it would reveal something about the author were one to note which practices are mentioned, which are esteemed, and which are denigrated, omitted, or poorly understood.

Some scholars believe that *Plum* posits a strong Confucian moral—the Ximen line is destroyed, the most comprehensive failure from a Confucian perspective. Others believe that such a reading ignores the explicit redemption provided the characters in the last chapter. One of the most notable arguments for the authorship of the novel and its overall vision has been made by David Tod Roy in the introduction to his translation of *Plum*. Roy makes a strong argument that the anonymous author of *Plum* affiliated himself with the philosopher Xunzi 荀子 (third century BCE; Introduction xxiv–xxvii, xxix–xxxii). The grand historian Sima Qian 司馬遷 (ca. 145–ca. 86 BCE) writes the following of the philosopher: "Xunzi hated the corrupt governments of his day, the decadent states and evil princes who did not follow the way but gave their attention to magic and prayers and believed in omens and luck" (荀卿嫉濁世之政, 亡國亂君相屬, 不遂大道而營於巫祝, 信機祥; *Selections* 74; *Shiji* 7.74.2852). The most famous tenet of Xunzi's philosophy is the notion that, although everyone has the capacity for goodness, human nature is basically evil and, if allowed to find expression without the conscious molding and restraint of ritual, is certain to lead the individual disastrously astray. It is this tenet, Roy maintains, that lies at the heart of the novel: the fact that the author of *Plum* "endorses this view should be apparent to even the most superficial reader, but he also makes it quite explicit by quoting in four different places in his novel, including the first chapter, a line that reads 'In this world the heart of man alone remains vile'" (Introduction xxv). Roy argues persuasively that the author of *Plum* was an adherent of Xunzi's philosophy in its entirety. But the novel's detailed descriptions of mantic arts, the invocation of spirits, and the various accurate prognostications of fortune and disaster seem to cast doubt on the author's complete adherence to Xunzi's beliefs.

Xunzi's work contains an entire chapter titled "Against Physiognomy" ("Fei xiang" 非相), and in another chapter we encounter the following claim:

> One performs the rain sacrifice and it rains. Why? I say, there is no special reason why. It is the same as when one does not perform the rain sacrifice and it rains anyway. . . . One performs divination and only then decides on important affairs. But this is not to be regarded as bringing one what one seeks, but rather is done to give things proper form. Thus the gentleman regards this as proper form, but the common people regard it as connecting with sprits.　　　　　　　　　　　(Hutton 179)

零而雨, 何也? 曰: 無佗也, 猶不零而雨也. . . . 卜筮然後決大事, 非以為得求也, 以文之也. 故君子以為文, 而百姓以為神.　　　　　　　　(Xunzi 273)

Xunzi concludes this thought by saying that "if one regards it as proper form, one will have good fortune. If one regards it as connecting with spirits, one will have misfortune" (以為文則吉, 以為神則凶也; Hutton 179; Xunzi 273). He acknowledges that it is fitting and proper to perform mantic arts, particularly at court, and particularly by those whose job it is to perform them. He writes, "The work of the hunchbacked shamans and lame-footed seers is to assess the yin and the yang, to divine the omens and portents, to drill the tortoise-shells and lay out the hexagrams, to preside over ceremonies for warding off ills, selecting lucky days and the five prognostications, and to know good and bad fortune, the auspicious and the inauspicious" (相陰陽, 占祲兆, 鑽龜陳卦, 主攘擇五卜, 知其吉凶妖祥, 傴巫跛擊之事也; Hutton 78; Xunzi 130). For Xunzi, there is good luck and there is bad luck, but the former is tempted by, and the latter averted by, proper ritual action, good intentions, and good behavior.

How is the reader to make sense of these views vis-à-vis *Plum*? The narrator and the story clearly criticize characters for their behavior. By extension, the society and court of the late Ming are criticized for the same selfish, decadent behavior that cause so much resentment in the world. The characters presented in *Plum* are squarely middlebrow—marginally literate, nouveau riche social climbers—perhaps not exactly the "common people" Xunzi refers to in his remarks, but certainly less wise than Confucian scholars and officials. But if fortune-telling is used in *Plum*, as it is often used in other fiction, as a foreshadowing device and to begin a conversation about fate, human nature, and individual agency, ghosts are decidedly real. Real ghosts and spirits may still serve as metaphors for the hauntings of guilt, a lustful heart, or the like, but they also really appear to characters, engaging them in conversation and warning them of what is to come. In fiction, communication with ghosts often occurs in dreams, which raises the possibility that it is imagined contact, but in *Plum*'s final chapter, a parade of the dead main characters appears before multiple witnesses, and each ghost explains their death and the circumstances of their rebirth. Moreover, in chapter 62, a Daoist priest summons a divine marshal who is on duty that day to inquire if there are supernatural forces at work in the illness of one of Ximen Qing's wives (4.62.62–63; 62.14a–14b; fig. 6). A genie-like Daoist deity

Figure 6. "Daoist Master Pan conjures up a yellow-turbaned warrior." *Qinggong zhenbao bi meitu* 清宮珍寶䀹美圖 (*Two Hundred Beautiful Paintings [Formerly] Treasured in the Qing Palace*), vol. 3, Qizhen gongshangshe, 1985?

that takes human form and serves its summoner presents itself in other fictional works, meaning that the author might have been borrowing from other literature, yet the author takes pains to describe the deity in detail and to have him report to the Daoist in the presence of Ximen Qing, which makes the marshal seem both original to the novel and real to the characters in it. *Plum* is a work of such sophistication that it would be obtuse to assert that it cannot contain contradictory or complicated attitudes toward divination or toward Xunzi or some similar moral vision, but the novel does impugn the assertion that the author followed or asserted the views of Xunzi wholesale. It also seems that Xunzi acknowledged divination as a fact of life and courting fortune as an unescapable paradigm regardless of one's social standing.

Apologies for *Plum*—whether in commentary editions, in prefatory essays, or in the text of the novel itself—tend to focus on the act of reading as a particular kind of seeing. Reading about debauched characters with a detached air of sympathy could lead to enlightenment, some claimed, while others warned that the allure of fictional representation would only entice naive readers to imitate what they encountered in the novel. Both apologies and accusations reinforced the notion that fiction was only for sophisticated readers, those who could look below the surface and read between the lines to appreciate the finely wrought structure of the novel, its devices, and its methods. Reading fortunes involved similar talent and implied dangers: whether it was reading facial features, images that corresponded to them, or dates and times of birth or interpreting obscure verses produced by an oracle, there were dire consequences for those who kept only to the surface.

We can learn a lot about divination from fiction. At the same time, there is also much to be learned about readers, authors, and editors of fiction by looking at divination. Issues relating to authorship, hermeneutics, literary history, or esoteric divinatory practices recorded in fictional texts may benefit in small ways from this type of investigation, but to my way of thinking, the most important aspect of mantic practices in fiction, and of divination in particular, is the implication of such practices for the concept of fate. Fictional texts foreshadow characters' fates using prognosticative methods, but they also consistently question the veracity or accuracy of those results, likely to retain some element of suspense. Narratives do not want to appear fatalistic to readers—they are motivated both to propagate divinatory practice through representation of practices of daily life and to call such practices into question. Fictional narratives routinely describe various mantic practices in loving detail. While the representation of a practice may be inaccurate, the text it creates is always true. This mantic text produced by divination puts characters in the position of readers. They must interpret the text to get at their fates. The reader of the novel, who struggles to understand the narrative text, thus relates to the character, who struggles to understand the mantic text, lest misreading lead to harm.[8]

We also learn from this discussion of divination and literature that fate makes room for human action. Realistic stories had to represent mantic and apotropaic practice, and the demands of fiction required prognostication to be tantamount to foreshadowing. But an interesting tale would be impossible without characters who not only misread or disbelieve their fates but also have the possibility to change their fates. The story knows that its readers, if not its characters, can discern the hidden meanings of oracular texts, be they verse or image, and had to provide those readers with the possibility of change. Hence, we have in *Plum* the repeated statement (at times quoted by Jinlian) that "you can know a man's fate, but not his actions" (算的著命, 算不著行; 3.46.127; 46.16a).[9] There are some stories that undermine fatalism through changing physiognomic features or the dates and times of birth, but, more often and more poignantly, fiction reminds readers of the limits of reading. That is, even if we divine correctly and interpret the signs or images or texts that are produced during divination, there is still the matter of multiple endings, whimsy, and the inscrutability of human behavior.

NOTES

[1] It is influential in Western literary history as well. Thinkers and authors from Gottfried Wilhelm Leibniz, Georg Wilhelm Friedrich Hegel, and Jacques Derrida to Philip K. Dick, John Cage, Jorge Luis Borges, and Hermann Hesse have used or discussed the *Yijing* in their work. Perhaps most famously, Carl Jung wrote about the *Book of Changes*, saying among other things that "[e]ven to the most biased eye, it is obvious that this book represents one long admonition to careful scrutiny of one's own character, attitude, and motives" (xxxiv).

[2] Unless otherwise noted, parenthetical citations refer to Roy's translation, *The Plum in the Golden Vase*, and to *Jin Ping Mei cihua* 金瓶梅詞話 (*Plum in the Golden Vase: A Ballad Tale*). In one of her essays in this volume, "Buddhist-Inflected Patterns of Characterization in *The Plum in the Golden Vase*," Maram Epstein discusses walking off the hundred illnesses.

[3] In early texts, Guigu zi 鬼穀子 is a personal name.

[4] Daily-use encyclopedias usually included twenty or thirty chapters devoted to medicine, culture, practical arts like agriculture or carpentry, and divination. For more on *Plum*'s use of these texts, see Shang, "Making."

[5] This method of fortune-telling is detailed in *The Purple Hairpins* (*Zichai ji* 紫釵記), a drama by Tang Xianzu 湯顯祖 originally completed in 1587 (author's preface dated 1595) and perhaps the source of information for *Plum*'s author. The Daoist nun who practices this art describes the method as follows: "On the painting, there are stories of joys and sorrows, and of departures and reunions. I tell the people what will happen to them according to where the tortoise goes on the painting." It is described unambiguously as a method to "fake an immortal's ability" (人道小仙才): "I have a lovely and clever tortoise, / with which I defraud people of some money" (這龜兒俊哉. 前去打光來). The stage directions indicated that the Daoist nun performing the divination "clumsily forces its crawling route on the painting" (捉龜兒錯走諢介; *Purple Hairpins* 346–48; 2554).

[6] In the *cihua* edition in the Waseda University library, a premodern reader has high-lighted Jinlian's quote about having a "short fate," suggesting that they were sensitive to the literary significance of this prediction.

[7] Ketu is the name of one of two imaginary "dark stars," or invisible planets, introduced into China during the T'ang dynasty through the translation of works on Indian astronomy, as part of a theory to account for lunar eclipses. In Chinese astrology and fortune-telling it was regarded as a baleful influence.

[8] See part 1, "Materials," for more on the harmful effects of misreading *Plum*.

[9] A similar phrase in *The Story of the Stone* (*Honglou meng* 紅樓夢) tells readers that "you can know a man's face, but never his heart" (知人知面不知心; Hawkes and Minford, *Story* [Fan Shengyu] 5: 334; 5: 335).

Filial Piety and *The Plum in the Golden Vase*

Maram Epstein

Given the lack of child-parent relationships depicted in *The Plum in the Golden Vase* (*Jin Ping Mei* 金瓶梅), the historical association between the novel and filial piety, the foundational virtue of the Confucian ethical system, may seem counterintuitive to modern readers. However, this association dates to the earliest theories of *Plum*'s composition and was later canonized in a prefatory essay to the novel entitled "On the Bitterness of Filial Sentiments" ("Kuxiao shuo" 苦孝說), written by Zhang Zhupo 張竹坡 (1670–98; ZZP 9b). Early readers of *Plum* considered filial piety central to the meaning of this literary masterpiece. For modern readers, the most meaningful way to understand the relationship between filial piety and *Plum* may derive from the long symbolic association between obscenity and perversions of ritual order in Chinese literature. Filial piety requires the restraining of personal desires in order to fulfill one's obligations to parents and patriline; in this sense, filial piety is the symbolic opposite of sexual self-indulgence.

Because filial piety (*xiao* 孝) includes such a broad range of meanings in premodern China, it is necessary first to define it before trying to understand its relevance to the fictional world depicted in *Plum*. In its earliest usage, the verb *xiao* referred to "making offerings to the dead" (Knapp 197–200). These early *xiao* rites were designed to ensure the happiness of the ancestors and thereby bring physical and political good fortune to their descendants. Even as its meanings broadened, filial piety retained its basic association with mourning rites: one of the most common meanings of *xiao* in premodern China was "to wear mourning robes" (*fuxiao* 服孝). The ritually proper observance of mourning rites was a basic expression of a person's commitment to the Confucian order during the imperial period. The meanings of filial piety extended far beyond its early emphasis on feeding the dead and came to refer to the treatment of one's living parents, including their feeding and support.

Confucius (551–479 BCE) expanded the meaning of *xiao* from the performance of ritual acts to an inner affective state of reverence: "The Master said: 'The *xiao* of today is called being able to feed [your parents]. But dogs and horses are both able to be fed. If there is no respect [*jing* 敬], what is the difference?'" (子曰: "今之孝者, 是謂能養. 至於犬馬, 皆能有養; 不敬, 何以別乎?"; 2.7). Mencius (391–308 BCE), the second most important early Confucian thinker, went further than the Confucian *Analects* in identifying filial piety as a moral instinct that is innate to human nature, and he identified it as the basis for ethical behavior: "Loving one's parents, that is humanity" (親親, 仁也; 7A.15). These two quotations taken from canonical Confucian texts explain how filial piety, the respectful and ritually proper treatment of one's parents, came to be understood as an essential expression of a person's basic moral nature.

The establishment of filial piety as a foundational virtue in China cannot be separated from the efforts of the Han court (206 BCE–220 CE) to legitimate their rule through the adoption of Confucianism as state ideology. The Han emperors canonized *The Classic of Filial Piety* (*Xiaojing* 孝經), a text that begins with an admonition against harming the body given by one's parents and goes on to argue that bringing honor to one's parents by rising through the ranks of the official bureaucracy is a core expression of filial piety (Rosemont). *The Classic of Filial Piety* established the norm still current today in East Asian cultures that dedication to studying and career success are matters of concern to the entire family, not just the individual. By the late sixteenth century, when *Plum* was written, a basic commitment to certain aspects of filial piety, no matter how individual men and women felt about their parents, was a normative and expected aspect of the image politics of the elite (Y. Zhang 18–22).

Filial piety had a universal appeal in traditional China, and both Buddhism and Daoism incorporated it as a central value. By the late sixteenth century, references to filial heroes from *The Twenty-Four Paragons of Filial Piety* (*Ershisi xiao* 二十四孝) were ubiquitous in both popular and elite culture ("*Twenty-Four Paragons*"). These exemplars were celebrated for a range of behaviors, from the extreme, most notably Guo Ju, who was willing to sacrifice his infant son to preserve the life of his aged mother during a famine, to the quotidian, such as the child Lu Ji, who saved two gifted oranges in his sleeve to give to his mother. Filial piety was so central a moral and affective value that references to a range of stereotyped filial behaviors were a normative component of any positive biography or character sketch. The lack of references to filial culture and the frequent inversions of filial norms in *Plum* must be read within this cultural context.

The moral chaos that defines the world of Ximen Qing (Hsi-men Ch'ing) stems from his lack of filial self-cultivation. The Confucian ritual order was actualized through the Five Cardinal Relationships: the relationship between emperor and subject, parent and child, husband and wife, older sibling and younger sibling, and friends. It was through these relationships that individuals could manifest the Three Cardinal Guides of loyalty, filiality, and chastity, or marital fidelity. With the exception of friendship, each of the relationships is explicitly hierarchical, its nature determined by the official status, age, and sex of the two people involved; in practice, friends frequently used kinship terms that encode status when addressing each other. The ritual texts that define the proper performance of these relationships emphasize the need to maintain distinctions and boundaries between the two roles. The person in the hierarchically inferior position was to defer to the authority of the person in the superior position in all matters and serve them loyally. This willingness to embrace a subordinate status was a key marker of personal virtue; even the emperor was expected to demonstrate filial devotion to his parents. Early Confucian philosophers highlighted the idea of "yielding" or "deferring" (*rang* 讓) as necessary to maintaining social order (Nylan 5–8); in popular literature of the sixteenth century, this value was also articulated as "keeping to one's place" (*shou benfen* 守本分).

The Five Relationships were generally thought of as parallel and mutually enhancing; a man's filial devotions to his parents were considered a reliable indicator of his ability to serve the state loyally. In this sense, the domestic world, rather than being a private space distinct from the public and subject to a more relaxed moral code, was viewed as a microcosm of the imperial court. As spelled out in the *Great Learning* (*Daxue* 大學), one of the Four Books of neo-Confucianism, failure to observe proper ritual order at the personal and domestic levels would lead to chaos in the social, political, and even cosmic realms (Plaks, *Four Masterworks* 156–63). Since a baby's first relationship was with their parents, being filial was considered foundational to the other virtues. As is obvious to most readers of *Plum*, the fundamental ritual and ethical values of knowing one's place, loyal service to one's superiors, and respect for the hierarchical nature of family and society are conspicuously missing from the fictional world of the novel.

Plum *as an Expression of Bitter Filial Sentiments*

Given that *Plum* continually inverts and denies the norms of filial culture, why then did Zhang Zhupo, the greatest and most influential interpreter of the novel, associate *Plum* with filial piety in the prefatory essays he included in his commentary edition? A first explanation derives from the earliest theories of authorship of the novel (see the introduction to part 1 of this volume). Two of the most popular theories link the novel to filial revenge; the best known of these suggests that the famous literatus Wang Shizhen (1526–96) put poison on the corner of each page of the manuscript, knowing that his intended victim, Yan Shifan (1513–65), was a devotee of pornography and licked his fingers to facilitate turning the pages as he read. Even though Zhang Zhupo denigrates this theory in his essay "How to Read the *Jin Ping Mei*" ("*Jin Ping Mei* dufa" 金瓶梅讀法), he confirms its importance in his detailed rejection of it.[1] Zhang's prefatory essay "On the Bitterness of Filial Sentiments" echoes these early theories of authorship in suggesting that the unnamed author had lost his father through some injustice and wrote *Plum* to vent his frustrated filial sentiments (*ZZP* 9b).

A second explanation for Zhang's desire to connect *Plum* to filial piety is his defense of the novel as a great work of literature despite its obviously obscene content. His defense of *Plum* is based on his intertwined arguments that the author wrote the novel to vent his frustrated filial sentiments and that therefore the author's intent was moral, and that the author had exquisite control over the aesthetic aspects of the novel and that only those readers who learn to appreciate the complex aesthetic features of the text are able to decode the author's moral intent. As Zhang argues in his "How to Read" essay, those who read the novel for pornographic titillation have not learned to read it properly ("How to Read the *Chin P'ing Mei*" 236–38; *ZZP* 22b–23b).

Zhang Zhupo's claim for the unnamed author's seriousness of purpose is anchored in the concept of frustrated filial sentiments that resulted in the buildup of "sour bile" (含此酸者) that could only be released through the act of writing (my trans.; *ZZP* 9b). The cultural logic behind this line of argumentation would have been obvious to any educated Ming reader. The great historian Sima Qian 司馬遷 (ca. 145–ca. 87 BCE), who chose castration over death to continue the textual project that was his father's life work, established the trope that creative genius derives from suffering (*fafen zhushu* 發憤著述). Morally charged bitter experiences endowed writers with a recognizable "moral, intellectual, and aesthetic authority" (W. Li, "Letter" 97). Sima Qian attributed the literary power of such writers to the release of their pent-up frustrations (Durrant 28). Zhang Zhupo draws repeated analogies between the author of *Plum* and Sima Qian; as Zhang writes, *Plum* "is characterized by an air of resentful indignation, but then its author is certainly a reincarnation of Sima Qian" ("How to Read the *Chin P'ing Mei*" 236; *ZZP* 22b). In one of Zhang's typical allegorical readings of *Plum*, he raises two relatively minor characters to central thematic importance by suggesting that the musical instruments they play reflect an intentional pun on *resentment*:

> The story begins with Meng Yulou playing the guitar (*tanyuan* 彈阮; puns with *tanyuan* 嘆冤, to sigh with resentment) and concludes with Han Aijie carrying her guitar (*baoyuan* 抱阮; puns with *baoyuan* 抱冤, to harbor resentment). This is because the author had a bellyful of outraged tears but no place to shed them. Therefore, he created *Plum* as an outlet for his tears.   ("How to Read the *Chin P'ing Mei*" 243)

> 以玉樓 彈阮起, 愛姐抱阮結, 乃是作者滿肚皮倡狂之淚沒處灑落, 故以《金瓶梅》為大哭地也.   (ZZP 25a)

Although Zhang's attempts to force a specific moral reading of *Plum* as the work of a frustrated filial son will likely strike modern readers as contrived, such allegorical readings were a long-established tradition of Confucian hermeneutics.[2] Moreover, because his commentary edition became the standard version of the text, Zhang's allegorical reading of *Plum* shaped the text's reception in China until the rediscovery of the *cihua* edition in the 1930s.

Inversions of Filial Piety in Plum

Zhang Zhupo's thematic identification of *Plum* with frustrated filial piety was also influenced by the fact that he was working with the abridged Chongzhen (*xiuxiang*) edition and not the *cihua* edition. As discussed in the introduction to this volume, in addition to cutting out much of the descriptive verse, the editor(s) of the Chongzhen text rearranged the order of the early chapters of the novel so that the first chapter begins not with an admonition about the dangers of lust but with an extended description of Ximen Qing swearing brotherhood with his shiftless band of friends. This scene does not appear in the *cihua* version, and the band of brothers is not introduced until the tenth chapter (1.10.200–01;

10.7a–7b).[3] Thematically, this scene alludes to the famous bond of sworn brotherhood among the three heroes that occurs in the first chapter of the canonical novel *Romance of the Three Kingdoms* (*Sanguo zhi yanyi* 三國志演義). By foregrounding the oath of brotherhood, the Chongzhen text shifts its thematic focus from the dangers of lust to the dangers of counterfeit relationships. As Zhang Zhupo expounds at some length in one of his prefatory essays, "Idle Musings" ("Zhupo xianhua" 竹坡閒話), the bonds of filial piety and brotherhood form the core of the Confucian ethical order:

> Of that which is the most true of all under Heaven, none surpasses the Five Relationships; of that which is false, none surpasses greed and lust. Of the Five Relationships, those between emperor and subject, friend and friend, husband and wife are established by contingency. But, the bonds between father and son and older and younger brother are like water flowing from the same source, or like tree trunks growing from the same root; no matter how they diverge, they are established by Heaven.   (my trans.)

> 天下最真者, 莫若倫常; 最假者, 莫若財色. 然而倫常之中, 如君臣, 朋友, 夫婦, 可合而成; 若夫父子, 兄弟, 如水同源, 如木同本, 溜分枝引, 莫不天成.
>
> (ZZP 4b)

In his "How to Read" essay, Zhang further expounds, "All the relatives of Ximen Qing described in the book are false relatives" (書內寫西門許多親戚, 通是假的; "How to Read the *Chin P'ing Mei*" 239; ZZP 23b). In his comments to the first chapter, Zhang negatively compares the relationship between Wu the Elder and Wu Song (Wu Sung), "brothers born to the same mother" (嫡親兄弟), to the motley group of acquaintances with whom Ximen Qing swears brotherhood (my trans.; ZZP 1.4b).

To those familiar with the conventions of Chinese narrative, the passage introducing Ximen Qing signals that he is to be understood as the mirror opposite of a filial son:

> It so happens that he was the decadent scion of a family of considerable wealth from whom he had inherited a wholesale pharmacy business located on the street that ran in front of the district yamen. He had been a dissolute young scamp since his youth and had acquired some skill in such martial arts as boxing and fencing with the quarterstaff. He also liked to gamble, and there was little he didn't know about backgammon, elephant chess, and the various word games played by breaking characters into their component parts. Now that he had come into an inheritance and had money of his own to spend, he had gone into cahoots with the officials and functionaries in the district yamen where he played the role of influence peddler, intervening in public business on people's behalf, for a fee. For this reason everyone in the whole district was rather afraid of him.

This man bore the double surname Ximen, and the single given name, Qing. He was an only son, so people had been in the habit of calling him Master Ximen, but now that he had come into his inheritance and had money of his own to spend they referred to him as the Honorable Ximen. Both his father and his mother were dead, and he had no siblings.

His first wife had died some time ago, leaving behind her only a single daughter. Recently he had been formally remarried to the daughter of battalion Commander Wu of the Qinghe Left Guard, but he was not above availing himself of the four or five serving maids in his establishment. Moreover, he had carried on an affair with a girl named Li Jiao'er from the licensed quarter for some time, and he had just arranged to take her into his household. (1.2.53)

原是清河縣一個破落戶財主, 就縣門前開著個生藥舖. 從小兒也是個好浮浪子
弟, 使得些好拳棒, 又會賭博, 雙陸象棋, 抹牌道字, 無不通曉. 近來發跡有
錢, 專在縣里管些公事, 與人把攬說事過錢, 交通官吏. 因此滿縣人都懼怕他.
那人複姓西門, 單名一個慶字, 排行第一, 人都叫他做西門大一郎. 近來發跡有
錢, 人都稱他做西門大官人. 他父母雙亡, 兄弟俱無. 先頭渾家是早逝, 身邊
只有一女. 新近又娶了清河左衛吳千戶之女, 填房為繼室. 房中也有四五個丫鬟
婦女. 又常與勾欄裡的李嬌兒打熱, 今也娶在家裡. (2.6a–6b)

According to the conventions of biography, subjects are typically placed in a genealogy that lists the names and places of origin of their parents and any prominent ancestors. Readers of *Plum* do not learn the name of Ximen Qing's father until chapter 39, and this is the only time his name is given (2.39.414; 39.6b).[4] Rather than situate him within his patriline, this introduction focuses on Ximen Qing's material wealth and his frivolous pursuits. One of the most influential pronouncements on filial piety was Mencius's statement that "[t]here are three ways of being unfilial; to be without heirs is the worst" (不孝有三, 無後為大; my trans.; 4A.26). Men who did not have a son by age forty were ritually justified in acquiring concubines to ensure the birth of a male heir to carry on the line of ancestor worship. Ximen Qing's introduction emphasizes his sexual pursuit of maids and prostitutes; even if any of these women were to bear a son, the child's paternity would be suspect. As Pan Jinlian (P'an Chin-lien) repeatedly comments, because Li Ping'er (Li P'ing-erh) married Ximen Qing immediately after divorcing Jiang Zhushan (Chiang Chu-shan), there is no reason to assume that Guan'ge (Kuan-ko) is Ximen Qing's son. Shockingly, when Wu Yueniang (Wu Yüeh-niang), Ximen Qing's formal wife and the preferred biological mother to any heirs, is close to her due date, Ximen Qing ignores her and can think only about his sexual pursuits of the wife of his manager Ben (Pen) the Fourth (4.78.584–85; 78.4a–4b); Lady Lin, the widowed mother of his sexual rival Wang the Third (4.78.591–96; 78.9a–11a); Lady Lan, the beautiful wife of He Yongshou (Ho Yung-shou), his new colleague (4.78.620–22; 78.28a–28b); and Wang Liu'er

(Wang Liu-erh), the wife of Han Daoguo (Han Tao-kuo), his manager (4.79.631–36; 79.4a–7b).

Another passage from Mencius lists five unfilial behaviors that undermine the respectful treatment of parents: physical laziness; gambling and a fondness for chess and drinking; greediness and an indulgence of one's wives and children; indulgence in sensual pleasures; and a fondness for bravado and brawling (4B.30). Ximen Qing engages in all these behaviors, and although this does not directly affect his treatment of his parents since they are already dead when the novel begins, Ximen fails to observe the customary rites associated with ancestor worship, such as making offerings to his parents' spirit altar at significant moments.[5] Ximen Qing's excessive mourning for Li Ping'er, a concubine, and for his son Guan'ge, a child who died before his first birthday, is symptomatic of his lack of concern for proper ritual order.

As the only son of his parents, Ximen Qing carries a particularly heavy filial burden: not only should he be focused on producing a son, he should also demonstrate respect for his parents by managing his patrimony and behaving in such a way that brings honor to the family name. The opening passage of the *Classic of Filial Piety* maintains that

> [i]t is filial piety that is the root of virtue and the source from which [moral] teachings are generated. . . . We receive our bodies, our hair and skin, from our parents; filial piety begins with taking care to avoid injury to your body. Establishing yourself through the way of filial piety, and elevating your name so it is known to future generations and thereby glorifies your parents, is the end point of filial piety.   (my trans.)[6]

> 夫孝, 德之本也, 教之所由生也 . . . 身體髮膚, 受之父母, 不敢毀傷, 孝之始也. 立身行道, 揚名於後世, 以顯父母, 孝之終也.   (*Xiaojing* 1.1)

Ximen Qing famously abuses his body by exhausting himself sexually and overindulging in rich foods. He also makes a mockery of any expectation that he should pursue an education, the most respected route to establishing fame. Not only is Ximen Qing unable to read official documents (3.48.169; 48.15a), he uses his library primarily as a site to pursue backdoor relations with officials and back-garden relations with his page boy and the wives of various employees.[7]

Ximen Qing's skill in the visual game of "breaking characters into their component parts" (*chai zi* 拆字) deserves special comment. Confucian thought posits the language of ritual texts as the foundation of moral order. Ritual texts delineate the proper hierarchical distinctions between the Five Cardinal Relationships by defining how people should behave. The Confucian precept of "the rectification of names" (*zhengming* 正名; "names" can also be translated as "nouns" or "social roles") requires people to evaluate their performance of a specific social role—whether as a parent, child, husband, or wife—and to "true" or "rectify" their behavior so that it aligns with the ritual ideal. As expressed in the hortative language of the Confucian *Analects*, the rectification of names places special emphasis on the relationships between emperor and subject and between father and son. Social order will be achieved when "the ruler acts as a ruler, the subject acts as a subject, the father acts as a father, and the son acts as a son" (君君, 臣臣, 父父, 子子; my trans.; 12.11). At no point in *Plum* does Ximen Qing act appropriately as either a son or a father. His penchant for confusing proper social roles, exemplified in his taste for having his lovers call him "daddy" while having sex, explicitly undermines any sense of proper order in the household.

Another important way that Ximen Qing's characterization as an inversion of a filial son informs *Plum*'s meaning derives from the special relationship among the Three Cardinal Guides of loyalty, filial piety, and female chastity. As mentioned, the *Classic of Filial Piety* established filial piety and loyalty as equivalent and intertwined virtues; the set phrase "loyal and filial" (忠孝) was commonly used to describe virtuous officials. None of these cardinal virtues is present in Ximen's household. Although political loyalty does not receive the same degree of attention as the other virtues, it is nonetheless an important theme in *Plum*. Midway through the novel Ximen Qing furthers the rot at the highest level of the imperial bureaucracy when he offers himself as an adopted son to the minister Cai Jing 蔡京 (Ts'ai Ching [1046–1126]) and presents substantial bribes, euphemistically referred to as "[filial] devotions" (*xiao jingyi* 小敬意), to further his own career (3.55.357; 55.7a).

After the imperial government institutionalized the cult of female chastity with a system of rewards to regulate it during the fourteenth century, female virtue in China became synonymous with a woman's chaste loyalty to her husband. Just as a virtuous man would serve only one father and one dynasty, a virtuous woman was to remain loyal to one husband her entire life. Once widowed, virtuous women eschewed sexual contact with any other man; the state honored those women who chose to commit suicide to demonstrate their absolute commitment to the chastity cult (Elvin 123–29). Pan Jinlian epitomizes the inversion of normative female virtues. Beyond her indifference to the concept of chastity, Jinlian is directly responsible for the death of three husbands as well as Ximen Qing's firstborn male heir (3.59.468; 59.11a). Not surprisingly, Pan Jinlian is equally indifferent to the norms of filial piety. As modeled by Lu Ji, providing one's parents with special foods, one of the twenty-four filial paragons, was a conventional filial act ("*Twenty-Four Paragons*"); when her mother is visiting, Jinlian first presents a variety of special fruits to her maid Chunmei (Ch'un-mei) before setting aside the leftovers for her mother (4.73.415; 73.19a). As other characters in the novel remark, all the other women in the household treat Jinlian's mother with some affection, while Jinlian is abusive toward her (4.78.607–08, 610–16; 78.18a–19b, 20b–25a). Jinlian's most shocking transgression of filial norms occurs after her mother's death. According to ritual norms, children should be so distraught after learning of a parent's death that they cannot eat for the first three days; two days after her mother dies, Jinlian fellates her son-in-law, Chen Jingji (Ch'en Ching-chi), when he sticks his penis out a window as she is passing by (5.82.25–26; 82.5b).

Filial Piety and Pornography

The hermeneutic role of filial piety in *Plum* extends beyond the creation of a didactic framework through which to interpret the various characters in the novel. Filial piety also performs an aesthetic function in establishing a symbolic binary anchored on one end by the self-restraint associated with filial piety and on the other with unbridled self-indulgence. Invoking either of these possibilities raises the specter of the opposing value. For example, the twenty-four positions depicted in the sex manual that Ximen Qing introduces to Pan Jinlian immediately call to mind *The Twenty-Four Paragons of Filial Piety*, one of the most popular texts on filial piety (1.13.271; 13.12b). That Chen Jingji, Ximen Qing's son-in-law, later tries out all twenty-four positions with Pan Jinlian makes the parallelism between the two texts explicit (5.83.49; 83.9a). The scene in which the naked Pan Jinlian chases mosquitoes on a hot night and then is aroused by the sight of Ximen Qing's penis evokes the filial Wu Meng, who slept naked near his parents' bed on summer nights to attract the mosquitoes away from them ("*Twenty-Four Paragons*"). Pan Jinlian's sucking wakes Ximen Qing and for the first time he refers to himself as "your dada" (你達達; 1.18.371; 18.10a). Pan Jinlian explicitly invokes *The Twenty-Four Paragons* when she calls Ximen Qing "another Wang Xiang, braving the frigid cold of the twelfth month and lying on the icy surface of that stone bench to prove your filiality" (你是王祥寒冬臘月行孝順, 在那石頭牀上臥冰哩) after he tells her he will sleep with Song Huilian (Sung Hui-lien) in the icy Hidden Spring Grotto (2.23.51; 23.6b). Because Wang Xiang's cruel stepmother craved fresh fish in the dead of winter, the filial Wang stripped off his shirt and lay down on a frozen river. After the heat of his tears and body melted a hole in the ice, two carp jumped out to reward his piety ("*Twenty-Four Paragons*").

Whereas the basic definition of pornography is "the explicit descriptions of sexual organs and sexual practices with the aim of arousing sexual feeling" (Hunt 10), the mode of pornography used in *Plum* and many of its source texts foregrounds ritual transgression. Though readers may endorse the depictions of sexual acts in *Plum* as a celebration of a natural sexuality unimpeded by cultural restraints, most depictions of sex acts in *Plum* emphasize perversion in the way they incorporate the erasure of normative architectural and ritual boundaries. As mentioned, one of the fundamental goals of Confucian ritual is the creation and maintenance of distinctions between the hierarchical status roles: these distinctions are marked by both status and the architectural boundary that separates the inner women's quarters from the outer areas of the household associated with the men.

Characters in *Plum* continually transgress boundaries: Ximen Qing jumps over garden walls to pursue illicit sexual relationships (1.13.262; 13.8b); he particularly enjoys seducing married women, including the wives of his servants and employees; Ximen Qing and Pan Jinlian have sex with their servants; and several of Ximen Qing's courtesan lovers approach Ximen Qing's wives to be adopted as daughters. As the narrator cautions:

> Gentle reader take note: The head of a household ought never to engage in compromising intimacies with the wives of his slaves or servants. Sooner or later such conduct:
> Confuses the distinction between high and low,
> Opens the doors to surreptitious abuses, and
> Poses a threat to public morality.   (2.22.36)

> 看官聽說: 凡家主切不可與奴僕并家人之婦苟且私押, 久後必紊亂上下, 竊弄
> 奸欺, 敗壞風俗.   (22.5a)

The porousness of the architectural and status boundaries in the household is reflected in the repeated descriptions of bystanders spying and eavesdropping on many of the scenes of transgressive sex.

In contrast to the general lack of respect for architectural and status boundaries shown by the members of Ximen Qing's household, a well-ordered household regulates the physical and social movements of the inhabitants so that the women are protected from any hint of sexual impropriety and so that everyone, especially the servants, keeps to their proper place. Keith McMahon refers to this idealized state as "containment" (*Causality* 2). Containment is a moral concept that connotes the ability to close oneself off from desires, especially the metonymic four vices of drunkenness, lust, avarice, and anger (or ego).[8] Traditional literary aesthetics typically show how a character's indulgence in any of the vices in the narrative results in images of loss or leaking on a number of interrelated levels: corporeal (i.e., bodily) leaking (1.1.27, 4.79.639; 1.10b–11a, 79.9b); architectural leaking (1.8.167–68, 1.13.264; 8.12a–12b, 13.7b); material loss or theft of physical items (3.43.46, 5.81.7; 43.3b, 81.5a); and, on the macrocosmic level, the weakening of the empire, illustrated by the passing of bribes (1.18.360, 3.55.356; 18.2b, 55.6b) and the invasion of barbarian troops (1.17.344, 5.100.396; 17.4b, 100.4a). The dissolution of Ximen Qing's household in the last twenty chapters of the novel is mirrored in the final chapter with the collapse of the Northern Song dynasty (960–1127) when the Jin (Chin) troops capture Emperors Huizong (Hui-tsung [r. 1100–26]) and Qinzong (Ch'in-tsung [r. 1126–27]; 5.100.402; 100.7a). The message is clear: transgressing ritual boundaries has serious, even deadly, consequences.

Sexual containment is one of the behaviors associated with filial piety. For example, avoiding contact with one's wife during the three years of mourning for a parent was one of the conventional markers of piety. The inversion of filial restraint is intergenerational incest. The Chinese term for incest, *luanlun* 亂倫, literally means "disordering the Five Relationships." Implicit in the character *lun*, which appears in the Chinese expression for the Five Cardinal Relationships, *wulun* 五倫, is the Confucian concern that all relationships should be defined by the system of hierarchical ethics known as ritual. As discussed, social order is actualized through the rectification of names when "the father acts as a father, and the son acts as a son." The complex structure of traditional Chinese elite households, home to multigenerational and frequently polygynous conjugal units as well as dozens of servants, employees, and retainers, necessitated a strict code of behavior to protect the chastity of the women and to reinforce the status distinctions between masters and servants, among relatives of proximate age who might belong to different generations, and between wives and concubines.

Plum foregrounds the theme of incest to an unusual degree (Plaks, "Problem" 126–31). Ximen Qing is sexually stimulated when his lovers call him "daddy": as he encourages Jinlian, "You little whore, devote yourself to wantonly calling me 'Daddy,' in order to coax out your daddy's spunk" (小淫婦兒, 你好生浪浪的叫著達達, 哄出你達達屜兒來罷; 3.52.257; 52.2b; see also 4.78.584; 78.4b). The rival courtesans Li Guijie (Li Kuei-chieh) and Wu Yin'er (Wu Yin-erh), both patronized by Ximen Qing, seek to integrate themselves into his family by becoming the adopted daughters of Wu Yueniang and Li Ping'er (2.32.245, 3.42.21; 32.3a, 42.2a). If it were not already enough of a subversion of social boundaries that prostitutes should enter the family of an official as adopted daughters, their new relationships establish them as Ximen Qing's daughters and lovers. The perspicacious Ying Bojue (Ying Po-chüeh) comments to Ximen Qing, "Now that you've acquired an adopted daughter to boot, in the future, if you sprinkle a little water on her, barren as she is, she may end up producing a juicy little niece or nephew for me" (這回子連乾女兒也有了. 到明日洒上些水, 看出汁兒來; 2.32.256; 32.9b).

While many of the sexual encounters in *Plum* evoke symbolic incest, it is Pan Jinlian's sexual relationship with her son-in-law, Chen Jingji, that counts as actual incest. When Chen Jingji plays the role of the bereaved filial son, the primary mourner, for Li Ping'er, it demonstrates his ritual integration into the family (4.63.89, 4.65.129; 63.4a, 65.5a). Jinlian initiates her incestuous affair with Jingji within a week of Ximen Qing's death, saying, "My son, today your mother will give you what you want" (我兒, 你娘今日可成就了你罷; 4.80.673; 80.4b). After Chen Jingji starts sneaking into her apartment for their sexual assignations, Pan Jinlian gives him Ximen Qing's bag of sex toys (5.83.49; 83.9a). The ease with which son(-in-law) displaces father would immediately remind Chinese readers of one of the most important source texts for *Plum*. The pornographic *Lord of Perfect Satisfaction* (*Ruyijun zhuan* 如意君傳) begins with a scene in which the crown prince, the future Emperor Gaozong 唐高宗 (r. 649–83), initiates an affair with his father's consort, as his father, Emperor Taizong 唐太宗 (r. 626–49), lies on his deathbed (Stone 134). *The Lord of Perfect Satisfaction* is a fictionalized rendering of historical fact; this woman, whom Gaozong raised to empress, later usurped the throne, established her own dynasty (the Zhou [690–705]) and ruled as Empress Wu Zetian 武則天 (r. 690–704). Although it often seems that no act can scandalize the go-betweens who populate the fictional world of *Plum*, when Chen Jingji tries to hire Auntie Xue (Hsüeh) to help him communicate with Jinlian, "she laughed out loud, saying, 'Whoever heard of a son-in-law making out with his mother-in-law? Such conduct is unheard of in this world'" (誰家女婿戲丈母? 世間那裡有此事; 5.85.81; 85.6a). It is utterly fitting that Jinlian's only pregnancy results from this incestuous coupling with her son-in-law; although she had been desperate to bear a child for Ximen Qing, as the inversion of a virtuous bride who is stereotypically rewarded with fertility, Jinlian aborts this child and throws his body into the privy (5.85.75; 85.3a).

Even in its absence, the concept of filial piety is a productive lens through which to understand the characterizations and plot of *Plum*. Filial children are willing to subordinate their ego and desires in order to serve the common good of the intergenerational family. As defined by ritual norms, the self was no more than one link in a chain that connected the ancestors to future generations. The proper form of sexuality within this family model was reproductive. It should be noted that traditional views of reproductive sex in China did not preclude physical pleasure or intimacy. This, however, is not the type of sexual activity represented in *Plum*. Once readers become aware of the extent to which the sexual acts depicted in *Plum* reflect ever more frenzied perversions of reproductive sex, it becomes increasingly challenging for us to read the pornographic scenes in the novel as a defense of sexual pleasure. That Ximen Qing's posthumous son, ironically named Xiaoge (Hsiao-ko, "Filial Brother"), becomes a monk seems a fitting conclusion to the orgy of nonreproductive modes of sexuality depicted in the narrative. This one surviving male heir marks the end of Ximen's lineage and illustrates the ultimate sterility of Ximen Qing's rejection of filial norms.

NOTES

[1] Two pieces of evidence that support this theory are that one of Yan Shifan's style names was "Eastern Tower" (Donglou 東樓), an obvious parallel to the protagonist's unusual family name, "Western Gate" (Ximen 西門), and that Shifan's childhood name was Qing'er 慶兒, which includes one of the same characters that appears in the name of Ximen Qing (西門慶). See Zhang Zhupo, "How to Read the *Chin P'ing Mei*" 222 and *ZZP* 15b. See part 1, "Materials," for a fuller account.

[2] For excellent discussions of Zhang Zhupo's reading of *Plum*, see N. Ding 117–40.

[3] Unless otherwise noted, parenthetical citations refer to Roy's translation, *The Plum in the Golden Vase*, and to *Jin Ping Mei cihua* 金瓶梅詞話 (*Plum in the Golden Vase: A Ballad Tale*).

[4] Significantly, the Chongzhen and Zhang Zhupo editions mention Ximen Qing's father by name and place of origin when Ximen Qing is first introduced (*XXP* 1.3a; *ZZP* 1.13a).

[5] By way of comparison, the first thing Han Daoguo, the husband of Wang Liu'er, does when he returns from a business trip is to bow to the spirit tablets of his ancestors (5.81.6; 81.4a).

[6] For a different translation, see Rosemont 105.

[7] "Back-garden" relations is a common expression for anal sex.

[8] The four vices are the topic of the prefatory lyrics attached to *Plum* (1.10–11; 1a–3b).

Games in *The Plum in the Golden Vase*

Paize Keulemans

A study of games may at first seem frivolous, but those who read the novel *The Plum in the Golden Vase* (*Jin Ping Mei* 金瓶梅) with care cannot help but note how often games appear. A look at some of the illustrations that accompany the Chongzhen (*xiuxiang*) edition underscores this point. Chapter 23, for instance, depicts three of the consorts of Ximen Qing (Hsi-men Ch'ing)—Li Ping'er (Li P'ing-erh), Pan Jinlian (P'an Chin-lien), and Meng Yulou (Meng Yü-lou)—gambling on the outcome of a board game (fig. 1).[1] Chapter 25 features the various ladies of Ximen's household, including the ill-fated Song Huilian (Sung Hui-lien), sporting on a swing (fig. 2). The illustration to chapter 15 shows, amid the New Year's revelries, not a single game but three (fig. 3). In the foreground Ximen Qing enjoys a game of kickball (*cuju* 蹴鞠) with his favorite courtesan, Li Guijie (Li Kuei-chieh). In the background are the remains of two other games: a game of backgammon (*shuanglu* 雙陸) on the table and a vase and arrow used for a game called pitch-pot (*touhu* 投壺) right next to it. Even when we least expect it, the novel includes references to games. Such is the case, for instance, in the notorious chapter 27 where Ximen Qing ties his consort Pan Jinlian to a grape trellis and throws chilled plums at her exposed vagina, a "game" he calls "flesh pot" (*rouhu* 肉壺), a pun on "pitch-pot," a game the two played only a few moments earlier (2.27.145; 27.11a; fig. 4).[2]

The way the novel exhaustively lists the various popular games of its time should not surprise us. Given that the novel describes the domestic lives of people who spend most of their time doing little or nothing, it is not shocking to find its characters indulging in games. As other essays in this volume point out, the novel is a veritable encyclopedia of late Ming pleasures suitable to the domestic life of Ximen Qing and his consorts. The novel includes endless sartorial depictions of fabrics, hairstyles, and shoes, just as it teaches us the details of wines, teas, and snacks, among many other culinary delicacies. The different games depicted in the novel arguably serve as merely one more aspect of the indolent lifestyle of the late imperial rich and famous that the novel describes with such loving detail.

That said, the very idleness of games as depicted in *Plum* also raises an important question: If games are so unimportant, then why mention them to begin with? In fact, we might ask this same question about the novel itself. Wherein lies the significance of a text that enjoys spending so much time on documenting activities that seem so indolent, wasteful, and insignificant? To answer these questions, I do not offer an encyclopedic overview of the various games in the novel, something impossible in an essay this short.[3] Instead, I focus on two of the many moments where games are featured in the novel. Through a reading of these two moments—one focusing on a game of dominoes, the other featuring

Figure 1. "Li Ping'er Loses a Board Game and Stands a Treat" (賭棋枰瓶兒輸鈔).

Figure 2. "Ladies Enjoy the Swing on a Spring Day" (吳月娘春畫鞦韆).

Figure 3. "Hangers-on Abet Debauchery in the Verdant Spring Bordello" (狎客幫嫖麗春院).

Figure 4. "Pan Jinlian Engages in a Drunken Orgy under the Grape Arbor" (潘金蓮醉鬧葡萄架).

a mere glimpse of a game of go (*weiqi* 圍棋)—I suggest that games in the novel function as a microcosm of the novel itself. What at first seems to be a simple, innocent, and mostly irrelevant pastime is shown to hold the potential for serious social perversion. At the same time, when viewed with a critical and distant eye, these games (and the novel) also offer the promise of redemption. Games may seem irrelevant, a mere frivolous detail in a novel already famous for its frivolous, if not simply dissolute, nature. Yet arguably it is precisely by paying attention to this seemingly unimportant and irrelevant detail that we can find its purpose. It is only by taking games (and the novel) seriously, while at the same time playing or reading without getting absorbed into the game or text itself, that we can turn the insignificance of games into a virtue and transform the possible harm of a popular but scurrilous novel into a moral critique of its indolent times.

A Game of Dominoes

The illustration that accompanies chapter 18 of *Plum* shows a merry domestic gathering of people who are centered around a game of dominoes (*yapai* 牙牌; fig. 5).[4] At the heart of the gathering, around a table with three hands of dominoes laid out, we find the people playing: the head mistress of the household, Wu Yueniang (Wu Yüeh-niang); her son-in-law, Chen Jingji (Ch'en Ching-chi); the third mistress of the household, Meng Yulou; and Chen Jingji's wife, Ximen Dajie (Hsi-men Ta-chie), who for the time being is happy to watch the proceedings from the sidelines. Meanwhile, drawn to the excitement of the game, we see on the left a fifth character drawing a curtain aside to enter the room—Ximen Qing's fifth consort, Pan Jinlian.

This is where the moral of the chapter enters as well. After all, even though this social gathering seems perfectly innocent—what could possibly be wrong with a few family members enjoying a friendly game of dominoes?—it is, of course, not. The party takes place in Wu Yueniang's inner chambers, and the presence of a son-in-law in the lady's bedroom is completely inappropriate. Though

Figure 5. "On Seeing Pan Jinlian, Chen Jingji Loses His Wits" (見嬌娘敬濟魂銷).

nothing will happen between Wu Yueniang and her son-in-law, this is not the case for Chen Jingji and his other mother-in-law, Pan Jinlian. For the two of them, this moment marks the beginning of a long incestuous relationship that will span much of the next sixty chapters of the novel and end in both characters' untimely deaths.

It is important to understand how this inappropriate social gathering (and hence the various immoral events that follow) is made possible by a seemingly insignificant detail, namely the game of dominoes. In the illustration, the game centers the story visually, drawing the viewer's eye to the upper right corner of the page, just as the game draws the various characters to the table on which the game is played. Moreover, by being positioned at the center of the picture, the game anchors the visual connections that are positioned slightly further away from the center in the margins. The entrance of Pan Jinlian in the upper left corner is echoed by the promise of the bedchamber in the upper right corner, both of which welcome the reader's eyes through drawn curtains, a symbol that is repeated in the felt cloth that covers the game table at the center. In the narrative itself, the game matches the visual architecture of the illustration acoustically and temporally. After all, it is only after hearing the sound of dominoes being played in the room next door that Chen Jingji's interest is piqued (1.18.367; 18.8a). It is the game that becomes the pretext that next allows him to be invited into the deepest recesses of Wu Yueniang's boudoir, where before long he finds himself at the heart of the action, joined by his future lover, Pan Jinlian (1.18.368; 18.8a). Simply put, the repercussions of the first, fateful meeting between Chen Jingji and his mother-in-law Pan Jinlian are extensive, but the series of events is introduced through an almost insignificant and playful detail, a game of dominoes.

Why is a game such an appropriate plot device for setting in motion the immensely immoral proceedings that follow? In the next section, I argue that it is precisely because games seem so inconsequential that the novel can create a finely woven narrative in which small, seemingly unimportant moral missteps ultimately lead to significant moral failures. Here I want to draw attention to another important function of games—that is, the way in which games promote sociability. This production of social relationships is, of course, crucial to the definition of games. As Johan Huizinga points out in his pathbreaking cultural history of games, play "promotes the formation of social groupings" (13). In the context of *Plum*, this social aspect of games should be understood in more literary terms. First, with respect to character, games represent one way in which narrative can bring different, often distant figures into intimate contact. And second, in terms of plot, such initial contact can lead to relationships that, in Huizinga's words, "tend to become permanent even after the play is over" (12).

Because *Plum* is a novel of moral corruption, this contact between characters and the action that follows is inevitably inappropriate. As the dominoes scene shows, people who should have stayed separate are brought together through the sociability produced by the game. In terms of gender this of course means that the sexes that should have remained segregated come together when they join each other around the table for a game of dominoes. Crucially, however, games also allow for other social transgressions, most notably the bringing together of people who belong to different classes. In chapter 18, for instance, we are told that, before Chen Jingji joined the game, Wu Yueniang's maid Yuxiao (Yü-hsiao) had been playing with the other wives, a detail that seems unimportant until we learn that the maid is so engrossed in the game that she fails to heed her mistress's call (1.18.357; 18.8a). Games, in short, threaten to extinguish the social differences that are so fundamental to early modern Chinese society. Once lost in play, the maid forgets that her mistress is her superior, and the son-in-law approaches his mother-in-law without paying attention to the least bit of ritual decorum.

In presenting games as a threat to social hierarchy, *Plum* merely gives literary form to a broader early modern anxiety about games. Sixteenth- and seventeenth-century Chinese texts are filled with anecdotes in which games, and in particular the gambling associated with games, erase the boundaries between social classes. As Chen Hsi-yuan points out in his study of the game of Mah-Jongg (*majiang* 馬將), the seventeenth-century scholar Wu Weiye 吳偉業 (1609–71) wrote an extensive critique of gambling—a biography wittily entitled *Ye gong zhuan* 葉公傳 (*The Biography of Mr. Ace*)—in which the loss of social distinction is explicitly spelled out: "[O]nce people take their seat [at the table to play cards], they no longer differentiate between old and young, superior and inferior" (入其坐者, 不復以少長貴賤為齒; my trans.; Chen Hsi-yuan 148). In other anecdotes, this socially transgressive nature of games is imagined as a contagion between classes and genders. Such is the case, for instance, in the writing of the scholar Dai Mingshi 戴名世 (1653–1713), who argued that the game of *madiao* 馬吊, a predecessor to the late-nineteenth-century game of Mah-Jongg, was first played by sedan chair carriers in the capital only to spread later to the grand scholars and their wives (Chen Hsi-yuan 147–48).

Games are of course not really to blame for the erasure of social boundaries in society at large. But players do tend to lose themselves in the game, just as games, at least for the duration of the game itself, call for the equal treatment of each player regardless of their actual social status. As a result, it is easy to see how games could become a powerful symbol of the loss of traditional social distinctions that defined the early modern world. Because of this, it is not difficult to see why *Plum* would employ games as one way of registering Ximen Qing's many social transgressions; is he not a vulgar merchant who fails to keep to his ordained social status (*bu shou benfen* 不守本分)? Nor is it surprising, as we shall see, why the novel would characterize its most transgressive characters as "players." Games, like novels, create imaginary spaces in which traditional ritual rules and social roles no longer hold, an idea both exhilarating and threatening at the same time.

Even though games threaten a loss of social distinction, when it comes to the reader of the novel and the characters, *Plum* also employs games to reinscribe such differences with a vengeance. Most notably, and rather ironically, the novel reinstates social hierarchies by allowing the reader to position themself with respect to the players in the novel as a more advanced connoisseur of games. In the case of the dominoes scene, for instance, this superior knowledge of the game is based on a metafictional, explicitly extradiegetic, and ultimately poetic understanding of the name of the particular combination of dominoes each player lays on the table. In the paragraph in which each hand is fully described, we read that

> Meng Yulou melded a double six, a one six, and a double one to produce the combination known as "Heaven and Earth Separated." Chen Jingji added a five-six and another double six to Yulou's double six to produce the combination known as "One Sport Short." Wu Yueniang put down a pair of double fours and a double three, attempting to make the combination known as "Eight that Don't Add Up."　(1.18.368)

> 玉樓出了個天地分; 經濟出了恨點不到頭; 吳月娘出了個四紅沉八不就.
> 　(18.8b)

Though the combinations here seem innocuous, what each of the names secretly hints at is the inappropriate nature of the social gathering.[5] In the absence of Ximen Qing, the patriarch whose own philandering and constant absence make all this hanky-panky possible, "Heaven and Earth" (i.e., male and female) are separated. Chen Jingji plays "One Sport Short," a hint that the one character still missing from the party, Pan Jinlian, will enter next. Finally, Wu Yueniang, who in her own muddleheaded way has produced this breach of propriety by inviting her son-in-law into the bedroom, plays "Eight that Don't Add Up."

The players themselves of course are fully unaware of the symbolic significance of these names. Given that they only care about calculating their temporary winnings and points, the poetic references and fateful implications of each combination of dominoes are lost on them. In contrast, the well-educated reader, intimately familiar with the various guidebooks that offered both the numerical combinations and the classic poetic references of each name, would have immediately realized the literary game being played. Simply put, both the reader of the novel and the characters in the novel play games. It is just that the games played are fundamentally different. Whereas the characters are distracted by the pleasures of the game (if only to move from the game to the distractions of the bedroom soon thereafter), the reader instead focuses on the hidden meanings, the clever wordplay, and the intricate literary strategies employed by the novel.

A Game of Go

For readers interested in games, a small detail in the illustration that accompanies chapter 97 cannot help but draw one's attention (fig. 6). While most viewers

Figure 6. "The Spurious Cousins Resume Their Clandestine Affair" (假弟妹暗續鶯膠).

will be distracted by the two naked lovers in the middle of a pavilion, the reader studying games will note that in the lower left corner the illustrator has included two stools flanking a table, on top of which we see a go-board and two jars holding the game pieces. The game is, of course, a mere detail. The text only mentions the game three times, very briefly, and amid events that include an important military commander being hoodwinked by his new wife and two old lovers engaging in a secret and illicit tryst while pretending to be cousins; as the novel slowly works its way to its dramatic end—that is, to the fall of the Northern Song dynasty—a few games of go seem to matter little. The game seems to be a mere descriptive, superfluous detail that serves no purpose.

That said, *Plum* is a text that enjoys its details. Indeed, when some scholars praise the novel for its unprecedented "realism," what they often mean is that the novel lavishes an overwhelming amount of detail on objects and events belonging to the realm of everyday life for what seems to be little reason. Material objects—interior decorations, the fabrics of clothing, even the architectural layout of the garden belonging to Ximen Qing's house—are all described in such detail that the reader can almost visualize the scene. Similarly, though the novel eventually ends with the fall of the Northern Song dynasty, it never really depicts battles at the frontier or intrigues at court. Instead, the narrative prefers the humdrum detail of wives chatting in bedrooms, husbands going on excursions to the pleasure quarter, or servants stealing silver from inattentive masters.

The interest in such seemingly insignificant, everyday detail can of course be read in different ways. As Naifei Ding has pointed out, the novel's dense visual descriptions do not represent a love of reality so much as they testify to a fetishization of language (189). Conversely, as Wai-yee Li points out in this volume, we can also read *Plum* as a text that deliberately divorces its material objects from any symbolic or romantic meaning, turning objects into nothing but material artifacts and people into little more than objects of exchange as a result. Elsewhere, Sophie Volpp argues that the novel's interest in depicting sartorial choices in such detail is the result of Ming dynasty sumptuary laws and the ways in which a merchant such as Ximen Qing breaks each one of the minute legal strictures of Ming society ("Gift"). Scholars clearly disagree on why and how the novel employs details, but they all agree that the novel seems to care about such trivia.

The textual detail of the game board in chapter 97 serves as one of those minutiae that at first seems insignificant or merely descriptive but that on closer examination suggests deeper meaning. In fact, the detail of the go-board arguably presents a kind of metacommentary on detail itself. Precisely because games seem so unimportant at first and precisely because here the game of go is presented as an easily overlooked detail, the novel ends up admonishing the reader to pay attention to precisely that detail, to find meaning amid the seemingly insignificant. Or, to paraphrase Roland Barthes, the French literary scholar who famously theorized what he called the "reality effect" of the seemingly superfluous detail in French realist fiction, *Plum* challenges us to find the significance of the insignificant ("Reality Effect").[6]

The novel finds such significance by emphasizing the game as the first step in an extended sequence that eventually ends in full-blown adultery. Indeed, like the illustration depicting the detail of the game board right next to the adulterous couple, the narrative establishes a connection between the game and the moment of sexual misconduct by placing the two in sequential order. In the span of a few lines, we read how the foreplay begins when the Chen Jingji and Pang Chunmei (P'ang Ch'un-mei) first exchange cup for cup ("first a cup for you, then a cup for me" [你一杯, 我一杯]), then play one game after another ("first a game for you, then a game for me" [你一盤, 我一盤]), until, before long, "girdle pendants are untied, jade bodies are disclosed, and ruby lips extended" (解佩露相如之玉, 朱唇點漢; 5.97.338–39; 97.6b–7a). Realism is arguably an effect here, but only a side effect. By including the detail of the game, the novel creates a convincing causal sequence of events where adulterous sex appears to be a logical result of a series of smaller moral missteps. To include an insignificant game of go as a first small step on the road to moral disaster seems somehow appropriate in a novel that for the most part depicts the domestic life of a provincial merchant but that ends with the fall of a dynasty.

This reading of the novel, which through a long causal chain intimately ties everyday behavior to larger questions of (political) life and death, is generally associated with the orthodox philosophy of the neo-Confucian school of thought. In his influential commentary to the Confucian classic *The Great Learning* (*Daxue* 大學), Zhu Xi 朱熹 (1130–1200) reminds readers that those who want to enlighten the world must first order the affairs of state; those who wish to order the affairs of state must first regulate their family life; the regulation of family life is dependent on self-cultivation, which in turn is preceded by rectifying one's heart and making one's thought sincere (Carlitz, *Rhetoric* 29–30). Neither family life, the individual, nor even one's inner thoughts are irrelevant in Zhu Xi's totalistic account. Through a finely woven net of synecdochic connections, these

details come to represent the basis of a well-ordered or, conversely, truly chaotic state. *Plum* is, of course, not a work of philosophy. Yet as a literary work the
novel offers a similar chain of cause and effect, though in a different form, namely
its plot. By carefully painting each link in the causal chain, from a game of go to
full-blown adultery, from provincial household to imperial capital, the novel illustrates with captivating detail how the morally dissolute life of an ostensibly
insignificant merchant is in fact tied to a larger, political dissolution that in the
end causes the fall of the Northern Song.

The game of go, which requires constant painstaking attention and in which
the key to winning or losing is often found in an early, seemingly insignificant
move, is of course the perfect metaphor for this philosophy. Played on a grid of
nineteen-by-nineteen lines, the game serves as a microcosm that emphasizes how
events, whether on the board or in life, are governed by a series of small decisions with large consequences. Indeed, this is how the game, with its apparently
infinite variety of moves, has often been understood throughout imperial history: as a mirror of the real world that can strategically guide its player to a better understanding of the endless intricacies of the battlefield, life, and arguably
the universe itself.[7]

When writing about such a game, premodern scholars often mimicked the
minute yet ever-expanding nature of the game. For instance, the Song dynasty
neo-Confucian philosopher Shao Yong 邵雍 (1011–77), in trying to capture the
significance of the game of go, could not help but write poems of unprecedented
length and complexity. At 180 couplets, 360 lines, and 1,800 characters, the
scholar's "Great Ode on Observing the Game of Go" ("Guan qi da yin" 觀棋大吟)
is the longest poem produced in premodern literature.[8] *Plum*, a novel of one
hundred chapters filled with countless characters and innumerable events told
in the most exquisite detail, offers a similar, minutely drawn mirror of life. Like
the game of go, the novel represents a microcosm whose very complexity challenges us to make out the rules and learn from observed mistakes.

Yet if the game of go teaches that one should pay attention to detail, it also
teaches that one should not lose oneself in such detail. Indeed, when emphasizing how the game of go should be viewed as a guide to understanding the cosmos, scholars also tended to carefully emphasize that the game's most valuable
lesson was perhaps learned by not getting distracted by the game to begin with.
Here we might recall the title of Shao Yong's poem, "The Great Ode on Observing the Game of Go." The point is not to play the game of go but to observe it,
preferably from a careful and critical distance.[9] Or, as one influential late Ming
author of moral scripts, Hong Yingming 洪應明 (late sixteenth century), summarized the popular idea in his educational tract, *A Discussion of Bitter Roots* (*Cai
gen tan* 菜根談), "The affairs of the world are like a game of chess; those who do
not make a move are its true masters" (世事如棋局. 不着的才是高手; my trans.; 83).

Simply put, when the novel juxtaposes the game of go with the pleasure of
sex, the text suggests that in both it is best to be strategic, not to lose oneself in

the moment but instead to pay careful attention to each and every move. Such a message is lost, of course, on the two lovers depicted in the illustration in chapter 97. Chen Jingji and Pang Chunmei are so captivated by their pursuit of pleasure that they fail to pay much attention to where their moral missteps might lead. Not surprisingly, such inattention soon leads to the lovers' demise. In chapter 99, Chen Jingji, once again finding himself in the embrace of Pang Chunmei, fails to notice that his intimate whispers are overheard by Zhang Sheng (Chang Sheng), who avenges himself on the hapless Jingji by decapitating him. One chapter later, Pang Chunmei, having failed to strategically conserve her life force, dies of sexual exhaustion. Perhaps the two would have fared better had they paid more careful attention to the lessons offered by the game of go instead of viewing it as an insignificant game.

When Ximen Qing is first officially introduced in the second chapter, the narrator adds to the protagonist's long list of moral failings the following: "He also liked to gamble, and there was little he didn't know about backgammon, elephant chess, and the various word games played by breaking characters down into their component parts" (又會賭博, 雙陸象棋, 抹牌道字, 無不通曉; 1.2.53; 2.6b). The phrase is of course a cliché, a brief summary of games that serves as shorthand for characterizing someone as an unreliable loafer. As such, other disreputable characters in the novel—Ximen Qing's son-in-law, Chen Jingji (1.18.367; 18.8a), Ximen Qing's notorious fifth consort, Pan Jinlian (1.3.65; 3.2a), and Ximen Qing's favorite hanger-on, Ying Bojue (Ying Po-chüeh; 1.10.200; 10.7b)—are described in almost exactly the same terms. That said, when *Plum* describes Ximen Qing as a player, the novel goes out of its way to insert the line within a description that is otherwise borrowed wholesale from the novel *Outlaws of the Marsh* (*Shuihu zhuan* 水滸傳). Though a mere cliché and a minor detail, the novel clearly has an interest in games that its literary predecessor does not share.

In *Plum*, the playful detail of the game matters. Though it might appear insignificant, it points to larger themes that are much easier to detect: the transgression of social mores, the loss of crucial hierarchical distinctions, the fear of losing self-control, and the moral vigilance that is demanded of people when they find themselves in an age plagued by ethical uncertainty. If games help us to discern some of the more important moral lessons of the novel, equally important is that the seeming insignificance of the games played allows us to understand some of the innovative aesthetics that define the novel, one of which is a remarkable eye for detail, which should not be understood, as others have argued, as a sign of incipient realism. Rather, it is better understood as a literary game suitable only for, supposedly at least, the superior moral and aesthetic mind of the elite reader. For late Ming readers who found themselves surrounded by a culture that seemed to pay attention only to the superfluous, the excessive, and the insignificant, and in an age when culture was ever more readily consumed by the "vulgar" lower classes, games served not only as a sign of the times but also as a way of establishing oneself as a superior mind, a tasteful reader as opposed to a crass player.

NOTES

[1] As elsewhere, the text of the novel merely mentions a "board game" and does not explicitly clarify whether the game is go (*weiqi* 圍棋), an elegant game typically associated with the well-educated, and a clear marker of class, or, alternatively, elephant chess (*xiangqi* 象棋), a less exalted game. The illustration has for a variety of reasons settled on the game of go. For more on the game of go as it appears in the illustration to chapter 97, see the last section of this essay.

[2] Unless otherwise noted, parenthetical citations refer to Roy's translation, *The Plum in the Golden Vase*, and to *Jin Ping Mei cihua* 金瓶梅詞話 (*Plum in the Golden Vase: A Ballad Tale*).

[3] A full list would include physical sports, such as kickball, swinging, and jump rope; games of cards and dominoes; more strategic games, such as the vulgar elephant chess and the more elegant game of go; and the ancillary practices associated with games such as gambling (e.g., dice, knucklebones, backgammon, and other board games), drinking (guess-fingers [a game not unlike rock-paper-scissors, where two players have to hold out a number of fingers and guess the combined number], among many other games), and sex (most notably pitch-pot). Finally, there are the many word games associated with several characters in the novel, most notably the figure of Ying Bojue, and that are also played by the text of the novel itself. Unfortunately, there is no English-language study that lists the various games in the novel, though David Roy does dutifully translate and explain each game. The best source in Chinese is Bai Weiguo's *Jin Ping Mei fengsu tan* (*A Discussion of Customs in* Plum in the Golden Vase), which spends over a hundred pages explaining the rules, history, and literary significance of most of the games played in *Plum*.

[4] Note that the novel, though clearly describing a game of dominoes, uses more generic terms for the game that can also be used for playing cards, a game closely related to dominoes. The term used above, *yapai*, is particular to the game of dominoes. See Lo, "China's Passion."

[5] The use of such names for domino combinations became increasingly generic. In the eighteenth-century *Story of the Stone* (*Honglou meng* 紅樓夢), a novel with an even larger number of games than *Plum*, such names can become the basis for all kinds of poetic games, as we see in chapter 40. The translator, David Hawkes, explains in an appendix the at times puzzling combinations and poetic names ("Threesomes").

[6] Roland Barthes's original observation is phrased as a question, namely, "What is the significance of insignificance?" ("Reality Effect" 143). Elsewhere, Barthes identifies these arresting details as the punctum of the image—that is, the point where the personal associations triggered by the detail in a photograph break through the studiously constructed overall lesson of the image ("Punctum" 43–45).

[7] Early myths about the genesis of the game attribute its invention to the mythical emperor Yao, who sought to instruct his middling son in the art of political rule. In later poetry, philosophy, and go manuals, the game board is often likened to the world or the universe. See Lo and Wang, "Spider Threads."

[8] This particular poem has not been translated. However, a translation of a shorter poem, "Guan qi chang yin" 觀棋長吟 ("The Long Ode on Observing the Game of Go"), can be found on Shao's *Wikipedia* page (en.wikipedia.org/wiki/Shao_Yong).

[9] Of course merely observing the game could also pose risks. One of the names for the game of go—*lanke* 爛柯, or "rotten handle"—is derived from a popular anecdote from the fifth century. *Tales of the Uncanny* (*Shu yi ji* 述異記), by Ren Fang 任昉 (460–508), tells of a woodcutter who, while watching a game of go played by immortals, loses track of time. When he awakes from his reverie, he finds his axe handle has rotted away. The idea remains the same: the player should not get lost in the game, just as the reader should not get lost in the novel.

Domestic Violence in a Premodern Context in *The Plum in the Golden Vase*

Ying Zhang

Violence is prevalent in *The Plum in the Golden Vase* (*Jin Ping Mei* 金瓶梅), the first Chinese novel centered on a fictional domestic sphere. The novel manages to display all the ills one could imagine in a morally corrupt world. To satisfy men's indulgence in sex, wealth, and power, violence serves as a common tool, as shown in *Plum*'s depiction of an unjust legal system, murderous adulteries, and the misogynist treatment of women. This essay looks at the violence perpetrated in domestic spaces by men, women, masters, and servants in *Plum*. Closely reading the details of instances of domestic abuse allows for a deeper appreciation of the complexity of the characters and their world and of the causes and forms of domestic violence in Ming China.

The analysis of and fight against domestic violence occupies a significant place in modern feminist activism and theories. *Plum* seems to be an obvious example of universal patriarchal oppression. Some scholars focus on the sexual interactions of *Plum*'s male protagonist, Ximen Qing (Hsi-men Ch'ing), with women in the novel and interpret these as abusive and symptomatic of male dominance beyond the realm of sex. Interestingly, although the novel sometimes shows how Ximen Qing mistreats his concubines, it does not devote much attention to this. More often, the reader encounters scenes in which women, for a variety of reasons, abuse other women within the Ximen family compound. Some see the story of the Ximen household as representative of premodern Chinese patriarchal families, in which a husband had an official wife and multiple concubines. Jealousy and competition were inevitable and manifested the brutality inherent in the

Chinese family structure (Yin 141). The novel's representation of violent female behavior has also been interpreted as a reflection of male authors' gynophobia in late imperial China (Cass, *Dangerous Women* 99–101).

How might we map history onto the novel's portrayal of deplorable human relations such as domestic violence without simplifying history or a literary work? On the one hand, as Katherine Carlitz has argued, the depiction of family relations in *Plum*, though to some extent reflective of late Ming historical conditions, should not be read literally, as such a depiction may serve a didactic purpose ("Family" 388–89). On the other hand, as Naifei Ding points out, the male-dominated literati tradition of *Plum* exegesis and its political ethics has continued in some manner in contemporary feminist scholarship. A feminist interpretation of this novel "interjects in its revisionary reading the shadow of its own historical moment and concomitant egalitarian-individualist common sense, just as it might well come to occupy a reformulated yet nonetheless authoritative position of reading" (Ding xxvii–xxviii). Keeping these insights in mind, I show that although we cannot assume that the novel's depiction of the Ximen family's relations is an accurate representation of broader Ming society, it is a meaningful exercise to read the characters' experience with domestic violence both as a literary trope and as a critical reflection on social relations.

Take the historical phenomenon of concubinage as an example.[1] Only five to ten percent of late Ming families could afford to take in concubines. Even fewer had the resources to keep multiple concubines, as Ximen does in the novel, although ample historical sources affirm the existence of such households. Therefore, the Ximen family structure only reflects a particular kind of historical reality. Nonetheless, the bloated scale of this fictional household does allow the author to fully develop his didactic agenda. For male readers in the Ming, the novel "could serve as a textbook about what can go wrong with polygamy" (McMahon, *Misers* 51) and, ultimately, about the abyss of desire and immorality.

Ming elite were concerned about maintaining domestic order in a time of material abundance. Women as wives, concubines, courtesans, and servants populated a gender-status continuum in which distinctions between objects and subjects were rigid only in name. Some Ming literati writers never questioned keeping concubines but warned against the likelihood of chaos and even scandal if too many women—daughters, daughters-in-law, female relatives, concubines, and a horde of maidservants—lived in the same household (Y. Zhang 63–64). In Ming China, the law reflected and protected the privileges of the patriarch and the wife vis-à-vis other women (Chen Baoliang 125–32). Although elite families more or less followed the Confucian idea of maintaining domestic harmony by requiring each family member to respect the hierarchical order and act in accordance with role expectations and behavioral propriety, the husband and his wife could abuse concubines without fear of legal consequences. While the legal distinction between the wife and the concubine was strict, the identity and roles of the concubine remained negotiable and could vary quite significantly from one situation to the next. In some cases, especially if she gave birth to a son, a concubine could garner so much respect and power in a family that she could seriously challenge the wife. But in other cases, her role resembled that of a maidservant. Historical sources present to us a range of possibilities—and sufferings, too—in the lives of concubines, maids who became concubines, and maids who were sexually involved with the patriarch (Yu Xinzhong 272–332). The characters who engage in and endorse domestic violence in *Plum* help us understand this complex historical reality. Furthermore, because the privileges of the concubines are amplified in *Plum*, their frequent maltreatment of maidservants may be understood as mirroring the abuse of real-world concubines at the hands of wives.

Most of the examples examined in this chapter may strike readers as realistic portrayals of violent expressions in everyday life. But it is useful to keep in mind Carlitz's caution against reading *Plum* too literally. I treat domestic violence in *Plum* as integral to the novel's literary and pedagogical agendas rather than reducing it to a collection of cases of patriarchal oppression. Specifically, I focus on how the author uses domestic violence to develop the characters and reveal their relations. I explore how domestic violence serves as a means of communication among the characters in their negotiation for power, status, and legitimacy.

Main Patterns of Domestic Violence

The first episode of domestic violence in the Ximen household, which takes place in chapter 11, demonstrates how domestic violence helps construct status distinctions and power relations. The beginning of this chapter describes a quarrel in the kitchen between Sun Xue'e (Sun Hsüeh-o), the fourth concubine, and Pang Chunmei (P'ang Ch'un-mei), a maid who first serves Ximen Qing's principal wife, Wu Yueniang (Wu Yüeh-niang), but is later reassigned to Pan Jinlian (P'an Chin-lien) after Jinlian enters the household as the fifth concubine. Xue'e is Ximen Qing's least favorite concubine and was originally a maidservant herself. She plays a unique role in the household, managing the kitchen with the help of the wives of the household retainers. The heavy traffic of maidservants to and from the kitchen brings all sorts of information to her. It also means that she has to take other concubines' food orders from maidservants whose status is officially lower than hers. She also participates in cooking. These factors make Xue'e gossipy, sensitive, and combative.

The quarrel between Xue'e and Chunmei in the kitchen ends with Xue'e backing down, but it also plants the seeds of a series of verbal and physical confrontations. Chunmei returns to her mistress, Jinlian, and makes a false claim that Xue'e had said Jinlian and Chunmei connived to share the patriarch's favors and keep him to their quarters. A few days later, Ximen Qing wants cakes and soup for breakfast and orders Chunmei to get them from the kitchen. Chunmei refuses to go. Jinlian adds that if Chunmei goes, some would say that she and her maid connive in keeping Ximen Qing's favors between themselves. Ximen Qing is persuaded. He tells another maid from Jinlian's quarters, Qiuju (Ch'iu-chü), to go to the kitchen. Unsurprisingly, Xue'e makes her wait. Meanwhile, back in Jinlian's quarters,

> [e]nough time went by in which to eat two meals; the woman had already set the table, but still no food was forthcoming. By this time Ximen Qing was getting very hot and bothered.
>
> When the woman saw that Qiuju had not returned she turned to Chunmei and said, "You go back there and see what's going on. That slave still hasn't come back. She must have:
>
>> Taken root and sent up sprouts,
>
> by now."
>
> Chunmei was rather out of sorts to begin with and marched off to the kitchen in a huff.
>
> When she saw that Qiuju was still waiting for the food, she started to curse at her, saying, "You lousy, sleepy-eyed slave! Mother's going to beat the legs right off you! 'Why haven't you come back?' she'd like to know. Father's being kept waiting. As soon as he's eaten he wants to go to the temple fair. There he is up front, anxious to be on his way, and getting increasingly hot and bothered. I've been sent to see if I can drag you back with me."
>
> If Sun Xue'e had not heard these words nothing might have happened, but having heard them, she became enraged and started to curse, saying, "You crazy little whore! You may think I'm like:
>
>> The Mohammedan bowing to Mecca;
>> So whoever shows up gets a bow.
>
> But:
>
>> The saucepan is beaten out of iron;
>> Things take a little time to make.
>
> The congee I had already prepared, he doesn't want to eat. Instead, all of a sudden, he comes up with a brand new idea, and expects me to start grilling cakes and making soup. How was I supposed to know what he wanted?"   (1.11.209–10)

約有兩頓飯時, 婦人已是把桌兒放了, 白不見拿來, 急的西門慶只是暴跳. 婦人見秋菊不來, 使春梅, 你去後邊瞧瞧, 那奴才只顧生根長苗的不見來. 春梅有幾分不順, 使性子走到廚下, 只見秋菊正在那里等著哩, 便罵道: 賊奴才, 娘要卸你那腿哩. 說你怎的就不去了, 爹等著吃了餅要往廟上去, 急的爹在前邊暴跳, 叫我採了你去哩. 這孫雪娥不聽便罷, 聽了心中大怒, 罵道: 怪小淫婦兒. 馬回子拜節, 來到的就是鍋兒. 是鐵打的, 也等慢慢兒的來. 預備下熬的粥兒, 又不吃, 忽剌入新興出來, 要烙餅做湯. 那個是肚裡蛔蟲.   (11.3a–3b)[2]

Ready to create a scene to avenge the fourth concubine and her verbal abuse, Chunmei returns, dragging Qiuju by the ear. Ximen Qing is fuming. He storms into the kitchen and beats Xue'e. Xue'e denies having said anything insulting to the maids, which invites another round of beating by Ximen Qing.

In this short section, the reader has already encountered two instances of physical violence, one by Chunmei toward another maid and one by the patriarch toward one of his concubines. Other instances soon follow. After her confrontation with Chunmei and beating by Ximen Qing, Xue'e complains to the principal wife, Wu Yueniang, in the hopes of gaining some leverage against Chunmei. But her complaint reveals not only her abusive attitude toward Chunmei but also her effort to create discord between the principal wife and the fifth concubine. The wife, however, refuses to intervene unless her own interest is threatened.

> "I don't remember your ever acting this way before," said Yueniang. "If he sent a maidservant from the front compound to ask for cakes, all you needed to do was to make them up as best you could and send him on his way. What need was there for you to start cursing her for no good reason?"
>
> "I will call her bald or blind if I like!" retorted Xue'e. "Just a little while ago, when that maidservant worked for you, if she refused to do as she was told when I was on duty in kitchen, I would give her a smack with the back of a knife. And you didn't say anything about it. But now that she's fallen into the hands of that other one, she's started to carry on as though she owned the place."   (1.11.213)

> 月娘道: 也沒見你. 他前邊使了丫頭要餅, 你好好打發與他去便了, 平白又罵他怎的. 孫雪娥道: 我罵他禿也瞎也來. 那頃這丫頭在娘房裡, 着緊不聽手, 俺沒曾在灶上把刀背打他, 娘尚且不言語. 可可今日輪他手裡, 便驕貴的這等的了.   (11.5a)

Overhearing this conversation, Jinlian comes in to argue with Xue'e. Yueniang "just sat there and let the two of them continue to trade insults, without saying a word" (那吳月娘坐著, 由看他那兩個你一句我一句, 只不言語). But now Ximen Qing comes home and learns about this dispute. He once again "descended upon the kitchen, seized Xue'e by the hair, and proceeded to beat her with a short stick as hard as he could" (一陣風走到後邊, 採過雪娥頭髮來, 儘力拿短棍打了幾下; 1.11.214; 3.5b–6a). Yueniang finally intervenes and saves the fourth concubine from further beating while also blaming her: "Why doesn't everyone take things a little easier? You're just upsetting the master of the house" (沒的大家省事些兒罷了, 好交你主子惹氣; 1.11.215; 11.6a).

These examples illuminate the main patterns of domestic violence in the novel. This is one of the few places in which the author directly describes Ximen Qing's use of force on the women in his household. Even though such descriptions appear infrequently throughout the novel, Ximen Qing looms large as the embodiment of male authority and violence. As Keith McMahon points out, Ximen

Qing "takes care of his women as long as they don't cross him by sleeping with other men or making too many demands upon him" (McMahon, *Misers* 49). Women respond with a strategy of self-preservation: "No matter how rough a man may be, he won't beat a wife who is diligent and knows what she's about. As a member of his household, if I manage to run a tight ship, so that words spoken inside don't get out, and words spoken outside do not get in, what can he do to me?" (男子漢雖利害, 不打那勤謹省事之妻. 我在他家把得家定, 裡言不出, 外言不入, 他敢怎的; 1.7.139; 7.13a).

Domestic violence among women—and the characters' attitudes toward it—reveals the complexity of these characters and their relations. Though she appears to be the most restless troublemaker in the household, Pan Jinlian might not be more evil than her quiet rivals are. Other women, including Wu Yueniang, who appear exemplarily virtuous but act on domestic disputes only selectively, are just as calculating and manipulative. The conversation between the wife, Wu Yueniang, and the fourth concubine, Sun Xue'e, quoted above shows that Wu Yueniang had previously endorsed Sun Xue'e's physical abuse of Chunmei. Wu Yueniang is aware of the prevalence of abuse in the household but chooses to act only when it helps her please the patriarch and secure her own superior status over other women. The conversation between Yueniang and Xue'e also demonstrates how concerns about status and legitimacy motivate these women and are communicated by them in the language of domestic violence.

In what follows I take a closer look at several instances of domestic violence in *Plum* to show how violence functions as an important narrative element and how it serves the author's pedagogical agenda.

The Shrews

Plum's depictions of domestic abuse reveal much about the women's characters and relations rather than simply representing them as stereotypical abusers. Chapter 29 provides a number of examples, including the following scene that sheds light on the layered privilege of using violence:

> Wearing nothing but short undershirts of thin floss silk, [Ximen Qing and Pan Jinlian] got onto the bed, where a bed table had been prepared for them, replete with wine and delicacies.
>
> "Bring some distilled spirits for your father to drink," the woman instructed Qiuju.
>
> She also took some stuffed pastries out of a square box on the shelf of her bed cabinet and gave them to Ximen Qing to eat, fearing he might have an empty stomach.
>
> It was some time before Qiuju reappeared with a silver flagon of wine. The woman was just about to pour it into a cup when she felt it and, finding it to be ice cold, threw the contents right into Qiuju's face, soaking her:
>
> > Head and face alike.

"Why you lousy dead duck of a slave!" she railed at her. "I told you to decant it for him, but how could you have brought cold wine for Father to drink? Who knows what you've got on your mind?"

"Drag this slave out to the courtyard for me," she told Chunmei, "and make her kneel down there."

"I had just gone out back," said Chunmei, "to roll up Mother's foot bindings for her. I was hardly out of the way for a moment, and you've already gotten into mischief."

Pouting with her lips, Qiuju mumbled to herself, "Father and Mother have been drinking iced wine every day. Who could have known that today they would change their tune?"

When the woman heard this, she cursed her, saying, "Why you lousy slave! What did you say? Drag her over here."

"Give her ten slaps on each side of her face," she ordered Chunmei.

"I wouldn't want to dirty my hands on that thick-skinned face of hers," said Chunmei. "Mother, just have her kneel down with a stone balanced on her head, that's all."

Thereupon: Without permitting any further explanation, she was dragged out to the courtyard and made to kneel with a large stone balanced on her head.
(2.29.192–93)

拭抹身體乾淨, 撤去浴盆, 止著薄纊短襦, 上床安放炕桌菓酌飲酒, 教秋菊, 取白酒來與你爹吃. 又拿果餡餅與西門慶吃, 恐怕他肚中饑餓. 只見秋菊半日拿上一銀注子酒來. 婦人纔斟了一鐘, 摸了摸冰涼的, 就照著秋菊臉上只一潑, 潑了一頭一臉, 罵道: 好賊少死的奴才. 我分付教你燙了來, 如何拿冷酒與爹吃. 你不知安排些甚麼心兒. 叫春梅, 與我把這奴才採到院子里跪著去. 春梅道: 我替娘後邊捲裏腳去來, 一些兒沒在跟前, 你就弄下碴兒了. 那秋菊把嘴谷都著, 口裡喃喃吶吶說道: 每日爹娘還吃冰湃的酒兒, 誰知今日又改了腔兒. 婦人聽見罵道:好賊奴才, 你說甚麼. 與我採過來. 教春梅每邊臉上打與他十個嘴巴. 春梅道: 皮臉, 沒的打污濁了我手. 娘只教他頂著石頭跪著罷. 于是不由分說拉到院子裡, 教他頂著塊大石頭跪著.
(29.42a–42b)

The physical punishment of a maid by the wife or mistress of the household was common in the Ming world. Here, however, the novel presents a more complex domestic relationship. Chunmei does not want to be Jinlian's tool of punishment. Instead, she suggests to the mistress a cruel method: making Qiuju kneel with a large stone balanced on her head. Jinlian follows the suggestion, as she does again later in the novel. This detailed account of domestic violence reveals not only the alliance between these two women but also the blurred boundaries between their status and roles.

We find another interesting example in chapter 41, in which the abuse of a maid literally serves as a weapon of domestic intrigue. Jealous of the sixth concubine, Li Ping'er, who has just given birth to a son, Jinlian lashes out at Qiuju, who was slow to open the gate for her:

[Jinlian] made Qiuju balance a flagstone on her head and kneel down in the courtyard until she had finished combing her hair. She then told Chunmei to pull down her trousers and bring [Jinlian] a heavy bamboo cane with which to flog her.

"What a filthy slave!" complained Chunmei. "If you have me pull down her pants, it will only dirty my hands."

She then went up front and called for the page boy Huatong to come and pull down Qiuju's drawers for her.

The woman then proceeded to cane her, cursing as she did so, "You lousy slave of a whore! Since when did you become so uppity? Other people may see fit to favor you, but I'll never favor you. Sister:

> You know it and I know it.

You'd do better to slack off a bit. What need is there for you to stick your neck out and put on airs for no good reason? Sister, you'd better give up any such presumptions. From now on, I'm going to keep my eyes peeled where you're concerned."

As she vilified her, she continued to beat her, and as the beating continued, she gave vent to further vilification. The caning continued until Qiuju:

> Howled like a stuck pig.   (3.41.15)

婦人把秋菊叫他頂著大塊柱石跪在院子裏跪的他. 梳了頭, 教春梅扯了他褲子, 拿大板子要打他. 那春梅道: 好乾淨的奴才, 教我扯褲子到沒的污濁了我的手. 走到前邊旋叫了畫童兒, 扯去秋菊底衣. 婦人打著他罵道: 賊奴才淫婦, 你從幾時就恁大來. 別人興你, 我卻不興你. 姐姐, 你知我見的, 將就膿著些兒罷了, 平白撐著頭兒逞什麼強. 姐姐你休要倚着我, 到明日洗著兩個眼兒看着你哩. 一面罵着又打, 打了又罵, 打的秋菊殺豬也似叫.   (41.6b–7a)

The real target of this abuse is Li Ping'er, whose quarters are adjacent to Jinlian's and who can therefore hear everything. As Jinlian expects, the noise startles the newborn next door, prompting Ping'er to send a servant to ask Jinlian to stop the beating. Hearing this,

[Jinlian] beat Qiuju all the harder, cursing as she did so, "You lousy slave! You'd think someone were sticking ten thousand knives into you, the way you scream for mercy. Well, it's just my temperament, but the more you scream, the harder I'll beat you. You've already succeeded in arresting the attention of a passerby, who's come to contemplate the sight of a maidservant being beaten. Well, my good Sister, you can always tell your husband about it, and get him to give me a hard time."

Li Ping'er, from her vantage point next door, understood perfectly well that Jinlian's abuse was really directed at her. She was so upset by it that her two hands turned cold.   (3.41.17)

金蓮聽了越發打的秋菊狠了, 罵道: 賊奴才! 你身上打着一萬把刀子, 這等叫饒? 我是恁性兒, 你越叫我越打. 莫不為你拉斷了路行人. 人家打丫頭, 也來看着你. 好姐姐, 對漢子說, 把我別變了罷. 李瓶兒這邊分明聽見指罵的是他, 把兩隻手氣的冰冷.　　　　　　　　　　　　　　　　　　　　(41.7a–7b)

Then Jinlian adopts Chunmei's method of punishment again: she has Qiuju kneel down in the courtyard with a stone on her head. Once again Chunmei does not want to touch Qiuju herself. Instead, she goes out of her way to fetch a male servant from another corner of the family compound to help strip Qiuju.

The intrigue against Li Ping'er escalates with the intensity of abuse. In chapter 58, unhappy about Ximen Qing's attention to Ping'er and her newborn, Jinlian lashes out, first at a dog and then at the maid Qiuju. Again, Chunmei not only acts as an accomplice of her mistress but also benefits from a flare-up:

> [A]mid the dark shadows, she stepped into a pile of dog shit with one of her feet. As soon as she got inside, she had Chunmei light a lamp to examine the damage and saw that the entire vamp of her brand new scarlet silk shoe had been soiled. Immediately, she:
>> Pricked up her willow brows,
>> Opened wide her starry eyes,
>
> called for Chunmei to bring a lantern, locked the postern gate, picked up a big stick, and proceeded indiscriminately to beat the offending dog, beating him until he howled outlandishly.
>
> Li Ping'er, in her adjacent quarters, sent Yingchun over to say, "My mistress says to tell you that the baby has just taken Dame Liu's medicine and fallen asleep, and asks that the Fifth Lady refrain from beating the dog any longer."
>
> Jinlian sat down and had nothing to say for some time, after which, she beat the dog a little more, opened the gate, and let him out. She then turned her attention to finding fault with Qiuju. When she examined her shoe, she was:
>> Angry on the left, and
>> Angry on the right.
>
> Calling Qiuju before her, she said, "If you consider the matter, by this time of day, the dog ought to have been let out. What were you keeping him in here for, anyway? I suppose, slave that you are, he serves you as a clandestine lover. By not letting him out, you caused him to leave his shit all over the place, so that by stepping into it, this brand new pair of shoes of mine, which, including today, I haven't worn for more than three or four days, is all covered with shit. You knew I would be coming home and should have lit a lantern and come out to meet me. How can you expect to get away with:
>> Pretending to be both deaf and dumb,
>
> and playing the fool this way?"

"I told her some time ago," said Chunmei, "you ought to take advantage of the fact that Mother isn't home yet to feed him and put him out in the back courtyard. But she pretended to be deaf and paid me no attention at all, even giving me a dirty look."

"There you are!" exclaimed Jinlian. "The lousy, audacious, death-defying slave! How is it that she's so reluctant to get her ass in motion? I'm aware that you think you're the boss around here. As they say, you're such a hardened convict that a beating no longer means anything to you."

Thereupon, she called her up in front of her and told Chunmei to bring a lamp over so she could see better, saying as she did so, "Just look at the filth on my shoe. It's a shoe that I just made, and one that I really liked, and now it's been ruined by a slave like you."

Having tricked her into lowering her head in order to see better, she took up the shoe by its heel lift and slapped her right in the face several times with the sole. She hit her so hard that Qiuju's lips were broken, and, rubbing away the blood with her hand, she stepped out of reach.

"You lousy slave!" the woman cursed at her. "Trying to get away, are you?"

"Drag her over here, and make her kneel down," she said to Chunmei. "Fetch the riding crop, and strip off her clothing for me. I'll give her a good thirty strokes with the whip before I'm through. Merely grabbing hold of her and giving her a few random strokes will hardly do the job."

Chunmei accordingly stripped off Qiuju's clothing. The woman then told Chunmei to tie her hands, after which she swung the riding crop into the air, and the strokes of the whip began to fall on Qiuju like rain. She whipped the slave girl until she:

> Howled like a stuck pig. . . .

She gave her a good twenty or thirty strokes with the riding crop and then finished her off with ten crisscross strokes of the cane. She beat her until:

> The skin was broken and the flesh was split,

before letting her up. She also used her sharp fingernails to gouge the cheeks of her face until they were a bloody mess.   (3.58.439–43)

黑影中躧了一腳狗屎. 到房中叫春梅點燈來看, 大紅緞子新鞋, 滿幫子都展污了, 登時柳眉剔竪, 星眼圓睜, 叫春梅打着燈, 把角門關了, 拿大棍把那狗沒高低只顧打, 打的怪叫起來. 李瓶兒使過迎春來說: 俺娘說哥兒纔吃了老劉的藥, 睡着了, 教五娘這邊休打狗罷. 潘金蓮坐着, 半日不言語, 一面把那狗打了一回, 開了門放出去, 又尋起秋菊的不是來. 看著那鞋, 左也惱, 右也惱, 因把秋菊喚至跟前說:這咱晚, 這狗也該打發去了, 只顧還放在這屋裡做甚麼. 是你這奴才的野漢子, 你不發他出去, 教他恁遍地撒屎, 把我恁雙新鞋兒, 連今日纔三四日兒, 躧了恁一鞋幫子屎. 知道我來, 你也該點個燈兒出來, 你如何恁推聾妝啞裝憨兒的. 春梅道: 我頭裡就對他說, 你趁娘不來, 早喂他些飯, 關到後邊院子裡去罷. 他伴打耳睜的不理我, 還拿眼兒瞅着我. 婦人道: 可又來, 賊膽大萬殺的奴才. 我知道你在這屋裡成了把頭, 把這打來不作准. 因叫他到眼前瞧躧的我這鞋上的齷齪. 哄得他低頭瞧, 提著鞋拽巴, 兜臉就是幾鞋底子, 打的秋菊嘴唇都破了, 只顧搵着抹血, 忙走開一邊. 婦人罵道: 好賊奴才, 你走了. 教春梅: 與我採過來跪着, 取馬鞭子來, 把他身上衣服與我扯了, 好好教我打三十馬鞭子便罷. 但扭一扭兒, 我亂打了不算. 春梅于是扯了他衣裳, 婦人教春梅把他手扭住, 雨點般鞭子打下來, 打的這丫頭殺豬也似叫 ... 打勾二三十馬鞭子, 然後又蓋了十攔杆, 打得皮開肉放出來, 又把他臉和腮頰, 都用尖指甲掐的稀爛.

(58.26b–27b)

Through repeated, detailed representations of domestic violence like this, the novel leads the reader to look deeper into the characters and their relations. In this bloody scene of midnight abuse, Chunmei not only assists Jinlian in beating Qiuju, thereby harassing the sixth concubine next door. More important, her accusation that Qiuju had ignored her order to let the dog out ignites Jinlian's anger. The novel's depictions of domestic violence repeatedly show how Chunmei establishes her own authority. She often joins Jinlian in scolding Qiuju. She provokes Jinlian to elevate the abuse to the level of physical violence, but she makes her own decisions about whether or not she wants to participate in the beating herself.

Innocent Women

At first glance, the physical abuse Qiuju is subjected to seems to present her as a hapless victim of the capricious behavior of her mistress and a superior maid. Details of the verbal and physical abuses inflicted on her may earn the reader's sympathy, but they also leave traces of Qiuju's own problems. Her innocence—and that of some of the other characters—is deceptive. The author quietly embeds such revelations in the noisy scenes of domestic conflicts. This is one of the ways in which the author leads us to contemplate the meaning of "truth."

A good example of this technique appears in the lengthy description of another episode of domestic violence in chapter 73, just a few chapters before Ximen Qing's death and the dissolution of his household. On the surface, this chapter narrates a typical day in the Ximen family, a day replete with sex, wine, and gossip among women living in or visiting the compound. But the gradual unfolding of this instance of domestic violence crystallizes some details critical to our understanding of the characters: Chunmei's sexual relationship with Ximen Qing, Pan Jinlian's reliance on Chunmei, and Qiuju's habits of stealing, lying, and sabotage.

Earlier that day, Jinlian sees Ximen Qing and Chunmei having sex in her room. She leaves them alone and goes to the rear section of the family compound to kill time with other women. Wasted and tired, she later returns to her own quarters:

[S]he had to call out for what seemed like half a day before the postern gate was opened for her by Qiuju, who was still rubbing the sleep out of her eyes.

"So, you lousy slave, you've been asleep have you?" the woman said to her accusingly.

"I haven't been to sleep," protested Qiuju.

"It's obvious that you've just gotten up," the woman said. "You're just trying to deceive me. You've been taking it easy, rather than thinking of coming back to the rear compound to get me."

She then went on to ask, "Has Father gone to bed yet?"

"Father's been asleep for some time already," responded Qiuju.

The woman then went into the room that was furnished with a kang, where she pulled up her skirt and sat down on the kang to warm herself, while calling for some tea.

Qiuju hastily poured out a cup of tea for her, but the woman said, "You lousy slave! You'd pour tea for me to drink with those dirty hands of yours, would you? I won't drink any of that stale tea that has been steeped for so long it smells of the pot. Go call Chunmei, and tell her to fill a little kettle with sweet water, put in an abundance of tea leaves, and boil it until it is good and strong, for me to drink."

"She's asleep in the other room with the bed in it," said Qiuju. "Wait till I call her to bring it for you."

"Don't call her, but let her sleep," the woman said.

Qiuju did not obey her but went into the other room, where she found Chunmei lying fast asleep at Ximen Qing's feet.

Shaking her awake, she said, "Mother has come back and wants some tea to drink. Haven't you even gotten up yet?"

Chunmei spat at her, and cursed, saying, "You slave! You've been seeing things! So Mother has come back. So what? Why should you be in such a frightful stew over it, for no good reason?"

She then proceeded to get up:

Just as slow and easy as you please,

stretched her waist, pulled on her trousers, and came to see the woman, still rubbing her eyes as she approached the kang.

The woman, for her part, chose to criticize Qiuju, saying, "That slave! You were fast asleep, and she woke you up."

. . . When the woman had finished her tea, she said to Chunmei, "A while ago, I brought back some fruit and candied sweetmeats in my sleeve, that had been given to me by Yu-hsiao for my mother to eat. I turned them over to this slave here to take inside for you to put away."

"I haven't seen anything of them," said Chunmei. "Who knows where she put them?"

The woman then called in Qiuju and asked her, "Where did you put that fruit?"

"It's here," responded Qiuju. "I put it in the cabinet."

So saying, she went and brought the things over to her.

The woman counted them over and, finding that a tangerine was missing, asked her what had happened to it.

"When Mother gave them to me," said Qiuju, "I brought them inside and put them in the cabinet. Surely you don't imagine I was suffering from such an avid craving as to blight my own mouth with it, do you?"

"You lousy slave!" the woman responded. "You still insist on talking back, do you? If you didn't snitch it, where did it go? I counted them with my own hand before turning them over to you. You lousy slave! You've simply been picking them up and secreting them for yourself, until only these measly:

>   Odds and ends,

are left. You've already consumed more than half of them. Under the circumstances, I'll have to teach you a lesson."

Then turning to Chunmei, she said, "You give that slave ten slaps on each side of her face."

"Those dirty cheeks of hers," responded Chunmei. "I'd only be dirtying this hand of mine."

"You drag her over to me, then," the woman said.

Chunmei pushed her over in front of the woman with both hands, and the woman pinched her cheeks, while taking her to task, saying, "You lousy slave! It was you who snitched this tangerine to eat, wasn't it? If you tell me the truth, I won't beat you. But if you don't, I'll get the riding crop, strip you naked, and whip you until I lose track of the strokes. No doubt, you thought I was drunk enough so that you could snitch it for yourself, while pulling the wool over my eyes, didn't you?"

She then turned to Chunmei and asked her, "Am I drunk, or not?"

"Mother is perfectly sober," replied Chunmei. "What does wine have to do with it? If you believe her, then she didn't eat it. But if you don't believe her, try groping inside her sleeve. I wouldn't be surprised if there were still tangerine peels in her sleeve."

The woman, then, pulled the sleeve over and started to grope inside it, but Qiuju tried to brush her aside with one hand, in order to prevent her from doing so. Chunmei, then, intervened by pulling her hand away and, sure enough, was able to grope out some remnants of tangerine peel.

The woman responded by pinching her cheeks twice, as hard as she could, and giving her two full-handed slaps on the face, as she reviled her, saying, "You lousy slave! You hopeless scamp of a slave! You're hardly good at anything else, but it seems you're proficient at telling tales and snitching food to eat. These tangerine peels in your sleeve constitute:

>   Irrefutable proof of your guilt,

so you can hardly try to blame anyone else. I would give you a whipping right now, but Father is asleep here, and it's not an appropriate time to whip you while;

>   Anticipating tea or recovering from wine.

Tomorrow, when I'm completely myself, I'll settle accounts with you."

"Mother," said Chunmei, "you ought not to be perfunctory about it tomorrow, but have her stripped completely naked, and get someone to give her a real shellacking, administering several tens of strokes with the bamboo. If she is made to suffer some real pain, it might throw some fear into her. If you merely touch her up with a few strokes of the rod, as if you were playing with a monkey, she won't take it to heart."

Qiuju's face was swollen from the pinches she had received at the woman's hands, and she took herself off to the kitchen with a pout on her lips.
(4.73.413–15)

金蓮坐不住, 去了, 到前邊叫了半日, 角門才開, 只見秋菊揉眼. 婦人罵道: 賊奴才, 你睡來. 秋菊道: 我沒睡. 婦人道: 見睡起來, 你哄我. 你到自在, 就不說往後來接我接兒去. 因問: 你爹睡了. 秋菊道: 爹睡了這一日了. 婦人走到炕房裡, 摟起裙子來就在炕上烤火. 婦人要茶吃, 秋菊連忙傾了一盞茶來. 婦人道: 賊奴才, 好乾淨手兒, 我不吃這陳茶, 熬的怪泛湯氣, 你叫春梅來, 叫他另拿小銚兒頓些好甜水茶兒, 多着些茶葉, 頓的苦艷艷我吃. 秋菊道: 他在那邊床房裡睡哩, 等我叫他來. 婦人道: 你休叫他, 且教他睡罷. 這秋菊不依, 走在那邊屋裡, 見春梅歪在西門慶腳頭睡得正好, 被他搖推醒了道: 娘來了, 要吃茶, 你還不起來哩. 這春梅嗐他一口罵道: 見鬼的奴才, 娘來了罷了, 平白唬人剌剌的. 一面起來, 慢條廝禮撒腰拉褲走來見婦人, 只顧倚著炕兒揉眼. 婦人反罵秋菊: 怎奴才, 你睡的甜甜兒的, 把你叫醒了.... 這婦人吃了茶, 因問春梅: 我頭裡袖了幾個菓子和蜜餞, 是玉簫與你姥姥吃的, 交付這奴才接進來, 你收了. 春梅道: 我沒見, 他知道放在那里. 婦人叫秋菊問他菓子在那裡, 秋菊道: 我放在揀妝內哩. 走去取來, 婦人數了數兒, 少了一個柑子, 問他那里去了, 秋菊道: 我拿進來就放在揀妝內, 那個害饞癆爛了口吃他不成. 婦人道: 賊奴才, 還溳嘴. 你不偷, 那去了. 我親手數了交與你的, 怎就少了一個. 原來只孝順了你. 教春梅: 你與我把那奴才一邊臉上打與他十個嘴巴子. 春梅道: 那齪臉彈子, 倒沒的齷齪了我的手. 婦人道: 你與我拉過他來. 春梅用雙手推顙到婦人跟前, 婦人用手撐着他腮頰, 罵道: 賊奴才, 這個柑子是你偷吃了不是. 你寔寔說了, 我就不打你, 不然取馬鞭子來, 我這一旋剝就打個不數. 我難道醉了, 你偷吃了, 一徑里鬼混我. 因問春梅: 我醉不醉. 那春梅道: 娘清省白醒, 那討酒來. 娘不信, 只掏他袖子, 怕不的還有柑子皮兒在袖子里哩. 婦人於是扯過他袖子來, 用手去掏, 秋菊慌用手撇着不教掏. 春梅一面拉起手來, 果然掏出些柑子皮兒來. 被婦人儘力臉上撐了兩把, 打了兩下嘴巴, 罵道: 賊奴才, 你諸般兒不會, 象這說舌偷嘴吃偏會, 真贓寔犯拿住, 你還賴那個. 我如今茶前酒後, 且不打你, 到明日清省白醒, 和你算帳. 春梅道: 娘到明日, 休要與他行行忽忽的, 好生旋剝了, 叫個人把他寔辣辣打與他幾十板子, 教他忍疼也懼怕些. 甚麼逗猴兒似湯那幾棍兒, 他才不放在心上. 那秋菊被婦人撐得臉脹腫的, 谷都着嘴往廚下去了.
(73.35b–37a)

This detailed instance of domestic violence completes the characters and constitutes a critical juncture in the novel: Pan Jinlian and Chunmei have become more equal, which anticipates Jinlian's reliance on Chunmei's mercy after Ximen Qing's death. Importantly, Qiuju's bad habits of stealing and lying finally come to light and partially explain Jinlian's attitude toward her. In addition, Qiuju's bold defiance of and hostility toward her mistress soon culminate in repeated attempts to bring down her mistress after the death of the patriarch.

There are other seemingly innocent women in the novel as well. Consider, for instance, chapters 72–73, where Pan Jinlian beats Ruyi (Ju-i), the wet nurse of Li Ping'er and Ximen Qing's son. This incident is interesting for our purposes not only because it is triggered by Qiuju's lies but also because it leads to a conversation about domestic violence between Wu Yueniang and Pan Jinlian that completely exposes the former's hypocrisy.

A fight breaks out over a stick-shaped laundry bat, which can be seen as a phallic symbol. After the deaths of both Li Ping'er and her son, Ximen Qing begins to sleep with Ruyi, the deceased boy's nanny. One day, Wu Yueniang asks Ruyi to help wash the patriarch's undergarments. Coincidentally, Chunmei is also doing laundry for Pan Jinlian but cannot find a laundry bat. She sends Qiuju to borrow one from Ruyi, but Ruyi refuses to lend it. Qiuju reports this to Chunmei with some exaggeration and misrepresentation. Jinlian, having been looking for an occasion to challenge Ruyi, dispatches Chunmei to demand the laundry bat: "Chunmei, who was in the prime of youth and needed no urging, set off in a fit of rage for Li Ping'er's quarters, where she arrived like a gust of wind, saying, 'Just who do you take to be an outsider in this household, anyway, that should refuse to let her have a laundry bat when she asks for it? It would seem that yet another mistress has emerged out of nowhere in these quarters'" (這春梅一沖性子就一陣風走來李瓶兒那邊説道: 那個是世人也怎的要棒槌借使使就不與, 如今這屋裡又鑽出個當家的來了; 4.72.344; 72.11b). As Ruyi tries to explain herself, Jinlian emerges and starts ranting:

> That's enough of your lip, woman! Since your mistress died, you act as though you have taken over her place in these quarters, and that Father won't be satisfied to have anyone but you take care of his intimate clothing for him. The rest of us wives might just as well be dead, since only you are fit to launder and starch his clothes for him. You think that by adopting this strategy you can lord it over the rest of us, do you?   (4.72.344)

> 你這個老婆不要說嘴. 死了你家主子, 如今這屋裡就是你. 你爹身上衣服, 不着你恁個人兒栓束. 誰應的上他那心. 俺這些老婆死絕了, 教你替他漿洗衣服. 你死拿這個法兒伏俺每.
> (72.11b)

Clearly, Jinlian considers it a (sexual) privilege to clean Ximen Qing's undergarments and therefore attempts to deprive Ruyi of this privilege. In her own defense, Ruyi argues that she is merely doing what the masters—both Ximen Qing and the principal wife—expect of her. But her self-defense only triggers more violent reactions from Jinlian:

"Fifth Lady, how can you say such a thing?" protested Ruyi. "If the First Lady had not instructed us to do so, do you really think we would have had to nerve to insist on being the only ones to take care of Father's things for him?"

"Why you lousy splay-legged, man-hunting whore!" exclaimed Jinlian. "You still insist on defending yourself, do you? Who is it that served Father with tea and adjusted his bedding for him in the middle of the night? And who talked him into having a jacket made for her? You think the things you're up to behind our backs are unknown to me, do you? Even if your furtive shenanigans should result in a pregnancy, I won't be intimidated by you."

"His legitimate consort and her son both came to grief," said Ruyi.

"Where can I hope to get to?"

If Jinlian had not heard these words nothing might have happened, but having heard them:

> A fire blazed up in her heart, and
> Her powdered face became suffused with red.

Striding forward, she grabbed hold of the woman's hair with one hand and proceeded to thump her in the belly with the other until Auntie Han intervened and succeeded in separating them.   (4.72.344)

如意兒道: 五娘怎的說這話. 大娘不分付, 俺們好意掉攬替爹整理的. 金蓮道: 賊歪剌骨雌漢的淫婦, 還溅說什麼嘴. 半夜替爹遞茶兒扶被兒是誰來, 討披襖兒穿是誰來, 你背地幹的那繭兒, 你說我不知道. 就偷出肚子來我也不怕. 如意道: "正經有孩子還死了哩, 俺每到的那些兒. 這金蓮不聽便罷, 聽了心頭火起, 粉面通紅, 走向前一把手把老婆頭髮扯住, 只用手摳他腹. 虧得韓嫂兒先向前勸開了.   (72.11b–12a)

Jinlian is fuming not only because Ruyi threatened to claim some sexual privilege but also and even more so because of her long-standing grudge against both the wife and the deceased concubine Li Ping'er. Jinlian believes that, because the wife has failed to discipline the maids or to take proper action when Ximen Qing became sexually involved with them, she herself has to keep an eye on and discipline these shameless women. She makes this clear to Meng Yulou (Meng Yü-lou), the third concubine, who arrives just in time to prevent her from beating Ruyi any further:

Have you ever seen the likes of our elder sister's irresponsibility? It's reminiscent of the way she indulged that lousy slave of a whore, Laiwang's wife, to the point where she lost all sense of decorum, with the result that the two of us ended up:

> Feeling resentment and harboring hostility,

toward each other. And after that, she had the nerve to besmirch me with the gross allegation that I was responsible for driving that slave out of the household. Now, once again, she's indulging this woman to the point that:

All the rules of propriety are turned upside down.

If you're a wet nurse, you ought to confine yourself to being a wet nurse, rather than being allowed to flaunt your:

Showy glamour and gaudy airs. . . .

You can tell from the way she carries on that she regards herself as a reincarnation of Li Ping'er. And meanwhile, our elder sister keeps to the rear compound:

Pretending to be both deaf and dumb,

and criticizing anyone who opens her mouth about it.   (4.72.347–48)

大姐姐也有些不是. 想着他把死的來旺兒賊奴才淫婦償的有些猖兒, 教我和他為冤結仇, 落後一染膿帶還垜在我身上, 說是我弄出那奴才去了. 如今這個老婆又是這般慣他, 慣的恁沒張倒置的. 你做奶子行奶子的事, 許你在跟前花黎胡哨.... 你看他如今別模改樣的, 又是個李瓶兒出世了. 那大姐姐成日在後邊, 只推聾兒裝啞的, 人但開口就說不是了.   (72.12b–13b)

It is interesting that Jinlian justifies her use of violence on Ruyi by blaming the principal wife. She adopts the rhetoric of "rules of propriety" and assumes the tone of the guardian of moral order. In a sense, her verbal and physical violence toward Ruyi exposes the hypocrisy of women who are thought to be virtuous, as shown in a conversation in the women's quarters about domestic violence that immediately follows this scene of beating. In this conversation, Yueniang fears that opposing Ximen's sexual engagement of the wet nurse—and other women in and outside the Ximen household—will cause him to react violently. Because of this, she tries to avoid provoking him. Astonished by Jinlian's open warning that Ximen Qing seems to treat the wet nurse as a replacement for the deceased sixth concubine, she tells Jinlian that the patriarch might beat her:

It seems to me that you took him to task somewhat too severely just now. As the saying goes:

The male of the species has dog's hair

growing on his face;

The woman of the species has the fleece

of a female phoenix.

He was drunk, after all. My fear is that if you irritate him to the point where he loses his temper:

If he doesn't beat you,

Should he beat the dog instead?

I actually broke into a sweat on your behalf, but it turns out you're enough of a minx to tough it out.   (4.73.399)

我見你頭裡話出來的忒緊了. 常言漢子臉上有狗毛, 老婆臉上有鳳毛. 他有酒的人, 一時激得惱了, 不打你, 打狗不成. 俺每倒替你捏兩把汗, 原來你到這等潑皮.

(73.33b)

In this conversation, Yueniang plays the role of an ideal virtuous wife by voicing her support of Jinlian and some of the other concubines. Her image would have resonated in elite Ming society, where the widespread practice of concubinage gave new urgency to the question of the relationship between a wife and a concubine (Chen Baoliang 132). However, her use of the language of domestic violence reveals that the wife in this novel—as in many elite Ming families—is not an innocent peacemaker. Yueniang selectively endorses women's violence against one another. She focuses all her energy on producing a legitimate heir to secure her own status in the family. In the meantime, she justifies the patriarch's use of physical violence, exploits the conflicts among other women, and benefits from their fierce competition.

Order

Plum's depictions of domestic violence not only play a role in character development but also serve didactic purposes by exposing the absurdity of order, as seen in Pan Jinlian's appropriation of the rhetoric of propriety. Some revealing examples of this can be found in the chapters following Ximen Qing's death, which brings with it the collapse of the old domestic order centered around the hopelessly corrupt patriarch. After Ximen Qing's death, Pan Jinlian becomes involved with Chen Jingji, the husband of Ximen's daughter with his principal wife and hence also Jinlian's son-in-law. In chapter 83, Jinlian's maid Qiuju discovers the affair and begins to spread gossip into the wife's quarters. It quickly reaches her mistress's ears—again through Chunmei—and gets her a round of relentless beating:

> When the cock crowed at dawn the next morning, [Qiuju] got up to urinate and suddenly heard the sound of the door being opened in the adjoining room. In the hazy moonlight, it had not yet stopped raining. On looking through the window, she saw someone draped in a red blanket on his way out the door.
>
> "That looks like Chen Jingji," she said to herself. "So it turns out that he's been sleeping with my mistress, night after night. She is forever protesting her own virtue in front of other people, while all the time she's been carrying on an affair with her son-in-law."
>
> That day, she went straight back to the kitchen in the rear compound and told Xiaoyu, thus and so, all about what she had seen.
>
> She did not anticipate that Xiaoyu, who was on friendly terms with Chunmei, would go tell her about it, saying, "That Qiuju from your place

says that your mistress is carrying on an affair with her son-in-law Chen Jingji. Yesterday, he spent the whole night in her room, and he only left this morning. His wife, Ximen Dajie, and Yuanxiao did not spend the night in the front compound."

When Chunmei returned to Jinlian's quarters, she told her all about it, word for word, and concluded, "If you don't give that slave a few strokes of the rod, but allow her to carry on this way with her:
> Deceitful mouth and duplicitous tongue,
you might as well be giving her the license to do you in."

On hearing this, Jinlian became enraged, summoned Qiuju into her presence, and made her kneel down before her. . . . [T]aking up a rod, she gave her thirty cruel strokes on the back with all her strength until she:
> Howled like a stuck pig,
and the skin on her body was broken.

At this point, Chunmei came over and said, "Mother, these few strokes that you've given her will do no more than scratch her where she itches. You ought to strip her naked, call in a page boy to give her twenty or thirty strokes with the heavy bamboo, and see if that will induce any fear in her."

(5.83.38)

到天明鷄叫時分, 秋菊起來溺尿. 忽聽那邊房內開的門響, 朦朧月色, 雨尚未止, 打窗眼看見一人披着紅卧單從房中出去了, 恰似陳姐夫一般. 原來夜夜和我娘睡, 我娘自來會撇清乾淨, 暗裡養着女婿. 次日逕支到後邊廚房裡, 就如此這般對小玉说. 不想小玉和春梅好, 又告訴與春梅說: 秋菊説你娘養着陳姐夫, 昨日在房裡睡了一夜, 今早出去了. 大姑娘和元宵又没在前邊睡. 這春梅歸房一五一十對婦人說: 娘不打與這奴才幾下, 教他騙口張舌, 葬送主子. 金蓮聽了大怒 . . . 拏棍子向他脊背上盡力狠抽了三十下, 打的秋菊殺豬也似叫, 身上都破了. 春梅走將來說: 娘沒的打他這幾下兒, 只好與他搔癢兒罷了. 旋剝了, 叫將小廝來, 拿大板子盡力砍與他二三十板, 看他怕不怕.

(83.17b–18a)

Determined to bring down her mistress, Qiuju is a strong-willed troublemaker in her own right. The frequent abuse inflicted on her not only fails to change her but also cements her determination to fight. After Ximen's death, she feels emboldened to act against her mistress in the name of defending domestic order. But her defiant and unpredictable actions have inconvenienced not only her mistress and Chunmei but also other women of the household.

Soon after the beating, Qiuju resumes her fight but this time by trying to directly report to Wu Yueniang that her mistress is having sex with the son-in-law. Yueniang overhears Quiju's gossip and decides to go over to check on Jinlian. Jinlian and her lover narrowly escape an exposure, partly because Yueniang would rather believe everything is in order in the family and therefore does not probe carefully.

Qiuju's third attempt at exposing the sexual scandal of her mistress, in the same chapter, ends with the principal wife's scolding and threat of violence: "Yueniang responded with a shout and cursed her, saying, 'You lousy slave, you're just trying to do your mistress in!'" (被月娘喝了一聲, 罵道: 胈弄主子的奴才). Yueniang "threatened Qiuju with a beating, but [Qiuju] was so intimidated that she fled back to the front compound and no longer dared to report anything to the rear compound" (於是要打秋菊, 說的秋菊在前邊疾走如飛, 再不敢來後邊說了; 5.83.52; 83.22b–23a). Although Qiuju has never before been hindered by beating, she gives up this time because she understands Yueniang's message behind the threat of violence. The stakes are high for Yueniang: after her husband's death, gossip about the household will ultimately jeopardize her own legitimacy. When Yueniang threatens to beat Qiuju, this is clearly not meant to protect the fifth concubine but to protect herself:

> [Yueniang] feared that if word of this got out, it would lead gossipers to say, "Although Ximen Qing was a person to be reckoned with during his lifetime, it did not take long after his death for the women in his household to end up:
> All at sevens and eights."
> "They may even suggest that this child of mine is:
> Of questionable origin." (5.83.42)

> 傳出去, 知道的是你這奴才葬送主子, 不知道的, 只說西門慶平日要的人強多了, 人死了多少時兒, 老婆們一個個都弄的七顛八倒, 恰似我的這孩子, 也有些甚根不正一般. (83.23a)

As these episodes of domestic violence make clear, the meaning of order varies from character to character depending on their personal agenda. For Yueniang, concerns about her status and the legitimacy of her child trump everything else. The novel's only explicit depiction of Yueniang's use of physical violence takes place precisely for this reason, when she hears from the wet nurse that her son-in-law, Chen Jingji, has said the following in public about Yueniang's son, who was born the moment Ximen Qing died: "This child behaves just as though I were his father, in that he does what I tell him to do" (這孩子倒相我養的, 依我說話; 5.86.98; 86.5b). On hearing this, Yueniang immediately faints. After she recovers consciousness, a plan to beat up and oust Chen Jingji ensues:

> Yueniang arranged to have seven or eight maids and servants' wives lie in wait, armed with sticks and cudgels, and then send the page boy Lai'an to trick Chen Jingji into coming into the rear compound for a talk.
> Once he was inside, and the ceremonial gate had been closed behind him, she ordered him to kneel down in front of her and demanded, "Do you acknowledge your crime?"

Chen Jingji refused to kneel and exhibited as haughty an air as ever, while Yueniang proceed to interrogate him. . . .

[She] directed the squad of women, including Sun Xue'e, Laixing's wife Hui-hsiu, Laizhao's wife "The Beanpole," Zhongqiu, Xiaoyu, to proceed, hugger-mugger, to hold Chen Jingji down on the floor and give him a drubbing with their sticks and cudgels. . . .

They beat the young scamp until, in desperation, he tore off his pants and exposed his organ, which was standing up as straight as a stick. This so startled the women that they dropped their sticks and cudgels and fled in all directions.

Yueniang, for her part, was both annoyed and amused by this display and berated him, saying, "What a fine phony of cuckold's spawn you are!"

(5.86.99–101)

月娘埋伏了丫鬟媳婦七八個人, 各拿短棍棒槌, 使小廝來安兒請進陳經濟來後邊, 只推説話, 把儀門關了, 教他當面跪下 ... 率領雪娥並來興兒媳婦、來昭妻一丈青、中秋兒、小玉、繡春眾婦人, 七手八腳, 按下地下, 拏棒槌短棍打了一頓. 西門大姐走過一邊, 也不來救. 打的這小伙兒急了, 把褲子脱了露出那直豎一條棍來. 諕的眾婦人看見都丟下棍棒亂跑了. 月娘又是那惱又是那笑, 口裡罵道: 好個沒根基的王八羔子.

(86.6b–7a)

Note the complete collapse of social hierarchy in this scene: wife, concubine, and maids join forces, and a man is beaten by women, including servants. But in Yueniang's mind, order has returned to the Ximen household. Ironically, it is Chen Jingji's dramatic exposure of his penis to these women that sends them into shock and scares them away. It signals the restoration of the authority associated with the phallus and male-centered order in the world of *Plum*.

In the remaining chapters, although women still commit domestic abuse, male violence and male-centered order become much more pronounced: Chen Jingji's violence toward his wife eventually leads to her death (chs. 89 and 92); Meng Yulou's new husband, who initially appears to be a decent man, beats a maid-turned-concubine (ch. 91). The turning point toward the surge of male violence, announced by Chen Jingji's penis in chapter 86, comes in chapter 87 with the return of the hero Wu Song (Wu Sung), the brother of Pan Jinlian's deceased husband, and his gruesome torture of Jinlian. After Jinlian confesses to murdering her former husband, Wu Song proceeds to dissect and kill her:

When the woman saw that the situation had taken a turn for the worse, she was about to cry out loudly, but Wu Song plucked up a handful of ashes from the incense burner and stuffed it into her mouth, so that she was unable to utter a sound, and then roughly doubled her over on the floor. The woman struggled so violently that the fret on her hair, and her pins and earrings, rolled off onto the ground.

Wu Song was afraid that she might succeed in struggling free, so he kicked her in the ribs with his waxed boots and then stamped on her two arms, saying, "You whore! It is said that you're really intelligent, but I don't know what sort of a heart you have, so I'm going to take a look at it."

So saying, he pulled open her bodice with one hand, and then:

> The telling is slow, but
>
> What happened was quick;

he took the dagger and cut open her pale and fragrant breast with a single slash, producing a blood-filled cavity from which fresh blood gushed out. As for the woman:

> Her starry eyes blinked half open,

and her two feet kicked spasmodically. Holding the dagger in his teeth, Wu Song then pulled open her breast with his two hands and, with a popping sound, tore her living heart and entrails, dripping with blood, out of the cavity, and laid them as a sacrifice before the spirit tablet. After which, with a single swipe of the dagger, he cut off her head, as a result of which:

> The flow of blood inundated the ground.   (5.87.127–28)

那婦人見勢頭不好, 才待大叫, 被武鬆向爐內摑了一把香灰塞在他口, 就叫不出來了, 然後劈腦揪番在地. 那婦人掙扎, 把鬆髻簪環都滾落了. 武鬆恐怕他掙扎, 先用油靴只顧踢他肋肢, 後用兩隻腳踏他兩隻肶膊, 便道:淫婦, 白說你伶俐, 不知你心怎麼生, 着我試看一看. 一面用手去攤開他胸脯, 說時遲, 那時快, 把刀子去婦人白馥馥心窩內只一剜, 剜了個血窟窿, 那鮮血就冒出來. 那婦人就星眸半閃, 兩隻腳只顧登踏. 武鬆口噙著刀子, 雙手去幹開他胸脯, 撲乞的一聲, 把心肝五臟生扯下來, 血瀝瀝供養在靈前. 後方一刀割下頭來, 血流滿地.   (87.19b–20a)

With this brutal murder, revenge is accomplished, and order seems to have been restored. Perhaps this scene serves the author's pedagogical purpose by showing the excessiveness of violence completing and complementing the excessiveness of the violence that Jinlian herself had perpetrated on others throughout the novel (N. Ding 221). But the reader might also wonder, Is the fictional world of *Plum* better as a result?

This essay has shown how *Plum* employs domestic violence as a means of developing the characters and the story line and as a way of executing a particular didactic agenda. It calls for a feminist reading that is not only methodologically sensitive to an exegesis tradition of moral judgment but also historically minded. The novel's detailed depictions of domestic violence, even though they do not accurately represent history, amplify the structure of violence that maintained patriarchal power relations in elite Ming households, relations in which women themselves participated. *Plum*'s characters, like people in the Ming, are not located within a simple moral hierarchy. This complexity compels us to consider the different ways domestic violence was used by men and women as a tool to negotiate status, access, and power.

NOTES

[1] Keith McMahon's essay in this volume discusses the question of concubinage more directly.

[2] Unless otherwise noted, parenthetical citations refer to Roy's translation, *The Plum in the Golden Vase*, and to *Xinke xiuxiang piping* Jin Ping Mei 新刻繡像批評金瓶梅 (*Newly Cut, Lavishly Illustrated, and Commented On* Plum in the Golden Vase).

Wives, Concubines, Prostitutes, and Other Men's Wives: The Portrayal of Sex in *The Plum in the Golden Vase*

Keith McMahon

The descriptions of sex in *The Plum in the Golden Vase* (*Jin Ping Mei* 金瓶梅) have made the anonymous novel notorious ever since readers first discovered it in the late 1500s. Even today the uncut version of the book cannot be legally sold in mainland China, though the parts that need to be cut according to current official standards only amount to about two percent of the novel's entire length. *Plum*'s descriptions of sex appear in two broad modes, one that consists of poetic or metaphoric language that is euphemistic and nonvulgar, the other direct and explicit, sometimes using vulgar and obscene language. The first mode had been used for centuries in Chinese literature and can be seen in the first description of the male protagonist, Ximen Qing (Hsi-men Ch'ing), and one of his concubines, Pan Jinlian (P'an Chin-lien), having sex: "Shoulder to shoulder, the mandarin ducks sport in the water; cheek to cheek, the phoenixes thread the flowers" (交頸鴛鴦戲水, 並頭鸞鳳穿花; 1.4.83 [trans. modified]; 4.2a).[1] This mode can be called the high erotic. The second mode, which began to appear sometime in the Ming before *Plum* was written, uses straightforward language to describe sexual scenes and sounds, as in the case of the monks who secretly listen to Pan Jinlian and Ximen Qing: "Her voice was trembling and soft; she sighed and moaned; there was panting and groaning" (顫聲柔氣, 呻呻吟吟, 哼哼唧唧; 1.8.167 [trans. modified]; 8.12a). In this scene, Jinlian is still supposed to be in mourning for her husband, Wu Da (Wu the Elder), whom she and Ximen Qing have just murdered. The monks are supposed to be chanting sutras for Wu's dead soul but are tantalized by what they hear from the other room. Whatever the mode of description, the description always comments on what is happening, whether subtly or directly. In other words, it always relates thematically to the moment in the narrative in which it appears. The euphemistic "mandarin ducks sport[ing] in the water" is an ancient expression referring to the elegant and harmonious love of a monogamous couple, mandarin ducks having been thought to mate for life. But the elegant words are ironic in that Ximen Qing and Pan Jinlian are now and will remain adulterous throughout the novel.

Is it fitting to label *Plum in the Golden Vase* a pornographic novel? The answer would seem to be yes, in part, though defining pornography is notoriously difficult and though much of what counts as pornography today hardly applies to the sixteenth-century novel. A statue of a naked Greek figure is generally not considered pornographic today, but in certain contexts or to certain mentalities it might be, just as a certain way of filming a scene of two people having sex under bedcovers might be. Some would say that the high-erotic description above hardly counts as pornography; it is not explicit enough, explicitness being a core element of what many consider pornographic. In my usage, *pornography* is a convenient label for roughly referring to extended portrayals of sex, whether elegant and suggestive or vulgar and graphic. (The meaning of "extended" remains open, of course, but it is something more than a few euphemistic words.) Other common assumptions are that pornography both describes and excites sexual arousal and that it must be considered offensive.[2] Pornographic literature is also supposedly intended for the titillation of—and consumption by—third parties, potentially great numbers of them, as in the case of *Plum* after its appearance as a published and marketed text. Readers are like the voyeurs often depicted in sexual scenes in *Plum* and in other texts, both past and present, from all over the world (Sullivan and McKee 4). By this broad definition, *Plum in the Golden Vase* is intermittently pornographic. One might imagine a modern-day film adaptation of *Plum* that contains full nudity and detailed portrayals of sexual arousal, whether male or female, hetero- or homoerotic, and an abundance of obscene language. To create a product with broader appeal, filmmakers might decide to downplay the sexuality of the source text, at least to a degree.

Although the novel was considered offensive from the start and has since been subject to censorship and abridgement, in both original and translated versions, its style is artful, energetic, and shameless. It is as if the author felt that it was natural to write in such a way and that only by writing in such a way could his talents be put to best use.[3] It is as if he were discovering a new, liberating way to write. *Plum*'s characters enjoy sex to the extreme, but the author also injects notes of humor, sarcasm, and irony, not to mention misogyny, the last of which can be seen in scenes of women's arousal that are sometimes tinged with elements of the grotesque. When Pan Jinlian is deliriously aroused, for example, her vagina is "like a snail secreting its slime" (如蝸之吐涎; 2.27.144; 27.10b).[4] Or was this in fact to some readers an artful, pleasing, or arousing image? When Ximen Qing fails to visit Pan Jinlian for too long a time, she is desperate to have sex and seduces a young servant boy, who leaves his "glob of donkey spunk" in her "jadelike body" (一滴驢精髓; 傾在金蓮玉體中; 1.12.233; 12.6b). As unheroic as Ximen Qing may be, he does not ejaculate "donkey spunk." The jarring contrast between "spunk" and Jinlian's "jadelike body" connotes that the wanton, ravenous, and ravishing Pan Jinlian, abandoned by the unfaithful Ximen Qing, cannot do without sex for long and must make do with this handsome young servant, whom she can dominate but who hardly matches the wealthy sexual master with whom she normally consorts.

Yet another common definition of pornography cites the relentless and obsessive attempt to portray sex in all its forms and even to go beyond what is humanly possible to create supernormal fantasies of sexual capacity and desire. In such a mode, the goal of pornography is to break all boundaries of decency and try to be as offensive, grotesque, and bizarre as possible.[5] *Plum* fits this definition in some ways, although it hardly counts as obsessive given that its focus on sex only takes up a small portion of the narrative. It is unlike other works written both before and after it in which sexual acts are the main focus. It sometimes ventures into the supernormal, especially after Ximen Qing acquires the monk's aphrodisiac, and it seems to delight in the bizarre. Ximen Qing and his sexual partners enjoy forms of repetition and combination and like to bend the limits of human capacity. Some say that pornography carries a utopian element in its portrayal of sexual ecstasy. Characters in *Plum* enjoy sex to an extreme degree, some passages describing undiluted sexual pleasure. As mentioned, the novel's pornography is nevertheless thematic: pornography conveys a message, and the author uses it to evaluate and comment on characters and situations. Humor and satire are ubiquitous, especially in those moments in which the novel undercuts Ximen Qing, the profligate man.

In the United States and elsewhere, pornography has come under attack because of its degradation of women. A similar treatment of women also appears in *Plum*, which portrays a dominant male protagonist with access to as many women as he wants. Ximen Qing inevitably satisfies his partners, the assumption being that in their eyes he is irresistibly powerful and arousing. In Ming society, in which polygamy was not only legal but also normal, women and individuals of lower status were the subjects of polygamist masters. They both willingly and unwillingly served men like Ximen Qing because of the benefits they could gain and for fear of the harm they might suffer if they refused. The novel points to such truths in its repeated portrayals of the impossibility of any one woman winning over Ximen Qing's heart. In one of its narrative asides, *Plum* warns, "Don't any human be a woman, for your every joy and sorrow will be at the will of another" (為人莫做婦人身, 百年苦樂由他人; 1.12.239 [trans. modified]; 12.10a). Ximen Qing's main wife, Wu Yueniang (Wu Yüeh-niang), once says that her husband can buy all the women he wants, and that no number is too many: "We're like women serving in the army, merely taking up space in the house and nothing more" (俺們多是老婆當軍, 在這屋裡充數兒罷了; 2.40.446 [trans. modified]; 40.5b). Since the seventeenth century, critics have reproduced the book's misogyny, especially in the characterization of Pan Jinlian as a wanton woman presumed to be innately base, immoral, and lascivious. Qing dynasty commentators typically present a woman such as Pan Jinlian as a kind of semihuman creature who, if not kept at a distance, will inevitably capture and destroy the unwitting man, who is nevertheless fascinated and even terrified by her.[6]

Besides the language of sexual description, at least three other issues are of interest in terms of the novel's portrayals of sex. The first of these is the institution of polygamous marriage, which affects the lives of all characters. Second, even though *Plum*'s language may often be elegant and sublime, there is no sublime love or grand love affair in the novel. As C. T. Hsia once wrote, all characters in *Plum* are "divested of heroism and grandeur," regardless of the context in which the novel portrays them (166). Third, readers may initially assume that sex is sex because humans are human, to put it simply. True as that may be in terms of the assumed biology of sex, the way characters have sex in *Plum* must be understood against the backdrop of the history of sexuality in China, in particular the long tradition of the art of sex, called the "art of the bedchamber" (*fangzhong shu* 房中術), which dates to at least the early Han dynasty (206 BCE–220 CE). No matter which of these three issues one considers—whether polygamy, the lack of heroic characters, or the tradition of the art of the bedchamber—each must be read in the context of Ming culture and society. Cultural norms and historical expectations inform the way people have sex, who can enjoy sex and who cannot, and the definition of sexual enjoyment, no matter the time period, culture, or narrative mode.

Polygamy and Plum

Plum's main setting—the marital household—is based on a form of polygamy that was prevalent among the elite in Ming China. In such a household, a man had one main wife—in this case Yueniang—as well as secondary wives or concubines. The first to enter the Ximen household as secondary wives are a former maid, Sun Xue'e (Sun Hsüeh-o), and, later, a former prostitute, Li Jiao'er (Li Chiao-erh). Then come three widows: Pan Jinlian, whose husband she and Ximen Qing murdered; Meng Yulou (Meng Yü-lou), who before entering the house was falsely told she would be Ximen's main wife; and Li Ping'er (Li P'ing-erh), the wife of Ximen's neighbor. Both Meng Yulou and Li Ping'er bring their riches with them and thus provide Ximen Qing with enormous wealth. Each woman has a numbered rank, though the ranking does not reflect the master's affections since Ximen Qing loves Number Six, Li Ping'er, the most. In theory, a man had concubines to increase his chances of bearing a son or sons. But in practice men took concubines because it pleased them to do so. These men also visited prostitutes, whom they might purchase as concubines or otherwise retain by paying long-term fees and visiting them periodically at the brothel, as Ximen Qing does. This type of prostitute was a kind of concubine away from home. In this way, the meaning of polygamy was in effect extended to include prostitutes as well.

Polygamy was a sign of high status. Emperors always had multiple wives, and in this sense men such as Ximen Qing can be understood as miniature emperors of sorts. Polygamy came with a set of principles and expectations, some of which changed over time.[7] The main wife was expected to live in the best part of the rear of the compound. This was where concubines went to kowtow to her when they first entered the house and where they often visited and gathered to pay respects, confer, and conduct household business. The main wife was in charge of the other wives and their children and was responsible for maintaining harmony and for preventing or settling disputes among the other wives. Though a concubine's status abruptly rose if she had a son, she still had to defer to the main wife and be careful not to offend the other wives. In addition to wives and concubines, maids were considered sexually available to the master, who might favor them by giving them special clothing and other gifts.

Plum's *Lack of Heroic Characters*

Plum's lack of heroic characters is especially apparent in the humor and sarcasm that the author injects into portrayals of sex. Ximen Qing is a wealthy upstart, one of whose main signs of success is the many women—his wife and the concubines, prostitutes, and other men's wives—with whom he consorts at will. Orthodox polygamy does not permit a man to have sex with other men's wives, but the most flagrant polygamists do. Ximen Qing also avails himself of his young, handsome male servants. His power and influence make it easy for him to enjoy so many partners, who relate to him sexually in ways that reflect their social status. Ximen Qing has sex more often with characters of lower status; those who depend on him more heavily or stand to gain more from him are willing to do more to please him, including engaging in unusual sexual practices. Such characters include his concubines, prostitutes, and servants, all of whom contrast with his main wife, Yueniang, to whom social standards assign a relatively more dignified role. The novel describes Ximen Qing having sex with her only once, using high-erotic language, an example of which is the following: they "gave free reign to: The oriole's abandon and the butterfly's pursuit" (一任其鶯恣蝶採; 2.21.7–8; 21.3b).[8] They enjoy voluptuous pleasure, but the author avoids portraying them in unusual sexual positions or having her involved in anything but vaginal sex. Ximen Qing in fact spends many nights with her, but the author provides no depiction of sex. In Chinese literature, main wives are generally less lustful than concubines, if lustful at all. Li Ping'er also enjoys greater privilege after she has a son, reflecting the ancient saying "the mother is prized who gives birth to a son" (*mu yi zi gui* 母以子貴). After she gives birth to her son, there are far fewer descriptions of sex between her and Ximen Qing. Yet Ximen Qing spends more time with her and less time with Pan Jinlian, whose jealousy grows fiercer until she finally manages to cause the deaths of both the child and Li Ping'er.

The novel's most graphic and extensive descriptions of sex involve sex with concubines, prostitutes, servants, and other men's wives, in particular the sex that Ximen Qing enjoys with the concubine Pan Jinlian and with the married woman Wang Liu'er (Wang Liu-erh). The latter is especially notable. By agreement of all three, Wang Liu'er's husband conveniently leaves the house to allow Ximen Qing to visit her for sex whenever he wishes. In return, Ximen Qing gives them money, protection, and favors, including helping them marry their daughter as a concubine to an important man in the capital. Wang adds variety to Ximen Qing's adventures because, as a relatively older woman of twenty-eight, she has sexual experience and know-how. She is sexually appealing and self-confident, immediately attracting Ximen Qing as someone who can offer exciting sex. The descriptions of their affair accord with these features: "It so happens," the narrator tells us, that "she suffered from a malady" (原來婦人有一件毛病; my trans.; 37.10b), a tongue-in-cheek reference to her fondness for anal intercourse, which, in combination with manual stimulation, is said to be the only way she can have an orgasm. Wang Liu'er has a second "malady," a love of fellatio. She likes to have a man's organ "in her mouth as long as possible, even all night is not enough" (常遠放在口裏, 一夜他也無個足處; my trans.; 37.10b).[9] This is an instance of ambiguous portrayal, in which her so-called "malady" could instead be her way of best pleasing the man to gain more profit from him. She and her husband illustrate a type of polyandry that was widespread in China at the time, in which for financial and other types of gain a couple prostituted the wife to a select man or men. The husband was in agreement, and, as is the case here, it was possible for the wife to initiate the affair herself (Sommer, *Polyandry* 56, 69).[10] Wang Liu'er and others like her—but again less so the main wife, Yueniang; the concubine Meng Yulou; and the concubine-mother Li Ping'er—compete for Ximen Qing's attention. In the case of Pan Jinlian, such competition means maligning, attacking, and even destroying other women in the process.

Giving Ximen Qing sexual pleasure is a professional skill in the case of the prostitutes whom he pays generously to serve him. But it is also the case for Pan Jinlian, Wang Liu'er, and the servant women he collects, including the wet nurse Ruyi (Ju-i). Pan Jinlian craves sex but will also suffer pain to please Ximen Qing and draw him closer. After being exposed and punished for her affair with the male servant, she "lowers herself to the most shameful acts, there being no length to which she will not go" (屈身忍辱, 無所不至; 1.12.241 [trans. modified]; 12.12a). Both she and Wang Liu'er submit to his practice of burning moxa on their bodies, including their genitals, which supposedly makes the woman writhe in pain, thus exciting the man (1.8.500n41). Like Wang Liu'er, Pan Jinlian is practiced at "playing the flute" (品簫), a euphemism for fellatio. Like prostitutes, Wang Liu'er and Pan Jinlian are expert at titillating Ximen Qing's "jade stalk" (玉莖), something that Yueniang is never shown doing and that the concubine-mother Li Ping'er no longer does either. Once while "playing the flute," rather than have Ximen Qing disengage to urinate, Pan Jinlian tells him to do so in her mouth. She wants nothing more than to "bore her way into his belly" (恨不得鑽入他腹中; 4.72.358; 72.11a)—that is to say, win him over completely. Anal intercourse is part of the same set of acts. Except for Wang Liu'er, the women are never portrayed as enjoying it, but like fellatio it delights and excites Ximen Qing: "My precious child," he says after Pan swallows his urine, "no one else cares for me as much as you do" (乖乖兒, 誰似你這般疼我; 4.72.358; 72.11a). Later, hearing that Pan Jinlian did such a thing, the wet nurse Ruyi does the same, having quickly learned how to curry favor with her master. After the deaths of Li Ping'er and her baby, Ruyi depends on Ximen Qing's favor to keep her place in his household. She would otherwise have to fend for herself as a far poorer woman. She becomes another of the always-ready sexual companions whom Ximen Qing collects after the death of Li Ping'er, for whom she becomes an emotional stand-in. Although Pan Jinlian is perhaps also always ready, she is a major personality, always full of demands, who dares to defy Ximen Qing and make herself heard. In contrast, Ruyi and another woman, Ye (Yeh) the Fifth, the wife of the servant Ben Dichuan (Pen Ti-ch'uan), immediately offer themselves when he arrives: "The two of them wasted no words, went into the inner room, where [Ye the Fifth] took off her clothes, undid her girdle, and lay down on the kang spreading her legs" (兩個也無閒話, 走到裏間內, 老婆脫衣解帶, 仰〈手扉〉擺炕上; 4.78.584 [trans. modified]; 78.4a). Later, Huiyuan (Hui-yüan), the wife of another one of Ximen Qing's servants, does the same (4.78.625).

The Art of the Bedchamber

The ancient art of the bedchamber is also relevant to a reading the novel, even though the characters are far from mirroring its logic or tone. A clue to the basic male perspective of the art of the bedchamber appears in one of the ways it was referred to in the Han dynasty, as the "art of riding women" (*yu nü zhi shu* 御女之術). Consisting of numerous texts from the Han to the Qing, the art of the bedchamber premises itself on the notion that the woman is superior to the man in sex, because of which he must learn how to master his sexual energy and read her signs of pleasure and arousal in order to satisfy her. According to the art of the bedchamber, one of the man's key methods of self-mastery is semen retention, something that Ximen Qing never practices. Semen retention is not merely meant to satisfy the woman but is also good for the man's health since excess ejaculation is said to be injurious, even fatal. *Plum* portrays Ximen Qing as someone who is already formidable in sex, never suffering from lack of confidence. Note, however, a detail in the first scene in which he appears naked, when he is already girded with a weapon that he will never do without: "About the base of his member he wore a clasp that had been: Beaten out of silver, and / Imbrued with drugs, / which had the effect of making that organ both large and long" (根下又帶着銀打就, 藥煮成的托子; 1.4.90; 4.5b). The silver clasp is one of several tools Ximen Qing relies on, storing them in Pan Jinlian's chambers, since it is with her that he usually has his most stimulating sex at home. In the art of the bedchamber, however, a man only needs such things if he is old or sexually weak, the implication being that a healthy man should not have to rely on them unless he goes to excess. Ximen Qing's other tools include ointments that combine stimulation and irritation, two kinds of dildos, and the so-called Burmese bell, all of which were available to people in those times who had the money to pay for them and the leisure to have concubines and consort with prostitutes. The Burmese bell is something that Li Ping'er owns because of her previous husband's eunuch uncle, who obtained it from the imperial palace. Worth four or five taels of silver, it is an object that is placed in the vagina to produce a numbing sensation and is not something a poorer woman such as Pan Jinlian could originally ever have owned or come across. But when she discovers it, she wants to try it, saying, "You've been experimenting with Li Ping'er, haven't you?" (你與李瓶兒也幹來; 1.16.325; 16.5b–6a).[11] Both the clasp and the bell allow Ximen Qing to "display his spearsmanship" (施逞鎗法; 1.6.123; 6.5a).

The reference to spearsmanship brings up the battle motif that appears throughout Chinese erotic literature and that also appears in ancient India and Rome. Spearsmanship appears explicitly in poems in *Plum* that accompany scenes depicting sex as battle. "Wielding his spear, he wants to penetrate / as far as the heart cavity; / The female commander is agitated; / Opening her orifice, she tries to swallow / her assailant, head and all" (使鎗只去扎心窩; 女帥心忙, 開口要來吞腦帶; 2.37.376; 37.10a). In another poem, each opponent is left wounded and exhausted, no one the victor: "Before long, behold, the ballista attacks have / reduced Crotch County to rubble, / Leaving each of them with bulging brows / and swollen eyes; / In no time, one perceives, the sparsely wooded / field is so gored with the spear, / That they are each left with split flesh and broken skin" (頃刻間只見這內襠縣, 乞砲打成堆, 個個皆腫眉[月-囊]膿眼; 霎時下則望那沙草場, 被鎗扎倒底, 人人肉綻皮開; 4.78.595; 78.10b).[12] In spite of the art of the bedchamber's premise about the woman's superiority over the man, its chief message is that of conservation of energy and achievement of harmony. Sex is like an artful calisthenic exercise or a musical performance that the man and woman carry out together, controlling pleasure rather than taking it to extremes.

Another topic of the traditional art of the bedchamber is positions of intercourse, which partners assume in playful variation. They are engaged in a kind of sport, as seen in expressions that mirror the moves of martial arts. Ximen Qing "assumes the position of 'inserting the arrow upside down'" (賣了個倒入翎花; 2.27.144 [trans. modified]; 27.10b), "assume" (*mai* 賣) being the same word for assuming a pose in martial arts. Shortly after, as he proceeds to lunge himself deep inside her, he tells Pan Jinlian, "Now I am going to play you the position of the 'old monk rings the bell'" (我要耍個老和尚撞鐘; 2.27.148 [trans. modified]; 27.12b). The first reference to positions occurs when Ximen Qing tells Pan Jinlian about his sex with Li Ping'er and pulls out an erotic album that he obtained from Li. Like the Burmese bell, the album is of exquisite quality, originally coming from the imperial palace and, also like the bell, inherited by Li Ping'er from her husband's eunuch uncle. It consists of a set of twenty-four illustrations of positions, which Ximen Qing and Li have been imitating, as he tells Pan. He and Pan place it open at their side as they have sex later that night (1.13.271–72).[13] Such albums still exist in museums and private collections around the world.

The two most common positions in the novel are "pok[ing] up the fire from the other side of the mountain" (隔山取火; 1.27.133; 27.5a) and "dousing the prone red candle" (倒澆紅蠟燭; 1.6.124 [trans. modified]; 6.7b). The first refers to the man penetrating the woman from behind and the second to the woman being on top of the man. The same positions occur in the art of the bedchamber, but with more elegant names. "Dousing the prone red candle" appears in other novels and tends to connote female dominance. In *Plum*, it appears, for instance, in the fateful scene in which Pan Jinlian rides the barely conscious Ximen Qing, whom she feeds an overdose of the powerful aphrodisiac, trying to get as much out of him as she can, but ends up giving an unquenchable erection that leads to his death.

A major turning point occurs midway through the novel when Ximen Qing acquires the marvelous aphrodisiac, which gives him extraordinary power. Like the art of the bedchamber, the use of aphrodisiacs goes back to ancient times, the two forming a neat contrast: On the one hand, individuals discipline themselves by following the procedures of the art of the bedchamber and in so doing reap the benefits of physical and spiritual well-being. On the other, they take shortcuts to guarantee pleasure by relying on drugs. It is commonly a Daoist or Buddhist adept who dispenses the drug. In the case of Ximen Qing, it is an Indian monk whose head looks like an engorged purple penis. *Plum*'s sexual descriptions enter new territory after Ximen Qing acquires the aphrodisiac, portraying a more aggressive character who shocks women with the size of his organ and ignores their pleas to go slower or finish sooner now that his new size causes them pain. When he does the "rear court flower," a euphemism for anal intercourse, with Pan Jinlian, she tells him to hurry and ejaculate because it hurts. To help persuade her, he says that he will buy her a new set of clothing. She bargains for a nicer set, then pretends to enjoy his painful thrusting by making wanton and lascivious sounds (3.52.256–58).

The scene in which the monks overhear Ximen Qing and Pan Jinlian having sex illustrates a motif that extends throughout the book and its uninhibited descriptions of sexual acts. The author is a voyeur and so are the readers. The combination of open description and complicit watching is both subtle and troubling. Ximen Qing is not an admirable character. It is true that he is generous with his partners and friends, never failing to reward them. But the author also portrays Ximen Qing as a person who surrounds himself with fawning male inferiors, curries favor with corrupt superiors, and indulges himself with women who compete, sometimes viciously, for his attention and favor. Ximen Qing assumes the privilege of having unrestrained sex without punishment. He is the local powerful man; to cross him can be dangerous and to please him can be profitable. He wears the silver clasp at all times and, after acquiring the monk's aphrodisiac, uses the drug from then on. Both the clasp and the aphrodisiac are examples of Ximen Qing's fraudulent appropriations of power. Such fraud parallels his reliance on bribery and collusion to extricate himself from predicaments and acquire immodest gain. Here it is fitting to return to the notion of pornographic description as a means of critical commentary. *Plum*'s pornographic scenes typically contain a hint of deprecation. At the same time, however, such explicit descriptions also tend to leave a remainder that produces an alternate flow of meaning. The remainder consists of the excitement and ecstasy of sex that overrides the voice of critical commentary, an excitement and ecstasy in which the author indulges while also constantly leaning on that critical voice.

NOTES

¹ Unless otherwise noted, parenthetical citations refer to Roy's translation, *The Plum in the Golden Vase*, and to *Jin Ping Mei cihua*金瓶梅詞話 (*Plum in the Golden Vase: A Ballad Tale*).

² Some would say that literature is erotic until it becomes grotesque and offensive, but I prefer to avoid the chore of fine-tuning the distinction between *erotic* and *pornographic*, though *pornographic* tends to sound stronger and harsher.

³ It is generally assumed that *Plum*'s author was a man, but of course this cannot be known for certain.

⁴ As Roy notes, the phrase "like a snail secreting its slime" is taken from the earlier novel *Ruyi junzhuan* 如意均轉 (*The Lord of Perfect Satisfaction*; 2.508n58).

⁵ See Hunt 39: "[S]pace and time only measure the repetition of sexual encounters, and bodies are reduced to sexual parts and to the endless possibilities of their variation and combination."

⁶ See N. Ding 160: "The narrative tends toward the seducer's (the man's) point of view. . . . This is a gendered narrative, telling a man's tale, whose projected reader must likewise be male."

⁷ For changes in the Ming, see McMahon, *Celestial Women* 75–157.

⁸ Other occasions provide no description (chs. 55 and 58).

⁹ For Roy's translation, see 2.37.377. See also N. Ding 160.

¹⁰ This arrangement can also be called "marital prostitution."

¹¹ Roy translates this as the "Titillating Bell" (1.16.324–25).

¹² For another example, see 2.29.192.

¹³ For a later appearance of the album, see 5.83.1201.

Trafficking Women
in *The Plum in the Golden Vase*
Siyen Fei

The Plum in the Golden Vase (*Jin Ping Mei* 金瓶梅) is known for its piercing gaze into late Ming society through its exploration of the rise and fall of the Ximen family. *Plum* is set in a market town along the Grand Canal. Trade in all forms (goods, political clout, information, etc.) dictates the terms of social life and serves as the novel's central node for a myriad of plotlines. Located at the center of all transactions, I argue, is the ultimate commodification of social relations—human trafficking. Indeed, the very formation of the Ximen household is itself the outcome of dozens of transactions in people. Trading people—especially women—is so central to *Plum*'s plot that we can read the entire novel through this lens: the compulsive purchase of women by the novel's protagonist, Ximen Qing (Hsi-men Ch'ing), drives the first half of *Plum*; in the second half of the novel, most of these women are sold off as Ximen's household falls apart. In this way, *Plum* presents the most searing exposition of how monetary transaction had infiltrated the very core of all social relations in imperial China—the family.

This emphasis on human trafficking in a family drama is not accidental. Despite its astonishingly realistic details, *Plum* is not a novel that passively observes. The world of Ximen Qing, who runs a local business while also serving in the government, provides the perfect basis for social and political critique. In Ximen Qing's world, bribery is taken as a given in the day-to-day operations of a yamen, and monetary influence infiltrates all levels of government. Such commentaries were not uncommon in the late Ming cultural world. *Plum* is different, however, in that it extends the story of money and power from the public domain into the realm of kinship and family. The victims of human trafficking constitute an integral element of the Ximen household. They suffer exploitation and find opportunity in it. Reading *Plum* through the lens of trafficking encourages readers to consider issues of social relations, value, and agency.

Ximen Qing as Women Trafficker

The prominent role of trafficking in *Plum* stems from the simple fact of failed biology: the swift growth of the Ximen household—one of the main themes in the first half of the novel—has little to do with familial procreation but rests instead on the purchase of people. Infertility is a shadow that looms over Ximen Qing's otherwise all-around success in bed, creating a need for more partners. Of the more than thirty transactions in people depicted in the novel, many are described in painstaking detail. The narrative first directs readers' attention to human trafficking through its seemingly repetitive reminder of Ximen's reputation as a charismatic womanizer and a trafficker.

In particular, the infamy of trafficking is evoked to foil Ximen's marriage proposition. When Meng Yulou (Meng Yü-lou) is considering marriage with Ximen Qing, her uncle, Zhang (Chang) the Fourth, comes to dissuade her. He makes a most serious accusation against Ximen, saying that he "is given to trading in human flesh. . . . Whenever his women displease him, even just the slightest, he calls in a matchmaker to sell them" (單管挑販人口, 打婦熬妻, 稍不中意, 就令媒人賣了; 1.7.138–39; 7.9a).[1] According to article 298 of the Ming legal codes, trafficking was a criminal offense punishable by one hundred strokes of beating and three years of penal servitude (Y. Jiang 164). Accusing Ximen Qing of human trafficking was not empty slander by Zhang the Fourth. In chapter 17, Jiang Zhushan (Chiang Chu-shan), in an effort to convince Li Ping'er (Li P'ing-erh) that he would make a far stronger husband, brings the same charge against Ximen Qing:

> Why would you want to marry him? I've often been called on to perform medical services in his household and know all about it. He's nothing but an influence peddler in the district yamen, and a loan shark as well. His home is a veritable flesh market. Not counting the maidservants, he's already got five or six bedmates, of higher and lower status, about the place, whom he subjects to a regular caning if they get out of hand. Whenever one of them fails to please him in any way, however slight, he calls in a go-between and disposes of her without more ado. He's:
>> The foreman of the wife-beaters,
>> The leader of the lotharios.
> It's a good thing you told me about it. Otherwise, if you had entered his household, it would have been like:
>> A moth darting into the flame.
> You would have been trapped, unable to escape in any direction, and it would have been too late to think better of it.   (1.17.352)

娘子因何嫁他? 小人常在他家看病, 最知詳細. 此人專在縣中事, 舉放私債; 家中挑販人口. 家中不算丫頭, 大小五六個老婆; 着緊打趙棍兒, 稍不中意, 就令媒出賣了. 就是打老婆的班頭, 坑婦女的領袖. 娘子早是對我說, 不然進入他家, 如飛蛾投火一上不上, 下不下, 那時悔之晚矣.   (17.9b)

The accusation convinces Li Ping'er to give up her plan to marry Ximen Qing, a decision that comes with substantial financial loss because a good portion of Li Ping'er's personal valuables are already in the Ximen household. In this sense, her decision shows how terrifying the charge made against Ximen Qing was to her. Yet Yulou was utterly unfazed; in fact, she made a forceful rebuttal. Why the drastically different responses? What did human trafficking mean to sixteenth-century Chinese men and women?

Teaching *Plum* through the lens of human trafficking is both rewarding and challenging. The novel's plot, which describes the rise and fall of a merchant family in a flourishing market town at the height of China's silver economy, resonates with our era of high capitalism. This timely connection allows students to relate to the predominant concerns of late Ming elites about money and its corrosive effect on society. In late Ming local gazetteers, literati produced lengthy treatises that established a correlation between thriving commerce and a disrupted social order.

Yet human trafficking in *Plum* also presents some anachronistic perils. It might be tempting to see repeated descriptions of Ximen Qing as a peddler of women as an indictment of women's commodification, but that is not necessarily the case. While the author and late Ming readers of *Plum* would have been accustomed to criticisms concerning the destructive power of money, they did not live in a postabolitionist world that viewed people who were bought and sold as having been deprived of meaningful relationships and social mobility—that is, as destined for social death. This gap between past and present opens a window for readers today to reflect on notions of servitude and slavery across cultures and time.

Throughout *Plum*, trafficking and marriage are closely intertwined. In both examples above, we learn that Ximen Qing sells the women in his household by calling in a marriage broker to manage the sale. As the line between transaction and marriage is blurred, trafficking becomes the means of kinship formation. By the end of *Plum*—literally the final paragraph—Ximen's bloodline has been extinguished, and Dai'an (Tai-an), who has been sold to Ximen, becomes his heir and is even given a new name, Honorable Young Ximen (Ximen xiao guan ren 西門小官人; 5.100.419; 100.16b). If the final act of *Plum* is to adopt a trafficked slave as the heir of the household, should we read this as a critique of the family system? an optimistic view of human trafficking? And, most important, to what extent is this conflation of transaction and kinship grounded in social reality?

I begin by considering the indictment of Ximen Qing as a peddler of women. Despite its realist literary style, *Plum* is never explicit about its message. Meaning is hidden among lavish descriptions of physical indulgence, layered deceptions, and plot twists. True to this style, the seemingly straightforward charge of Ximen's women trafficking belies the tension between legal and social connotations. Careful contextualization helps elucidate the intersection between kinship and trafficking that lies at the heart of *Plum*'s exposition on social conditions and relationships (*shiqing* 世情 ["ways of the world"]).

A Women Trafficker Who Never Sells Women

The first layer of deception is that, while *Plum* tells its reader everyone in town knows Ximen Qing as a women trafficker, he never actually sells any women. Jiang Zhushan's and Zhang the Fourth's claims that Ximen sells women on a whim is only a possibility, one that is certainly within Ximen Qing's power but that never materializes. But this fact does not necessarily make the accusation false, at least in a strict legal sense. Under Ming law, human trafficking included both the act of purchase and that of sale and was deemed a crime even with mutual consent. According to article 298 of the Ming legal codes:

> In the case of enticing others [to agree to be taken into the offenders' households] or, with mutual agreement, selling honorable persons as slaves, the offenders shall be punished by 100 strokes of beating with the heavy stick and penal servitude for three years. If [they take them] as wives, concubines, sons or sons' sons, they shall be punished by 90 strokes of beating with the heavy stick and penal servitude for two and one-half years.
>
> (Y. Jiang 164)

In consenting to their sale, the persons being sold are also at fault, though the penalty was somewhat lighter: for the persons who were enticed, the law maintains that "the penalty shall be reduced." The law also sees minors under the age of ten as incapable of giving consent, meaning that sales in such cases are treated as kidnapping (164).

Therefore, although Ximen Qing never forces anyone into such a sale, his compulsive acquisition of women, be it maidservants or concubines, makes him a trafficker in the eyes of the law. The purchase of Pang Chunmei (P'ang Ch'unmei), for example, violates the law that one cannot take honorable persons as slaves.[2] In this sense, the perception of Ximen as a trafficker of women stands, since the expansion of the Ximen household is grounded in its massive acquisition of people.

However, this legal interpretation might not be what Zhang the Fourth and Jiang Zhushan have in mind. In late imperial China, a wide gap existed between law and social practice. While it was illegal for nonofficials to purchase and keep slaves, it had become a common practice by the time *Plum* was written, a fact attested to by anecdotal evidence as well as the many extant contracts of sale. The ownership of slaves or bond servants would have been seen more as a status symbol than as incriminating evidence (*Ming Qing Huizhou* 551; *Huizhou qiannian* 37). So, what exactly is Zhang the Fourth referring to? How did Ximen Qing cross the line from wealthy merchant to women trafficker?

Meng Yulou's rebuttal offers an important clue. In chapter 7, in response to her uncle's accusation of Ximen, Meng Yulou replies:

> [Y]ou're mistaken. No matter how rough a man may be, he won't beat a wife who is diligent and knows what she's about. As a member of this household, if I manage to run a tight ship, so that:
> Words spoken inside do not get out, and
> Words spoken outside do not get in,
> What can he do to me? If a wife:

> Likes to eat but hates to work,
> Has a big mouth and a long tongue, and
> Devotes herself to stirring up trouble,

then:

> If her husband doesn't beat her,
> Should he beat the dog instead?

(1.7.139)

四舅, 你老人家差矣. 男子漢雖利害, 不打那勤謹省事之妻. 我到他家, 把得家定, 里言不出, 外言不入, 他敢怎的? 為女婦人家, 好吃懶做, 嘴大舌長, 招是惹非; 不打他, 打狗不成?

(7.9a–9b)

Meng Yulou does not dispute the trafficking accusation but argues instead that if she fulfills her wifely duty, there is no reason for Ximen Qing to use violence in any form (beating, selling) against her. In other words, Yulou declares that women were not passive victims but could preempt domestic violence through their own action. It is her, not Ximen, who gets to draw the line between trafficking and marriage.

This one declaration sheds light on Yulou as someone who takes control of her fate. And her argument appears to be persuasive: Zhang the Fourth gives up and moves on to his next line of attack on Ximen Qing (i.e., the problem with Ximen's unmarried daughter). Yulou stands her ground with the firm moral conviction that by acting within the realm of propriety, she can be in charge of her destiny. Indeed, by the end of the novel, she is the only wife who is not sold out of the Ximen household. She exits the Ximen family on her terms, for a loving marriage. Li Ping'er, in contrast, fails to grasp the power of women's moral agency. In her desperation, she abandons the original plan to marry Ximen Qing and props up Jiang Zhushan as a clone of the former, a gambit that ends in devastating humiliation: ultimately, Ping'er must beg her way back into the original marriage plan and throw herself at the mercy of Ximen Qing.

Taken together, the drama surrounding Ximen the women trafficker boils down to the tangled mess of marriage and transaction. For Li Ping'er, the terror of slipping from marriage to trafficking is so overpowering that she runs away. Yulou, however, insists that such slippage can be prevented through sheer moral power. *Plum* does not tell us who has the better answer, but it repeatedly casts light on this tangled mess that was not uncommon in late Ming life.

The tangling of marriage and trafficking had an ironic footing in Ming anti-trafficking laws created to separate the two. Despite the state's explicit intention against monetarizing social bonds, it was far from successful in stemming the tide of human trafficking. Most wealthy households, like Ximen's, would have had dozens of servants through written contracts of sale.[3] Despite its failure, the law did effect changes to social practice that are visible in extant Ming contracts. The trafficking contracts that survive today mostly came from Huizhou, an inland province that, like the Qinghe of the novel, was well known for its active commerce. One fascinating feature of these sales contracts is their blatant conflation of *maishen wenshu* 賣身文書, a contract by which one sells oneself or a member of one's family, and *hunyin wenshu* 婚姻文書, a contract of marriage where prospective buyers were referred to as *qinjia* 親家, or in-laws. These contracts are common enough that we find a sample format in popular almanacs—guidebooks for daily use for middlebrow people:

> ___(seller) sign the contract of marriage. Now for inability to afford daily food, I volunteer to give my son/daughter___, age___, via matchmaker to___(buyer) as adopted son/daughter in receiving cash gift___taels of silver. From now on [sold son/daughter] will follow the order and never return home. If people from outside or inside tempt them [sold son/daughter] to make trouble, this contract will be the basis of arbitration. Hereby we establish the contract of marriage with handprints of boy/girl to be kept by the Master. (my trans.)

> 立婚書某, 今因日食無度, 自願將男、女名某, 年命某生, 憑媒與某名下為義男、女, 得受財禮紋銀若干, 自後聽從使喚, 永不歸家. 如內外人等生端引誘, 憑從證理, 致立婚書並男、女手印, 付主存照. (Xie Guozhen 204)

The content of this contract is clearly about the sale of children, with specific details about the commodity under sale (age, sex, price) and the terms of the sale (obedience to the master and termination of family ties). While the sale is disguised as adoptive kinship (*yi nan* 義男 or *yi nu* 義女), the contract itself is referred to as a contract of marriage. This deliberate conflation, historians believe, is a product of Ming laws that specifically forbade nonofficial families from purchasing slaves or bond servants. As a result, sales contracts for servants, including concubines, were often rendered (i.e., masked) as marriage contracts.

This conflation is not just wordplay used to bypass the law. It weaves together two realms—kinship formation and monetary transaction. As seen in many late Ming critiques, social relations had become more and more commodified, and marriage increasingly took traits of monetary transaction. But the infiltration went both ways: the transaction of people had to be conducted through the veins of kinship and, as a result, was bound by familial proprieties.

With this in mind, I return to the question raised earlier: Is Zhang the Fourth correct in calling Ximen Qing a women trafficker? While Ximen Qing clearly breaks the law by purchasing commoners as bond servants, the practice was so common at the time that owning slaves would have been seen more as a status symbol than as material for slander. The accusation that Ximen "is given to trading in human flesh" and that "[w]henever his women displease him, even just the slightest, he calls in a matchmaker to sell them" (打婦煞妻, 又管挑販人口, 稍不中意, 就令媒婆賣了) is based not on the act of buying and selling but on Ximen's unjustified selling of women. In other words, Ximen Qing would have been considered within his rights were he to sell women who committed serious offenses—as in the case of the maid Xiahua (Hsia-hua).

Of the over three dozen purchases detailed in *Plum*, readers will find only one instance where Ximen Qing actually intends to sell a woman. This comes in chapter 44, when he finds out that the maid Xiahua is responsible for stealing a gold bracelet. The disappearance of this expensive bracelet (worth fifty to sixty taels of silver, ten times the price of maidservants) causes a big fuss in the household as Ximen Qing interrogates all servants and gets into a fight with Pan Jinlian (P'an Chin-lien). When Ximen Qing finally discovers that Xiahua is the real culprit, he declares that she should be sold off. But this seemingly justified sale does not materialize. Ximen Qing is talked down by Li Guijie (Li Kuei-chieh), a courtesan he keeps outside his household. Guijie intervenes because she does not want to be tainted through kinship association. Xiahua was a maid to her aunt, Li Jiao'er (Li Chiao-erh). A disgraced maidservant reflected poorly on her master and, by extension, the master's niece, Guijie:

> If you don the black livery of a servant,
> You must cling to even the blackest post.
> If you weren't assigned to her quarters, it wouldn't matter, but when you are subjected to the third degree the way you just were, how do you suppose it reflects on your mistress's standing in the household?   (3.44.77)

穿青衣, 抱黑柱. 你不是他這屋裡人? 就不管他? 剛纔這等掠掣着你, 你娘臉上有光沒光?   (44.6b)

The concern here is obviously not the maid's welfare but the the mistress's dignity. It is interesting, moreover, to observe how this shame and humiliation travels across class lines and along the veins of kinship. Nevertheless, were it not for the family politics among women, the sale of Xiahua would have surely gone through and have been considered legitimate. Conversely, were the woman to be sold not at fault, the sale would have been deemed improper and Ximen Qing would have been condemned as a women trafficker. Therefore, in chapter 86, on hearing the news that she is about to be sold, Pan Jinlian vehemently protests this, arguing that the sale is not justified:

> "How long has it been since my husband died?" said Jinlian. "As for me:
> What fault have I committed;
> What offense am I guilty of?
> Why should I be driven away for no good reason?"   (5.86.104)

我漢子死了多少時兒, 我為下甚麼非, 作下甚麼歹來? 如何憑空發我出去?
                                   (86.10b)

Here Pan Jinlian invokes the rules of familial propriety and her right as a concubine to stay in the house. But it only brings humiliation as Yueniang publicly denounces Jinlian's incestuous adultery with Chen Jingji and forces her into submission. To Jinlian's protest Yueniang responds with the following:

> Don't you:
>> Feign being more silly than you are,
>> Pretending to be both dumb and deaf.
> It has always been true that:
>> When a snake makes a hole for itself
>> It knows where it is.
>> Whatever a person sees fit to do,
>> Is clear in the mind of the doer.
> Jinlian, you had better not:
>> Disguise your perfidy by playing dumb,
>> Showing an innocent face to both sides.
>> Praising here and faultfinding there.
> In my hands you can dispense with your:
>> Clever words and deceptive phrases,
>> Apple polishing and favor currying.
> It has always been true that:
>> There is no party that does not come to an end.
>> The beam that projects is the first one to rot.
>> Just as a man has his reputation,
>> A tree has its shadow.
>> Flies don't cluster on eggs
>>> unless they're cracked.
> You had better not assume that you can continue to support yourself by committing adultery. And right now, I'm going to send you off to oblivion.
>> (5.86.104–05)

你休稀裡打哄, 做啞裝聾. 自古蛇塼鑽窟礲蛇知道, 各人乾的事兒, 各人心裡明白! 金蓮, 你休呆裡撒奸, 兩頭白麵, 說長並道短! 我手裡使不的你巧語花言, 幫閒鑽懶! 自古沒個不散的筵席, 出頭緣兒先朽爛. 人的名兒, 樹的影兒, 蒼蠅不鑽沒縫兒彈. 你休把養漢當飯! 我如今要打發你上陽關!

> (86.10b)

What Pan Jinlian is guilty of is not just adultery, an offense she was already caught committing early in the novel but from which she emerged unscathed. Now she is guilty of committing adultery with her son-in-law—incest—a crime that violated the core tenet of kinship. For that she must go. If Jinlian had held her moral ground as Meng Yulou does, she would have been able to resist Yueniang, who is driven by vengeance to evict her. Once she loses her place in kinship relations, Jinlian is taken into the circuit of trafficking, and her fate is left in the hands of Dame Wang in an ensuing bidding war. The swiftness of Jinlian's fall attests to the deep infiltration of commercial forces into the institution of marriage.

Between Kin and Sold People

And this—the close intertwining of kinship and trafficking—is the point of *Plum*'s repeated invocation of Ximen Qing as women trafficker. The point is delivered from both sides: the narrative reveals a world in which money governs social relations and in which kinship has become so fragile that it can be terminated at any moment through trafficking deals. The author drives this point home through repeated warnings of Ximen Qing's reputation as a women trafficker to Meng Yulou and Li Ping'er—while both women enjoy respectable social and economic standing, in entering the Ximen household, they subject themselves to this precarious slippage between kinship and trafficking.

Just as kin could be sold, people who were sold could also become kin. The reason that the warning is only delivered to Li Ping'er and Meng Yulou is because Ximen's other wives are already part of the trafficking circuit. Pan Jinlian, for example, is sold twice by her own mother—first at the age of nine and again at the age of fifteen—before being gifted as a wife to Wu the Elder, with the implicit understanding that she will be sexually available to her former master. Ximen Qing's second wife, Li Jiao'er, marries in from a brothel, while the fourth wife, Sun Xue'e (Sun Hsüeh-o), enters the Ximen household as a maidservant who was part of a dowry gift. These women already live in a space defined by the intermixing of marriage and trafficking. The proximity of kin and sold people allows *Plum* to advance a deeper critique of money power in late Ming society.

The Rise

How does *Plum* describe the rise of Ximen Qing through his acquisition of not only assets but also people? This idea foregrounds a crucial fact, namely that these two forms of acquisition were not independent from each other: the women acquired by Ximen Qing constitute one of the main sources of his wealth, their acquisition representing some of his most successful deals.

Given that trafficking had become a fact of late Ming life, readers of the time wouldn't have been surprised that most of Ximen Qing's women come to him through trafficking circuits. What is radical and provocative is the bluntness with which *Plum* lays bare the transactional nature of the two conventional marriages. Ximen Qing treats his marriage to Li Ping'er and Meng Yulou first and foremost as business transactions. Before Li Ping'er enters the Ximen household, most of her assets have already been transferred to her new house. The incentive behind Zhang the Fourth's slandering of Ximen Qing is, by his own admission, Yulou's property. As a remarrying widow, Meng Yulou has no claim over immobile assets such as real estate or land. But mobile valuables, usually stored in chests and boxes in the inner chamber, follow her to her new husband's household.

In fact, Yulou's wealth is what prompts the marriage proposal. Although the author stresses that it is Yulou's mastery of the moon guitar that touches Ximen Qing's heart, the matchmaker opens her sales pitch with mention of Yulou's wealth before beginning to describe her looks:

> The young lady in question is someone you probably already know about, sir. She's the legitimate widow of the owner of the Yang family's textile business outside the South Gate, and she's got a tidy sum of money at her disposal. She owns two Nanking beds, with retractable steps; four or five trunks full of clothing for all four seasons, figured gowns and so forth, packed so tightly you can't stick your hand into them; and pearl headbands and earrings, gold jewelry set with precious stones, and gold and silver bracelets and bangles, it goes without saying. In ready cash alone, she has more than a thousand taels of silver at her disposal. And she has two or three hundred bales of fine cotton drill as well. (1.7.126)

> 說起來你老人家也知道, 是咱們南門外販布楊家的正頭娘子. 手裡有一分好錢. 南京拔步床也有兩張. 四季衣服, 妝花袍兒, 插不下手去也有四五隻箱子. 珠子箍兒, 胡珠環子, 金寶石頭面, 金鐲銀釧不消說, 手裡現銀子, 他也有上千兩. 好三梭布也有三二百筒. (7.1b)

Yulou's assets, which have been stored in her chamber trunks, soon became the focus of dispute. Having failed to dissuade Yulou from marrying Ximen, Zhang the Fourth moves to plan B: to create a disruption on the wedding day and grab the trunks during the chaos. However, the support of Aunt Yang, Yulou's maternal aunt, successfully foils the plot. Since a widow is entitled take her dowry with her if she remarries, the maternal aunt is the right kind of authority to assert Yulou's right to take her trunks. Here readers will realize why the matchmaker would bring Ximen Qing to bribe Aunt Yang even before she introduces Meng Yulou to her future husband. The elaborate strategizing involved in matchmaking is certainly impressive. As the terms of the arrangement are discussed, the transactional nature of marriage is foregrounded in a narrative aside: "Gentle reader take note: In this world, money is like the brain and spinal cord of man in that it is one indispensable thing that governs his every move" (看官聽說: 世上錢財, 乃是眾生腦髓, 最能動人; 1.7.130; 7.4a). It is also important to note that marriage, as a form of transaction, involved the transfer not only of assets but also of people in the roles of servants. With each new concubine Ximen Qing takes in, the household grows accordingly. The rich concubines bring their own servants as dowry: Meng Yulou and Li Ping'er, for instance, bring their own servants. Ownership of attractive servants in fact enhanced the value of marriage deals. One of the appeals of Li Ping'er is her attractive young maid-servant, who catches Ximen Qing's eye and prompts him to move forward with the marriage proposition.

The less well-off concubines, in contrast, rely on Ximen Qing to do the purchase. For example, when Pan Jinlian marries in, Ximen Qing lays out five taels of silver to buy a young maidservant to wait on Yueniang (the black lacquer bedstead Ximen Qing bought for Jinlian, in comparison, costs sixteen taels) so he can reassign Chunmei from Wu Yueniang's chamber to Jinlian and a further six taels of silver to buy a scullery maid named Qiuju (1.9.171).[4] Ximen Qing asks Chunmei "to serve her new mistress diligently and address her as Mother" (令他伏侍金蓮, 趕著叫娘; 1.9.171; 9.2a).

Either way, with each marriage, more people are trafficked into the household. Monetary transaction morphs into kinship formation. Moreover, it is this sense of kinship that gives the mistress claim to ownership of these servants. At the end of the novel, when Li Jiao'er remarries after the death of Ximen Qing, she wants to bring her maidservants along, and she would have succeeded had she not been taking them into a brothel, which Yueniang resists fiercely:

> Wu Kai, as the occupant of an official post, was reluctant to express an opinion on the matter, one way or the other, but after negotiating for what seemed like half a day, he suggested that Yueniang should let her keep all the clothing, jewellery, luggage, bedding, and other accessories from her quarters, and send her on her way, but not permit her to take the maidservants Yuanxiao and Xiuchun with her.
>
> Li Jiao'er, however, really wanted to retain the two maidservants, but Yueniang adamantly refused to allow this, saying, "You must only want to procure them in order to make prostitutes out of them." This accusation threw the procuress into such consternation that she did not dare to utter another word on the matter. (4.80.681)

> 吳大舅居著官, 又不敢張主, 相講了半日, 教月娘把他房中衣服、首飾、箱籠、床帳、家活盡與他, 打發出門. 只不與他元宵、繡春兩個丫頭去. 李嬌兒生死要這兩個丫頭. 月娘生死不與他, 說道: "你倒好, 買良為娼." 一句慌了鴇子, 就不敢開言. (80.8b)

Parallel to the novel's depiction of a series of transactions of women is a gift economy of people, mostly boys. As Ximen Qing grows more powerful, he begins to receive boys as gifts. In chapter 31, Ximen Qing finally ascends the social ladder and enters officialdom. To celebrate his assumption of office, Magistrate Li

> sent someone to deliver the traditional congratulatory gifts of mutton and wine to Ximen Qing. Magistrate Li also sent him, along with his card, a young man to wait upon him. He was just seventeen years old and was a

native of Changshu district in Suzhou prefecture. His nickname was Little
Zhang Song, and he had begun his career as a "gate-boy" in the district
yamen. He had a naturally clear-cut appearance:
>   His face looked as though it were powdered,
>   His teeth were white and his lips were red.
Moreover:
>   He knew how to read and write,
and was good at:
>   Singing southern-style songs.
He was wearing a long gown of black chiffon, sandals, and white socks.
When Ximen Qing saw how accomplished the young man appeared to be,
he was utterly delighted. He sent a card expressing his appreciation to Magistrate Li, agreed to retain the young man in his service, and changed his
name to Shutong, or Book Boy. He had a complete outfit of clothes made
for him, including new boots and a new hat, and did not have him accompany him when he went out on horseback, but put him in charge of his
studio, where he was responsible for his social correspondence, and gave
him custody of the key to the garden gate.

Ximen Qing's crony, Zhu Rinian, also recommended a fifteen-year-old
page boy to wait on him. His name was changed to Qitong [Ch'i-t'ung], or
Chess Boy. Every day he and Qintong [Ch'in-t'ung] were deputed to carry
his letter case and card case and accompany him when he went out on
horseback.   (2.31.220)

差人送羊酒賀禮來. 又拿帖兒送了一名小郎云來答應, 年方一十六歲, 本貫蘇
州府常熟縣人, 喚名小張松. 原是縣中門子王出身, 生的清俊, 面如傅粉, 齒白
唇紅, 又識字會寫, 善能歌唱南曲. 穿着青銷直掇, 京鞋淨襪. 西門慶一見小郎
伶俐, 滿心歡喜. 就拿拜帖回覆李知縣, 留下他在家答應, 改換了名字, 叫做書
童兒. 與他做了一身衣裳, 新靴新帽. 不教他跟馬, 教他專管書房收禮帖, 拿花
園門鑰匙. 祝日念又舉保了一個十四歲小廝來答應, 亦改名棋童, 每日派定和
琴童兒兩個背書袋、夾拜帖匣, 跟馬.   (31.4b–5a)

Ximen Qing's collection of beautiful boys starts to form a pattern. In chapter 55,
Squire Miao also sends two boys to cement his connection with Ximen Qing.
These boys, so favored and close to Master Ximen, wield such power of influence that Wang Liu'er (Wang Liu-erh), Ximen Qing's lover, sends in her brother
as a servant boy to strengthen her connection to Ximen.

Plum deliberately engenders its presentation of transaction in people. Consider
Zhu Yun (Chu Yün), a girl who is bought for ten taels of silver and trained as a
courtesan to be gifted to Ximen Qing so that the buyer, Miao Qing (Miao Ch'ing),
can purchase Ximen Qing's influence in the local government in order to evade
a murder and robbery charge. Like the young boys, Zhu Yun is intended as a
gift, but it is only Zhu Yun whose price is revealed. This is clearly a deliberate
narrative device: while all transactions involving women are detailed in terms

of price, prices are revealed for virtually none of the transactions involving men. And this is the case despite the fact that, through sales contracts, we know that just as many boys as girls were transacted. Why does *Plum* do this? To what end? The same gendered lens is applied in the second half of the novel, which is dedicated to the outgoing members of the Ximen household. When Ximen Qing dies, these boys simply leave or submit themselves to new masters, and readers are not privy to any of the transactional details. In contrast, women exit the Ximen household by means of various forms of transaction that are elaborated into dramas of mobility, justice, and kinship. This gendered narrative choice, as we will see, is less a reflection of historical reality than of the author's social critique.

The Fall

The rapid expansion of the Ximen household is rooted in Ximen's failure to procreate. The central irony of the story is that despite having endless sex throughout the novel, Ximen Qing is left with no blood descendants: one son dies, one daughter commits suicide, and one son becomes a monk. This narrative design makes two things possible: First, it separates sex from its moral purpose of sustaining patrilineage, the foundation of social order. Second, it allows the author to advance his unconventional take on kinship. After a hundred chapters of elaborate, extreme corporeal indulgence, the Ximen family is purged of all its biological members and left with only those who were either purchased or gifted into the family. Despite Ximen's reputation as a women trafficker, the sale of the women in his household takes place only after he dies. In fact, the drama surrounding these transactions dominates the post–Ximen Qing plotline. Repeatedly, readers are struck by the ease with which these women slip back into the trafficking circuit.

The endless stream of women being sold out of the Ximen household puts to test the moral precept enunciated by Meng Yulou in the beginning of the book. Is there a distinction between marriage and trafficking, one that can be upheld through wifely virtue? That is, if a woman fulfills her duty, is she able to gain control of her fate and avoid becoming a commodity? This appears to work for Meng Yulou, who is the only wife who is not sold after Ximen's death. Yet the author complicates the seemingly clear moral lesson with the exit of Li Jiao'er.

Immediately after Ximen Qing dies in chapter 79, as a means of planning her own exit from the household, the second wife, Li Jiao'er, begins to steal money from the first wife, Wu Yueniang. To enhance the dramatic effect, Li Jiao'er plans her exit on the very day Ximen Qing is buried. Li Guijie, Li Jiao'er's niece and Ximen's favorite courtesan, stands by Ximen Qing's grave and propositions Jiao'er:

> Mother [i.e., the madam of the brothel] says that you ought to consider the fact that since you no longer have anything of value in your hands, there is no reason for you to remain any longer in his household. You have no sons

or daughters, so what is there to keep you there? She suggests that you initiate a quarrel that will give you an excuse for breaking clear of the
place.   (4.80.680)

媽說你, 摸量你手中沒甚細軟東西, 不消只顧在他家了. 你又沒兒女, 守甚麼?
教你一場嚷亂, 登開了罷.   (80.8a)

In fact, a plan has been prepared for Li Jiao'er to marry a wealthy local official
willing to pay five hundred taels of silver for a second wife who will take charge
of the household. Following the plan, Li Jiao'er picks a fight with Wu Yueniang.
Threatening suicide, Jiao'er forces Yueniang to negotiate with Auntie Li the
Third, the madam of the Li family bordello. Apprehensive that Jiao'er might be
forced to leave all her clothes and jewelry behind, Auntie Li drives a hard bargain with Wu Yueniang and her brother. While it must be clear to both parties
that Jiao'er sees no future in the Ximen household and decides to leave the family
for a better life in the brothel, in negotiating the terms of Jiao'er's leave, Auntie
Li demands payment for Jiao'er's emotional labor during her tenure at the Ximen household:

> This kinswoman of mine, while here, has been forced to:
> >   Humble herself and experience humiliation,
> >   Taking the blame for the faults of others.
> If you insist on severing the relationship, hard as it may be for her, you
> ought to offer her the sum of several tens of taels of silver to compensate
> her for her embarrassment.   (4.80.681)

我家人在你這裡做小伏低, 頂缸受氣, 好容易就開交了罷? 須得幾十兩遮羞
錢!   (80.8b)

This bold request effectively redefines Li Jiao'er's role in the Ximen household.
Instead of being a kinswoman who should bear all emotional suffering as part
of her wifely duty, Jiao'er sees her time with Ximen Qing as a service, rendered
in the form of emotional labor, that should be compensated. Once out of the
Ximen household, Li Jiao'er is able to secure three hundred taels—the highest bridal price in *Plum*. This shows us that trafficking is not always about sub-
jecting women to bondage. For Sun Xue'e, the move from kinship to trafficking
is punishing, but for Li Jiao'er it offers a means of mobility.

Another good example is Chunmei, who does not opt out of the household
voluntarily like Li Jiao'er but is sold off as punishment. Yet despite this humiliation, Chunmei is able to move up the social ladder as a result of this transaction.
The sale of Chunmei and Pan Jinlian in chapter 85 is triggered by Yueniang's
discovery of Jinlian's affair with her son-in-law, Chen Jingji. Yueniang first calls
in the matchmaker, Auntie Xue, who brokered Meng Yulou's deal and the initial

purchase of Chunmei. Yueniang accuses Chunmei of acting as a go-between for Jinlian's adultery and decides to sell her off:

> "Originally," said Yueniang, "I purchased her from you for sixteen taels of silver, and now you can have her back for the same sum of sixteen taels of silver."
>
> She then turned to Xiaoyu, and said, "You go out front with her to take care of things, and see that she leaves empty-handed. Don't let her take any clothing with her other than what she has on."
>
> Auntie Xue then proceeded out front and told the woman, thus and so, "The First Lady has sent me to take Sister Chunmei away. She told me that you and she had been:
>> Colluding in chicanery,
>
> in order to facilitate your clandestine adultery, and that she:
>> Didn't care about the rights and wrongs,
>
> of the situation, but only wanted to recover the original price she had paid for Chunmei."
>
> When the woman heard that she was going to take Chunmei away in order to be sold, she opened her eyes wide and was unable to say a word for what seemed like half a day. (5.85.86)

> "那咱原是你手裡十六兩銀子買的, 你如今拿十六兩銀子來就是了." 吩咐小玉: "你看着, 到前邊收拾教他罄身兒出去, 休要他帶出衣裳去了." 那薛嫂兒到前邊, 向婦人如此這般: "他大娘教我領春梅姐來了. 對我說, 他與你老人家通同作弊, 偷養漢子. 不管長短, 只問我要原價." 婦人聽見說領賣春梅, 就睜了眼, 半日說不出話來. (85.9b)

The sale is meant as a punishment in that Yueniang strips Chunmei of her personal belongings and moves the transaction toward sale and away from marriage:

> "It's outrageous!" exclaimed Auntie Xue. "The First Lady is making a mistake to act this way. To send off an attractive young woman who has been favoured by her husband without allowing her to take a trunkful of her belongings with her, or even an outfit of clothing, but requiring her to leave emptyhanded, will not seem right in the eyes of the neighbours." (5.85.87)

> 薛嫂道, "可又來, 大娘差了! 爹收用的佶個出色姐兒, 打不與, 又不許帶一件衣服兒, 只教他罄身兒出去, 隣舍也不好看的!" (85.10a)

Thanks to the broker's skimming, Chunmei, purchased at the price of seventeen taels, is sold for thirteen—a price that, in the world of Ximeng Qing, is not enough to throw a banquet. In spite of this indignity, the sale eventually helps Chunmei ascend the social ladder and fulfills Immortal Wu's prediction that she will be the only woman in the Ximen household "to wear a pearl-decked cap and receive a title of nobility" (戴珠冠; 2.29.185; 29.10a). At the time, Yueniang disputes Immortal Wu's prophecy:

> It indicates that at an early age she will wear a pearl-decked cap.
> If one's gait resembles an immortal in flight,
> And the sound of one's voice is ethereal and clear,
> She is sure to benefit her husband and gain wealth,
> Obtaining a title of nobility at twenty-six.   (2.29.182)

> 早年必戴珠冠. 行步若飛仙, 聲喃神清, 必盆夫而得祿, 三九定然封贈.
> (29.9b)

Yet it is ultimately Yueniang's sale of Chunmei that fulfills this prophecy. Ximen Qing only manages to acquire a post of the fifth rank, whereas Chunmei's husband dies on the battlefield and receives a posthumous first-rank title, leaving Chunmei with the title of "Lady" (夫人). The reversal of status between kin and sold people is a crucial thread that peaks in *Plum*'s ending. Dai'an, Ximen Qing's closest servant, is also a sold person. Like all men in the Ximen household, the story of his sale and the amount paid for him are not made known. Dai'an shadows Ximen Qing everywhere and acquires intimate knowledge (probably more than Ximen Qing himself) of the Ximen enterprise. After Ximen's death, with no blood descendent left in the family, Dai'an becomes Ximen's heir and is given the master's name. There can be no more drastic demonstration of mobility within bondage.

Justice and Market

Trafficking also allows the author a very different take on the intertwined link between money and justice, an issue central to *Plum*. Ximen Qing, a peddler of influence, uses money to manipulate the local yamen to his benefit in every way possible: from exiling Wu Song to bribing the tax bureau to expedite the processing of his cargo. On the surface, the realization of justice is constantly obstructed by money. However, the most foundational justice of *Plum* is also delivered through the market: it is, after all, an open bidding war that allows Wu Song to avenge his brother's death, the act of justice that readers have been waiting for throughout *Plum*.

Immediately after Chunmei is sold, Dame Wang is called in to take Pan Jinlian away. A bidding war ensues among Chunmei, Pan Jinlian's former maidservant; Chen Jingji, Jinlian's lover; and Wu Song, the avenger. Compared with the specific instructions she gave for the sale of Chunmei, Yueniang's order for Jinlian is ambiguous. She says to the matchmaker-broker:

You are the one who produced this problem,
You should be the one who eliminates it.
One guest does not trouble two hosts.
I would, therefore, prevail upon you to take her away again and either
marry her off to someone else, or dispose of her in a way that allows her to
continue:
Eating the bread of idleness.
Now that my husband is dead, I can no longer afford to maintain such
people as this. Needless to say, that dead devil of mine spent vast sums of
money on her; enough to cast a silver figurine to match her dimensions. If
you give me back whatever you manage to marry her off for, I can use it to
hold a sutra recitation for my husband, so some good may come of it.

(5.86.104)

今來是是非人, 去是是非者, 一客不煩二主, 還起動你領他出去, 或聘嫁, 或打
發, 教他吃自在飯去罷. 我男子漢已是沒了, 招攬不過這些人來. 說不的當初
死鬼為他丟了許多錢底那話了, 就打他佶個銀人兒也有. 如今隨你聘嫁多少
兒, 交得來, 我替他爹念個經兒, 也是一場勾當.   (86.10a)

Yueniang uses this transaction to settle scores and attain justice for herself.
But she has a hard time determining the monetary value of her revenge
because Jinlian is the only woman who entered the Ximen household without
a price tag. The best Yueniang can do is to cite her dead husband's investment
in Jinlian (jewels, furniture, etc.) as grounds for compensation. It is Dame
Wang, the broker, who is familiar with the market, who gives Jinlian a price of
105 taels (and only reimburses Yueniang twenty). But to potential buyers,
Dame Wang announces an asking price of one hundred taels from Wu Yueniang. She receives a bid of seventy taels from a silk merchant and eighty from
Chunmei's agent. Chen Jingji is willing to pay the asking price but needs to
leave town to raise the money. Despite Chunmei's desire to make a higher offer, her servant still loses the bid because he insists on bargaining down the
price—ironic, seeing that Chunmei herself drove hard bargains in her purchase of maidservants. Between Chen Jingji's promise of money and the ready
cash offered by Wu Song, Dame Wang decides to sell Jinlian to Wu Song. The
sale to the highest and speediest bidder, Wu Song, seals the fates of Jinlian
and Dame Wang; both are brutally killed by Wu Song as revenge for his brother's
murder.

The bidding war over the sale of Pan Jinlian presents an innovative take on
the intersection of market and morality. In Ming vernacular novels, markets usually cause ruin, and only through retribution can justice be restored. *Plum*
opens with the murder of Wu the Elder and delays the delivery of justice until
almost the very end. While Wu Song's murder of Pan is confirmation of social

justice and karma, it is achieved through the market mechanism of women trafficking.

Indeed, the fates of so many of *Plum*'s main characters are tied to this bidding war: if Chen Jingji had won, the two incestuous adulterers might have had a happy ending; if Chunmei had won, Jinlian would have married a high-ranking officer. Instead, the plot plays out according to pure market logic—the person who wins is the highest bidder with ready cash, Wu Song. The trafficking chain continues: as Chunmei fails to save Jinlian, she exacts her revenge by selling Sun Xue'e, who instigated the sale of Jinlian in the first place, into prostitution.

What Is a Woman's Worth?

The circuits of kinship and trafficking, as Ming law envisioned, should run parallel but separate courses. However, in the Ximen household, they are so closely intertwined that their crossover dictates the fates of men and women tied to Ximen Qing. *Plum*'s deliberation of *shiqing* 世情 ("ways of the world") is a double-edged sword: while it exposes the deep penetration of monetary transactions in family formation, it also shows how the logic of kinship inflects the terms of human trafficking.

In the late Ming world, the corrosive power of money was well recognized by ruling elites. When *Plum* declares in chapter 7 that money governs human action as if it is the brain and spinal cord (1.7.130; 7.4a), it reads like a reiteration of a common criticism. Yet the meaning of this analogy, as unveiled through one hundred chapters, goes much deeper. *Plum* creates a microcosm of society in the form of the Ximen household, where women enter and exit with a specific sales value. In other words, it was not money that corrupted an existing ideal social hierarchy; rather, transaction in people became a constitutive element of family and kinship. Monetary forces were as organic and endogenous to Ming society as the brain and spinal cord are to human bodies.

Through painstaking details on transactions involving people, most of whom are women, *Plum*'s author asks readers to contemplate the issue of value, in particular the gap between market price and human value. In a world built on monetary transaction, women do not command a high price when compared with Ximen Qing's major business ventures (table 1).

While being sold marks women's entry into and exit from the Ximen household, it by no means defines their social relations. Ximen Qing does not choose his sex partners according to their sales price. Pan Jinlian's alter ego, Song Huilian, is brought into the Ximen household through her marriage to a servant for five taels—a price even lower than that of Qiuju, the maidservant at the bottom of the Ximen household who is beaten endlessly by Pan Jinlian.[5] Yet Huilian is not affected. She parades herself around, relying on her beauty, wit, and sexuality. She manages to achieve a higher status with her cooking skills and, more effec-

Table 1. Relative Prices for Objects and People in *Plum in the Golden Vase*

Person or Item for Sale	Price	Chapter
Pang Chunmei	16 taels	85
Chunmei buys Sun Xue'e after the latter is convicted of a crime and auctioned off by local government	8 taels	90
The maid Xiaoyu to wait on Yueniang	5 taels	9
The scullery maid Qiuju for Jinlian	6 taels	9
A twelve-year-old maid for Li Jiao'er	5 taels	24
A fourteen-year-old maid (Xiahua) for Li Jiao'er, bargained down from the asking price of seven taels and five candareens	7 taels	30
Pan Jinlian, sold by Dame Wang to the highest bidder (Wu Song)	100 taels	86
Ruyi, the wife of a poor soldier, assigned to be Guan'ge's wet nurse	6 taels	30
The fourteen-year-old Han Aijie, as concubine (with possibility of procreation) for Master Zhai Qian	20 taels	37
A monthly fee to maintain Li Guijie as Ximen's mistress	20 taels	20
A monthly fee to maintain Li Guijie as the mistress to the third son of Imperial Commmissioner Wang	30 taels	69
The maid Jin'er for Wang Liu'er	4 taels	37
A bribe for the coroner, He the Ninth, to cover up Wu the Elder's murder	10 taels	6
A bribe to the district magistrate to ensure Wu Song is not treated leniently	50 taels	10
A bribe to the Minister of the Right to change Ximen's name on the bill of impeachment	500 taels	48
A donation to repair the Temple of Eternal Felicity	500 taels	28
The eunuch director's mansion on Main Street	700 taels	14
Hua Zixu's modest house next to Ximen Qing's	540 taels	14
Han Daoguo's house on the east side of the stone bridge on Lion Street, with twelve-foot-wide frontage and four interior courtyards. The second courtyard is occupied by a passageway in addition to a nine-foot-wide reception room. The third courtyard consists of a three-foot-wide anteroom for the display of Buddhist effigies and ancestral tablets and a six-foot-wide living apartment, in the interior of which are the usual recessed kang frame and, across from it, a fire pit for burning charcoal, all of which has been newly replastered. The fourth courtyard, in addition to a six-foot-wide kitchen, contains a three-foot-wide storage room for charcoal and space in the rear for a latrine.	120 taels	39
A titillating bell or Burmese bell (Ximen Qing's favorite sex toy)	5 taels	16
A jade girdle	70 taels	31
A blue woman's jacket of Hangzhou chiffon, a green pongee skirt, a pale blue blouse of cloud-patterned silk, a red satin jacket, a skirt of white pongee, a gosling-yellow satin jacket, a long robe of lavender-colored pongee, and several items of coarse cotton clothing	6 ½ taels	56
A black-lacquer bedstead, adorned with gold tracery; bed curtains of scarlet silk; a dressing case; and a complete complement of tables, chairs, and porcelain taborets embossed with patterns of ornamental brocade for Jinlian	16 taels	9
A mother-of-pearl alcove bedstead for Jinlian like the one Li Ping'er has	60 taels	29

Table 1. (continued)

Person or Item for Sale	Price	Chapter
A jug of Jinhua wine, two roast ducks, two chickens, fresh fish, a leg of pork, stuffed cream puffs, and fruit-flavored sweet rolls	1 ½ taels	34
A banquet so lavish it elevates Qinghe County and even makes Shandong famous	1,000 taels	49
A horse	70 taels	38
A coffin for Li Ping'er	350 taels	62

tively, through sexual service to Ximen Qing. If she had not committed suicide, she might well have become his sixth concubine.

Here we again are reminded of the fact that those living in late Ming China did not harbor ideological objections against human trafficking as we do today. Trafficking was a crime, but it was also a constitutive element of social reality. Being sold did not mean social death but rather the beginning of new social relations. No sold woman in *Plum* is denied power, intellect, ambition, or, above all, upward mobility. The same, however, cannot be said of sold men. As has been noted, the author shies away from naming the price for the sale of men while meticulously listing transaction details for women. Why this gendered treatment? Does it mean that men were above monetary transaction? Was it more difficult for the author to divulge the prices of men when his readers were mostly men? Or could it be the opposite—that men were of less value, meaning that their prices bore no significance in the fictional or real worlds? No matter the reason, when contrasted with the complicated friendships, allegiances, and rivalries among women in the novel, male relationships in *Plum* appear superficial. That should not surprise us: in a novel structured around monetary transactions, the comparative lack of mention of men's prices renders their relationships and emotions opaque.

And this is where *Plum* is most subversive: through details of women trafficking—and sparing no particulars as to their abuse and suffering—the novel opens and concludes with scathing critiques of two essential myths of masculinity: brotherhood and patrilineage. *Plum* begins with a banquet celebrating the commitment to one another of a new band of ten sworn brothers, which unfolds into a mockery of the very notion of brotherhood. Some readers will recognize the close kinship between *Plum* and *Outlaws of the Marsh* (*Shuihu zhuan* 水滸傳), a novel founded on the ironclad bond between sworn brothers. Yet from the very first chapter, *Plum* subverts the core tenet of its literary predecessor. In *Plum*, this sworn brotherhood becomes a means through which women are trafficked in and out of the Ximen household. Ying Bojue pimps women for Ximen Qing in exchange for favors and money, and as soon as Ximen Qing dies, he facilitates the selling off of the women in Ximen's household and brokers the dissolution of the household. The chilling turnabout of Ximen's "brotherhood" deserves a close reading:

Originally, Ximen Qing had been so close to Ying Bojue that they were:
    Like glue and like lacquer,
more intimate with each other than brothers. Hardly a day passed during
which [Ying Bojue] failed to sponge off [Ximen Qing], wear something of
his, or benefit from his largesse; but soon after his death, while his body
was still warm, he committed a series of unrightful acts. Truly:
        In painting a tiger, you can paint the skin,
            but you can't paint the bones;
        In knowing people, you can know their faces,
            but you can't know their hearts.
There is a poem that testifies to this:
        In former years their friendship for each other
            was like gold or orchids;
        He did everything he could to toady up to him,
            leaving no stone unturned.
        But today, no sooner is Ximen Qing's body
            safely buried in the grave,
        Than he does his best to induce his concubines
            to sleep with someone else.   （4.80.687–88)

當初西門慶待應伯爵如膠似漆, 賽過同胞弟兄, 那一日不吃他的, 穿他的, 受用
他的? 身死未幾, 骨肉尚熱, 便做出許多不義之事! 正是: 畫虎畫皮難畫骨, 知
人知面不知心. 有詩為證: 昔年義氣似金蘭, 百計趨承不等閑. 今日西門身死
後, 紛紛謀妾伴入眠.   （80.13a)

In its ending, *Plum* delivers a different critique of family and kinship and turns
Dai'an, Ximen Qing's closest servant—and a sold person—into Ximen Qing's
heir. No blood descendants remain, and Dai'an, who has learned the ins and outs
of Ximen's ways of making money and conducting himself, is anointed Honorable Young Ximen and the successor to the Ximen household. This seemingly
anticlimactic ending calls our attention to the ultimate irony between master and
slave: the master delegates labor so thoroughly that he himself becomes replaceable. Sold people replace kin—the most radical criticism on social relations
Plum could possibly deliver.

NOTES

I want to thank Andrew Schonebaum, Keith McMahon, and the anonymous reviewers
for their careful reading and thoughtful comments and suggestions. The price data were
compiled with the assistance of the LoGart team at the Max Planck Institute for the History of Science.

[1] Unless otherwise noted, parenthetical citations refer to Roy's translation, *The Plum
in the Golden Vase*, and to *Jin Ping Mei cihua* 金瓶梅詞話 (*Plum in the Golden Vase: A
Ballad Tale*).

² In his conversation with the matchmaker Auntie Xue (Hsüeh), Ximen Qing mentions that he just bought Chunmei from her last year and that he still owes the matchmaker "several bolts of muslin on that deal" (許了我幾疋大布, 還沒與我; 1.7.132; 7.6a).

³ It is curious that of all *Plum*'s detailed depictions of trades in people, only toward the end is such a contract mentioned. In chapter 94, a contract is drawn in the final sale of Sun Xue'e. Later we again see Chunmei draw up a contract when she purchases another maid, having bargained down the price from five to three taels. No mention is made of contracts for Ximen Qing's many purchases since he is probably too powerful a local strongman to ever need a contract to secure his purchases.

⁴ Wai-yee Li discusses this bed in her essay in this volume.

⁵ Song Huilian's original name is Song Jinlian, but since Pan Jinlian has a higher status in the family, Song Jinlian, a maidservant, must change her name to Huilian.

Sexual Acts and
the Articulation of Norms and Hierarchies
in *The Plum in the Golden Vase*

Matthew H. Sommer

In this essay I examine sexual encounters between males in *The Plum in the Golden Vase* (*Jin Ping Mei* 金瓶梅) to demonstrate how the novel uses male-male sexual acts and relationships to map certain hierarchies and to show how these acts help drive the narrative as a whole. To understand the symbolic role of anal intercourse between males in this novel, it is necessary to grasp the underlying assumption, common to many premodern societies, that any act of intercourse is an act of domination and subordination that is defined by (and helps define) hierarchies of gender, status, power, and (between males) age.

The organization of male same-sex desire and relationships according to age, with an older masculinized subject penetrating a younger feminized object, is, historically, a widespread pattern both in China and elsewhere. This pattern in no way precluded dominant males, such as *Plum*'s protagonist, Ximen Qing (Hsi-men Ch'ing), from the pursuit of women. Generally inspired by Michel Foucault, many scholars have argued that it is only in the modern era, with the general decline of rigidly hierarchical ideologies and social structures and with the emergence of relatively egalitarian patterns of gender relations, that a new paradigm for sexual relations has taken shape, one that places exclusive priority on the sex of one's object of desire. It is this modern, egalitarian paradigm of sexual orientation that has defined people's social identities as either homosexual or heterosexual, regardless of their role in sexual acts. In much of the world, this modern paradigm has increasingly supplanted the older pattern of a gendered hierarchy of sexual roles in a stereotyped act of penetration.

This logic elucidates the way in which *Plum* employs sexual relations between males to plot individuals on hierarchies of status, power, and gender that are quite independent of sex. These same hierarchies, and the phallocentric logic that organizes them, are at work in the novel's male-female relations as well, yet they are even more obvious in the context of male same-sex desire.

The Libertine's Bisexual Object Choice

The sexual relations between the protagonist, Ximen Qing, and his teenage page Shutong (Shu-t'ung, or "book boy") illustrate the irrelevance of modern notions of sexual orientation to the novel's phallocentric logic. Both figures are male, yet the transgressive, emphatically masculine character of the powerful libertine contrasts sharply with the subordinate, feminized character of the object of his possessive desire. In fact, Ximen Qing is the most famous libertine in all Chinese literature, and his insatiable, omnivorous sexual behavior provides the template for all subsequent incarnations of this literary stereotype (Sommer, *Sex* 140–41; Vitiello, *Libertine's Friend* 93–97).

In terms of the object of his desire, Ximen Qing is bisexual, although his primary obsession is women: in Giovanni Vitiello's words, "Ximen Qing is first and foremost a penetrator—mostly of women, occasionally of boys"; significantly, his own masculinity "is predicated on his own sexual impenetrability" (*Libertine's Friend* 94). The danger to social order that the libertine represents is not his eclecticism but rather his incorrigible pursuit of sexual objects. Thus, when Ximen Qing penetrates Shutong, the episode serves to underscore his indiscriminate self-indulgence. Far more dangerous, however, is the protagonist's promiscuous seduction of other men's wives, which leaves a series of wrecked households in its wake. Likewise, in the seventeenth-century comic-erotic novel *The Carnal Prayer Mat* (*Rouputuan* 肉蒲團), by Li Yu 李漁 (1611–80?), when the hero, Vesperus, finds no female vessel at hand, he substitutes the "south gate" (i.e., the anus) of one of his male pages (180). But Vesperus's energies are also spent primarily in the pursuit of other men's wives. Both novels present their heroes' transgressive overindulgence as harmful to their own physical health. More important, though, is that such overindulgence ruptures the boundaries that frame familial and social order.[1]

The corollary to the fictional libertine's bisexual object choice is the eroticization of the young male as an object of possessive desire. Fiction aside, there is widespread evidence of such eroticization in legal texts and other sources from the same era (Sommer, *Sex* 141–43). To serve the aggressive penetrator in Ming-Qing fiction, the young male is cast in the female role as a penetrated object. In fact, one of the oldest Chinese terms for male-male anal intercourse defined that act simply as "to use a male as a female" (*jiang nan zuo nu* 將男作女; Sommer, *Sex* 121). The penetrator seems attracted to the same kinds of feminized features regardless of the sex of the individual who possesses them.

Thus, in *Plum in the Golden Vase*, males who play the penetrated role are uniformly eroticized for their youth and feminine refinement. For example, an encounter between Ximen Qing and Shutong begins thus: "Shutong had been drinking wine, so his fair face was glowing; his lips were red and fragrant, and his teeth were as white as grains of glutinous rice—how could one not be enchanted? At once, Ximen Qing's lust was aroused" (西門慶見他吃了酒, 臉上出紅白來紅馥馥唇兒, 露着一口糯更牙兒, 如何不愛, 于是淫心輒起). While they engage in intercourse, Ximen Qing addresses the boy as "my child" (*wo de er* 我的兒), and Shutong calls him "Daddy" (*die* 爹)—a term also used by Ximen's concubines when he has sex with them (my trans.; 34.11b–12a).[2]

Later in the novel, in chapter 93, we find the following account of the attraction of a Daoist priest, Jin Zongming (Chin Tsung-ming), to the males he penetrates:

Under his supervision he had two novices who were fresh, clean, and young, and who shared his bed; but this had gone on for some time, and he was getting bored of them. He saw that Jingji had white teeth and red lips, and his face was as white as if it had been powdered; he looked fresh, refined, and charming, with lively eyes. So the priest arranged for Jingji to stay in the same room with him.   (my trans.)[3]

手下也有兩箇清紫年小徒弟, 同舖歇臥, 日久絮繁, 因見經濟生的齒白唇紅, 面如傳粉, 清俊乖覺, 眼裡說話, 就纏他同房居住.   (93.10a)

The novel notes that Jin Zongming also "was in the habit of maintaining singing girls from the local brothels as his mistresses, and was a libertine devoted to wine and sex" (常在娼樓包占樂婦, 是箇酒色之徒; 5.93.260; 93.10a).

In *The Carnal Prayer Mat*, Li Yu explains the hero's sexual attraction to his pages in similar terms. The boys—whose nicknames, Satchel and Sheath, seem appropriate for those cast in the role of penetrated object—are described as follows: "Both boys were attractive; indeed, apart from their big feet, they were on a par with the most beautiful women." The hero prefers Satchel because he is the more "artful" and "coquettish" of the two and can manipulate his buttocks "like a woman" (120–22). In "A Male Mencius's Mother," Li Yu presents the young male hero as embodying an ideal femininity more natural and alluring than that of a genuine woman. The willow-waisted boy Ruilang is described as "a woman of peerless attraction," but when he begins to develop masculine attributes (his genitals are growing and he feels an insatiable penetrative lust), he castrates himself to retain the characteristics that make him attractive to his "husband" (Volpp, "Discourse" 119).

In both texts, the male sex object appears attractive to the extent that he possesses a certain feminized standard of beauty. Youth, whiteness, cleanliness, clarity of complexion, red lips, white teeth, and a willowy physique—all these features are conflated and eroticized.[4] It seems that biological sex matters less than these gender features do when it comes to the aggressive penetrator's attraction to the object of his desire.

Homoerotic Vogue among Elite Men

As many scholars have documented, a distinctive feature of elite male culture in China during the period in question was the erotic connoisseurship of young males, most famously the cross-dressing actors who played female roles in opera (Volpp, "Classifying Lust" and "Literary Circulation"; Wu Cuncun). This vogue was prominent especially among the literati of the sixteenth and seventeenth centuries, although it peaked again later in the nineteenth century with the maturity and enormous popularity of Beijing opera. Such connoisseurship played an important role in elite-male bonding and was expressed through shared poetry and an avid fan literature that ranked boys and young men by their feminine beauty, charm, and talent. In effect, the erotic appreciation and exploitation of subordinate youths was one way that elite men performed a refined homosociality, one that had both aesthetic and carnal dimensions. As part of this trend, it was not uncommon for wealthy men of fashion to maintain attractive page boys among their servants and to exploit them for sex. Some maintained their own household opera troupes, which included teenage boys who played female roles (Goldman 98–102).

Ximen Qing's indulgence in same-sex relations and, specifically, the role played by the page boy Shutong in the novel should be understood against this backdrop. Homoerotic indulgence emerges as a prominent theme just as Ximen's social and financial fortunes begin to improve dramatically, and it features prominently in his corrupt networking with the powerful officials whose patronage he seeks. It is no accident that Shutong is originally given to Ximen as a present by a magistrate who seeks his favor or that one of the boy's chief talents is to dress up as a girl and sing female roles in "the southern style."[5] The most elaborate example of this homoerotic socializing appears in chapter 36, where Ximen Qing has Shutong and two other cross-dressing boys entertain Principal Graduate Cai and Metropolitan Graduate An, and the two guests are absolutely enchanted (2.36.350–59). As Vitiello suggests, "[I]t appears that Ximen Qing's adopting of a homoerotic sensibility is directly related to his desire to rise in the ranks of the elite and meet its aesthetic and cultural standards. . . . [This episode's] place in the fictional narrative encourages us to read sex with boys as denoting elite taste, as a sign of Ximen Qing's newly achieved distinction in the social arena" (*Libertine's Friend* 94).

The Stigma of Being Penetrated

If homoerotic connoisseurship is a status symbol that signals Ximen Qing's upward mobility, then by contrast the penetrated sexual role conveys a profound stigma. It is no accident that the penetrated role was strongly associated with those individuals, such as slaves, servants, and actors, who were either unfree or who occupied an otherwise inferior social status. How was the stigma of being penetrated understood in the late Ming?

The portrayal of male same-sex acts in Chinese law contemporary with the novel provides important clues. Anal intercourse between males was prohibited from at least the mid–sixteenth century on, although such prohibitions do not seem to have inhibited the lifestyle or tastes of elite men, whose flouting of convention was a hallmark of their privileged status (Brook 231–32; Volpp, "Classifying Lust" 81–87). To my knowledge, the earliest Chinese law explicitly banning anal intercourse between males dates from the Jiajing reign (1522–67) of the Ming dynasty—that is, shortly before *Plum* was written. The Ming legal code includes a chapter prohibiting crimes of "illicit sexual intercourse" (*jian* 姦), but that chapter contains no reference to same-sex acts; its focus is extramarital sexual acts, both consensual and coerced, between men and women of free-commoner status, and its fundamental purpose is to control sexual access to "wives and daughters of good family" (*liangjia funu* 良家婦女) in order to keep descent lines clear. In that context, homosexual acts are irrelevant (Sommer, *Sex* 119–20). The Jiajing prohibition of anal intercourse between males appears elsewhere in the code, in a supplementary set of "statutes applied by analogy" (*bi yin lu* 比引律), each of which cites a preexisting measure to be applied to offenses not covered in the code proper.[6] The statute pertaining to anal intercourse between males states that "[w]hoever inserts his penis into another man's anus for lascivious play [*jiang shenjing fang ru ren fenmen nei yinxi* 將腎莖放入人糞門內淫戲] shall receive 100 blows of the heavy bamboo, in application by analogy of the statute on 'pouring foul material into the mouth of another' [*huiwu guan ru ren kou* 穢物灌入人口]" (my trans.; Huang Zhangjian 2: 1068).

This statute contrasts sharply with those against heterosexual offenses found in the chapter of the Ming code that deals with illicit sex. This statute could hardly be more explicit about the physical act of being punished, and it is far more explicit than are the statutes against illicit sex, which use the legal term *jian* 姦 ("illicit sexual intercourse") to stress extramarital context without reference to specific gestures or anatomy. In contrast, the Jiajing statute never mentions *jian*, let alone the legal term for sodomy, *ji jian* 雞姦, used in the Qing dynasty.

Moreover, the Jiajing statute against male-male anal intercourse does not employ the dichotomy between coercion and consent that Chinese legal codes had used to define sex offenses since antiquity. While the statute's analogy to assault might seem to imply coercion, my only example of this law's use in practice involves the punishment of a man who had consented to being penetrated (Zhang Weiren 40-73; Sommer, *Sex* 122–23).[7] Ming lawmakers may have simply assumed that it was impossible to rape a man—an assumption that continued, with some qualification, to inform Chinese law in later centuries (Sommer, *Sex* 132–38). At any rate, the penalty prescribed by the statute—"100 blows of the heavy bamboo"—approximated contemporary penalties for consensual heterosexual offenses (eighty to one hundred blows) but was far less severe than strangulation, the penalty for heterosexual rape (Xue Yunsheng 366-00).[8]

The most significant feature of the statute is its analogy between anal penetration and a crime described in the "fighting" (*dou ou* 鬭歐) chapter of the Ming code as "pouring foul material into the mouth of another person" (*huiwu guan ru ren kou* 穢物灌入人口; Xue Yunsheng 302-00). Lawmakers evidently considered this form of assault a more exact analogy to male-male anal intercourse than any of the heterosexual offenses in the Ming code's chapter on illicit sex. But the code's "fighting" chapter lists dozens of crimes, so this choice of analogy begs analysis. It contains three key elements: penetration of the body, use of "foul material" to do so, and targeting the mouth. Such assault could surely cause physical injury, but "foul material" suggests pollution and humiliation more than physical danger. It is also a universal theme of human cultures to associate the head and face with personal dignity. In other words, pollution and humiliation were more important than battery was to defining the crime of anal penetration. Moreover, the act of anal penetration is portrayed as having a clearly hierarchical division of roles, in which subject acted on object so that only the penetrated person suffered pollution and humiliation: it was the instance of being penetrated that corresponded to having foul material poured into one's mouth; the stigma attached itself to the penetrator no more than foul material would contaminate the assailant who poured it.

The logic of this legal analogy is clearly reproduced in *Plum*'s portrayal of Shutong. The other members of the household are perfectly aware that Shutong is Ximen Qing's catamite, and they scorn and bully Shutong for that reason, causing him shame and resentment. For example, in the scene from chapter 34 in which Ximen sodomizes Shutong, the servants Ping'an (P'ing-an) and Huatong (Hua-t'ung) listen outside the studio window and hear everything that transpires within. When Ximen is finished, Shutong emerges from the studio to fetch water so that Ximen can wash himself. Catching sight of the other two servants, Shutong realizes they have been eavesdropping, and "his face turned crimson with embarrassment" (把臉飛紅了; 2.34.299; 34.12a). In chapter 52, Ximen Qing proposes that he and one of his concubines, Pan Jinlian (P'an Chin-lien), engage in anal intercourse, telling her that "[t]oday your daddy would like to pluck the flower in your rear courtyard. Are you willing to agree to that?" (你達今日要和你幹個後庭花兒, 你肯不肯?). Jinlian retorts, "What an utterly shameless lover you are! After screwing around with that page boy Shutong until you're tired of it, you've come to pester me. Just continue carrying on with that slave, why don't you?" (好個沒廉恥冤家, 你成日和書童兒小廝幹的不值了, 又纏起我來了, 你和那奴才幹去不是; 3.52.256; 52.1b).

The most revealing scene, however, is a scuffle between Shutong and his fellow servant Dai'an (Tai-an) in which the latter makes direct, insulting references to Shutong's penetrated sexual role in his relations with their master, Ximen Qing. The encounter begins when Dai'an finds Shutong drinking wine and says teasingly, "What a fine wanton you are, what are you doing here?" (好淫婦, 你在這里做甚麼; 3.50.207; 50.3b). It is probably no coincidence that the term David Roy translates as "wanton"—*yin fu* 淫婦—literally means "licentious wife" and is one of Ximen Qing's favorite bedroom names for Pan Jinlian. When Shutong asks in a flippant manner what Dai'an wants him for, Dai'an responds, "I was looking for you so I could fuck you in the ass!" (我尋你要肏你的屁股; 3.50.207; 50.3b), and then roughly kisses him on the mouth, hurting Shutong's teeth and knocking off his hat. Shutong pushes him away, cursing him; angered, Dai'an again calls Shutong "*yin fu*" and "lifted him up by the legs, forced him down onto the *kang*, and spit a mouthful of saliva into his mouth as hard as he could" (掀起腿把他按在炕上, 儘力向他口裏吐了一口唾沫; 3.50.207–08; 50.4a). Shutong counters with the following: "A game's a game; a joke's a joke, but you've spit a mouthful of filthy jizz [*song shuizi* 屎水子] all over me!" To this Dai'an responds, "As though this were the first time you've ever swallowed jizz [*song* 屎]. From first to last, who knows how much jizz [*song* 屎] you may have swallowed?" (耍便耍, 咳便咳, 臜剌剌的屎水子, 吐了人恁一口. 玳安道, 賊秫村村, 你今日纔吃屎?你從前已後, 把

屍不知吃了多少!; 3.50.208; 50.3b–4b). A similar episode of bullying appears in the next chapter, when Dai'an again calls Shutong "*yin fu*," forces him down on the ground, and spits in his mouth (3.51.250; 51.19b).

Central to an understanding of this dialogue is a double entendre: the word *song* 屍, which appears three times in the interchange between Shutong and Dai'an, was a nasty term for either saliva or semen (Bai, Jin Ping Mei *cidian* 505), though, somewhat misleadingly, Roy translates *song* as "jizz" in all three instances. In Shutong's comment, it refers to Dai'an's saliva, whereas in Dai'an's retort, it refers to Ximen Qing's semen, which Shutong repeatedly consumes in his role as catamite.

A number of interesting details stand out in this episode. Dai'an's repeated use of the epithet *yin fu* emphasizes the feminization that Shutong has suffered by virtue of his sexual role vis-à-vis their master. When angered, Dai'an reinforces that message with a kind of physical bullying that is heavily homoerotic in its implications. But Dai'an clearly does not worry that his gestures, including kissing, might compromise his own masculinity in any way—in fact, it is very much a macho performance for the two other men watching the scuffle. On the contrary, this interaction reveals a gendered homoerotics of (masculine) domination and (feminine) subordination, in which Dai'an overpowers and humiliates Shutong to remind him of his place: as a "wanton" who is "fuck[ed] . . . in the ass" and who "swallow[s]" their master's "jizz."

Dai'an's final gesture of spitting recalls the Jiajing statute's analogy between anal penetration and "pouring foul material into the mouth of another person." This hardly seems accidental: Dai'an's act of spitting is most certainly a sly reference to the statute since it acts out that very analogy. The connection is underscored by Shutong's characterization of Dai'an's saliva as "filthy" (*za lala* 臢剌剌). Spitting in Shutong's mouth after forcing him down on the bed is an explicit imitation of sodomy, designed to humiliate and insult Shutong, an effect reinforced by the accusation that "swallow[ing] jizz" is no new experience for the boy.

Chen Jingji's Fate

If Ximen Qing's acquisition and penetration of Shutong signal his upward mobility into the rarefied stratum of elite homoerotics, then by the same logic the decline in fortune of Ximen Qing's son-in-law, Chen Jingji (Ch'en Ching-chi), later in the novel is marked by the latter's tragicomic reversal of sexual roles. Jingji's descent maps the hierarchy of sexual roles and opportunities against social stratification in a way that perfectly captures the Ming-Qing understanding of sexual penetration (Sommer, *Sex* 158–62).

In chapter 82, shortly after Ximen Qing's death, Chen Jingji begins an incestuous affair with Ximen's newly widowed concubine, Pan Jinlian. When Jinlian's chambermaid, Pang Chunmei (P'ang Ch'un-mei), interrupts their intercourse, Jinlian makes her have sex with Jingji as well; in this way, Jinlian enlists Chunmei as a coconspirator and is thereby able to ensure her silence. From then on, the three carry on a ménage à trois. In these episodes, Jingji plays the role of consummate penetrator: a great deal of attention is paid to his penis—by Jinlian, Chunmei, and the narrative voice (fig. 1).

Some chapters later, however, Jingji loses both his fortune and his wife and becomes homeless. He takes refuge with a gang of beggars who sleep in a night-watch shed—*leng pu* 冷舖, which Roy translates as "homeless shelter" (5.93.246; 93.2a)—and their leader sodomizes him, apparently as a condition for being accepted by the gang. (At night, Jingji dreams of the good old days with Jinlian and bursts into tears when he awakes to find himself surrounded by filthy beggars.) Next, Jingji takes refuge as a novice in a Daoist temple, where he shares a bed with the priest Jin Zongming:

Figure 1. "Chen Jingji Enjoys One Beauty and Makes Out with Two" (陳敬濟弄一得雙). Illustration from chapter 82 of the *xiuxiang* edition.

At first, they slept head to foot and foot to head, but [Jin Zongming] objected to the smell of Chen Jingji's feet and had him come share the same pillow with him. But before they had been asleep very long, he complained about Chen Jingji's breath, and had him turn over so that his bottom ended up against his belly. Chen Jingji pretended to be asleep and paid no attention to him, but [the priest] went on to manipulate his organ until it rose up as hard and straight as a stick, rubbed some saliva on the head of his glans, and proceeded to thrust it into [Chen Jingji's] anus. It so happens that when Chen Jingji had been residing in the homeless shelter, the beggar boss Hou Lin, whose nickname was Flying Demon, had sodomized him, so that his anus was already enlarged. As a result, Jin Zongming's organ had penetrated him before he knew it.

As for Chen Jingji:

From his mouth no word was uttered, but

In his heart he thought to himself,

"This rascal is asking for it; he is trying to take such egregious advantage of me. Who does he take me for?"   (5.93.260–62)

初時兩頭睡, 便嫌經濟腳臭, 叫過一箇枕頭上睡, 睡不多回又說他口氣噴着, 令他吊轉身子, 屁股貼着肚子, 那經濟推睡着不理他, 他把那話弄得硬硬的, 直豎一條棍, 抹了些唾津在頭上, 往他糞門裡只一頂, 原來經濟在冷舖中, 被花子飛天鬼侯林兒弄過的, 眼子大了, 那話不覺就進去了, 這經濟口中不言, 心內暗道, 這廝合敗, 他討得十分便宜多了, 把我不知當做甚麼人兒.

(93.10a–10b)

Chen Jingji's fate epitomizes the ironic logic and black humor of *Plum in the Golden Vase*. A major theme of the novel is karmic retribution, which visits each of its villains in turn. (In the novel's penultimate chapter, after many other vicissitudes, Jingji is finally murdered.) Jingji's downfall with respect to his sexual roles symbolizes and parallels the karmic decline in his fortunes: this rich, arrogant penetrator of other men's wives ends up playing the female role himself, in ignominious service to beggars and clergy. Jingji's descent into this Hobbesian world of marginal males requires him to submit to make the best of a bad situation. In each instance there is a quid pro quo: the beggars give Jingji shelter and sustenance to survive the winter, while the Daoist becomes his patron and protector within the temple.

In an earlier scene, Chen Jingji prepares to be fellated by Pan Jinlian in the following manner: he "manipulated his organ until it rose up as hard and straight as a stick" (他把那話弄得硬硬的, 直豎一條棍; 5.82.25; 82.5b). In chapter 93, in the passage quoted above, the very same words are used to describe Jin Zongming's preparation to penetrate Jingji's anus. As Roy points out, such strategic repetition of words and images is a standard device in the novel, an internal echo that underscores parallels between characters and links cause with effect (Introduction xxvii–xxix). Here, such repetition adds ironic emphasis to Jingji's role reversal: what is now being done to him by the dissolute priest is precisely what Jingji himself has done to others in the past.

Moreover, Jingji—an adult man of twenty-four *sui* (twenty-two or twenty-three years old by a Western reckoning)—is caricatured in his new sexual role as a feminized youth. Jin Zongming's lust is aroused when he notices that Chen Jingji's "teeth were white and his lips were red, his face looked as though it were powdered" (齒白唇紅, 面如傅粉; 5.93.260; 93.10a). The original woodblock illustration of this scene depicts the penetrated Jingji as a beardless youth, an image that contrasts with that of the full-bearded priest (fig. 2). The term used in the caption for "acolyte," *di* 弟, literally

Figure 2. "Daoist Jin Opts to Sodomize a Youthful Acolyte" (金道士變淫少弟). Illustration from chapter 93 of the *xiuxiang* edition.

means "younger brother." Jingji's reversal of sexual roles is a direct consequence of his loss of wealth, status, and power and is confirmed by a corresponding loss of masculine maturity and agency. His fate sums up the Ming-Qing understanding of phallic penetration.

Historically, sexual relations between males have often served as a sort of blank screen on which societies project their fantasies and anxieties about heterosexual relations. The gendered hierarchy of roles in a stereotyped act of penetration is perhaps the most obvious and pervasive example of this larger tendency. This is the context for understanding the portrayal of male same-sex acts and relations in *Plum in the Golden Vase*. The novel employs such episodes to plot individuals on hierarchies of status, power, and gender that are quite independent of sex itself. These same hierarchies, and the phallocentric logic that organizes them, are at work in the novel's heterosexual relations as well, yet they appear all the more starkly and with even greater clarity in the same-sex context.

NOTES

An early version of this essay was presented at the annual meeting of the Association for Asian Studies in Boston in 2000 as part of a panel on *Plum* chaired by David Roy and organized by Tina Lu and me. Some parts of this essay also recapitulate material first presented in Sommer, *Sex* 114–65; see also Sommer, "Dangerous Males" and "Scandal." Unless otherwise noted, all translations are from Roy's *The Plum in the Golden Vase*. In-text citations for passages from the Chinese text refer to *Jin Ping Mei cihua* 金瓶梅詞話 (*Plum in the Golden Vase: A Ballad Tale*).

[1] See Roy's analysis of "the causes of social disintegration" in *Plum* (Introduction xxix–xxxi) and Hanan's discussion of the fictional libertine (Li Yu, *Carnal Prayer Mat* vii–ix).

[2] For Roy's translation, see 2.34.298–99. See also the novel's first description of Shutong (2.31.220).

[3] For Roy's translation, see 5.93.260.

[4] In the same way, pornographic prints from the same era often depict both women and penetrated males with lighter skin and less facial and body hair when compared with their masculine partners.

[5] Here and elsewhere in the novel, references to "the south" are puns that imply a taste for male love, because in Chinese "south" (*nan* 南) is a homonym for "male" (*nan* 男).

[6] This supplement systematized the long-standing practice of judgment by analogy (Bodde and Morris 32, 228), meaning that the punishment of male-male intercourse may predate its Jiajing codification.

[7] Cases in Zhang Weiren are cited by serial number.

[8] Statutes and substatutes in Xue Yunsheng are cited by serial number.

Popular Songs and Drama
in *The Plum in the Golden Vase*

Catherine Swatek

Of the four great Ming novels, only *The Plum in the Golden Vase* (*Jin Ping Mei* 金瓶梅) has an urban setting; its action unfolds in the household of a wealthy merchant, the brothels he visits, the business establishments he owns, and, on occasion, the residences of officials whose patronage he cultivates in the capital, Kaifeng. The novel depicts a world of extravagant material comforts, in which performances of all kinds function both as everyday entertainment and as the lubricant of social relationships and official connections. In chapter 20, as the main narrative gets underway, Ximen Qing (Hsi-men Ch'ing) hires Li Ming, the brother of his Second Lady Li Jiao'er (Li Chiao-erh), to teach four of his maidservants how to sing so that they can entertain his guests. Singing was an important part of a prostitute's training, and the novel depicts performances by prostitutes as well as by Ximen Qing's household performers, both maidservants trained in the home and professionally trained male servants. The first of these performances takes place in a brothel in chapter 11, when a young prostitute, Li Guijie (Li Kuei-chieh), sings for Ximen Qing just before he deflowers her; thenceforth she and other prostitutes often perform at banquets in Ximen Qing's home, bantering with his guests in ways that the maidservants cannot. In almost all cases, the songs performed were not composed by the author but adapted from plays and songbooks that were popular in his day.

Among Ximen Qing's wives, only Pan Jinlian (P'an Chin-lien) has extensive knowledge of these songs (*qu* 曲) by virtue of her early training as a household entertainer, and we sometimes see her accompanying herself when alone on the *pipa* 琵琶, a four-stringed plucked instrument sometimes referred to as the "Chinese lute." More often, we see her using her knowledge of songs to discomfit rivals or score points against them with Ximen Qing. In this way the author captures a dimension of the intensely theatrical culture of the late Ming. The author uses songs to engage his reader, and he expects the reader to work out how they function in their new contexts, much as the novel's characters are called on to do. This exercise has both a playful and a serious side, as becomes apparent when one considers the many rhetorical uses of the song repertoire made by the author.

The author incorporates other performance genres into his novel as well—storytelling, religious narratives, farcical skits, and puppet plays, among others. This essay focuses on plays and popular songs, which were sung in a variety of musical styles, the Haiyan 海鹽 regional style being the one most often mentioned in the novel. *Qu* were composed to set tunes (*qupai* 曲牌) identified by their titles, and new lyrics were written by "filling in the words" (*tian ci* 填詞). *Qu* were composed as independent songs (*xiaoling* 小令), suites of songs (*sanqu* 散曲), and dramatic scenes built around suites of songs (*juqu* 劇曲). There is considerable slippage between these forms of *qu*, since a song from a play might be performed as a *xiaoling*, and scenes once detached from their play were published alongside *sanqu* in songbooks.

All these forms of *qu* are found in *Plum*. Roughly 280 songs or song suites appear in the text in various ways, in fifty-nine of the eighty-nine chapters written by the author, and are one of his trademarks.[1] One of the pedagogical challenges of *Plum* is to get students unaccustomed to verse of any kind in fiction to engage with the songs and explore how they contribute to the novel's dense narrative texture. The most useful guide to them is David Roy's notes to his translation; another engaging resource for students who can read Chinese is a set of recently published reading notes, arranged by chapter, which include discussions of some of these songs.[2] Relying especially on Roy's notes, this essay endeavors to help instructors make *Plum*'s songs more accessible for novice readers by exploring their multifarious uses.

The first challenge for any reader is one of identification, since other kinds of verse are also incorporated into the novel. *Shi* 詩, poems with five or seven characters per line, and *ci* 詞, an earlier song form that was no longer performed in the late Ming but still written, were used in earlier vernacular novels and short stories, generally to describe a scene or character or to provide narrative commentary, but the author of *Plum* was the first to also make use of *qu*. However, *ci* and *qu* are difficult to distinguish in a printed text because both are typically introduced by their titles using similar formulas, and because it is presumed that readers will know which is which. Most late Ming readers would have known the difference. Indeed, the editors of the Chongzhen (*xiuxiang*) edition of *Plum* removed many of the *qu* while retaining the *ci*, streamlining the novel and, in the process, rejecting some of the author's experiments with *qu* (Rolston, "Oral Performing Literature" 47).

Roy performs a service by distinguishing *qu* and *ci* for his readers, using "song" for *qu* and "lyric" for *ci* when translating the introductory formulas for them. In what follows I explore how the novel's uses of *qu* make *Plum* a "landmark of the Chinese novel" and throw light on its author's narrative technique (Hanan, "Landmark"). I begin with nondramatic songs before turning my attention to songs excerpted from plays.

Nondramatic Songs

The distinction between *ci* and *qu* matters because in the world of *Plum qu* were often sung, while *ci* no longer were. Although the novel is set in the Song dynasty (960–1279), when *ci* was a popular song form, the society it depicts is that of the late Ming, by which time *qu* had supplanted *ci* as popular entertainment. The author's use of *qu* is thus deliberately anachronistic.

Roy devotes an article to nondramatic songs in *Plum*, limiting his discussion to occasions where song lyrics have been copied into the novel from other sources or from memory.[3] The vast majority of nondramatic songs—seventy-two instances—are performed on demand by professional entertainers, either in private or in a brothel, and are concentrated in the novel's middle chapters (chs. 27–79). The remainder are sung as a form of self-expression, for the purpose of communication between characters, or are used by the narrator to provide description and commentary. Many songs feature Pan Jinlian and characters associated with her, reflecting Jinlian's importance in the novel and immersion in the song culture of Ximen Qing's world (and knowledge of *qu* that equals his).

Xiaoling

Chapter 8 provides several noteworthy examples of the novel's use of nondramatic songs. Eight songs are quoted in that chapter, just as the narrative is breaking free from *Outlaws of the Marsh* (*Shuihu zhuan* 水滸傳), an earlier Ming vernacular novel for which *Plum* is a sequel. Chapter 7, the first chapter written by the author of *Plum* that is independent from the story line of *Outlaws*, depicts Ximen Qing's pursuit of the wealthy widow Meng Yulou (Meng Yü-lou), who becomes his Third Lady. It is written in a style typical of the Ming vernacular short story and contains comparatively little verse apart from opening and concluding *shi* poems (one in the voice of a matchmaker, the other in the voice of the narrator) and a set piece of parallel prose that describes Meng Yulou through Ximen Qing's eyes. The contrast between chapter 7 and chapter 8, which returns the focus to Pan Jinlian, is pronounced, as if to signal to readers that they have exited the world of *Outlaws* and entered that of *Plum*. Four songs in this chapter are *xiaoling*, or independent songs; the remainder are part of a set of four *xiaoling* written to the same set tune. As Roy's notes to chapter 8 indicate, it is likely that the author borrowed all these songs from the same source, a sixteenth-century anthology titled *Songs of a Harmonious Era*

(*Yongxi yuefu* 雍熙樂府; 1.496–98 [nn 6, 9, 11, and 20]).[4] These appropriated songs are put to various uses, providing an early glimpse of the author's methods when it comes to *qu*.

Three songs are written to "Sheep on the Mountain Slope" ("Shanpoyang" 山坡羊), a song popular in the late Ming that is frequently used by *Plum*'s author. Twenty-one versions of it crop up in chapters 1, 8, 33, 44, 46, 50, 59, 61, 89, and 91, and eleven of these instances are clustered in chapters 8, 33, and 89. All eleven of the latter are associated with Pan Jinlian in some fashion, making "Sheep on the Mountain Slope" her leitmotif. At the beginning of chapter 8, Ximen Qing, who is now pursuing Meng Yulou, has ceased visiting Jinlian. Hoping to learn when he will next come to her, Jinlian uses her shoes to cast "love hexagrams" (*xiangsigua* 相思卦), and two songs set to "Sheep on the Mountain Slope" are quoted at this point (1.8.148–50; 8.2a). In the first of these songs, imagery of shoes and lotus roots conveys the tangled emotions of a woman longing for an absent lover. Both songs exhibit the subjective intensity for which this song was known, as does another appearance of the song in chapter 1, where Jinlian laments the misery of her marriage to Wu Da (Wu the Elder) while accompanying herself on the *pipa* (1.1.28; 1.11b–12a).[5] These uses of "Sheep on the Mountain Slope" add a dimension to Jinlian's character not found in novels that predate *Plum* and set Jinlian apart from the stereotypical licentious women (*yinfu* 淫婦) of *Outlaws*. Although the versions of "Sheep on the Mountain Slope" in these two chapters are not borrowed from plays, their presence reflects influence from the Chinese dramatic form known as southern drama (*chuanqi* 傳奇), where it was sometimes sung to convey a character's feelings directly to the audience, as a soliloquy.[6]

In chapter 8, Jinlian does not sing "Sheep on the Mountain Slope," as she does in chapter 1; instead, the two songs "testify to" her feelings (*you "Shanpoyang" wei zheng* 有山坡羊為証; 1.8.148; 8.2a). Rendering the narrator's commentary as verse is common in earlier vernacular fiction, but the author of *Plum* frequently uses *qu* for this purpose instead of *shi* or *ci*, blurring the line between narrative commentary and a character's self-expression. Moments later in chapter 8, Jinlian again sings to "Sheep on the Mountain Slope" as she complains to Ximen Qing's servant Dai'an (Tai-an) about Ximen's neglect of her to elicit Dai'an's sympathy and help (1.8.153; 8.3b–4a). This marks another experiment by the author, since dialogue in vernacular fiction took the form of song only rarely. The fourth song in this chapter, set to the tune "Mistletoe" ("Jishengcao" 寄生草), also breaks new ground: Jinlian writes a note to Ximen Qing, matching her words to the tune of this song (1.8.153–54; 8.4b). There are four other occasions, utilizing eight songs, when notes are written as song lyrics, and most feature Jinlian as the writer or recipient (chs. 12, 82, 83, and 85). Later in chapter 8, as her frustration deepens, Jinlian again sings a set of four songs to the tune "Making Silk Floss" ("Miandaxu" 綿搭絮; 1.8.155–57; 8.5b–6a). Between the first two songs she sings in this chapter and these last four, the author depicts Jinlian abusing her stepdaughter capriciously by stripping her naked, beating her with a riding crop, and gouging her cheeks with her fingernails. The effect of such juxtaposition is that Pan Jinlian's image of herself as "a languishing beauty pining away from the neglect of her lover" (Roy, "Use" 114) belies the viciousness of her actions, in the reader's mind at least. This technique, whereby a sentimental stereotype from popular culture is rendered absurd in its new setting, is often resorted to by the author of *Plum*.

Independent songs appear mainly in the first twenty and final twenty chapters of the novel, usually alone but sometimes in clusters of two songs or more written to the same tune, what Roy refers to as "sets." In addition to the expressive use of such songs to convey a character's strong emotion, *xiaoling* are sometimes employed to describe (e.g., a brothel in chapter 11, "cribbers" and "ball clubbers" in chapter 15) or comment (e.g., on the just-consummated affair of Pan Jinlian and Chen Jingji [Ch'en Ching-chi] in chapter 80, on the couple's intercourse in chapter 82). Here the function of songs differs little from that of *ci* in earlier vernacular fiction, though the tone is more facetious and jocular, in keeping with *qu*'s popular origins. After self-expression by important characters, the second most common appearance of *xiaoling* is as entertainment, when they are sung on demand by professionally trained performers at banquets (e.g., in chs. 11, 35, 45, 50, 60, 61, 65, 93, 94, and 96). I have already cited examples of *qu* as a form of written communication, but songs are also employed as dialogue: Ximen Qing and a brothel madam's quarrel is presented as an exchange of songs set to the same tune (ch. 20); Pan Jinlian and Chen Jingji sing to the same tune while making love (ch. 82); Ximen Qing sings to Wu Yueniang (Wu Yüeh-niang) on his deathbed, and she responds in kind (ch. 79); a quack doctor sings his prescription for aborting a fetus (ch. 85); a concubine pleads not to be sent away (ch. 91); and Chen Jingji tells his life story in the form of a song (ch. 93). Many of these innovations were cut by the editor of the Chongzhen edition.[7]

Clusters of *xiaoling*, usually four, appear thirteen times in the novel. These song sets are distinct from song suites, which were composed to different set tunes of the same musical mode in a fixed order, but like the suites they generally occur in the novel's middle chapters (chs. 8, 32, 33, 35, 38, 46, 49, 61, 68, 74, 75, and 96). Twice they are they used expressively when Pan Jinlian sings in chapters 8 and 38. Otherwise they are performed on demand—by professional singers summoned to entertain Ximen Qing's family and their guests, by servants in Ximen Qing's household, and once by Chen Jingji at Pan Jinlian's behest (ch. 33). Their themes are conventional and their language formulaic. Almost invariably they are in the voice of a person, usually a woman, longing for an absent lover, and when performed they often include a playful and intimate interplay between singer and listener that was intrinsic to this kind of song.

In chapter 33, for example, Chen Jingji adopts the voice of a neglected woman while singing four songs to "Sheep on the Mountain Slope," whose lyrics pun lasciviously on the terminology of fruits and flowers, silver and coinage (2.33.269–73; 33.6a–6b). This set tune, and Chen Jingji's ability to sing, link him to Pan Jinlian, who has demanded that he sing four songs for her before she will return his keys; the witty wordplay continues a flirtation begun in chapter 19. In chapter 35, Ximen Qing's crony Ying Bojue (Ying Po-chüeh) amuses himself by making Ximen Qing's servant Shutong (Shu-t'ung) dress as a woman and sing a set of songs to "Jade Lotus Blossoms" ("Yufurong" 玉芙蓉; 2.35.330–34; 35.14b–16b); this becomes an occasion for homosocial bonding among the men present. In chapter 49, Shutong once again sings four songs to "Jade Lotus Blossoms" for a corrupt official whom Ximen Qing is entertaining in his garden (3.49.187–89; 49.9a–10a). The voice of the songs' persona is that of a lovesick man pursuing a coquettish beauty, and as Shutong's performance concludes, Censor Cai (Ts'ai) takes to his bed one of the prostitutes Ximen Qing has hired to entertain him.

A noteworthy use of this form of *qu* comes in chapter 38, where Pan Jinlian performs a set of three songs, "River Water, with Two Variations" ("Er fan Jiang'ershui" 二犯江儿水; 2.38.394–400; 38.8b–10b). This performance is different compared with Jinlian's singing of "Making Silk Floss" in chapter 8. On that occasion she sings uninterrupted, while in chapter 38 segments of straight narration mixed with dialogue and other kinds of verse, formulaic language, and interior monologue are inserted between the songs, prolonging the sequence. Roy finds the influence of southern drama here and praises the segment for how it enriches the depiction of Pan Jinlian's character ("Use" 114–24).[8]

Sanqu

In chapters 21–79, as Ximen Qing's fortunes are on the rise, we increasingly see him hobnobbing with powerful officials and eunuchs and entertaining them in his home. Accordingly, performances by trained entertainers come to the fore in these chapters, and song suites (*sanqu*) are mentioned more frequently than independent songs (*xiaoling*). *Sanqu* differ formally from song sets in that the author's uses of them are more often rhetorical. In other words, the reader is expected to recognize a disjunction between a *sanqu*'s conventional or original meaning and the meaning it assumes in the context of the novel.

Of the forty occasions I have identified in twenty-six chapters where performances of *sanqu* are depicted, twenty-four quote only the opening line of the opening song, sometimes with and sometimes without that song's title. This reflects how *sanqu* would have been requested by those familiar with the song repertoire, people such as Ximen Qing, Pan Jinlian, Ying Bojue, and some of Ximen Qing's guests. Of the song suites requested by citing opening lines only, Roy provides a complete translation of all but one (in chapter 31) in the appendixes to volumes 1 and 2 of his translation, thereby providing his reader with knowledge of the song repertoire that many late Ming readers likely would have possessed. As Roy points out in his notes to these *sanqu* and their sources, these performances often reflect either on the person requesting them or on the person to whom they are addressed, in ways apparent to anyone who knows the song suite.

A song suite performed in chapter 15 illustrates this rhetorical use of songs. The occasion is the Lantern Festival, which marks the end of the New Year's celebrations. Two prostitutes entertain Ximen Qing and his sworn brothers by performing a *sanqu* that celebrates the beauties of spring in the capital. The song begins with the line "The fair weather is balmy" (霄景融和) and concludes with the line "May the good fortune and long life of our Sage Sovereign equal Heaven" (聖主福壽天齊; 1.15.312; 15.9a). Because they appear in a chapter that depicts Ximen Qing and his ladies' lavish celebration of the New Year, the lyrics encourage readers to compare Ximen Qing to the emperor. *Sanqu* expressing congratulations or gratitude to the emperor are performed on five other occasions to similar effect (chs. 21, 43, 46, 60, and 78).

In chapter 21, at a banquet celebrating a reconciliation between Wu Yueniang and Ximen Qing after a period of estrangement, four of Ximen Qing's maidservants perform a song suite requested by Pan Jinlian that begins with the line "It was the night of their assignation" (佳期重會; 2.21.14; 21.8b). Ximen Qing takes immediate exception, accusing Jinlian of "[f]ool[ing] with the branches and tug[ging] at the leaves" (胡枝扯葉; 2.21.15; 21.8b). His reaction prompts the reader to supply the words not given in the text, which are sung in the voice of a woman anxiously awaiting her lover in her garden. Jinlian's request of this particular song suite mocks Yueniang's pretense that her prayers for Ximen Qing were uttered in private rather than staged for him to overhear. This jibe is lost on the other ladies, Yueniang included, and Ximen Qing must explain what happened to Meng Yulou a few pages later. Jinlian is adept at the veiled attack; songs are her medium, and Wu Yueniang is a favorite target. In chapter 20 she again upsets Yueniang by pointing out that a scene from a southern play, *The Gaily Colored Tower* (*Cailou ji* 彩樓記), performed at a wedding feast for Li Ping'er (Li P'ing-erh), insults Yueniang by implying that Ximen Qing favors his new concubine over Yueniang, his principal wife (1.20.417–18; 20.10b). It is as if the author is alerting his reader at the threshold of the main narrative to this particular use of popular songs and plays.

Other such disjunctions occur when someone fails to make appropriate use of songs on occasions where they are being performed as entertainment. In chapter 31, for instance, satire is directed at eunuchs invited to Ximen Qing's home when they repeatedly request inauspicious songs at a party celebrating Ximen's official appointment and his newborn son's first month. In chapters 41, 42, and 43, scenes from inappropriate plays are sung at occasions marking the betrothal of Guan'ge (Kuan-ko). Examples such as these depict how songs were performed in households, where such mistakes were apt to be made. In the brothel most everyone present would have been in the know.[9]

Sanqu whose lyrics are quoted in the text are concentrated in the chapters leading up to the novel's climax in chapter 79. Many of these *sanqu* contribute to a feverish (*renao* 熱鬧) atmosphere in these chapters: five are performed on festivals (chs. 42, 43, 44, 46, and 61), three on birthdays (chs. 58, 72, and 73), two at banquets for high officials (chs. 49 and 65), one at an informal gathering (ch. 52), and one in a brothel (ch. 77). Some go on for pages in translation, including one in chapter 52 that stretches over seven pages and includes copious interpolated dialogue as Ying Bojue provides droll commentary on the lyrics being sung by Li Guijie, in a witty send-up of the courtesan's lament. Several chapters are so packed with performances that they become "baggy monsters," trying the patience of modern readers unaccustomed to such varied fare in a novel (Rolston, "Oral Performing Literature" 51).[10]

Some performances of song suites reflect how they were enjoyed in the late Ming, while others reflect on the characters who request them in pointed ways. In chapter 61, on the Double Yang Festival, Li Ping'er requests that Second Sister Shen perform a song suite with an autumn theme that begins with the tune "A Variation on a Sprig of Flowers" ("Zheyao yizhi hua" 折腰一枝花; 4.61.18–21; 61.11b–12b). Ping'er's choice contains lines that foreshadow her impending death, as does the despondency of the singer's persona, which matches Ping'er's own. Likewise, in chapter 73, a *sanqu* performed at Ximen Qing's request on Meng Yulou's birthday finds him still grieving for Li Ping'er, to Jinlian's chagrin (4.73.388–92; 73.3b–4a). In chapter 65, two suites of songs are performed at a lavish banquet hosted by Ximen Qing in honor of a notoriously corrupt eunuch, Director-in-Chief Huang Jingchen (Huang Ching-ch'en). The first of these suites, performed but not quoted, is a scene from a southern drama, *The Return of the Belts* (*Huandai ji* 還帶記), and the second is a *sanqu* by Zhu Youdun 朱有燉 (1379–1439), a scion of the Ming ruling family, whose opening song, "A Sprig of Flowers" ("Yizhi hua" 一枝花), is quoted in the text (3.65.146–47; 65.13b–14a). Both the play and the song reflect ironically on host and guest, the former by alluding to a dramatic character whose worldly and spiritual merit belie the corrupt behavior of Ximen Qing, the latter doing the same for Huang Jingchen by effusively praising an official whose "sole endeavor is to clarify the laws and transform the people" (正直也則是清懲化民; 4.65.147; 65.14a). In chapter 77, a song suite that opens with the tune "Green Jacket" ("Qingna'ao" 青衲襖), performed for Ximen Qing at a brothel, resonates portentously with his circumstances (4.77.557–60; 77.8a–9b). Written in the voice of a lovesick man who anticipates a happy reunion with the woman he loves (Li Ping'er, as hinted at by several lines in the song), it is performed in the depths of winter, hours before Ximen Qing will die a gruesome death brought on by his sexually rapacious concubine.

Songs performed ostensibly as entertainment also begin to take on a metaphoric dimension as the novel approaches its midpoint (Chang 28–31). This is especially true of the song sets and song suites, whose length allows for the inclusion of more elaborate imagery. Beginning around the fifth decade of chapters (41–50), after the quarrel between Pan Jinlian and Li Ping'er becomes an open one, images of cats and flowers crop up in songs sung by Li Guijie and Li Ming, foreshadowing the death of Guan'ge in chapter 52 after he is traumatized by the trained cat of Pan Jinlian, whose given name, Jinlian, contains the name of a flower (i.e., a lotus). Soon after, imagery of dropped vases (*ping* 瓶), broken mirrors (symbolizing separation), and withered flowers foreshadows the death of Guan'ge's mother, Li Ping'er, and in chapter 61 a song set titled "The Four Dreams and Eight Nothings" ("Si meng ba kong" 四夢八空) is performed by Second Sister Shen at Ximen Qing's request, as Li Ping'er slowly bleeds to death in her room (4.61.27–29; 61.17a–17b). In chapters 65–77, imagery of plum blossoms and snow crops up in songs, portending the death of Ximen Qing, the rise of Pang Chunmei (P'ang Ch'un-mei, "Spring Plum"), and the subsequent dissolution of Ximen Qing's household in the novel's concluding chapters.

Dramatic Songs and References to Drama

Distinctions between nondramatic *qu* and dramatic *qu* are blurred in *Plum*; by the time the novel was written, scenes from plays were often performed separately, as "scene selections" (*zhezixi* 折子戲), and the same song suites were used in both subgenres of *qu*. As such, detached scenes were anthologized together with *sanqu* and when stripped of their dialogue, as was often the case, became virtually indistinguishable from them.[11] This can pose challenges for those unfamiliar with the song repertoire, as demonstrated in chapter 31 when Eunuch Director Liu twice requests song suites from plays inappropriate to the occasion (2.31.238–39; 31.14b–15a). Another instance occurs in chapter 43, when Madame Qiao (Ch'iao), the wife of Ximen Qing's neighbor, requests the performance of a scene from a play about illicit love, *Tale of a Shoe Left Behind* (*Liuxie ji* 留鞋記), at a banquet celebrating her infant daughter's betrothal (3.43.62; 43.13b). On occasions when songs from plays are quoted in the text, they are requested in the same way as *sanqu* are—by the first line of the first song, with or without mentioning the song's title; in only one case is the play also mentioned, when Metropolitan Graduate An requests that an actor sing a song from *The Story of the Jade Ring* (*Yuhuan ji* 玉環記), a southern drama (2.36.354–55; 36.5b–6a).[12] References to plays are not limited to occasions where songs from plays are performed. In the novel's middle chapters especially, plays are sometimes mentioned in passing by their titles, either by the narrator or in conversations between characters. Passages from plays other than songs also appear in the text on occasion, and some plot details resemble those from well-known plays.

In the appendix to her book *The Rhetoric of* Chin p'ing mei, Katherine Carlitz identifies twenty-five plays alluded to in the novel (147–50). Fifteen of them are named in the text, songs from ten others are quoted without the play being named, and some plot details resemble incidents from plays. These plays include eleven *zaju* 雜劇, a style originating in North China in the Yuan dynasty that was rarely performed in the late Ming; twelve southern dramas; and two *xiwen* 戲文, folk precursors to southern drama. Plays form part of the novel's backdrop and are also used by the author to signal his moral and political concerns to his readers. These elliptical references to a variety of plays make the novel's allusions to drama more complicated than its allusions to popular songs and more difficult for modern readers to decode.[13]

Dramatic Allusion as a Framing Device

References to plays sometimes bracket important moments in the novel in a way that comments on these moments. One example of this is the impromptu betrothal of Ximen Qing's son, Guan'ge, in chapter 41, which coincides with an elaborate observance of the Lantern Festival that spans six chapters (chs. 41–46). Three plays are mentioned in these chapters. In chapter 40, Ximen Qing plans a party on the eve of the festival and commissions a performance of a *zaju*, *Romance of the Western Chamber* (*Xixiang ji* 西廂記), which is mentioned again in chapter 42, though no songs from it are quoted. In chapter 41, Yueniang arranges Guan'ge's betrothal, and to mark the moment a suite of songs from act 3 of *Two Lives of Love* (*Liangshi yinyuan* 兩世姻緣), another *zaju*, is sung for the ladies present and quoted in the text (3.41.6–9; 41.4a–5a). In chapter 43, a party marking Guan'ge's betrothal and celebrating the birthday of his mother, Li Ping'er, takes place on the day of the Lantern Festival. On this occasion, Madame Qiao, the mother of Guan'ge's future bride, calls for a performance of another romantic *zaju*, *Tale of a Shoe Left Behind*, which is performed though no songs are quoted (3.43.62; 43.13b).

This concentration of romantic dramas about illicit love affairs at the moment when a marriage is being contracted improperly—Yueniang acts on an impulse, and no matchmakers are used—during a festival synonymous with danger and transgression invites the reader to consider how these plays inform this plot development. Carlitz makes a persuasive case that the numerous references to romantic dramas at this point call attention to the impropriety of the betrothal and, by extension, to mismanagement in Ximen Qing's household (*Rhetoric* 102–05). By extension they also allude to a failure of state governance, since Ximen Qing is allegorically linked to the emperor, here and elsewhere in the novel. The song suite from act 3 of *Two Lives of Love* quoted in chapter 41 resonates suggestively with the context, since the suite is laced with references to illicit love affairs and is sung in the voice of the play's heroine, who is encountering her lover from her former life and fearful that his intentions in seeking to marry her are not honorable.

Dramatic Allusion as a Reflection on Characters

As is the case with *sanqu*, songs excerpted from plays sometimes comment on characters by confronting the reader with incongruities—contrasts so marked as to border at times on the preposterous or grotesque. The targets of this kind of irony are male, and the plays alluded to are usually *chuanqi* rather than *zaju*, one reason being that most *chuanqi* are concerned with public morality and typically depict young scholars confronting official abuse. The world of romantic *chuanqi*—the kind of play alluded to most often in *Plum*—presents a decided contrast to the morally compromised world of *Plum* presided over by Ximen Qing and his associates.

In chapter 27 songs from an early Ming southern play, *The Lute* (*Pipa ji* 琵琶記), are sung as Ximen Qing disports himself with two of his concubines in his garden on a hot summer day. He first makes tender love with Li Ping'er and then engages in rough and prolonged sex with Pan Jinlian, who has provoked him with jealous comments at Li Ping'er's expense and then arouses him by stripping naked (except for her shoes). In between these bouts of sex, three songs from scene 21 of *Pipa ji* are sung as Li Ping'er and Meng Yulou depart the garden (2.27.138–40; 27.7a–7b). The songs make delicate reference to lovemaking between the hero of the play, Cai Bojie (Ts'ai Po-chieh), and the woman he has been forced to marry against his will but nonetheless loves. Famous for their depiction of Cai's conflicted feelings (he misses his first wife while making love to his second), these songs assume a different significance when transposed to *Plum*, heightening by contrast the depiction of Ximen Qing's flagrant and rampant sexuality and reflecting negatively on his abusive relationships with the women in his household. (He engages in painful sex with Li Ping'er early in her pregnancy.)

In chapter 36 Ximen Qing hires actors to entertain two freshly minted examination candidates who are about to embark on their official careers. The paired songs that each man calls for at the banquet are from *chuanqi* and are quoted in the text (2.36.353–55; 36.5a–6a). The first play, *The Scent Bag* (*Xiangnang ji* 香囊記), is about a virtuous scholar, Zhang Jiucheng (Chang Chiu-ch'eng), who is persecuted by a powerful official despite passing the examinations as principal graduate (*zhuangyuan* 狀元). The second play, *The Story of the Jade Ring* (*Yuhuan ji* 玉環記), also centers on a virtuous scholar, Wei Gao (Wei Kao), who falls in love with a pure-hearted singing-girl, Yuxiao (Yü-hsiao), who dies but is eventually reincarnated and becomes his concubine. Each pair of songs requested by Ximen Qing's guests can be understood as reflecting sardonically on the men who requested them, who in no way resemble the heroes of the respective plays. In the first instance, the request made by Principal Graduate Cai Yun (Ts'ai Yün) suggests that he is not at all self-reflective since his success in the examinations is the result of fraud rather than talent. In the second case, the fit between the play and the novel is "preposterously bad" (Carlitz, *Rhetoric* 116), since the songs exchanged between the play's hero and his bride express lifelong devotion, while in the novel Shutong, Ximen Qing's servant and catamite, sings the chaste bride's part while seated on the lap of Metropolitan Graduate An Chen (An Ch'en), who will bed him after the banquet concludes. David Rolston ("Oral Performing Literature" 20) and Katherine Carlitz (*Rhetoric* 96) also discuss how *Yuhuan ji* is used in other chapters to comment on the world of *Plum* in terms of its similarity to *Yuhuan ji*. In chapters 63 and 64, for example, references to some of the play's characters and details suggest parallels between the family depicted in the play, whose head believes the slander directed at his daughter, and Ximen Qing, who is similarly deluded on countless occasions about what is going on in his chaotic household.

In these examples, songs are quoted in the text, but the plays from which they are taken are not named. It is likely that the author expected his readers to know the origin of these songs and to consider how they resonated in their new contexts. Rolston cements his case for irony by pointing out that characters in the novel themselves sometimes use plays in this allusive way ("Oral Performing Literature" 21). Pan Jinlian requests songs from plays to get at her rivals, expecting Ximen Qing to recognize the game she is playing, and he does.

The Particular Importance of
The Story of the Precious Sword (Baojian ji 寶劍記)

Of the twenty-five plays alluded to in *Plum*, most are mentioned, or songs from them are quoted, in one or two chapters at most, but three plays crop up in several chapters: *The Story of the Jade Ring* (nine), *Romance of the Western Chamber* (eight), and the southern drama *The Story of the Precious Sword* (*Baojian ji* 寶劍記; seven). Even though *Precious Sword* is never once mentioned by its title and figures only in the novel's second half, Patrick Hanan has proposed that it is "infinitely more important than any of the other plays used" ("Sources" 50). Carlitz also affirms its importance, concluding her examination of drama in *Plum* with a discussion of it. Written by Li Kaixian 李開先 (1501–68) in 1547, *Precious Sword*, like *Plum*, is based on *Outlaws* and depicts the adventures of Lin Chong (Lin Ch'ung), one of the novel's 108 martial heroes (*haohan* 好漢). The play's subject—Lin Chong's persecution by and revenge against a corrupt military official, Gao Qiu (Kao Ch'iu 高俅 [d. 1126])—is close to that of *Plum*, as becomes evident in the ways that references to the play are transposed to several chapters in *Plum*. Carlitz observes that each substantial borrowing from *Precious Sword* comes at a critical moment in the novel, linking Li Kaixian's political and ethical concerns to the those of *Plum*'s author (*Rhetoric* 123–26).

In chapters 61 and 79, respectively, Li Ping'er and Ximen Qing are on their deathbeds, and in both chapters passages from *Precious Sword* have been inserted, with modifications to fit the context.[14] In chapter 61, the author borrows three segments from scene 28 that describe a visit by a quack doctor as Ximen Qing attempts to save Li Ping'er, who hovers near death (4.61.36, 38, and 39; 61.22b, 23a–23b, and 24a). In chapter 79, in analogous fashion, Immortal Wu's predictions concerning Ximen Qing's fortune, which take the form of a quatrain and six lines of rhymed verse, are borrowed from scene 10 as Wu Yueniang attempts to save Ximen Qing, who hovers near death; a comment by the narrator in the form of a quatrain is also likely taken from this scene (4.79.653 and 654–55; 79.18b–19a and 19b). Both chapters depict doomed efforts to save dying patients, borrowing stock comic characters (a doctor and a fortune-teller, respectively). It is conceivable that such borrowings would have prompted late Ming readers to associate a widely popular play with these incidents in the novel and to ponder how the allusions to the play comment sardonically on the deaths of these principal characters.[15]

Chapter 67 borrows from scene 33 on the occasion of a snow-viewing party in Ximen Qing's garden. Images of snow describe a wintry scene as Ximen Qing's servant Chunhong (Ch'un-hung) sings two songs to the tune "Stopping the Horse to Listen" ("Zhuma ting" 駐馬聽; 4.67.190–91 and 193; 67.11b and 13a). The disparity between the circumstances of Lin Chong, who sings these songs in scene 33 while suffering in exile, and Ximen Qing, who enjoys their performance while playing a game of dice with his cronies, draws attention to Ximen Qing's hedonism when compared with the suffering of *Precious Sword*'s righteous hero.

Other uses of *Precious Sword* in chapter 70 have attracted the most attention from critics. In this chapter, the author borrows a soliloquy in parallel prose from scene 3 and combines it with a suite of songs from scene 51 (4.70.298–301; 70.12b–13b). The long soliloquy, spoken in the play by a retainer in the household of Gao Qiu, the play's villain, condemns Gao's opulent lifestyle; in *Plum*, this soliloquy becomes a set piece that describes the fabulous wealth of Defender-in-Chief Zhu Mian (Chu Mien 朱勔 [1075–1126]), known to history as one of "six traitors" (*liu zei* 六賊) who served Emperor Huizong (Hui-tsung 宋徽宗 [r. 1100–25]).[16] In this chapter Ximen Qing travels to the Song capital to accept a promotion and attends a banquet feting Zhu, who has just been promoted to the post of grand guardian to the heir apparent. Set amid an account of the banquet that goes on for eight pages in Roy's translation, the song suite, performed by actors at the banquet and addressed to Zhu Mian, sits oddly here, with its scathing condemnation of extravagance and official malfeasance. So incongruous are these fragments from the play in their new context that the reader is compelled to see them as a biting attack, directed not only at Zhu Mian but also at Ximen Qing, Zhu's protégé. Such placement of these passages from *Precious Sword*, Hanan concludes, "can only be a deliberate statement of the author's own attitude" ("Sources" 52–53).[17]

Songs, Plays, and the Composition of Plum

While scholars have been slow to recognize *Plum*'s artistic and rhetorical uses of drama and popular song, they were quick to praise the novel for its detailed and realistic portrayal of late Ming performance culture. By the sixteenth century drama had become an important part of elite culture; literati wrote plays and enjoyed performances of them in their homes, and wealthy merchants followed their lead. Ximen Qing is a wealthy merchant who consorts with powerful officials and eunuchs; two of his six wives are trained performers, as are the prostitutes he patronizes. Entertainment is an important part of both his private life and his public life and is densely woven into the novel's fabric.

While praising *Plum*'s realistic evocation of late Ming daily life and culture, early scholars deplored the author's extensive borrowings from other genres and saw this as evidence of the poverty of his imagination. In his pioneering chapter on the novel, C. T. Hsia describes the author dismissively: "[H]e appears to us as a perverse writer who apparently prizes his ingenuity as much as, if not more than, his creativity. Despite his manifest talent for realistic fiction, he tampers with it so as to impress a special audience who will applaud his cleverness in offering other kinds of borrowed attractions" (170). In Hsia's view, both the author and the readers he had in mind were people of "low culture and ordinary mentality" who enjoyed *Plum* as a compendium of plays, songs and jokes, mundane Buddhist tales, and adapted stories (168). More recently, Shang Wei has suggested that *Plum*'s relationship to oral literature is mediated through late Ming print culture—through song anthologies, joke books, drama miscellanies, and other popular genres. Shang sees the novel as an "encyclopedic narrative of the everyday" ("'Jin Ping Mei'" 189), influenced by the daily-life encyclopedias (*riyong leishu* 日用類書) that circulated widely in the late Ming. Such popular works were multivocal and hybrid, fragmented rather than unified, and so too is the novel, a "book of books" that lacks a consistent viewpoint (195). Shang argues that the disparate works incorporated into *Plum* are not fully assimilated but "carry with them the specific approaches, forms of thinking, nuances, and accents of the given genres" (210).

These appraisals go hand in hand with a view, entertained especially in the 1950s and 1960s, that *Plum* emerged from a milieu of popular storytelling and remained close to its oral roots. The narrator, the argument goes, poses as a professional entertainer and intrudes from time to time to offer comments, recite poems, and, on occasion, break into song. This simulated context of professional storytelling lent support to the view that *Plum*, like its progenitor *Outlaws of the Marsh*, emerged by accretion from a mélange of stories circulating about Ximen Qing and his scandalous affairs. Some still entertain this view of collective authorship of the novel, but it has largely given way to an opposing view, namely that the novel is the work of a highly educated author broadly conversant with the literary culture of his day who sought to weave the full range of available genres, both classical and vernacular, into his narrative. In doing so he transmuted the texts he borrowed to achieve a variety of effects. In support of this argument, scholars such as Roy and Andrew H. Plaks have turned to a seventeenth-century commentator on the novel, Zhang Zhupo 張竹坡 (1670–98), who made the case for *Plum* as a masterwork (*qishu* 奇書) in an edition of the novel he published in 1695. I am indebted to the work of Roy and Plaks and their students, who in turn have benefited from Zhang's commentary and the pioneering work of Chinese scholars who go unmentioned here.

NOTES

[1] Chapters 1–6 are largely lifted from an earlier novel, *Outlaws of the Marsh* (*Shuihu zhuan* 水滸傳), and chapters 53–57 are not by the author of the remaining chapters. However, the author of *Jin Ping Mei* adds a *xiaoling* to chapters 1, 4, and 6, respectively, among other interpolations to these borrowed chapters.

²See Tian Xiaofei. A drawback is that the author uses the Chongzhen (*xiuxiang*) edition of the novel, which omits many of the songs found in the Wanli edition, on which Roy's translation is based.

³See Roy, "Use." See also Chang. Discrepancies between lyrics in songbooks and those in the novel suggest that the author was often quoting from memory. See Hanan, "Sources" 63.

⁴Unless otherwise noted, parenthetical citations refer to Roy's translation, *The Plum in the Golden Vase*, and to *Jin Ping Mei cihua* 金瓶梅詞話 (*Plum in the Golden Vase: A Ballad Tale*).

⁵The use of this song in chapter 1 represents an addition to the *Outlaws* text.

⁶For example, when Du Liniang (Tu Li-niang) sings to "Sheep on the Mountain Slope" in scene 10 of *Peony Pavilion* (*Mudan ting* 牡丹亭), or when the nun Sekong (Se-k'ung) does the same in *Longing for Worldly Pleasures* (*Sifan* 思凡). Both *Peony Pavilion* and *Longing for Worldly Pleasures* belong to the Kun operatic tradition.

⁷For the parodic nature of duets in *Plum*, see Rolston, "Oral Performing Literature" 28–29, which cites from Carlitz, *Rhetoric* 118. For the cutting of songs by the Chongzhen editor, see also Rolston, "Oral Performing Literature" 47.

⁸Rolston points out that *Plum*'s author here follows the orthographic conventions of printed plays when representing interpolated dialogue (*daibai* 帶白; "Oral Performing Literature" 30–31). See chapters 33, 35, 49, 52, and 96 for other examples of singing mixed with dialogue.

⁹Rolston points out that the songs requested by the eunuchs in chapter 31 are multivalent, revealing the eunuchs' mental world while also foreshadowing future plot developments ("Oral Performing Literature" 19).

¹⁰See, for example, chapters 61, 73, 82, and 83. Hanan points out that these uses of *sanqu* reflect practices current at the time the novel was written ("Sources" 57–58). Once Li Ping'er dies in chapter 61, they largely cease while funerary rituals are conducted in chapters 62–66.

¹¹In his notes to his translation, Roy often points out that a song or suite of songs quoted from a play is closer to an anthologized version than to the version in the complete play. Hanan lumps such excerpts together with *sanqu* for this reason, citing their "independent life" apart from the mother play ("Sources" 49).

¹²For other examples in which scenes or songs from plays are quoted in the text, see chapters 11, 27, 36, 41, 61, 67, 70, 71, 74, and 83.

¹³The discussion that follows is indebted to Carlitz's *Rhetoric*, especially chapters 5 and 6 (95–127) and the endnotes included in these chapters.

¹⁴Roy's translation makes note of such modifications. For modifications made in chapter 61, see 4.702 (nn 91, 94, 95); for those made in chapter 79, see 4.847n45 and 4.848 (nn 49, 50).

¹⁵For the author's modeling of some characters after the clown (*chou* 丑) role in Chinese drama, see Hanan, "Sources" 55; for an explication of the ironies involved in the transposition, see Carlitz, *Rhetoric* 123–26.

¹⁶This presents another anachronism since the Embroidered Uniform Guard was a Ming institution.

¹⁷Carlitz adds that *Precious Sword* was understood at the time it appeared as a statement of Ming outrage, a "living articulation of contemporary grievances," and so too, she suggests, was *Plum* (*Rhetoric* 122–23).

The Emergence of the Novel:
From *Outlaws of the Marsh* to *The Plum in the Golden Vase*

Shang Wei

The late Ming (1550–1644) has long been seen as the golden age of traditional Chinese novels, as exemplified by *Romance of the Three Kingdoms* (*Sanguo yanyi* 三國演義), *Outlaws of the Marsh* (*Shuihu zhuan* 水滸傳), and *The Plum in the Golden Vase* (*Jin Ping Mei* 金瓶梅). However, such an indiscriminate extension of the generic concept of the novel to early modern China (1550–1919) is not without problems.[1] When these distinctive Chinese works of different origins are lumped together under this modern European rubric, the accepted scholarly convention is merely followed for the sake of convenience without questioning the relevance of the rubric, much less inquiring about the issues at stake in a particular literary work.

With its earliest extant edition dated to 1618, *Plum* stands out among these late Ming works in a number of respects. For one, it seems modern in its representation of its male protagonist, Ximen Qing (Hsi-men Ch'ing), a self-made merchant whose fortune is no longer determined by kinship, status, and tradition. Tracing the trajectories of Ximen Qing's relentless financial adventures and sexual conquests, the novel explores the themes of desire, unbridled ambition, and moral corruption, showing how these lead to the protagonist's ultimate self-destruction. David Roy, known for his complete English translation of *Plum*, tends to read the novel with reference to Charles Dickens's *Bleak House* in the light of what is usually called realism. Often Roy has James Joyce's *Ulysses* in mind, seeing *Plum* as a linguistic labyrinth that requires patient and careful decoding to navigate it (Introduction xxvii–xxix, vlvii).

Whether or not one adopts such a comparative approach, it seems reasonable to suggest that *Plum* is probably the only one of the above Ming dynasty works that can be said to approximate a novel as understood in the early modern European tradition. *Plum* breaks new ground for long-form Chinese fiction, most noticeably in its dramatic departure from the literary tradition of grand narrative, featuring instead ordinary men and women as its protagonists; it is also recognized for its elaborate rendering of the new tempo of quotidian experiences in a commercial urban setting.

This said, *Plum* did not come from nowhere. Marthe Robert's comment on early modern European novels seems applicable here: "In fact, the novel achieved its devastating success as an upstart. All things considered, its victories were mainly due to its encroachments on the neighboring territories it surreptitiously infiltrated, gradually colonizing almost all of literature" (4). This remark helps highlight the affinity between *Plum* and its male protagonist. Not unlike Ximen Qing, *Plum* is a latecomer and upstart in the realm of literary production; it builds its own narrative by encroaching on the territories of all the neighboring forms and genres. More specifically, *Plum* feeds on *Outlaws* by recycling and reconfiguring the latter's rhetoric and motifs as part of its raw materials, but it does so only to demonstrate a process through which it deviates from the literary tradition to which *Outlaws* belongs.

As indicated by the word *biography* (*zhuan* 傳) in its title (which is omitted from the English translation), *Outlaws* originates in historical narrative through both written and oral sources. It is known primarily for its account of legendary, larger-than-life heroes whose deeds contribute, in one way or another, to the rise and fall of a dynasty. For too long, *Outlaws* has been misclassified as a novel, but even if it is read through the lens of European literature, it would seem to make more sense to compare it to historical romance and heroic saga. And it is precisely by rejecting the narrative model represented by *Outlaws* that *Plum* comes to claim its own distinctive identity. In this sense, *Plum* is like *Don Quixote*, arguably the first European novel to provide a ravaging parody of chivalric romance by recycling and reappropriating the genre's language, tropes, and motifs. *Plum* stands in the same relationship with *Outlaws* as *Don Quixote* does with chivalric romance. Even more important, *Plum* not only constitutes the emergence of what may be called the novel in Chinese literary history but also turns its own rise into a subject for representation and commentary—hence, it is a novel about the beginning of the novel that invites scrutiny and reflection.

Set in the Northern Song (960–1127), *Plum* offers a comprehensive and meticulous account of the rise and fall of Ximen Qing and his family. Thematically and stylistically, the appearance of *Plum* marks a new era in the history of Chinese fiction. However, this masterpiece of one hundred chapters does not construct its plotline independently. Rather, the first ten chapters of *Plum* build on scenes in chapters 23 to 26 of *Outlaws*, wherein Wu Song (Wu Sung), a valiant man of honor, beats a tiger to death bare-handed and then slaughters his sister-in-law, Pan Jinlian (P'an Chin-lien), and Ximen Qing in revenge for his elder brother's wrongful death. *Plum* rewrites the ending of this story of revenge by allowing the adulteress Pan Jinlian and Ximen Qing to escape Wu Song's vengeance, thereby ushering in the main characters for its own narrative. In other words, the author of *Plum* takes *Outlaws* as the starting point, drawing on it as raw material to initiate a new narrative on its own terms. Without *Outlaws*, *Plum* would not have been possible.

As the first Chinese novel noted for its concrete and lively reflection of the everyday lives of ordinary men and women, *Plum* has also been lauded as an example of literary realism. Much ink has been spilled over the verisimilitude it manages to achieve through its combination of diverse narrative devices. Its author's effective portrayal of what are typically understood as round characters serves to further distinguish *Plum* from historical romances and sagas. However, *Plum*'s narrative account of real life is mediated by an exceedingly broad range of literary and nonliterary genres and forms and countless pieces of ready-made material pulled from the commercial publications of the day (Shang, "'Jin Ping

Mei'"). It is impossible to verify the extent to which *Plum*'s representation is realistic by comparing it with so-called reality. Realism is primarily a matter of representation, and *Plum* develops its own representation of reality through contrast with the narrative world of *Outlaws*. Its textual entanglement with *Outlaws* only serves to highlight the texts' striking differences in focus, concerns, and general orientation.

A What-If Narrative

In *Outlaws* Wu Song is recognized as a hero (*haohan* 好漢) and appointed as a police officer in the county government after killing a tiger. This not only forces him to temporarily settle into a residential life but also confronts him with a series of unforeseeable intrigues involving adultery, bribery, and corrupt legal procedures. With no other options, he resorts to savage violence for justice, then flees to join like-minded comrades who are also branded as outlaws. *Plum*, however, turns Wu Song's fate upside down. No longer a dauntless idol, Wu Song is portrayed as a reckless boor. Instead of killing off the villains once and for all, *Plum*'s Wu Song is so blinded by his rage that he misses his target, Ximen Qing, and ends up slaying Li Waizhuan (Li Wai-ch'uan, "Li the Squealer"), a local government runner, by mistake. He is therefore apprehended by police and endures physical torture. As a potentially fatal threat to Ximen Qing and Pan Jinlian, Wu Song must be sent away for *Plum* to begin. On hearing the long-awaited news of Wu Song's exile, Ximen Qing holds a banquet in chapter 10 of *Plum* to entertain his wife and concubines. This is how the author ushers in the female protagonists of the novel; it also allows him to bid farewell to *Outlaws* while celebrating the true beginning of his own novel.

Plum is a novel about Ximen Qing and Pan Jinlian, who have survived Wu Song's slaughter only by chance. Unlike *Outlaws*, whose heroes are constantly on the open road, *Plum* shows no interest in following Wu Song into exile. Instead, its narrator decides to stay put and turn his attention to the world left behind, a world of urban residential life fraught with money, power, and sexual and financial adventures. Along with this drastic shift in focus comes an entirely different perspective. It seems as if the novelist is wondering aloud about what could have happened to Ximen Qing and Pan Jinlian and what kind of lives they would have lived had they managed to escape Wu Song's killing spree. In this sense, *Plum* conjures up a what-if narrative about a hypothetical scenario foreclosed by *Outlaws*. In so doing, it also explores the intricacies of the mundane experiences that elude historical sagas and heroic romances altogether.

The transition from *Outlaws* to *Plum* signifies a shift from romance to novel. This shift is demonstrated by the rise of *Plum* in place of *Outlaws*, and it occurs within *Plum* in metafictional terms through the devices of reappropriation, revision, and displacement. It is unnecessary to look elsewhere for evidence of how this happens, as *Plum* itself is capable of both representing and reflecting on the rise of the novel through its own narrative.

We can thus interpret the first ten chapters of *Plum* as a transition to a brave new world that has not previously lent itself to long-form fictional representation. And it soon becomes clear that the socioeconomic power Ximen Qing stands for prevails over the moral codes embodied by *Outlaws*'s Wu Song. Accordingly, the narrative logic Wu Song acts on in *Outlaws* can no longer make sense of Ximen Qing's personal life and social networks. Ximen Qing, a marginal figure who functions merely as a foil for martial heroes in *Outlaws*, looms large and becomes a dominant character in *Plum*. Hailing from a non-gentry family, he runs a wholesale pharmaceutical business, but his financial success offers him a springboard to political standing. The fact that Ximen Qing becomes the protagonist of *Plum* reflects broader social changes that were taking place in the late Ming: the flow of silver contributed to the flourishing of a monetary economy in Jiangnan in particular and other national markets by extension,[2] consumer culture took shape in tandem with the rise in literacy and wide spread of popular knowledge through the printing industry, neo-Confucian orthodoxy and moral teaching lost its grip on individuals' leisure activities, and the local order of elite dominance gave way to more fluid and dynamic urban spheres. Many historical forces account for the emergence of *Plum*, but the virtue of the novel lies in the internal perspective it provides to elucidate those changes.

Plum gives the nobodies in *Outlaws* a chance to play out their joys and sorrows in ill-defined arenas of everyday politics. In the absence of Wu Song, the novelist relies on the textual and cultural resources of the time to experiment with a new way of observation, narration, and writing. The persona of Ximen is prefigured in chapter 2 of *Outlaws*, where the evil minister Gao Qiu (Kao Ch'iu) strikes readers as a stereotypical profligate. Gao perfectly fits the label of a "dissolute young fellow" (*fulang zidi* 浮浪子弟) skilled at a wide range of pastimes, from the traditional high arts of the musical instrument *qin* 琴 (seven-string zither), the strategy game go, calligraphy, and painting to ball-kicking, stone-shooting, singing, and dancing (Shi and Luo, *Marshes* 1: 29). *Plum* develops the narrative potential of *zidi* 子弟, a category of people loaded with cultural symbolism, to the extent that Ximen Qing organizes the knowledge and practice of how to be a *zidi* along the arc of commercial pursuit. His mentality, dispositions, habits, skills, dress, and other features are derived from a knowledge system shared by many texts contemporary with *Plum*. In particular, by situating the emblem of *zidi* in late Ming print culture, we find in many daily-use encyclopedias (*riyong leishu* 日用類書) the related rubrics of *zidi*, a category that encompasses knowledge of sexual techniques, drug prescriptions, and banquet games for private and public consumption (Shang, "Making"). The pronounced profile of *zidi* embodied by *Plum*'s Ximen Qing thus thematizes the encyclopedic discourse of daily practice and pleasure and partakes of the changing frame of reference detached from official-elite learning. Following the plotline of Ximen Qing, readers not only learn how *zidi* behave in everyday life but also discern what is at stake in their aspirations and lust.

As an outsider, Ximen Qing dreams of becoming an official through bribery and succeeds in doing just that, but ultimately his success brings disaster to both the elite world and his own family. The disruptions caused by the alliance of money and power manifest themselves in nearly all aspects of political and socioeconomic life. And the premature death of Ximen's son, Guan'ge (Kuan-ko, the "Boy, an Official to Be"), is a portent for what is to occur later to his family at large. Just like Ximen Qing, who leaves behind no offspring to inherit his wealth, his story becomes a singular one incapable of self-reproduction.

Following the revised Wu Song episode with its own story about Ximen Qing, *Plum*, however, does not let *Outlaws* go. *Plum*'s textual entanglement with its predecessor stretches throughout. If the exile of Wu Song marks the real beginning of *Plum*, his return in chapter 87 is equally consequential, allowing him to fulfill his aborted mission of revenge. Before his arrival, Ximen Qing has died of sexual indulgence, but Pan Jinlian, one of the female protagonists of the novel, is meant to be killed by her brother-in-law, as promised by *Outlaws*. Her death is postponed but not prevented. In this sense, the male and female protagonists of *Plum* can be said to live in the time they borrow from *Outlaws*, time that allows their stories to fully unfold instead of being cut short too early, as in *Plum*'s parent text. However, these characters also live in a doomed story whose ending is already written and remains unchanged. By finally beheading Pan Jinlian, one of *Plum*'s title characters, Wu Song brings this what-if narrative close to its end while returning readers to chapter 26 of *Outlaws*. Indeed, with Jinlian's death, *Plum* resumes the original timeline of Wu Song's adventure in *Outlaws*, at least in theory. Readers can pick up *Outlaws* again and continue to read it after going through the long digressive detour taken by *Plum*.

In this way, *Plum* functions as a supplement to *Outlaws* within the framework provided by the latter. The idea of supplementary writing is deeply rooted in Chinese literary tradition; this type of writing is meant to reconstruct an earlier piece of writing that has been destroyed or lost. However, the term *supplement* may also describe a literary work that elaborates an alternative scenario to that presented by an existing story or drama. The best-known example of this kind of supplementary writing is perhaps Dong Yue's *A Supplement to the* Journey to the West (*Xiyou bu* 西遊補), dated to 1640. This sixteen-chapter novel develops its own narrative that Monkey goes astray and becomes entangled in dreams and desires while escorting his master on an arduous journey to fetch Buddhist sutras, whereas his counterpart in *The Journey to the West* (*Xiyou ji* 西遊記), attributed to Wu Cheng'en, is famous for his indifference to sexual temptation and his lack of introspection, if not his lack of interiority altogether (A. Yu). Dong Yue seeks to supplement what he finds lacking in the parent text. By deriving his narrative from chapter 61 of *The Journey to the West*, he takes readers on a long detour before returning to *The Journey*. Composed much earlier, *Plum* initiates this type of supplementary narrative, drawing inspiration in part from the proliferation of contemporaneous paratexts, including commentaries, prefaces, prefatory notes, and so on. The commentators, editors, and publishers of the time often saw in an existing narrative opportunities to experiment with alternative or additional scenarios by means of redaction and rewriting. Viewed through this lens, supplementary writing can be said to present readers' audacious intervention into an established work, or rather, the extension of their participatory reading through fiction writing. Whereas *A Supplement to the* Journey to the West plunges its protagonist into a land of fantasies, *Plum* resorts to a subjunctive mode of writing only to confront readers with the specificities of day-to-day experience, therefore enacting the dialectics of real and unreal, true and fictional. Thus, the creativity *Plum* registers in its compositional strategy heralds *The Story of the Stone* (*Shitou ji* 石頭記 or *Honglou meng* 紅樓夢), otherwise known as *Dream of the Red Chamber*, a mid-eighteenth-century masterpiece that knits together the particularities of a material world within its metafictional and self-referential frames of illusion-making.

Plum does not end right after Pan Jinlian's death; instead, it continues for thirteen chapters. The final part of the novel is concerned primarily with the disintegration of the Ximen household. Chen Jingji (Ch'en Ching-chi), Ximen Qing's son-in-law, steps into Ximen Qing's shoes, trying in vain to bring the family together again. In the end, the Ximen family's collapse coincides and merges with the crumbling of the Northern Song Empire. In this way, *Plum* finally returns to *Outlaws*, which concludes its narrative with the end of the Song dynasty. However, *Plum*'s author also offers his own interpretation of the parent text: instead of being preoccupied with historical personas and legendary heroes, his story about the Ximen family serves as a proper supplement to *Outlaws* by offering a compelling illustration of a specific amalgamation of social and economic forces that contributes to the dynasty's ultimate downfall.

Reconfiguring Desire

Plum's indebtedness to *Outlaws* transcends the former's beginning and ending. Its author extracts motifs, symbols, images, metaphors, and expressions from *Outlaws* and incorporates them into the narrative of *Plum* through multilayered reconfiguration. And he never misses an opportunity to develop imagined links between *Plum* and *Outlaws* in mutually constructive ways. As a result, the interpretative approaches to both texts are altered to accommodate the reciprocal connection built into the conditions of signification. A reading of one text inevitably modifies or enhances an analytical avenue into the other. Their interrelationship enables a unique contemplation of the compositional principles and techniques of early modern Chinese fiction in ways that may shed new light on an understanding of transtextuality.

The visual configuration of the female body through the lens of male desire is one means of understanding the interconnection between the two works. As mentioned, the narrative focus of *Plum* shifts from lofty exploits to domestic particularities imbued with corporal and mercantile values. Symptomatic of this shift is the changing image of Pan Jinlian. Whereas Pan is wiped away as a wanton adulteress after a transitory appearance in *Outlaws*, in *Plum* she is fleshed out with painstaking attention to her actions and emotions, which promotes her to the status of a main character. At the same time, the narrator of *Plum* does not abandon the descriptive phrases and passages *Outlaws* mobilizes to evoke Jinlian's image as a femme fatale. Pan Jinlian's debut in chapter 2 of *Plum* bears a striking resemblance to the repertoire of expressions with which *Outlaws* stages the seductive:

> [Ximen Qing], on whose head the forked stick had fallen, stopped in his tracks and was about to make trouble; but when he looked around to see who was responsible he found, to his surprise, that it was a beautiful and seductive woman. Behold, she has:
>> Glossy, black, raven's feather tresses;
>> Dark, curved, new moon eyebrows;
>> Clear, cold, almond eyes;
>> Redolently fragrant cherry lips;
>> A straight, full, alabaster nose;
>> Thickly powdered red cheeks;
>> A handsome, silver salver face;
>> A light, lissome, flowerlike figure;
>> Slender, jade-white, scallion-shoot fingers;
>> A cuddlesome, willow waist;
>> A tender, pouting, dough-white tummy;
>> Tiny, turned-up, pointed feet;
>> Buxom breasts; and
>> Fresh, white legs.
> And there is something else as well:
>> Tight and squeezy,
>> Red and wrinkly,
>> Pale and fresh,
>> Black and cushioned;
>> Who can tell what it might be?   (1.2.50)

這個人被叉竿打在頭上, 便立住了腳. 待要發作時, 回過臉來看, 卻不想是個美貌妖嬈的婦人. 但見她: 黑鬒鬒賽鴉翎的鬢兒, 翠彎彎的新月的眉兒, 清冷冷杏子眼兒, 香噴噴櫻桃口兒, 直隆隆瓊瑤鼻兒, 粉濃濃紅艷腮儿, 嬌滴滴銀盆臉兒, 輕嬝嬝花朵身兒, 玉纖纖葱枝手兒, 一捻捻楊柳腰兒, 軟濃濃白麪臍肚兒, 窄多多尖趫腳兒, 肉奶奶胸兒, 白生生腿兒. 更有一件緊揪揪、緊擖擖、紅皺皺、白鮮鮮、黑裀裀, 正不知是什麼東西.   (2.4b–5a)[3]

This portrayal of Pan Jinlian from Ximen's perspective is colloquially suggestive, moving the focus from her hair to her countenance, the features of her body, and her garments. Notably, the adjectives used to describe Pan are rather general. Collectively they evoke a sense of bodily hyperbole that adds up to bawdy expressiveness. A juxtaposition of Pan Jinlian's image with the pattern by which an alluring woman comes into view in *Outlaws* shows that the above passage is by no means a distinctive invention on the part of *Plum*'s author. This passage corresponds closely to the passage describing how Pan Qiaoyun, another enticing wife, is perceived by her husband's sworn brother Shi Xiu in chapter 44 of *Outlaws* (Shi and Luo, *Marshes* 3: 20–21). In *Outlaws*, Pan Qiaoyun is the daughter of a butcher and is remarried to the martially mighty Yang Xiong, who works as an executioner in the local government. Shi Xiu is invited by Yang to stay with his family and take care of the family business, only to discover the adultery between Pan Qiaoyun and a lustful monk. To cover up the crime, Pan takes measures to set Shi Xiu up, but her trick backfires. Eventually, in the name of masculine fraternity and honor, Shi Xiu and Yang Xiong murder and chop up Pan Qiaoyun in a notoriously violent manner. *Plum* appropriates the visual representations of Pan Qiaoyun in *Outlaws* to reconfigure the perceptual experience of Ximen Qing. The point of view from which Shi Xiu beholds Pan Qiaoyun is transferred to Ximen Qing with slight modification.

Accordingly, the contextual discrepancies between Shi Xiu's and Ximen Qing's visual sensitivities entail rereadings of the two texts. In *Outlaws*, only by overcoming desire can a warrior prove his heroic qualities and his loyalty to the homosocial ties of sworn brotherhood. By contrast, Ximen Qing turns sex from a test of self-denial into a battlefield of lust and indulgence in *Plum*. He embarks on a very different journey driven by, rather than insulated from, the desire for sexual conquest. In this sense, *Plum*'s story of Ximen Qing is a parody of the heroic deeds elaborated on in *Outlaws*. However, the way Ximen Qing takes Pan Jinlian's sensuous appearance as the visual cue for his sexual conquest also casts a shadow over Shi Xiu's motivation for killing in *Outlaws*. Ximen Qing's case provides a retrospective angle from which Shi's righteousness, seemingly immune to Pan Qiaoyun's seduction, is called into question. A short story by the modern novelist Shi Zhecun 施蟄存 (1905–2003) entitled *Shi Xiu zhi lian* 石秀之戀 (*The Love of Shi Xiu*) exploits the subtext of Shi Xiu's sadism in a psychoanalytical vein. Shi's modern rendering returns us to the moment when Pan Qiaoyun is first introduced in *Outlaws* and suggests great interpretative ambiguities already embedded in the narrator's configuration of her impression. Ironically, the suppressed desire hinted at in passing in *Outlaws* finds its outlet in *Plum*, where sexual drive, violence, and death loom large as recurrent motifs through repetitions and variations. In this regard, the intertextual connection that *Plum* builds up through the recycling of visual representation in *Outlaws* affords new possibilities for understanding each work.

Reappropriating Outlaws, *Rewriting* Outlaws

The multilayered interconnection between *Plum* and *Outlaws* carves out an imaginary space of convergence, wherein the novels' unfolding plots intertwine in both time and place. Moments of overlap show how *Plum* weaves together different threads, events, and characters from *Outlaws* in the most intriguing ways. This also helps set *Plum* apart from other fictional works that fall into the same category of supplementary writing, as its narrative often runs across the story line of its parent text, forcing us to reexamine the relationship between these two texts in spatiotemporal terms.

Besides Pan Jinlian, a few other characters who play important parts in Ximen Qing's life are presumably linked to *Outlaws* in one way or another. Wu Yueniang (Wu Yüeh-niang), Ximen's wife, is a case in point. After her husband's death, she decides to make a pilgrimage to Mount Tai to fulfill the oath she took while he was ill. As she chances on the Qingfeng stronghold, the bandit-heroes who guard it as their own territory detain her and her entourage. Were it not for Song Jiang (Sung Chiang), the head of the Liangshan bandit-heroes who comes to her rescue, Yueniang would have lost her life in their hands. Interestingly, Song Jiang claims that Wu Yueniang was the wife of his former colleague in the same country administration, a colleague with whom he was "slightly acquainted" (有一面之識; 5.84.70; 84.9a). Song Jiang's rescue of Yueniang is nowhere to be found in *Outlaws*. Instead of taking its parent text as given, *Plum* ends up rewriting it. *Plum* assumes that *Outlaws*'s narrative continues to develop concurrently with its own, and their episodes occasionally intersect when characters venture out of their usual setting and step into *Outlaws*'s territory. Wu Yueniang's foray into *Outlaws* turns out to be a perilous adventure, but its ramifications go beyond the fortune of an individual character. *Outlaws* continues to hover as a potential threat, as Wu Yueniang proves to be yet another character in *Plum* whose life and story would be cut short, if not terminated altogether, by *Plum*'s predecessor.

Li Ping'er (Li P'ing-erh), one of *Plum*'s main female characters who marries into Ximen Qing's household as a concubine, offers another instance of *Plum*'s retrospective intervention in *Outlaws*. Although she is never explicitly mentioned in *Outlaws*, Li is identified by the narrator of *Plum* as a survivor of the violence traceable to *Outlaws*. In chapter 10 of *Plum*, the narrator introduces Li Ping'er as a former concubine of Secretariat Liang (Liang Zhongshu), the son-in-law of Grand Preceptor Cai Jing (Ts'ai Ching). Li Ping'er flees the Liang household when the Liangshan band raids Daming Prefecture, taking a substantial fortune with her (1.10.199). The raid happens in chapter 66 of *Outlaws*, much later than Wu Song's revenge in the story's original timeline. In that raid, the outlaws wipe out the entire family except for the Liang couple. *Plum* not only reshuffles that story but also invents the character of Li Ping'er altogether: to reappropriate *Outlaws*, *Plum* must first rewrite it.

The fact that *Plum* inserts Li into the narrative trajectory in a way that allows her to outlive the havoc wreaked by the Liangshan heroes is thought-provoking—in metaphoric terms, she stands for the fictional alternative to the life-and-death world of *Outlaws*. Only in *Plum* is her story rendered possible and endowed with otherwise unimaginable significance. Accordingly, *Plum* comes to define itself as a novel that outlives *Outlaws*.

Li's story is just as important in terms of how *Plum* builds its narrative around tropes and manages to sustain that narrative by weaving together fragments appropriated from *Outlaws*. Ximen woos Li Ping'er as her husband, Hua Zixu (Hua Tzu-hsü), falls ill, promising to marry her soon. After Hua's passing, Li Ping'er longs for Ximen day and night. To use her own words, Li sees Ximen as "the medicine to cure my sickness" (醫奴的藥; 1.17.340; 17.2b), a medicine she is addicted to.[4] However, because of the lawsuit against his son-in-law's family in the capital, Ximen shuts himself off without giving Li any explanation. In sheer desperation, Li starts to harbor delusions and loses her vitality to haunting fox spirits. It is at this point, in chapter 17, that Dr. Jiang Zhushan (Chiang Chu-shan) appears. He claims to be a palace physician, or more accurately a member of the Imperial Academy of Medicine, but the novel provides no means of verifying this. He is an enigmatic loner who seems to come from nowhere, with no family or social relationships to help pin him down. He is invited to Li's inner chamber to diagnose her illness, but it takes only one meeting for him to seal a marriage deal and move into Li Ping'er's household. This marriage does not last long. Halfway through chapter 19 he is driven away, leaving no traces of his presence behind.

How can we make sense of Jiang Zhushan's phantom appearance and disappearance? One way of answering this question is to see how Jiang replaces Ximen Qing, carrying out the latter's role as Li Ping'er's "cure" in his self-proclaimed capacity as a physician. Li is no passive participant in her relationship with Jiang: She subtly initiates the conversation about marriage and takes Jiang in as her new husband immediately after he proposes. She later sponsors his medical and medicinal trade, enabling him to open his own pharmacy, which is in competition with the one owned by Ximen Qing. She even goes so far as to model him on Ximen Qing: she buys Jiang a donkey, allowing him to ride on it while showing off on the street, with a swaggering gait identical to that of Ximen on horseback (1.17.355). Soon after, in chapter 19, Li Ping'er expels him from her household, and then resumes her relationship with Ximen Qing while reiterating her description of him as her "cure" (1.19.399).

Viewed within this symmetrical frame, Jiang's very existence takes on structural significance. First, in the temporary absence of Ximen Qing, Jiang Zhushan becomes a fictional stand-in, an allegorical substitute for Ximen Qing. He acts out what Ximen is expected to do, delivering the promised marriage while offering Li a sense of physiological security that she desperately needs. Second, Jiang Zhushan is more a mental projection of Li Ping'er's desire than a three-dimensional character capable of acting on his own. She summons him into being in service of her needs. The marriage is doomed to fail in the first place: a homophone for his name, *jiang zhu san* 將逐散 ("to be driven out"), prefigures his transience.

It is particularly interesting that Jiang Zhushan's exit from the novel allows the memory of *Outlaws* to resurface. In chapter 19 of *Plum*, on learning of Li Ping'er's marriage to Jiang, Ximen Qing hires two local thugs to harass and penalize him. The two ruffians—"Snake in the Grass" ("Caoli she" 草裡蛇) Lu Hua and "Street-Skulking Rat" ("Guojie shu" 過街鼠) Zhang Sheng (Chang Sheng)—mimic the hotheaded warriors of *Outlaws* both in name and in conduct. Particularly, Lu Hua is reminiscent of Lu Da, who not only makes a fool of the notorious butcher Zhen Guanxi but also beats him to death for his violence against the weak and poor in chapter 3 of *Outlaws*. The way the two thugs handle Jiang Zhushan is also familiar: they first ask for nonexistent pharmaceuticals, then threaten him with a piece of fake documentation, forcing him to repay money he never owed. In the end, Lu Hua deliberately spurs Jiang into an altercation, and then gives him a preplanned beating in response: "When Lu Hua heard these words he reacted with outrage. From the other side of the narrow counter he sent a clenched fist whistling across that flew right into Jiang Zhushan's face, knocking his nose to one side. At the same time, he started pulling the pharmaceuticals off the shelves and hurling them into the street" (魯華聽了, 心中大怒, 隔着小櫃, 颼的一拳去, 早飛到竹山面門上, 就把鼻子打歪在半邊, 一面把架上藥材撒了一街; 1.19.387; 19.7b). The language used by the narrator to describe this scene bears a remarkable resemblance to the way *Outlaws* renders Lu Da's vengeance against Zhen Guanxi: "He struck him another blow, right on the nose, so that the blood came flooding out and the nose was knocked sideways. For the butcher it was as if he had opened a sauce and vinegar shop: salty, sour, and hot all mixed up together!" ((魯達)撲的只一拳, 正打在鼻子上, 打得鮮血迸流, 鼻子歪在半邊, 卻便似開了油醬鋪, 鹹的、酸的、辣的, 一發都滾出來). By comparing the taste of blood to sauce and vinegar, the narrator of *Outlaws* assimilates the vernacular vocabulary and sensibility of urban peddlers and merchants in a comic vein. The metaphors describing how Zhen Guanxi suffers Lu Da's deadly punches go on, likening Zhen Guanxi's physical pain to the spectacle of opening on his face "a brocade shop" (彩帛鋪; *Marshes* 1: 77; *Shuihu zhuan* [Renmin wenxue chubanshe] 1: 50). They amount to a sequence of tropes about the intensifying symptoms of Zhen Guanxi's physical suffering, including his burst eyeballs and damaged head. If we follow closely the language Ximen Qing uses to anticipate how Jiang Zhushan is beaten up in *Plum*, we find that the vendor metaphor returns. At one point, Ximen informs Pan Jinlian, "You may have heard that Dr. Jiang Zhushan has opened a pharmaceutical shop right under my nose. Well, one of these days, you can rely upon it, he's going to look as though he's opened a fruit shop on his own face" (你道蔣太醫開了生藥鋪, 到明日, 管情教他臉上開果子鋪出來; 1.19.384; 19.5b). To some extent, this metaphor exaggerates Ximen's revenge on economic grounds. The pharmaceutical shop endangers his own business, and thus Ximen intends not only to smash Jiang's physical shop but also to beat him black and blue. In this regard, the metaphoric language derived from *Outlaws* penetrates *Plum*, highlighting the discrepancies of the contexts of the two novels.

It is therefore clear that *Plum* cannot be read as a self-contained text. Rather, it develops many links to *Outlaws* in both structure and details. The figurative language that underlies Jiang Zhushan's story illustrates the polytextual nature of *Plum*, by which I refer to the interweaving of expressions and tropes across textual boundaries. Although Lu Hua punishes Jiang Zhushan in the same manner in which Lu Da takes revenge on Zhen Guanxi, the justifications for their actions are completely different. Whereas Lu Da steps forward in *Outlaws* as a dauntless hero to give Zhen Guanxi a thrashing he deserves, Lu Hua works for hire and becomes an accomplice in Ximen Qing's coercive evil plot. More specifically, he serves to deflate Lu Da's heroic deed while foregrounding Ximen Qing's crafty appropriation of the textual resources from *Outlaws*. Ximen Qing's verbal prediction of the revenge scene extends the array of metaphors centering on comedic violence to Jiang Zhushan, his foredoomed double who is summoned only to be eliminated.

Even before this incident, the relationship between Li Ping'er and Jiang Zhushan has turned sour, in part because Li is disappointed by Jiang's inability to live up to her expectations. She begins to calculate what she has gained and what she has lost as a result of her investment in him, and it becomes evident that Ximen's revenge plot has turned him into a liability:

> "Just who do you think you are?" she demanded. "You might as well regard the whole episode as a fit of delirium on my part, and those thirty taels of silver as the fee for your treatment. The sooner you move out of here the better. If I let you stay any longer, I'm likely to discover that even the value of this house of mine will not suffice to pay off your debts."
>
> (1.19.391)

> 你還欠那人家的? 只當奴害了汗病, 把這三十兩銀子問你討了藥喫了. 你趁早與我搬出去罷! 再遲些時, 連我這兩間房子, 尚且不夠你還人!　　(19.10a)

Li Ping'er's repurposing of the trope of the therapeutic "cure" strips the trope of its veil of warmth and intimacy by disclosing the hidden aspect of her relationship with Jiang. Reluctantly, she admits that she has suffered a "fit of delirium" for which she must pay her physician for the prescribed medicines. Underlying the same trope are the financial transactions between a physician and his client. Once Li Ping'er pays her medical bills, it is time for him to leave:

> Jiang Zhushan realized that they had come to a parting of the ways and hobbled off on his painfully wounded legs, weeping and wailing, to look for a place to stay. He had to leave behind all the stock that had been purchased with his wife's money. She pressed him to remove the medical supplies, mortar and pestle, pharmacological sieve, and other impedimenta that he had brought with him, and the two severed their relationship forthwith. At their final parting, as he was on his way out the door, the woman even sent Old Mother Feng to dip up a pewter basin full of water and throw it after him, saying: "At last my enemy has been removed from my sight."
>
> (1.19.392)

這將竹山自知存身不住, 哭哭啼啼, 忍着兩腿疼, 自去另尋房兒. 但是婦人本錢置買的貨物都留下, 把他原舊的藥材、藥碾、藥篩、箱籠之物, 即時催他搬去, 兩個就開交了. 臨出門, 婦人還使馮媽媽舀了一錫盆水, 趕着潑去, 說道: "喜得冤家離眼前!" 當日打發了竹山出門.　　(19.10a)

In this moment, Jiang proves to be nothing more than a set of medical supplies; as a cure for Li Ping'er's illness, he is utterly ineffective. The term *enemy* (*yuanjia* 冤家), which Li Ping'er uses in bidding farewell to Jiang, is noteworthy, as its connotations range from "foe" to "sweetheart." Two chapters earlier, she uses the same phrase when addressing Ximen Qing and comparing him to her cure.

This example showcases how deftly the author of *Plum* develops the Jiang Zhushan episode by setting into motion a single trope while revealing its multiple layers of significance through the unfolding narrative. To sustain his narrative, the author again employs the rhetoric of reappropriation, conjuring up a verbal wonder by knitting together the phrases, metaphors, and motifs he extracts from *Outlaws*.

From Military Adventure to Sexual Adventure

Despite its drastic departure from *Outlaws* in theme and focus, *Plum* inherits, on a fundamental level, the former's motif and rhetoric of adventure writ large. Individual adventures and chance encounters on the open road are salient features of heroic sagas, and, invariably, these adventures and encounters lead to collective activities and military campaigns closely associated with the fortune of the empire, as shown in *Outlaws*. At the center of this grand narrative are the heroic struggle and sacrifice that speak to dynastic governance and its legitimacy. By contrast, Ximen Qing settles down in an urban sphere devoid of expeditions and warfare. The spatial movement that occurs with adventure and peril are by and large absent from his everyday life. As the male protagonist of a domestic fiction, he is the opposite of Wu Song. However, closer inspection reveals that *Outlaws*'s trademark motif of adventure does infiltrate *Plum*, fueling it with narrative energy while transmuting its figures of speech. *Plum*'s transtextual strategy boils down to a rewriting of the adventure narrative.

To start with, Ximen Qing, the most prominent power broker in his hometown district, is a parody of the figure of the hero-adventurer in *Outlaws*. As someone of humble origins and with no known family lineage, Ximen Qing climbs the social ladder in the most transgressive manner. He gambles on his financial success, bribes his way into the proximity of the central authority that extends its power down to the local government through empire-wide bureaucratic networks, and thus cashes in on his acquired status. As an upstart and a merchant-turned-official, Ximen is constantly on an upwardly mobile trajectory, crossing distinct social spheres occupied respectively by elite-officials, fellow businessmen, peddlers, whoremongers, and good-for-nothing local *zidi*. At the same time, he embarks on a series of sexual adventures and conquests out of proportion to his physical capacity. From the furtive rendezvous with his sworn brother's wife, Li Ping'er, to the aggressive lovemaking with Lady Lin, the widow of Imperial Commissioner Wang Yixuan (Wang I-hsüan), Ximen Qing spares no effort, having sex with every woman he can lay his hands on. In due course, he dies of the overconsumption of that which he wins by conquest. Not unlike Song Jiang's inherent dilemma of fighting for the unattainable recognition of an established order in *Outlaws*, Ximen Qing strives to subjugate a world to which he does not belong. His self-made fortune violates the social norm, and his premature and unnatural death leaves no legacy for a household already torn apart by distrust, hypocrisy, and incest. Beyond the organic, communal relationship of a Confucian society, Ximen Qing's story offers no prospect for self-reproduction.

To appropriate the theme of military adventure, the narrator of *Plum* constantly switches the narrative focus between the public life and private life of Ximen Qing in accordance with the protagonist's increasingly accelerated quest for riches, prestige, and women. The pace of narration does not lend itself to a static sphere of domestic clichés and daily routine. New encounters bring in new characters and move the plotline forward in a suspenseful fashion. At one point, the narrator confronts Ximen Qing with the personification of the protagonist's own libido, revealing the dark force that motivates his impulse toward success and self-destruction. This occurs in chapter 49 when Ximen Qing encounters a foreign monk, symbolic of Ximen's own penis, at the Yongfu Temple, where Ximen will be buried after death. Earlier, readers learn that Ximen has reached the height of his career thanks to his ties with Prime Minister Cai Jing and his close connections with other officials. On his visit to the temple, he arouses the grotesque monk, whom he thought to be a divine master, and procures from him the "medication to enhance the performance of the arts of the bedchamber" (房術的藥; 3.49.199; 49.16a). The encounter and dialogue between Ximen Qing and the monk reads as an exceptional allegory of desire:

> Ximen Qing:
> Without premeditation or forethought,
> strolled inside to take a look and noticed a monk whose physique was out of the ordinary, and whose appearance was grotesque. His leopard-shaped head with its sunken eyes was the color of purple liver and was crowned with a cock's comb-like chaplet. He wore a long flesh-colored gown. The whiskers beneath his chin bristled unevenly, and he had a shiny annular ridge around the base of his head. Truly, he was:
> An authentic arhat, of the most
> extraordinary aspect;
> A one-eyed dragon, undivested of
> his fiery temperament.
> He had fallen into a trance on his meditation couch, so that his head was drooping, his neck had subsided into his upper trunk, and a trickle of jade-white mucus was dribbling from his nostrils.

When Ximen Qing had finished observing him:

> From his mouth no word was uttered, but
>
> In his heart he thought to himself,

"This priest must surely be a monk of high attainments, possessed of extraordinary powers. If not, how could he exhibit such an unusual appearance? I might as well wake him up and ascertain the truth of the matter."

Thereupon, raising his voice, he called out to the monk, "Where do you come from, and what temple are you attached to, that you have arrived here in the course of your peregrinations?"

The first time he called out to him, there was no response; and the second time, he also failed to reply; but the third time, behold, that monk on his meditation couch jerked himself erect, gave his torso a stretch, opened his one good eye, sprang up from his relaxed position, nodded his head toward Ximen Qing, and said, in a coarse voice, "Why are you interrogating me?

> I neither alter my given name when abroad,
>
> Nor change my surname when at home.

I am a foreign monk from the land of India in the Western Regions, who has descended into the mundane world from Cold Shivers Temple, beneath Navel Waist Peak, in Dense Sperm Forest. Having come here in the course of my peregrinations I plan to distribute medicine in order to cure people. In calling upon me this way, sir, what have you got to say?"

"Since you plan to distribute medicine in order to cure people," said Ximen Qing, "were I to ask you for some restorative medication, might you have such a thing, or not?"

"I do! I do!" exclaimed the monk.

Ximen Qing then went on to ask, "Were I to invite you to my home, would you come, or not?"

"I'll come! I'll come!" asseverated the monk.   (3.49.193–95)

西門慶不因不由, 信步走入裡面觀看, 見一個和尚, 形骨古怪, 相貌搊搜: 生的豹頭凹眼, 色若紫肝; 戴了雞蠟箍兒, 穿一領肉紅直裰; 頦下髭鬚亂拃. 頭上有一溜光簷. 就是個形容古怪真羅漢, 未除火性獨眼龍. 在禪床上旋定過去了: 垂着頭, 把脖子縮到腔子裡, 鼻口中流下玉箸來. 西門慶口中不言, 心內暗道: "此僧必然是個有手段的高僧, 不然, 如何有此異相? 等我叫醒他, 問他個端的." 於是揚聲叫那位僧人: "你是那裡人氏, 何處高僧, 雲遊到此?" 叫了頭一聲, 不答應; 第二聲, 也不言語; 第三聲, 只見這個僧人在禪床上把身子打了個挺, 伸了伸腰, 睜開一隻眼, 跳將起來, 向西門慶點了點頭兒, 粗聲應道: "你問我怎的? 貧僧行不更名, 坐不改姓, 乃西域天竺國密松林齊腰峰寒庭寺下來的胡僧, 雲遊至此, 施藥濟人. 官人, 你叫我有甚話說?" 西門慶道: "你既是施藥濟人, 我問你求些滋補的藥兒, 你有也沒有?" 胡僧道: "我有! 我有!" 又道: "我如今請你到家, 你去不去?" 胡僧道: "我去! 我去!"   (49.13a–13b)

Without doubt, the foreignness of the monk, as perceived by Ximen Qing, embodies the enchanting power elicited by unrestrained human desire. By describing the monk as "[a] one-eyed dragon, undivested of his fiery temperament," the narrator adds an air of exoticness to Ximen Qing's interlocutor and proxy. Ximen Qing is caught bewildered. Blinded by desire, he fails to recognize the incarnation of his own lust; instead, he makes endless inquiries about the anonymous monk's origin and identity. The monk's responses to Ximen's questions are ambiguous, mixing irreverent generalization ("I am a foreign monk from the land of India") with the minutest details ("in the Western Regions, who has descended into the mundane world from Cold Shivers Temple, beneath Navel Waist Peak, in Dense Sperm Forest"). In this way, the narrative is imbued with and driven by allegorical impulse.

Most striking in this passage is how the narrator calls attention to the monk's enormous physical strength while also highlighting his verbal impotence. After introducing himself in an almost arrogant manner as an Indian monk who intends to distribute healing medication, the monk replies to Ximen Qing's further request with minimal utterances. The repetition of straightforward subject-predicate combinations—"I do! I do!" and "I'll come! I'll come!"—problematizes his ability to self-narrate. Desire does not lend itself to verbal articulation. As an embodiment of desire, the monk is at a loss for words. In contrast, once awakened by Ximen Qing, the monk avails himself of his unbridled propensity for action. He not only "jerk[s] himself erect" and "spr[ings] up from his relaxed position" in front of Ximen Qing, he is also blessed with superhuman energy and speed. At the invitation of Ximen Qing, the monk walks to Ximen's mansion faster than his host, who rides a donkey, and feels at ease as he overindulges himself in uncontrolled drinking and eating in a hall decorated with sexually suggestive symbols. Ximen Qing hence gives in to the monk's power in ways acutely captured in allegorical narrative.

Ximen Qing's unsuccessful race with the monk anticipates his own destiny. He inadvertently awakens his monstrous carnality but lacks the means to bring it under control. The therapeutic prescription the monk bestows on Ximen eventually backfires on him. Notably, the motif of awakening can be traced to the mythological moment when Song Jiang receives the Black Goddess's prophetic instruction in chapter 42 of *Outlaws*, an equally symbolic encounter that guides him toward self-redemption. This is the moment when Song Jiang becomes aware of his own mission. However, the path the goddess of war points out to him does not elevate him above the existing sociopolitical order; nor does it lead him toward a peaceful reconciliation with it. Before her departure, the goddess leaves him with a "heavenly book" (天書) to consult at the moment of crisis while advising him not to share it with others. According to the goddess, Song Jiang has not cleansed his "evil heart" (魔心) entirely (Shi and Luo, *Marshes* 2: 409; *Shuihu zhuan* [Renmin wenxue chubanshe] 1: 559). In order to return to heaven, he must continue to exercise caution in self-cultivation without the slightest slip. As the turning point in his lifelong odyssey, Song's dreamlike encounter with the goddess is paradoxically illuminating and misleading with respect to his self-awareness. From this perspective, *Outlaws* provides an indispensable reference point for complicating our interpretation of Ximen Qing's allegorical contact with the monk. Granted, the Indian monk is incommensurate with the goddess of war. Although Ximen Qing worships him as a godlike figure, he is merely a disguised prophecy of Ximen's unchecked self, portending the indescribable terror of sexual appetite and conquest. Nevertheless, not unlike the goddess, the monk does not forget to give Ximen verbal admonition. He makes explicit toward the end of the episode that the aphrodisiac he prescribes—a token of sexual enlightenment—should not be overdosed. As the monk sheds his responsibility for the most likely consequences, he also abandons Ximen to the impossible struggle of coping with his own thirst for bodily pleasure that will end with a gruesome death.

Despite his persistent attempt to win the recognition of the imperial court and society, Song Jiang hardly succeeds in reining in his own rebellious, violent impulse, an idea embodied by his sworn brother Li Kui, both a foil to pretense and a menace to the civilized order (Hsia 75–114). Song Jiang's struggle to silence Li Kui turns out to be part of the former's self-censorship. Only when Song Jiang lets his guard down does he slur out a verse testifying to his ambition to dethrone the emperor through bloodshed, which perfectly echoes Li Kui's frequent assertions. The Indian monk who makes only a transitory appearance in *Plum* resembles Li Kui to some extent, but unlike Song Jiang, Ximen Qing fails to recognize him, much less to exercise any conscious control over him. Allowing lust to dominate his life, Ximen Qing is a slave to an insatiable master to whom he owes nothing less than his life.

It is possible to argue that *Plum* presents its male protagonist, Ximen Qing, as the personification of its own narrative adventures. Compared with the heroes of historical romances and heroic sagas, Ximen is a latecomer; with an obscure family background and no lineage, he seems to come from nowhere. However, he is also a self-made man capable of creating his own financial empire, and he succeeds as a conqueror by appropriating the property of others. *Plum* is fully aware of its belatedness in developing its own narrative, which takes the form of supplementary writing; it ushers in a new paradigm of what may be called novel writing through its constructive and multilayered appropriation of *Outlaws* and a multiplicity of other fictional and nonfictional contemporaneous texts. It transforms themes, tropes, and expressions derived from *Outlaws* into a polytextual narrative frame while also interweaving what-if scenarios. Much like *Don Quixote*, *Plum* represents the thematic transition from legendary saga to ordinary life through narrative innovation. Accordingly, an array of figural devices and rewriting techniques are employed to forge intertextual connections between *Outlaws* and *Plum* in terms of structure and language. As Jorge Luis Borges acutely points out, "The fact is that every writer creates his own precursors. His work modifies our conception of the past, as it will modify the future" (192). By extracting new meaning from *Outlaws* through the devices of substitution, alteration, and parody, *Plum* refashions the way readers make sense of its predecessor. Although *Plum*'s author apparently positions *Outlaws* as its precursor in diachronic terms, he also manages to knit the textural elements of *Outlaws* into a synchronic space, thereby accommodating the latter's grand narrative of heroic adventures to the values of commerce. By virtue of polytextual configuration, *Plum* defines itself as an encyclopedic novel, as a book of books, one that predicates the mechanism of signification on all the strands incorporated into and reconfigured within its own narrative fabric.

NOTES

I want to thank Yifan Zhang for his assistance with this essay and a much longer version published in Chinese in 2016: Shang Wei 商偉, "Fushi xiaoshuo de goucheng: cong *Shuihu zhuan* dao *Jinpingmei cihua*" 複式小說的構成: 從《水滸傳》到《金瓶梅詞話》 ("The Formation of a Polytextual Novel: From *Outlaws of the Marsh* to *Plum in the Golden Vase: A Ballad Tale*"), *Fudan daxue xuebao* 復旦大學學報 (*Fudan Journal* [Social Sciences Edition]), 2016, no. 6, pp. 30–58.

[1] Leaving aside the question of translation for the time being, what is referred to as a novel can hardly be taken as given. The genre has its own complex history in early modern Europe. Once described by Virginia Woolf as the "most pliable of all forms," the novel seems to have always defied exact definition (84). With this caveat in mind, I do not advocate a comparative study of novels across time and space. Rather, I draw on early modern European novels only as part of my frame of reference to help throw into relief some of *Plum*'s salient features.

[2] Jiangnan (literally, "South of the Yangtze") is a historically prosperous geographic area referring to lands immediately south of the lower reaches of the Yangtze River, including the important cities Hangzhou, Nanjing, and Suzhou.

[3] Unless otherwise noted, parenthetical citations refer to Roy's translation, *The Plum in the Golden Vase*, and to *Jin Ping Mei cihua* 金瓶梅詞話 (*Plum in the Golden Vase: A Ballad Tale*).

[4] Roy renders this phrase differently: "You're just what the doctor ordered" (1.17.340, 1.19.399).

The Plum in the Golden Vase
and The Story of the Stone

Mary Scott

The great Chinese literati novels, taken as a group, are pervasively, imaginatively intertextual. Just as the author of *The Plum in the Golden Vase* (*Jin Ping Mei* 金瓶梅) borrowed the story of Wu Song (Wu Sung), Pan Jinlian (P'an Chinlien), and Ximen Qing (Hsi-men Ch'ing) from *Outlaws of the Marsh* (*Shuihu zhuan* 水滸傳), the great eighteenth-century novel *The Story of the Stone* (*Honglou meng* 紅樓夢), by Cao Xueqin 曹雪芹 (1715?–63), clearly shows the author's familiarity with *Plum*. Because the story of the historical Cao family's fall from grace is so easily framed as a cautionary tale about the consequences of both sexual and financial excess, *Plum*—in the commentary edition of the great seventeenth-century critic Zhang Zhupo 張竹坡 (1670–98), the one that circulated in Cao's lifetime—must have been a particularly suggestive guide to the art of writing fiction for Cao.

Plum is the most technically and thematically innovative of the great works of Chinese fiction before *Stone*. It initiated a shift in the concerns of fiction from public life to private life: from questions of power, status, loyalty, and honor among men to the increasingly pressing question of desire (*qing* 情) in the private lives of men and—for the first time—women. Unlike its predecessors, *Plum* is only minimally based on earlier materials, and where its predecessor novels are essentially episodic, *Plum* is a tightly constructed whole that focuses on Ximen Qing, his six wives, and their servants, lovers, neighbors, patrons, and dependents. As Zhang Zhupo puts it, "The hundred chapters of this work constitute a single chapter. Only if you expand your view until you can read it as a single chapter will you be able to appreciate its overall structure" (一百回是一回, 必須放開眼光, 作一回讀, 乃知其起盡處.; "How to Read the *Chin P'ing Mei*" 224; *ZZP* 24b). This sustained focus puts a premium on the art of managing many narrative lines simultaneously and developing characters incrementally over a long period. Zhang devotes his commentary to showing how skillfully the author does this and what his motives might have been.

Stone's author learned from *Plum* to advance a narrative by alternating depictions of a complementary pair of women, often through their surrogates. Like *Plum*, *Stone* has two major—and very different—female characters, Lin Daiyu and Xue Baochai, who compete for the favor of the male protagonist, Jia Baoyu. Zhang Zhupo describes this technique as follows:

> [The writer] depicts a Pan Jinlian and then goes on to depict a Li Ping'er [Li P'ing-erh]. This could be described as repetitive, yet from first to last, whether they are together or apart, there is never the slightest confusion

between them in their words or acts. . . . All of these are examples of the marvelous way in which the author purposely duplicates characters and yet succeeds in individualizing each character so that they all remain distinct.   ("How to Read the *Chin P'ing Mei*" 226)

寫一金蓮. 更寫一瓶兒. 可謂犯矣. 然又始終聚散. 其言語舉動又各各不亂一絲.... 皆特特犯手. 卻又個個一款. 絕不相同.   (ZZP 25a)

Zhang notes how the depictions of the main female characters are amplified by surrogates:

Li Guijie [Li Kuei-chieh] and Wu Yin'er [Wu Yin-erh] are purposeful duplications of Pan Jinlian and Li Ping'er, respectively, demonstrating that by taste and affinity the latter pair are indistinguishable from prostitutes and that though they may never have actually engaged in that trade, their wantonness and depravity are such that they not only show the same proclivities as prostitutes, but will go even further than they do.
                                    ("How to Read the *Chin P'ing Mei*" 213)

而於中寫桂姐, 特犯金蓮; 寫銀姐特煩瓶兒; 又見金, 瓶 二人, 其氣味聲息, 已全通娼家. 雖未身為倚門之人, 而淫心亂行, 實臭味相投, 彼娼婦猶步後塵矣.   (ZZP 20a)

Zhang Xinzhi 張新之 (fl. 1828–50), one of the most thoughtful of the later *Stone* critics, and who was especially interested in textual patterning, describes the alternation and contrast of the main female characters and their surrogates in *Stone* in similar terms:

In this book Baochai and Daiyu are presented in tandem with each other. The maids Aroma and Skybright are the "shadows" of these two characters. At every point where a scene involving Baoyu and Daiyu is presented, it is always Baochai who is taken up for treatment immediately after. When scenes involving Baoyu and Baochai are depicted it is always Daiyu who is taken up for treatment immediately after. Failing that, Aroma may be used as a substitute for Baochai, or Skybright may be used to substitute for Daiyu, while occasionally attention is turned to a third party, but such cases are never far removed from the original situation. This is a major compositional principle of the entire text from which the author never strays by even as much as a hair, retaining it firm and unshakeable.
                                    (Plaks, "How to Read" 330–31)

是書釵, 黛為比肩, 襲人, 晴雯乃二人影子也. 凡寫寶玉同黛玉事跡, 接寫者必是寶釵; 寫寶玉同寶釵事跡, 接寫者必是黛玉. 否則用襲人代釵, 用晴雯代黛. 間有接以他人者, 而仍不脫本處. 乃是一絲不走, 牢不可破, 通體大章法.
                                    (Zhang Xinzhi 65)

The symmetry between the major characters' acts and their consequences in the novel, which expresses a principle of retributive justice shared by all three of the major religious traditions of China, is echoed and underlined by the minor, surrogate characters' violations of propriety. If the reader apprehends this pattern—expressed in the proverb "If the upper beam is not straight, the lower ones will certainly be crooked" (上樑不正下樑歪)—they can see past the intricate, dazzling surface of the narrative to grasp its moral implications.[1]

Plum evokes the world of seventeenth-century life so persuasively that some have read it as a roman à clef, as some have read *Stone*. Zhang Zhupo cautions us against such readings: "If you read [*Plum*] as a description of actual events you will be deceived by it. You must read it as a work of literature in order not to be deceived by it" (看金瓶, 把他當事實看便被他瞞過, 必須把他當文章看, 方不被他瞞過也. 四十; "How to Read the *Chin P'ing Mei*" 224; *ZZP* 24b).

In *Plum*, the expressive range of language in the novel is substantially broadened to include everything from the coarsest vernacular to subtle chains of metaphors to quotations from plays, Buddhist scripture, and legal documents. Zhang Zhupo's "Witty Turns of Phrase in *Jin Ping Mei*, the First Marvelous Book" ("Diyi qishu *Jin Ping Mei* qu tan" 第一奇書金瓶梅趣談) lists examples of *Plum*'s pathbreaking realism in the use of vivid vernacular speech (*ZZP* 10a–11a), but Zhang is even more interested in figurative language as a technique for narrative management. In "A Theory of Hidden Meanings" ("Yuyi shuo" 寓意說) he explicates *Plum*'s use of figurative language: puns and double entendres on the names of characters, places, and objects meant to link the characters' actions and their outcomes across a wide expanse of narrative time (6a–10a). Reading its title as a rebus of the names Jinlian ("Golden Lotus"), Ping'er ("Lady of the Vase"), and Chunmei ("Spring Plum"), Zhang extends the image of plum blossoms in a golden vase to other major characters through puns and linked images from well-known lines of poetry. He points out foreshadowing devices that take the form of horoscopes, medical prescriptions, dominoes, wine games, and other kinds of riddling language; notes the ways that the writer uses gatherings on birthdays and symbolically significant holidays to contrast certain characters and show the consequences of passing time; and expresses a connoisseur's delight in quotations from songs and plays that provide ironic commentary or prefigure events to come.

Stone uses all these devices with—if anything—an even richer and more subtle patterning. Chapter 5 is the best-known example: the Fairy Disenchantment's cryptic registers of the young women in Jia Baoyu's life foreshadow their eventual fates in much the same way that—as Zhang Zhupo points out—Wu the Immortal's horoscopes for Ximen Qing's wives do in chapter 29 of *Plum*. *Stone*'s use of the omniscient, itinerant Buddhist and Daoist, who periodically appear to make oracular pronouncements that are borne out once they have vanished, also recalls Zhang's comment on such figures in *Plum*:

First Wu the Immortal surveys Ximen Qing's household at its height, then Huang Zhen-ren [His Holiness Huang] sustains it somewhat in its decline [chapter 66], and finally Master Pujing purges the sins of the main characters [chapter 100]. The ways in which these episodes are correlated are highly significant.   ("How to Read the *Chin P'ing Mei*" 202)

先是吳神仙總覽其盛, 後是黃真人少扶其衰, 末是普淨師一洗其業, 是此書大照應處.   (ZZP 16b)

Like the social world it depicts, *Plum* is saturated with theatrical performances, not just in its frequent citations from plays but also in its adoption of some of the narrative conventions of the theater. The characters in both *Stone* and *Plum* habitually quote from and comment on plays in their conversations, as Baoyu and Daiyu do with their favorite lines from the romantic dramas *Western Chamber* (*Xixiangji* 西廂记) and *Peony Pavilion* (*Mudanting* 牡丹亭), or even burst into song themselves, as Ximen Qing and Wu Yueniang (Wu Yüeh-niang) do while he is on his deathbed. *Stone* conspicuously shares such theatrical conventions as the garden setting where valuables and love tokens are lost or stolen or misplaced or found anew, propelling the narrative forward. Dropped handkerchiefs and lost hairpins abound in both novels, each signaling a violation of the moral order by characters distracted by money or sexual desire.

Zhang Zhupo's prefatory essay "Ximen Qing's Compound" ("Ximen Qing fangwu" 西門慶房屋) emphasizes the garden's importance in determining the story's course. Zhang notes that

> [i]n reading [*Plum*] we must pay attention to the significant features of the spatial setting. These include the location of Pan Jinlian and Chunmei in one place and Li Ping'er in another and the placing of all three of them in the single larger setting of the front garden. The fact that Pan Jinlian and Chunmei are placed together accentuates the isolation of Li Ping'er. The fact that Pan Jinlian and Li Ping'er live close to each other in the garden allows their jealousy to flourish, while the fact that Wu Yueniang lives far removed from them gives Chen Jingji his chance to get at Pan Jinlian.
> ("How to Read the *Chin P'ing Mei*" 205)

讀金瓶, 須看其大間架處, 則分金, 梅在一起, 分瓶兒在一處, 又彼合金, 瓶, 梅在前院一處. 金, 梅合而瓶兒孤, 前院近而金, 瓶妒, 月娘遠而經濟得以下手也.   (ZZP 17b)

Plum's garden setting is a particularly obvious inspiration for *Stone*, several of whose later commentators include detailed essays on *Stone*'s garden. In both novels the garden is built and occupied by the main characters during the first twenty chapters and is gradually abandoned to ruin in the last twenty chapters. Its seasons are a vehicle for the motif of hot and cold, for linked metaphors involving plants and flowers, and for references to all the implications of the word *chun* 春, which means not only "springtime" but also "youth," "sex," and "fecundity." The garden is a place that creates the illusion that time has stopped and the consequences of one's actions have been suspended, a place where the protagonist's desires can be indulged without restraint. Like Ximen Qing's garden, which incorporates the garden that once belonged to the adulterous Li Ping'er and her first husband, Hua Zixu (Hua Tzu-hsü), *Stone's* Prospect Garden incorporates an earlier garden already tainted by sexual misconduct.[2]

The trope of the extravagant pleasure garden that ends in ruin is very old. *Plum* includes ominous direct references to one of the most famous ones, the twelfth-century Emperor Huizong's proverbially extravagant garden, which is causally linked in the folk-historical imagination to the events described in the last chapters of *Plum*, in which Wu Yueniang is caught up in the tide of refugees when an invasion topples the dynasty. The emperor's garden is figuratively linked to Ximen Qing's garden through his many corrupt dealings with the imperial court and by court eunuchs' and officials' repeated visits to the garden (Plaks, *Four Masterworks* 55–180). The link between *Stone's* Prospect Garden and imperial favor are obvious: the garden is built to celebrate the elevation of the Jias' eldest daughter to the rank of imperial concubine, and it dwindles into ruin after the Jias' corrupt dealings are exposed and their holdings confiscated by the court.

Many scenes in *Stone* resemble scenes in *Plum*. The commentator known by the pseudonym Red Inkstone (Zhiyanzhai 脂硯斋) compares chapter 28 of *Stone*, when Baoyu joins the loutish Xue Pan and his friend Feng Ziying to drink and play wine riddles with a singing-girl, to Ximen Qing's revels in chapters 11 and 12 of *Plum* (Yu Pingbo 400). Grandmother Jia's prayer for her children and grandchildren in chapter 106 of *Stone* resembles Yueniang's prayer in chapter 21 of *Plum* that Ximen Qing will eventually have children, and commentators reproach both women for favoritism and lax household governance. There are similar scenes of witchcraft motivated by jealousy: In chapter 25 of *Stone*, Zhao Yiniang enlists Mother Ma to cast a spell on Baoyu and Wang Xifeng, which parallels the spell Jinlian casts on Li Guijie in chapter 12 of *Plum*. Xia Jingui's vicious quarrel with her mother-in-law, Madame Xue, in chapter 83 of *Stone* resembles the quarrel between Jinlian and Wu Yueniang in chapter 75 of *Plum*. Pang Chunmei (P'ang Ch'un-mei) is evicted from Ximen Qing's household just as Baoyu's maid Skybright is evicted from the Prospect Garden, signaling in both cases that the novel's garden world has begun to disintegrate. Many other patterns in *Stone* also suggest an indebtedness to *Plum*: dreams that express the psychology of the dreamer; the mostly offstage presence of the Zhen family, whose story parallels the Jia family's story in the same way that the rise of the Qiao family is linked to that of Ximen's household. Corrupt eunuchs, falsely pious Buddhist nuns, temperamental female performers, sycophantic dependents, and backstabbing friends play similar roles in both novels.

In particular, the narrative in chapters 63–69 of *Stone* that describes Wang Xifeng's marriage to Jia Lian, her jealousy about his multiple affairs, and her vengeance on his secret concubine, You Erjie, depicts a jealous triangular relationship that strongly resembles the one that dominates *Plum* from chapter 13 to chapter 63. Xifeng, whose sharp-tongued wit and talent for social manipulation owe a good deal to *Plum*'s depiction of Pan Jinlian, has power over the household finances, and it becomes clear early in the novel that she is involved in bribery and loan-sharking. Her servant and right-hand man is given the same name as Ximen Qing's manservant Laiwang (Lai-wang). Xifeng's husband, Jia Lian, is a libertine whose amours with Mistress Duo and Bao Er's wife echo Ximen Qing's affairs with his servants' wives. Jia Lian's clandestine second household with You Erjie, whose gentleness, passivity, and somewhat tarnished sexual history strongly recall Li Ping'er, ends when Xifeng causes You Erjie's suicide with a calculating cruelty reminiscent of Pan Jinlian's vicious maneuvers against her rival, Ping'er. Meanwhile, a servant's opinion sheds new light on a major character: cynical comments made by Ximen Qing's manservant Dai'an (Tai-an) about his master's affection for Li Ping'er mirror those made by Jia Lian's manservant about Wang Xifeng's malevolence and Erjie's kindness.

The first to comment on the resemblance between *Stone* and *Plum* was Red Inkstone, one of several people close to Cao Xueqin who wrote comments on the latter's manuscript even as it was being written and circulated in fragmentary form in the mid–eighteenth century. In commentary to chapter 13, Red Inkstone maintains that *Stone* is "[w]ritten so that every detail strikes home and without a single facile word, profoundly capturing the hidden shape of *Plum in a Golden Vase*" (寫個個皆到, 全無安逸之筆, 深得金瓶梅壺奧; my trans.; Yu Pingbo 164).

Much of chapters 10–13 of *Stone* deals with Qinshi's mysterious wasting illness and subsequent death from it. Qinshi, whose surname puns on the word for passionate love (*qing* 情), is the much-beloved young daughter-in-law of the Ning household, in whose room Baoyu dreams of a visit to the Fairy Disenchantment's garden that culminates in his sexual dream-encounter with the fairy's little sister Jianmei, who eventually emerges in Baoyu's dream-logic as Qinshi herself (ch. 5). In a conspicuous excess of grief at Qinshi's death, her father-in-law, Jia Zhen, vows to spare no expense for the funeral. Red Inkstone's comment comes when Jia Zhen accepts Xue Pan's offer of a set of outrageously expensive coffin boards, a clear violation of ritual propriety for an extremely junior family member, as Xue Pan's cousin Jia Zheng points out. Jia Zhen also purchases official rank for his son, Jia Rong, to enhance the funeral's splendor. In an example of what Zhang Zhupo would have called *yaodui* 遙對, "matching from a distance," Qinshi's egregiously grand funeral is mirrored in chapter 110 of *Stone* with the funeral of Grandmother Jia, the most senior member of the family, which is rushed, inadequate, and altogether ritually inappropriate to her rank. Red Inkstone's comment shows not only that he was familiar with *Plum* but also that he assumed *Plum* had a "hidden shape" that the writer of *Stone* was trying to capture in his own writing, and that he succeeded with Qinshi's story, which is ultimately about the consequences of violating proper family relations (Plaks, *Archetype* 208).

Red Inkstone's comments show that some of *Stone*'s earliest readers insisted on excising certain details from the text to avoid exposing a case of incest in Cao Xueqin's own family thirty years earlier. In that version, now lost, Qinshi hangs herself in the Ning family garden out of shame over her incestuous affair with Jia Zhen. Some details from the original version remain, notably the servant Jiao Da's drunken accusation that Jia Zhen "pokes in the ashes," meaning that the latter has committed incest with his daughter-in-law:

> "Who would ever have believed the Old Master could spawn this filthy lot of animals?" he bawled. "Up to their dirty little tricks every day. I know. Father-in-law pokes in the ashes. Auntie has it off with nevvy. Do you think I don't know what you're all up to? Oh, we 'hide our broken arm in our sleeve'; but you don't fool me."
>
> (Hawkes and Minford, *Story* [Fan Shengyu] 1: 185)

> 哪裏承望到如今生下這些畜生來！每日偷勾戲雞，爬灰的爬灰，養小叔子的養小叔子，我什麼不知道？咱們 '胳膊折了袖子裡藏'！   (1: 184)

All this strongly resembles the decline and death of Li Ping'er (*Plum* chs. 61–64), Ximen Qing's favorite wife, the wife of his sworn brother Hua Zixu until Ximen's flagrant affair with her (*Plum* ch. 13). Li Ping'er's funeral, with its extravagant coffin boards and inappropriate use of honorifics to add prestige to her funeral banner, is far out of proportion to her low status as Ximen Qing's dubiously acquired sixth wife. Ximen Qing's own death follows not long afterward. His funeral is much less grand and carefully planned when compared with Ping'er's funeral, with far fewer mourners, and when he is scarcely cold in his grave his wives, friends, and servants almost instantly steal from him, betray him sexually, renege on debts, or simply disappear (Plaks, *Four Masterworks* 72–120).

Like *Plum*, *Stone* focuses above all on violations of family hierarchy and ritual propriety, acts that erase distinctions between elders and juniors, masters and servants, husbands and wives, wives and courtesans. Zhang Zhupo's "Theory of Outraged Filial Piety" ("Ku xiao shuo" 苦孝说) equates such violations of family hierarchy with *Plum*'s repeated examples of official corruption, which link Ximen Qing's household to the highest levels of the imperial court, making it clear that this family is a metonym for the entire empire's misrule (*ZZP* 12a–12b; Plaks, *Four Masterworks* 156–80).

All this is true of *Stone* too. Qinshi, Jia Zhen, Wang Xifeng, and Jia Lian are the most flagrant examples, but in *Stone* proper hierarchical relations are routinely violated, whether by seniors who show favoritism or abdicate responsibility for their younger family members—Grandmother Jia and Jia Jing come to mind here—or by overly lenient masters and overweening maids, or by lecherous masters who prey on their servants, or by masters who use their power and wealth to corrupt justice. In *Stone*, as in *Plum*, the family's corruption is marked by the flow of eunuch staff members of the imperial household, imperial regalia, and objects made in palace workshops into the family's house and garden. As Zhang Zhupo explains in "General Outline" ("Da lue" 大略), one of his prefatory essays to *Plum*:

> Nothing in the world is more genuine than the canonical human relationships, and nothing is more false than money and sex. . . . With fathers and sons, or elder and younger brothers, it's like water from the same source, different branches of the same stream, which can be drawn on in a completely natural way. But if there really is a corrupt intention that leads to false fathers and false sons, false elder and younger brothers—if that can be false, then what cannot be false? If one could genuinely treat wealth and high rank as false and illusory, then those who suffer real poverty and disgrace could also [understand it as] false. Wealth and rank are hot. When one is hot, one accepts it as reality. Poverty and humble status are cold. When one is cold, then wealth that had once been real turns out to be an illusion. Unexpectedly, the words "hot" and "cold" turn out to reverse the categories "real" and "illusory," and once one has reached that point, there's no certainty about either "hot" or "cold." If today's cold becomes tomorrow's heat, then today's reality has been rendered illusory and one's illusions about tomorrow have become reality.　　　　　　　(my trans.)

> 天下最真者莫若倫常. 最假者莫若財色 . . . 若夫父子兄弟如水同源, 如水同, 流分枝引, 莫不天成. 乃竟有假父假弟之蕫意, 此可假孰不可假. 將富貴而假者可真, 貧賤而真者亦假. 富貴熱也. 熱則無不真. 貧賤冷也. 冷則無不假. 不謂冷熱二字顛倒真假. 一至於此, 然而冷熱亦無定矣. 今日冷而明日熱, 則今日真者假, 而明日假者真.　　　　　　　(*ZZP* 4b)

In this passage Zhang equates "heat" with wealth, high social status, and abundant social connections, while "cold" is associated with poverty, disgrace, and isolation. Both are ultimately transient and illusory, but, as in *Stone*, "heat" is an illusion that can seem all too real. Kin relations—which can be denied or falsified when family hierarchy and ritual propriety are violated by individual desires for money or sex—are no guarantee against eventual "cold" consequences. For example, in chapter 1 of Zhang's commentary edition of *Plum*, the chapter title "Ximen Qing Warmly Entertains Ten Sworn Brothers / Wu the Second Has a Cold Encounter with His Own Brother's Wife" (西門慶熱接十兄弟／武二郎冷遇親哥嫂) sets up the expectation that "hot" will turn "cold" and establishes the motif of false kin relations that will be developed through the rest of the novel.

Stone also uses images of heat and cold to show the vagaries of fate. Chapter 1 plays on the contrast between a long, hot summer day, when Zhen Shiyin has a mysterious dream, a harbinger of his fall from contented prosperity to ruin, and the icy cold night of the Lantern Festival, when Zhen's baby daughter is kidnapped, his house burns down, and he becomes a half-mad wandering Daoist.

Meanwhile, Zhen's impoverished friend Jia Yucun has passed the examinations and risen to the pinnacle of wealth and worldly success. Chapter 2 introduces a minor character who first describes the Jia family to Jia Yucun. This man's unusual surname, Leng 冷, or "cold," which subtly contradicts his personal name, Zixing 子興, "a son emerges" or "a seed sprouts," epitomizes the story of the family's decline, which he sees as a consequence of their moral decay and fiscal indiscipline. Cold details are interspersed with hot ones in both texts, often in seasonal scenes in the garden, where Jia Baoyu's presence among the girls is itself a violation of conventional family ritual decorum.

Some nineteenth-century *Stone* commentators not only echo Zhang Zhupo's comments on narrative technique and figurative language but also read *Stone* as a further working out of *Plum*'s themes. Zhang Xinzhi, for example, remarks that

> [t]he [*Stone*] conceals within itself a [*Plum*]. That is why [Baoyu is said to indulge in] "excess of the mind" [*yiyin* 意淫]. For [*Plum*] we have the theory of frustrated filiality [*ku xiao shuo* 苦孝說]; accordingly that book concludes explicitly with the concept of filial piety. This book, on the other hand, concludes with a vague implication of filiality. As for the hidden suffering contained in this work, it is far deeper than that of the author of [*Plum*]. [*Plum*] works out the concepts of "cold" and "heat." This book also works out the concepts of "cold" and "heat." [*Plum*] works out the concepts of money and sex. This book also works out the concepts of money and sex.   (Plaks, "How to Read" 327–28)

> 《石頭記》是暗《金瓶梅》, 故曰 "意淫".《金瓶梅》有苦孝說, 因明以孝字結;《石頭記》則暗以孝字結. 至其隱痛, 較作《金瓶梅》者尤深.《金瓶梅》演冷熱, 此書亦演冷熱;《金瓶梅》演財色. 此書亦演財色.
>   (Zhang Xinzhi 63–64)

Zhang Xinzhi warns, moreover, that "[*Stone*] goes even further than [*Plum*] in producing dangerous effects, in that readers are prone to recognize only its immediate surface, failing to perceive what lies on the other side" (石頭記一書, 不惟膾炙人口, 亦且鑴刻人心, 移易性情, 較金瓶梅尤造孽, 以讀者但知正面, 而不知反面也; Plaks, "How to Read" 323; Zhang Xinzhi 63–64). Here Zhang refers to chapter 12 of *Stone* and its story of Jia Rui's death by masturbatory excess after disregarding a Daoist's repeated warnings not to turn over the magic mirror that shows the image of a memento mori, a human skull, on the reverse side. Instead, he gazes insatiably on the alluring figure of Wang Xifeng on the forbidden side of the mirror. The mirror is a figure for the mind, encompassing both the perfect clarity with which the mind can reflect the world as well as the passionate illusions that can cloud the mind. The comment, which takes this mirror as a metaphor for the novel itself, reminds us that at least some readers took these novels seriously, as exercises in the cultivation of the mind. As one nineteenth-century *Stone* commentator put it, "Confucian scholars 'rectify the mind,' Daoists 'refine the mind,' Buddhists 'discipline the mind.' Clearly 'mind' is everywhere and enters into everything, and the single fear is that it will enter irrecoverably into wrongdoing; thus they 'rectify,' 'refine,' and 'discipline' in order to restrain it" (儒家正心, 道者煉心, 釋輩戒心. 可見此心無有不到, 無不能入者, 獨畏其入於邪而不反, 故用正煉戒以縛之; my trans.; Yu Pingbo 158). And the "dangerous effects"? Zhang Xinzhi recognized, perhaps, that *Stone*'s sorrowful, nostalgic tone has far more emotional appeal than does *Plum*'s brilliant but ice-cold moralism, and that *Stone* is therefore all the less likely to free the reader from the illusions of *qing* ("love" or "passionate feeling"). *Plum* announces itself at the outset as a book about the dangers of passionate feeling, but for all that, its characters have little *qing* for one another: there is plenty of lust but not much love. Ximen Qing learns nothing from his sexual adventures. Even his attachment to Li Ping'er, though apparently heartfelt, does not make him a wiser or more moderate man. Instead, it is the reader who can either vicariously wallow in Ximen Qing's lust or avoid Ximen Qing's fate by heeding the novel's warning against the consequences of lust. When Ximen Qing's posthumous son and reincarnation, Xiaoge (Hsiao-ko, "Filial Son" or "Mourning Son"), born at the moment of Ximen Qing's death, is wafted away by Wu the Immortal to expiate his father's life of sexual excess, it is the reader, not Xiaoge, who takes the lesson to heart.

Near the end of *Stone*, when Baoyu wordlessly meets and bows to his father in a farewell gesture of filiality (*xiao* 孝), the reader shares the suffering that has brought Baoyu to that point. *Stone*, like *Plum*, is about the difference between passionate feeling (*qing* 情) and sexual excess (*yin* 淫), but it distinguishes the two with far more delicacy than *Plum* does, often through the intersection of the world of Wang Xifeng, Jia Lian, and other adults outside the garden, who are motivated by money and sex, and the world of the young people in the garden, especially Baoyu and Daiyu, whose innocent love expresses itself in their avatars, the Stone and Flower of chapter 1 of *Stone*. The world of Baoyu and Daiyu is more like the romantic vision of the seventeenth-century playwright Tang Xianzu's *Peony Pavilion*, in which the heroine wastes away and dies of love but is eventually resurrected through the power of love itself. Daiyu sees the world that way, as shown by her tacitly self-referential quotation from *Peony Pavilion* in the famous flower-burying scene (*Stone* ch. 23)—and so does Baoyu, at least at first.

In chapter 5 of *Stone*, the Fairy Disenchantment accuses Baoyu of *yiyin* 意淫 ("lust of the mind") and arranges his dream-encounter with Qinshi to shock him into awareness of love's consequences, to no immediate avail. Another possible translation of *yiyin* is "will to excess," which extends the term beyond mere sexual desire to encompass both romantic love and the human desire for more of everything, including life itself. This is the dilemma of *qing*.

Plum unambiguously affirms the need to discipline passionate feeling for the sake of social order. *Stone* can be read that way too, but it has often been read as affirming love in the face of repressive social convention. Baoyu's decision, after Daiyu's death, to abandon his family for the life of a wandering monk seems to affirm the desires of the self over the demands of civilization. Yet Baoyu's choice to abandon his worldly self and worldly desires can be read as selfishness, itself a form of desire. He has carried out his social obligations by passing the examinations and fathering a son, gestures that are simultaneously filial and renunciatory, but what of the parents, wife, and son he has left behind?

Readers have succumbed now and then to the temptation to treat these characters as real people, even in the knowledge that the vivid mimetic quality of both novels is the result of symmetry and mirroring at many levels through an intricate network of puns and metaphors that can only be partially rendered in translation. Mimesis, then, is the front of the Daoist's mirror, but it is delusory. The patterns on the mirror's reverse side, figurative language itself, are more real, if only by comparison. A second reading—or the help of a commentator—may convince the reader that *Stone*'s evocations of *Plum* are not merely imitations of *Plum*'s mimetic surface but also an important thread in the tapestry of *Stone*'s language.

NOTES

[1] This well-known phrase, which illustrates the principle that bad behavior of those in authority is imitated by their subordinates, appears in chapters 26 and 78 of *Plum*: "If the ridgepole is not straight, / The rafters will be crooked" (上梁不正下梁歪; Roy, *Plum* 2.26.171–72, 4.78.585; *JPMCH* 26.8b, 78.5a). Roy notes seven different sources in drama, stories, and *baozhuan* (Buddhist tales) where this phrase is used (*Plum* 4.78n11).

[2] See Plaks, *Archetype* 146–211 for an extended discussion of the allegorical dimensions of the Chinese literary garden.

Digital Approaches
to *The Plum in the Golden Vase*

Paul Vierthaler

The Plum in the Golden Vase (*Jin Ping Mei* 金瓶梅) is a complex and nuanced novel that rewards the close reader. Yet after hundreds of years of careful reading, qualitative analyses, and even attempts at small-scale quantitative analyses, the text still hides many mysteries. Some are exceedingly difficult to solve, such as the identity of the author. Others are better understood but open to additional lines of evidence: How unique is *Plum*'s style? What are its sources and what do these tell us about its creation? The digitization of the novel and the recent development of computational tools offer a unique set of approaches that complement traditional research and that may help unravel *Plum*'s remaining secrets.

In this essay I introduce a variety of resources and tools that will be of interest to readers and students of *Plum in the Golden Vase*. Projects in the digital humanities, a field that encompasses a wide variety of approaches (Terras et al.), generally fall into three categories: presentation, access, and analysis. The presentation of digital information through websites and curated museum exhibits is how most engage with the digital humanities, but access to digital materials and to the possibilities of digital analysis are the core concern for the digital scholar of *Plum*.

Digital repositories of Chinese texts are rapidly expanding and provide access to both image scans and full-text versions of early editions of *Plum*, opening new avenues of content analysis for scholars. Digital tools are also quickly developing, and even the most basic of these can be extremely powerful. Scholars can use highly customizable searches to find textual patterns. They can leverage text-alignment algorithms to highlight minute differences in different editions. Readers can enhance their qualitative appreciation of style with a quantification of the style of a document. More ambitious researchers can use machine-learning techniques that aggregate large amounts of information to categorize documents and potentially uncover the novel's author. Many of these methods are easy to use and accessible, while others have a steeper learning curve and require significant investment in acquiring technical skills. Some tools are highly refined and are based on methods developed in the early twentieth century, while others are still only experimental. The primary downside of digital tools and resources is that some may have a short shelf life and may eventually become defunct or obsolete. All these approaches and materials, however, can help us better understand *Plum* on its own, in relation to its multiple editions, and in comparison with a larger corpus of Chinese texts.

Digital Editions

Access to high-quality electronic editions of Chinese texts is a necessary pre-condition for conducting accurate and meaningful digital studies of *Plum in the Golden Vase*. Fortunately, there has been a proliferation of digital editions over the last several decades, but this expansion comes with some caveats. Academic databases, for example, contain faithful reproductions of many pre-1911 Chinese texts. Extracting texts for analysis, however, is difficult; many academic databases require paid subscriptions and prohibit bulk analysis of materials. Open-source repositories, on the other hand, make their contents freely available. Some free collections of texts, particularly those created by avid nonspecialist fans of Chinese literature, are vaguely sourced and may contain inaccurate and poorly transcribed texts. Other collections are developed with the careful input of individual experts but contain fewer documents. The repositories maintained by individual scholars, and other free sources, continue to improve and are the most useful for the would-be digital scholar of *Plum*.[1]

Paramount among large-scale pre-1911 Chinese corpora compiled by scholars is the *Kanseki Repository* (www.kanripo.org), created by Christian Wittern at Kyoto University. It is designed with both careful readers and text miners in mind. It contains thousands of editions of premodern Chinese literature that have been vetted by scholars. Texts available through the *Kanseki Repository* are carefully checked and accurately reflect the original documents on which they are based. There is also a shadow repository that allows users to download the entire corpus, minus markup, in bulk (github.com/kr-shadow/kr-shadow .github.io). Due to the historical origins of the repository in Wittern's work, however, this corpus may not be as useful for the student of the Chinese novel; the repository currently lacks any novels (and by extension *Plum in the Golden Vase*).

The *Chinese Text Project* (ctext.org) is another important resource for pre-1911 Chinese texts that also provides basic analytic tools. This project, developed and maintained by Donald Sturgeon, includes a large collection of full-text Chinese works, with a heavy focus on early philosophical documents. It now contains a large corpus of scanned documents from the Harvard-Yenching Library that is fully searchable using optical character recognition (OCR). The quality of this OCR varies across text, but Sturgeon continues to improve its functionality, and users of the website have hand-corrected some documents. The primary disadvantage of the *Chinese Text Project* for would-be text miners is that, unless one is at an institution with a subscription, extracting multiple texts for analysis is not possible due to bandwidth issues.

Somewhat more useful for those interested in large-scale text mining, but of more dubious fidelity to original sources, are the various websites that provide free access to very large digital Chinese corpora. Websites like zh.wikisource .org, guoxue123.com, and even gutenberg.org offer readers transcribed copies of both the *cihua* and Chongzhen editions of *Plum in the Golden Vase*. In many cases, these websites seem to be sharing identical versions of the novel, but the origin of the original transcription of these works is unclear. Spot checks indicate that the text files are, for the most part, reasonable facsimiles of the documents they claim to represent.

Plain-text versions of *Plum* are common on the internet, but there are also efforts being made to provide access to high-quality image-based versions. Some libraries, like the Harvard-Yenching Library, are making scanned versions of their rare books available online. Other scholars are building platforms that display digital editions and make contributing commentary and translations easy. The Mellon-funded *Ten Thousand Rooms Project*, run by Tina Lu and Mick Hunter at Yale University, uses an image viewer based on Stanford University's Mirador viewer. The project hopes to democratize access to rare versions of Chinese texts by building a platform that allows for collaborative analysis and translation (tenthousandrooms.yale.edu/). The project hosts, for example, high-quality scans of David Tod Roy's personal copy of the *cihua* edition of *Plum in the Golden Vase*, complete with Roy's handwritten annotations.

A *Digital* Plum in the Golden Vase

Access to a digital transcription of *Plum in the Golden Vase* opens a wide array of new analytic approaches. A digital transcription makes it possible to search the text, extract information, perform statistical analyses, and compare the text with other documents of interest. Such analyses become progressively more complex as the size of the corpus being considered increases, but much can be uncovered with just the novel itself.

Regular Expressions

Basic searching is the obvious way to begin working with a digital copy of *Plum in the Golden Vase*. Finding the phrase "it is said" (*huashuo* 話說) and studying how it is used in context is only a search away. Regular expressions, however, allow scholars to quickly assess much more complex issues by finding patterns within a document. Mastering regular expressions, or regexes, is the single most effective way to open digital possibilities, since such expressions offer a highly customizable and precise search tool.

The applicability of regular expressions to research is most aptly illustrated with an example. Scholars have long felt that chapters 53–57 of *Plum* were likely inserted by someone other than the author of the rest of the novel. Patrick Hanan argues that the terms used for "I" or "we" are irregular in these chapters ("Text" 30–31). The terms *wo* 我, *women* 我們, *zan* 咱, *zamen* 咱們, *an* 俺, and *anmen* 俺們 are all used to mean "I" or "we," but occurrences of each vary depending on chapter. Hanan also notes that the plural suffix *men* 們 is used interchangeably with the plural suffix *mei* 每 throughout the novel (30). Tracking these terms by hand is difficult, and it can be easy to miss a few instances when tabulating

Table 1. Common Special Characters in Regular Expressions

SPECIAL CHARACTER	MATCHES
.	Anything except a newline character
\d	Any number
\D	Anything not a number
+	One or more of the last term, will find the longest match possible
*	Zero or more of the last term, will find the longest match possible
?	When placed after + or *, find the shortest match possible
[ ]	Enclosing characters in brackets makes them optional
\s	White space
\S	Not white space
\b	Word boundary
\n	New line
{2}	Match the last term twice
{2,4}	Match the last term at least twice, but no more than four times
{2,}	Match the last term at least twice
^	When at the beginning of regex, find match at beginning of line
$	When at the end of regex, find match at end of the line
[^]	Negate the term inside brackets
( )	Find the term inside parentheses, capture, and return as a group
( )?	Makes the term inside the parentheses optional
(?:)	Makes it so the group does not capture anything
\	Escape character, used to search for the literal version of special characters. \. finds a full stop

them across the entire work. One could search for each of these terms individually, count them, and subtract occurrences of *wo* when it occurs with *women* (for example), but with a regular expression, one can quickly find every example of these terms with no duplication.

Regular expressions are a powerful and complex concept, but they are useful with just a few basic constructs. Most plain-text editors, such as BBEdit or Notepad++, support regular expression searches by default. In most cases, they are activated with a "regular expression" or "GREP" option in the search dialogue. The power of regular expressions comes from the special characters that can be inserted into search terms to match patterns. Table 1 contains some of the most important special characters. Table 2 presents examples of regular expressions and the text that these expressions would find.

Regular expressions can be combined using the find-and-replace function to quickly and easily mark up documents:

Table 2. Examples of Useful Regular Expressions

PATTERN TO FIND	REGULAR EXPRESSION	EXAMPLES OF MATCHING TEXT
Arabic numeral of any length	\d+	10000424 8 1099
Four-digit Western year	\d{4}年	1617年 2017年
Single Chinese numbers	[一二三四五六七八九十零百千萬亿]	三 七 九
Multiple Chinese numbers	[一二三四五六七八九十零百千萬亿]+	五 四千七百九十三
A term and the preceding seven characters	.{7}西門慶	問他怎的?」 西門慶
A term and the subsequent seven characters	西門慶.{7}	西門慶說:「我和你
A term and seven characters of context	.{7}西門慶.{7}	問他怎的?」 西門慶說: 「我和你
"Ximen," wherever it is not followed by "Qing," and the following two characters	西門[^慶]{2}	西門大姐
"There is a poem/ci that proves this:"	有[詩詞]為證	有詩爲證 有詞爲證
"There is . . . that proves this"	有.為證	有詩爲證 有曲爲證

Find: (西門慶)
Replace: <maincharacter>\1</maincharacter>[2]
Results: "西門慶" becomes "<maincharacter>西門慶</maincharacter>"

We can now return to Hanan's original observation that variation in the use of singular and plural terms for "I" and "we" offers insight into textual authenticity. Instances of "I" and "we" are easy to find with this regular expression:

[我咱俺][們每]?

Wo 我, *za* 咱, and *an* 俺 inside the first square brackets matches either *wo*, *zan*, or *an*. *Men* 們 and *mei* 每 inside the next square brackets, followed by a "?," indicates that either *men* or *mei* can optionally follow the first set of characters. This will find every instance of these terms and evaluate the validity of Hanan's claims, provided one has accurate digital copies of the manuscripts that Hanan was working with.

Basic Text Analysis

After searching, the next logical step is to consider aggregating the results of a search. Counting the occurrences of terms is a basic step in natural language processing, and there are many tools that offer quick overviews of term frequencies. Google's Ngram Viewer, which allows users to search for term frequencies across a large corpus of texts that have been digitized by Google, is a famous example of such a tool.

An *n*-gram is simply a sequence of words or characters of *n* length. When dealing with Chinese literature it often makes most sense to work with character-based *n*-grams because of unique linguistic considerations that do not affect those who work on Western literature. Most quantitative textual analyses of this type in Western languages use word-frequency counts and depend on punctuation and white space to find words. In Chinese there is often no logical divider along which to break a text. As such, *n*-gram analyses that divide a text into overlapping chunks of some length *n* are often the most useful. 1-grams, or single characters, are quite useful given their proximity to words in classical Chinese, but larger *n*-grams can be used to take context into account.

Voyant Tools, an easy-to-use online software platform for basic text analysis, is the simplest way to begin exploring *Plum in the Golden Vase*. Uploading the text and visualizing it is fast and straightforward but does require some preprocessing for works written in Chinese. Dividing the texts into 1-grams is simple with regular expressions (find: (\S), replace: _\1_, where an underscore is a space). Selecting the "Whitespace Only" tokenization option when uploading the text allows the researcher to quickly see how different characters are used throughout the novel (fig. 1). This view provides a cloud visualization, the text itself, word frequencies, some descriptive statistics, and a keyword-in-context, or KWIC, viewer. Voyant Tools can also visualize the use of the terms for "I" across the entire text (fig. 2). This visualization shows, by chapter, how often *wo* 我, *an* 俺, and *za* 咱 appear throughout the text. By default, Voyant Tools will divide a text into equal segments, unless it is provided with multiple documents. (To create this visualization, I put each chapter in an individual file.) As the visualization shows, the term *wo* 我 is by far the most common term for "I."

Possibilities expand greatly with a small amount of programming knowledge. Complex research is possible with enough knowledge to remove unwanted characters and words with string methods and the ability to do basic math and plotting.[3] In the last several years the R statistical programming language has exploded in popularity, and Python offers highly flexible natural language and data processing tools.[4]

These programmatic tools allow one to further scrutinize Hanan's claim that certain terms for "we," like *women* 我們 and *womei* 我每, are evidence that chapters 53 to 57 were written by a second author (fig. 3).[5] Hanan is correct that *women* and *womei* are rarely used throughout the novel. Chapter 54, which Hanan considers to be of suspect provenance, clearly stands out, with thirteen appearances of *women*. This more than quadruples the frequency for any chapter that is not significantly derived from *Water Margin* (*Shuihu zhuan* 水滸傳). The other suspect chapters, chapters 53 and 55, do not use *women* or *womei* at a rate that clearly diverges from those chapters thought to be authentic. Each of

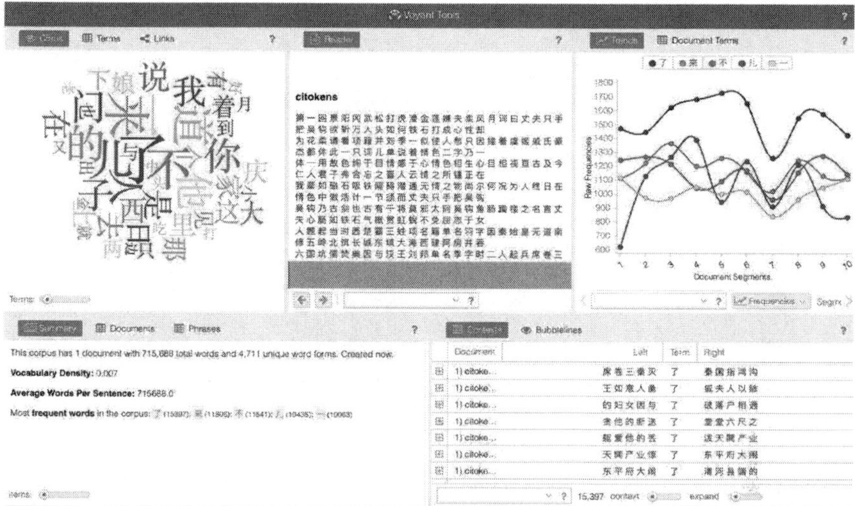

Figure 1. Voyant Tools default view of the *cihua* edition of *Plum*.

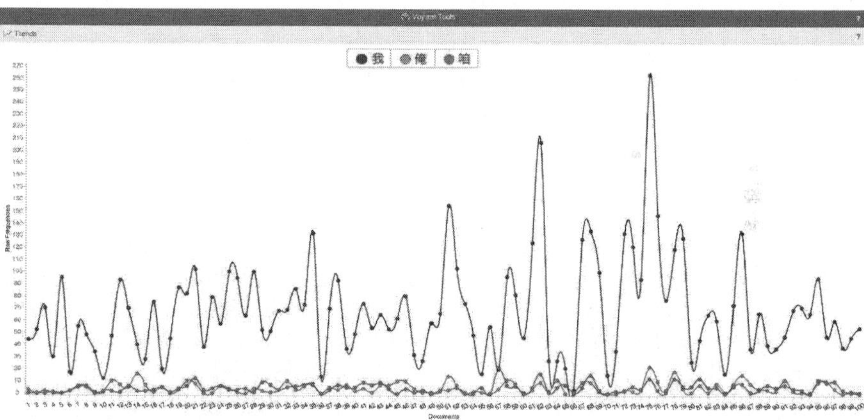

Figure 2. Raw counts of different terms for "I" in *Plum*.

these chapters uses *women* or *womei* three times, which is more than normal, but chapter 21 does as well. The use of such terms alone is not enough to determine if these chapters are inauthentic. Hanan makes a strong case that chapters 53 to 57 are not original to the novel, but variant "we"-usage does not contribute significantly to his argument. By analyzing many terms simultaneously, one can build on Hanan's argument to make a stronger claim about the authenticity of these chapters.

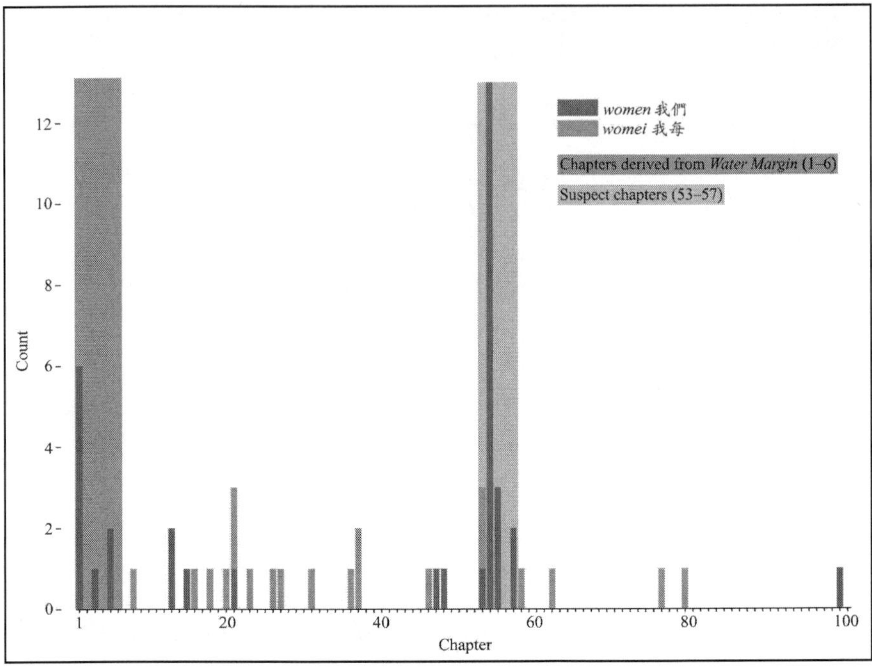

Figure 3. Use of *women* 我們 and *womei* 我每 for "we" in *Plum*.

Comparisons among Digital Editions

More complexity and nuance can be added either methodologically or with the introduction of electronic versions of multiple editions of *Plum*. Analyzing variations between editions of texts is an important component of the study of Chinese literature, and *Plum* is no exception. Scholars who have studied *Plum*, such as Hanan and Xiaofei Tian, have identified a vast array of major and minute changes from the *cihua* edition of the novel, now considered the earlier version, to the Chongzhen edition, which was popular throughout the Qing dynasty (Hanan, "Text"; Xiaofei Tian, "Preliminary Comparison"). For readers of the novel, major changes are easy to identify. Small changes in word choice, deletions, modifications, and elaborations, all of which affect the narrative and nuance of the text, are more difficult to spot. Studying the extensive variation among multiple editions of any document in a fully analog setting is a difficult and complicated process. With digital copies, however, we can use a computer to align different versions of the text to quickly spot differences.[6]

Sequence Alignment

Scholars of Chinese literature need not reinvent the wheel in developing tools to aid detailed edition analysis. Sequence alignment is an important problem in many fields, such as biology. As more living creatures' genomes are sequenced, it is increasingly useful to align base pairs of DNA to detect areas of high homology within a genome. Many techniques have been developed by biologists, some of which are optimized for speed and others for accuracy. There are also various types of alignments, depending on the relationship between the two strings being compared.

Global Alignment

Highly similar strings can be compared using global alignments methods. These global methods score one complete sequence against another complete sequence, applying a penalty to the alignment score if the first and last characters of each sequence do not line up. In the following example, which presents the title of the first chapter of *Plum*, the first line is correct, but the second line has two deletions, a typo, and an insertion:

景陽岡武松打虎　潘金蓮嫌夫賣　風月[7]
景陽　武宋打虎　潘　蓮嫌夫賣了風月

Semiglobal Alignment

Semiglobal alignment is most useful when the sequences are largely the same but the beginning or end might be quite different. This is the alignment type most effective for comparing the *cihua* and Chongzhen editions of *Plum in the Golden Vase* because of the extensive edits to the opening chapter. In the following example, the second line is missing some initial characters and has one deletion, but the gap at the beginning of the sequence is not penalized:

景陽岡武松打虎　潘金蓮嫌夫賣風月
　　松　虎　潘金蓮嫌夫賣風月

Local Alignment

Local alignment finds and aligns small sequences of similar characters in two larger sequences that aren't necessarily alike:

　　景陽岡武松打　虎
你知道　　　武松打了虎麼？[8]

Aligning Manuscripts

Modified so that differences at the beginning and end of sequences are not penalized, the Needleman-Wunsch Algorithm works well for aligning different editions of *Plum* (Needleman and Wunsch). The algorithm is slow but will find an optimal alignment. (In many cases there are multiple possible optimal alignments.) The mechanics of the alignment depend on something known as dynamic programming. An optimal alignment between two strings is found using a scoring

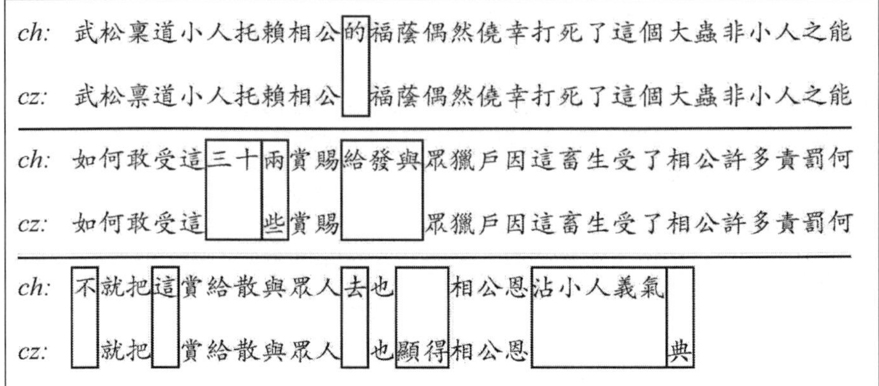

Figure 4. Sample character alignment for the *cihua* (*ch*) and Chongzhen (*cz*) editions of *Plum* using the Needleman-Wunsch Algorithm.

matrix in which each row corresponds with a character in one edition, and each column with a character in another edition. Positive scores are given for matching characters, and negative scores are assigned to mismatched characters (mutations) and gaps (places where there was either an insertion or deletion in one of the texts). Once the matrix is created, the optimal alignment is found by working backward from the highest score in the final row or final column to the highest score in the first row or first column.

Aligning editions of *Plum* offers students an opportunity to clearly grasp the kinds of changes made by the editor of the Chongzhen edition. An aligned section from early in the first chapter of the *cihua* edition and late in the first chapter of the Chongzhen edition is instructive (fig. 4). When presented in this fashion, insertions, deletions, and mutations are immediately obvious. The passage from the *cihua* edition reads as follows:

> Wu Song said respectfully, "It is only owing to Your Honor's benevolent deeds that I have had the accidental good fortune to kill this tiger. It is due to no merit of mine. How could I accept this reward? These thirty taels of silver ought to go to the licensed hunters who have suffered so much at your hands on account of this beast. Why not divide up the reward among them as a demonstration of Your Honor's graciousness and of my own public spirit?" (Roy, *Plum* 1.1.23)

> 如何敢受這三十兩賞賜? 給發與眾獵戶, 因這畜生, 受了相公許多責罰. 何不就把這賞給散與眾人去? 也相公恩沾, 小人義氣. (*JPMCH* 1.17b–18a)

Compare this with the same passage from the Chongzhen edition, which reads quite differently:

"By your Honour's leave," said Wu Song, "I owe my victory over the tiger more to good fortune than to than to ability. I have no right to this reward. The hunters here have incurred your Honour's displeasure on account of this same brute, and I shall be grateful if you will give them the silver rather than myself."   (Egerton and Lao 1.1.48)

如何敢受這些賞賜! 眾獵戶因這畜生, 受了相公許多責罰, 何不就把賞給散與眾人, 也顯得相公恩典.   (*XXP* 1.34a–34b)

With the various types of edits highlighted, it is evident what sorts of editorial choices were made by the compiler of the Chongzhen edition. Most were deletions that seem aimed at tightening the prose, but there are also several insertions placed for emphasis. This arrangement makes it easier to perceive the changes and to understand their nuance.

Plum in the Golden Vase *in a Digital Comparative Context*

The next step is to compare *Plum* not just against itself but also against a large corpus of documents of interest. In this section I explore several potential avenues through which digital research can expand our understanding of *Plum*: comparing it stylistically with other late Ming works, discussing digital efforts to unmask its author, and finding the source of quotations within the novel.

Stylometric Analysis

Stylometric analysis offers an interesting opportunity to understand how *Plum's* style compares with that of similar documents, such as novels. There are many ways of qualitatively understanding style through meter, allusion, tone, and so forth, but it is also possible to develop a quantitative understanding of style. The theoretical underpinning of this idea has been explored by J. Berenike Herrmann, Karina van Dalen-Oskam, and Christof Schöch, who argue that "style is a property of text constituted by an ensemble of formal features which can be observed quantitatively or qualitatively" (44).

The stylometric approach I use boils down to an elaboration of the basic term counting discussed earlier. Breaking texts into quantifiable units, a process known as tokenizing, enables an analysis of how tokens are used in different frequencies in the documents being compared. Thus, documents can be modeled based on relative counts of *n*-grams.[9] The simplest but by no means only method is known as a bag-of-words model. Instead of studying the frequency of individual terms of interest, a bag-of-words model calculates the frequency of *n*-grams within every document in a corpus. Each document is represented as a list, or vector, consisting of its internal *n*-gram frequencies. This list usually contains a subset of all *n*-grams appearing in the corpus, often the most common one hundred to one thousand *n*-grams (particularly when studying authorship or genre).

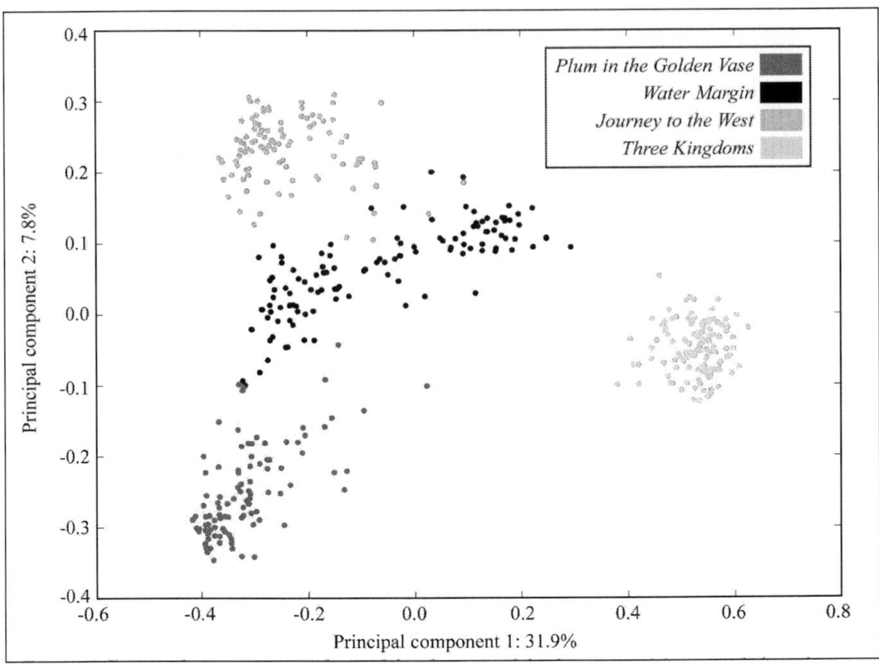

Figure 5. Principal component analysis of the chapters of the four major Ming novels based on one thousand most frequent characters.

This is known as a vector space model (Turney and Pantel). Simple comparisons are done by measuring the distance between each document, commonly with Euclidean distance and cosine similarity (Schöch). Linear algebra's principal component analysis is a popular method of visualization that shows the relationships among texts on a scatter plot based on variance within the data (Binongo and Smith).

These methods are valuable for identifying language unique to a given set of texts. Principal component analysis makes the relationships among the four major Ming novels clear (fig. 5). In figure 5, each dot represents a chapter. Based on quantitative stylistics of 1-grams, *Plum in the Golden Vase* contains sections that are remarkably similar to *Water Margin* and to a lesser extent *Journey to the West* (*Xiyou ji* 西遊記), while *Romance of the Three Kingdoms* (*Sanguo yanyi* 三國演義), written in a simplified classical style, is stylistically most distinct. The principal component loadings, which show how characters influence the results, help us interpret what is happening (fig. 6). The farther a character is from the center of the plot, the more influence that character has on the variance. There is a clear x-axis differentiation between vernacular characters on the left and classical ones on the right. Names are influential here as well. For instance, Ximen Qing's name plays an important role in pulling *Plum* down on the y-axis. Plots

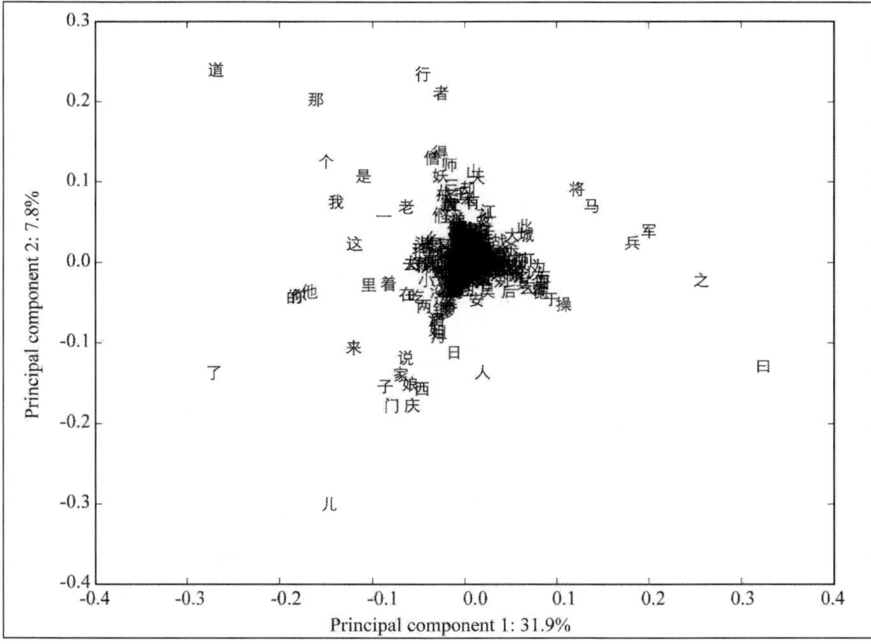

Figure 6. Principal component loadings.

such as these offer broad overviews of stylistic relationships and help identify individual chapters that are of interest.

Machine Learning and Authorship

The quantitative models built to represent Chinese literature (through bag-of-words or some other representation) can be elaborated and then further leveraged with machine learning. Machine learning offers scholars an interesting new opportunity to approach age-old issues related to the novel. Among the most famous of these is the authorship of *Plum in the Golden Vase*. Who was Lanling Xiaoxiao Sheng, "the Laughing Scholar of Lanling," the pseudonym adopted by *Plum*'s author? It seems hard to conceptualize this question in a way that has not been considered before, but digital methods help uncover new lines of evidence, though whether they offer new answers is still an open question.

Some elements of authorial style can be quantified, but drawing meaningful conclusions about authorship requires researchers to consider many features at once and is exceedingly difficult. Quantitative methods aimed at authorship attribution have been applied to Chinese literature in the past: *The Story of the Stone* (*Honglou meng* 紅樓夢), also known as *Dream of the Red Chamber*, has been subjected to this treatment multiple times to determine if the last forty chapters were written by Cao Xueqin 曹雪芹 (1715?–63). In 1986 Bing Chan analyzed part-of-speech frequency across the novel and concluded that the entire novel was most likely written by a single author (84). Debate continues, despite the high quality of Chan's work, because of the inherent limits of this type of work: it is complex, probabilistic, and conclusions are only possible in terms of likelihood. Discussion is further fueled by disagreements over what features best predict authorship. In 2013 Hsieh-Chang Tu and Jieh Hsiang argued that if one chooses a different set of features, which Tu and Hsiang generate using a text-mining algorithm, the last chapters appear to be written by someone else (1). Unsurprisingly, scholars continue to use new quantitative methods to rehash this old question.

The approach I take to studying *Plum*'s authorship is an extension of these earlier approaches and leverages machine-learning techniques developed and refined by computer scientists over the last decade or so. Machine-learning algorithms simplify the process of picking the best features to accurately differentiate authorship by taking in all available data on labeled documents, from word count to text size to any other additional features one chooses to add, and then attempting to distinguish among the documents based on the input.[10] Machine-learning algorithms essentially generate a set of rules to make a decision based on available evidence. There are many algorithms that do this, and their efficacy with regard to authorship attribution is highly variable. These algorithms differ with respect to their treatment of the data and the assumptions they make about it. Few have been rigorously tested on premodern Chinese texts, but Matthew Jockers and Daniela Witten have evaluated how they perform in English and found that some perform quite well.

Attempting to identify *Plum*'s author is straightforward: If we have a large corpus of documents written by people who were alive when *Plum* was written, we can take those documents with known authors and compare them with *Plum*. By feeding these documents into a machine-learning algorithm, we can create a classifier. This will predict which other documents' style—and by extension which author's style—is most like *Plum*'s. This analytical approach depends on a major assumption, namely that the corpus used to train the classifier contains a text by the author of *Plum*. Variations in the frequency of the most common 1-grams in the corpus seem to offer the best results in determining the most likely author. Based on analysis I've conducted using corpora and methods available in 2014 and 2015, Wang Shizhen 王世貞 (1526–90) seems to be the most likely candidate.[11]

The main drawback of a machine-learning approach is that it is often unclear why the model categorizes Wang's writing as more similar to *Plum*'s than the writing of Tang Xianzu 湯顯祖 (1550–1616), for example. Such an approach depends on similarities between Wang's and *Plum*'s respective use of certain terms, but it is not clear which terms are most important, although variation in common terms, such as the possessive markers *zhi* 之 and *de* 的, probably play a significant role. Empirically, authorship attribution also works much better when used within the same genre. Comparing plays with novels is extremely difficult because variation in terms is much larger between genres than it is between authors, meaning that stylistic variations attributable to genre can obscure variations attributable to the author. This is problematic in *Plum*'s case because some potential authors only wrote plays, making the authors inherently difficult to compare with the author of *Plum*.

The applicability of machine learning to Chinese literature is not limited to questions of authorship. It is useful for developing any categorization schema, whether this means grouping documents by genre, by the gender of the author, by subject matter, or by date of original compilation. Machine learning can also be used to study more abstract concepts; for example, if we wanted to evaluate Roy's claim that "[Xunzi's] Philosophy [Is] a Key to the Novel" (Introduction xxiv), we might use topic modeling, an unsupervised machine-learning method designed to extract latent topics from a set of documents (Blei), to analyze a corpus of philosophical and other relevant texts, making sure Xunzi and other competing philosophers are represented. In doing so, we could develop a topic model of philosophical texts that could then be applied to *Plum* to evaluate which philosopher's "topics" are closest to those found in *Plum*.

Fuzzy Quote Matching

One of the most intriguing aspects of *Plum in the Golden Vase* is its use of text from other works. A quick perusal of the endnotes to Roy's translation offers a glimpse into the complexity of the source material, a subject that scholars like Hanan and Shang Wei have studied at length (Hanan, "Text"; Shang, "'Jin Ping Mei'"). Identifying which sections of the novel come from other works is difficult using traditional research methods but relatively easy with access to digital corpora. By scanning the novel and finding fuzzy, or approximate, matches of text in other works, it is now possible to identify all occurrences of direct textual influence (assuming the corpus one uses contains all *Plum*'s sources).

There are a variety of ways to implement this type of method, and an experimental version called COMPARATIVUS has now been developed for the MARKUS online platform (dh.chinese-empires.eu/beta/). Another tool called Philologic, created by Jeff Tharsen, is being used at the University of Chicago (Tharsen and Gladstone). The basic principle used by COMPARATIVUS is simple: scan through a text such as *Plum* in small chunks and search for these chunks in the larger corpus (Vierthaler and Gelein). When found, matches can be extended and then compared using Levenshtein distance, a measure of how many edits would change one string into another. Figure 7 illustrates the results of an experimental version of this process, showing the percentage of text in chapters in *Plum* that is easily identified in earlier texts. The first five chapters and to a lesser extent the sixth chapter are heavily based on *Water Margin*. Chapter 5 stands out as the only chapter that is over ninety percent attributable to earlier works. Most chapters are between one and ten percent quotations.

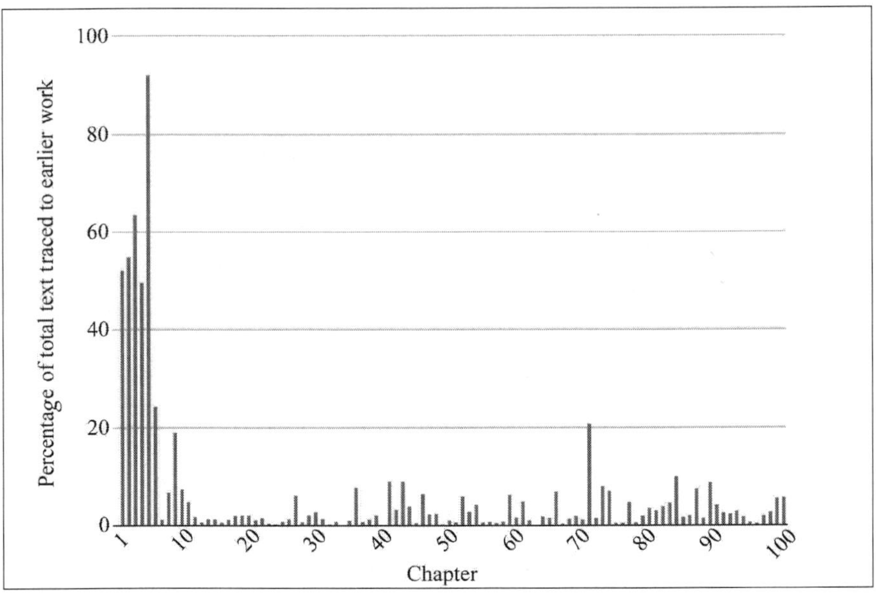

Figure 7. Proportion of each chapter of *Plum* attributable to an earlier work.

Future Directions

This essay outlines a few ways that digital analyses can help us more clearly understand *Plum in the Golden Vase*, its multiple editions, and its place within the larger context of sixteenth- and seventeenth-century textual production. Currently, conducting all manner of digital analysis is limited by the availability of high-quality corpora that accurately reflect the texts as they were originally written or printed. This, however, is becoming less of a problem every day. At the same time, new tools are being developed to help scholars leverage digital tools for their own work.

In many ways, the tools I discuss here are all an elaboration of one another. Machine learning builds on the structures in the bag-of-words model to add decision-making logic based on extensive information. The bag-of-words model is an elaboration of the basic word counts that tools like Voyant Tools make available. Word counts, in turn, are based on the ability to find specific patterns in text. All these tools, and other ancillary ones like sequence alignment and quote mining, help us study the macrostructure of *Plum* when considered both alone and in relation to an outside corpus.

The opportunities that digital tools provide for reading and analyzing *Plum in the Golden Vase* are extensive and not limited to the primarily text-based tools I have introduced here. Network analysis and geographical analyses, for example, are also well-suited to an analysis of the novel. Using a simple list of characters in the novel, network analysis makes it possible to find each instance when one character interacts with every other character. A study like this would enable a researcher to build full character networks, networks of enemies, and networks of friends and allies. Doing this for multiple texts would further allow the reader to understand if, as is often claimed, *Plum* is as unusual as it seems. The primary innovations afforded by the digital are flexibility, rapidity of analysis, and the possibility for replication. Digital methods are also useful when it comes to spotting larger trends that can then guide close readings. For students new to the novel, digital methods encourage interaction with the work at varying scales that reveal new and unexpected frontiers for study. The future is bright for digital analysis of *Plum in the Golden Vase* and for Chinese literature in general.

NOTES

[1] I should caution that some may be unstable; those that lack institutional support may disappear in the future.

[2] The "\1" syntax works in some text-editing programs, such as BBEdit. Others use a slightly different syntax, such as "$1." This approach is most useful for adding XML or XHTML markup.

[3] A string is a sequence of characters treated like language by a computer program.

[4] For an introduction to using R in the humanities, see Arnold and Tilton. For those interested in text mining with Python, see Bird et al.

[5] Hanan's claim that *zan* is only used as a first-person singular pronoun in the suspect chapters, which appears with his discussion of *women* and *womei* ("Text" 29–31), is not as amenable to digital analysis: it is difficult to computationally ascertain singular versus plural usage (of which there are many). I also ignore the distinction between "we"-inclusive and "we"-exclusive because there are too few examples for the difference to be useful.

[6] It is important to bear in mind that the copies of these texts available today are not perfect representations of the original documents from the seventeenth century. However, they are close, and their contents are instructive.

[7] This is the title of chapter 1 in the *cihua* edition (*JPMCH* 1.3a), which Roy translates as "Wu Song Fights a Tiger on Jing-Yang Ridge; Pan Jinlian Disdains Her Mate and Plays the Coquette" (*Plum* 1.1.12).

[8] This is a corruption of the title that might appear in an unreliable but hypothetical digital version meaning roughly "Did You Know that Wu Song Fought the Tiger?"

[9] For an overview of this approach in the Chinese context, see Vierthaler.

[10] That being said, tossing all available information into an algorithm is not a recipe for success. Good results depend on extensive curation of features and adjustment of the models.

[11] For a detailed engagement with this, see "Digital Research."

Katherine Carlitz served as assistant director for academic affairs at the Asian Studies Center of the University of Pittsburgh until her retirement in May 2016. She also served as adjunct professor in the University of Pittsburgh's Department of East Asian Languages and Literatures, where she taught courses on Ming dynasty fiction and drama, on Chinese law, and on Chinese religious traditions.

Maram Epstein is professor of Chinese at the University of Oregon. She is the author of *Competing Discourses: Orthodoxy, Authenticity, and Engendered Meanings in Late-Imperial Chinese Fiction* and *Orthodox Passions: Narrating Filial Love during the High Qing* as well as many articles focused on reading Ming-Qing novels within their specific cultural and aesthetic contexts. Two of her essays appear in *Approaches to Teaching* The Story of the Stone (Dream of the Red Chamber).

Siyen Fei is associate professor of history at the University of Pennsylvania. Her work to date is primarily concerned with the political and cultural activism of sixteenth- and early-seventeenth-century Ming dynasty China. Her first book, *Negotiating Urban Space: Nanjing and Late Ming Urbanization* (2010), argues that urbanism in late imperial China was intricately defined by the distinct vision of each dynastic empire. Her current book project, *Sexuality and Empire: Female Chastity and Frontier Societies in Ming China, 1368–1644*, tells a story about a time when familiar concepts such as empire and identity were unavailable and, in that absence, how the commemoration of chaste heroines—women who martyred themselves to preserve their chastity—became a venue for negotiating destabilized frontier identities and reimagining the Chinese world.

Paize Keulemans is associate professor of East Asian studies at Princeton University. Keulemans's research interests focus on the interaction between oral and written literature. His book, *Sound Rising from the Paper: Nineteenth-Century Martial Arts Fiction and the Chinese Acoustic Imagination* (2015), pursues this topic from an acoustic angle, investigating how a plethora of sound effects (onomatopoeia, dialect accents, vendor calls, etc.) turn the silent pages of printed novels into a lively acoustic spectacle. His second research project, tentatively entitled *Idle Chatter: The Productive Uses of Gossip and Rumor in Seventeenth-Century Chinese Literature*, explores the relationship between oral and written literature from a different point of view, the seemingly endless production of printed hearsay, rumor, and gossip in late Ming and early Qing novels, short stories, and operas.

Ling Hon Lam is associate professor in the Department of East Asian Languages and Cultures at the University of California, Berkeley. His research and teaching interests cover premodern drama and fiction, sex and gender, media culture, and critical theories. He is the author of *The Spatiality of Emotion in Early Modern China: From Dreamscapes to Theatricality* (2018). Other publications include "The Matriarch's Private Ears: Performance, Reading, Censorship, and the Fabrication of Interiority in *The Story of the Stone*," published in the *Harvard Journal of Asiatic Studies*; "Reading off the Screen: Toward Cinematic Il-literacy in Late 1950s Chinese Opera Film," which appeared in *Opera Quarterly*; and "Allegory and the 'World' Formation in *The Journey to* *the West,"* published in *A Companion to World Literature*. His current research focuses on the historical ontology of media in early modern to twentieth-century China.

Wai-yee Li is 1879 Professor of Chinese Literature at Harvard University. Li's research topics range from early Chinese thought and narrative to late imperial Chinese literature and culture. Her recent publications include *The Readability of the Past in Early Chinese Historiography* (2007) and *Women and National Trauma in Late Imperial Chinese Literature* (2014). Her coedited volume of translations of ten influential plays from the thirteenth and fourteenth centuries, *The Columbia Anthology of Yuan Drama*, was also published in 2014. Her annotated translation of *Zuozhuan*, in collaboration with Stephen Durrant and David Schaberg, was published in 2016. *The Zuo Tradition / Zuozhuan Reader*, a topical study of *Zuozhuan* based on the translation, was published in 2020. Other recent publications include a coauthored book, *Sima Qian and the Letter to Ren An* (2016); *The Oxford Handbook of Classical Chinese Literature* (2017), which Li coedited with Wiebke Denecke and Tian Xiaofei; *Keywords in Chinese Culture* (2020), which she coedited with Yuri Pines; and her translation of two memoirs about courtesans, Plum Shadows *and* Plank Bridge (2020).

Tina Lu is Colonel John Trumbull Professor of East Asian Literatures at Yale University. She specializes in fiction and drama of the Ming and Qing dynasties. She is the author of *Persons, Roles, and Minds: Identity in* Peony Pavilion *and* Peach Blossom Fan and of *Accidental Incest, Filial Cannibalism, and Other Peculiar Encounters in Chinese Literature*. She is coeditor of *Approaches to Teaching* The Story of the Stone (Dream of the Red Chamber*)* and the author of a chapter on the late Ming in *The Cambridge History of Chinese Literature*. Lu currently has three major research projects: a monograph on how seventeenth-century people conceived of and defended materiality, a group-authored book on the sixteenth-century artist and playwright Xu Wei, and a digital initiative that will enable collaborative philological work.

Keith McMahon is professor of Chinese at the University of Kansas. He studies the history of sexuality in China from ancient times to the verge of modernity, including most recently the history of imperial women from the Han to the Qing. Recent publications include *Women Shall Not Rule: Imperial Wives and Concubines in China from Han to Liao* and *Celestial Women: Imperial Wives and Concubines in China from Song to Qing*, a two-volume history of imperial marriage and women rulers. A forthcoming book is *Saying All That Can Be Said: The Art of Describing Sex in* Jin Ping Mei (Harvard U Asia Center).

Andrew Schonebaum is associate professor of Chinese studies at the University of Maryland, College Park. He specializes in traditional Chinese culture and literature and the history of daily life in China. His recent works include *Novel Medicine: Healing, Literature, and Popular Knowledge in Early Modern China* (2016) and *Approaches to Teaching* The Story of the Stone (Dream of the Red Chamber), coedited with Tina Lu. Other publications include "Lust and Love in English Translation: *Plum in the Golden Vase* and *The Story of the Stone*," in *A Companion to World Literature*. His next book, *Classifying the Unseen: Curiosity, Fantasy, and Common Knowledge in Early Modern China*, is forthcoming from the University of Washington Press.

Mary Scott is professor of humanities at San Francisco State University. She teaches interdisciplinary courses on Beijing, Shanghai, and traditional and modern Chinese literary culture. In addition to *The Story of the Stone* (*Honglou meng* 紅樓夢) and *The Plum in the Golden Vase* (*Jin Ping Mei* 金瓶梅), her research interests include the realist novel in China and Europe, modern Chinese literary history, and comparative literary theory.

Shang Wei is professor of Chinese literature and chair of the Department of East Asian Languages and Cultures at Columbia University. He specializes in premodern Chinese literature and culture, especially fiction and drama of the Ming and Qing dynasties. Additional research interests include print culture, book history, and intellectual history of the same era as well as medieval poetry. His publications include *"Rulin Waishi" and Cultural Transformation in Late Imperial China* (2003), *Tixie mingsheng: Cong Huanghe lou dao Fenghuang tai* 題寫名勝: 從黃鶴樓到鳳凰台 (*Writing on Landmarks: From Yellow Crane Tower to Phoenix Pavilion* [2020]), and articles on a wide range of topics in both English and Chinese. He is also a contributor to *Approaches to Teaching* The Story of the Stone (Dream of the Red Chamber).

Matthew H. Sommer is Bowman Family Professor of Chinese history at Stanford University. His research focuses on sexuality, gender relations, chosen kinship, and law during the Qing dynasty. The main sources of his work are legal cases from central and local archives in China. His first book, *Sex, Law, and Society in Late Imperial China*, is primarily a legal history, but more recent projects use legal cases to explore sociohistorical topics as well. His second book, *Polyandry and Wife-Selling in Qing Dynasty China: Survival Strategies and Judicial Interventions*, was published in 2015. He is now completing a third book, which analyzes male same-sex relations and masculinity in eighteenth-century China on the basis of some seventeen hundred relevant cases.

Catherine Swatek is associate professor emeritus of Chinese language and premodern literature at the University of British Columbia. She is primarily interested in Chinese vernacular literature of the late imperial period, both fiction and drama. She has published work on Ming dynasty drama, especially *The Peony Pavilion* (*Mudan ting* 牡丹亭), and on uses of dialect humor in performances of Kun operas.

Michael Szonyi is Frank Wen-hsiung Wu Memorial Professor of Chinese History and director of the Fairbank Center for Chinese Studies at Harvard University. A social historian of the Ming dynasty and the twentieth century, he is the author of *The Art of Being Governed: Everyday Politics in Late Imperial China* (2017) and *Cold War Island: Quemoy on the Front Line* (2008). He is also the editor of *A Companion to Chinese History* (2017) and coeditor, with Jennifer Rudolph, of *The China Questions: Critical Insights into a Rising Power* (2018). He is currently writing a history of rural China in the twentieth century.

Paul Vierthaler is assistant professor of Chinese studies at the College of William and Mary. He formerly taught digital humanities at Leiden University, where he helped found the Leiden University Centre for Digital Humanities. He has held the An Wang Postdoctoral Fellowship at Harvard University and the digital humanities postdoctoral fellowship at Boston College. He is currently working on a monograph about the movement of historical information through novels, drama, and unofficial histories in late Ming and early Qing China. He has published work on late imperial printing trends and computational textual analysis in journals such as the *Harvard Journal of Asiatic Studies* and the *Journal of Cultural Analytics*.

Y. Yvon Wang is associate professor of history at the University of Toronto. They are the author of *Reinventing Licentiousness: Pornography and Modern China* (2021), which explores the intersections of pornography, sexuality, print culture, law enforcement, and cultural authority in early modern and twentieth-century urban China. They have published articles on pornography, sodomy, and "hooligans" in *Modern China, The Journal of Asian Studies*, and *Nan nü*. They are currently translating and editing a collection of memoirs and oral histories from the Small Third Front military-industrial campaign that took place between the 1960s and the 1980s.

Ying Zhang is associate professor of history at Ohio State University. She is particularly interested in exploring the history of Ming politics, of Confucianism, of Chinese religion, and of gender and family in China. She is the author of *Confucian Image Politics: Masculine Morality in Seventeenth-Century China* (2016) and *Religion and Prison Art in Ming China, 1368–1644* (2020).

Lisa Zunshine is Bush-Holbrook Professor of English at the University of Kentucky, a former Guggenheim Fellow (2007), and the author and editor of eleven books, including *Strange Concepts and the Stories They Make Possible: Cognition, Culture, Narrative* (2008), *Getting Inside Your Head: What Cognitive Science Can Tell Us about Popular Culture* (2012), and *The Oxford Handbook of Cognitive Literary Studies* (2015). She serves on the editorial board of *Cognitive Poetics* 认知诗学.

WORKS CITED

Editions of *Jin Ping Mei*

Lanling Xiaoxiao Sheng 蘭陵笑笑生. *Gaohe Tang piping diyi qishu* Jin Ping Mei 皋鶴堂批評第一奇書金瓶梅 [Plum in the Golden Vase: *The First Marvelous Book, with Gaohe Tang Commentary*]. Commentary by Gaohe Tang 皋鶴堂 [Zhang Zhupo 張竹坡], 1695. *Waseda University Library*, www.wul.waseda.ac.jp/kotenseki/html/he21/he21_03765/index.html.

———. *Huiping huijiao* Jin Ping Mei 會評會校金瓶梅 [*Variorum* Plum in the Golden Vase]. Edited by Liu Hui 劉輝 and Wu Gan 吳敢, Tiandi tushu gongsi, 1998. 5 vols.

———. *Jin Ping Mei cihua* 金瓶梅詞話 [*Plum in the Golden Vase: A Ballad Tale*]. 1617–18. *National Central Library*, rbook.ncl.edu.tw/NCLSearch/Search/SearchDetail?item=6b1544b218634be48c8aa83ac4986bb2fDg2ODk0Ng2&image=1&page=&whereString=&sourceWhereString=&SourceID=.

———. *Xinke xiuxiang piping* Jin Ping Mei 新刻繡像批評金瓶梅 [*Newly Cut, Lavishly Illustrated, and Commented On* Plum in the Golden Vase]. 1628–44. *National Archives of Japan Digital Archive*, www.digital.archives.go.jp/das/meta/F1000000000000107682.html.

Translations of *Jin Ping Mei*

Egerton, Clement, and Lao She, translators. *The Golden Lotus*. By Lanling Xiaoxiao Sheng 蘭陵笑笑生, edited and introduced by Robert Hegel, Tuttle, 2011. 2 vols.

Kuhn, Franz, translator. Kin Ping Meh; *oder, Die abenteuerliche Geschichte von Hsi Men und seinen sechs Frauen*. By Lanling Xiaoxiao Sheng 蘭陵笑笑生, Insel Verlag, 1931.

Miall, Bernard, translator. Chin P'ing Mei: *The Adventurous History of Hsi Men and His Six Wives*. By Lanling Xiaoxiao Sheng 蘭陵笑笑生, introduction by Arthur Waley, John Lane, 1939.

Roy, David Tod, translator. The Plum in the Golden Vase; *or, Chin P'ing Mei*. By Lanling Xiaoxiao Sheng 蘭陵笑笑生, Princeton UP, 1993–2013. 5 vols.

Critical Works

Abel-Rémusat, Jean-Pierre. *Livre des récompenses et des peines.* Paris, Antoine-Augustin Renouard, 1816.

Alemán, Mateo. *The Life and Adventures of Guzman D'Alfarache, or the Spanish Rogue.* 1599–1604. Translated by John Henry Brady. Longman, Hurst, Rees, Orme, Brown, and Green, 1823.

Armstrong, Nancy. *How Novels Think: The Limits of Individualism from 1719–1900.* Columbia UP, 2005.

Arnold, Taylor, and Lauren Tilton. *Humanities Data in R: Exploring Networks, Geospatial Data, Images, and Text.* Springer, 2015.

Bai Weiguo 白維國, editor. Jin Ping Mei *cidian* 金瓶梅詞典 [*A Dictionary of* Jin Ping Mei]. Zhonghua Shuju, 1987.

———. Jin Ping Mei *fengsu tan* 金瓶梅風俗譚 [*A Discussion of Customs in* Plum in the Golden Vase]. Shangwu yinshuguan, 2015.

Barthes, Roland. "Punctum." *Camera Lucida*, translated by Richard Howard, Hill and Wang, 1980, pp. 43–46.

———. "The Reality Effect." *The Rustle of Language*, translated by Richard Howard, U of California P, 1989, pp. 141–48.

Beijing Municipal Police. "Bao'an madui guanyu zun ling zhuahuo Zhang Peilin deng shoumai yinshu yi an de cheng" 保安馬隊關於遵令抓獲張霈霖等售賣淫書一案的呈 ["Report from the Mounted Constabulary about Arresting Zhang Peilin and Others Selling Licentious Books as Ordered"]. 15 Dec. 1918. Beijing Municipal Archives, file number J181-019-22193.

———. "Beijing shi jingcha ju gaodeng zhentan shi guanyu Lang Baoqi shoumai chunshu yi an de cheng" 北京市警察局高等偵探室關於郎寶棋售賣春書一案的呈 ["Report from the Beijing Municipal Police Bureau Superior Detective Office about Lang Baoqi Selling Spring Books"]. 15 Mar. 1938. Beijing Municipal Archives, file number J181-023-04473.

———. "Jingshi jingcha ting nei you yi qu quanyu Zhang Peilin shoumai yinshu yi an de cheng" 京師警察廳內右一區關於張霈林售賣淫書一案的呈 ["Report from the Inner Right First District Police about Zhang Peilin and Selling Licentious Books"]. 27 May 1919. Beijing Municipal Archives, file number J181-019-29847.

———. "Jingshi jingcha ting nei zuo si qu quanyu Gao Jie shoumai weijin xiaoshuo yi an de cheng" 京師警察廳內左四區關於高傑售賣違禁小說一案的呈 ["Report from the Inner Left Fourth District Police about Gao Jie Selling Banned Novels"]. 22 Sept. 1918. Beijing Municipal Archives, file number J181-019-22190.

———. "Jingshi jingcha ting nei zuo yi qu biao song Li Sixun shoumai yinshu yi an cheng" 京師警察廳內左一區表送李思勳售賣淫書一案呈 ["Report from the Inner Left First District Police about Li Sixun Selling Licentious Books"]. 25 May 1920. Beijing Municipal Archives, file number J181-019-57016.

———. "Jingshi jingcha ting wai you yiqu fengqu biao song Liu Honglin shoumai Yulou chun gezhong yinshu qing jiu yi an" 京師警察廳外右一區分區表送劉洪林售

賣玉樓春各種淫書請究一案 ["Report from the Outer Right First District Police about Liu Honglin Selling *Yulou chun* and Assorted Licentious Books and Invitation for Sentencing"]. 2 Oct. 1922. Beijing Municipal Archives, file number J181-019-35958.

"Beijing nanzi si yin *Jin Ping Mei* beifa yiwan yuan" 北京男子私印《金瓶梅》被罚 1 万元 ["Beijing Man Fined Ten Thousand Yuan for Secretly Printing *Jin Ping Mei*"]. *China.com*, 19 May 2016, economy.china.com/news/11173316/20160509/22610520.html.

Benjamin, Walter. "The Work of Art in the Age of Mechanical Reproduction." *Illuminations: Essays and Reflections*, edited by Hannah Arendt, translated by Harry Zohn, Schocken Books, 2007, pp. 217–51.

Binongo, J. N. G., and M. W. A. Smith. "The Application of Principal Component Analysis to Stylometry." *Literary and Linguistic Computing*, vol. 14, 1999, pp. 445–66.

Birch, Cyril, translator. *The Peony Pavilion: Mudan ting*. By Tang Xianzu 湯顯祖, introduction by Catherine Swatek, 2nd ed., Indiana UP, 2002.

———. Peony Pavilion; or, Return of the Soul. By Tang Xianzu 湯顯祖. *Renditions*, no. 3, autumn 1974, pp. 149–73, www.cuhk.edu.hk/rct/pdf/e_outputs/b03/v03p149.pdf.

Bird, Stephen, et al. *Natural Language Processing with Python*. O'Reilly, 2009, www.nltk.org/book.

Blei, David. "Probabilistic Topic Models." *Communications of the ACM*, vol. 55, no. 4, 2012, pp. 77–84.

Blum, Jeremy. "Erotic Film Broadcast to Hundreds outside Railway Station." *South China Morning Post*, 1 July 2013, www.scmp.com/news/china/article/1273029/erotic-film-broadcast-hundreds-outside-railway-station.

Bodde, Derk, and Clarence Morris. *Law in Imperial China: Exemplified by 190 Ch'ing Dynasty Cases (Translated from the* Hsing-an hui-lan). U of Pennsylvania P, 1967.

"Book Dealer Summoned." *The New York Times*, 17 July 1931, p. 24.

Borges, Jorge Luis. "Kafka and His Precursors." *Labyrinths*, edited by Donald A. Yates and James E. Irby, New Directions, 2007, pp. 190–93.

Braester, Yomi. *Witness against History: Literature, Film, and Public Discourse in Twentieth-Century China*. Stanford UP, 2003.

Brook, Timothy. *The Confusions of Pleasure: Commerce and Culture in Ming China*. U of California P, 1998.

Cahill, James. *Pictures for Use and Pleasure: Vernacular Painting in High Qing China*. U of California P, 2010.

Cai Qiong 蔡瓊. "Mao Zedong lun *Jin Ping Mei* ji dui qi yanjiu de yiyi" 毛澤東論《金瓶梅》及對其研究的意義 ["Mao Zedong's Comments on *The Plum in the Golden Vase* and Their Significance for Its Study"]. *Mao Zedong sixiang luntan* 毛澤東思想論壇 [*Forum on Mao Zedong's Thought*], no. 2, 1994, pp. 63–65.

Cao Pi 曹丕. "Scholar T'an." Translated by Dennis T. Hu. *Traditional Chinese Stories: Themes and Variations*, edited by Y. W. Ma and Joseph S. M. Lau, Columbia UP, 1978, p. 387.

Cao Xueqin 曹雪芹. Honglou meng *bashi hui jiaoben* 紅樓夢八十回校本 [*The Eighty-Chapter* Dream of the Red Chamber, *Critically Collated Edition*]. Edited by Yu Pingbo 俞平伯 and Wang Xishi 王惜時, Zhonghua shuju, 1985. 2 vols.

Carlitz, Katherine. "Family, Society, and Tradition in *Jin Ping Mei*." *Modern China*, vol. 10, no. 4, Oct. 1984, pp. 387–413.

———. "Mourning, Personality, Display: Ming Literati Commemorate Their Mothers, Sisters, and Daughters." *Nan Nü: Men, Women and Gender in Early and Imperial China*, vol. 15, no. 1, 2013, pp. 30–68.

———. *The Rhetoric of* Chin p'ing mei. Indiana UP, 1986.

———. *The Role of Drama in the* Chin P'ing Mei: *The Relationship between Fiction and Drama as a Guide to the Viewpoint of a Sixteenth-Century Chinese Novel*. 1978. U of Chicago, PhD dissertation.

Cass, Victoria. *Dangerous Women: Warriors, Grannies, and Geishas of the Ming*. Rowman and Littlefield, 1999.

———. "Revels of a Gaudy Night." *CLEAR: Chinese Literature: Essays, Articles, Reviews*, vol. 4, no. 2, July 1982, pp. 213–31.

Chan, Bing C. *The Authorship of the* Dream of the Red Chamber: *Based on a Computerized Statistical Study of Its Vocabulary*. Joint Publishing, 1986.

Chan, Wing-tsit, translator. "Daxue/Great Learning." *Sources of Chinese Tradition*, edited by Chan et al., Columbia UP, 1960, pp. 113–17.

Chang, K'ang-i Sun. "Songs in the *Chin P'ing Mei Tz'u-hua*." *Journal of Oriental Studies*, vol. 18, nos. 1–2, 1980, pp. 26–34.

Chen Baoliang 陳寶良. "Zheng ce zhi bie: Mingdai jiating shenghuo lunli zhong zhi qiqie guanxi" 正側之別:明代家庭生活倫理中之妻妾關係 ["The Difference between Main Wife and Concubines: The Relationship of Wives and Concubines in the Lives of Ming Dynasty Families"]. *Zhongguo shi yanjiu* 中國史研究 [*Research on Chinese History*], vol. 3, 2008, pp. 123–44.

Chen Hsi-yuan 陳熙遠. "Cong madiao dao majiang—Xiao wanyi yu da chuantong wenzhi de yiduan lishi yinyuan" 從馬吊到馬將—小玩意與大傳統交織的一段歷史因緣 ["From *madiao* to *majiang*: The Historical Affinity Binding a Great Tradition and an Irrelevant Pastime"]. *Zhongyang yanjiuyuan Lishi yuyan yanjiusuo jikan* 中央研究院歷史語言研究所集刊 [*Journal of the History and Language Institute, Academia Sinica*], vol. 1, no. 3, 2009, pp. 137–96.

Chin, Tamara T. *Savage Exchange: Han Imperialism, Chinese Literary Style, and the Economic Imagination*. Harvard U Asia Center, 2014.

Clunas, Craig. *Superfluous Things: Material Culture and Social Status in Early Modern China*. U of Hawai'i P, 2016.

Comber, Leon. *The Strange Cases of Magistrate Pao: Chinese Tales of Crime and Detection*. Charles Tuttle, 1964.

Confucius. *The Analects: The Simon Leys Translation, Interpretations*. W. W. Norton, 2014.

"Digital Research into the Authorship of the *Jin Ping Mei*." *YouTube*, uploaded by CESTA Stanford, 15 Feb. 2017, www.youtube.com/watch?v=hZYiDdYyYlc. Accessed 31 Mar. 2022.

Dikötter, Frank. *Sex, Culture and Modernity in China*. Hong Kong UP, 1995.

Ding, Naifei. *Obscene Things: Sexual Politics in* Jin Ping Mei. Duke UP, 2002.

Ding Yaokang 丁耀亢 . *Flower Shadows behind the Curtain:* Ko Lien Hua Ying, *A Sequel to* Chin P'ing Mei. Translated by Vladimir Kean, Pantheon Books, 1959.

———. *Gelian huaying* 隔簾花影 [*Flower Shadows behind the Curtain*]. 1935. *Harvard Library*, iiif.lib.harvard.edu/manifests/view/drs:49802772$1i.

———. *Xu* Jin Ping Mei 續金瓶梅 [*Sequel to* Plum in the Golden Vase]. *Guben xiaoshuo jicheng* 古本小說集成 [*Collection of Classic Novels*]. Shanghai guji chubanshe, 1994.

Don Juan of China: An Amour from the "Chin P'ing Mei." Retold in pictures and text by Kwan Shan-mei, translated by Samuel Buck, Tuttle, 1960.

Dong, Madeleine Yue. *Republican Beijing: The City and Its Histories.* U of California P, 2003.

Dong Yue 董說. *The Tower of Myriad Mirrors: A Supplement to* Journey to the West. Translated by Larry J. Schulz and Shen-fu Lin, Asian Humanities Press, 1978.

Durrant, Stephen W., et al. *The Letter to Ren An and Sima Qian's Legacy.* U of Washington P, 2016.

Eagleton, Terry. *William Shakespeare.* Blackwell Publishing, 1986.

Eco, Umberto. *The Name of the Rose.* Mariner Books, 2014.

Elvin, Mark. "Female Virtue and the State in China." *Past and Present*, vol. 104, 1984, pp. 111–52.

The Epic of Gilgamesh. Translated and edited by Benjamin R. Foster, W. W. Norton, 2001.

Epstein, Maram. *Competing Discourses: Orthodoxy, Authenticity, and Engendered Meanings in Late-Imperial Chinese Fiction.* Harvard U Asia Center, 2001.

Fang Man, composer. *Golden Lily* 金蓮. Libretto by Guo Jie. *Fang Man Music*, 2020, www.fangmanmusic.com/opera.

Feng Xiaogang 馮小剛, director. *Wo bu shi Pan Jinlian* 我不是潘金蓮 [*I Am Not Pan Jinlian*]. Performance by Fan Bingbing 範冰冰, Beijing Sparkle Roll Media et al., 2016.

Film poster for *The Notorious Concubines ("The Golden Lotus"). Eiga Wiki*, eiga .fandom.com/wiki/The_Notorious_Concubines?file=The_Notorious_ Concubines.jpg. Accessed 19 Aug. 2021.

Fogel, Joshua A., and Peter Gue Zarrow, editors. *Imagining the People: Chinese Intellectuals and the Concept of Citizenship, 1890–1920.* M. E. Sharpe, 1997.

Forsythe, Michael. "China's Chief Justice Rejects an Independent Judiciary, and Reformers Wince." *The New York Times*, 18 Jan. 2017, www.nytimes.com/2017/ 01/18/world/asia/china-chief-justice-courts-zhou-qiang.html.

The Fragrant Flower: Classic Chinese Erotica in Art and Poetry. Translated by N. S. Wang and B. L. Wang, Prometheus Books, 1990.

"From the *Jin Ping Mei* to the School Book." *Tales of Manchu Life*, 26 Jan. 2016, talesofmanchulife.wordpress.com/2016/01/26/from-the-jin-ping-mei-to-the -school-book/. Accessed 30 Apr. 2018.

Furth, Charlotte. "Androgynous Males and Deficient Females: Biology and Gender Boundaries in Sixteenth- and Seventeenth-Century China." *Late Imperial China*, vol. 9, no. 2, Dec. 1988, pp. 1–31.

Gamble, Sidney D. *Peking: A Social Survey*. George H. Doran, 1921.

Gardner, Daniel K. *Confucianism: A Very Short Introduction*. Oxford UP, 2014.

Gardner, Daniel K., and Mark C. Carnes. *Confucianism and the Succession Crisis of the Wanli Emperor, 1587*. 3rd ed., W. W. Norton, 2014.

Ge, Liangyan. *Out of the Margins: The Rise of Chinese Vernacular Fiction*. U of Hawai'i P, 2001.

Gimm, Martin. *Hans Conon von der Gabelentz und die Übersetzung des chinesischen Romans* Jin Ping Mei. Harasowitz Verlag, 2005.

Goldman, Andrea S. *Opera and the City: The Politics of Culture in Beijing, 1770–1900*. Stanford UP, 2012.

Goldman, Merle, and Elizabeth J. Perry, editors. *Changing Meanings of Citizenship in Modern China*. Harvard UP, 2002.

Goodrich, L. Carrington, and Chaoying Fang, editors. *Dictionary of Ming Biography*. Columbia UP, 1976. 2 vols.

Haenisch, Erich. *Mandschu-Grammatik*. Verlag Enzyklopädie, 1961.

Hanan, Patrick D. "A Landmark of the Chinese Novel." *University of Toronto Quarterly*, vol. 30, no. 3, July 2015, pp. 325–35.

———. "Sources of the *Chin P'ing Mei*." *Asia Major*, new series, vol. 10, no. 1, 1963, pp. 23–67.

———. "The Text of the *Chin P'ing Mei*." *Asia Major*, new series, vol. 9, no. 2, 1962, pp. 1–57.

The Harem of Hsi Men: The Complete Adventures of a Dissolute Mandarin, His Six Wives, His Concubines, His Singing Girls and Flower Maidens—Told with Unblushing Frankness and Rich Humor!. Royal Books, 1960s?

Hargett, James M. "Huizong's Magic Marchmount: The Genyue Pleasure Park of Kaifeng." *Monumenta Serica*, vol. 38, 1988, pp. 1–48.

Harootunian, Harry. *Marx after Marx: History and Time in the Expansion of Capital*. Columbia UP, 2015.

Harvey, David. *Marx, Capital, and the Madness of Economic Reason*. Oxford UP, 2018.

Hawkes, David. "Threesomes with the Dominoes." Appendix II. *The Crab-Flower Club*, by Cao Xueqin 曹雪芹, translated by Hawkes, Penguin Books, 1977, pp. 586–87. Vol. 2 of *The Story of the Stone*.

Hawkes, David, and John Minford, translators. *The Story of the Stone*. By Cao Xueqin 曹雪芹, Penguin Books, 1973–86. 5 vols.

———, translators. *The Story of the Stone*. By Cao Xueqin 曹雪芹, edited by Fan Shengyu, bilingual ed., Shanghai Foreign Language Education Press / Penguin Books, 2014. 5 vols.

He Xiangjiu 何香久. Jin Ping Mei *chuanbo shihua—yibu qishu zai quanshijie de qiyu* 金瓶梅傳播史話——一部奇書在全世界的奇遇 [*The History of* The Plum in the Golden Vase*'s Dissemination—An Extraordinary Book's Extraordinary Encounters around the World*]. Zhongguo wenlian chuban gongsi, 1998.

Hegel, Robert. "General Introduction." *The Golden Lotus*, vol. 1, by Lanling Xiaoxiao Sheng 蘭陵笑笑生, translated by Clement Egerton and Lao She, edited and introduced by Hegel, Tuttle, 2011, pp. 5–21.

Herrmann, J. Berenike, et al. "Revisiting Style, a Key Concept in Literary Studies." *Journal of Literary Theory*, vol. 9, no. 1, 2015, pp. 25–52.

Ho, Ping-ti. "The Salt Merchants of Yang-Chou: A Study of Commercial Capitalism in Eighteenth-Century China." *Harvard Journal of Asiatic Studies*, vol. 17, nos. 1–2, 1954, pp. 130–68.

Hockx, Michael. *Questions of Style: Literary Societies and Literary Journals in Modern China, 1911–1937*. Brill, 2003.

Hogan, Patrick Colm. *Sexual Identities: A Cognitive Literary Study*. Oxford UP, 2017.

Hong Yingming 洪應明. *Cai gen tan* 菜根譚 [*A Discussion of Bitter Roots*]. Commentary by Yang Chunqiao 楊春俏, Zhonghua shuju, 2013.

Hou Zhongyi 侯忠義 and Wang Rumei 王汝梅, editors. Jin Ping Mei *ziliao huibian* 金瓶梅資料匯編 [*Collected Materials on* The Plum in the Golden Vase]. Beijing daxue chubanshe, 1985.

Houses of Joy. Olympia Press, 1965.

Hsia, C. T. *The Classic Chinese Novel: A Critical Introduction*. Columbia UP, 1968.

Hu, Siao-Chen. "In the Name of Correctness: Ding Yaokang's *Xu Jin Ping Mei* as a Reading of *Jin Ping Mei*." *Snakes' Legs: Sequels, Continuations, Rewritings, and Chinese Fiction*, edited by Martin W. Huang, U of Hawai'i P, 2004, pp. 75–97.

Hu Wenbing 胡文彬, editor and compiler. Jin Ping Mei *shulu* 金瓶梅書錄 [*A Plum in the Golden Vase Bibliography*]. Liaoning renmin, 1987.

Hua, Wei. "How Dangerous Can the *Peony* Be? Textual Space, *Caizi Mudan ting*, and Naturalizing the Erotic." *The Journal of Asian Studies*, vol. 65, no. 4, Nov. 2006, pp. 741–62.

Huang Lin 黃霖. Jin Ping Mei *jiangyan lu* 金瓶梅講演錄 [*Lectures on* The Plum in the Golden Vase]. Guangxi shifan daxue, 2008.

Huang, Martin. *Desire and Fictional Narrative in Late Imperial China*. Harvard U Asia Center, 2001.

Huang, Philip. *Civil Justice in China: Representation and Practice in the Qing*. Stanford UP, 1996.

Huang, Ray. *1587: A Year of No Significance: The Ming Dynasty in Decline*. Yale UP, 1982.

———. "The Lung-ch'ing and Wan-li Reigns, 1567–1620." *The Ming Dynasty, 1368–1644*, edited by Frederick W. Mote and Denis Twitchett, Cambridge UP, 1988, pp. 511–84. Vol. 7, part 1 of *The Cambridge History of China*.

Huang Zhangjian 黃彰健, editor. *Mingdai lulihuibian* 明代律例彙編 [*Compendium of Ming Dynasty Statutes and Substatutes*]. Zhongyang Yanjiuyuan Lishi Yuyan Yanjiusuo, 1994. 2 vols.

Huizhou qiannian qiyue wenshu 徽州千年契約文書 [*A Thousand Years of Contracts from Huizhou*]. Vol. 1, Huashan wenyi chuban she, 1991.

Huizinga, Johan. *Homo Ludens: A Study of the Play-Element in Culture*. 1949. Martino Publishing, 2014.

Hunt, Lynn, editor. *The Invention of Pornography: Obscenity and the Origins of Modernity, 1500–1800*. Zone Books, 1993.

Hutton, Eric L., translator. *Xunzi* 荀子, by Xunzi 荀子. Princeton UP, 2016.

Idema, Wilt L. *Judge Bao and the Rule of Law: Eight Ballad-Stories from the Period 1250–1450*. World Scientific, 2010.

Idema, Wilt L., and Beata Grant. *The Red Brush: Writing Women of Imperial China*. Harvard UP, 2004, digital.wustl.edu/r/red/.

Jiang Ruizao 蔣瑞藻, editor. *Xiaoshuo kaozheng* 小說考證 [*Research on Fiction*]. Shang wu yin shu guan, 1919.

Jiang, Yonglin, translator. *The Great Ming Code: Da Ming lü*. U of Washington P, 2005.

Jiang, Yonglin, and Yanhong Wu. "Satisfying Both Sentiment and Law: Fairness-Centered Judicial Reasoning as Seen in Late Ming Casebooks." *Thinking with Cases: Specialist Knowledge in Chinese Cultural History*, edited by Charlotte Furth et al., U of Hawai'i P, 2007, pp. 31–61.

"*Jin Ping Mei* yan liangxiang Nanjing 'Pan Jinlian' shuixiu qingwan duancha songshui" 金瓶梅宴亮相南京 "潘金蓮"水袖轻挽端茶送水 ["A *Jin Ping Mei* Banquet Appears in Nanjing, and 'Pan Jinlian' Delicately Rolls Her Sleeves to Pour Tea"]. *Sina .com.cn*, 12 Jan. 2004, news.sina.com.cn/s/2004-01-12/13192610636.shtml. Accessed 10 Feb. 2022.

Jockers, Matthew L., and Daniela M. Witten. "A Comparative Study of Machine Learning Methods for Authorship Attribution." *Literary and Linguistics Computing*, vol. 25, no. 2, 2010, pp. 215–23.

Jung, Carl. Foreword. *I Ching: The Richard Wilhelm Translation*, translated by Cary F. Baynes, Princeton UP, 1961, pp. xxi–xxxix.

Keane, Webb. *Ethical Life: Its Natural and Social Histories*. Princeton UP, 2016.

Keown, Damien. *Buddhism: A Very Short Introduction*. Oxford UP, 2013.

Knapp, Keith N. "The Ru Reinterpretation of *Xiao*." *Early China*, vol. 20, 1995, pp. 195–222.

Ko, Dorothy. "The Written Word and the Bound Foot: A History of the Courtesan's Aura." Widmer and Chang, pp. 74–100.

Kuhn, Philip. *Soulstealers: The Chinese Sorcery Scare of 1768*. Harvard UP, 1990.

Langlois, John. "Ming Law." *The Ming Dynasty, 1368–1644*, edited by Denis Twitchett and Frederick Mote, Cambridge UP, 1998, pp. 172–220. Vol. 8, part 2 of *The Cambridge History of China*.

Laufer, Berthold. "Skizze der manjurischen Literatur." *Revue Orientale*, vol. 9, 1908, pp. 1–53.

Law, Clara, director. *Pan Jinlian zhi qianshi Jinsheng* 潘金蓮之前世今生 [*Reincarnation of Golden Lotus*]. Performances by Joey Wong et al., Youhe Film Production, 1989.

Lazarillo de Tormes. 1554. Edited and translated by Ilan Stavans, W. W. Norton, 2016.

Lee, Haiyan. "Measuring the Stomach of a Gentleman with the Heart-Mind of a Pipsqueak: On the Ubiquity and Utility of Theory of Mind in Literature, Mostly." *Poetics Today*, vol. 41, no. 2, 2020, pp. 205–22.

———. "Response to the Panel on Cognitive Approaches to Chinese Literature." MLA Annual Convention, 4 Jan. 2018, New York City.

———. *Revolution of the Heart: A Genealogy of Love in China, 1900–1950*. Stanford UP, 2007.

———. *The Stranger and the Chinese Moral Imagination*. Stanford UP, 2014.

Lévy, André. "Introduction to the French Translation of *Jin Ping Mei cihua*." Translated by Marc Martinez. *Renditions*, no. 24, autumn 1985, pp. 109–29.

Li Mengyang 李夢陽. *Kongtong Ji* 空同集 [*The Collected Works of Master Kongtong*]. Zhu Mujie, 1552. *Harvard Library*, iiif.lib.harvard.edu/manifests/view/drs:51492726$1i.

"Li Mengyang (Li Meng-yang)." Goodrich and Fang, 1: 841–45.

Li, Wai-yee. "The Late Ming Courtesan: Invention of a Cultural Ideal." Widmer and Chang, pp. 46–73.

———. "The Letter to Ren An and Authorship in the Chinese Tradition." Durrant et al., pp. 96–123.

———, translator. Plum Shadows *and* Plank Bridge. By Mao Xiang 冒襄 and Yu Huai 餘懷, Columbia UP, 2020.

Li Yu 李漁. *The Carnal Prayer Mat*. Translated by Patrick Hanan, U of Hawai'i P, 1990.

Li Yu 李玉. "A Handful of Snow." Translated by Tina Lu. *Hawai'i Reader in Traditional Chinese Culture*, edited by Victor Mair et al., U of Hawai'i P, 2005, pp. 517–24.

———. *Yipeng xue* 一捧雪 [*A Handful of Snow*]. *Yi'li an si zhong qu* 一笠庵四种曲 [*Four Kinds of Qu from Master of the Shrine of the Single Bamboo Hat*], Baoyanzhai, 1794.

Lin Yutang 林語堂. "Tan Laolunsi" 談勞倫斯 ["On Lawrence"]. *Lin Yutang piping wenji* 林語堂批評文集 [*The Critical Essays of Lin Yutang*], compiled and edited by Shen Yongbao 沈永寶, Zhuhai chubanshe, pp. 310–16.

Link, Perry. "The Wonderfully Elusive Chinese Novel." *The New York Review of Books*, 23 Apr. 2015, www.nybooks.com/articles/2015/04/23/wonderfully-elusive-chinese-novel/.

Liu Cunren 柳存仁. "Lundun suojian Zhongguo xiaoshuo shumu tiyao" 倫敦所見中國小說書目提要 ["Bibliography of Chinese Novels Seen in London"]. Jin Ping Mei *ziliao huibian* 金瓶梅資料彙編 [*A Compendium of Materials on* The Plum in the Golden Vase], edited and compiled by Zhu Yixuan 朱一玄, Nankai daxue, 2002, pp. 168–73, 708–11.

Liu Jixing 劉繼興. *Mao Zedong yishi* 毛澤東軼事 [*Anecdotes about Mao Zedong*]. Zhongguo wenshi chubanshe, 2011.

Liu Zhenyun 刘震云. *I Did Not Kill My Husband*. Translated by Howard Goldblatt and Sylvia Li-chun Lin, Arcade, 2014.

———. *Wo bu shi Pan Jinlian* 我不是潘金蓮 [*I Am Not Pan Jinlian*]. Changjiang wenyi chubanshe, 2012.

Lo, Andrew. "China's Passion for Pai: Playing Cards, Dominoes, and Mahjong." Mackenzie and Finkel, pp. 216–32.

Lo, Andrew, and Tzi-cheng Wang. "Spider Threads Roaming the Empyrean: The Game of *Weiqi*." Mackenzie and Finkel, pp. 186–201.

Lopez, Donald S., Jr. *The Heart Sutra Explained: Indian and Tibetan Commentaries*. State U of New York P, 1988.

The Love Pagoda: The Amorous Adventures of Hsi Men and His Six Wives. Introduction by Albert Ellis, Brandon House, 1967.

Lu, Tina. "The Literati Culture of the Late Ming (1573–1644)." *The Cambridge History of Chinese Literature*, vol. 2, edited by Kang-I Sun Chang and Stephen Owen, Cambridge UP, 2011, pp. 63–151.

Lu Xun 魯迅. *A Brief History of Chinese Fiction*. Translated by Yang Xianyi and Gladys Yang, Foreign Languages Press, 1976.

———. "Di shijiu pian Ming zhi renqing xiaoshuo (shang)" 第十九篇明之人情小說 ["Chapter Nineteen: Ming-Period Novels of Manners, Part One"]. *Zhongguo xiaoshuo lüe* 中國小說史略 [*A Brief History of Chinese Fiction*]. *Jin Ping Mei ziliao huibian* 金瓶梅資料彙編 [*A Compendium of Materials on* The Plum in the Golden Vase], edited and compiled by Zhu Yixuan 朱一玄, Nankai daxue, 2002, pp. 685–88.

———. *A Madman's Diary: English and Chinese Bilingual Edition*. Translated by Paul Meighan, CreateSpace, 2014.

Luma ding sheng sijue 祿馬定生死訣 [*Instructions on How to Determine Survival or Death by Means of Emolument and Horse*]. East Asia Department, Berlin State Library, Prussian Cultural Heritage Foundation (Staatsbibliothek zu Berlin—Preussischer Kulturbesitz). Slg. Unschuld 8806. Medical manuscript.

Luo Guanzhong 羅觀眾. *Sanguo yanyi* 三國演義 [*Romance of the Three Kingdoms*]. Renmin wenxue chubanshe, 2005. 2 vols.

———. *Three Kingdoms: A Historical Novel*. Translated by Moss Roberts, U of California P, 1991.

Ma, Ning. *The Age of Silver: The Rise of the Novel East and West*. Oxford UP, 2017.

Mackenzie, Colin, and Irving Finkel, editors. *Asian Games: The Art of Contest*. Asia Society, 2004.

Mair, Victor, editor. *The Columbia Anthology of Traditional Chinese Literature*. Columbia UP, 1996.

Mann, Susan, and Yu-Yin Cheng, editors. *Under Confucian Eyes: Writings on Gender in Chinese History*. U of California P, 2001.

Marx, Karl. *Capital*. Translated by David Fernbach, Penguin Books, 1978. 3 vols.

———. *Grundrisse: Foundation of the Critique of Political Economy (Rough Draft)*. Translated by Martin Nicolaus, Penguin Books, 1993.

McDermott, Joseph P. "The Chinese Domestic Bursar." *Ajia bunka kenkyuu*, Nov. 1990, pp. 15–52.

McMahon, Keith. *Causality and Containment in Seventeenth-Century Chinese Fiction*. Brill, 1988.

———. *Celestial Women: Imperial Wives and Concubines from Song to Qing*. Rowman and Littlefield, 2016.

———. *Misers, Shrews, and Polygamists: Sexuality and Male-Female Relations in Eighteenth-Century Chinese Fiction*. Duke UP, 1995.

Mencius. *Mencius*. Translated by Irene T. Bloom, edited by Philip J. Ivanhoe, Columbia UP, 2009.

Meng, T'ien-p'ei, and Sidney D. Gamble. *Prices, Wages, and the Standard of Living in Peking, 1900–1924*. Peking Express, 1926.

Miao Huaiming 苗懷明 and Song Nan 宋楠. "Guowai shoubu *Jin Ping Mei* quanyiben de faxian yu tanxi" 國外首部金瓶梅全譯本的發現與探析 ["An Analysis of the First Complete Edition of *The Plum in the Golden Vase* Abroad"]. *Shanghai shifan daxue xuebao (zhexue shehui kexue ban)* 上海師範大學學報 (哲學社會科學版) [*The Journal of Shanghai Normal University (Philosophy and Social Sciences Edition)*], vol. 44, no. 6, 2015, pp. 88–96.

Miller, Patricia H., et al. "Thinking about People Thinking about People Thinking about . . . : A Study of Social Cognitive Development." *Child Development*, vol. 41, no. 3, Sept. 1970, pp. 613–23, https://doi.org/10.2307/1127211.

Ming Qing Huizhou shehui jingji ziliao congbian 明清徽州社會經濟資料叢編 [*Collection of Sources in Society and Economics of Ming Qing Huizhou*]. Zhongguo she hui ke xue yuan, 1988.

Moretti, Franco, editor. *History, Geography, and Culture*. Princeton UP, 2007. Vol. 1 of *The Novel*.

Naquin, Susan. *Peking: Temples and City Life, 1400–1900*. U of California P, 2001.

National Statistics Bureau of the People's Republic of China. *Guanyu 1993 nian guomin jingji he shehui fazhan de tongji gongbao* 關於 1993 年國民經濟和社會發展的統計公報 [*Public Statistical Report on the National Economy and Social Development for the Year 1993*]. *National Bureau of Statistics*, 28 Feb. 1994, www.stats.gov.cn/tjsj/tjgb/ndtjgb/qgndtjgb/200203/t20020331_30007.html.

Needleman, Saul, and Christian Wunsch. "A General Method Applicable to the Search for Similarities in the Amino Acid Sequence of Two Proteins." *Journal of Molecular Biology*, vol. 48, no. 3, Mar. 1970, pp. 443–53.

Niu Seng-ju 牛僧孺. "Scholar Ts'ui." Translated by Donald E. Gjertson. *Traditional Chinese Stories: Themes and Variations*, edited by Y. W. Ma and Joseph S. M. Lau, Columbia UP, 1978, pp. 413–15.

Nylan, Michael. "Confucian Piety and Individualism in Han China." *Journal of the American Oriental Society*, vol. 116, no. 1, 1996, pp. 1–16.

Ong, Walter J. *Orality and Literacy: The Technologizing of the Word*. 3rd ed., Routledge, 2012.

Ouyang Yuqian 歐陽予倩. *Pan Jinlian* 潘金蓮. Huaxia chubanshe, 1999.

Owen, Stephen, editor and translator. *An Anthology of Chinese Literature: Beginnings to 1911*. W. W. Norton, 1996.

Pan Guangdan 潘光旦. "Yixu" 譯序 ["Translator's Preface"]. 1944. *Xing xinlixue* 性心理學 [*Studies in the Psychology of Sex*], by Havelock Ellis, translated by Pan 潘, Sanlian shudian, 1987, pp. 1–7.

Perry, Elizabeth. *Rebels and Revolutionaries in North China, 1845–1945*. Stanford UP, 1980.

Petrovic, Misha, and Gary Hamilton. "Making Global Markets: Wal-Mart and Its Suppliers." *Wal-Mart: The Face of Twenty-First-Century Capitalism*, edited by Nelson Lichtenstein, W. W. Norton, 2006, pp. 107–42.

Plaks, Andrew. *Archetype and Allegory in* Dream of the Red Chamber. Princeton UP, 1976.

———. *The Four Masterworks of the Ming Novel*. Princeton UP, 1987.

———, translator. "How to Read the *Dream of the Red Chamber*." By Zhang Xinzhi 張新之. Rolston, *How to Read*, pp. 323–40.

———. "The Novel in Premodern China." Moretti, pp. 181–213.

———. "The Problem of Incest in *Jin Ping Mei* and *Honglou meng*." *Paradoxes of Traditional Chinese Literature*, edited by Eva Hung et al., Chinese UP, 1994, pp. 123–46.

———. "Toward a Critical Theory of Chinese Narrative." *Chinese Narrative: Critical and Theoretical Essays*, edited by Plaks, Princeton UP, 1977, pp. 309–52.

Posner, Richard. *Law and Literature*. 3rd ed., Harvard UP, 2009.

Postone, Moishe. "Marx, Temporality and Modernity." *East-Asian Marxisms and Their Trajectories*, edited by Joyce C. H. Liu and Viren Murthy, Routledge, 2017, pp. 29–48.

Qi, Lintao. Jin Ping Mei *English Translations: Texts, Paratexts and Contexts*. Routledge, 2018.

Qian Xuantong 錢玄同. Letter to Hu Shih. 1917. *Wenxue gailiang chuyi* 文學改良芻議 [*Tentative Proposals for Literary Reform*], Zhongguo banben tushugan, 2003, p. 25. Vol. 1 of *Hu Shih wencun* 胡適文存 [*The Works of Hu Shih*].

"Refuses to Indict in Book Case." *The New York Times*, 22 Jan. 1932, p. 7.

Ricoeur, Paul. *Time and Narrative*. Translated by Kathleen McLauglin and David Pellauer, U of Chicago P, 1984–88. 3 vols.

Robbins, Joel, and Alan Rumsey. "Introduction: Cultural and Linguistic Anthropology and the Opacity of Other Minds." *Anthropological Quarterly*, vol. 81, no. 2, 2008, pp. 407–20.

Robert, Marthe. *Origins of the Novel*. Indiana UP, 1972.

Rolston, David L., editor. *How to Read the Chinese Novel*. Princeton UP, 1990.

———. "Introduction: *Jin Ping Mei* Chapters 1 and 100: Zhang Zhupo Commentary." *Renditions*, nos. 81–82, 2014, pp. 13–27.

———. "Oral Performing Literature in Traditional Chinese Fiction: Nonrealistic Usages in the *Jin Ping Mei cihua* and Their Influence." *Chinoperl Papers*, vol. 17, 1994, pp. 1–110.

———. *Traditional Chinese Fiction and Fiction Commentary: Reading and Writing between the Lines*. Stanford UP, 1997.

Ropp, Paul S. "Ambiguous Images of Courtesan Culture in Late Imperial China." Widmer and Chang, pp. 17–45.

Rosemont, Henry. *The Chinese Classic of Family Reverence: A Philosophical Translation of the* Xiaojing. U of Hawai'i P, 2009.

Roy, David Tod. "Appendix I: Translator's Commentary on the Prologue." *The Gathering*, Princeton UP, 1993, pp. 429–36. Vol. 1 of The Plum in the Golden Vase; or, Chin P'ing Mei.

———. "The Case for T'ang Hsien-Tsu's Authorship of the *Jin Ping Mei*." *CLEAR: Chinese Literature: Essays, Articles, Reviews*, vol. 8, nos. 1–2, July 1986, pp. 31–62.

———. "Chang Chu-P'o's Commentary on the *Chin P'ing Mei*." *Chinese Narrative: Critical and Theoretical Essays*, edited by Andrew Plaks, Princeton UP, 1977, pp. 115–23.

———. "*Chin P'ing Mei.*" *The Indiana Companion to Traditional Chinese Literature*, edited by William Neinhauser et al., Indiana UP, 1986, pp. 287–91.

———. Introduction. *The Gathering*, Princeton UP, 1993, pp. xvii–xlviii. Vol. 1 of The Plum in the Golden Vase; *or,* Chin P'ing Mei.

———. "The Use of Songs as a Means of Self-Expression and Self-Characterization in the *Chin P'ing Mei.*" *CLEAR: Chinese Literature: Essays, Articles, Reviews*, vol. 20, Dec. 1998, pp. 101–26.

Satyendra, Indira Suh. *Toward a Poetics of the Chinese Novel: A Study of the Prefatory Poems in the "Chin P'ing Mei tz'u-hua."* 1989. U of Chicago, PhD dissertation.

Saussy, Haun. *The Ethnography of Rhythm: Orality and Its Technologies.* Fordham UP, 2016.

Schöch, Cristof. "Beyond the Black Box; or, Understanding the Difference between Different Various Statistical Distance Measures." *The Dragonfly's Gaze*, 3 Aug. 2012, dragonfly.hypotheses.org/101. Accessed 16 May 2017.

Schonebaum, Andrew. Introduction. Schonebaum and Lu, pp. 5–69.

———. *Novel Medicine: Healing, Literature, and Popular Knowledge in Early Modern China.* U of Washington P, 2016.

Schonebaum, Andrew, and Tina Lu, editors. *Approaches to Teaching* The Story of the Stone (Dream of the Red Chamber). Modern Language Association of America, 2012.

Scott, Mary. "*The Story of the Stone* and Its Antecedents." Schonebaum and Lu, pp. 258–73.

Shang Wei. "'Jin Ping Mei' and Late Ming Print Culture." *Writing and Materiality in China: Essays in Honor of Patrick Hanan*, edited by Judith T. Zeitlin and Lydia H. Liu, Harvard U Asia Center, 2003, pp. 187–231.

———. "The Making of the Everyday World: *Jin Ping Mei cihua* and Encyclopedias for Daily Use." *Dynastic Crisis and Cultural Innovation: From the Late Ming to the Late Qing and Beyond*, edited by David Der-wei Wang and Shang, Harvard U Asia Center, 2006, pp. 63–92.

Shanghai Social Bureau. "Shanghai shehui ju guanyu chajin *Xiyang* Jin Ping Mei deng yinhui zhoukan ji gudi huishu tan tong jingcha ji zhoukan faxing she de laiwang wenshu" 上海社會局關於查禁《西洋金瓶梅》等淫穢週刊及取締穢書攤同警察及週刊發行社的來往文書 ["Correspondence with Municipal Police and Periodical Printers on Banning *Xiyang* Jin Ping Mei and Other Licentious, Filthy Weekly Periodicals and Eliminating Licentious Bookstalls"]. 22 Aug. 1946. Shanghai Municipal Archives, file number Q6-12-170-14.

———. "Shanghai shehui ju guanyu *Yuhai qingchao* deng huangyinshu ji" 上海社會局關於《欲海情潮》等荒淫書籍 ["Report on *Yuhai qingchao* and Other Licentious Books"]. 1940s? Shanghai Municipal Archives, file number Q6-12-170-39.

Shi Nai'an 施耐庵 and Luo Guanzhong 罗贯中. *The Marshes of Mount Liang: A New Translation of the* Shuihu Zhuan *or* Water Margin. Translated by John Dent-Young and Alex Dent-Young, Chinese UP, 1994–2003. 5 vols.

———. *Outlaws of the Marsh.* Translated by Sidney Shapiro, Foreign Languages Press, 2001.

———. *Shuihu zhuan* 水滸傳 [*Outlaws of the Marsh*]. Renmin wenxue chubanshe, 1997. 2 vols.

———. *Shuihu zhuan* 水滸傳 [*Outlaws of the Marsh*]. Zhonghua shuju, 1958. 4 vols.

Shi Yukun 石玉昆. *Tales of Magistrate Bao and His Valiant Lieutenants: Selections from* Sanxia wuyi. Translated by Susan Blader, Chinese UP, 1998.

Shi Zhecun 施蟄存. *Shi Xiu zhi lian* 石秀之恋 [*The Love of Shi Xiu*]. Renmin wenxue chubanshe, 1991.

Sima Qian 司馬遷. *Selections from Records of the Grand Historian*. Translated by Gladys Yang and Yang Xianyi, Foreign Languages Press, 2002.

———. *Shiji: Dian jiaoben ershisi shi xiuding ben* 史記：點校本二十四史修訂本 [*Records of the Grand Historian: Revised, Commented, Twenty-Four History Edition*]. Zhonghua shuju, 2014. 10 vols.

Simon, Julien J. "Contextualizing Cognitive Approaches to Early Modern Spanish Literature." *Cognitive Approaches to Early Modern Spanish Literature*, edited by Isabel Jaén and Simon, Oxford UP, 2016, pp. 13–33.

Slingerland, Edward. "Cognitive Science and Religious Thought: The Case of Psychological Interiority in the *Analects*." *Mental Culture: Towards a Cognitive Science of Religion*, edited by Dimitris Xygalatas and Lee McCorkle, Acumen Publishing, 2013, pp. 197–212. Religion, Cognition and Culture.

Smith, Richard J. "Divination: Science, Technology, and the Mantic Arts in Traditional China." *Encyclopaedia of the History of Science, Technology, and Medicine in Non-Western Cultures*, edited by Helaine Selin, Springer, 2008, pp. 684–92.

Sommer, Matthew H. "Dangerous Males, Vulnerable Males, and Polluted Males: The Regulation of Masculinity in Qing Dynasty Law." *Chinese Femininities/Chinese Masculinities: A Reader*, edited by Susan Brownell and Jeffrey Wasserstrom, U of California P, 2002, pp. 67–88.

———. "The Penetrated Male in Late Imperial China: Judicial Constructions and Social Stigma." *Modern China*, vol. 23, no. 2, 1997, pp. 140–80.

———. *Polyandry and Wife-Selling in Qing Dynasty China: Survival Strategies and Judicial Interventions*. U of California P, 2015.

———. "Scandal in the Garden: *The Story of the Stone* as a 'Licentious Novel.'" Schonebaum and Lu, pp. 186–207.

———. *Sex, Law, and Society in Qing Dynasty China*. Stanford UP, 2000.

Spence, Jonathan D. "Remembrance of Ming's Past." *The New York Review of Books*, 23 June 1994, www.nybooks.com/articles/1994/06/23/remembrance-of-mings -past/?lp_txn_id=1046089.

———. *The Search for Modern China*. W. W. Norton, 2013.

Stember, Nick. "Jin Porn Mei: Comic Book Adaptations of the Chinese Novel." *Nick Stember*, 15 May 2014, www.nickstember.com/jin-porn-mei-comic-book -adaptations-chinese-novel/. Accessed 10 Mar. 2017.

Stone, Charles R. *The Fountainhead of Chinese Erotica:* The Lord of Perfect Satisfaction (Ruyijun zhuan). U of Hawai'i P, 2003.

Sullivan, Rebecca, and Alan McKee. *Pornography: Structures, Agency and Performance*. Polity Press, 2015.

Sun Shuyu 孫述宇. Jin Ping Mei de yishu: Jiushu xindu zhi er 金瓶梅的藝術:舊書新讀之二 [*The Art of* Plum in the Golden Vase: *A New Reading of Old Books, Part 2*]. Shibao wenhua chuban shiye youxian gongsi, 1978.

Swatek, Catherine, translator. *P'an Chin-lien. Twentieth-Century Chinese Drama: An Anthology*, edited by Edward M. Gunn, Indiana UP, 1983, pp. 52–75.

Tang Xianzu 湯顯祖. *Caizi* Mudan ting 才子牡丹亭 [*The Genius* Peony Pavilion]. Commentary by Cheng Qiong 程瓊, edited by Hua Wei 華瑋 and Jiang Jurong 江巨榮, Taiwan xuesheng shuju, 2004.

———. *Mudan ting* 牡丹亭 [*The Peony Pavilion*]. Dongwen shuju, 1886.

———. *The Purple Hairpins*. Translated by Wang Rongpei. *The Complete Dramatic Works of Tang Xianzu*, edited by Wang Rongpei and Zhang Ling, Bloomsbury China, 2018, pp. 189–412.

———. *Wu Wushan sanfu heping* Mudan ting *huanhunji* 吳吳山三婦合評牡丹亭還魂記 [*The Three Wives of Wu Wushan's Commentary on* The Peony Pavilion]. Shanghai guji chubanshe, 2008.

———. *Zichai ji* 紫釵記 [*The Purple Hairpin*]. *Tang Xianzu ji* 湯顯祖集 [*The Collected Works of Tang Xianzu*], edited by Xu Shuofang 徐朔方, vol. 5, Shanghai guji chubanshe, 2015, pp. 2257–603.

Teiser, Stephen F. *The* Scripture on the Ten Kings *and the Making of Purgatory in Medieval Chinese Buddhism*. U of Hawai'i P, 1994.

Terras, Melissa, et al., editors. *Defining Digital Humanities*. Routledge, 2014.

Tharsen, Jeffrey, and Clovis Gladstone. "Using Philologic for Digital Textual and Intertextual Analyses of the *Twenty-Four Chinese Histories* 二十四史." *Journal of Chinese History*, vol. 4, no. 2, 2020, pp. 558–63.

Tian, Xiaofei. "A Preliminary Comparison of the Two Recensions of *Jinpingmei*." *Harvard Journal of Asiatic Studies*, vol. 62, no. 2, 2002, pp. 347–88.

Tian Xiaofei 田曉菲. *Qiushuitang lun* Jin Ping Mei 奇秋水堂論金瓶梅 [Qiushuitang on *The Plum in the Golden Vase*]. Revised ed., Tianjin renmin chubanshe, 2003.

Tsing, Anna Lowenhaupt. *The Mushroom at the End of the World: On the Possibility of Life in Capitalist Ruins*. Princeton UP, 2015.

Tu, Hsieh-Chang, and Jieh Hsiang. "A Text-Mining Approach to the Authorship Attribution Problem of *Dream of the Red Chamber*." 2013, pp. 1–6, www.digital.ntu.edu.tw/hsiang/pdf/A%20Text-mining%20Approach%20to%20the%20Authorship%20Attribution%20Problem%20of%20Dream%20of%20the%20Red%20Chamber.pdf.

Turney, Peter, and Patrick Pantel. "From Frequency to Meaning: Vector Space Models of Semantic Meaning." *Journal of Artificial Intelligence Research*, vol. 37, 2010, pp. 141–88.

"*The Twenty-Four Paragons of Filial Piety* [*Ershisi Xiao*]." *Rice University*, www.ruf.rice.edu/~asia/24ParagonsFilialPiety.html. Accessed 9 Jan. 2018.

Unschuld, Paul U., and Jinsheng Zheng. *Chinese Traditional Healing: The Berlin Collections of Manuscript Volumes from the Sixteenth through the Early Twentieth Century*. Brill, 2012.

Vierthaler, Paul. "Fiction and History: Polarity and Stylistic Gradience in Late Imperial Chinese Literature." *Journal of Cultural Analytics*, vol. 1, 2016, https://doi.org/10.22148/16.003.

Vierthaler, Paul, and Mees Gelein. "A BLAST-Based, Language-Agnostic Text Reuse Algorithm with a MARKUS Implementation and Sequence Alignment Optimized for Large Chinese Corpora." *Journal of Cultural Analytics*, vol. 1, no. 2, 18 Mar. 2019, https://doi.org/10.22148/16.034.

Vinograd, Richard Ellis. *Boundaries of the Self: Chinese Portraits, 1600–1900.* Cambridge UP, 1992.

Vitiello, Giovanni. "Exemplary Sodomites: Chivalry and Love in Late Ming Culture." *Nan Nü*, vol. 2, no. 2, Jan. 2000, pp. 207–57.

———. *The Libertine's Friend: Homosexuality and Masculinity in Late Imperial China.* U of Chicago P, 2011.

Volpp, Sophie. "Classifying Lust: The Seventeenth-Century Vogue for Male Love." *Harvard Journal of Asiatic Studies*, vol. 61, no. 1, 2001, pp. 77–117.

———. "The Discourse on Male Marriage: Li Yu's 'A Male Mencius's Mother.'" *Positions*, vol. 2, no. 1, 1994, pp. 113–32.

———. "The Gift of a Python Robe: The Circulation of Objects in *Jin Ping Mei*." *Harvard Journal of Asiatic Studies*, vol. 65, no. 1, June 2005, pp. 133–58.

———. "The Literary Circulation of Actors in Seventeenth-Century China." *The Journal of Asian Studies*, vol. 61, no. 3, 2002, pp. 949–84.

Von Glahn, Richard. *Fountain of Fortune: Money and Monetary Policy in China, 1000–1700.* U of California P, 1996.

Wakamatsu, Koji, director. *Kinpeibai* 金瓶梅 [*The Notorious Concubines*]. Boxoffice International, 1968.

Waley, Arthur. Introduction. Chin P'ing Mei: *The Adventurous History of Hsi Men and His Six Wives*, by Lanling Xiaoxiao Sheng 蘭陵笑笑生, translated by Bernard Miall, John Lane, 1939, pp. vii–xviii.

Wang, David Der-wei. *Fin-de-Siècle Splendor: Repressed Modernities of Late Qing Fiction, 1849–1911.* Stanford UP, 1997.

Wang Feng-Chow. *The Adventures of Hsi Men Ching.* Translated by Chu Tsui-Jen, Library of Facetious Lore, 1927.

Wang Guoxuan 王國軒, editor. *Da Xue, Zhong Yong* 大學, 中庸 譯註 [*The Great Learning*]. Zhonghua shuju, 2006.

Wei Minglun 魏明伦. *Pan Jinlian: The History of a Fallen Woman.* Translated by David Williams and Xiaoxia Williams. *Theater and Society: Anthology of Contemporary Chinese Drama*, edited by Haiping Yan, M. E. Sharpe, 1998, pp. 123–88.

———. *Pan Jinlian: The Story of One Woman and Four Men—A New Sichuan Opera.* Translated by Shiao-ling Yu. *Asian Theatre Journal*, vol. 10, no. 1, spring 1993, pp. 1–48.

———. *Pan Jinlian: Yige nuren de chenlun shi* 潘金蓮: 一個女人的沉淪史 [*Pan Jinlian: The History of a Woman's Downfall*]. Beifang wenyi chubanshe, 1987.

Widmer, Ellen, and Kang-I Sun Chang, editors. *Writing Women in Late Imperial China*. Stanford UP, 1997.

Wilhelm, Richard, and Cary F. Baynes, translators. *The* I Ching; *or,* Book of Changes. Princeton UP, 1967.

Wolfendale, Stuart. "But It's Not Porn, Officer." *South China Morning Post*, 28 Mar. 1993, www.scmp.com/article/23978/its-not-porn-officer.

Woolf, Virginia. *A Room of One's Own*. Grafton, 1977.

Wright, Arthur F., editor. *The Confucian Persuasion*. Stanford UP, 1960.

Wu Cuncun. *Homoerotic Sensibilities in Late Imperial China*. RoutledgeCurzon, 2004.

Wu Gan 吳敢. *Ershi shiji* Jin Ping Mei *yanjiu shi changbian* 二十世紀金瓶梅研究史長編 [*Long Version of the History of the Study of* The Plum in the Golden Vase *in the Twentieth Century*]. Wenhui chubanshe, 2003.

Wu Han 吳晗. "*Jin Ping Mei* de zhuzuo shidai ji qi shehui Beijing" 金瓶梅的著作時代及其社會背景 ["The Historical and Social Backgrounds of the Production of *The Plum in the Golden Vase*"]. 1934. *Du shu zhai ji* 讀書齋集 [*Records from the Reading Studio*], by Wu 吳, Sanlian, 1957, pp. 1–38.

Wu Xiaoling 吳曉鈴. "*Jing Ping Mei cihua* li de Qinghe ji yi Jiajing shiqi de Beijing wei moxing chutan" 金瓶梅詞話裡的清河即以嘉靖時期的北京爲模型初探 ["A Preliminary Study of the Fact that Qinghe in *Plum in the Golden Vase: A Ballad Tale* Is Modeled on the Beijing of the Jiajing Reign Period"]. *Zhongwai wenxue* 中外文學 [*Chinese and Foreign Literature*], vol. 18, no. 2, 1989, pp. 107–22.

Wu, Yi-Li. *Reproducing Women: Medicine, Metaphor, and Childbirth in Late Imperial China*. U of California P, 2010.

Xiaojing 孝經 [*Classic of Filial Piety*]. *Chinese Text Project*, ctext.org/xiao-jing/zh. Accessed 19 June 2021.

Xie Guozhen 謝國楨, editor. *Mingdai shehui jingji shiliao xuanbian* 明代社會經濟史料選編 [*Selected Collection of Primary Sources regarding Ming Social and Economic History*]. Fujian ren min chu ban she, 2004.

Xu Wei 徐渭. "Di mu Miao yiren mu zhi ming" 嫡母苗宜人墓誌銘 ["Epitaph of Lady Miao"]. *Xu Wei ji* 徐渭集 [*Collected Works of Xu Wei*], Zhonghua shu ju, 2008, pp. 631–32.

Xu Zhen 徐㽘. *Shagou ji* 殺狗記 [*Record of Killing a Dog*]. Zhonghua shuju, 1960.

Xu Zhongming 徐忠明. "*Jin Ping Mei* gong'an yu Mingdai xingshi xusong zhidu chutan" 金瓶梅"公案"與明代刑事訴訟制度初探 ["Preliminary Discussion of the Cases in *The Plum in the Golden Vase* and the Criminal Lawsuit System in Ming"]. *Bijiao fa yanjiu* 比較法研究 [*Journal of Comparative Law*], no. 1, 1996, pp. 44–58.

Xu Zhongming 徐忠明 and Du Jin 杜金. "Tang-Ming lüli xingxun guiding zhi yitong" 唐明律例刑訊規定之異同 ["A Comparison of the Regulations concerning Judicial Torture in Tang and Ming Law"]. *Beijing daxue xuebao* 北京大學學報 [*Journal of Beijing University*], vol. 46, no. 4, 2009, pp. 40–48.

Xue Yunsheng 薛允升. *Du li cun yi chong kan ben* 讀例存疑重刊本 [*Lingering Doubts while Perusing the Substatutes, Newly Edited Version*]. Punctuated and edited by Huang Jingjia 黃靜嘉, Chinese Materials and Research Aids Service Center, 1970. 5 vols.

Xunzi 荀子. *Xunzi* 荀子. Edited by Fang Yong 方勇 and Li Bo 李波, Zhonghua shuju, 2011.

Yang Jiyun 楊霽雲. "Yibu dazhongyu xiecheng de xiaoshuo—*Jin Ping Mei*" 一部大眾語寫成的小說《金瓶梅》 ["A Work of Fiction Composed in Popular Language—*The Plum in the Golden Vase*"]. *Shehui yuebao* 社會月報 [*Society Monthly*], vol. 1, no. 3, 1934, pp. 59–82.

Yang, Lien-sheng. "Economic Justification for Spending: An Uncommon Idea in Traditional China." *Harvard Journal of Asiatic Studies*, vol. 20, nos. 1–2, June 1957, pp. 36–52.

Yang Muzhi 楊牧之. "Chuban shi shang de yiduan gushi—*Jin Ping Mei, Chatailai furen de qingren* chuban faxing de ganxiang" 出版史上的一段故事—《金瓶梅》《查泰萊夫人的情人》出版发行的感想 ["A Tale from the Annals of Publishing—Thoughts on the Publication of *The Plum in the Golden Vase* and *Lady Chatterley's Lover*"]. *Zhonghua dushu bao* 中華讀書報 [*Chinese Reader*], 30 Oct. 2013, p. 5.

Yin Gonghong 尹恭弘. Jin Ping Mei *yu wan ming wenhua*: Jin Ping Mei *zuowei "xiao" shu de wenhua kaocha* 《金瓶梅》與晚明文化—《金瓶梅》作為"笑"書的文化考察 [The Plum in the Golden Vase *and Late Ming Culture: A Cultural Investigation of* The Plum in the Golden Vase *as Joke Book*]. Huawen chubanshe, 1997.

Yu, Anthony, translator. *The Journey to the West*. U of Chicago P, 1977–1983. 4 vols.

Yu Pingbo 俞平伯, editor. *Zhiyan zhai* Honglou meng *jiping* 脂硯齋紅樓夢輯評 [*Collated Comments from the Red Inkstone Commentaries on* Dream of the Red Chamber]. Taiping Book Company, 1979.

Yu Xinzhong 餘新忠. *Ming Qing shiqi* 明清時期 [*Ming and Qing Periods*]. *Zhongguo jiating shi* 中國家庭史 [*A History of Families in China*], vol. 4, edited by Zhang Guogang 張國剛, Renmin chubanshe, 2013.

Zeitlin, Judith T. "Shared Dreams: The Story of the Three Wives' Commentary on the *Peony Pavilion*." *Harvard Journal of Asiatic Studies*, vol. 54, no. 1, 1994, pp. 127–79.

———. "*Xiaoshuo*." Moretti, pp. 249–61.

Zhang Weiren 張偉仁, editor. *Zhongyang Yanjiuyuan Lishi Yuyan Yanjiusuo xian cun Qing dai Neige Daku yuan cang Ming-Qing dang'an* 中央研究院歷史語言研究所現存清代內閣大庫原藏明清檔案 [*Ming-Qing Documents from the Qing Grand Secretariat Archive in the Possession of the History and Language Research Institute, Academia Sinica*]. Academia Sinica, 1986. 324 vols.

Zhang Xinzhi 張新之. *Miaofu xuan xuanping* Shitou ji 妙複軒評石頭記 [*The Miao-fu Pavilion Commentary on* Story of the Stone]. *Chinese Text Project*, 2021, ctext.org/library.pl?if=gb&file=92836&page=1&remap=gb.

Zhang, Ying. *Confucian Image Politics: Masculine Morality in Seventeenth-Century China*. U of Washington P, 2017.

Zhang Zhongmin 張仲民. *Chuban yu wenhua zhengzhi: Wan Qing de "weisheng" shuji yanjiu* 出版與文化政治: 晚清的 "衛生" 書籍研究 [*Publishing and Cultural Politics: A Study on "Hygiene" Books of the Late Qing*]. Shanghai shudian, 2009.

Zhang Zhupo 張竹坡. "How to Read the *Chin P'ing Mei* (*The Plum in the Golden Vase*)." Translated by David T. Roy. Rolston, *How to Read*, pp. 202–43.

———. "How to Read *Jin Ping Mei*." Translated by David T. Roy. *Renditions*, no. 24, autumn 1985, pp. 63–101, www.cuhk.edu.hk/rct/pdf/e_outputs/b24/v24p063 .pdf.

———. "*Jin Ping Mei* Chapters 1 and 100: Zhang Zhupo Commentary." Translated by Xiaofei Tian. *Renditions*, nos. 81–82, 2014, pp. 29–128.

Zhao Xingqin 趙興勤 and Zhao Wei 趙韡. "*Shenbao* suo zai wanqing minguo *Jin Ping Mei* de liubo" 申報所載晚清民國金瓶梅的流播 ["Transmission of *The Plum in the Golden Vase* as Documented in *Shen Bao*"]. *Shehui kexue luntan* 社會科學論壇 [*Social Science Forum*], vol. 3, 2016, pp. 169–88.

Zheng Xuan 鄭玄 et al., editors. *Fushiyin Liji zhushu* 附釋音礼记注疏 [*Annotation and Commentary of the Li Ji with Accompanying Notes*]. Revised by He Shen 和珅, vol. 14, 1795.

Zheng Zhenduo 鄭振鐸. "Tan *Jin Ping Mei cihua*" 談金瓶梅詞話 ["On the *Cihua* Edition of *The Plum in the Golden Vase*"]. *Xidi shuhua* 西諦書話 [*Xidi's Book Talks*], Sanlian shudian, 1998, pp. 71–90.

Zhong Yang 鐘揚. "Chen Duxiu de 'Jinxue' guan yu Wusi Xinwenhua yundong zhong de 'xiaoshuo zhi zheng'" 陳獨秀的 "金學" 與五四新文化運動中的 "小說" 之爭 ["Chen Duxiu's '*Plum*-ology' and the 'Novel Debate' in the May Fourth New Culture Movement"]. *Anqing shifan xueyuan xuebao (shehui kexue ban)* 安慶師範學院學報 (社會科學版) [*Journal of Anqing Teachers College (Social Science Edition)*], vol. 26, no. 6, 2007, pp. 47–49.

Zhou Yueran 周越然. "Waiguo *Jin Ping Mei*" 外國金瓶梅 ["Foreign *Plum in the Golden Vase*"]. *Yulin* 語林 [*Forest of Words*], no. 1, 1944, pp. 77–80.

———. "Yu zhi goushu jingyan" 余之購書經驗 ["My Book-Buying Experiences"]. *Jiushi shufang* 舊時書坊 [*Old-Time Booksellers*], edited by Qiu He 秋禾, Sanlian shudian, 2005, pp. 282–90.

Zhu Yixuan 朱一玄, editor. Jin Ping Mei *ziliao huibian* 金瓶梅資料彙編 [*Collection of Materials on* The Plum in the Golden Vase]. Nankai daxue, 2002.

Žižek, Slavoj. *Living in the End Times*. Expanded ed., Verso, 2011.

Zunshine, Lisa. "From the Social to the Literary: Approaching Cao Xueqin's *The Story of the Stone* (*Honglou meng* 紅樓夢) from a Cognitive Perspective." Zunshine, *Oxford Handbook*, pp. 176–96.

———. "Introduction to Cognitive Literary Studies." Zunshine, *Oxford Handbook*, pp. 1–9.

———, editor. *The Oxford Handbook of Cognitive Literary Studies*. Oxford UP, 2015.

———. *The Secret Life of Literature*. MIT Press, forthcoming.

———. "Theory of Mind and Fictions of Embodied Transparency." *Narrative*, vol. 16, no. 1, 2008, pp. 65–92. *JSTOR*, www.jstor.org/stable/30219272.

———. "'Think What You're Doing, Or You'll Only Make an Ugly Reputation for Yourself': *Chin P'ing Mei* (金瓶梅), Lying, and Literary History." *Cognitive Poetics* 認知詩學, vol. 4, Dec. 2017, pp. 44–62.

———. "What Mary Poppins Knew: Theory of Mind, Children's Literature, History." *Narrative*, vol. 27, no. 1, 2019, pp. 1–29.

———. *Why We Read Fiction: Theory of Mind and the Novel*. Ohio State UP, 2006.